HALLIWELL'S
TELEGUIDE

THE ADVENTURES OF DON QUIXOTE. Frank Finlay and Rex Harrison clearly personify the spirit of adventure which is appropriate to actors trying to cram a multi-volume classic novel into the narrow and limited confines of a TV movie. The result, alas, was just a little dull.

LESLIE HALLIWELL

HALLIWELL'S TELEGUIDE

GRANADA
London Toronto Sydney New York

Published by Granada Publishing 1979

Granada Publishing Limited
Frogmore, St Albans, Herts AL2 2NF
and
3 Upper James Street, London W1R 4BP
866 United Nations Plaza, New York, NY 10017, USA
117 York Street, Sydney, NSW 2000, Australia
100 Skyway Avenue, Rexdale, Ontario, Canada M9W 3A6
PO Box 84165, Greenside, 2034 Johannesburg, South Africa
CML Centre, Queen & Wyndham Streets, Auckland 1, New Zealand

Copyright © Leslie Halliwell 1979

ISBN 0 246 11090 2

Filmset in Great Britain by
Richard Clay (The Chaucer Press), Ltd,
Bungay, Suffolk,
and printed by Fletcher & Son, Ltd,
Norwich

Granada
Granada Publishing ®

Contents

This book is for my son
CLIVE
to whom television has
brought continual delight

Explanatory Notes

Television is a vast and frightening wasteland in which occasional treasures are to be found by the keen explorer. This book is intended to be a catalogue of the treasures.

What is not covered? Foreign-speaking programmes unless they have been well exposed in Britain or America. News and magazine items. Sports coverage. Music and arts compilations. Live or tape shows which have not been preserved: pointless, usually, to record something which the student can no longer consult, when so much else is pressing for inclusion. (This last consideration means that many programmes are recorded simply because they are on film, not because they are any worthier than the thousands of programmes the reader will seek for in vain. Sorry.)

It's a start. Approximately four thousand items about a new art (all right, craft) which has had little written about it beyond fan effusions and technical text books. Yet it must be important enough for a book because it affects so many of our lives. If the attitudes to it in this volume are not by general consent the right ones, hopefully so many people will write to the author and say so that he will do better in the second edition. Bouquets and brickbats, please, to him c/o Granada TV, 36 Golden Square, London W1, England.

If a programme is well enough documented, its details are set out in a form similar to that of my *Film Guide*. Some long-running shows, however, change their personnel and length so frequently that a simple descriptive paragraph must suffice. As in the *Film Guide*, up to four asterisks are used to denote historical interest/general worthiness; contributions of especial merit are printed in small capitals in the programme entries (but not under people, where the description should give sufficient emphasis). I have tried to make sure that all series or single items which have genuinely widened the boundaries of television are included, but of course I have failed at this first attempt. I know that film series and TV movies are the best covered items, light entertainment and arts probably the least: the balance will improve next time.

There isn't much cross-referencing. If you are looking up a programme, most of the important contributors will have their own items. If you are looking up a person, the more important television productions in which he has appeared will also be separately treated. If a contributor has also had an extensive film career, I have not given details as these are covered in other reference books, in particular my *Filmgoer's Companion*.

Under programmes, I have intended to show only the contributors who are constant throughout the series. *Wagon Train* probably employed forty different directors: I have not even tried to indicate them. On the other hand, in television the producer is usually the most important, and constant, creative force, so I have given his name wherever possible; also that of the 'creator', the man who devised the format.

The cut-off date for entries is roughly June 1978, i.e. the end of the 1977–8 season, though I have added brief indications of many programmes due to begin in the autumn of 1978.

Archives in America and Britain have been steadily collecting and preserving television programmes for many years now. I trust that this book may be of value not only to the general viewer in search of instant nostalgia but to the student who pores over cassettes of those programmes in the year 2000 and after.

What is included

TV MOVIES: hopefully all which have been produced. A TV movie is something which fills a slot of 90 minutes or more. I give the actual length, not the slot length, and the main lengths (74m for a 90m slot, 96m for a 120m slot) are standardized even though some films may vary by a minute or two.

TV SERIES: virtually all which have been preserved (which usually means they're on film) or of which episodes at least will be found in archives.

INDIVIDUAL PROGRAMMES if they have historic or artistic significance.

PEOPLE who have made significant creative contributions to television. (Executives don't normally count.) The people entries are deliberately brief, mainly because the subjects tend to have been involved in so many programmes that it is impossible to finalize an accurate list or to find space for it if one did. Work in TV series only has therefore been noted (unless a single performance is especially distinguished). Reference is made to a film career, if any, so that the reader can look it up himself in my *Filmgoer's Companion* or other reference book.

TECHNICAL AND TRADE TERMS OF INTEREST

How the information is presented

The items are in strictly alphabetical order.

The arrangement of facts for TV movies and series is similar to that of the *Film Guide* (from which all the TV movie entries have been transferred). Special merit/artistic or historical interest is denoted by one to four asterisks.

First line: *Alternative title*, if any (aka). *Country and year of origin.*
> For series the end date is that of the last September season start.
> For single items I aim to give the year of first transmission.
> *Running time.* (Note that 'one-hour' slot programmes have been rationalized at 50m, though they may run as much as 52m or as little as 46m. 'Half-hours' are normally given as 25m, though if they are made for prime access time or Saturday morning there will be more commercials and the actual running time will be 22m.)

Colour or black-and-white.

If a TV movie (TVM).

Second line: *Production credits.* 'Jones/Bloggs' indicates equal partnership; a producer in brackets is an employee. Executive producers are often shown, as in some cases they are the people with the real influence; but situations vary immensely. Production companies are shown rather than distributors, as the latter tend to vary from continent to continent. In the case of American programmes I have had to show the network (CBS, ABC, NBC) commissioning the production.

Then: *Synopsis.*

Appraisal.

Writer (*w*), director (*d*), photographer (*ph*), music (*m*), musical director (*m/d*), art director (*a/d*), where available. In the case of series they often vary so much that there is no point in trying to give them. I have tried however always to give the creator (*cr*), i.e. the fellow who put the format together.

Selected cast. Again, in series, only the regular cast is shown.

Critical quotes, if any can be found. *Additional notes of interest* (†).

The author's request to the reader

Please be indulgent. Trying to pull together millions of possible facts about television, and to select the most useful, is a marathon task.

Here's to good viewing.

L.H., September 1978

A

Aaker, Lee (1943–). American child actor of the fifties who had a long run in *The Adventures of Rin Tin Tin*.

The Abbott and Costello Show: see Abbott, Bud

Abbott, Bud (1895–1974) (William Abbott). Veteran vaudevillian crosstalker famed for his partnership with Lou Costello. In 1953, after the decline of their Hollywood careers, they reunited for a half-hour TV series (52 episodes) which revamped all their old routines and was still being played 25 years later.

ABC (US). America's 'third network' which in the seventies, by a remarkable spurt, became number one in the ratings. (Its competitors are CBS and NBC.) ABC was formed in the forties by a merger between United Paramount Theatres and the proprietor of Life Savers. Its guiding spirit has been Leonard Goldenson, now chairman, and its most successful programme developments have included *The Wonderful World of Disney*, *Cheyenne* and *Maverick*, Movie of the Week, Monday night football and *Roots*.

ABC (GB). Independent TV contractor, an offshoot of the ABC theatre chain in which the major shareholders were ABPC (a production company) and Warners (who were bought out in the fifties). From 1955 ABC's territory was the North of England at weekends, but as a result of the ITA's 1968 reshuffle it became leading partner, with Associated Rediffusion, in Thames TV, the London weekday company.

The Abduction of St Anne *
US 1975 74m colour TVM
Quinn Martin

A private eye is asked by a bishop to investigate the reported sainthood of a gangster's daughter.
This is called having it all ways. Oddly, the mixture works well enough in the revered Hollywood manner.
w Edward Hume, *novel The Issue of the Bishop's Blood* by Thomas Patrick McMahon *d* Harry Falk

Robert Wagner, E. G. Marshall, Lloyd Nolan, William Windom, Kathleen Quinlan, James Gregory

Academy Awards Telecast. TV's bow towards the movies, this top-rating annual show, usually seen at the beginning of April, is networked live from Los Angeles and has been known to run more than three hours. The fact that it is staged for TV has made it rather a bore for those who actually attend, but it has its historical appeal as America's major annual gathering of film stars, with nostalgia its trump card. The statuette awarded is known as Oscar, and awards began in 1927.

Academy of Television Arts and Sciences. America's group of TV professionals who annually present their version of Oscar, called Emmy by derivation from the image orthicon tube. Awards began in 1949 and are usually televised.

Acapulco
US 1960 8 × 25m bw
NBC/UA/Libra

Veterans of the Korean war live it up in a ritzy resort. Flop series attempting a sub-Hemingway approach to post-war wanderers.

James Coburn, Ralph Taeger, Allison Hayes

Accidental Family
US 1968 16 × 25m colour
Sheldon Leonard

A widowed California farmer is joined by his son. Forgettable schmaltz.

Jerry Van Dyke, Teddy Quinn, Lois Nettleton

Ace, Goodman (1899–). Outstanding American comedy writer for radio and TV, who in the fifties provided smart scripts for Milton Berle, Perry Como and Sid Caesar.

Ackerman, Harry S. (1912–). American executive who after work in an advertising agency and with CBS programme development was supervisor and often creator of Screen Gems' output in the sixties.

Adam Adamant. BBC 50m tape show of the early sixties in which Gerald Harper played a period hero thawed out in the 20th century to pit his wits against modern evils. As a Saturday night time-filler, it had class.

Adam Smith *
GB 1972 39 × 25m colour (VTR)
Granada (June Howson)

After the death of his lady, a Presbyterian minister seeks the meaning of life while continuing to help his parishioners.

Gritty, determined and well-meaning combination of drama and religion, rather doleful to watch.

w Ben Rae

Andrew Keir, Tom Conti, Kara Wilson, Brigid Forsyth

Adam 12 *
US 1968–75   150 × 25m   colour
NBC/Universal/Jack Webb (James Doherty)

Incidents in the lives of urban police officers in a cruiser car.
Popular, easy-going attempt to humanize the cops. Worth comparing with the much tougher British *Z Cars*, which uses exactly the same premise except for taking 50 minutes to tell one story rather than 25 to tell four.

cr Jack Webb, Robert Cinader

Martin Milner, Kent McCord

The Adams Chronicles **
US 1975   13 × 50m   colour (VTR)
WNET (Jac Venza)

How succeeding generations of the John Quincy Adams family influenced American history.
Stalwart saga produced by public TV with the aid of grants: above the heads of the mass audience but with many pleasures, good historical sense, and the correct measured pace.

story editor Anne Howard Bailey

William Daniels, George Grizzard, John Houseman, Nancy Coleman, David Birney, JOHN BEAL, Wesley Addy, Leora Dana

Adams, Don (1927–) (Donald James Yarmy). American entertainer, former impressionist who hit it big on the *Tonight* show and later (1965–70) as the bumbling spy in *Get Smart*.

Adams, Nick (1931–68) (Nicholas Adamschock). American actor, young in the fifties, who starred in series *Saints and Sinners* and *The Rebel*.

Adams of Eagle Lake. An American series for ABC which never got off the ground, despite several efforts in 1975, when a TV movie, *Winter Kills*, and two one-hours were made, all based on the country sheriff played by James Garner in the cinema film *They Only Kill Their Masters*. In 1978 Andy Griffith, around whom the TV series was to be built, was still trying, with a slightly different character, in such TV movies as *The Girl in the Empty Grave* and *Deadly Game*. All were MGM productions.

Adam's Rib
US 1973   13 × 25m   colour
ABC/MGM (Peter Stone, Peter H. Hunt)

Married lawyers are at odds both at home and in court.

Unsuccessful copy of a successful film, with willing leads no substitute for Tracy and Hepburn.

cr Peter Stone

Blythe Danner, Ken Howard

Adamson, Peter (1930–). British character actor who since 1960 has played (exclusively) the rough diamond Len Fairclough in *Coronation Street*.

The Addams Family **
US 1964–5   64 × 25m   bw
ABC/Filmways

Daily doings of a macabre family based on the Charles Addams cartoons in the *New Yorker*.
A sophisticated black comedy idea became an un-expected popular success, largely owing to a catchy theme tune, a succession of good gags and snappy production values. *The Munsters*, a similar idea aired during the same season, was also popular but played more for sympathy.

John Astin (Gomez), Carolyn Jones (Morticia), Jackie Coogan (Uncle Fester), Ted Cassidy (Lurch)

Adventure at Scott Island: see Harbormaster

The Adventurer
GB 1972   24 × 25m   colour
ITC

A cloak and dagger series made on 16mm for an American prime-time access slot, with Gene Barry as a debonair villain-catcher against jetset backgrounds. It didn't catch anyone's imagination, despite the stalwart support of Stuart Damon, Barry Morse and Catherine Schell.

m Jerry Goldsmith

Adventures in Paradise
US 1959–61   91 × 50m   bw
ABC/TCF (Martin Manulis)

Adam Troy runs a small schooner in the South Pacific.
Mindless adventures inspired by James Michener stories. The star, a sailing enthusiast, subsequently made a movie called *I Sailed to Tahiti with an All-Girl Crew*, which suggests the level of the series.

Gardner McKay

Adventures in Rainbow Country
Canada 1972   26 × 25m   colour
CBC/Manitou

A 14-year-old boy has fun growing up near Lake Huron.
Unexceptional, and rather boring, open-air series for youngsters and indulgent adults.

Billy Williams, Lois Maxwell

Adventures of a Jungle Boy
GB 1957   13 × 25m   colour
ABC/Gross–Krasne

A young Tarzan lives with a friendly cheetah in East Africa.
Harmless, unimaginative, plagiaristic nonsense.

Michael Carr Hartley

The Adventures of Aggie. An independent British half-hour comedy series of the fifties with Joan Shawlee as a fashion designer on international assignments.

The Adventures of Black Beauty *
GB 1972   26 × 25m   colour
London Weekend/Freemantle

Two well-brought-up children, a horse, and a country estate in Victorian days.
Pleasantly made adventures with no relation to Anna Sewell's book.

William Lucas

The Adventures of Champion: see Champion the Wonder Horse

The Adventures of Don Quixote *
GB 1972   98m   colour   TVM
BBC/Universal

Easily assimilated but quite unremarkable compression of Cervantes's great novel.

w Hugh Whitemore, *novel* Cervantes *d* Alvin Rakoff

Rex Harrison, Frank Finlay, Rosemary Leach

The Adventures of Hiram Holliday *
US 1958   26 × 25m   bw

A meek little reporter on a world tour has various adventures.
Modest comedy series from a Paul Gallico character, which confirmed the stardom of Wally Cox after *Mr Peepers*.

Wally Cox

The Adventures of Jim Bowie
US 1957–8   78 × 25m   bw
ABC/Louis Edelman

A frontiersman journeys to Texas after the Louisiana Purchase.
Elementary western adventures for the family.

Scott Forbes

The Adventures of Judge Roy Bean
US 1955   39 × 25m   bw
Barrett/Quintet

Exploits of a rascally judge in the old west.

Acceptably amusing studio-bound western series.

Edgar Buchanan, Jack Beutel

The Adventures of Kit Carson
US 1952–4   104 × 25m   bw
Universal

Travels of a western scout.
Ho-hum family western series.

Bill Williams, Don Diamond

The Adventures of Long John Silver *
Australia 1955   26 × 25m   colour
Isola del'Oro

Cramped, studio-bound adventures of a rascally pirate, notable chiefly for preserving a famous star performance.

Robert Newton, Connie Gilchrist, Kit Taylor

The Adventures of Nick Carter
aka: *Nick Carter*
US 1972   73m   colour   TVM
Universal (Stanley Kallis)

A private detective gets into colourful company when investigating the death of a friend.
Another attempt to revivify one of the longest-lasting detectives of all; plot and cast are uneasy, the nineties setting really does not help.

w Ken Pettus   d Paul Krasny

Robert Conrad, Shelley Winters, Brooke Bundy, Dean Stockwell, Pat O'Brien, Broderick Crawford, Neville Brand, Pernell Roberts

The Adventures of Ozzie and Harriet *
US 1952–65   435 × 25m   bw (last 26 in colour)
ABC/Stage Five (Ozzie Nelson)

Archetypal domestic family comedy: so bland was the concept that the hero's occupation was never mentioned in fourteen years, but America lapped it up.

Ozzie Nelson, Harriet (Hilliard) Nelson and their children David, Rick, June and Kris

†A feature film, *Here Come the Nelsons*, was made in 1951.

The Adventures of Rin Tin Tin *
US 1954–6   52 × 25m   bw
ABC/Columbia

A dog is a great asset at Fort Apache in the 1880s.
Often enjoyable family western.

Lee Aaker, Jim Brown, Joe Sawyer

The Adventures of Robin Hood **
GB 1955–9   143 × 25m   bw
ITC/Sapphire ((Hannah Weinstein)

Robin outwits the wicked sheriff and thwarts King John.

Generally spirited extensions of a favourite legend; they certainly hit the target at the time.

Richard Greene, John Arnatt, Archie Duncan, Alexander Gauge

The Adventures of Sherlock Holmes
US 1955   39 × 25m   bw
Sheldon Reynolds

Sloppy retreads of great stories, ill-cast and poorly filmed.

Ronald Howard, Howard Marion-Crawford

The Adventures of Sir Lancelot
GB 1956   30 × 25m   bw
ITC/Sapphire

Legends of the court of King Arthur.
Adequate, unexciting production.

William Russell, Jane Hylton, Ronald Leigh-Hunt

The Adventures of Superman*
US 1953–5   104 × 25m   bw (52), colour (52)
Lippert/National Periodical Publications

A superbeing from the planet Krypton poses on earth as Clark Kent, a mild-mannered reporter, but zooms into action whenever the innocent need help.
Crude but likeable serial from a thirties comic strip. Superman had previously featured in a couple of low budget theatrical features and a serial, *Atom Man vs Superman*; in the sixties he became a cartoon character in *The Batman–Superman Hour* and *Super Friends*. 1978 revived him as the hero of a super-budget feature.

George Reeves, Phyllis Coates, John Hamilton

The Adventures of the Falcon
US 1954   39 × 25m   bw
Bernard Schubert

Mike Waring takes on hazardous assignments.
Roughneck version of the more famous film series.

Charles McGraw

Adventures of the Queen
US 1975   99m   colour   TVM
TCF (Irwin Allen)

A mad bomber is loose on an ocean liner.
Overstretched failed pilot shot on the *Queen Mary* at Long Beach. Plot and performances make it very ho-hum.

w John Gay   *d* David Lowell Rich

Robert Stack, Ralph Bellamy, David Hedison, Bradford Dillman, Sorrell Booke, Burr de Benning, John Randolph

Adventures of the Sea Hawk
US 1958   26 × 25m   bw
Wesmore, Inc

Scientists travel in a floating electronics lab.
Palatable early evening adventures, filmed in Bermuda.

John Howard, John Lee

Adventures of the Seaspray
Australia 1965   32 × 25m   colour
Columbia/Roger Mirams

An 83-foot schooner sails the South Pacific.
Moderate family fare.

The Adventures of Tugboat Annie
Canada 1956   39 × 25m   bw
Normandie

Tugboat captains enjoy a friendly feud.
Watchable extension of the feature film characters created by Norman Reilly Raine.

Minerva Urecal, Walter Sande

The Adventures of William Tell*
GB 1957   39 × 25m   bw
ITC

The legendary Swiss folk hero defeats the evil Gessler. Or, Robin Hood in the Alps. A location-filmed series with more than a spark of vitality.

Conrad Philips, Jennifer Jayne, Willoughby Goddard

AES Hudson Street. US 1978: a shortlived half-hour tape comedy series about a black doctor (Gregory Sierra) in an incompetently run emergency hospital.

The Affair*
US 1973   74m   colour   TVM
ITC/Spelling–Goldberg

Extrovert lawyer falls in love with reclusive polio victim, but it doesn't work.
Watchable modern soap opera.

w Barbara Turner   *d* Gilbert Cates   *ph* Jerry Hirschfeld

Natalie Wood, Robert Wagner, Bruce Davison, Kent Smith, Pat Harrington

† A theatrical version was released at 92m.

affiliate station. A local American station which contracts with a network to take a proportion of its programmes.

The AFI Salute. The American Film Institute has taken to hosting an annual dinner at which a famous star or director of yesteryear is toasted. The resulting festivals of nostalgia, filled with star tributes and film clips, have invariably been televised. Recipients have included John Ford, Alfred Hitchcock, James Cagney, Orson Welles, William Wyler, Bette Davis and Henry Fonda.

Africa**
US 1967 200m colour
ABC News (James Fleming, Blaine Littell)

Milestone four-hour documentary examining the new independent states of Africa; still one of the longest single programmes ever made for TV. Despite much ballyhoo, the public switched to other channels and the experiment was not repeated.

narrator Gregory Peck *m* Alex North

African Patrol
GB 1957 39 × 25m bw
Gross–Krasne

A mobile policeman in East Africa.
One of the shoddier adventure series of its time.

John Bentley

An Age of Kings**. Ambitious BBC attempt (1965) to make historical and dramatic sense of all Shakespeare's British-set historical plays by weaving them into a continuing series.

Ain't No Time for Glory
US 1957 74m bw TVM
Columbia/Playhouse 90

During the Battle of the Bulge, an American officer talks a German commander into surrender.
Dull and respectable.

d Oscar Rudolph

Barry Sullivan, Gene Barry, John Drew Barrymore, Bruce Bennett

Airport*
GB 1978 3 × 50m colour
BBC (Shirley Fisher)

A documentary triptych showing in detailed and assured style how a major international airport (Heathrow) really works.

reporter Harold Williamson

Akins, Claude (1918–). American character actor, a heavily-built, slow-moving fellow who throughout his Hollywood career was usually cast as a villain. TV, however, redeemed him, and after many guest star roles he starred in 1974 as the kindly truck-driving hero of the two-season series *Movin' On*, and in 1979 as the evil sheriff of *BJ and the Bear*.

The Alaskans
US 1959 36 × 50m bw
ABC/Warner

Adventures in the 1898 gold rush.
As tatty-looking and badly acted a series as ever came out of a major studio.

Roger Moore, Jeff York, Dorothy Provine

Alberg, Mildred Freed (19 –). American drama producer associated with *Playhouse 90*, and in the seventies two religious specials, *The Story of David* and *The Story of Jacob and Joseph*.

Albert, Eddie (1908–) (Eddie Albert Heimberger). Genial American actor, usually in light roles. A frequent guest star who also had two long-running series, *Green Acres* and *Switch*.

Albertson, Jack (1910–). American vaudevillian familiar for many years as straight man to Phil Silvers and Milton Berle; he subsequently enjoyed moderate success on Broadway and in Hollywood. In his later years he became a popular TV star in such series as *Ensign O'Toole, Dr Simon Locke, Chico and the Man* and *Grandpa Goes to Washington*.

Albright, Lola (1925–). American leading lady who after a rather disappointing movie career in wisecracking roles became a TV star in *Peter Gunn*.

Alcatraz Express**
aka: *The Big Train*
US 1960 96m bw TVM
Paramount/Desilu/Quinn Martin

An attempt is made to rescue Al Capone on his way by train to Alcatraz.
Excellent suspense thriller made from two episodes of *The Untouchables*.

w William Spier *d* John Peyser

Robert Stack, Neville Brand, Bruce Gordon, Paul Picerni, Nicholas Georgiade, Abel Fernandez

Alda, Alan (1936–). American leading actor, son of Robert Alda. His great success has been on TV as Hawkeye in *M*A*S*H*, throughout the long run of which he proved himself a star of the first magnitude. Also on TV in *That Was the Week that Was* (US version), *The Glass House, Kill Me If You Can* (as Caryl Chessman).

Alderton, John (1940–). British juvenile lead who matured into a quirky character comedian. He didn't make it in films, but TV kept him busy in *Emergency Ward Ten, Please Sir, Upstairs Downstairs, No Honestly, The Upchat Line* and *Thomas and Sarah*.

The Aldrich Family. A domestic comedy from the early days of US TV, this live half-hour series ran on and off from 1949 to 1953 and was based on the well-known Henry Aldrich teenage character created by Ezra Stone, a mid-America stereotype not far removed from Andy Hardy. In this version were Bob Casey, House Jameson and Barbara Robins.

Alexander, Ben (1911–69). American actor, a former child star of the cinema who in later life played a second lead cop in *Dragnet* and *The Felony Squad*.

Alexander: The Other Side of Dawn
US 1977   96m   colour   TVM
Douglas Cramer

A teenage male prostitute tries to reform.
Vaguely repellent quasi-documentary.

w Walter Dallenbach   *d* John Erman

Leigh J. McCloskey, Eve Plumb, Alan Feinstein, Earl Holliman, Juliet Mills, Jean Hagen, Frances Faye

Alfred Hitchcock Presents***
US 1955–61   268 × 25m   bw
CBS (later NBC)/Universal/Shamley (Norman Lloyd)

An anthology of twist-in-the-tail suspensers, usually with a dash of comedy. Because the villains often got away with their nefarious schemes, the moral code obliged Hitchcock to sign off in person with a throwaway moral ending, and these tit-bits, plus corresponding openings and a catchy theme tune, made the show phenomenally popular, though Hitch himself directed fewer than 20 episodes. The stories, often drawn from semi-classic sources, were always impeccably presented. In 1962–4 the series moved from CBS to NBC and became an hour for 93 episodes, but many of these were unsatisfactory and almost all seemed padded.
† The catchy theme tune was *Funeral March of a Marionette*.

Alias Smith and Jones*
US 1970   74m   colour   TVM
Universal (Frank Price, Glen Larson)

Two bandits come to an arrangement with the government.
Comedy western, clearly modelled on *Butch Cassidy and the Sundance Kid*; it spawned a successful series.

w Glen Larson   *d* Gene Levitt   *m* Billy Goldenberg

Pete Duel, Ben Murphy, Susan St James, James Drury, Forrest Tucker, Earl Holliman

Alias Smith and Jones*
US 1970–1   48 × 50m   colour
ABC/Universal

The series ran pretty true to the pilot, but the high spirits eventually proved no substitute for dramatic action, and westerns were in any case declining in audience appeal.

Pete Duel (who died after 37 episodes and was replaced by Roger Davis), Ben Murphy

Alice
US 1976–   × 25m   colour
Warner/David Susskind

A widow works in a hash-house and brings up her teenage son.

ALIAS SMITH AND JONES. Pete Duel and Ben Murphy brought some cheerfulness to the roles of young outlaws with hearts of gold, but they clearly saw themselves as player kings, knowing that *Butch Cassidy and the Sundance Kid* had already played the aces.

Moderate transcription of the restaurant sequences from the film *Alice Doesn't Live Here Any More*.

cr Robert Getchell

Linda Lavin, Alfred Lutter, Vic Tayback

Alistair Cooke's America ****
GB 1974   13 × 50m   colour
BBC

Brilliantly-filmed historical documentaries in which the knowledgeable and urbane Mr Cooke wanders across his adopted land and, aided by a first-class camera crew, picks up all the strands which have made up the present-day nation. Not only the series, but the book based on it, was a bestseller.

All Creatures Great and Small *
GB 1974   96m   colour   TVM
EMI/Venedon (for Hallmark Hall of Fame)

Adventures of a country vet in Yorkshire of the thirties.
Unadventurous crowd-pleaser based on the autobiographical books of James Herriot. A theatrical sequel followed under the title *It Shouldn't Happen to a Vet* (US: *All Things Bright and Beautiful*); and see below for TV series.

w Hugh Whitemore   *d* Claude Whatham   *ph* Peter Suschitzky   *m* Wilfred Josephs

Simon Ward, Anthony Hopkins, Lisa Harrow, Freddie Jones, Brenda Bruce

All Creatures Great and Small
GB 1977–   × 50m   colour (VTR)
BBC

A popular extension of the above.

Christopher Timothy, Robert Hardy, Carol Drinkwater

All Gas and Gaiters *. Enjoyable BBC character comedy of the sixties which broke new ground in allowing one to laugh gently at the clergy. It starred William Mervyn (the bishop), Robertson Hare (the archdeacon), Derek Nimmo (the curate). Nimmo went on to become a comic monk in the equally long-running *Oh Brother!*

All In the Family ****
US 1971–7   160 approx × 25m   colour (VTR)
CBS/Norman Lear

A working-class bigot continually gets his comeuppance but never learns his lesson.
A revolutionary comedy, adapted from BBC's *Till Death Us Do Part*; watching it quickly became a national pastime, and it played no small part in encouraging viewers to think about contemporary issues. It also killed the old gentle style of American domestic comedy which had been handed down from the clean-living families of the Hardys, the Aldriches and the Nelsons, introducing a raucous acid note, bad language and the discussion of ethnic, moral and religious topics. By 1977, however, it had served its purpose.

cr Norman Lear, Bud Yorkin

Carroll O'Connor, Jean Stapleton, Sally Struthers, Rob Reiner, Betty Garrett, Beatrice Arthur

† Spin-offs included *Maude* and *The Jeffersons*.

All My Children. American daytime soap opera which began on ABC in 1970 and shows no sign of being replaced. It concerns the tribulations of two middle-class families, and stars Ruth Warrick and Mary Fickett.

All My Darling Daughters *
US 1973   74m   colour   TVM
Universal (David Victor, David J. O'Connell)

A widower discovers that his four daughters want to get married at the same time.
Amiable sentimental nonsense which needed firmer control.

w John Gay   *d* David Lowell Rich

Robert Young, Raymond Massey, Eve Arden, Darleen Carr, Judy Strangis, Sharon Gless

† See also the following.

All My Darling Daughters' Anniversary
aka: *My Darling Daughters' Anniversary*
US 1974   74m   colour   TVM
Universal (David Victor, David J. O'Connell)

Inevitable sequel to the above: all the girls have babies at the same time.
Dim.

w John Gay   *d* Joseph Pevney

Robert Young, Raymond Massey, Ruth Hussey, Darleen Carr, Judy Strangis, Sharon Gless

All Our Yesterdays. A British documentary series from Granada which ran from 1960 to 1973, usually in 20m form. By use of theatrical newsreels, each weekly issue covered the events of 25 years ago. Regular presenter: Brian Inglis. Chief producers: Tim Hewat, Douglas Terry. 638 programmes were made in all.

All the Kind Strangers
US 1974   74m   colour   TVM
Cinemation/Jerry Gross

Seven orphans decoy strangers to their lonely farmhouse: some of the adults disappear.
Nuthatch melodrama with a certain amount of pizazz.

w Clyde Ware   *d* Burt Kennedy

Stacy Keach, Samantha Eggar, John Savage, Robby Benson

All Together Now
US 1975   74m   colour   TVM
RSO (Ron Bernstein)

A teenage boy proves to the court that he and his young brother and sisters can make it on their own.
Adequate sentimental stuff.

w Jeff Andrus, Rubin Carson   *d* Randall Kleiser

John Rubenstein, Glynnis O'Connor, Brad Savage, Bill Macy, Jane Withers, Helen Hunt

All You Need is Love **
GB 1977   13 × 50m   colour
LWT/Theatre Projects

A history of the popular music of the 20th century. Often disappointing, sometimes brilliantly assembled and presented, this solidly researched series covered its ground thoroughly and included much rare footage as well as rounding up for interview all the big surviving names. Historically, a most valuable project.

p/d Tony Palmer

Allen, Dave (1934–). Irish cabaret comedian whose speciality is religious jokes told from a high stool while he plays with a cigarette. Popular in Britain and Australia from the mid-sixties, in the mid-seventies he branched out less successfully as a TV traveller and interviewer of eccentrics. First TV drama appearance: *One Fine Day* (1979).

Allen, Fred (1894–1956) (John F. Sullivan). Mournful-looking American radio comedian famous for his feud with Jack Benny. He never quite made it in the movies, and although he appeared frequently on TV from 1950 until his death it is for radio that he will be remembered.

Allen, Irwin (1916–). American film producer who made some rather clodhopping fantasy spectaculars and then, with remarkable success for a time, adapted the same genre for TV. Series include *Voyage to the Bottom of the Sea*, *Lost in Space*, *Time Tunnel*, *Land of the Giants*, *The Swiss Family Robinson* and *The Return of Captain Nemo*.

Allen, Patrick (1927–). British leading actor, a lantern-jawed tough guy who became famous as Crane; subsequently the voice of innumerable commercials.

Allen, Steve (1921–). American general purpose comedian, commentator and panellist of the fifties, still seen occasionally as talk show host.

All's Fair
US 1976   23 × 25m   colour (VTR)
Norman Lear

An emancipated woman and her reactionary husband find marriage an enjoyable strain.
Talky comedy which didn't quite hit the jackpot.

cr Rod Parker, Bob Schiller, Bob Weiskopf   *d* Bob Claver

Richard Crenna, Bernadette Peters

Allyson, June (1917–) (Ella Geisman). American leading lady of the forties and fifties who also tried TV with a drama anthology, *The June Allyson Show*. Cuteness and charm were her forte. She still plays guest star roles.

Aloha Means Goodbye
US 1974   100m   colour   TVM
Universal (Sam Strangis)

A girl in hospital discovers that if she dies she may become a heart donor for the surgeon's son.
Icky medical melodrama.

w Dean Riesner, Joseph Stefano, *novel* Naomi A. Hentze   *d* David Lowell Rich

Sally Struthers, James Franciscus, Joanna Miles, Henry Darrow, Larry Gates

Along Came a Spider **
US 1972   74m   colour   TVM
TCF (Alan A. Armer)

The widow of a scientist killed in an accident plots revenge on his careless colleague.
Efficient suspenser shot on a university campus.

w Barry Oringer   *d* Lee H. Katzin

Suzanne Pleshette, Ed Nelson, Andrew Prine, Richard Anderson, Brooke Bundy

The Alpha Caper *
GB theatrical title: *Inside Job*
US 1973   74m   colour   TVM
Universal/Silverton (Aubrey Schenck)

A parole officer, unjustly retired, plots a 30-million-dollar robbery with one of his protégés.
Reasonably entertaining comedy drama.

w Elroy Schwartz   *d* Robert Michael Lewis   *ph* Enzo Martinelli   *m* Oliver Nelson

Henry Fonda, Leonard Nimoy, James McEachin, Larry Hagman, Elena Verdugo, John Marley, Noah Beery

'There's a good thesis to be written on the hermetic aesthetics of the TV movie: every element seems to follow a pre-ordained pattern whose points of reference are always other movies rather than real experience.' – *Monthly Film Bulletin*

The Alternative
Australia 1978   74m   colour   TVM
Paramount

An unmarried mother chooses between her ex-lover and a new protector.
Ho-hum Peg's Paper character drama.

w Tony Morphett   *d* Paul Eddey

Wendy Hughes, Peter Adams, Tony Bonner, Carla Hoogeveen

Alvin and the Chipmunks*
aka: *The Alvin Show*
US 1961   26 × 25m   bw
CBS/Ross Bagdasarian

Cartoon series featuring the producer's then-popular characters who (via electronic trickery) sang en masse in a high-pitched version of the producer's own voice.

Amahl and the Night Visitors***.
Gian-Carlo Menotti's opera about the shepherds welcoming the birth of Christ was written especially for TV and first produced by NBC in 1951. For many years, in various productions, it was an annual Christmas offering.

The Amazing Howard Hughes*
US 1977   2 × 96m   colour   TVM
EMI/Roger Gimbel (Herbert Hirschman)

The life of the millionaire aviator, inventor, film producer and recluse.
Informative and watchable biopic, rather slackly handled and with a disconcerting habit of stopping for a commercial break in the middle of a scene, then going on with something quite different.

w John Gay   *d* William A. Graham   *m* Laurence Rosenthal

TOMMY LEE JONES, Ed Flanders, Carol Bagdasarian, James Hampton

The Amazing Spiderman: see Spiderman (1978)

The Amazing World of Kreskin
US/Canada 1972–3   ? × 25m   colour (VTR)

Audience participation show featuring a genuinely bewildering bespectacled magician and mind reader.

Amelia Earhart*
US 1976   150m   colour   TVM
Universal/NBC (George Eckstein)

A biography of the American woman flyer of the thirties who disappeared over the Pacific.
Standard biopic, quite well done in television terms, with good performances, aerial sequences and music; but too long.

w Carol Sobieski   *d* George Schaefer   *costumes* Edith Head   *m* David Shire   *aerial sequences* Frank Tallman

SUSAN CLARK, John Forsythe, Stephen Macht, Susan Oliver, Catherine Burns, Jane Wyatt, Charles Aidman

America: see Alistair Cooke's America

An American Family**
US 1973   12 × 50m   colour (VTR)
PBS (Craig Gilbert)

For one year, TV cameras invaded the home of a well-to-do Californian family and patched together from the resulting miles of film 12 hours of what purported to be an intimate glimpse into their real, unadulterated private life, warts and all. The series caused furious discussion, but by any measurement was a television first. A year later the BBC made its own variation, this time using a working-class family from Reading: they quickly became national figures.

The American Girls
GB title: *Have Girls, Will Travel*
US 1978   11 × 50m   colour
Columbia (Harve Bennett, Harris Katleman)

Two girl reporters travel the US in a camper.
By *Charlie's Angels* out of *Route 66*, this derivative but trend-conscious series set out to peddle glamour and sex with a soupçon of social awareness.

Priscilla Barnes, Debra Clinger, David Spielberg, Dana Andrews

An American in Pasadena*
GB title: *Gene Kelly's Dancing Years*
US 1977   50m   colour (VTR)
Viacom

From-the-stalls record of a charity show in which Gene Kelly and guests talk, sing and dance through his career. Irresistible material, disappointingly staged and shot.

pd Marty Pasetta   *w* Buz Kohan

guests Frank Sinatra, Liza Minnelli, Lucille Ball, others

Ames, Leon (1903–) (Leon Waycoff). American character actor, in movies from the early thirties, usually in smooth, silent and not very interesting roles. He became a popular TV star in *Life With Father*, *Father of the Bride* and *Mister Ed.*

Amos Burke Secret Agent: see Burke's Law

Amos 'n' Andy. A famous radio comedy series in which caricatured black men were impersonated by whites, its translation to TV in 1951 was a brave attempt, but within two years it had been withdrawn because of protests from various organizations. The bewildered actors, who had been on radio since 1925, were Charles Correll and Freeman F. Gosden.

Ampex. The first successful brand of videotape was invented for the Ampex Corporation by Charles Ginsberg and Ray Dolby. Its acceptance by the TV industry in 1956 marked the end of live TV.

Amsterdam, Morey (1914–). American nightclub comedian chiefly familiar on TV as the hero's friend in *The Dick Van Dyke Show.*

anchorman. The chairman or question master of a panel game, or the studio announcer in a current affairs show, linking together various reports and interpreting them for the viewers.

AND MOTHER MAKES ... three or five, according to where you came in. This picture shows cameras with a touch of Big Brother in their design keeping an eye on Charlotte Mitchell, Wendy Craig, Richard Coleman and Tony Britton.

And Mother Makes Three. British (Thames) sitcom of the early seventies, written by Richard Waring, produced and directed by Peter Frazer-Jones, and starring Wendy Craig as a frantically coping mum. The show stemmed from another called *Not in Front of the Children*, and was eventually transformed into *And Mother Makes Five*.

And No One Could Save Her
GB 1972 73m colour TVM
Associated London (Robert Stigwood)

An American girl seeks her husband in Dublin; but there is no trace of him, so could he be a figment of her imagination?
Bunny Lake Is Missing all over again; not badly done.

w Anthony Skene *d* Kevin Billington

Lee Remick, Milo O'Shea, Frank Grimes, Jennie Linden

Anderson, Barbara (1945–). American leading lady, former beauty queen; became familiar as assistant to Raymond Burr in *Ironside*.

Anderson, Eddie (1905–77). Black American character actor familiar in Hollywood as the archetypal frightened manservant and on radio and TV as Jack Benny's disgruntled manservant Rochester. Black self-consciousness in the sixties made the stereotype unacceptable, and when Rochester reappeared on a Benny special in 1970 and was asked to fetch the car, he made the famous retort: 'Massah Benny, we don' do dat no mo'!'

Anderson, Gerry (1929–). American producer in Britain, specializing in stylish action hokum, usually enacted by puppets. Series include *Four Feather Falls*, *Supercar*, *Stingray*, *Captain Scarlet*, *Joe 90*, *Thunderbirds*, *UFO* (live action), *Space 1999* (live action).

Anderson, Richard (1926–). American second lead/character actor, familiar on TV as Oscar Goldman in *Six Million Dollar Man* and *Bionic Woman*.

Anderson, Warner (1911–76). American character actor, familiar on TV in *The Doctor*, *The Line Up*, *Peyton Place*.

The Andersonville Trial *
US 1972   120m   colour (VTR)
KCET Los Angeles/Stanley Kramer

The trial in the 1860s of Henry Wirtz, camp command-
ant accused of the deaths of many Unionist prisoners.
Solid docu-drama.

w Saul Levitt   d George C. Scott

Richard Basehart, Buddy Ebsen, Cameron Mitchell,
William Shatner

Andrews, Eamonn (1922–   ). Irish sports commentator who came to Britain and became popular, despite
his lack of conversational ability, as host and linkman
(*What's My Line?*, *The Eamonn Andrews Show*,
Tonight, *This is your Life*, *Time for Business*). He is
now looking back on nearly 30 years of such success.

Andrews, Julie (1934–   ) (Julia Wells). A British
child singer who after success on Broadway and
in Hollywood became a top international star and married Blake Edwards. An occasional TV guest star; see
also *The Julie Andrews Hour*.

Andrews, Tige (c 1923–   ). American character
actor, real name Andropoulos; chiefly familiar on TV
as cop in *The Detectives* and *The Mod Squad*.

The Andros Targets *
US 1977   13 × 50m   colour
CBS (Bob Sweeney, Larry Rosen)

Adventures of an investigative journalist.
A smooth, snappy dramatic show inspired by *All The
President's Men*. It failed because the masses found it
too serious, while the intelligentsia were annoyed by its
silly plots.

cr Frank Cucci

James Sutorius

The Andy Griffith Show *
aka: *Andy of Mayberry*
US 1960–8   249 × 25m   bw (last 100 in colour)
CBS/Mayberry

Adventures of a small-town sheriff.
Mid-American comedy, full of crackerbarrel philosophy
and rural types. (It continued as *Mayberry RFD* when
its star moved on to become *The Headmaster*.)

Andy Griffith, Don Knotts (in first 160), Ronny
Howard

† *The New Andy Griffith Show* was unsuccessful.

Angel *
US 1960   39 × 25m   bw
CBS

Tribulations of a young architect with a charming but
scatterbrained French wife.

Pleasing comedy of its time with just a touch of sophistication.

Annie Fargé, Marshall Thompson, Doris Singleton,
Don Keefer

Angels. Sporadic British (BBC) tape hour of the seventies, about a group of young nurses in a big hospital.
For home consumption; producers and directors various.

Anglia TV. British commercial station responsible for
Norfolk, Cambridge and Suffolk; internationally it is
chiefly known for the wild life series *Survival*.

Animal Doctor
aka: *Woobinda, Animal Doctor*
Australia 1968   39 × 25m   colour
Freemantle

Adventures of a vet in the outback.
Passable filler for young people.

Don Pascoe, Bindi Williams

Animal, Vegetable or Mineral. British (BBC)
panel game of the fifties, in which eminent university
dons and scientists, including Mortimer Wheeler and
Glyn Daniel, were asked to identify odd museum
pieces and archaeological artefacts.

The Ann Sothern Show *
US 1958–61   93 × 25m   bw
CBS/Anso Productions

Problems of running a New York hotel, with the star
as assistant manager.
Lightly likeable sitcom, with the star fighting her waist-
line.

Ann Sothern, Don Porter, Ernest Truex

Anna and the King *
US 1972   13 × 25m   colour
CBS/TCF (Gene Reynolds)

In Victorian times, the King of Siam hires an English
governess to tame his many offspring.
Reasonably careful and engaging extension of the films
Anna and the King of Siam and *The King and I*. It failed
because the network placed it badly and wouldn't give
it a second chance.

Yul Brynner, Samantha Eggar, Keye Luke, Eric Shea

The Annan Committee. Appointed by the British
government to pronounce on the future of TV, this
group under Lord Annan disgorged itself in 1977 of a
long and unwieldy report which more or less recommended the offering of the fourth channel to the IBA as
a holding point for independent producers. By the time
the decision is made, however, its recommendations are
likely to have been forgotten.

Annie Oakley
US 1953-7   80 × 25m   bw
ABC/Flying A Productions

Adventures of a female sharpshooter in the old west.
Annie Get Your Gun without the music; not very lively.

Gail Davis, Brad Johnson, Jimmy Hawkins

Another Sunday and Sweet FA*
GB 1972   52m   colour (16mm)
Granada (Peter Eckersley)

Rivalries between two small football teams come to violence on the field.
Amusing north country comedy.

w JACK ROSENTHAL   *d* Michael Apted

DAVID SWIFT, Duggie Brown

† Critics' Circle Award.

Another World. This title was used both by Granada TV for a travel and nature series produced by Dr Tom Harrisson, and by the NBC network for a one-hour soap opera which began in 1963 and is still going strong.

Ansara, Michael (1922–).   Heavy-featured American character actor often seen as Latin or Indian villain. In TV, played leads in *Law of the Plainsman* and *Broken Arrow*.

answer print. The first available print on which sound and vision have been combined (though the quality may be capable of improvement).

anthology. A dramatic series without a continuing character (though there may be a host).

Antony and Cleopatra. ATV's 1974 version of Shakespeare's tragedy, starring Richard Johnson and Janet Suzman, and directed by Jon Scoffield, was chosen by BAFTA as best play of the year.

Any Second Now
US 1959   98m   colour   TVM
Universal (Gene Levitt)

A would-be wife murderer is on the run in Mexico.
Thinly stretched suspenser with attractive backgrounds.

w/d Gene Levitt

Stewart Granger, Lois Nettleton, Joseph Campanella, Dana Wynter, Katy Jurado, Tom Tully

Apple's Way
US 1974   24 × 50m   colour
CBS/Lorimar (Lee Rich)

Tired of the rat race, a Los Angeles architect moves his family to a small town in Iowa.
Fashionable anti-urban family series in which the people were just too nice to be human.

Ronny Cox, Lee McCain, Malcolm Atterbury

Appointment With Destiny*
US 1971-3   7 × 50m   colour
David Wolper

A series of historical reconstructions which were staged and acted, then made to look like actuality film. The format was much criticized, though the films were exciting. Subjects: *The Crucifixion of Jesus, Showdown at OK Corral, Surrender at Appomattox, The Plot to Murder Hitler, The Last Days of John Dillinger, Peary's Race to the North Pole* and *They've Killed President Lincoln.*

Aquaman. A cartoon character created in 1970 by Filmation. Son of a lighthouse keeper and a lady from Atlantis, he found himself in command of all sea creatures. His seven-minute adventures featured in *The Superman–Aquaman Hour.*

The Aquanauts
aka: *Malibu Run*
US 1960   13 × 50m   bw
CBS/UA/Ivan Tors

Adventures of professional divers in Honolulu.
Thin hokum with glamour backgrounds.

Keith Larsen, Jeremy Slate, Ron Ely

The Aquarians
US 1970   96m   colour   TVM
Universal (Ivan Tors)

Underwater scientists fight sharks, earthquakes and each other.
Routine ocean depths hokum, professionally but boringly handled.

w Leslie Stevens, Winston Miller   *d* Don McDougall   *m* Lalo Schifrin

Ricardo Montalban, Jose Ferrer, Leslie Nielsen, Kate Woodville

Aquarius. British arts programme, LWT's very variable bid for culture on a Saturday night, marred by a succession of supercilious presenters. In 1978 it was succeeded by the *South Bank Show*, with a more down-to-earth approach.

Archard, Bernard (1922–).   Aquiline British character actor whose moment of fame came in the fifties when for several seasons he played Colonel Oreste Pinto in *Spycatcher.*

Archer
US 1975   7 × 50m   colour
NBC/Paramount

Adventures of Ross MacDonald's detective hero Lew Archer among California's idle rich.
A damp squib of a series, following the pilot *The Underground Man.* It seems the star just wasn't at ease.

Brian Keith, John S. Ryan

Arden, Eve (1912–) (Eunice Quedens). American character comedienne who graduated from the chorus, spent her Hollywood career as the heroine's tall, cool, wisecracking friend, then became a TV star in three successful series: *Our Miss Brooks*, *The Eve Arden Show* and *The Mothers in Law*.

Are You Being Served? *
GB 1974–8   40 approx. × 30m   colour (VTR)
BBC (David Croft)

Misadventures in the clothing section of a department store.

A single-set farce series relying heavily on outrageous characters and double entendres. A great success, it temporarily made a household word of John Inman as the gay Mr Humphreys.

w Jeremy Lloyd, David Croft

MOLLIE SUGDEN, JOHN INMAN, FRANK THORNTON, ARTHUR BROUGH, Trevor Bannister, Wendy Richard, HAROLD BENNETT, Arthur English

† A feature film version was made in 1977.

Armchair Theatre. Umbrella title for ABC (GB)'s highly commercial one-hour Sunday night plays in the fifties.

The Army Game *
GB 1957–62   153 × 25m   bw (VTR)
Granada (Peter Eton)

Archetypal army farce series which was enormously popular in the UK and made stars of BERNARD BRESSLAW, ALFIE BASS and BILL FRASER (the latter pair went on to become *Bootsie and Snudge*). Charles Hawtrey and Michael Medwin were also involved, and in the first two years William Hartnell was the sergeant. A film version was made in 1958 under the title *I Only Arsked*.

Arnaz, Desi (1915–) (Desiderio Alberto Arnaz y de Acha). Diminutive but explosive Cuban singer who became a bandleader, made a few films, married Lucille Ball, founded Desilu Studios, and starred with Lucy in the phenomenally successful comedy series *I Love Lucy*. Later divorced Lucy. Autobiography 1976: *A Book*.

Arness, James (1923–) (James Aurness). Long, lean American actor, brother of Peter Graves; after small film roles became enormously successful as star and owner of *Gunsmoke*; reappeared, rather more grizzled, in 1976 as star of *How the West Was Won*.

THE ARMY GAME. The over-age national servicemen in this unlovely group are Alfie Bass, Ted Lune, Harry Fowler and Mario Frabizi, under the beady eye of Bill Fraser as Sgt Major Snudge.

Arnie*
US 1970–1 58 × 25m colour
CBS/TCF (Rick Mittleman)

Slightly ethnic sitcom about a Greek–American blue collar worker suddenly promoted to managerial status. Moderate wit and pace made it appealing.

cr Rick Mittleman *ph* Leon Shamroy

Herschel Bernardi, Sue Anne Langdon, Tom Pedi, Roger Bowen, Herb Voland

Around the World in Eighty Days. A rather feeble Australian half-hour cartoon series was made in 1972 but was not well received.

Arquette, Cliff (1905–). American character comedian who has appeared on TV for many years as rustic philosopher Charlie Weaver.

Arrest and Trial*
US 1963 30 × 74m bw
ABC/Universal

Crime series with a dour tone and an exploratory format: each story was in two halves, the first showing cops tracking down a suspect, the second the DA's success or failure in prosecuting him. The public seems to have found it complicated, but it was a clear step towards longform TV movies, needed to replenish the dwindling Hollywood variety.

Ben Gazzara, Chuck Connors

The Art of Crime
US 1975 100m colour TVM
Brut

A girl is kidnapped by an escaped mental inmate, and falls in love with him.
Wouldn't you just know?

novel Welcome to Xanadu by Nathaniel Benchley *d* Lee Phillips

Linda Blair, Martin Sheen, Jeanne Cooper

Arthur, Beatrice (1924–). Self-confident, abrasive American character comedienne. A hit as cousin Maude in *All In the Family*, she quickly gained her own long-running series *Maude* in which much fun was poked at the American middle class. (Serious problems such as abortion were also tackled.)

Arthur, Jean (1905–) (Gladys Greene). Squeaky-voiced American leading lady of many important American films in the thirties and forties. Her sole excursion into series television, *The Jean Arthur Show*, was not a success.

Arthur of the Britons
GB 1972 26 × 25m colour
Harlech TV (Patrick Dromgoole)

Realistic treatment of the legend of King Arthur.

Oliver Tobias

As the World Turns. Long-running American soap opera, on CBS since 1956, about the residents of a middle-class suburb and their secrets.

The Ascent of Man*
GB 1974 13 × 50m colour
BBC/Time Life

Inspirational account by Dr Jacob Bronowski of the philosophies evolved by man throughout history. Sharp control gave the series strong visual appeal, and Bronowski proved himself a TV star.

Ashley, Ted (1922–). American executive, former head of Ashley Famous Agency and president of Warner Brothers.

Ask the Family. BBC quiz game of the sixties and seventies in which two families pit their wits against each other to answer questions which demand a high degree of intelligence. Quizmaster: Robert Robinson.

Askey, Arthur (1900–). Diminutive British music hall comedian who was a TV regular throughout the fifties and still makes frequent appearances.

Aspen
GB title: *The Aspen Murder*
US 1977 6 × 95m colour
Universal/Roy Huggins (Jo Swerling Jnr)

A young attorney investigates a murder at a ski resort. Mindless cobbling together, for the Best Sellers series of novelizations, of two flashy novels showing the rich at play.

w/d Douglas Heyes *novels Aspen* by Bert Hirschfield and *The Adversary* by Bart Spicer *ph* Isidore Mankowy *m* Tom Scott, Mike Melvoir

Sam Elliott, Perry King, Michelle Phillips, John McIntyre, Gene Barry, Bo Hopkins, Tony Franciosa, Joseph Cotten, John Houseman

'Enough purple passion and rampant victimizing to turn all that snow into slush.' – *Daily Variety*.
'*Aspen* is love! *Aspen* is mystery! *Aspen* is glamour! *Aspen* is murder! A jet-set killing at a glamorous ski capital . . . and the shocking, headline-making trial that followed!' – publicity

The Asphalt Jungle
US 1960 13 × 50m bw
ABC/MGM

Cops against crime in the big city.
Little relation to the famous film.

Jack Warden, Arch Johnson, Bill Smith

Assault on the Wayne
US 1970 74m colour TVM
Paramount

Enemy agents try to seize a top secret device from an atomic submarine.

Standard excitements, quite professionally put together.

d Marvin Chomsky

Joseph Cotten, Leonard Nimoy, Lloyd Haynes, Dewey Martin, Keenan Wynn, William Windom

Assignment Foreign Legion
US 1956   26 × 25m   bw
CBS/Anthony Bartley

A female foreign correspondent seeks the stories behind the men of the foreign legion.
Unintentionally hilarious hokum with the star out of her depth amid production values decidedly below her norm.

Merle Oberon

Assignment Munich
US 1972   96m   colour   TVM
MGM

A shady American saloon owner in Germany helps the US Army find loot stolen during World War II.
Pilot for a short-lived series which turned up as *Assignment Vienna*. (Vienna gave more facilities.) The aim was for a cross between *Casablanca* and *The Third Man*, but what came on the screen was pure hokum.

w Eric Bercovici, Jerry Ludwig   *d* David Lowell Rich

Roy Scheider, Richard Basehart, Lesley Warren, Werner Klemperer, Robert Reed, Pernell Roberts, Keenan Wynn

† The series, *Assignment Vienna*, ran eight episodes in rotation with *The Delphi Bureau*, under the umbrella title *The Men*.

Associated Rediffusion. British ITV company which owned the weekday London franchise from 1954 but merged – and was submerged – with ABC to become Thames in the 1968 reshuffle.

Astaire, Fred (1899–) (Frederick Austerlitz). American star dancer, singer and light romantic lead who after a dazzling Hollywood career turned to TV with a memorable series of specials and in the late sixties played an engaging old rogue in many episodes of *It Takes a Thief*.

Astin, John (1930–). Heavily-moustached American comedy character actor, less successful in films than in TV, where he has starred in such series as *I'm Dickens He's Fenster*, *The Addams Family* and *Operation Petticoat* as well as in TV movies like *Evil Roy Slade*.

Astin, Patty Duke: see Duke, Patty

Astro Boy. Half-hour cartoon series produced in Japan in 1963, about a robot boy who fights evil in the 21st century.

Asylum for a Spy
US 1967   74m   colour   TVM
Universal

A spy suffers a mental breakdown and a counterspy goes undercover in the hospital to pick his brains.
Tedious, talky suspenser, originally a Chrysler Theatre two-parter.

w Robert L. Joseph   *d* Stuart Rosenberg

Robert Stack, Felicia Farr, Martin Milner, George Macready

Atom Ant and Secret Squirrel
US 1965   26 × 25m   colour
NBC/Hanna–Barbera

A cartoon series from this studio's better days. Atom Ant, like Mighty Mouse, was a take-off of Superman;

THE AVENGERS. Patrick MacNee admitted borrowing his concept of the elegant spy Steed from Ralph Richardson's delightful performance in a pre-war movie called *Q Planes*; but he made it all his own.

Secret Squirrel, a spy, was seen in a separate section with his friend Squiddly Diddly.

Attack on Terror
aka: *The FBI versus the Ku Klux Klan*
US 1975 198m (two parts) colour TVM
Warner/Quinn Martin

The alternative title says it all.
Flat, overlong cops and robbers in a very familiar vein.

w Calvin Clements *d* Marvin Chomsky

George Grizzard, Rip Torn, Dabney Colman, Andrew Duggan, L. Q. Jones, Marilyn Mason, Peter Strauss, Wayne Rogers, Ed Flanders

Attenborough, David (1926–). British producer of innumerable international wild life series. In the mid-sixties became Controller of BBC2, then the BBC's director of programmes, but in 1972 returned to his favourite preoccupation.

ATV (Associated Television). British commercial company which until 1968 operated in the midlands on weekdays and in London at weekends; subsequently ran a seven-day midlands operation. ATV's guiding light was originally Norman Collins, then master showmen Val Parnell and Lew Grade took over. Lew Grade has now virtually deserted TV for movie-making, but during his 20 or so years as ATV's programme chief he staged a wide variety of light entertainment, including *Sunday Night at the London Palladium*, several Anglo-American series such as those starring Julie Andrews and the Muppets, upwards of a dozen Gerry Anderson puppet series, and mid-Atlantic crime series shot expensively on 35mm film. Among the latter are *The Saint, Danger Man, The Prisoner, Man in a Suitcase, The Persuaders* and *Space 1999*.

Aubrey, James (1918–). American executive, former salesman and station manager, who in 1959 became president of CBS and was known as the smiling cobra for his competitiveness and ruthlessness. Hints of scandal caused his downfall; he went briefly to MGM but was subsequently little heard from.

Audubon Wildlife Theatre. A Canadian half-hour series (78 episodes) made in 1970, showing the survival of rare birds and mammals; based on the researches of the famous naturalist.

Aurthur, Robert Alan (1922–). American writer, a graduate of the 'golden age' of TV drama, best remembered for *A Man Is Ten Feet Tall*.

Australia. Four major channels are available, three commercial and one (ABC) government-sponsored and

THE AVENGERS. The final (we presume) incarnation of this long-running and influential series came in 1976, when it was called *The New Avengers*. A more mature Steed was joined by Gareth Hunt as Gambit and Joanna Lumley as Purdey, but although they all performed gamely the moment seemed to have passed.

much akin to Britain's BBC. Home-produced product is variable at best, and all channels lean heavily on imports.

The Autobiography of Miss Jane Pittman **

US 1973 109m colour TVM
Tomorrow (Robert W. Christiansen, Rick Rosenberg)

In 1962, a 110-year-old negress in a southern state reflects on her early life as a slave and takes a drink from the 'Whites Only' fountain.
Ambitous and careful TV movie which did much in America to raise the sights of the genre.

w Tracy Keenan Wynn, *novel* Ernest J. Gaines d John Korty ph James Crabe m Fred Karlin pd Michael Haller

CICELY TYSON, Michael Murphy, Richard A. Dysart, Katherine Helmond

Autry, Gene (1907–). American singing cowboy who after a long film career produced and starred in a popular half-hour series featuring himself, Pat Buttram and Champion the wonder horse (85 episodes between 1950 and 1953). He later became a station owner.

The Avengers***. This influential comedy suspense series actually began as a serial melodrama called *Police Surgeon*, made by Britain's ABC in 1960.
This starred Ian Hendry as a man avenging his wife's murder, but a supporting character which caught the eye was that of Patrick MacNee as a dandified secret service agent (bowler hat and cane borrowed from a performance by Ralph Richardson in the film *Q Planes*). When Hendry wouldn't continue, MacNee became the lead of a retitled one-hour series, with Honor Blackman as his aide. Her judo and leather outfits became talking points, but she left the show after one series when it was still on black-and-white VTR. Thereafter *The Avengers* not only went on to colour film but gained an American network sale and lasted three seasons, two with Diana Rigg and one with Linda Thorson; MacNee was in every episode. It had developed into a secret agent spoof, with fantasy violence, zany villains and macabre plots solved by amusing and ambiguous leading characters whose hair never even got ruffled. The writer most responsible for its image was Philip Levene.
In 1976 Albert Fennell and Brian Clemens, who had been much involved with the production and writing of the old series, put together *The New Avengers*, with MacNee assisted by Joanna Lumley and Gareth Hunt, but the spark was fitful and the production beset by financial problems. It ran 26 episodes.

B

Ba Ba Black Sheep
US 1976–8   1 × 95m, 35 × 50m   colour
Universal (Stephen J. Cannell)

Adventures of 'Pappy' Boyington and his unconventional air crews during World War II in the Pacific.
Boisterous sentiment and melodrama amplify routine service antics in a rather dislikeable series which struggled over two seasons, latterly as *Black Sheep Squadron*.

w/cr Stephen J. Cannell   *d* Russ Maybury   *flying sequences* Tallmantz Aviation

Robert Conrad, Simon Oakland, Dana Elcar, Dirk Blocker

Babe *
US 1975   100m   colour   TVM
MGM/Norman Felton, Stanley Rubin

The story of woman athlete Babe Didrikson and her battle with cancer.
Careful but essentially tedious American hero-worship in the wake of *Sunshine*, *It's Good to be Alive*, etc.

SUSAN CLARK, Alex Karras, Slim Pickens, Jeanette Nolan, Ellen Geer

Baby, I'm Back
US 1978   × 25m   colour (VTR)
CBS/Charles Fries

A long-lost husband returns to disturb his wife's second marriage.
Black version of an old routine.

Desmond Wilson, Denise Nicholas, Ed Hall, Helen Martin

'The writers never exercise judgment at the expense of a joke.' – Robert Mackenzie, *TV Guide*

Bachelor Father *
US 1957–61   157 × 25m   bw
CBS/Universal

A bachelor lawyer is guardian to his teenage niece.
One of the more pleasing sitcoms of its era, with a smooth star performance.

John Forsythe, Noreen Corcoran, Sammee Tong

Backtrack
US 1968   97m   colour   TVM
Universal

Adventures of four Texas Rangers.
Poor pilot for *Laredo*.

d Earl Bellamy

Neville Brand, Doug McClure, Peter Brown, James Drury

Backus, Jim (1913–). American character comedian with a fruity voice well known in cartoons and commercials; the voice of Mr Magoo. TV series include *I Married Joan*, *The Jim Backus Show*, *Gilligan's Island*, *Blondie*.

Bad Ronald
US 1974   74m   colour   TVM
Lorimar

A teenage killer is hidden in the attic by his mother. When she dies, new tenants find him still there.
Silly, tasteless melodrama, put over with some style.

w Andrew Peter Marin, *novel* John Holbrook Vance
d Buzz Kulik

Kim Hunter, Scott Jacoby, Pippa Scott, Anita Sorsaut, John Larch

Badel, Alan (1923–). Incisive, aquiline British leading actor whose TV appearances have been surprisingly rare but include a series, *The Count of Monte Cristo*, Pinter's *The Lover* (BAFTA award 1964), *Trilby* and *The Winslow Boy*.

The Badge or the Cross
aka: *Sarge: The Badge or the Cross*
US 1971   98m   colour   TVM
Universal (David Levy)

When his fiancée is killed by a bomb meant for him, a cop becomes a priest, in which guise he later solves the crime.
Heavy-going pilot for a short-lived series. Another pilot was *The Priest Killer*.

w Don M. Mankiewicz   *d* Richard A. Colla

George Kennedy, Ricardo Montalban, Diane Baker, Larry Gates

Badge 714: see Dragnet

Baer, Max Jnr (1937–). Giant-size American actor, seen almost exclusively as Jethro in the long-running *Beverly Hillbillies*.

Baffled!
GB 1971 96m colour TVM
ITC/Arena (Philip Leacock)

A racing driver has a prophetic dream which leads him into a very involved murder plot.
Weird and fathomless hotchpotch which wastes a lot of talent.

w Theodore Apstein d Philip Leacock ph Ken Hodges m Richard Hill

Leonard Nimoy, Susan Hampshire, Vera Miles, Jewel Blanch, Rachel Roberts, Valerie Taylor, Ray Brooks, Angharad Rees

BAFTA: see British Academy of Film and Television Arts

Bailey, Raymond (1904–). American character actor who after playing innumerable small film roles became a nationally known character as the harassed banker Mr Drysdale in *The Beverly Hillbillies*.

The Baileys of Balboa
US 1964 39 × 25m bw
CBS/Richelieu (Bob Sweeney)

Episodes in the life of a beachcombing family.
Disappointing comedy series: no laughs.

Paul Ford, Judy Carne, Sterling Holloway, John Dehner

Baily, Leslie (1906–). British producer, remembered for his nostalgic 'Scrapbook' series on radio and TV.

Bain, Barbara (1932–). Cool American leading lady who starred with some success in *Mission Impossible* and with less in *Space 1999*.

Baird, John Logie (1888–1946). British inventor of the first mechanical system of television, also later of a colour system and videodisc.

The Bait *
US 1972 74m colour TVM
Spelling–Goldberg

An undercover policewoman lures a girl-killer into a trap.
Smart suspenser which oddly failed as a pilot; two years later along came *Police Woman*.

w Don M. Mankiewicz, Gordon Botler d Leonard Horn

Donna Mills, Michael Constantine, William Devane, June Lockhart

Baker, Hylda (1909–). Jerky little British character comedienne, at her most exuberantly typical in *Nearest and Dearest*.

Baker, Richard (1925–). British newsreader and presenter, a sympathetic and familiar presence of the sixties and seventies.

Baker, Robert S. (1916–). British executive producer who with his partner Monty Berman was responsible for most of ATV's filmed adventure series: *The Saint, Gideon's Way, The Baron, The Persuaders*, etc.

Baker, Tom (1941–). Gaunt character actor who in the mid-seventies took over the title role in the long-running *Dr Who*.

Bakewell, Joan (c 1942–). British presenter and interviewer whose greatest hour was on BBC2's *Late Night Line Up* during the late sixties.

balance. Material added to a schedule to give seriousness.

Ball Four
US 1976 5 × 25m colour (VTR)
CBS (Don Segall)

Life in the locker room of a baseball club.
Awesomely unfunny comedy series.

cr Jim Bouton, Marvin Kitman, Vic Ziegel

Jim Bouton, Jack Somack, David-James Carroll

Ball, Lucille (1910–). America's favourite female clown, who became nationally loved for her willingness to have a go at everything, even to fit her baby into the dictates of a weekly series. With her then husband Desi Arnaz she founded Desilu Studios and became her own producer and distributor; her comedy shows under various titles turned simple situations and knockabout into high art. *I Love Lucy, Here's Lucy, The Lucy Show*, plus innumerable specials and guest appearances. A two-hour special, *CBS Salutes Lucy*, was shown in 1977 and encapsulates her career.

Banacek: see Mystery Movie and Detour to Nowhere

Banana Splits *
US 1968–70 125 × 25m colour
Hanna–Barbera

Freewheeling miscellany for children: cartoons and a live adventure serial, hosted by a puppet rock group. Some bright ideas.

Banjo Hackett
US 1976 99m colour TVM
Columbia

Adventures of a wandering cowboy and a small orphan boy.
A failed pilot, and no wonder: aimless, slow-moving sentimental goo.

LUCILLE BALL, an always-likeable light comedienne, unexpectedly became one of the queens of TV and allegedly one of the richest women in America. All the top names appeared on her shows: here she indulges in slapstick with John Wayne and in song-and-dance with George Burns.

w Ken Trevey   *d* Andrew V. McLaglen

Don Meredith

Banner, Bob (1921–   ). American producer, mainly of musical specials: Carol Channing, Dinah Shore, Peggy Fleming, Liberace, etc.

Banner, John (1910–73). Austrian–American character actor, a chubby comedian or sometimes a heavy villain. TV series: *Hogan's Heroes, Chicago Teddy Bears*.

Banyon *
aka: *Walk Up and Die*
US 1971   97m   colour   TVM
Warner (Richard Alan Simmons)

Adventures of a Los Angeles private eye of the thirties. Smart-looking nostalgia and not a bad plot for a pilot; but the hero is humourless and the show was short-lived (running only 13 episodes), as four years later was its almost indistinguishable successor *City of Angels*, which even used the same building for the hero's office.

w Ed Adamson   *d* Robert Day

Robert Forster, Jose Ferrer, Darren McGavin, Herb Edelman

Barbary Coast *
GB title: *In Old San Francisco*
US 1975   74m or 98m (two versions)   colour   TVM
Paramount (Douglas Heyes)

A police detective with a penchant for disguise blackmails a saloon proprietor into helping him.
Ambitious pilot for a rumbustious nineties series. Alas, the elements did not jell.

w Douglas Heyes   *d* Bill Bixby

William Shatner, Dennis Cole, Lynda Day George, Charles Aidman, Michael Ansara

†Dennis Cole may have been all at sea, but his replacement, Doug McClure, was merely stolid, and the show, retitled *Cash and Cable*, folded after 13 × 50m episodes. Producer: Cy Chermak.

Barbeau, Adrienne (1947–   ). American leading lady with sharp edges. A hit in *Maude*; later in demand as guest star.

Barefoot in the Park
US 1970   12 × 25m   colour
ABC/Paramount

Life for young marrieds in a New York cold water flat.
Neil Simon's amusing play is rather pointlessly given a black cast. Nobody cheered.

Scoey Mitchell, Tracey Reed, Thelma Carpenter

Baretta*
US 1975–7   82 × 50m   colour
ABC/Universal/Public Arts–Roy Huggins (Jo Swerling Jnr)

A redrafting of *Toma* when the star refused to continue. The new man is still a plainclothes cop with a penchant for disguise; this time he has a pet parrot and the urban milieu is overpowering; also, from the first episode he's hot to get the gangsters who shot his girl in mistake for him. (See *The Badge or the Cross*.) The mixture turned out to have great appeal to the young.

cr Stephen J. Cannell

Robert Blake, Tom Ewell, Dana Elcar, Michael D. Roberts

Barker, Ronnie (1929–). Cheerful, avuncular British character comedian; with Ronnie Corbett one of *The Two Ronnies,* and remarkable for his precision, his enunciation, his characterizations and his ability to smile his way through dubious material and make maiden aunts love it. Also popular solo as the old lag in *Porridge* and *Going Straight*.

The Barkleys
US 1972   26 × 25m   colour
NBC/Hanna–Barbera

Adventures of a family headed by a loud-mouthed suburbanite; they just happen to be dogs. A take-off of *All in the Family* which didn't quite work.

Barkworth, Peter (1929–). Leading British character actor, always in well-bred surroundings, sometimes as sympathetic silly ass but often with deeper meaning. 1979 series: *Telford's Change*.

Barmitzvah Boy**
GB 1976   75m   colour (VTR)
BBC

Tensions rise in a Jewish family as a teenager disappears on his barmitzvah day.
Amusing, warmly written but very slight comedy which was a great popular success.

w Jack Rosenthal   *d* Michael Tuchner

Jeremy Steyn, Bernard Spear, Maria Charles, Adrienne Posta

Barnaby Jones*
US 1972–   ? × 50m   colour
CBS/Quinn Martin (Philip Salzman)

A retired private detective takes over the practice when his son is killed.
Griff had the same idea at precisely the same time, but Lorne Greene flopped in one season while his rival has so far carried through seven seasons with ease. Neat, interesting mysteries with high life settings, adequately produced and with a highly personable old star.

Buddy Ebsen, Lee Meriwether

Barney Miller*
US 1975–   ? × 25m   colour (VTR)
ABC/Columbia/Danny Arnold (Chris Hayward)

'Realistic' but funny episodes in a New York police precinct house.
Raucous and often penetrating humour with tragic undercurrents give this series much in common with *M*A*S*H* and *All in the Family,* but it travels somewhat less well.

Hal Linden, Barbara Barrie, Abe Vigoda, Jack Soo, Max Gail, Ron Glass, James Gregory

† In 1977 Abe Vigoda left the show and appeared in a spin-off, *Fish,* creators Danny Arnold, Theodore Flicker.

The Baron
GB 1965   30 × 50m   colour
ITC (Robert Baker, Monty Berman)

An antique dealer is really an undercover agent.
Routinely glossy adventures, pleasingly implausible plots, mid-Atlantic atmosphere, vaguely based on the John Creasey character.

script supervisor Terry Nation

Steve Forrest, Sue Lloyd

Barr, Patrick (1908–). British character actor, a popular TV leading man of the fifties.

Barr, Robert (–). British writer and producer who had much to do with the shape of *Spycatcher* and *Z Cars.*

Barratt, Michael (1928–). British linkman; formerly an investigative TV journalist.

Barrett, Rona (–). American columnist who covers Hollywood in print and latterly on TV.

Barry, Gene (1921–) (Eugene Klass). American entertainer and light actor who made his greatest mark on TV in a series of impeccably dressed roles with just the right amount of cuff showing. *Bat Masterson, Burke's Law, The Name of the Game, The Adventurer.*

Bass, Alfie (1920–). Diminutive British cockney actor who during the sixties was a national figure on TV as 'Excused Boots' Bisley, though when that particular star waned he found no further leading roles and returned to the stage. Series: *The Army Game, Bootsie and Snudge,* later episodes of *Till Death Us Do Part.*

The Bastard
US 1978   2 × 95m   colour
Universal for Operation Prime Time (John Wilder)

A combination of unlikely circumstances sends a French peasant boy of the 1780s to fame and fortune in America.

GENE BARRY always seemed concerned to have the right amount of cuff showing, and profited from this image through several series. Here he lords it over a magazine empire in *The Name of the Game*.

Stiff historical charade, from the first in a whole dynasty of novels. The actors appear to have been only recently introduced to their clothes, and for the first hilarious half-hour all speak with ze French accent.

w Guerdon Trueblood, *novel* John Jakes *d* Lee H. Katzin *ph* Michael Hugo *m* John Addison

Andrew Stevens, Patricia Neal, Lorne Greene, Tom Bosley, Buddy Ebsen, William Daniels, James Gregory, Olivia Hussey, Cameron Mitchell, Henry Morgan, Eleanor Parker, Donald Pleasence, Barry Sullivan, William Shatner, Keenan Wynn

'As a serious contender in the field of telefilms, it falls on its face ... as bloodless and unconvincing as a school pageant.' – *Daily Variety*

† The film was shot in six weeks at a cost of three million dollars.

Bat Masterson*
US 1958–60 108 × 25m bw
United Artists

Adventures of a dandified gunfighter.
Silly but mildly amusing exploits which made a star of Gene Barry.

Bate, Anthony (1928–). British character actor with a slightly supercilious air; his best chance came with the lead in *Intimate Strangers*.

Bates, Richard (1937–). British producer. *Please Sir, Public Eye, A Man of Our Times, Helen – A Woman of Today, Intimate Strangers, Love for Lydia, The Prime of Miss Jean Brodie*, etc.

Batman*
US 1965–7 120 × 25m colour
ABC/TCF/Greenway (William Dozier)

The first 'camp' TV series, based on the old comic strip by Bob Kane about the 'caped crusader' who dashes around in his Batmobile saving society from such supercriminals as the Riddler, the Joker and the Penguin. Adults soon tired of the stereotyped spoof, clearly shot on a shoestring, but kids enjoyed it, especially when exclamations such as Splat! and Zowie! appeared onscreen during the fight scenes.

Adam West, Burt Ward, Yvonne Craig, Alan Napier; with frequent guests Frank Gorshin, Cesar Romero, Burgess Meredith

† The production was spurred by the theatrical re-release of the old *Batman* serials, which were a great hit with campus audiences. In 1966 a movie feature was made.

Battered
US 1977 96m colour TVM
Charles Fries

A frustrated husband whose job is threatened becomes a wife-beater.
Exploitative social drama.

w Richard and Esther Shapiro *d* John Llewellyn Moxey

Dennis Weaver, Sally Struthers, Tyne Daly, Larry Hagman, Melvyn Douglas

Battlestar Galactica *
US 1978   140m   colour
ABC/Universal/Glen Larson (Leslie Stevens)

Survivors from a distant galactic war work their way towards earth, hampered by the Cylons whose aim is to destroy mankind.
Lumbering, humourless space fantasy in the wake of *Star Wars*: the hardware is the undoubted star, but even that becomes repetitive, and the actors and script are boring.

w/d Richard A. Colla, Glen Larson   *sp* JOHN DYKSTRA, Joe Goss, Karl Miller   *costumes* Jean-Pierre Dorleac

Lorne Greene, Dirk Benedict, Richard Hatch

Batty, Peter (1931–   ). British historical documentarist who after long experience with BBC and ATV went independent and regularly turns out such features as *The Battle of the Bulge*, *The Birth of the Bomb* and *Operation Barbarossa*.

Baxter, Raymond (1922–   ). British sports and news commentator, long with BBC; in the sixties became best known for introducing a weekly science programme, *Tomorrow's World*.

Baxter, Stanley (1929–   ). Scottish comedian and mimic who had a rather unsatisfactory career as a film star but in the mid-seventies became nationally known for his annual comedy spectaculars in each of which he plays scores of roles. His talent is undeniable, though he relies overmuch on blue material.

Bayldon, Geoffrey (1924–   ). Ascetic looking British actor, best known on TV in the title role of *Catweazle*.

BBC (British Broadcasting Corporation). The 'voice of London' is not state controlled, but was founded by royal charter in 1927 and exists by virtue of a licence fee collected from all who have receivers on their premises. It now operates two TV channels and four national radio channels as well as local radio. In the days of its first director general, John Reith, it was undoubtedly puritanical and maiden-auntish, but the advent of commercial TV made BBC1 at least very competitive for top ratings.

BBC3: see That Was the Week that Was

The Beachcomber
US 1960   39 × 25m   bw
Filmaster

A businessman throws up his career and goes to the South Seas in search of truth.
Vaguely inspirational dramas which don't really have enough punch.

Cameron Mitchell

Beachcombers
Canada 1972–4   39 × 25m   colour
CBC

Children help a middle-aged man who prefers to live a rugged existence on the beaches north of Vancouver.
Moderately pleasant open-air series for young people.

Beacon Hill
US 1975   13 × 50m   colour (VTR)
CBS/Robert Stigwood (Jacqueline Babbin, Beryl Vertue)

Life in an upper-class Boston home during the first part of the century.
An attempt to re-create the British success *Upstairs, Downstairs* for American audiences. It failed.

w Sidney Carroll   *m* Marvin Hamlisch

Steven Elliott, Nancy Marchand, George Rose, Beatrice Straight, Don Blakely, Roy Cooper, David Dukes, Edward Herrmann

Bean, Orson (1928–   ) (Dallas Burrows). American comedian and talk show host, popular on TV from the mid-fifties to the mid-sixties.

Beany and Cecil
US 1961–2   78 × 25m   colour
Bob Clampett

Adventures of a boy who can fly and a serpent who gets seasick.
Smoothly animated cartoon adventures.

The Bearcats *
US 1971   13 × 50m   colour
CBS/Filmways (David Friedkin, Morton Fine)

In 1914, two freelance investigators roam the southwest in a Stutz Bearcat.
Ambitious semi-western which didn't quite work: too many Mexican accents, perhaps.

cr/executive producer Douglas Heyes

Rod Taylor, Dennis Cole

† See also *Powder Keg*, which was the pilot.

The Beasts Are on the Streets
US 1978   95m   colour   TVM
NBC/Hanna–Barbera (Harry R. Sherman)

Wild animals escape from a safari park.
Predictable panic and suspense movie, rather tortuously plotted and at its best when the beasts are in close-up.

w Laurence Heath   *d* Peter Hunt   *ph* Charles G. Arnold   *m* Gerald Fried

Carol Lynley, Dale Robinette, Anna Lee, Billy Green Bush, Philip Michael Thomas

The Beatles
US 1965   39 × 22m   colour
King Features

Fragmented adventures and singalongs with the mop-headed quartet, quite well animated by Halas and Batchelor.

Beauty and the Beast *
US 1976   76m   colour (VTR)
Hallmark Hall of Fame/Palm Productions (Thomas M. C. Johnston)

A more or less faithful version of the classic fairy tale, with scenes filmed in England. Somewhat uninspired.

w Sherman Yellen   *d* Fielder Cook   *m* Ron Goodwin

George C. Scott, Trish Van Devere, Virginia McKenna, Bernard Lee

Beauty, Bonny, Daisy, Violet, Grace and Geoffrey Morton. Prizewinning (BAFTA 1974) Thames TV documentary about the rearing of farm horses, directed by Frank Cvitanovitch.

Beavers, Louise (1902–62). Big, warm-hearted, black character actress who in 1960 starred in the series *Beulah*.

Beckinsale, Richard (1945–79). British light leading man of the new school, familiar on TV in the series *The Lovers*, *Rising Damp* and *Porridge*.

Beeny, Christopher (1941–   ). Self-effacing British light character man, former child actor. *Upstairs, Downstairs*, *The Rag Trade*.

Beery, Noah Jnr (1913–   ). Dependable American character actor who graduated from rustic types to genial uncles. TV series include *Circus Boy*, *Hondo*, *Doc Elliott*, *The Rockford Files*.

Beg Borrow or Steal
US 1973   74m   colour   TVM
Universal (Stanley Kallis)

Three disabled men plan a museum heist.
Modest caper yarn which becomes tasteless in its effort to be different.

w Paul Playdon   *d* David Lowell Rich

Mike Connors, Kent McCord, Michael Cole, Russell Johnson, Joel Fabiani, Henry Beckman

THE BEATLES were discovered through television, though they later treated it warily. Here around 1962 they perform in a Granada TV late-night show. Left to right Ringo Starr, George Harrison, Paul McCartney, John Lennon.

Behind Closed Doors (US 1959). A half hour anthology series allegedly revealing secrets of naval intelligence in World War II. Narrator: Bruce Gordon.

Bell, David (1936–). British light entertainment producer who has successfully handled Danny La Rue, Stanley Baxter, Bruce Forsyth and Benny Hill.

The Bell Telephone Hour. A splendid example of enlightened sponsorship, this show has been a leading provider of light culture – ballet, opera, music – to the American networks for nearly 30 years. In 1976, to celebrate the centenary of the telephone, a superb variety special, *Jubilee*, was mounted by Gary Smith and Dwight Hemion; Bing Crosby and Liza Minnelli introduced many famous stars.

Bellamy, Ralph (1904–). Veteran American character actor who played second leads in Hollywood from the early thirties, became a stage star, and remains in demand for TV guest spots. Series include *Man Against Crime, The Eleventh Hour, The Most Deadly Game, The Survivors, Hunter, Wheels.*

Ben Casey *
US 1960–5   153 × 50m   bw
ABC/Bing Crosby Productions (James E. Moser)

Cases of a tough, intense young doctor on the staff of a big hospital.
A downbeat show which succeeded partly because of its air of startling realism, and partly from the appeal of its young and old leads.

cr James Moser

Vince Edwards, Sam Jaffe

'It has become popular because so many like to hear others talk about their operations.' – Don Miller

Ben Hall
GB–Australia 1975   13 × 50m   colour (VTR)
BBC–ABC

Stories of an Australian outlaw.
Modest, forgettable action series.

p Neil McCallum

Jon Finch, John Castle

RALPH BELLAMY had one of the longest careers in Hollywood, and even in his seventies seemed never to refuse a TV role. Here in *The Survivors* (with Lana Turner) he plays the ailing head of a banking empire.

Ben Spray. A TV play by Peter Nichols about a sacked schoolteacher who goes to a hilarious party with a girl he has just met. In the *Lucky Jim* tradition. Originally produced by Granada in 1961 (Ian Hendry); revived by LWT in 1972, with John Alderton.

Benaderet, Bea (1906–68). American TV comedienne, the perfect neighbour for Gracie Allen in many seasons of *The Burns and Allen Show* and later the star of her own *Petticoat Junction*.

Bennett, Alan (1934–). British revue star (*Beyond the Fringe*) whose work as a TV writer is always interesting if widely spaced: *A Day Out, Famous Gossips, Sunset Across the Bay*, etc. Contributed six plays to LWT's 1978–9 season.

Bennett, Harve (*c* 1925–) (Harvey Fischman). American series producer who concocted *Six Million Dollar Man* and *Bionic Woman*.

The Benny Hill Show. An occasional one-hour show from Thames TV in which the star writes and performs all his own material, usually consisting of very old jokes turned into doggerel song, impressions of celebrities, and moderately blue sketches. Over the years his chief aides have been Bob Todd and Patricia Hayes, with John Robins as most frequent director. BAFTA award 1971, best light entertainment.

Benny, Jack (1894–1974) (Benjamin Kubelsky). American stand-up comedian who made international trademarks of his meanness and his 'slow burn'. Admired everywhere, he had a reasonably distinguished film career but was if anything even more distinguished in radio and TV, both in situation comedy and musical specials, and became a national monument.

Bentine, Michael (1922–). Anglo–Peruvian comedian who has purveyed zany nonsense for 20 years in recurring series such as *The Goon Show, It's a Square World* and *Potty Time*.

Bentley, John (1916–). Stalwart British leading man of the fifties, of the strong silent type. Little TV between *African Patrol* in the fifties and *Crossroads* in the seventies.

Berg, Gertrude (1899–1966) (Gertrude Edelstein). Amply proportioned American character actress famous as Molly in *The Goldbergs*, which began on radio in the forties and on TV in various forms up to 1956. There was also a movie version in 1951. See also *Mrs G. Goes to College*.

Berle, Milton (1908–) (Mendel Berlinger). Brash, disarming American vaudevillian who never quite managed movie fame but in the fifties became Mr Television and indulged in every known form of slap-

stick and schmaltz. His later career was sketchy but he never gave up guest appearances.

Berlin Affair
US 1970   97m   colour   TVM
Universal (E. Jack Neuman, Paul Donnelly)

A professional killer loses his value when he falls in love.
Complex, rather unpleasant international suspenser.

w Peter Penduik, E. Jack Neuman   *d* David Lowell Rich

Darren McGavin, Fritz Weaver, Brian Kelly, Claude Dauphin, Pascale Petit

Berman, Monty (1913–). See Baker, Robert S.

Bernardi, Herschel (1923–). American character actor, usually in sympathetic but lugubrious ethnic roles; a Broadway hit as star of *Fiddler on the Roof*. TV series: *Peter Gunn, Arnie*.

Berns, Seymour (1914–). American executive producer and ideas man, latterly with Four Star and Columbia; formerly in radio and director of a wide range of shows.

Bernstein, Sidney (Lord Bernstein) (1899–). British tycoon, founder of Granada Television.

LORD BERNSTEIN. One of the most impressive success stories in television was his founding of Granada TV as a major British station and his preservation of it as essentially a family business.

Berry, Ken (c 1929–   ). American comic actor of the meek and mild type. Series include *F Troop*, *Mayberry RFD*.

Bert D'Angelo, Superstar
US 1976   13 × 50m   colour
Quinn Martin (Mort Fine)

Clumsily titled and generally unhappy spin-off from *Streets of San Francisco*, with Paul Sorvino as a belligerent New York cop on loan-out.
The spin-off episode generated good tension between him and the regulars, but in the series he badly needed someone to spark with.

Beryl's Lot (GB 1973–6). Fitfully scheduled working-class series from Yorkshire TV, varying from 25 to 50 minutes, about a milkman's wife trying to better herself; with Carmel McSharry.

The Best of Families*
US 1977   8 × 50m   colour (VTR)
PBS/Children's Television Workshop (Gareth Davies)

In New York between 1880 and 1900, the fortunes of three families, of very different social backgrounds, intermingle.
Social history rather than drama, this stylish production was surprisingly badly received by the critics.

cr Naomi Foner   *w* Corinne Jacker and others

William Prince, Milo O'Shea, Guy Boyd, Victor Garber, William Hart

Best Sellers. Umbrella title devised by Universal in 1976 to cover the novelizations, in various shapes and sizes, which followed *Rich Man, Poor Man*. They were *Captains and the Kings*, *Once an Eagle*, *The Rhinemann Exchange*, *Seventh Avenue*, *79 Park Avenue*, *Aspen*, *Wheels*, *The Dark Secret of Harvest Home*, *Brave New World* and *Women in White* and all are noted separately in this volume.
A separate series, commissioned for syndicated stations, was called *Operation Prime Time*, and the first four novels under this heading were *Testimony of Two Men*, *The Bastard*, *Evening in Byzantium* and *The Immigrants*.

The Betrayal
aka: *The Companion*
US 1974   74m   colour   TVM
Metromedia

A girl takes a job as companion to a lonely widow and sets her up as a robbery victim.
Fairly well characterized suspenser which runs out of steam.

w James Miller   *d* Gordon Hessler

Amanda Blake, Tisha Sterling, Dick Haymes, Sam Groom

The Betty Hutton Show: see Goldie

The Betty White Show*
US 1977   ?22 × 25m   colour
Viacom/MTM

A middle-aged TV actress makes a police woman series with her ex-husband as producer.
Wisecracking comedy, smartly performed; but the public maintained its tradition of not liking backstage shows.

Betty White, John Hillerman

The Beverly Hillbillies*
US 1962–70   212 × 25m   106 bw, 106 colour
Filmways (Al Simon)

The Clampetts strike oil and move into Beverly Hills.
A hokey idea which surprised everyone by working at full steam for several years before the strain began to show: the Clampetts became America's favourite family.

cr Paul Henning

Buddy Ebsen, Irene Ryan, Donna Douglas, Max Baer Jnr, Raymond Bailey, Nancy Kulp

Bewes, Rodney (1937–   ). British light comic actor, familiar as one of *The Likely Lads*. Also played solo in *Dear Mother, Love Albert*.

Bewitched*
US 1964–71   252 × 25m   colour
ABC/Columbia (Harry Ackerman/Bill Asher)

An attractive witch gets married and has a family, but is unable to resist the temptation to turn the magic on by twitching her nose.
Tolerable and popular fantasy comedy enlivened by the number of older stars who popped in occasionally as magical uncles and aunts.

cr William Dozier, Harry Ackerman

Elizabeth Montgomery, Dick York (five seasons), Dick Sargent (thereafter), Agnes Moorehead, Maurice Evans, Marion Lorne, George Tobias

Beyond the Bermuda Triangle
US 1975   74m   colour   TVM
Playboy (Ron Roth)

Sequel to *Satan's Triangle*: a businessman searches for friends who have disappeared in the fatal area.
Open-air melodramatic nonsense: quite watchable.

w Charles A. McDaniel   *d* William A. Graham

Fred MacMurray, Sam Groom, Donna Mills, Suzanne Reed

Biff Baker USA
US 1953   26 × 25m   bw
Universal

An American couple travels behind the Iron Curtain.
Ingenuous cold war thick-ear.

Alan Hale Jnr, Randy Stuart

Big Blue Marble*. American children's series showing how experience can be enjoyably enlarged; basically a magazine format with *Sesame Street* trimmings. Created and produced by Henry Fownes; musical director Norman Paris; animation by Ron Campbell; produced weekly from 1974 for the ITT Corporation.

Big Breadwinner Hog
GB 1969 8 × 50m bw (VTR)
Granada

An evil young London gangster stops at nothing to get his way.
Tawdry mixture of *Scarface* and *Brighton Rock*, much criticized for its violence.

w/p Robin Chapman

Peter Egan

Big Eddie
US 1975 9 × 25m colour
CBS/Deezdemandoze/Persky–Denoff (Hy Averback)

Family problems of the owner of a New York arena.
Forgettable comedy.

cr Bill Persky, Sam Denoff

Sheldon Leonard, Sheree North, Quinn Cummings, Alan Oppenheimer

Big G: see Empire

Big Hawaii
GB title: *Danger in Paradise*
US 1977 13 × 50m colour
Filmways (Perry Lafferty)

A wanderer returns to the family's Hawaii ranch to help his ailing father.
Bland, uninteresting series developed from a promising pilot, *Danger in Paradise*. The scenery is all that's worth watching.

Cliff Potts, John Dehner, Bill Lucking

'A rebel son and his brawling buddy take on all comers in a turbulent drama set against the allure of the islands' – publicity

The Big Rip Off
US 1974 97m colour TVM

A gambling con-man confounds his enemies and solves a murder.

BIG HAWAII. The smiles quickly faltered, along with the series, but for a while it looked as though a new television family had been created. John Dehner, Lucia Stralser, Bill Lucking, Cliff Potts.

Slick, fairly entertaining pilot for a *Mystery Movie* segment (McCoy).

w Roland Kibbee, Dean Hargrove   *d* Dean Hargrove

Tony Curtis, Roscoe Lee Browne, Larry Hagman, John Dehner, Brenda Vaccaro

Big Rose
US 1974   74m   colour   TVM
TCF

Adventures of a middle-aged lady private eye.
Not unentertaining for a failed pilot.

w Andy Lewis   *d* Paul Krasny

Shelley Winters, Barry Primus, Lonny Chapman, Peggy Walton, Joan Van Ark

The Big Time: see Rantzen, Esther

Big Town
US 1952–7   169 × 25m   bw

Adventures of a crusading magazine editor.
Routine time-filler, syndicated under various titles including *Heart of the City*, *By-Line Steve Wilson*, *Headline* and *City Assignment*.

Mark Stevens

The Big Valley *
US 1965–8   112 × 50m   colour
ABC/Four Star

Tales of a California ranching family in the 1870s.
Cleanly made stories, mostly domestic, with plenty of guest stars.

Barbara Stanwyck, Richard Long, Peter Breck, Linda Evans, Lee Majors

Bilko: see You'll Never Get Rich

Bill Brand *
GB 1976   11 × 50m   colour (VTR)
Thames/Stella Richman

Problems of a radical left-wing MP.
Downbeat dramatic series, revered by the critics but rejected by the public.

w Trevor Griffiths   *d* Michael Lindsay-Hogg

Jack Shepherd

The Bill Cosby Show (US 1969).
Syndicated NBC half-hour which ran two seasons. The star played the athletic coach at a Los Angeles high school, and the emphasis was on warmth rather than comedy. Also starred: Joyce Bullifant, Lee Weaver.

The Bill Dana Show (US 1965).
NBC half-hour comedy with the star in his familiar portrayal of Latin immigrant Jose Jiminez, here a bellboy in a New York hotel. It ran one-and-a-half seasons, and featured Don Adams, Jonathan Harris and Gary Crosby.

Billy Liar (GB 1973–4).
The young northern fantasist created for novel and film by Keith Waterhouse and Willis Hall was turned by them quite successfully into TV situation comedy. A minor stir was created by Dad's bad language, but generally speaking the half-hour series was popular even though it clearly lacked originality. Produced and directed by Stuart Allen, with Jeff Rawle and George A. Cooper. An American version was mooted in 1977 but didn't happen.

Billy, Portrait of a Street Kid
US 1977   96m   colour   TVM
Mark Carliner

A black ghetto youth finds his problems overwhelming and attempts suicide.
Slow, downbeat and not especially well made, this tedious movie offers neither entertainment nor uplift.

w/d Steve Gethers   *book* *Peoples* by Robert C. S. Downs   *ph* William J. Jurgensen   *m* Fred Karlin

LeVar Burton, Tina Andrews, Michael Constantine, Ossie Davis

The Bing Crosby Show
US 1964   28 × 25m   bw
ABC/Bing Crosby Productions

Domestic comedy about a middle-aged couple with two teenage daughters and a long-staying friend.
Moderately pleasant but entirely unremarkable.

Bing Crosby, Beverly Garland, Frank McHugh

Bionic Woman *
US 1976–7   35 × 50m   colour
MCA (Harve Bennett)

After the six-million-dollar-man, a badly injured girl is scientifically reconstructed and put to work for the CIA.
Initially much effort was made to inject warmth and humanity into this comic strip idea, but within a season our heroine had become just another dumb dame who could run fast and lift weights, with dialogue to match. She and her bionic boyfriend were cancelled by the network in April 1978.

Lindsay Wagner, Richard Anderson

† Also in for guest shots during the series were *Bionic Boy* (played by Vincent Van Patten) and *Bionic Dog*.

Birch, Paul (*c* 1904–   ).
Canadian actor who in 1958 starred as the burly truck driver in *Cannonball*.

bird.
Slang term for satellite.

Birdman
US 1967   26 × 22m   colour
NBC/Hanna–Barbera

An explorer is helped and blessed by the Egyptian sun god, and finds he has special powers to combat evil.
Derivative cartoon series.

THE BIONIC WOMAN and THE SIX MILLION DOLLAR MAN ran successfully in harness for a while, but bad scripts rather than electronic failure were responsible for their demise. Lindsay Wagner, Lee Majors.

The Birdmen
aka: *Escape of the Birdmen*
US 1971 96m colour TVM
Universal (Harve Bennett)

Prisoners of war escape from the Nazis by building a glider and soaring down from the castle parapets into Switzerland.
By *Colditz* out of *The Flight of the Phoenix*: phoney-looking but otherwise passable fantasy.

w David Kidd   *d* Philip Leacock

Doug McClure, Chuck Connors, Richard Basehart, René Auberjonois, Don Knight, Max Baer, Tom Skerritt

Birds of Prey **
US 1972 81m colour TVM
Tomorrow (Alan A. Armer)

A helicopter pilot on traffic duty tracks down an armoured car hold-up.
Smoothly-made actioner with pretensions.

w Robert Boris   *d* William Graham

David Janssen, Ralph Meeker, Elayne Heilveil

Birney, David (1944–). American leading man who became known via *Bridget Loves Bernie*, in which he met his wife Meredith Baxter Birney, then known as Meredith Baxter. Later TV series: *Serpico*.

The Birth of Television **
GB 1977 90m colour/bw (VTR)
BBC

A memoir of TV's early days, with extracts from programmes and interviews with survivors. A valuable research tool.

w/p Bruce Norman

Gracie Fields, Dinah Sheridan, Arthur Askey, Cyril Fletcher, Leslie Mitchell

Bishop, Joey (1918–) (Joseph Abraham Gottlieb). American nightclub comedian who had sporadic success in TV. See *The Joey Bishop Show*.

Bixby, Bill (1934–). Unassuming American light leading man, one of the most familiar faces on TV. Series include *My Favorite Martian, The Courtship of Eddie's Father, The Magician, The Incredible Hulk*.

The Black and White Minstrel Show. Long-running fast-moving BBC variety show, created by George Inns. Comedy turns alternated with medleys from the George Mitchell singers. Racial groups objected to the men's blackface make-up, but this added immeasurably to the old-fashioned style of the enterprise, and the show was an immense hit throughout the sixties, stimulating several touring versions of the show and creating such stars as Dai Francis, Tony Mercer and John Boulter. It lasted 21 seasons, from 1958 to 1978.

BBC copyright

THE BLACK AND WHITE MINSTREL SHOW gave traditional pleasure to millions for over twenty years, and the BBC turned a deaf ear to complaints about its 'racist' tendencies. Dai Francis, pictured here, was the undoubted star.

Black Beauty: see The Adventures of Black Beauty

Black, Cilla (1943–). British pop vocalist who since 1968 has had her own winter series of Saturday specials, in which she carefully nurtures her Liverpool accent and working-class gaucherie.

black crushing. Technical term for unsatisfactory lighting, under-exposed so that everything dark merges into one colour.

Black Market Baby
US 1977   96m   colour   TVM
ABC

A pregnant but unmarried college student plays into the hands of a 'babies for sale' racket.
Yucky teenage melodrama.

Desi Arnaz Jr, Linda Purl, Bill Bixby, Jessica Walter, Tom Bosley, David Doyle

'She loves him and wants their baby, but a ruthless adoption ring wants it more!' – publicity

Black Noon *
US 1971   73m   colour   TVM
Columbia (Andrew Fenady)

In the old west, a young minister and his wife arrive at a remote town run by diabolists.
Preposterous nonsense with a winning way.

w Andrew J. Fenady   d Bernard Kowalski

Roy Thinnes, Ray Milland, Yvette Mimieux, Gloria Grahame, Lynn Loring, Henry Silva

Black Saddle
US 1958–9   44 × 25m   bw
ABC/Four Star

A gunfighter turned lawyer tours the southwest after the Civil War.
Adequate western time-passer.

Peter Breck, Russell Johnson

Black Water Gold
US 1969   75m   colour   TVM
Metromedia

A scuba diver finds lost treasure from a Spanish galleon, but has trouble profiting from it.

31

Naïvely made and written adventure piece.

w/d Alan Landsburg

Bradford Dillman, Aron Kincaid, Keir Dullea, Ricardo Montalban, France Nuyen

Blackman, Honor (1926–). British leading lady from the Rank charm school; after years as an English rose, she blossomed forth in 1961 as the leather-garbed, judo-kicking Cathy Gale in the early series of *The Avengers*; subsequently her best chances were in the theatre.

Blacks in TV. Black actors have always had a place in TV, albeit an inferior one in the fifties, when *Amos 'n' Andy*, played by two whites in blackface, caused protests and had to be taken off the air. Subsequently blacks could be starred, but usually playing servants as in *Beulah*, or assistants as in *East Side West Side*, and *NYPD*. The breakthrough came in 1967 with *I Spy*, in which Bill Cosby was seen as Robert Culp's absolute equal in girl chasing as well as spy catching. Thereafter blacks were seen doing just as well as whites in *The Mod Squad, Mission Impossible, Hogan's Heroes, The Silent Force, The Young Lawyers, Julia, Tenafly* and many others. From 1970 on the success of *Sanford and Son* made all-black shows popular, and there have subsequently been two or three always on the air: *That's My Mama, Barefoot in the Park, Good Times, The Jeffersons*. The ultimate tribute was paid when TV movie specials began to atone for hundreds of years of black subordination: *The Autobiography of Miss Jane Pittman, Roots, King*.

The Blackwell Story
US 1957   74m   bw   TVM
Columbia/Playhouse 90

In the 1830s America's first woman doctor gains respect.
Very modest TV movie from the struggling early days.

d James Neilson

Joanne Dru, Dan O'Herlihy, Marshall Thompson, Charles Korvin, Keith Larsen

Blair, Janet (1921–) (Martha Lafferty). American leading lady of the forties whose chief TV outing was as Henry Fonda's wife in *The Smith Family*.

Blake, Amanda (1929–) (Beverly Louise Neill). American leading lady of the fifties who after a desultory career in films and TV landed the role of Miss Kitty in *Gunsmoke* and played it for 19 years.

Blake, Robert (1934–) (Michael Gubitosi). American character who started with Our Gang and developed along the lines of a Dead End Kid, finally discovering his star niche in *Baretta*.

Blakely, Susan (1949–). American leading lady, former model, who came to the fore in *Rich Man, Poor Man*.

Blansky's Beauties
US 1977   13 × 25m   colour
Paramount/Garry Marshall

A moral guardian is appointed to look after Las Vegas showgirls.
Fairly dire comedy series which gave its star no room to breathe.

cr Garry Marshall, Bob Brunner, Arthur Silver

Nancy Walker

† The format was tried again in 1978 as *Legs* (changed in mid-season to *Who's Watching the Kids?*).

bleeding whites. Technical term for photography so over-exposed that white sections become 'hot' and run off into other areas.

Bless This House. An absolutely straightforward British (Thames) family sitcom of the seventies which provided Sid James with his last good role, coping with teenage children and his own incompetence. Produced and directed by William G. Stewart for Thames TV, with Diana Coupland, Sally Geeson, Robin Stewart.

Blondie
US 1968   26 × 25m   colour
King/Kayro

The farcical adventures of the Bumstead family, so popular as a comic strip and in the movies, did not work on TV: either the timing was wrong or the new cast failed to appeal.

Will Hutchins, Pat Harty, Jim Backus

Blood Sport
US 1973   74m   colour   TVM
Danny Thomas

A college boy fights his father's wish to make him a football star.
Predictable character melodrama.

w/d Jerrold Friedman

Ben Johnson, Gary Busey, David Doyle, Larry Hagman

The Bloxham Tapes *
GB 1976   50m   colour (VTR)
BBC

An account of the British hypnotist who can project selected subjects back into previous lives; two of them bring back details from 11th-century York and medieval France.
If it's a con trick, it's a good one, and the programme is valuable as a record of what appears to have happened.

The Blue Angels
US 1960   39 × 25m   bw
NTA/Sam Gallu

Exploits of a naval four-man precision flying team. Standard action series of its time.

Mike Galloway, Don Gordon, Dennis Cross, Warner Jones

The Blue Knight*
US 1973   195m approx   colour   TVM
Lorimar (Walter Coblenz)

The life of a Los Angeles cop on the beat.
The first superlength TV movie: the length is wasted on this mundane material, which resists all efforts to give it status.

w E. Jack Neuman, *novel* Joseph Wambaugh   d Robert Butler   ph Michael Margulies

William Holden, Lee Remick, Sam Elliott, Eileen Brennan, Joe Santos

The Blue Knight
US 1975   74m   colour   TVM
Lorimar

Second try for the above: this time the pilot, though shorter, was even slower and duller, and the consequent series had a brief life.

w Albert Rueben   d J. Lee-Thompson

George Kennedy, Alex Rocco, Glynn Turman, Verna Bloom

† The one-hour series which ensued from the George Kennedy pilot was less than a spectacular success and ran 13 episodes. Produced by Joel Rogosin for Lorimar; music by Henry Mancini.

The Blue Light
US 1965   17 × 25m   colour
ABC/TCF

An American spy insinuates himself into Nazi Germany during World War II.
Poorly conceived tall stories.

Robert Goulet

† Four episodes were cobbled together for theatrical release under the title *I Deal in Danger*.

Blue Peter. BBC1's half-hour magazine programme for young people has been a fixture most of the year since the mid-fifties, sometimes appearing twice a week.

Bob and Carol and Ted and Alice
US 1973   12 × 25m   colour
ABC/Columbia/Mike Frankovich (Jim Henerson)

Flabby attempt to translate the wife-swapping film to TV without any wife-swapping.

cr Larry Rosen, Larry Tucker

Bob Urich, Anne Archer, David Spielberg, Anita Gillette

The Bob Crane Show
US 1975   13 × 25m   colour
MTM/NBC (Norman S. Powell, Martin Cohan)

A 42-year-old insurance salesman quits to pursue a medical career.
An interesting comedy with a point to make. It didn't make it.

Bob Crane, Trisha Hart, Ronny Graham, Todd Susman, James Sutorius

The Bob Cummings Show*
US 1961   22 × 25m   bw
CBS/Revue

The star in his last major series played an adventurer and troubleshooter with a choice of personal planes.
Cummings was more at home with the farce comedy of his earlier series.

Robert Cummings, Roberta Shore, Murvyn Vye

'If all his efforts to keep fit lead only to TV shows such as this, he might just as well let himself go to pot.' – Don Miller

The Bob Newhart Show
US 1972–7   104 approx × 25m   colour
CBS/Mary Tyler Moore (David Davies)

A psychiatrist has his own family problems.
Agreeable but unexciting sitcom with a grain of something more serious in it.

Bob Newhart, Suzanne Pleshette, Peter Bonerz

Bolam, James (c 1939–). Leading British character actor, familiar as one of *The Likely Lads*, and in more serious vein as the lead in three seasons of *When the Boat Comes In*, a one-hour serial about the depression years on Tyneside.

The Bold Ones*
US 1969–71   98 × 50m   colour
NBC/Universal (Roy Huggins/Cy Chermak/Jack Laird)

Interesting but unsatisfactory attempt to present rotating dramas about some of the pillars of our society. Hal Holbrook was a senator (pilots, *The Whole World is Watching*, *A Clear and Present Danger*, *A Continual Roar of Musketry*). E. G. Marshall, David Hartman and John Saxon were doctors (pilot, *Five Days in the Death Of Sergeant Brown*). Burl Ives and James Farentino were lawyers (pilots, *The Sound of Anger*, *The Long Morning After*). Leslie Nielsen was a police chief and Hari Rhodes a DA (pilot, *Deadlock*). George Kennedy was a cop turned priest (pilots, *The Badge and the Cross*, *The Priest Killer*). The one-hour series turned out to be a prestige offering which didn't grip the public imagination, and only doctors, lawyers and a DA were involved.

'The common theme is the contemporary world. The lawyer, the doctor, the urban situation and law-and-

order .... we focus on the young people in life who are trying to take over.' – Herb Schlosser, vp NBC.
'What will actually emerge from this smorgasbord is impossible to predict.' – Dave Kaufman.

Bold Venture
US 1959   39 × 30m   bw
United Artists

An adventurer and his pretty young ward live on a hotel boat in Trinidad.
Unremarkable hokum based on a radio series.

Dane Clark, Joan Marshall

Bolger, Ray (1904–). Amiable eccentric dancer who after careers on Broadway and in Hollywood came to TV in 1953 as star of *The Ray Bolger Show*, in which he played a hoofer in a touring company. It ran 59 episodes.

Bomba. In 1949 the old 'Bomba the Jungle Boy' films starring Johnny Sheffield were edited to make 13 TV hours under the title *Ziv Bomba*.

Bonanza ∗∗
US 1959–71   310 × 50m   colour
NBC (David Dortort)

Adventures of the Cartwright family on their Ponderosa ranch near Virginia City.
Supremely popular and often engaging western series in which the action elements were mainly subordinated to soap opera. Women especially liked it because there was a man for most types: grizzled, wise Ben (LORNE GREENE) and sons Adam (Pernell Roberts, who left after six seasons), the enormous, slow-thinking Hoss (DAN BLOCKER, who died in 1972), and fresh-faced Little Jo (MICHAEL LANDON). David Canary joined later, and Sen Yung was around as the Chinese cook. The studio look didn't seem to matter.

cr David Dortort   *story editor* John Hawkins
m DAVID ROSE

Bond, Julian (1930–). British writer responsible for *A Man of Our Times*, *Who Pays the Ferryman*, *Wings*, *Love for Lydia*, etc.

Bond, Ward (1903–60). Veteran American character actor who after a lifetime in Hollywood became a TV star as Major Adams in *Wagon Train*, which began in 1957. When he died in mid-season, John McIntire took over.

Boney
Australia 19   26 × 50m   colour (16mm)
Global/STV/John McCallum

Cases of an Aborigine detective.
Slow-paced stories with a flaw at the centre, i.e. the lead is played by a white man in blackface.

w from books by Arthur Upfield

James Laurenson

Bono, Sonny (1936–). American singer who, with or without his ex-wife Cher, has had several series on American TV.

Boone, Pat (1934–). Gentle-mannered American singer who had his own show on American TV as early as 1957, and made a seventies comeback with his family.

Boone, Richard (1917–). Craggy-featured American character actor who had mixed success on TV. Series include *Medic*, *Have Gun Will Travel*, *The Richard Boone Show*, *Hec Ramsey*.

Booth, Shirley (1907–) (Thelma Ford Booth). American character actress who had a brief career in Hollywood after much Broadway success. TV series include *Hazel*, *A Touch of Grace*.

Boots and Saddles
US 1957   39 × 25m   bw
NBC

Life in the fifth cavalry during the 1870s.
Mildly likeable western filler.

Jack Pickard, Pat McVey

Bootsie and Snudge. British comedy series. These caricatured fugitives from *The Army Game*, skiving private and bullying sergeant, got themselves demobbed in 1960 and for several seasons (100 × 25m shows) worked in a club to general approbation. Joining Alfie Bass and Bill Fraser in the taped series were Clive Dunn and Robert Dorning, and the producer was Peter Eton. In 1974, after a ten-year lay-off, Bootsie and Snudge were briefly reunited, but the effect wasn't the same, and only six episodes were transmitted.

Borge, Victor (1909–). Danish pianist–comedian, for many years an international TV and stage favourite with his one-man show.

The Borgia Stick ∗∗
US 1967   98m   colour   TVM
Universal (Richard Lewis)

An innocent-seeming suburban couple are blackmailed employees of a powerful and mysterious crime syndicate.
Well-paced and intriguingly unfolded thriller, one of the best of the early TV movies.

w A. J. Russell   *d* David Lowell Rich

Don Murray, Inger Stevens, Fritz Weaver, Barry Nelson, Sorrell Booke

† The film was also released theatrically.

Borgnine, Ernest (1915–) (Ermes Borgnino). Star American character actor who has been solidly busy throughout middle age, going to Hollywood in the fore-

WARD BOND. With a few wagons and a lot of process work he was able to give some idea of the indomitable spirit of the old west in the long-running *Wagon Train*, which never recovered from his sudden death.

BOOTSIE AND SNUDGE. Rather more amiable than Abbott and Costello, this ill-assorted pair were originally intended to turn up in various historical guises, but in fact settled down in the more economic venue of a London club which had seen better days. Robert Dorning, Bill Fraser (Snudge), Patricia Clapton, Alfie Bass (Bootsie), Clive Dunn.

front of the TV invasion of the fifties, to star in *Marty*. TV work has included many guest roles and two series: *McHale's Navy*, *Future Cop*.

Born Free*
US 1974   13 × 50m   colour
Columbia/David Gerber (Paul Radin)

Agreeable TV adaptation of Joy Adamson's books and films about game wardens and a lion in East Africa. Unfortunately the network couldn't play it before 8 pm, which was too late for the family audience, and its ratings disappointed.

Gary Collins, Diana Muldaur, Hal Frederick

Born Innocent
US 1974   74m   colour   TVM
Tomorrow

Problems of a 14-year-old girl in a tough detention centre.
Television thought it had grown up because the heroine was raped with a broom handle. Ho hum.

w Gerald di Pego   *d* Donald Wrye

Linda Blair, Joanna Miles, Kim Hunter, Richard Jaeckel, Mitch Vogel

† This film, unfortunately first transmitted in the US at 8 pm, is credited with assisting the anti-violence pressure groups which in 1976 were able to bring about 'family time' up to 9 pm and a stiff reduction in cop and crime shows after that. From this blow American TV took more than two years to recover.

The Borrowers
US 1973   74m   colour (VTR)   TVM
TCF/Walt de Faria (Warren J. Lockhart)

A small girl finds that little people live under her kitchen floorboards.
Slow-moving family larks based on Mary Norton's book; good trick effects.

Eddie Albert, Tammy Grimes, Judith Anderson, Beatrice Straight, Barnard Hughes

Bosley, Tom (1927–). Roly-poly American character actor who apart from film work has been much in evidence in TV series *The Debbie Reynolds Show*, *Happy Days*.

Boston Blackie
US 1951–2   58 × 25m   bw
United Artists

Underworld adventures of the crook with a heart of gold.
Flatly handled variation on the long-running film series.

Kent Taylor, Lois Collier, Frank Orth

Bough, Frank (1933–). British sporting commentator who also appears on *Nationwide*. BAFTA Richard Dimbleby Award 1976.

The Bounty Man
US 1972   74m   colour   TVM
Spelling–Goldberg

A hunter falls for the girl friend of his quarry.
Glum pocket western.

w Jim Byrnes   *d* John Llewellyn Moxey

Clint Walker, Richard Basehart, John Ericson, Margot Kidder, Gene Evans, Arthur Hunnicutt

Bouquet of Barbed Wire *
GB 1976   6 × 50m   colour (VTR)
LWT (Tony Wharmby)

A father's obsessive love for his married daughter leads to tragedy.
Kinky saga which was much discussed and provoked a less satisfactory sequel, *Another Bouquet* (*p/d* John Frankau). Well made and acted, but less than convincing.

w Andrea Newman   *d* Tony Wharmby

Frank Finlay, Susan Penhaligon, James Aubrey, Sheila Allen

Bourbon Street Beat
US 1959   39 × 50m   bw
ABC/Warner

Exploits of two private eyes in New Orleans.
Old-fashioned mysteries, adequately produced.

Richard Long, Andrew Duggan, Van Williams

The Boy in the Plastic Bubble *
US 1976   96m   colour   TVM
Spelling–Goldberg/ABC (Joel Thurm, Cindy Dunne)

A boy without immunities has to live in a sterile environment.
Unusual and moving but inevitably over-extended fable.

w Douglas Day Stewart   *d* Randal Kleiser

John Travolta, Glynnis O'Connor, Robert Reed, Diana Hyland

Boyd Q.C. An early staple (from 1956) of British independent TV, this half-hour series by Associated Rediffusion cast Michael Denison as a barrister and Charles Leno as his clerk. Like Perry Mason, Boyd always won, but the court procedure was often intriguing.

Boyd, William (1895–1972). Mature American leading man, familiar through films of the thirties and forties as the black-garbed Hopalong Cassidy. Edited for TV, these were a sensational success, and Boyd became a folk hero. See *Hopalong Cassidy*.

Bozo the Clown. A character created in 1959 by Larry Harmon. Actors were trained to play him in local shows for children, and cartoons featuring him had to be included. As merchandising schemes go, this certainly had the old one-two.

Bracken's World *
US 1969–70   41 × 50m   colour
NBC/TCF (Stanley Rubin)

How a big movie studio operates. In the first few episodes Bracken, the tycoon, was seen only as a hand and a cigar, but those who imagined Darryl F. Zanuck would not be far wrong. The series had a few interesting insights, but not surprisingly got itself bogged down in soap opera.

cr Dorothy Kingsley

Eleanor Parker (in first 16), Elizabeth Allen, Leslie Nielsen, Peter Haskell, Linda Harrison

'We deal with people at the workaday level, where there is identification.' – Stanley Rubin

Braden, Bernard (1916–). Canadian host and light actor who with his wife Barbara Kelly had varied success in Britain, notably as panellist and latterly host of a consumer guidance show, *On The Braden Beat*.

The Brady Bunch
US 1969–73   117 × 25m   colour
ABC/Paramount (Sherwood Schwartz)

A widower with three sons marries a widow with three daughters.
Yes, that old chestnut. Cheerful and sudsy, it worked well enough: the family even turned into a variety act

and – in 1972 – sparked off a cartoon series, *The Brady Kids*, which ran 52 episodes.

cr Sherwood Schwartz

Robert Reed, Florence Henderson, Ann B. Davis . . . plus six kids, one dog and one cat

Bragg, Melvyn (1939–). Nasal-accented British host of various literary and art series in the seventies.

The Brains Trust. This radio-talk-in with intellectual giants was invented by Howard Thomas for BBC radio during World War II and proved an astonishing success. Tried out on TV during the early days, it never seemed to work, but it must have had vast influence on a hundred later shows of the type.

Brambell, Wilfrid (1912–). British character actor specializing in dirty old men, e.g. the elder Steptoe in *Steptoe and Son*.

A Brand New Life*
US 1972 74m colour TVM
Tomorrow

A middle-aged wife discovers she is pregnant.
Well acted but fairly predictable domestic drama.

w Jerome Kass, Peggy Chantler Dick *d* Sam O'Steen
m Billy Goldenberg

Cloris Leachman, Martin Balsam, Wilfrid Hyde White, Mildred Dunnock, Gene Nelson, Marge Redmond

Branded
US 1964–5 48 × 25m bw (35 in colour)
NBC/Goodson–Todman

In the old west, a West Point graduate is cashiered as a coward and seeks to prove himself.
Good standard western.

Chuck Connors

Brasselle, Keefe (1923–). Gangling young film actor who became a TV producer for James Aubrey and CBS and formed Richelieu Productions. When hints of scandals cancelled the projects, he wrote a satirical novel called *The CanniBalS*.

Brave Stallion: see Fury

The Bravos
US 1971 100m colour TVM
Universal

Post-Civil War problems of an army officer.
Adequate, overlong mini-western.

w Christopher Knopf *d* Ted Post

George Peppard, Pernell Roberts, Belinda Montgomery, L. Q. Jones, Bo Svenson

The Breaking Point*
US 1963–4 52 × 50m bw
ABC/Bing Crosby Productions

Psychiatric case histories.
At least a bid towards adult drama at a time when it was sorely needed. The atmosphere however was a little too rarefied.

Ralph Bellamy, Wendell Corey

Breakout
US 1967 97m colour TVM
Universal (Richard Irving)

Escaped convicts in a blizzard stop to help a small boy.
Ripe Hollywood corn and not much action.

w Sy Gomberg *d* Richard Irving

James Drury, Kathryn Hays, Woody Strode, Sean Garrison

Breck, Peter (1930–). American 'second lead' who had a fair crack at series: *Black Saddle*, *The Big Valley*.

Brenda Starr, Girl Reporter*
US 1975 74m colour TVM
David Wolper

An intrepid newspaperwoman defends a millionaire from voodoo villains.
Comic strip derivative which did not quite take, but provides some fair fun along the way.

w George Kirgo, *comic strip* Dale Messick *d* Mel Stuart

Jill St John, Jed Allan, Victor Buono, Sorrell Booke, Joel Fabiani

Brennan, Walter (1894–1974). American character actor with a long and honourable Hollywood history including three Academy Awards; for the roles he played, he often did not require his teeth. He remained busy on TV to an advanced age, in long-running series: *The Real McCoys*, *To Rome with Love*, *Tycoon*, *The Guns of Will Sonnett*. He also starred in TV movies, notably *The Over the Hill Gang*.

The Brian Keith Show
aka: *The Little People*
US 1972–3 48 × 25m colour
NBC/Warner

Easy-going comedy about a pediatrician in Hawaii.

Brian Keith, Shelley Fabares, Victoria Young, Roger Bowen, Nancy Kulp

Brian's Song*
US 1971 73m colour TVM
Columbia (Paul Junger Witt)

The true story of Brian Piccolo, a baseball star who died of cancer.

In the tradition of *The Pride of the Yankees*, this earnest sentimental piece was a big hit in its home country, and won a few plaudits for telemovies, but other countries saw it as one long cliché.

w William Blinn   *d* Buzz Kulik   *m* MICHEL LEGRAND

James Caan, Jack Warden, Billy Dee Williams, Bud Furillo, Shelley Fabares, Judy Pace

Bridger
US 1976   100m   colour   TVM
Universal (David Lowell Rich)

Adventures of a mountain man around 1830.
Fairly pleasing western pilot which didn't make it.

w Merwin Gerard   *d* David Lowell Rich

James Wainwright, Ben Murphy, Dirk Blocker, Sally Field, William Windom

Bridges, Alan (1927–   ). British director whose most lauded television plays include *The Lie* and *The Traitor*.

Bridges, Lloyd (1913–   ). Reliable American star actor whose physique belies his years. Apart from a successful film career he may well hold the record for TV guest shots and series. Among the latter: *Sea Hunt, The Loner, Water World, The Lloyd Bridges Show, San Francisco International, Joe Forrester, How the West was Won*.

Bridget Loves Bernie*
US 1973   24 × 25m   colour
CBS/Columbia/Douglas S. Cramer (Arthur Alsberg, Bob Nelson)

New York comedy: wealthy Irish Catholic girl falls for a Jewish cab driver.
Surprisingly agreeable updating of *Abie's Irish Rose*: it was popular enough, but network pressures caused its demise.

cr Bernard Slade

Meredith Baxter, David Birney (the stars later married in real life), Harold J. Stone, Bibi Osterwald, Audra Lindley, David Doyle, Ned Glass, Robert Sampson

Brief Encounter
GB 1975   74m   colour   TVM
ITC/Carlo Ponti/Cecil Clarke (Duane C. Bogie)

A suburban wife falls for an unhappily married doctor she meets on her weekly shopping trip.
Almost a word-for-word remake of the successful film, but with the wrong talent off form. A disaster.

w John Bowen   *d* Alan Bridges

Richard Burton, Sophia Loren, Jack Hedley, Rosemary Leach, Anne Firbank, John Le Mesurier

Briers, Richard (1934–   ). Dithery British light comedy actor, an engaging silly ass who appeared in several series as a young and not so young husband:

Brothers in Law, The Marriage Lines, The Good Life, The Norman Conquests, The Other One.

Briggs, Professor Asa (1921–   ). British TV historian.

Bringing Up Buddy
US 1960   34 × 25m   bw
CBS/MCA/Kayro

A young bachelor is cared for by his maiden aunts.
Mildly appealing comedy.

cr Joe Connelly, Bob Mosher

Frank Aletter, Doro Merande, Enid Markey

Brinkley, David (1920–   ). American commentator and anchorman, half (with Chet Huntley) of a famous newscasting team on NBC from 1956.

British Academy of Film and Television Arts (BAFTA). The organization which gives annual merit awards. Formerly known as the British Film Academy, then as the Society of Film and Television Arts. It is operated from club premises in Piccadilly, London.

British Broadcasting Corporation: see BBC

Britton, Tony (1924–   ). Leading British actor, too often allocated roles lighter than his potential. Series: *The Nearly Man, Robin's Nest*.

Broadside
US 1964   32 × 25m   bw
ABC/Universal

Adventures of four Waves in the Pacific war.
Flimsy service comedy.

Kathy Nolan

'Of genuine laughter there is little, of novelty none.' – Don Miller

Brock's Last Case*
US 1972   98m   colour   TVM
Universal (Roland Kibbee)

A New York detective retires to a Californian citrus ranch but finds himself still up to his neck in murder.
Competent movie serving as the pilot for a series which later switched back to New York and the title of its original inspiration, *Madigan*.

w Martin Donaldson, Alex Gordon   *d* David Lowell Rich   *m* Charles Gross

Richard Widmark, Will Geer, John Anderson, Michael Burns, Henry Darrow

Brodkin, Herbert (1912–   ). American executive producer who won much respect for such projects as *The Defenders, Holocaust, Studs Lonigan*. Originally a scenery designer.

Broken Arrow
US 1956–7 72 × 25m bw
ABC/TCF

An Indian agent tries to bring peace with the Apaches.
Contrived and rather glum rip-off of the famous film.

John Lupton, Michael Ansara (as Cochise)

Brolin, James (1941–). American general purpose
leading man who appeared regularly in *The Monroes* and
rose to fame as the junior doctor in *Marcus Welby MD*.

Bronco
US 1958–61 68 × 50m bw
ABC/Warner

An ex-Confederate officer brings law to the west.
Below par spin-off from *Cheyenne*, one of a nap hand
of hour westerns held by Warner at this period
(*Maverick*, *Sugarfoot*, etc.).

Ty Hardin

Bronk
US 1975 74m colour TVM
MGM

A homicide detective on suspension tracks down a narcotics ring.
Utterly predictable crime hokum resting on its star,
who carried the subsequent 50m series for 24 episodes.

w Ed Waters, Al Martinez, Carroll O'Connor, Bruce
Geller *d* Richard Donner

Jack Palance, David Birney, Tony King, Joanna
Moore, Henry Beckman

† The series was produced by Bruce Geller.

Bronowski, Jacob (1902–76). British philosopher
and historian whose great TV achievement was his 13-
hour film series *The Ascent of Man*, aired by the BBC in
1975.

Bronson, Charles (1922–) (Charles Buchinski).
Steely-eyed American star actor who before his
Hollywood eminence was in two TV series: *Man with a
Camera*, *The Travels of Jamie McPheeters*.

The Brontës of Haworth *
GB 1973 5 × 50m colour (VTR)
Yorkshire TV (Marc Miller)

A fresh look at the lives of the Victorian novelist sisters
and their dissolute brother.
Excellent semi-documentary drama with a genuine feeling for the period.

w Christopher Fry *d* Marc Miller

Alfred Burke, Michael Kitchen, Vickery Turner,
Rosemary McHale, Ann Penfold

Brooke-Taylor, Tim (1940–). British lightweight
comedy and cabaret actor, since 1970 one of *The
Goodies*.

Brooks, Mel (1927–) (Melvin Kaminsky).
American jokester who made a big killing in Hollywood
in the seventies when there was a lack of anyone with a
sharper sense of humour. His previous TV career included co-scripting *Get Smart* and having the original
idea for *When Things were Rotten*.

The Brotherhood of the Bell *
US 1971 100m colour TVM
Cinema Center (Hugh Benson)

A secret fraternity takes stern measures against the enemies of its members.
Unusual mystery, quite watchable and well done.

w David Karp *d* Paul Wendkos *ph* Robert Hauser
m Jerry Goldsmith

Glenn Ford, Dean Jagger, Maurice Evans, Rosemary
Forsyth, Will Geer, Eduard Franz, William Conrad

The Brothers. Long-running BBC 50m VTR serial of
the seventies, about a family of brothers in the trucking
business and their domination by their widowed
mother. For a while it was a Sunday night must, but its
appeal suddenly waned. Jean Anderson, Jennifer
Wilson, Richard Easton, Robin Chadwick, Patrick
O'Connell and Kate O'Mara were involved.

The Brothers Brannigan
US 1960 39 × 25m bw
CBS/Wilbur Stark

Two private eyes are based in Phoenix.
Adequate, forgettable crime filler of its time.

Steve Dunne, Mark Roberts

Brothers, Joyce (1928–). American psychiatrist
who had her own series in the fifties and sixties after
winning top prizes on two quiz shows and becoming a
national celebrity.

Brown, Robert (*c* 1931–). Stalwart American
leading man, seen in *Here Come the Brides* and *Primus*.

Brush, Basil. A foxy glove puppet familiar on British
screens from the early sixties. The combination of an
aristocratic voice, good jokes and catchphrases like
'Boom Boom' has endeared the simple entertainment
to adults and children alike.

The Buccaneers
GB 1956 39 × 25m bw
ATV/Sapphire

In the 1620s, an ex-pirate protects British interests on
the high seas.
Cut-price swashbuckler.

Robert Shaw

Buchanan, Edgar (1902–). American character
actor who vied with Walter Brennan for country philos-

opher roles and later made an equal killing in TV with roles in long-running series: *Judge Roy Bean, Petticoat Junction, Cade's County.*

Buck Rogers in the 25th Century
US 1950 39 × 25m bw
ABC

In 1919 a mining engineer is rendered unconscious by a mountain gas and awakes in 2430, helping to save his new society from evil forces.
A long-lost series version of the comic strip.

Ken Dibbs, Lou Prenis, Harry Deering

† In the wake of *Star Wars*, Universal in 1978 revived the project, but the intended series was turned into a single expensive feature film.

Buckskin *
US 1958 39 × 25m bw
NBC/Betford/Revue

Life in a Montana town in wild west days.
Rather pleasing minor western series, too gentle to last.

Tommy Nolan, Sally Brophy

Budgie
GB 1971–3 30 approx × 50m colour (VTR)
Thames (Verity Lambert)

Adventures of a London spiv.
Occasionally likeable but not especially interesting comedy dramas.

w Keith Waterhouse, Willis Hall

Adam Faith, Ian Cuthbertson, Georgina Hale

Buffalo Bill Jnr
US 1955 40 × 25m bw
Flying A (Gene Autry)

Self-explanatory meek-and-mild western.

Dick Jones, Nancy Gilbert

The Bugaloos
US 1970–1 17 × 25m colour
NBC/Sid and Marty Krofft

Adventures of a group of singing insects and their evil nemesis Benita Bizarre.
Screechy kiddy show in which most of the characters are played by puppets.

m Charles Fox

Martha Raye, Caroline Ellis, Wayne Laryea, John Philpott, John McIndoe

Bugs Bunny. Warners' famous cartoon rabbit has been well exposed on TV via various groupings of the old films. In the seventies several newly animated specials were made, but they were never up to the old standard.

Bullwinkle. A dumb moose cartoon character created by Jay Ward for innumerable segments of a long-running series usually called *The Rocky Show*, though Bullwinkle was certainly the more striking character. The cartoons originally appeared in the fifties, linked to such other segments, all quite wittily scripted, as *Peabody's Improbable History* and *Fractured Fairy Tales* (narrated by Edward Everett Horton).

† When Jay Ward later made *Fractured Flickers*, it was officially introduced as 'the biggest waste of time since *The Bullwinkle Show*'.

Burke, Alfred (1918–). British character actor with a wry look, most memorably cast in *Public Eye* as the private detective who was always behind the eight ball.

Burke, Paul (1926–). Serious-looking leading man who scored handsomely as the young cop in *Naked City* but subsequently found work a little scarce. Other series: *Noah's Ark, 12 O'Clock High.*

Burke's Law *
US 1963–5 81 × 50m bw
ABC/Four Star/Barbety (Aaron Spelling)

Murder cases of an elegant and eligible police chief.
A genial send-up of who-done-its which never quite managed enough wit and tended to waste its vast supply of guest stars, but created an engaging central character and a mind-boggling Beverly Hills atmosphere with an endless helping of glamour girls.

cr Ivan Goff, Ben Roberts (after a Four Star Theatre film by Ernest Kinoy)

Gene Barry, Gary Conway, Regis Toomey

† Ill-advisedly, the format was changed in 1965 to *Amos Burke Secret Agent*, the atmosphere becoming more that of James Bond, with Carl Benton Reid as spymaster. The new show lasted 13 episodes.

Burnet, Alastair (1929–). British journalist and former newspaper editor, he now heads Independent Television News.

Burnett, Carol (1934–). American lady comic, the plain Jane's Lucille Ball. Much loved by the American public and practically unknown elsewhere, she has had her own weekly variety show throughout the seventies.

Burnett, Hugh (*c* 1913–). British documentary producer. *Face to Face, Lifeline, Panorama,* etc.

Burnley, Fred (1933–73). British producer, a promising career cut short. *The Dream Divided* (BFA 1969), *Down These Mean Streets* (BFA 1969), *The Search for the Nile,* etc.

The Burns and Allen Show **
aka: *The George Burns and Gracie Allen Show*
US 1950–7 239 × 25m bw
CBS/McCadden

The celebrated comics used a simple format, starting and ending with a chat to the audience: she was scatty, he was indulgent, and in the central sketch their long-suffering neighbours got involved. (The format was being imitated as late as the seventies by Britain's *No, Honestly*.) It worked beautifully, to the satisfaction of an entire nation.

George Burns, Gracie Allen, Fred Clark/Larry Keating, Bea Benadaret, Harry Von Zell

† After eight seasons, Gracie retired; in 1958 *The George Burns Show* was moderately successful, with son Ronnie Burns playing a major role.

Burr, Raymond (1917–). Heavyweight American character actor who unexpectedly became a major TV star in a succession of popular crime series: *Perry Mason, Ironside, Kingston Confidential*.

Burrud, Bill (1925–). American anchorman, former child star, who from the fifties hosted many travel and adventure series, sometimes from his own experience but often bought in.

Burton, Humphrey (1931–). British anchorman associated with several arts programmes, *Omnibus, Aquarius*, etc.

Bus Stop*
US 1961   25 × 50m   bw
ABC/TCF/Roy Huggins (Robert Blees)

Strangers passing through a small town find their personal dramas coming to a head in the bus stop café.
An unlikely premise, vaguely derived from the William Inge film, produced a very variable but usually watchable semi-anthology.

Marilyn Maxwell, Joan Freeman, Richard Anderson, Rhodes Reason

† The violence of one episode, starring Fabian Forte as a teenage tough, is alleged to have caused the downfall of a network president.

'Inge is "story consultant" for the series but if he has personally approved any of the episodes presented thus far, he must have done so while thinking about something else.' – Don Miller

Busting Loose
US 1977   ?13 × 30m   colour
Paramount/Mark Rothman, Lowell Ganz (Lawrence Kasha)

A young Jew determines to set up house away from his mama.
Raucous ethnic comedy which succeeds, more or less, on a hit or miss principle.

cr Mark Rothman, Lowell Ganz

Adam Arkin, Jack Kruschen, Pat Carroll, Barbara Rhoades

But I Don't Want to Get Married
US 1970   72m   colour   TVM
Aaron Spelling

A widower is inundated with candidates to be the mother of his family.
Pleasant comedy which is neither quite funny nor quite moving enough.

w Roland Wolpert   *d* Jerry Paris

Herschel Bernardi, Kay Medford, Shirley Jones, Sue Lyon, Nanette Fabray

Butch Cassidy and the Sundance Kids
US 1973   13 × 22m   colour
Hanna–Barbera

Four members of a rock group are actually spies.
Inept cartoon masquerading under a come-on title.

Buttons, Red (1919–) (Aaron Schwatt). American nightclub comic who had moderate success in TV and movies. Series: *The Red Buttons Show, The Double Life of Henry Phyfe*.

Bygraves, Max (1922–). British cockney singer and entertainer, famous for his easy manner, his family humour and his waving hands. TV shows: mostly variety specials.

Byington, Spring (1893–1971). Favourite American character actress who made a big hit on TV in *December Bride* and was later featured in *Laramie*.

Byrne, Peter (1928–). Pleasing British second lead whose main success was as Jack Warner's son-in-law in the long-running *Dixon of Dock Green*.

C

cablevision. Improved method of TV transmission in which ground cables give a better defined picture in difficult reception areas. Big business in America, where it is controlled independently of the networks.

Cabot, Sebastian (1918–77). Bulky British character actor, from the mid-fifties in great demand on American TV. Series: *Checkmate, Family Affair, Ghost Story.*

Cade's County*
US 1971   24 × 50m   colour
CBS/TCF/David Gerber (Charles Larson)

Cases of a New Mexico sheriff.
Well-made modern western which surprisingly ran only one season, perhaps because in recommended TV fashion the hero was given neither home nor personal life, appearing to exist only in his office (a device which did work for Jack Lord in *Hawaii Five-O*).

Glenn Ford, Edgar Buchanan, Peter Ford

Caesar, Sid (1922–). American revue comic who never really recovered from being the toast of the nation in the fifties in *Your Show of Shows*. Between 1954 and 1958 he had his own domestic comedy series *Caesar's Hour*, his 'wives' including Nanette Fabray and Janet Blair. A fairly frequent guest artist.

The Caesars**
GB 1968   7 × 50m   bw (VTR)
Granada (Philip Mackie)

A history of the machinations which led to the decline and fall of Rome.
Freehand version of well-known historical facts, wittily written and incisively acted in a stylish studio production. At least the equal of the later *I, Claudius.*

w Philip Mackie   *d* Derek Bennett

Freddie Jones (Claudius), André Morell (Tiberius), Ralph Bates (Caligula), Sonia Dresdel (Livia), Barrie Ingham, Roland Culver

Cage without a Key
US 1975   100m   colour   TVM
Columbia/Douglas S. Cramer

A girl teenager is wrongly convicted of murder and sent to a penal institution.
By *Born Innocent*, out of *Caged* and *Woman's Prison* . . . every scene has been seen before.

w Joanna Lee   *d* Buzz Kulik

Susan Dey, Michael Brandon, Jonelle Allen, Sam Bottoms

Cain's Hundred
US 1961   30 × 50m   bw
NBC/MGM (Paul Monash)

A young lawyer heads a government law enforcement agency, after being a legal adviser for the mob.
Smartish crime series somewhat handicapped by a cold lead.

Mark Richman

'Having accumulated damning data on an even hundred of the nation's top gangsters, he brings one to justice each week, unless the show is pre-empted by a special.' – Don Miller

Calhoun, Rory (1922–) (Francis Timothy Durgin). American hero of co-features in the fifties; never made it big in TV but did star in *The Texan*.

The California Kid*
US 1974   74m   colour   TVM
Universal (Paul Mason)

The brother of a victim corners a psychotic small-town sheriff who forces speeders off the road to their deaths.
Oddball mixture of *Duel* and *Bad Day at Black Rock*; not unentertaining.

w Richard Compton   *d* Richard Heffron

MARTIN SHEEN, Vic Morrow, Michelle Phillips, Stuart Margolin, Nick Nolte

The Californians
US 1957–8   69 × 25m   bw
NBC/Louis F. Edelman

A young marshal has trouble in San Francisco in the 1850s.
Acceptable gold rush semi-western with plenty of rough stuff.

Richard Coogan, Adam Kennedy

Call Her Mom
US 1972   74m   colour   TVM
Columbia (Herb Wallerstein)

A glamorous waitress becomes house mother for a college fraternity and sharpens up the ideas of the members.

Easy-going collegiate nonsense.

w Kenny Solms, Gail Parent   *d* Jerry Paris

Connie Stevens, Van Johnson, Charles Nelson Reilly, Jim Hutton, Cyd Charisse, Corbett Monica, Gloria de Haven

Call My Bluff. A panel game: devised by Mark Goodson and Bill Todman for NBC in 1965, it became a much longer runner on the BBC, with sides captained by Patrick Campbell and Frank Muir, and Robert Robinson as compere. Three panellists give a definition of an obscure word; the other side has to decide which is telling the truth.

The Call of the Wild
US 1976   96m   colour   TVM
Charles Fries/NBC (Malcolm Stewart)

Adventures of a dog which belongs to a Klondike gold prospector.
It moves in fits and spurts, but the scenery is great and it's reasonably faithful to Jack London's book.

w James Dickey   *d* Jerry Jameson

John Beck, Bernard Fresson, Donald Moffat

Call to Danger
US 1972   74m   colour   TVM
Paramount

Adventures of an elite squad for the Justice Department.
Warmed-over crime busting in a failed pilot designed as a follow-up to *Mission Impossible*.

w Laurence Heath   *d* Tom Gries

Peter Graves, Clu Gulager, Diana Muldaur, John Anderson, Tina Louise

Callan**
GB 1967–73   52 × 50m   colour (VTR and film)
Thames TV

A cold-blooded secret service agent has his own standard of ethics.
If only as a corrective to the James Bond brand of spy glamour, this deserved to be a success, and was. It was also very influential, so that rather too many bleak and violent spy melos followed.

cr James Mitchell

Edward Woodward, Michael Goodliffe, Russell Hunter

CALLAN. Edward Woodward (right) looks characteristically scared and scruffy in this tense series which appeared as a corrective to the theory advanced by the James Bond films that spying was all girls and glamour. With him, Anthony Valentine.

Callan, Michael (1935–) (Martin Caliniff). American light leading man of the sixties. TV series include *Occasional Wife*.

Calling Doctor Gannon: see Medical Center

Calucci's Department
US 1973   13 × 25m   colour (VTR)
CBS/Sullivan

Frustrations of a state unemployment office.
Claustrophobic studio comedy which proved unsympathetic.

James Coco, Candy Azzara, Jose Perez, Jack Fletcher

Calvert, Phyllis (1915–) (Phyllis Bickle). British leading lady of the forties; later became a TV star in *Kate*.

Camera in Action**
GB 1965   4 × 25m   bw
Granada

Four historical documentaries using the rostrum camera technique to animate old photographs. (See *City of Gold*.) The titles were *Uprooted, A Prospect of Whitby, War of the Brothers, Photographer*.

Cameron, James (1911–). Distinguished British journalist and traveller, frequently on TV as current affairs commentator.

Cameron, Rod (1910–) (Nathan Cox). Tough-looking American co-feature star of the forties who was popular in early TV series: *City Detective, Coronado 9, State Trooper*.

Camp Runamuck
US 1965   26 × 25m   colour
NBC/Columbia (David Swift)

Boys' and girls' summer camps are just across the lake from each other.
Flat comedy vaguely inspired by *The Happiest Days of Your Life*.

cr David Swift

David Ketchum, Arch Johnson, Dave Madden, Frank De Vol

Campanella, Joseph (1927–). American character actor. TV series: *Guiding Light, The Nurses, Mannix, The Bold Ones*.

Can Ellen Be Saved?
US 1974   74m   colour   TVM
ABC Circle

A private eye rescues a teenager from a strange religious sect.

Adequate melodrama, treated rather more weirdly than it warrants.

w Emmett Roberts   *d* Harvey Hart

Leslie Nielsen, Michael Parks, John Saxon, Kathy Cannon, Louise Fletcher

Canadian Broadcasting Corporation: see CBC

Canary, David (1938–). Stalwart American actor who was added to the star line-up of *Bonanza* during its last few seasons.

Candid Camera. An American studio half-hour which originated in the fifties (host: Allen Funt) and lasted on and off for 20 years. (The English version was at its best when hosted by Jonathan Routh.) The format was to stage impossible situations – e.g. a car turns up at a garage without an engine – and film, by hidden cameras, people's bewildered reactions.

Cannon
US 1970   100m   colour TVM
CBS/Quinn Martin

A fat private eye investigates a murder and finds small-town corruption.
Adequate, padded mystery serving as pilot for a successful series.

w Edward Hume   *d* George McCowan

WILLIAM CONRAD, Barry Sullivan, Vera Miles, J. D. Cannon, Lynda Day, Earl Holliman

† The series lasted five seasons. (120 × 50m episodes).

Cannon, J. D. (1922–). Mean-faced American actor. TV series: *McCloud*.

Cannonball
Canada 1958   39 × 25m   bw
Robert Maxwell

Adventures of a team of truck drivers plying between Canada and the US.
Acceptable comedy dramas, pleasantly played.

Paul Birch, William Campbell

The Canterville Ghost*
GB 1974   50m   colour (VTR)
HTV–Polytel (Joseph Cates)

A 17th-century earl is walled up alive in his own castle and comes back 200 years later as a benign ghost.
Careful and well-cast version of the Oscar Wilde story.

w Robin Miller   *d* Walter Miller

David Niven, Flora Robson, James Whitmore, Audra Lindley, Maurice Evans

Cantor, Eddie (1892–1964) (Edward Israel Itskowitz). Ebullient American star of Broadway and

J. D. CANNON. Here backing up Dennis Weaver as the familiar Marshal McCloud, Cannon is one of those actors vital to television who always gives good value and is welcomed by the audience but never seems to merit a show of his own.

the movies who in later life turned successfully to radio and TV, in the latter medium usually as host of specials and discoverer of young talent.

Capra (US 1978). A new 50m show about a lawyer who spends less time in court than outside solving weird murder mysteries. Another try at the Ellery Queen–Columbo genre.

The Captain and Tennille. A singing act which came to the fore in 1976 and briefly starred in their own weekly one-hour variety show for ABC. They are Daryl Dragon and Toni Tennille.

Captain David Grief
US 1956   39 × 25m   bw
Jack London Productions/Guild Films

Adventures of a South Seas trader.
It seemed tolerable at the time.

Maxwell Reed

Captain Gallant
US 1955–6   65 × 25m   bw
Frantel

Foreign Legion adventures, filmed in North Africa. If revived, they could become a cult.

Buster Crabbe, Fuzzy Knight

† Also known as *Foreign Legionnaire* and *Captain Gallant of the Foreign Legion.*

Captain Kangaroo. An early morning studio show for small children, hosted since 1953 by Bob Keeshan. Two generations of American kids have grown up with it.

Captain Midnight
Syndicated title: *Jet Jackson, Flying Commando*
US 1954   39 × 25m   bw
CBS/Screen Gems

A former air ace commands the Secret Squadron, a government organization designed to combat evil. Ingenuous hokum which filled a need.

Richard Webb, Sid Melton, Olan Soule

Captain Nice
US 1966   15 × 25m   colour
NBC (Buck Henry)

A secret formula turns a mild-mannered chemist into a crime fighter.
Unfunny attempt in a familiar mould.

William Daniels, Alice Ghostley

'Seems to have been concocted on the principle that if you make something sufficiently absurd people will laugh it to scorn.' – Jack Edmund Nolan

Captain Noah and his Floating Zoo*
GB 1972   25m   colour
Granada (Douglas Terry)

The ark story, very stylishly animated.

w Michael Flanders   d/animation Brian Cosgrove,
Mark Hall   m Joseph Horowitz

Captain Scarlet and the Mysterons*
GB 1967   32 × 25m   colour
ATV/Gerry Anderson

Martians invade the earth. Spectra combats them.
Superior puppet series.

Captains and the Kings
US 1977   12 × 50m   colour
MCA/Universal/Public Arts (Roy Huggins, Jo
Swerling Jnr)

A boy who arrives in the US as an orphan immigrant
starts an important political dynasty.
Hastily pasted together mini-series from a novel based
on the Kennedy family. Only occasionally compulsive;
structure weak and make-up especially poor in the later
sequences.

w/d Douglas Heyes, Allen Reisner, novel Taylor
Caldwell

Richard Jordan, Barbara Parkins, Vic Morrow, Joanna
Pettet, Ray Bolger, Celeste Holm, Ann Sothern, Pernell
Roberts, Robert Vaughn, Burl Ives, Jane Seymour

Captains Courageous
US 1977   93m   colour   TVM
Norman Rosemont

A rich boy, nearly drowned, is rescued by New England
fishermen.
An old chestnut, rather stolidly recreated, and certainly
no match for the MGM 1937 version.

w John Gay, story Rudyard Kipling
d Harvey Hart   ph Philip Lethrop   m Allyn Ferguson

Karl Malden, Jonathan Kahn, Johnny Doran, Neville
Brand, Fred Gwynne, Charles Dierkop, Jeff Corey,
Fritz Weaver, Ricardo Montalban

Car 54, Where Are You?**
US 1961–2   60 × 25m   bw
NBC/Euopolis

Misadventures of a precinctful of New York cops.
A crack comedy series with real control in the writing
and excellent characterizations.

cr Nat Hiken

Fred Gwynne, Joe E. Ross

'The funniest film show currently on the air.' – Don
Miller, 1962

The Cara Williams Show
US 1964   39 × 25m   bw
CBS

In a company which prohibits the employment of married couples, a scatterbrained young woman tries to
hide her marriage to the efficiency expert.
Mild comedy which soon ran out of steam when the
secret had to be revealed.

Cara Williams, Frank Aletter, Paul Reed

Carey, Macdonald (1913–). American second lead
who after a fair innings in movies came to TV in the
fifties in *Dr Christian* and *Lock Up*; ten years later
settled in a long-running soap opera, *Days of Our
Lives*.

Carey, Phil (1925–). American second lead who
never quite made it in pictures but appeared in several
TV series: *77th Bengal Lancers*, *Philip Marlowe*,
Laredo.

Cargill, Patrick (1918–). Accomplished British
farceur of the sixties and seventies. Series: *Father Dear
Father*, *Ooh La La*, *The Many Wives of Patrick*.

Caribe
US 1975   13 × 50m   colour
ABC/Quinn Martin (Anthony Spinner)

Adventures of a law enforcer in the Caribbean.
Dismally routine crimebuster with star and stories alike
uneasy.

Stacy Keach, Carl Franklin, Robert Mandan

Carlson, Richard (1912–77). American second lead
who from the fifties alternated movies with acting in,
and sometimes directing, TV series: *I Led Three Lives*,
McKenzie's Raiders.

Carmichael, Ian (1920–). British light comedy star
whose TV series (from the mid-sixties) have included
The World of Wooster, *Bachelor Father* and *Lord Peter
Wimsey*.

Carne, Judy (1939–). Vivacious British leading
lady in Hollywood. Series include *The Baileys of
Balboa*, *Love on a Rooftop*, *Laugh-In* (in which she was
the sock-it-to-me girl).

Carney, Art (1918–). American comedy actor who
began on TV as Jackie Gleason's stooge in *The
Honeymooners* and in the sixties emerged as a star in his
own right, especially in movies. Series: *Lanigan's
Rabbi*.

The Carol Burnett Show: see Burnett, Carol

Carpenter, Richard (c 1933–). British writer of
series for imaginative older children: *Catweazle*, *The
Ghosts of Motley Hall*. Began as an actor in Granada's
Knight Errant.

Carradine, David (1940–). Lean, thoughtful American actor, son of John Carradine. Pursues an eccentric movie career and has starred in two TV series: *Shane*, *Kung Fu*.

Carrillo, Leo (1880–1961). Mexican character actor who after a long career in films was seen on TV in the fifties as Pancho in the long-running *Cisco Kid* series.

Carroll, Leo G. (1892–1972). British character actor who after many years in Hollywood brought his dry personality to TV in three series: *Topper*, *Going My Way* and *The Man from UNCLE*.

Carson, Jeannie (1928–) (Jean Shufflebottom). Vivacious British star who scored a great hit in one American series of the fifties, *Hey Jeannie!*

Carson, Johnny (1925–). American stand-up comedian turned anchorman; breezy host of the *Tonight* show since 1962. Previously anchorman of *Who Do You Trust?*, *Earn Your Vacation* and *The Johnny Carson Show*.

Carson, Violet (*c* 1901–). British pianist and character actress who came to stardom in 1960 as the formidable Ena Sharples in Granada's long-running soap opera *Coronation Street*.

Carter's Army

US 1969 72m colour TVM
Thomas–Spelling

During World War II a white southern officer is given a black platoon to help in a dangerous assignment. Formula action hokum.

w Aaron Spelling, David Kidd   d George McCowan

Stephen Boyd, Robert Hooks, Susan Oliver, Roosevelt Grier, Moses Gunn, Richard Pryor, Billy Dee Williams

Cartier, Rudolf (1908–). Austrian man of many talents who joined the BBC drama department in 1952 and became its best-known director for programmes like *The Quatermass Experiment*, *1984*, *The Queen and the Rebels*, *Mother Courage*, *A Midsummer Night's Dream*, *The Aspern Papers*, *The Frog*, *An Ideal Husband*, *Lady Windermere's Fan*.

VIOLET CARSON proved, by her long run in *Coronation Street* as Ena Sharples, that youth and beauty are not essential to stardom. Another favourite old trouper in this shot is Jack Howarth (closest to her) who has played Albert Tatlock for eighteen years.

Casablanca. In 1955 eight 50m episodes were made for a rotating series called *Warner Brothers Present*. It had the ambience of the movie though the stories were weak; Charles McGraw played Rick.

Casanova *
GB 1971   6 × 50m   colour (VTR)
BBC

The life of Casanova.
Eyebrows were raised at language, nudity and sexual writhings in this otherwise downbeat though well-acted historical reconstruction.

w Dennis Potter   *d* John Glenister

Frank Finlay

Case, Allen (*c* 1937–). American 'second lead' who appeared in two western series, *The Deputy* and *The Legend of Jesse James*.

A Case of Rape *
US 1974   98m   colour   TVM
Universal

A rape victim finds the legal system works against her.
Spirited warming over of documentary facts.

w Robert E. Thompson   *d* Boris Sagal

Elizabeth Montgomery, Ronnie Cox, Cliff Potts, William Daniels, Rosemary Murphy

The Case of the Dangerous Robin
US 1960   38 × 27m   bw
Ziv

Cases of an insurance investigator.
Oddly titled but otherwise quite forgettable crime series.

Rick Jason, Jean Blake

Casey Jones *
US 1957   32 × 25m   bw
Columbia/Briskin

Adventures of a train driver in the wild west.
Lively adventure series which lingers pleasantly in the memory.

Alan Hale Jnr, Bobby Clark, Mary Laurence, Dub Taylor

Cash and Cable: see Barbary Coast

Cassidy, David (1951–). American pop singer of the seventies, one of the children of Jack Cassidy and Shirley Jones, who rocketed to solo stardom after *The Partridge Family*.

Cassidy, Shaun (1956–). Another Cassidy brother who appeared as one of *The Hardy Boys*.

Cassidy, Ted (1932–79). Hulking seven-foot American character actor who played Lurch the butler in *The Addams Family* and later provided menace in *The New Adventures of Huck Finn*.

Castle, Roy (1933–). British comedian, light entertainer and dancer of the fifties and sixties.

The Cat Creature
US 1973   74m   colour   TVM
Columbia/Douglas S. Cramer

Death from a supernatural feline follows a stolen Egyptian amulet.
Poorly made, sluggishly written horror hokum which wastes its cast.

w Robert Bloch   *d* Curtis Harrington

Meredith Baxter, Stuart Whitman, Gale Sondergaard, Keye Luke, David Hedison, John Carradine

The Catcher
US 1971   98m   colour   TVM
Columbia/Herbert B. Leonard

An ex-police detective offers his services in tracking down fugitives.
Tedious pilot which not surprisingly didn't get anywhere.

w David Freeman   *d* Allen H. Miner

Michael Witney, Jan-Michael Vincent, Tony Franciosa, Catherine Burns, David Wayne, Alf Kjellin, Anne Baxter

Catholics **
GB 1973   74m   colour   TVM
CBS/Harlech TV

A remote abbey insists on sticking to the Latin mass and a young priest is sent to talk to the abbot.
Absorbing drama of ideas with splendid Scottish island backgrounds.

w BRIAN MOORE   *d* JACK GOLD   *ph* Gerry Fisher   *m* Carl Davis

TREVOR HOWARD, MARTIN SHEEN, Cyril Cusack, Andrew Keir, Michael Gambon

Cathy Come Home **
GB 1966   95m   bw
BBC (Jeremy Sandford)

Documentary play dramatizing the plight of homeless young mothers.
A low-life saga which became one of TV's most discussed dramas.

CAROL WHITE, RAY BROOKS

Cattanooga Cats
US 1969   17 × 22m   colour
Hanna–Barbera

Adventures of a feline rock group (and other segments: *Auto Cat and Motor Mouse, Phileas Fogg Jnr, It's the Wolf*).
Unremarkable Saturday morning cartoon fare.

Catweazle*
GB 1970   26 × 25m   colour
LWT

An 11th-century wizard accidentally transports himself
to the 20th century and is helped by a small boy.
Imaginative comedy series for children, but in the final
analysis it lacks charisma despite an excellent star performance.

w Richard Carpenter

Geoffrey Bayldon

Cavett, Dick (1933–). American talk show host of
the sixties and seventies, probably the most intelligent
of his breed. A former actor.

Cawston, Richard (1923–   ). British documentary
producer, long with BBC. Highlights include *This Is the
BBC* and *Royal Family*.

CBC. Canadian Broadcasting Corporation, the official
TV channel in that country, founded on similar lines to
the BBC.

CBS. The Columbia Broadcasting System has nothing
to do with Columbia Pictures. Beginning in 1927 as a
chain of independent radio stations, and controlled
from 1929 by William S. Paley, it grew into the most
trusted and conservative of the American TV networks,
managing in the sixties to be leader in entertainment
too.

Ceefax. The BBC's form of data transmission system,
providing instant access to a wide range of printed information.

Celebrity Squares. British title for *Hollywood
Squares*; hosted since 1976 by Bob Monkhouse.

Centennial*
US 1978   2 × 140m, 10 × 93m   colour
NBC/Universal/John Wilder (Howard Alston)

Episodes adapted from James Michener's immense
novel, bringing the story of a western town from Indian
times to the present day.
A mammoth undertaking just fails to be the white
man's *Roots*, which was clearly the intention.

w John Wilder and others   *d* Virgil Vogel and others
ph Duke Callaghan   *m* John Addison

Robert Conrad, Richard Chamberlain, David Janssen,
Raymond Burr, Sally Kellerman, Michael Ansara

† NBC called the series 'the longest motion picture ever
made'.

The Century Turns
aka: *Hec Ramsey*
US 1971   97m   colour   TVM
Universal (Jack Webb, William Finnegan)

An ex US marshal solves the double murder of a home-
steading couple.
Tolerable pilot for a series which became part of
Mystery Movie, about a western detective using scientific methods.

w Harold Jack Bloom   *d* Daniel Petrie

Richard Boone, Rick Lenz, Sharon Acker, Harry
Morgan, Robert Pratt

The Chadwick Family
US 1974   74m   colour   TVM
Universal (David Victor)

A writer discovers family problems when he is offered
an important new job which involves a move.
Ho-hum domestic drama.

w John Gay   *d* David Lowell Rich

Fred MacMurray, Kathleen Maguire, Darleen Carr,
Barry Bostwick, John Larch, Margaret Lindsay

The Challenge
US 1970   74m   colour   TVM
TCF

To avoid a nuclear war, two countries poised to strike
each other agree to settle their differences by an unarmed contest between one man from each side.
Silly panic button melodrama.

w Marc Norman   *d* Alan Smithee

Darren McGavin, Mako, Broderick Crawford, Paul
Lukas, James Whitmore, Skip Homeier

The Challengers
US 1968   96m   colour   TVM
Universal (Roy Huggins)

International racing drivers compete in the Grand
Prix.
You can compute this one before you switch on.

w Dick Nelson   *d* Leslie H. Martinson

Darren McGavin, Sean Garrison, Nico Minardos,
Anne Baxter, Richard Conte, Farley Granger, Juliet
Mills, Sal Mineo, Susan Clark

Chamberlain, Richard (1935–). Handsome,
thoughtful American leading man who sprang to fame
as TV's *Dr Kildare*.

Champion
US 1955   26 × 25m   bw
Flying A (Gene Autry)

A small boy befriends the leader of a pack of wild
horses.
Unexceptional, rather dull children's western.

Barry Curtis, Jim Bannon

Champion the Wonder Horse
aka: *The Adventures of Champion*
US 1956   ? × 25m   bw
CBS

A once wild horse befriends a 12-year-old boy in the 1880s southlands.
Adequate children's adventure, much revived.

Barry Curtis, Jim Bannon

The Champions
GB 1967   30 × 50m   colour
ATV

A secret agent team is composed of three people with supernormal skills and powers.
Cheerful nonsense which seemed rather childish at the time, which was before the advent of *Six Million Dollar Man* and *Marvel Superheroes*.

script supervisor Dennis Spooner

Stuart Damon, Alexandra Bastedo, William Gaunt

Channing
US 1963   26 × 50m   bw
ABC/Universal

A young college professor finds he has much to learn from an older colleague.
Dr Kildare transferred to the campus, with less happy results.

Jason Evers, Henry Jones

Charlie Brown. The hero of the Snoopy cartoons, created by Charles M. Schultz, has appeared in a number of 25m cartoon specials since 1973, all written by the original author and produced by Lee Mendelson and Bill Melendez, with music by Vince Guaraldi. They are *Charlie Brown's Thanksgiving, Charlie Brown's Christmas, It's a Mystery Charlie Brown, It's the Easter Beagle Charlie Brown, Be My Valentine Charlie Brown, It's the Great Pumpkin Charlie Brown, It's Arbor Day Charlie Brown, Happy Anniversary Charlie Brown.*

Charlie Chan: Happiness is a Warm Clue
US 1971   96m   colour   TVM
Universal (Jack Laird)

A famous detective emerges from retirement to solve murders aboard a yacht.
Dismal comeback for a famous screen character: desperately poor writing, total lack of pace and unsuitable casting made sure that no series ensued.

w Gene Kearney   *d* Daryl Duke

Ross Martin, Leslie Nielsen, Virginia Lee, Rocky Gunn

† See also *The New Adventures of Charlie Chan.*

The Charlie Farrell Show
US 1956 and 1960   ? × 25m   bw
CBS

An ex-actor runs the Palm Springs Racquet Club.
In fact this ex-actor is the Mayor of Palm Springs, so the show went down well there, but not anyplace else.

Charlie Farrell, Charles Winninger, Richard Deacon, Anna Lee, Marie Windsor, Jeff Silver, Kathryn Card

Charlie's Angels **
US 1976   74m   colour   TVM
Spelling–Goldberg (Ivan Goff, Ben Roberts)

Three gorgeous girls with special skills work undercover on expensive, impossible cases for an employer they never see.
If it's smooth Hitchcockian hokum you are after, a very good pilot for a series that did make it. The plot is borrowed from all kinds of other movies including *Dark Waters*, the pace is snappy and the spirit of *The Avengers* and *Mission Impossible* hovers at hand.

w Ivan Goff, Ben Roberts   *d* John Llewellyn Moxey

Kate Jackson, Farrah Fawcett-Majors, Jaclyn Smith, Diana Muldaur, Bo Hopkins, David Doyle, David Ogden Stiers

† The 50m series which followed was the hit of the 1976 season, to the despair of all intelligent telewatchers. In its second season Farrah Fawcett-Majors was replaced by Cheryl Ladd.

Chase
US 1973   74m   colour   TVM
Universal/Jack Webb

Four Los Angeles police officers, with special skills and motor cycles, form an elite squad.
The mixture as before; it doesn't rise.

w Stephen J. Cannell   *d* Jack Webb

Mitch Ryan, Reid Smith, Michael Richardson, Brian Fong

† The 50m series which followed ran 24 episodes and was not accounted a success.

Chataway, Christopher (c 1926–). British long-distance runner of the forties. He came into TV as an anchorman and commentator, then went into politics.

Chayevsky, Paddy (1923–). Star American TV dramatist of the fifties. His *Marty, The Catered Affair, The Bachelor Party* and *Middle of the Night* were all made into movies. He went to Hollywood and seemed to lose most of his flair.

The Cheaters
GB 1960   × 25m   bw

An insurance investigator exposes defrauders.
Average comic series.

John Ireland, Robert Ayres

Checkmate
US 1959–61   70 × 50m   bw
CBS/Universal

Adventures of three assorted private detectives in San Francisco.

CHARLIE'S ANGELS. Three attractive girls rather than the sub-Hitchcock plots were the mainstay of this popular series, which was accused (rather unfairly) of relying on 'T and A' and 'the jiggle factor' for its appeal. Jaclyn Smith, Kate Jackson, Farrah Fawcett-Majors.

Elementary but reasonably competent mystery series with a hero for each age group.

cr Eric Ambler

Anthony George, Sebastian Cabot, Doug McClure

Chelsea at Nine (GB 1957–64). A sophisticated variety show originated by Granada TV from the Chelsea Palace. American directors were employed to give the latest transatlantic look to the show, and many American acts were imported.

Cher (1946–) (Cherilyn Sarkisian). Armenian–American singer who has starred in variety series of the seventies both with and without her ex-husband Sonny Bono.

Chertok, Jack (*c* 1910–). Independent producer (*My Favorite Martian*, *The Lone Ranger*, etc).

The Chester Mystery Plays ∗∗
GB 1976   150m   colour (VTR)
BBC (Cedric Messina)

A compilation of scenes from the 14th-century religious plays originally performed by the craft guilds of Chester.
A marvellous rendering of these crude but vigorous playlets, with much use of chroma-key enabling actors

to play against backdrops which look like a brightly illuminated medieval manuscript.

modern version Maurice Hussey   *d* Piers Haggard   *m* Guy Wolfenden   *designer* Stuart Walker

Michael Hordern (as God), Tom Courtenay (as Christ), Brian Glover, Joe Gladwin, Christine Hargreaves, Christopher Guard

'A superb example of a fusion of all the crafts.' – *Guardian*

Cheyenne*
US 1955–62   107 × 50m   bw
ABC/Warner

Adventures of a frontier scout.
Marathon western series in which right always prevailed and many episodes were cutdown variants on popular Warner movies, using the original stock footage. In general, satisfying to all classes, with a new giant star.

Clint Walker (as Cheyenne Bodie)

'No different from the low-budget westerns that kids used to see in movie theatres on Saturday afternoons.' – Don Miller, 1957

Chicago Teddy Bears*
US 1971   13 × 25m   colour
CBS/Warner

The owner of a Chicago restaurant in the twenties has trouble with gangsters.
Quite a lively comedy spoof of the *Untouchables* era, this amiable series failed to make its mark with the public.

Dean Jones, Art Metrano, John Banner, Marvin Kaplan, Jamie Farr, Huntz Hall, Mike Mazurki, Mickey Shaughnessy

Chico and the Man*
US 1974–7   approx. 75 × 25m   colour (VTR)
NBC/Wolper/Komack (James Komack)

A crotchety old garage owner is helped and hindered by a young Chicano.
Phenomenally successful comedy series relying on characterization. When 'Chico' died in 1977, other young Chicanos were used in approximations of the role.

Jack Albertson, Freddie Prinze

Child, Julia (1912–). American cookery expert who has starred in several series.

Child of Glass
US 1978   96m   colour   TVM
Walt Disney (Jan Williams, Tom Leetch)

A family moving into an old house finds in possession the ghosts of a Victorian child and her dog.
Moderate ghost story for children, rather similar to the cinema film *The Amazing Mr Blunden*. Produced for *The Wonderful World of Disney*.

w Jim Lawrence, *novel The Ghost Belonged to Me* by Richard Park   *d* John Erman   *ph* William Cronjager   *m* George Duning

Barbara Barrie, Biff McGuire, Anthony Zerbe, Nina Foch, Katy Kurtzman, Steve Shaw

Children's Television Workshop. A non-profit, independently funded organization headed by Joan Ganz Cooney and dedicated to better TV for children. From its New York studios it has produced since 1967 *Sesame Street*, *The Electric Company* and special events such as *The Best of Families*.

The Chinatown Murders
US 1974   98m   colour   TVM
Universal

Kojak tangles with Chinese Tongs when a top gangster is kidnapped.
Tedious Kojak double entry.

w Jack Laird   *d* Jeannot Szwarc

Telly Savalas, Dan Frazer, Kevin Dobson, George Savalas, Michael Constantine, Sheree North

CHiPs
US 1977–   × 50m   colour
MGM (Cy Chermak)

Adventures of two motorcycle cops in the California Highway Patrol.
What might have made an acceptable half-hour series is relentlessly padded both with talk and with irrelevant action, and generally operates at a low level of intelligence.

cr Rick Rosner

Larry Wilcox, Erik Estrado, Robert Pine

Chomsky, Marvin (–). American TV director who has acquired a reputation for efficient if not very stylish presentations of epic mini-series, notably *Roots* and such TV movies as *Attack on Terror*, *Danger in Paradise* and *Victory at Entebbe*.

Chopper One
US 1974   13 × 25m   colour
ABC/Spelling–Goldberg (Ronald Austin, James Buchanan)

Adventures of a helicopter patrol team in the Los Angeles Police.
Acceptable crime hokum with good photography and plenty of action.

James McMullen, Dirk Benedict

The Christians*
GB 1977   13 × 50m   colour
Granada (Norman Swallow, Mike Murphy)

The history of Christianity.
Basically a coffee-table series, pretty to look at but with

CHOPPER ONE. An undemanding police show about a helicopter team, this fitted so snugly into international schedules that buyers wondered why it was allowed to expire so young.

insufficient hard information. Bamber Gascoigne proved less than hypnotic both as writer and as linkman.

A Christmas Carol**
GB 1971   25m   colour
Chuck Jones, Richard Williams

A cartoon version of Dickens's story of Scrooge.
A potted but effective cartoon achievement, with drawings in the style of Victorian illustrations.

d Richard Williams   *md* Tristam Cary

voices Alastair Sim, Michael Redgrave, Michael Hordern

The Christmas Coal Mine Miracle*
US 1977   96m   colour   TVM
TCF (Lin Bolen)

An account of a 1951 disaster in Pennsylvania, when a mine was rocked by explosions but miraculously no one was killed.
Good solid drama of a kind rarely encountered these days.

w Dalene Young   *d* Jud Taylor   *ph* Terry Meade

Mitch Ryan, Kurt Russell, Barbara Babcock, Don Porter, Andrew Price, John Carradine

chroma key. An electronic device which allows a background studio space, by blue saturation, to be filled by a moving picture from another source. Much used in news broadcasts.

Chronicle. A BBC occasional one-hour series of the seventies, relating and updating archaeological discoveries.

Chuckleheads. 150 × 5m bw comedies edited down in the fifties from two-reelers featuring Ben Turpin, Snub Pollard, etc. Distributor: Adrian Weiss.

Churchill, Donald (1930–). British light actor who has also written dozens of equally light TV plays.

Churchill's People
GB 1975   26 × 50m   colour (VTR)
BBC/MCA

Stories from British history.
A genuinely disastrous attempt to breathe flesh into Churchill's *History of the English-Speaking Peoples.* A pretentious embarrassment.

Cimarron City
US 1958   26 × 50m   bw
NBC/Universal/Mont

The mayor keeps the peace in a western town.
Watchable *Destry*-style western.

George Montgomery, Audrey Totter, John Smith

THE CHRISTIANS. An ambitious and costly series which didn't quite hit the mark, possibly because it strove too hard to avoid commitment. Here Bamber Gascoigne surveys St Peter's in Rome.

Cimarron Strip
US 1967   23 × 74m   colour
CBS (Philip Leacock)

A marshal keeps the peace between Kansas and Indian territory.
Standard, overlong western episodes.

Stuart Whitman, Percy Herbert, Randy Boone, Jill Townsend

Cinema. * Long-running (1964–72) British film magazine show, a weekly half-hour from Granada, in which new releases were related to old clips linked by theme, star or director. Successive hosts were Bamber Gascoigne, Derek Granger, Mark Shivas, Michael Scott, Michael Parkinson, Clive James.

A Circle of Children *
US 1977   96m   colour   TVM
TCF/Edgar J. Scherick

Problems of a teacher of autistic children.
An earnest and well-written piece, but *A Child Is Waiting* was better.

w Steven Gethers, *book* Mary McCracken   d Don Taylor   ph Gayne Rescher   m Nelson Riddle

Rachel Roberts, Jane Alexander, David Ogden Stiers

Circle of Fear: see Ghost Story

Circus Boy *
US 1956–7   49 × 25m   bw
NBC/Columbia/Herbert B. Leonard

A boy is adopted by a circus troupe.
Well-made children's drama series with a lively background.

Noah Beery Jnr, Robert Lowery, Guinn Williams, Mickey Braddock

The Cisco Kid
US 1951–5   156 × 25m   colour
Ziv

Adventures of the masked rider of the old west.
Standard children's western.

Duncan Renaldo, Leo Carrillo

Cities at War **
GB 1968   3 × 50m   bw (16mm)
Granada (Mike Wooller)

Documentary reconstructions of life in Leningrad, Berlin and London during World War II.
Excellent, straightforward history on film.

w (respectively) Bruce Norman, Annemarie Weber, Bruce Norman   d Michael Darlow

The City *
US 1971   95m   colour   TVM
Universal (Frank Price)

The Indian mayor of a southwestern city wages a political war while he pursues a mad bomber.
Well made telemovie set in Albuquerque, the pilot for a shortlived series.

w Howard Rodman   d Daniel Petrie   m Alex North

ANTHONY QUINN, Skye Aubrey, Robert Reed, E. G. Marshall, Pat Hingle

City Beneath the Sea
GB theatrical release title: *One Hour to Doomsday*
US 1970   98m   colour   TVM
Warner/Kent/Motion Pictures International (Irwin Allen)

An undersea city is threatened by an errant planetoid.
Futuristic adventure from a familiar stable; it will satisfy followers of *Voyage to the Bottom of the Sea.*

w John Meredyth Lucas   d Irwin Allen   ph Kenneth Peach   m Richard La Salle   ad Roger E. Maus, Stan Jolley

Stuart Whitman, Robert Wagner, Rosemary Forsyth, Robert Colbert, Burr de Benning, Richard Basehart, Joseph Cotten, James Darren, Sugar Ray Robinson, Paul Stewart

City Detective
US 1953–4   65 × 25m   bw
MCA/Universal

Stereotyped private eye series.

Rod Cameron

City of Angels
US 1976   13 × 50m   colour
Universal/Public Arts (Jo Swerling Jnr)

Cases of a Los Angeles private eye in the thirties.
More effort went into the period detail than into the plots, and the films looked unattractive, which is unforgivable.

cr Jo Swerling Jnr

Wayne Rogers, Clifton James, Elaine Joyce

† The first three episodes were cobbled together and released in theatres as *The November Plan.*

City of Gold **
Canada 1957   22m   bw
National Film Board

Pierre Berton, born in the Yukon, re-creates life there around the turn of the century by the use of still photographs.
Pioneer example of the use of the rostrum camera, and a highly successful and delightful one.

w Pierre Berton

Civilization ***
GB 1969   13 × 50m   colour (VTR)
BBC

Imposing documentary series, by and with Kenneth Clark, tracing the arts which have shaped western man.

clapperboard. Hinged board clapped together to mark synchronization at beginning of filmed action. Also *Clapperboard* is the title of Granada's weekly half-hour on the cinema, compiled since 1970 by Graham Murray and introduced by Chris Kelly.

Clark, Dane (1913–) (Bernard Zanville). American leading man, mildly popular at the end of the forties. A frequent TV guest actor; series include *Wire Service*, *Bold Venture*, *The New Perry Mason*.

Clark, Dick (1929–). American game show host and linkman, famous since his pop music programmes of the fifties.

Clark, Kenneth (1903–) (Lord Clark). British art critic and connoisseur who has fronted many TV documentaries including *Civilization*.

Class of '63
US 1973   74m   colour   TVM
Metromedia/Stonehenge (Dick Berg)

Old passions flare up at a college reunion.
Adequate mini-drama.

w Lee Kalcheim   *d* John Korty

Joan Hackett, James Brolin, Cliff Gorman, Ed Lauter

Clayhanger*
GB 1976   26 × 50m   colour (VTR)
ATV/Stella Richman

Two generations of a Potteries family, a step or two down from the Forsytes.
Impeccably made but rather boring family saga.

m Douglas Livingstone, *novels* Arnold Bennett   *d* John Davies, David Reid

Harry Andrews, Janet Suzman, Peter McEnery, Joyce Redman

A Clear and Present Danger*
US 1969   100m   colour   TVM
Universal (William Sackheim)

A senator's son determines to do something about smog.
Mildly enjoyable socially-conscious drama.

w A. J. Russell, Henri Simoun   *d* James Goldstone

Hal Holbrook, E. G. Marshall, Jack Albertson, Joseph Campanella, Pat Hingle, Sharon Acker, Mike Kellin

Cleaver and Haven: see Future Cop

Cleese, John (1939–). Tall, angular, eccentric British comedy actor, an essential ingredient of *Monty Python* and his own manic man in *Fawlty Towers*.

Clemens, Brian (1931–). British writer–producer, associated with *The Avengers*, *The Persuaders* and *Thriller* (GB).

Clement, Dick (1937–). British comedy scriptwriter, with Ian la Frenais. Series: *The Likely Lads*, *Porridge*, *Going Straight*.

Clews, Colin (19 –). British director, mainly of light entertainment shows (Palladium, Morecambe and Wise, etc). BAFTA award 1964.

cliffhanger. Unresolved situation (e.g. the hero hanging off a cliff) at the end of an episode of a serial, designed to persuade viewers to tune in next week.

Climb an Angry Mountain*
US 1972   97m   colour   TVM
Warner/Herb Solow

A local sheriff trails an Indian escaped convict to the top of Mount Shasta.
Overlong but generally enjoyable location melodrama which failed to spark a series.

w Joseph Calvelli, Sam Rolfe   *d* Leonard Horn

Fess Parker, Arthur Hunnicutt, Marj Dusay, Barry Nelson, Stella Stevens

Clipper Ship
US 1957   74m   bw   TVM
Columbia/Playhouse 90

On a ship returning to South America a girl falls for a condemned prisoner.
Talky melodrama with back-projected sails.

d Oscar Rudolph

Charles Bickford, Jan Sterling, Steve Forrest, Helmut Dantine, Evelyn Ankers

Clouds of Glory*
GB 1978   2 × 50m   colour (16mm)
Granada (Norman Swallow)

The lives of the Wordsworths and Coleridge.
Historical re-creations with the director on top technical form, but also with some exploitation and distortion of fact. The Coleridge episode, *The Rime of the Ancient Mariner*, is to say the least eccentrically told, but it looks good.

w Melvyn Bragg, Ken Russell   *d* KEN RUSSELL   *pd* Michael Grimes   *ph* DICK BUSH

David Warner, Felicity Kendal, David Hemmings

Coca, Imogene (1908–). American eccentric revue comedienne associated in the early fifties with Sid Caesar and *Your Show of Shows*. In 1954 she had her own variety hour, *The Imogene Coca Show*. Never subsequently found a niche except in *Grindl*, which lasted only one season, and the abysmal *It's About Time*.

57

Coco, James (1929–). Chubby American comic actor with stage, screen and TV credits. Series: *Calucci's Department*.

Code Name: Diamondhead
US 1977 74m colour TVM
Quinn Martin/NBC

Adventures of a US counter-intelligence agent in Hawaii.
A predictable pilot which didn't sell.

w Paul King *d* Jeannot Szwarc *ph* Jack Whitman *m* Morton Stevens

Roy Thinnes, France Nuyen, Zulu, Ian MacShane

Code Name: Heraclitus
GB 1967 88m colour TVM
Universal

A war veteran dies briefly on the operating table; revived, he is emotionless and so makes an ideal spy.
So who said the six million dollar man was a new idea?

w Alvin Sapinsley

Stanley Baker, Ricardo Montalban, Jack Weston, Leslie Nielsen, Sheree North, Kurt Kasznar

Code R
US 1977 13 × 50m colour
Warner (Ed Self)

Adventures of an emergency rescue service on a Californian island (Catalina).

Simple-minded action for children, tourists and dogs.

cr Ed Self

James Houghton, Martin Cove, Tom Simcox, Susanne Reed

Code Three
US 1956 39 × 25m bw
Hal Roach

Cases of the Los Angeles County Sheriff's office.
Below par crime filler.

Richard Travis

Coe, Fred (1914–). American producer associated with TV's 'golden age' of the fifties: many plays; series includes *Mr Peepers*.

Coffee, Tea or Me?*
US 1973 74m colour TVM
Mark Carliner

An airline stewardess has one lover in London and another in Los Angeles.
So what else is new? Agreeable daffy comedy.

d Norman Panama

Karen Valentine, John Davidson, Michael Anderson Jnr

Cold Comfort Farm*
GB 1968 3 × 50m bw (VTR)
BBC

COLDITZ. A prisoner of war series which was accused of reviving old Anglo-German feuds; but in fact the Germans came out as by far the most interesting characters. Dan O'Herlihy, Edward Brooks, Anthony Valentine, Paul Chapman, Jack Hedley.

A young woman finds her country relations to be grotesque caricatures of the popular urban conception of country folk.

Stella Gibbons's wryly amusing novel of the twenties, a splendid corrective to *The Archers*, was subtly transferred to TV in this memorable adaptation.

dramatized by David Turner

Alastair Sim

COLDITZ. Nominal stars of the series were Robert Wagner and David McCallum.

A Cold Night's Death*
US 1972 73m colour TVM
Spelling–Goldberg (Paul Junger Witt)

In a snowbound laboratory scientists are experimenting on apes . . . and someone is experimenting on *them*.
Reasonably tart and chilling sci-fi.

w Jarrold Freeman *d* Christopher Knopf

Robert Culp, Eli Wallach, Michael C. Gwynne

Colditz*
GB 1972–3   28 × 50m colour
BBC/Universal

Incidents during World War II in the crack German prisoner-of-war camp.
A good intelligent series which proved highly popular in the UK but was never even screened in the US.

Robert Wagner, Bernard Hepton, David McCallum, Anthony Valentine

Cole, Dennis (*c* 1941–). Bland American juvenile lead, in series *The Felony Squad*, *Bracken's World*, *Bearcats*.

Cole, Nat King (1919–65) (Nathaniel Coles). Black American pianist and singer. In 1957 he was to have his own series, but it was cancelled, because southern stations threatened a boycott.

Coleman, David (*c* 1927–). British sports commentator, longtime host of *Sportsnight*.

The Collaborators
Canada 1975–6   × 50m colour
CBC

Stories of the pathologists who assist police work.
The stories in fact became very miscellaneous, and the series petered out, but essentially it was a competent imitation of American standards.

College Bowl. American quiz show of the fifties, with college teams competing to answer difficult general knowledge questions. From it the British *University Challenge* was drawn.

Collingwood, Charles (1917–). American international correspondent, long with CBS.

Collins, Gary (*c* 1935–). Unassuming American leading man. Series include *The Wackiest Ship in the Army*, *Iron Horse*, *The Sixth Sense*, *Born Free*.

Collins, Norman (1907–). British executive instrumental in the creation of ITV and the founding of ATV. Also author of the novel *London Belongs to Me* (serialized in 1977).

Collision Course **
US 1976   100m   colour   TVM (tape)
David Wolper

The conflict between President Truman and General MacArthur which led to the latter's resignation.
Dogged dramatized documentary with some splendid moments between the padding.

w ERNEST KINOY   d Anthony Page

E. G. MARSHALL, HENRY FONDA, John Randolph, Andrew Duggan, Barry Sullivan, Lloyd Bochner, Lucille Benson, Ann Shoemaker

Colonel Flack
US 1953   × 25m   bw
CBS/Wilbur Stark

An elderly confidence trickster constantly eludes the law.
Mild but surprisingly popular comedy of its time.

Alan Mowbray, Frank Jenks

Colonel March of Scotland Yard
GB 1953   26 × 25m   bw
Sapphire

Stories of the Department of Queer Complaints, from the novels by Roy Vickers.
Despite its star, a tacky series in which the sets always seemed about to fall apart.

Boris Karloff

Colorado C.1
US 1978   50m   colour
CBS/Quinn Martin/Woodruff (Philip Salzman)

Two brothers lead an elite state police force.
Competent standard cop show pilot which wasn't signed on.

w Robert W. Lenski   d Virgil W. Vogel   ph Jacques R. Marquette   m Dave Grusin

John Elerick, Marshall Colt, L. Q. Jones, Laurette Spang, Christine Belford, David Hedison

Colossus: The Ship That Lost a Fortune *
GB 1978   2 × 50m   colour (16mm)
BBC (Tony Salmon)

An account of the reconstruction of rare Greek vases which were smashed and lost in a 1798 shipwreck off the Scillies.
Precise and painstaking documentary paying as much attention to diving as to museum work. The kind of film report that only the BBC would mount.

narrator Dr Ann Burchall

colour. America began a colour system in 1953, Britain not until 1968, when technology was much more advanced and the system more satisfactory, with subtler tones and a much wider range. In each case colour sets were expensive and slow to sell, but by the mid-seventies were in the majority.

Colt 45
US 1958–9   67 × 25m   bw
ABC/Warner

In the old west, a gun salesman is actually a government agent.
Passable western.

Wayde Preston, Donald May

Columbia Broadcasting System: see CBS

Columbo: see Mystery Movie

Combat! *
US 1962–6   152 × 50m   bw (last 25 in colour)
ABC/Selmur

Adventures of an infantry platoon in the European theatre during World War II.
Smartly tooled films, much appreciated by war veterans, and of a high standard of scripting.

Rick Jason, Vic Morrow

Come Dancing. A perennial BBC series culminating in an annual ballroom dancing championship.

The Comedians. An influential format created by Granada TV. The acts of stand-up comics were sliced into individual jokes and re-edited into a shaped half-hour with musical bridges. It lasted well for two seasons before talent became scarce. Creator: John Hamp. With Bernard Manning, Charlie Williams, Tom O'Connor, Mike Reid, Ken Goodwin, Frank Carson, Duggie Brown.

The Comedy Company
US 1978   93m   colour   TVM
CBS/MGM/Merrit Malloy/Jerry Adler

Would-be comics at a try-out club save the owner from a takeover.
Rather woebegone modern treatment of an old-hat theme; not very entertaining.

w Lee Kalcheim   d Lee Phillips   ph Matthew F. Leonetti   m Tom Scott

Jack Albertson, GEORGE BURNS, Lawrence-Hilton Jacobs, Susan Sullivan, Abe Vigoda, Michael Brandon, Herb Edelman

Como, Perry (1912–) (Nick Perido). Easy-going Italian–American ballad singer, a TV staple through the fifties and sixties, especially on *Kraft Music Hall*.

Compact. Popular BBC soap opera of the sixties, set in the offices of a magazine for women.

COLUMBO. Who would have thought that a short, shapeless, cast-eyed not-too-good-looking character actor in a rumpled old raincoat could endear himself to a nation and become television's highest-paid actor? It happened to Peter Falk.

THE COMEDIANS. A simple but effective idea which proved influential in the early seventies. Take a dozen stand-up comics and intercut their jokes. But make sure you've an ample supply of gag books to start with.

Companions in Nightmare *
US 1967 99m colour TVM
Universal (Norman Lloyd)

Murder at a group therapy session.
Slightly offbeat, rather pretentious whodunnit.

w Robert L. Joseph *d* Norman Lloyd

Melvyn Douglas, Gig Young, Anne Baxter, Patrick O'Neal, Dana Wynter, Leslie Nielsen

Company of Killers
US 1969 87m colour TVM
Universal

A psychopathic killer is at large in the city.
Adequate chase thriller.

w E. Jack Neuman *d* Jerry Thorpe

Van Johnson, Ray Milland, Robert Middleton, John Saxon, Susan Oliver, Clu Gulager, Brian Kelly, Fritz Weaver, Diana Lynn

compilation. Programme made up chiefly from segments of other programmes, stock shots or library film.

Confession
US 1957 74m bw TVM
Columbia/Playhouse 90

A reporter discovers that the public idol who is his subject had feet of clay.
Familiar exposé stuff, adequately put over.

d Anton M. Leader

Dennis O'Keefe, June Lockhart, Paul Stewart, Romney Brent

Conflict. Umbrella title used for a suspense anthology segment of *Warner Brothers Present*, a one-hour series aired in 1955.

COMPANY OF KILLERS. When TV movies were released theatrically, the advertising usually showed them up as decidedly routine.

Congratulations, It's a Boy
US 1971 73m colour TVM
Aaron Spelling

A swinging bachelor's life changes when his grown son turns up.
Modest comedy with a few laughs.

w Stanley Cherry *d* William A. Graham

Bill Bixby, Diana Baker, Jack Albertson, Ann Sothern, Karen Jensen

Congressional Investigator
US 1959 26 × 25m bw
Sandy Howard

Government investigators uncover evidence for congressional hearings.
Syndicated series, a rare example of an attempt to make entertainment out of politics (not forgetting a little thick-ear).

Edward Stroll, William Masters, Stephen Roberts, Marion Collier

The Connection *
US 1973 74m colour TVM
Phil D'Antoni/Metromedia

A tough reporter mediates between jewel thieves and insurance companies.
Complex, New York based thriller which resolves itself into a pretty good chase comparable with the same producer's *The French Connection*.

w Albert Ruben *d* Tom Gries

Charles Durning, Ronnie Cox, Zohra Lampert, Dennis Cole, Dana Wynter, Howard Cosell, Mike Kellin

Connelly, Christopher (1941–). American leading man, who became known in *Peyton Place* and later played the lead in *Paper Moon*.

Connors, Chuck (1924–) (Kevin Connors). Lean, mean-looking action star, former sportsman, who enjoyed a fairly successful film career but did even better in TV. Series: *Rifleman*, *Arrest and Trial*, *Branded*, *Cowboy in Africa*, *The Thrill Seekers*.

Connors, Michael (1925–) (Kreker Ohanian). Armenian–American leading man who after a mild film career became a top TV star in the action series *Tightrope* and *Mannix*.

Conrad, Robert (1935–) (Conrad Robert Falk). American leading man. Series include *Hawaiian Eye*, *The DA*, *The Wild Wild West*, *Assignment Vienna* and *Baa Baa Black Sheep*.

Conrad, William (1920–). Portly American character actor, the original Matt Dillon on radio. Often a director for TV, but most famous as the long-running *Cannon*.

Conspiracy of Terror *
aka: *Enter Horowitz*
US 1975 74m colour TVM
Lorimar

A man-and-wife detective team encounter diabolism in the suburbs.

COMPILATIONS. Television documentaries used historical footage as the cinema never would, and caused the newsreel libraries to take good care of their negatives. Here Hitler is seen planning his campaign against Russia in 1941.

Curious mix of Jewish humour and macabre goings-on; a failed pilot.

w Howard Rodman d John Llewellyn Moxey m Neal Hefti

Michael Constantine, Barbara Rhoades, Mariclare Costello, Logan Ramsay

Conspiracy to Kill *
aka: *The DA: Conspiracy to Kill*
US 1970   97m   colour   TVM
Universal/Jack Webb

The DA of a small community tries a case involving a local chemist who is also a fence.
One or two failed pilots for the same non-series (see *The DA: Murder One*). Quite watchable.

w Stanford Whitmore, Joel Oliansky d Paul Krasny

Robert Conrad, William Conrad, Belinda Montgomery, Don Stroud, Steve Ihnat

Constantine, Michael (1927–) (Constantine Joanides). Familiar rumpled-looking American character actor who had a leading role in *Room 222*; also appeared in *Hey Landlord*.

Conti, Tom (1941–). Leading British character actor, usually in single plays apart from *Adam Smith*, *The Glittering Prizes* and *The Norman Conquests*.

Contract on Cherry Street
US 1977   148m   colour   TVM
NBC/Artanis/Columbia (Renee Valente)

A police lieutenant starts a private war on the Mafia in revenge for the death of a pal.
Overlong, repetitive and ordinary cop saga, *Madigan*-style, in which Sinatra saw fit to make a comeback.

w Edward Anhalt d William E. A. Graham ph Jack Priestley m Jerry Goldsmith

Frank Sinatra, Martin Balsam, Verna Bloom, Harry Guardino, Henry Silva, Martin Gabel

'The cop show pattern emerges all too soon, and even Sinatra can't stem the tedium.' – *Daily Variety*

contrast. The relationship between the lightest and darkest areas in a TV picture.

convergence. Superimposition during transmission of various colours of the picture over each other. Bad convergence is almost always a malfunction of the set.

Converse, Frank (1938–). Thoughtful American leading man who has had a sporadic TV career. Series: *Coronet Blue, Movin' On*. Also appeared in *A Tattered Web* and *Dr Cook's Garden*.

Convoy
US 1965   13 × 50m   bw
NBC/Universal

World War II adventures in the North Atlantic.
Uninteresting war series with the chill wind of failure about it.

John Gavin, John Larch, Linden Chiles

Conway, Gary (1938–) (Gareth Carmody). Adequate American leading man who was briefly popular in the series *Burke's Law* and *Land of the Giants*.

Conway, Russ (1924–) (Trevor Stanford). British pianist popular during the fifties and sixties, especially in the Billy Cotton Band Show.

Conway, Shirl (1914–) (Shirley Crossman). American character actress, on the lighter side, who scored an unexpected hit in the series *The Nurses*.

Conway, Tim (*c* 1928–). American comic actor and writer. Rose to fame in *McHale's Navy*, briefly had a series of his own in 1970, joined Carol Burnett in 1975.

Coogan, Jackie (1914–). American actor who made a great hit in 1921 as a child star and is still around in TV, where he scored his biggest hit as the grotesque Uncle Fester in *The Addams Family*.

Cook, Fielder (1923–). TV director of the fifties whose *Patterns* took him to Hollywood for the film version. Later career interesting but sporadic.

Cook, Peter (1937–). British writer and performer of undergraduatish humour, moderately popular with Dudley Moore in a sporadic cabaret style sixties series called *Not Only But Also*.

Cooke, Alistair (1909–). Respected Anglo-American journalist and commentator who adds incisive wit to his urbane manner. Many TV appearances as host and commentator, mostly in America; his major project, however, was his 13-hour series *America*, which he wrote and narrated for BBC.

Cool Million
US 1971   97m   colour   TVM
Universal (David J. O'Connell)

A private eye whose fee per case is one million dollars locates a missing heiress.
Slick, glamorous and empty pilot for a shortlived (only four episodes) addition to *Mystery Movie*.

w Larry Cohen   *d* Gene Levitt

James Farentino, Lila Kedrova, Patrick O'Neal, Christine Belford, Barbara Bouchet, John Vernon, Jackie Coogan

Cooney, Joan Ganz (1930–). American executive and pioneer of Children's Television Workshop, which produces *Sesame Street*.

Cooper, Jackie (1921–). American ex-child star who pursued a varied adult career as executive, producer and occasional actor. Features vividly in *Only You Dick Daring*. Series: *The People's Choice, Hennessy*.

Cooper, Joseph (1912–). Diffident British musical expert who chairs BBC2's occasional *Face the Music* series.

Cooper, Tommy (1921–). Giant-size, fez-topped British comedian who makes a speciality of getting magic tricks wrong. A star since the mid-fifties, almost always in a variety format.

The Cop and the Kid
US 1975   × 25m   colour
NBC/Paramount/Playboy (Jerry Davis)

A bachelor policeman fosters an unruly orphan and his dog.
Ho-hum sentimental comedy which didn't last.

cr Jerry Davis   *m* Jerry Fielding

Charles Durning, Tierre Turner, Patsy Kelly

co-production. One financed and produced jointly by more than one company, usually in different countries. The danger of such enterprises is that the flavour of compromise may be the predominant one.

Corbett, Harry (1918–). Cheerful Yorkshire puppeteer, one of Britain's longest-running TV personalities. Created the famous glove puppet Sooty.

Corbett, Harry H. (1925–). Burly British character actor whose finest hour was as the younger Steptoe in the innovative comedy series *Steptoe and Son*.

Corbett, Ronnie (1930–). Diminutive Scottish comedian who has had several series of his own but is best known as one of *The Two Ronnies*.

Corey for the People
US 1977   74m   colour   TVM
Columbia/Jeni (Buzz Kulik, Jay Daniel)

A young assistant DA prosecutes a socialite for murder.
Competent standard courtroom stuff: no series resulted.

w Alvin Boretz   *d* Buzz Kulik

John Rubenstein, Eugene Roche, Carol Rossen, Ronny Cox, Joseph Campanella

Corey, Wendell (1914–68). Reliable American actor who usually played the other man or the deceived husband. TV series: *Harbor Command, Peck's Bad Girl, The Eleventh Hour.*

Coronado 9
US 1959   39 × 25m   bw
Universal

A former Naval Intelligence officer operates as a private eye.
Routine mysteries agreeably set on the Coronado peninsula.

Rod Cameron

Coronation Street. Long-running British soap opera set in a terraced street in industrial Lancashire. Granada have made two half-hours a week since 1960, with the help of many producers and writers, though H. V. Kershaw has been the most consistent guiding light and the original format was devised by Tony Warren. Characters who became household names include Ena Sharples (Violet Carson), Elsie Tanner (Pat Phoenix),

Minnie Caldwell (Margot Bryant), Albert Tatlock (Jack Howarth), Annie Walker (Doris Speed) and Hilda and Stan Ogden (Jean Alexander and Bernard Youens). Arthur Lowe as Mr Swindley also gained his last step to stardom in the series.

Coronet Blue
US 1966   13 × 50m   colour
CBS/Plautus/Herb Brodkin

An amnesiac seeks to uncover his past.
Promising series which was never allowed to get going.

Frank Converse, Brian Bedford, Joe Silver

Cosa Nostra, Arch Enemy of the FBI
US 1966   97m   colour   TVM
Quinn Martin

A contract killer murders a grand jury witness.
Muddled cops and robbers, as cumbersome as its title, put together from two episodes of *The FBI*.

w Norman Jolley   *d* Don Medford

Efrem Zimbalist Jnr, Walter Pidgeon, Celeste Holm, Philip Abbott, Telly Savalas, Susan Strasberg

CORONATION STREET. This long-running twice-weekly serial began in 1960 and this was the roll call for the first episode. Little did some of these people know that they were in for a twenty-year sentence.

Back row, left to right: IVAN BEAVIS, Harry Hewitt; JACK HOWARTH, Albert Tatlock; ERNEST WALDER, Ivan Cheveski; PHILIP LOWRIE, Dennis Tanner; ALAN ROTHWELL, David Barlow; ARTHUR LESLIE, Jack Walker; WILLIAM CROASDALE (an extra, no name); FRANK PEMBERTON, Frank Barlow; NOEL DYSON, Ida Barlow; MARGOT BRYANT, Minnie Caldwell.

Front row: DORIS SPEED, Annie Walker; BETTY ALBERGE, Florrie Lindley; ANNE CUNNINGHAM, Linda Cheveski; PATRICIA PHOENIX, Elsie Tanner; VIOLET CARSON, Ena Sharples; CHRISTINE HARGREAVES, Christine Hardman; WILLIAM ROACHE, Kenneth Barlow; PATRICIA SHAKESBY, extra; PENNY DAVIES, extra; LYNNE CAROL, Martha Longhurst.

Cosby, Bill (1938–). Black American actor and comedian who made a major breakthrough in *I Spy* as the first black to get equal star billing in a series. Subsequently most effective as guest artist, though he has been involved in a couple of series, *Cos* and *Fat Albert and the Cosby Kids*, with special appeal to children.

Costello, Lou (1906–59) (Louis Cristillo). American comedian, the chubby half of Abbott and Costello (see Abbott, Bud).

Cotton, Billy (1900–69). Cheerful British bandleader who would have a go at anything and hosted a long-running BBC variety show with the emphasis on comedy. His son, Bill Cotton Jnr, subsequently became controller of BBC1.

Count Dracula
GB 1977   approx. 160m   colour (VTR)
BBC (Gerald Savory)

An elongated and sex-ridden version of the classic vampire yarn, with too much unpleasant horror to sustain the romantic gothic mood which it obviously seeks, and too little room for its star to manoeuvre.

w Gerald Savory, *novel* Bram Stoker   *d* Philip Saville

Louis Jourdan, Frank Finlay, Susan Penhaligon

The Count of Monte Cristo
GB 1955   39 × 25m   bw
ATV

Adventure series vaguely based on the Alexandre Dumas classic.

George Dolenz, Nick Cravat, Fortunio Bonanova

The Count of Monte Cristo
GB 1975   96m   colour
ITC/Norman Rosemont

A man unjustly imprisoned escapes and revenges himself on his enemies.
Competent rather than inspired version; one longs for the Robert Donat version.

w Sidney Carroll   *d* David Greene

Richard Chamberlain, Tony Curtis, Trevor Howard, Louis Jourdan, Donald Pleasence, Kate Nelligan, Dominic Guard

The Counterfeit Killer
aka: *The Faceless Man*
US 1968   95m   colour   TVM
Universal

A cop with a criminal background goes undercover to solve the mystery of corpses being washed ashore.
Underdeveloped and rather boring mystery pilot.

w Harold Clements, Stephen Bochco   *d* Josef Leytes

Jack Lord, Shirley Knight, Charles Drake, Jack Weston, Mercedes McCambridge, Joseph Wiseman

Counterspy
US 1958   39 × 25m   bw
Screen Gems

Adventures of a governmental counter-intelligence agent.
Routine syndicated series which later spawned a couple of feature films, *David Harding Counterspy* and *Counterspy Meets Scotland Yard*.

Don Megowan

The Country Husband*
US 1957   74m   bw   TVM
Columbia/Playhouse 90

A middle-aged executive wonders whether to leave his wife and family for a young girl.
Routine domestic drama, quite well acted.

w Paul Monash, *story* John Cheever   *d* James Neilson

Frank Lovejoy, Barbara Hale, Felicia Farr, Kerwin Mathews

Country Matters**
GB 1972   13 × 50m   colour (16mm)
Granada (Derek Granger)

An anthology of superior dramas linked only by their setting in the English countryside; drawn from the stories of H. E. Bates and A. E. Coppard.

'Consistently superb.' – *The Times*

The Couple Takes a Wife
US 1972   73m   colour   TVM
Universal (George Eckstein)

An au pair girl becomes rather too well entrenched.
Simple domestic comedy.

w Susan Silver   *d* Jerry Paris

Bill Bixby, Paula Prentiss, Myrna Loy, Nanette Fabray, Valerie Perrine, Robert Goulet, Larry Storch

The Courage and the Passion
US 1978   96m   colour   TVM
Columbia/David Gerber

The private lives of officers at an air force base.
Unsuccessful pilot for a soap opera series which didn't happen. Good flying sequences are submerged by half-a-dozen trivial sex plots.

w Richard Fielder   *d* John Moxey   *ph* John M. Nickolaus   *m* Richard Shores

Vince Edwards, Desi Arnaz Jnr, Trisha Noble, Linda Foster, Robert Hooks, Paul Shenar, Monty Hall, Don Meredith, Robert Ginty

† Previously known as *Joshua Tree*; aka *The Power and the Passion*.

Courageous Cat. A five-minute cartoon series spoofing Batman, syndicated in the US in 1961, with music by Johnny Holiday.

Court Martial *
GB 1966   26 × 50m   bw
ITC/Roncom (Robert Douglas, Bill Hill)

Cases of two officer–lawyers in the US Army during World War II.
Brisk, efficient and slightly unusual series made by Lew Grade for the ABC network.

Peter Graves, Bradford Dillman

The Court Martial of George Armstrong Custer
US 1977   93m   colour   TVM
Norman Rosemont

An imaginary reconstruction of the trial which would have happened had Custer survived the battle of Little Big Horn.
Rather flat considering the possibilities.

w John Gay, *book* Douglas C. Jones   d Glen Jordan   m Jack Elliott

James Olson, Brian Keith, Ken Howard, Blyth Danner, J. D. Cannon, William Daniels, Stephen Elliott, Biff McGuire

The Court of Last Resort
US 1957   26 × 25m   bw
ABC/Paisano

A seven-man court of do-gooders aims to free prisoners wrongfully convicted.
Modest mystery series, based on a real organization founded by Erle Stanley Gardner.

Lyle Bettger, Paul Birch (as Gardner)

The Courtship of Eddie's Father
US 1969–71   78 × 25m   colour
ABC/MGM (James Komack)

A small precocious boy tries to get his widowed father remarried.
Popular but rather trying sentimental comedy.

Bill Bixby, Brandon Cruz, Miyoshi Umeki, James Komack

Cousteau, Jacques (1910–). French undersea explorer who from the mid-sixties appeared in a long-running documentary series for Metromedia.

Cover Girls
US 1977   74m   colour   TVM
Columbia/David Gerber/NBC

Two glamorous fashion models are espionage agents.
Desperate flim-flam in the wake of *Charlie's Angels*.

w Mark Rodgers   d Jerry London

Cornelia Sharpe, Jayne Kennedy, Vince Edwards, Don Galloway, George Lazenby

Cowboy in Africa
US 1967   26 × 50m   colour
ABC/Ivan Tors

A rodeo star is hired to capture and domesticate African wild animals.
Moderately pleasing variation on *Daktari*, from the pilot film *Africa Texas Style*.

Chuck Connors, Tom Nardini, Ronald Howard

The Cowboys
US 1974   13 × 25m   colour
ABC/Warner

Seven boys help a widow run her ranch.
Disappointing extension of a popular western film.

Moses Gunn, Diana Douglas, Jim Davis

Cox, Brian (1946–). British character actor, notable on TV as Henry II in *The Devil's Crown*.

Cox, Ronny (1938–). American character actor who starred in the series *Apple's Way*.

Cox, Wally (1924–76). Bespectacled American comedy actor who made a hit as *Mr Peepers* and *Hiram Holliday* in the fifties.

CPO Sharkey
US 1977   × 25m   colour
R and R (Aaron Ruben, Gene Marcione)

A petty officer commands a training unit at the San Diego Naval Station.
Another service comedy which doesn't travel.

cr Aaron Ruben   d Peter Baldwin

Don Rickles, Elizabeth Allen, Harrison Page

Craig Kennedy, Criminologist
US 1952   26 × 25m   bw
Adrian Weiss

Adventures of a scientific detective.
Sherlock Holmes need have no fear.

Donald Woods

Craig, Wendy (1934–). British comedy actress, popular in domestic comedy series starting with *And Mother Makes Three* and carrying on from there.

Crane. British one-hour series of the early sixties, with Patrick Allen as an adventurer abroad.

Crane, Bob (1929–78). Wry-faced American leading man, former drummer and radio comic. Most popular in *Hogan's Heroes*.

Crawford, Broderick (1910–). Burly American character actor, son of Helen Broderick. His lengthy film career included an Academy Award for *All the King's Men*. TV series include *Highway Patrol*, *King of Diamonds*, *The Interns*.

Crawford, Michael (1942–) (Michael Dumble Smith). British light leading man and comedian, former child actor. After being accepted in a variety of roles he shot to fame as the accident-prone hero of *Some Mothers Do 'Ave 'Em*, an extreme characterization which may have prevented his finding another vehicle.

crawl. The roll-up credits which end most TV shows.

Crawlspace*
US 1971 74m colour TVM
Viacom/Titus

A lonely middle-aged couple take in a dangerous young man who comes to repair their furnace.
Unusual suspenser which keeps the interest.

w Ernest Kinoy, *novel* Jerbert Lieberman *d* John Newland

Teresa Wright, Arthur Kennedy, Tom Harper, Gene Roche

Crenna, Richard (1926–). Busy American leading man whose film career was desultory but who was popular enough on TV to star in several series: *Our Miss Brooks*, *The Real McCoys*, *Slattery's People*, *All's Fair*.

The Crezz*
GB 1977 12 × 50m colour (VTR)
Thames (Paul Knight)

An interesting but unsuccessful attempt at a light-hearted *Peyton Place* set in a genteel London suburb. Marks for trying rather than achievement.

w Clive Exton

Joss Ackland, Hugh Burden, Peter Bowles, Elspet Gray

Crime Club*
US 1972 74m colour TVM
CBS/Glicksman–Larson

A private detective investigates the fatal car crash of an old friend.
Entertaining mystery pilot which never got anywhere.

d David Lowell Rich

Lloyd Bridges, Barbara Rush, Victor Buono, Paul Burke

Crime Club
aka: *The Last Key*
US 1975 74m colour TVM
Universal (Matthew Rapf)

A Washington DC club comprises specialists who band together to combat crime.

Another failed attempt to promote this famous title into a series.

w Gene R. Kearney *d* Jeannot Szwarc

Robert Lansing, Scott Thomas, Eugene Roche, Barbara Rhoades, Biff McGuire

Crime Sheet. A half-hour British series of the early fifties introducing Raymond Francis as Lockhart of Scotland Yard. After a period under the title *Murder Bag*, the show became the long-running one-hour *No Hiding Place*.

Crisis. International title for the *Bob Hope Chrysler Theatre*, an anthology of 114 50m film dramas made between 1963 and 1966 by Universal.

Crisis at Sun Valley
US 1978 96m colour TVM
Columbia/Barry Weitz

A skier becomes a sheriff in Sun Valley.
Casual coupling of two unsold pilots for a series variously touted as *Stedman* and *Deadly Triangle*. Barely watchable.

w Carl Gottlieb, Alvin Boretz *d* Paul Stanley *ph* Al Francis *m* Dick de Benedictis

Dale Robinette, Bo Hopkins, Tracy Brooks Swope, Paul Brinegar, Taylor Lacher, John McIntire, Ken Swofford

Criss Cross Quiz. British title of *Tic Tac Dough*, a popular long-running quiz of the fifties in which correct and incorrect answers scored noughts or crosses on an electronic game board. Chief host: Jeremy Hawk.

Cronkite, Walter (1916–). American star newsman and commentator, with CBS from 1962.

The Crooked Hearts
US 1972 74m colour TVM
Lomar

A policewoman goes undercover to catch a suave murderer who preys on wealthy members of a lonelyhearts club.
Rather unattractive comedy-drama, interesting for its stars.

w A. J. Russell *d* Jay Sandrich

Douglas Fairbanks Jnr, Rosalind Russell, Maureen O'Sullivan, Ross Martin

Crosbie, Annette (1934–). British character actress, popular in a few films but mainly notable on TV: *The Six Wives of Henry VIII* (as Catherine of Aragon: BAFTA award 1970), *Katherine Mansfield*, *Edward the Seventh* (as Queen Victoria: BAFTA award 1975).

Crosby, Bing (1901–77). American crooner and light actor. One of the most memorable entertainers of his time, Bing made many guest appearances on TV and for many years up to his death provided a Christmas special. His only film series, a domestic comedy called *The Bing Crosby Show*, was not a great success when it aired in 1964.

Crosscurrent *
aka: *The Cable Car Murders*
US 1971 96m colour TVM
Warner (E. Jack Neuman)

The San Francisco police investigate when a man is found dead on a cable car.
Good competent police mystery.

w Herman Miller *d* Jerry Thorpe

Robert Hooks, Jeremy Slate, Robert Wagner, Carol Lynley, Jose Ferrer, Simon Oakland, John Randolph

Crossfire
US 1975 75m colour TVM
Quinn Martin

A police volunteer for undercover work is 'caught' peddling drugs and ostracized by his colleagues.
Routine hokum, well enough made.

w Philip Saltzman *d* William Hale

James Farentino, John Saxon, Roman Bieri, Patrick O'Neal, Pamela Franklin, Frank de Kova

Crossroads. British soap opera set in a midlands motel. ATV have networked four half-hours a week, more or less, since 1964, and the series has been continuously derided by the press and lapped up by the public. The continuing star has been Noele Gordon.

Crowhaven Farm *
US 1970 72m colour TVM
Aaron Spelling (Walter Grauman)

Local witches terrify a New York wife when she inherits a Connecticut farm.
Genuinely frightening supernatural high jinks in the *Rosemary's Baby* arena.

w John McGreevey *d* Walter Grauman

Hope Lange, Paul Burke, Lloyd Bochner, John Carradine, Virginia Gregg

Crown Court. A long-running British daytime series of the seventies, produced by Granada TV. Based on *The Verdict is Yours*, but with a rehearsed script, it gets through a court case in three half-hours, and is more entertaining than many peak-time offerings.

Crowther, Leslie (1933–). British comedy actor, the perpetual innocent. Series include *Crackerjack, My Good Woman, My Wife Next Door.*

Cruickshank, Andrew (1907–). British character actor who made his greatest mark in TV as Dr Cameron in *Dr Finlay's Casebook* in the mid-sixties.

Cruise into Terror
US 1978 96m colour TVM
Aaron Spelling, Douglas Cramer (Jeff Hayes)

Passengers on a pleasure ship are menaced by evil spirits surrounding an Egyptian sarcophagus.
Lethargic nonsense with the usual quota of semi-stars and an unseaworthy script.

w Michael Braverman *d* Bruce Kessler

Hugh O'Brian, Ray Milland, John Forsythe, Dirk Benedict, Christopher George, Lynda Day George, Frank Converse, Lee Meriwether, Stella Stevens, Marshall Thompson

Crunch and Des
US 1955 39 × 25m bw
NTA

Adventures of two owners of a charter boat.
Predictable adventures in the studio tank.

Forrest Tucker, Sandy Kenyon, Joanne Bayes

Crusader
US 1955–6 52 × 25m bw
Universal

A current affairs reporter has a mission to right international wrongs.
Implausible thick-ear.

Brian Keith

A Cry for Help **
aka: *End of the Line*
US 1975 74m colour TVM
Universal/Fairmont-Foxcroft (Richard Levinson, William Link)

A cynical disc jockey desperately tries to help a suicidal girl who phones in.
Character drama with sufficient suspense.

w Peter S. Fischer *d* DARYL DUKE

ROBERT CULP, Elayne Heilveil, Ken Swofford, Chuck McCann

A Cry in the Wilderness
US 1974 74m colour TVM
Universal/Lou Morheim

Bitten by a rabid skunk, a man chains himself in the barn while his wife fetches medical help. His home is then threatened by a flood . . .
Absurd piling-up of disaster situations: more laughs than suspense.

w Stephen and Elinor Karpf *d* Gordon Hessler

George Kennedy, Joanna Pettet, Lee H. Montgomery, Collin Wilcox-Horne

Cry Panic *
US 1974 74m colour TVM
Spelling–Goldberg

In an unfamiliar town, a motorist accidentally kills a pedestrian. The body then disappears . . .
Efficient what-the-hell-happened melodrama with echoes of *Bad Day at Black Rock*.

w Jack Sowards   *d* James Goldstone

John Forsythe, Earl Holliman, Anne Francis, Ralph Meeker, Claudia McNeil

Cry Rape*
US 1974   74m   colour   TVM
Warner

Various points of view on the trying of rape cases.
Dramatized documentary: nothing new, but persuasive.

w Will Lorin   *d* Corey Allen

Peter Coffield, Andrea Marcovicci, Patricia Mattick

CTV. Canadian channel of independent commercial stations, akin to Britain's ITV.

The Cuckoo Waltz*
GB 1976   19 × 25m   colour (VTR)
Granada (Brian Armstrong)

Two impecunious young marrieds have his rich friend as boarder.
Modestly pleasing comedy series which never quite got to first base.

w Geoffrey Lancashire

Diane Keen, David Roper, Lewis Collins

Culloden***
GB 1964   70m   bw   (16mm)
BBC

A brilliantly re-created, low-budget docu-drama account of the Battle of Culloden, presented as though modern TV cameras were on the spot. Vivid, exciting and highly influential.

w/d PETER WATKINS   *ph* DICK BUSH   *ed* MICHAEL BRADSELL

Culp, Robert (1931–   ). Tall, wolfish, American leading actor whose main TV success was the series *I Spy*. (He had previously starred in *Trackdown*.)

THE CUCKOO WALTZ. Domestic comedy never seems to wear out its welcome. This one provided contrast by adding the husband's rich friend as a temporary lodger. Diane Keen, David Roper.

Cummings, Robert or **Bob** (1908–). American light leading man who after a moderate Hollywood career became a popular TV star in the fifties, usually as a harassed executive. *Love That Bob*, *The Bob Cummings Show*, *My Hero*, *My Living Doll*, etc.

Curse of the Black Widow
US 1978 96m colour TVM
ABC Circle (Steven North)

Murders are committed by a giant spider.
Nonsense mystery which passes the time.

w Robert Blees, Earl Wallace *d* Dan Curtis

Tony Franciosa, Donna Mills, Patty Duke Astin, June Allyson, Sid Caesar

Curtis, Dan (1926–). American independent producer who, after his success with the serial *Dark Shadows*, has concentrated on TV movies with a horror theme: *The Night Stalker*, *Dracula*, *Scream of the Wolf*, etc. 1978: *When Every Day was the Fourth of July*, *Supertrain*, etc.

Curtis, Ken (1916–) (Curtis Gates). American character actor, a *Gunsmoke* regular.

Curtis, Tony (1925–) (Bernard Schwarz). Popular second level film star of the fifties who in middle age managed only occasional character roles. In TV, he played a number of guest roles, and co-starred in *The Persuaders* and *McCoy*.

Cushing, Peter (1913–). British leading actor and horror star who in the mid-sixties, with fair success, played Sherlock Holmes in a long BBC tape series.

Custer
aka: *The Legend of Custer*
US 1967 17 × 50m colour
ABC/TCF (Frank Glicksman, Robert Jacks)

Legendary western exploits of the famous American general.
A fair western series which somehow failed to connect with the public, perhaps because Custer was presented as a whitewashed hero.

m Elmer Bernstein

Wayne Maunder, Peter Palmer, Slim Pickens, Michael Dante, Alex Davion, Robert F. Simon

Cutter*
US 1973 74m colour TVM
Universal (Richard Irving)

Private eye seeks missing football player.
Snazzy black-oriented mystery pilot that didn't make it.

w/d Dean Hargrove

Peter De Anda, Cameron Mitchell, Barbara Rush, Gabriel Dell, Robert Webber, Archie Moore

Cutter's Trail*
US 1969 100m colour TVM
CBS/John Mantley

Adventures of the Marshal of Santa Fe in 1873.
Standard western pilot that wasn't picked up.

w Paul Savage *d* Vincent McEveety

John Gavin, Marisa Pavan, Joseph Cotten, Beverly Garland

D

The DA
US 1971   13 × 25m   colour
NBC/Universal/Jack Webb

The problems of a conscientious district attorney.
A series which followed two successful pilots (see
Conspiracy to Kill and *The DA: Murder One*) but failed
to take off.

Robert Conrad, Henry Morgan

The DA: Murder One
US 1969   97m   colour   TVM
Universal (Harold Jack Bloom)
The District Attorney traps a homicidal nurse.
One of two competent pilots (see *Conspiracy to Kill*)
made for a series that didn't go.

w Harold Jack Bloom   *d* Boris Sagal

Robert Conrad, Howard Duff, Diane Baker, J. D.
Cannon, David Opatoshu

Dad's Army***
GB 1967–77   50 approx. × 30m   colour (VTR)
BBC

Adventures of a platoon of over-age local defence vol-
unteers (Home Guard) in a small southern town in
Britain during World War II.
At its best, an inimitable character comedy with a
splendid company of old timers dispensing essentially
British, throwaway humour.

w/cr David Croft, Jimmy Perry

Arthur Lowe, John Le Mesurier, Clive Dunn, John
Laurie, Ian Lavender, Arnold Ridley, James Beck,
Frank Williams, Bill Pertwee

† A feature film version was made in 1971.

Dagmar (*c* 1930–) (Virginia Ruth Enger).
American vaudeville artist who traded on her super-
structure in TV variety shows of the fifties.

Dailey, Dan (1914–78). American dancing hero of
many a forties musical. Turned to TV in character
roles, and series include *The Four Just Men, The Governor
and J.J., Faraday and Company*.

The Dain Curse*
US 1978   3 × 96m   colour
CBS/Martin Poll

A private eye in the twenties seeks missing diamonds
and finds himself on a murder trail.

Atmospheric film version of a classic mystery novel of
considerable plot complication; but far too long for the
material.

w Robert Lenski, *novel* Dashiell Hammett   *d* E. W.
Swackhamer   *ph* Andrew Laszlo   *m* Charles Gross

JAMES COBURN, Jean Simmons, JASON MILLER, Hector
Elizondo, Paul Stewart, Beatrice Straight, David
Canary, Paul Harding, Roland Winters

'Lush, thought-provoking . . . a fine puzzler.' – *Daily
Variety*

The Dakotas*
US 1962   19 × 50m   bw
ABC/Warner

Four men fight corruption after the Civil War.
An appropriately dour, tough western which didn't
please generally but certainly created an atmosphere of
its own.

Larry Ward, Jack Elam, Chad Everett, Mike Greene

Daktari*
US 1966–8   89 × 50m   colour
CBS/MGM/Ivan Tors

Adventures centring on an African animal welfare com-
pound.
Popular family series from the pilot *Clarence the Cross-
Eyed Lion* which was released theatrically.

Marshall Thompson, Cheryl Miller, Hari Rhodes,
Hedley Mattingley

† *Cowboy in Africa* and *Keeper of the Wild* (a 1978 failed
pilot) adopted an almost identical format.

Dallas*
US 1978   × 50m   colour
Lorimar (Leonard Katzman)

Two Texas ranching families, long antagonistic, are reluctantly joined by marriage.
Good-looking but cliché-strewn family saga in the wake
of *Giant* and *Romeo and Juliet*. Not bad for those who
like this kind of thing.

cr/w David Jacobs   *d* Robert Day (pilot)

Barbara Bel Geddes, Jim Davis, Larry Hagman, Patrick
Duffy, Victoria Principal, David Wayne, Tina Louise,
Charlene Tilton, Linda Grey

'A limited series with a limited future.' – *Daily Variety*

Daly, James (1918–78). Incisive American character actor, in a few films. TV series: *Foreign Intrigue*, *Medical Center*.

Damon Runyon Theater
US 1954   39 × 25m   bw
CBS/Columbia

Anthology of low-life New York stories.

Host: Donald Woods

Dan August*
US 1970   26 × 50m   colour
ABC/Quinn Martin (Adrian Samish)

Cases of a police detective in California.
One of the better mystery series, from the pilot *The House on Greenapple Road* which however had Chris George in the lead. Despite its star, snappy pace and good production quality it failed to score high numbers.

Burt Reynolds, Richard Anderson, Norman Fell

Dan Raven
US 1960   43 × 50m   bw
NBC/Columbia

Cases of a police detective whose beat is Sunset Strip. Fair cop show which failed to take off.

Skip Homeier

Danger Has Two Faces
US 1967   89m   colour   TVM
TCF

A much disliked executive in Berlin is shot in mistake for an American agent, who promptly takes his place. Re-edited episodes from *The Man Who Never Was*, a series which had nothing except the title to do with its movie namesake.

w Merwin Gerard, Robert C. Dennis, Judith and Robert Guy Barrows   *d* John Newland

Robert Lansing, Dana Wynter, Murray Hamilton

Danger in Paradise
US 1977   98m   colour   TVM
CBS/Filmways/Perry Lafferty

An ailing Hawaiian rancher has to accept the help of his estranged ne'er-do-well son.
Expensive but muddled pilot which looked fine but had too many sub-plots including the Mafia and a wicked stepmother. It led to a shortlived (13 × 50m) series, *Big Hawaii* (*Danger in Paradise* in GB).

w William Wood   *d* Marvin Chomsky

Cliff Potts, John Dehner, Ina Balin

Danger Man***
GB 1959   26 × 25m   bw
GB 1961–2   45 × 50m   bw (2 in colour)

Adventures of an independent spy working for the British Secret Service.
Crisp, sophisticated James Bondery with a star who had a clipped style of his own.

Patrick McGoohan

†The 50m films were known in the US as *Secret Agent*.

The Dangerous Days of Kiowa Jones
US 1966   100m   colour   TVM
MGM/Max E. Youngstein, David Karr

Adventures of an ex-lawman in the old west.
Dreary, talkative western which seems desperate to fill up its allotted time and go home.

w Frank Fenton, Robert E. Thompson, *novel* Clinton Adams   *d* Alex March   *ph* Ellsworth Fredericks   *m* Samuel Matlovsky

Robert Horton, Diane Baker, Sal Mineo, Nehemiah Persoff, Gary Merrill, Robert H. Harris, Royal Dano

Daniel Boone
US 1964–9   165 × 50m   colour (29 bw)
NBC/Arcola/Felspar/TCF (Aaron Rosenberg)

Adventures of the frontiersman of revolutionary days. Rather sloppy adventure series with too much use of the studio backlot; but the kids lapped it up year after year.

story editor D. D. Beauchamp

Fess Parker, Patricia Blair, Ed Ames

†In 1977 an attempt was made to revive the character as *Young Dan'l Boone*.

Daniel, Glyn (*c* 1900–). British archaeologist and Cambridge don who became one of Britain's first TV stars after his appearances on *Animal, Vegetable or Mineral*.

Daniels, William (1927–). Neat-featured American character actor who apart from a few films has been seen in TV series as *Captain Nice* and as the detective in *Soap*.

Danner, Blythe (*c* 1945–). Leading American TV actress chiefly notable in series *Adam's Rib* and in *A Love Story*.

The Danny Thomas Show: see Make Room for Daddy

Dante
US 1960   26 × 25m   bw
NBC/Four Star

A nightclub owner has his heart in the right place though he's always in trouble with the cops.
Or, Everybody Comes to Rick's. In this case the formula didn't work as well as in *Casablanca*.

DANGER MAN. Patrick McGoohan as John Drake was always in command of the situation, and pretty girls like Susan Hampshire didn't influence him one way or the other.

Howard Duff

† From a character played by Dick Powell in *Four Star Playhouse*.

The Dark Secret of Harvest Home
US 1978   1 × 96m, 1 × 145m   colour
MCA/Universal (Jack Laird)

A family of city dwellers move to the country but find themselves the object of dark satanic rites.
Protracted tarradiddle with no narrative grip and not much in the way of characterization; but it occasionally looks good.

w Jack Guss, *novel Harvest Home* by Thomas Tryon   d Leo Penn

Bette Davis, David Ackroyd, Joanna Miles, Rosanna Arquette, René Auberjonois

Dark Shadows*. A mark for trying is deserved by this curious daily soap opera which between 1966 and 1970 notched up nearly a thousand VTR half-hours on ABC. Centring on a spooky New England house, it mixed vampires into its romantic brew and even tried to take them seriously. Those involved included Jonathan Frid, Joan Bennett and Mitch Ryan; creator was Dan Curtis.

Dark Victory
US 1975   150m   colour   TVM
Universal

A socialite finds she is dying of a brain tumour.
Absurdly extended remake of the 1939 film, which proved to be way out of fashion when remade in 1963 as *Stolen Hours*.

w M. Charles Cohen   d Jules Irving

Elizabeth Montgomery, Anthony Hopkins, Michele Lee

The DA's Man
US 1958   26 × 25m   bw
NBC/Universal/Jack Webb

Adventures of an undercover agent working for the DA.
Forgettable crime series.

John Compton

Dastardley and Muttley in Their Flying Machines*
US 1969   17 × 22m   colour
CBS/Hanna–Barbera

In World War I, an incompetent spy and his dog try to prevent American messages from getting through.
Rather a bright and original cartoon series.

voices Paul Winchell, Dick Messick   *m* Hoyt Curtin

A Date with Judy
US 1951–2   39 × 25m   bw
ABC

Adventures of a spoiled but lovable teenage girl in Santa Barbara.
A pre-Gidget Gidget, from the film and radio series.

Patricia Crowley, Judson Rees, Anna Lee

A Date with the Angels
US 1957   39 × 25m   bw
ABC

The trials and tribulations of young marrieds.
Unsurprising domestic comedy.

Betty White, Bill Williams, Russell Hicks, Isobel Elsom, Burt Mustin

Daughter of the Mind**
US 1969   74m   colour   TVM
TCF (Walter Grauman)

An international scientist believes that the ghost of his dead daughter is appearing to him, but the FBI exposes the trickery as the work of foreign agents.
Chilling little mystery which plays reasonably fair with the audience and works up quite a bit of excitement.

w Luther Davis, *novel The Hand of Mary Constable* by Paul Gallico   *d* Walter Grauman

Ray Milland, Gene Tierney, Don Murray, George Macready

The Daughters of Joshua Cabe
US 1972   74m   colour   TVM
Spelling–Goldberg

A grizzled westerner finds that he will lose his property unless his three daughters to whom it is entailed come to live on it. He cannot reach them, so he recruits three more . . .
Rather boring open-air comedy drama, like a heavy-handed *Petticoat Junction.*

w Paul Savage   *d* Philip Leacock

Buddy Ebsen, Sandra Dee, Karen Valentine, Lesley Warren, Jack Elam, Leif Erickson

†Sequels: *The Daughters of Joshua Cabe Return, The New Daughters of Joshua Cabe.*

The Daughters of Joshua Cabe Return
US 1975   74m   colour   TVM
Spelling–Goldberg

One of the daughters is blackmailed by her own father.
Another attempt to turn a pilot into a series, with a new cast. No livelier than the first. (A third pilot appeared in 1976, and again failed: see *The New Daughters of Joshua Cabe.*)

w Kathleen Hite   *d* David Lowell Rich

Dan Dailey, Christine Hart, Dub Taylor, Carl Betz, Ronne Troup, Brooke Adams, Kathleen Freeman

David Copperfield*
GB 1975   6 × 50m   colour (VTR)
BBC/Time-Life (John McRae)

A solid, sensible serial version of Dickens's novel, with all the favourite characters well preserved.

w Hugh Whitemore   *d* Joan Craft

Jonathan Kahn/David Yelland (David), Arthur Lowe (Micawber), Patricia Routledge (Mrs Micawber), Patience Collier (Betsey Trotwood), Martin Jarvis (Uriah Heep), Timothy Bateson (Mr Dick), Ian Hogg (Mr Peggotty), Pat Keen (Peggotty)

Davidson, John (*c* 1945–   ). Young American leading man of the seventies. TV series: *The Girl with Something Extra.*

Davies, Dickie (*c* 1942–   ). British sports commentator, long on ITV's *World of Sport.*

Davies, John Howard (1939–   ). British comedy director, former child star.

Davies, Rupert (1916–76). Solidly-built British character actor who after years of small parts, and indifferent series such as *Sailor of Fortune*, became a star as the pipe-puffing *Maigret*, a role which unfortunately typed him and harmed his later career.

Davies, Windsor (1930–   ). Welsh supporting actor who made a hit as the bellowing sergeant-major of *It Ain't Half Hot, Mum.*

Davis, Ann B. (1926–   ). Wry-faced American supporting comedienne. Series include *The Bob Cummings Show, The Brady Bunch.*

Davis, Joan (1908–61). Rubber-faced American eccentric comedienne who after a solid film career became a TV star in *I Married Joan.*

Davy Crockett. Five one-hour segments of Disney's *Frontierland*, made in 1954 and 1955, were subsequently combined into two feature films, *Davy Crockett* and *Davy Crockett and the River Pirates*, which were theatrically released. The five titles were *Davy Crockett Indian Fighter, Davy Crockett Goes to Congress, Davy Crockett at the Alamo, Davy Crockett's Keelboat Race* and *Davy Crockett and the River Pirates.*

Dawn: Portrait of a Teenage Runaway
US 1976 96m colour TVM
Douglas S. Cramer/NBC

A 15-year-old girl runs away and becomes a prostitute. Exploitation masquerading as social conscience. Dreary, too.

w Dalene Young d Randal Kleiser m Fred Karlin

Eve Plumb, Bo Hopkins, Leigh McCloskey

Dawson, Les (1933–). Glum Yorkshire comedian at his best in a variety format; pessimism is his forte, and he also does a passable impression of W. C. Fields.

Day, Dennis (1917–) (Owen Patrick Denis McNulty). High-voiced American comedian and singer, long associated with Jack Benny in radio and TV.

day for night. Method of shooting night scenes in daytime and then darkening them in the lab. The system gives far more clarity than the more 'realistic' method of shooting at night, which all too often results in all the blacks 'crushing' into each other.

Day, Robin (1923–). Formal British anchorman and interviewer, long associated with *Panorama*.

The Day the Earth Moved*
US 1974 74m colour TVM
ABC Circle

Aerial photographers track an incipient earthquake and try to persuade local townfolk to evacuate.
Fairly smart low-budget disaster movie.

w Jack Turley, Max Jack d Robert Michael Lewis

Jackie Cooper, Stella Stevens, Cleavon Little, William Windom, Beverly Garland

The Day War Broke Out*
GB 1975 50m colour
Thames (John Robins)

Memories of World War II are revived by film clips and interviews with Ronnie Aldrich, Bing Crosby, George Elrick, Margaret Lockwood, Tommy Trinder, Jack Warner, etc.
A pleasant piece of social history.

Days of Hope**
US 1976 four films: 99m, 103m, 77m, 132m colour
BBC/Polytel (Tony Garnett)

Four socialist-oriented plays tracing events in Britain between 1916 and 1926, through the lives of three poor people.
Hard tack, vigorously presented in grainy semi-documentary style. Not exactly entertaining, but compulsive once one gets into the mood.

w Jim Allen d Ken Loach

Paul Copley, Nikolas Simmonds, Pamela Brighton, Norman Tyrrel, Gary Roberts, Edward Underwood, John Phillips

'It made much else on television seem amateur and effete.' – *The Times*

Days of Our Lives. American soap opera which has run five times a week on NBC from 1965. Those involved include Macdonald Carey, Susan Flannery and Susan Seaforth.

De Camp, Rosemary (1913–). American character actress adept at pleasant understanding wives. TV series include *Dr Christian*, *The Bob Cummings Show*, *That Girl*.

De Cordova, Frederick (1910–). American director of innumerable star comedy half-hours in the fifties and sixties.

The Dead Don't Die*
US 1975 74m colour TVM
Douglas S. Cramer

A man wrongly executed becomes a zombie and helps find the real murderer.
Interesting low-budget attempt to reproduce a thirties horror thriller such as *The Walking Dead*. Script not quite good enough.

w Robert Bloch d Curtis Harrington

George Hamilton, Ray Milland, Ralph Meeker, Linda Cristal, Joan Blondell, James McEachin

Dead Man on the Run
aka: *New Orleans Force*
US 1975 74m colour TVM
Bob Sweeney

The head of an elite squad of federal investigators investigates his predecessor's murder.
Unnecessarily muddled and unrefreshing cop show.

w Ken Pettus d Bruce Bilson

Peter Graves, Pernell Roberts, Diana Douglas, Katherine Justice

Dead Man's Curve
US 1978 96m colour TVM
EMI (Pat Rooney)

Two fifties rock-and-roll singers are drowned while surfing.
Dreary youth-oriented biopic of Jan Berry and Dean Torrence.

w Dalene Young d Richard Compton ph William Cronjager m Fred Karlin

Richard Hatch, Bruce Davison, Pam Bellwood, Floy Dean

'Facile approach to real-life drama.' – *Daily Variety*

Dead Men Tell No Tales*
US 1971 74m colour TVM
TCF (Walter Grauman)

A travelling photographer in Los Angeles is hunted by professional killers who have mistaken him for someone else.
Quite smartly-made chase mystery.

w Robert Dozier, *novel* Kelly Roos *d* Walter Grauman

Christopher George, Judy Carne, Patricia Barry, Richard Anderson

Dead of Night
US 1977 74m colour TVM
Dan Curtis/NBC

A trilogy of supernatural stories . . .
. . . none of them very good.

w Richard Matheson *d* Dan Curtis

Joan Hackett, Lee Montgomery, Horst Buchholz, Anjanette Comer, Patrick MacNee, Ed Begley Jnr, Ann Doran, Christina Hart

Dead on Target
US 1977 74m colour TVM
TCF (Stanley Colbert)

An oil executive is kidnapped.
Feeble sequel to the theatrical features about *Our Man Flint*. No series.

w Norman Klenman

Deadline
US 1959 39 × 25m bw
Official

Anthology of dramatic stories about newspapermen.
Adequate late-night filler.

narrator Paul Stewart *m* Fred Howard

Deadlock
US 1969 96m colour TVM
Universal (William Sackheim)

The police chief and district attorney of a large city disagree violently over the best means of solving local murders and preventing mob action.
Sobersided, socially conscious pilot for a series that didn't go.

w Chester Krumholtz, Robert E. Thompson, William Sackheim *d* Lamont Johnson

Leslie Nielsen, Hari Rhodes, Aldo Ray, Ruby Dee

The Deadly Dream*
US 1971 73m colour TVM
Universal (Stan Shpetner)

A weird dream about a death sentence begins to turn into reality.

A sufficiently engaging suspenser with an unconvincing outcome.

w Barry Oringer *d* Alf Kjellin

Lloyd Bridges, Janet Leigh, Leif Erickson, Carl Betz, Don Stroud, Richard Jaeckel

Deadly Harvest*
US 1972 73m colour TVM
CBS/Anthony Wilson

An East European defector in California finds himself the target for an assassin's bullet.
Efficient suspenser.

w Anthony Wilson, *novel Watcher in the Shadows* by Geoffrey Household *d* Michael O'Herlihy

Richard Boone, Patty Duke, Michael Constantine, Murray Hamilton

The Deadly Hunt*
US 1971 74m colour TVM
Four Star

A young couple on a forest holiday become unwitting targets for paid killers, and a forest fire helps them escape.
Silly but watchable action suspenser.

w Eric Bercovici *d* John Newland

Tony Franciosa, Peter Lawford, Anjanette Comer, Jim Hutton

The Deadly Tide
US 1975 98m colour TVM
Spelling–Goldberg

Jewel thieves vanish into thin air from a waterfront warehouse . . . they become scuba divers.
Fragmented adventures of the *SWAT* team originally shown in two parts.

w Ben Masselink *d* Gene Levitt

Steve Forrest, Christopher George, Lesley Warren, Sal Mineo, Don Stroud, Susan Dey, Phil Silvers

The Deadly Tower*
US 1975 100m colour TVM
MGM

The capture of the University of Texas sniper who in 1966 caused many casualties before being caught by a single policeman.
Good documentary-style re-creation of an awesome event.

w William Douglas Lansford *d* Jerry Jameson

Kurt Russell, Richard Yniguez, Ned Beatty, John Forsythe, Pernell Roberts

Deadly Triangle
US 1977 74m colour TVM
Columbia

An Olympic skier becomes sheriff of Sun Valley.

Familiar crime stuff with unfamiliar but limiting background.

w Carl Gottlieb d Charles S. Dubin

Dale Robinette, Robert Lansing, Maggie Willman, Taylor Lacher

†See also *Crisis at Sun Valley*.

The Dean Martin Show*. A one-hour comedy variety spectacular which ran on NBC from 1965 to 1973. The star kidded himself and his friends, and was backed by a chorus line called The Gold Diggers.

Dear Phoebe
US 1954 39 × 25m bw
NBC/Chrislaw

A male reporter writes the Lonelyhearts column.
Passable comedy series.

Peter Lawford

Death Among Friends
aka: *Mrs R*
US 1975 74m colour TVM
Warner/Douglas S. Kramer

A lady cop solves a Beverly Hills murder.
Talkative whodunnit.

w Stanley Ralph Ross d Paul Wendkos

Kate Reid, Martin Balsam, Jack Cassidy, Paul Henreid, Lynda Day George

Death and the Maiden: see Hawkins on Murder

Death at Love House*
US 1976 74m colour TVM
Spelling–Goldberg (Hal Sitowitz)

A long-dead silent film star appears to haunt her Beverly Hills mansion.
Engaging supernatural nonsense with a most agreeable cast entering into the spirit of the thing.

w Jim Barnett d E. W. Swackhamer

Robert Wagner, Kate Jackson, Marianna Hill, Sylvia Sydney, Joan Blondell, Dorothy Lamour, John Carradine

Death Be Not Proud**
US 1975 100m colour TVM
Westfall Productions/Good Housekeeping (Donald Wrye)

An account of the death of journalist John Gunther's son from a brain tumour.
Extremely well-made and acted wallow in a real-life tragedy, for those who can take it.

w/d Donald Wrye, *book* John Gunther

Arthur Hill, Jane Alexander, ROBBY BENSON, Linden Chiles

Death Cruise
US 1974 74m colour TVM
Spelling–Goldberg

Holidaymakers on a luxurious cruise are systematically murdered.
Mildly engrossing murder mystery on the lines of *And Then There Were None*.

w Jack Sowards d Ralph Senensky

Edward Albert, Kate Jackson, Richard Long, Polly Bergen, Celeste Holm, Tom Bosley, Michael Constantine, Cesare Danova

A Death in Canaan*
US 1978 120m approx. colour TVM
Warner/Robert W. Christiansen, Rick Rosenberg

A teenage boy is accused of his mother's murder.
Draggy fictionalization of a real-life case, with vivid scenes and good acting but too many unanswered questions.

w Thomas Thompson, Spencer Eastman, *novel* Joan Barthel d Tony Richardson ph James Crabe m John Addison

Stefanie Powers, Tom Atkins, Jacqueline Brookes, Paul Clemens, Brian Dennehy, Kenneth McMillan

'The areas between fact and fiction are lamentably fuzzy.' – *Daily Variety*

A Death of Innocence*
US 1971 74m colour TVM
Mark Carliner

A small-town woman goes to New York for her daughter's murder trial.
Emotional character drama, well presented.

w Zelda Popkin, from her novel d Paul Wendkos

Shelley Winters, Arthur Kennedy, Tisha Sterling, Ann Sothern

The Death of Me Yet*
US 1971 74m colour TVM
Aaron Spelling

A Russian spy who has apparently defected to California turns out to have been a US agent all the time.
Confused but watchable suspense drama.

w A. J. Russell, *novel* Whit Masterson d John Llewellyn Moxey

Richard Basehart, Doug McClure, Darren McGavin, Rosemary Forsyth, Meg Foster

Death Race*
US 1973 74m colour TVM
Universal (Harve Bennett)

In the Libyan desert during World War II, two grounded US pilots are relentlessly pursued by a German tank commander.

Fairly gripping war action suspenser.

w Charles Kuenstle   d David Lowell Rich

Lloyd Bridges, Roy Thinnes, Eric Braeden, Doug McClure, Brendan Boone

Death Scream*
US 1975   100m   colour   TVM
RSO (Ron Bernstein)

The case history of a woman who was fatally stabbed in view of neighbours who ignored her cries for help. Dramatized documentary about an American malaise – the 'don't get involved' syndrome.

d Richard T. Heffron

Raul Julia, Cloris Leachman, John Ryan, Nancy Walker, Philip Clark, Lucie Arnaz, Art Carney, Diahann Carroll, Kate Jackson, Tina Louise

Death Sentence*
US 1974   74m   colour   TVM
Spelling–Goldberg

A woman juror who discovers the truth about a murder case is threatened by the real killer – her husband. Good watchable suspenser.

w John Neufeld, novel After the Trial by Eric Roman   d E. W. Swackhamer

Cloris Leachman, Laurence Luckinbill, Nick Nolte, Alan Oppenheimer, William Schallert

Death Squad*
US 1973   74m   colour   TVM
Spelling–Goldberg

The police commissioner hires a tough ex-cop as under-coverman to expose a renegade policeman. Good gritty cop show.

w James David Buchanan, Ronald Austin   d Harry Falk

Robert Forster, Melvyn Douglas, Michelle Phillips, Claude Akins

Death Stalk*
US 1974   80m   colour   TVM
David Wolper/Herman Rush (Richard Caffey)

Escaped convicts abduct the wives of two campers, and an overland chase ensues. Good outdoor suspenser.

w Stephen Kandel, John W. Bloch   d Robert Day

Vince Edwards, Anjanette Comer, Robert Webber, Carol Lynley

Death Takes a Holiday
US 1971   73m   colour   TVM
Universal (George Eckstein)

Death comes to earth in handsome form, and falls in love.

Curious, would-be fashionable, tricksily photographed and mainly flat-footed updating of a dated concept.

w Rita Lakin, play Alberto Cosella   d Robert Butler

Melvyn Douglas, Myrna Loy, Monte Markham, Yvette Mimieux, Maureen Reagan

Death Valley Days*.
A half-hour western series sponsored and owned by the makers of Twenty Mule Team Borax. It has gone through over 600 episodes since 1952, and before that was on radio for 20 years. Hosts have included Robert Taylor, Dale Robertson, Ronald Reagan, and Stanley Andrews ('The Old Ranger'). aka: Call of the West.

The Debbie Reynolds Show
US 1969   26 × 25m   colour
NBC/Filmways/Harmon (Jess Oppenheimer)

Adventures of a scatty suburban housewife.
The star seems to have thought of herself as a second Lucille Ball, but the viewers had other ideas.

cr Jess Oppenheimer

Debbie Reynolds, Don Chastain, Tom Bosley, Patricia Smith

December Bride*
US 1954–8   146 × 25m   bw
CBS/Desilu

An elderly widow thinks of herself as eligible.
Amusing comedy with pleasing characters.

Spring Byington, Frances Rafferty, Dean Miller, Verna Felton, Harry Morgan (as Pete)

†Pete's wife Gladys was never seen, but in the spin-off series she was played by Cara Williams.

Decoy*
aka: Police Woman Decoy
US 1957   39 × 25m   bw
Pyramid

Adventures of an undercover police woman.
A smart suspense series of its time with an attractive lead.

Beverly Garland

The Defection of Simas Kudirka*
US 1978   96m   colour   TVM
Paramount/Jozak (Gerald I. Eisenburg, Gerald W. Abrams)

A Lithuanian radio operator on a Soviet fishing vessel leaps hopefully to freedom in a Massachusetts harbour.
Arresting, sober docu-drama from a true incident.

w Bruce Feldman   d David Lowell Rich   ph Jacques Marquette   m David Shire

Alan Arkin, Richard Jordan, Shirley Knight, Donald Pleasence, John McMartin, George Dzundza

The Defenders***
US 1961–4 132 × 50m bw
CBS/Plautus/Herb Brodkin (Robert Markell)

Cases of a father–son lawyer team.
Superior courtroom drama, usually with serious issues at stake. A milestone in TV series.

cr Reginald Rose

E. G. Marshall, Robert Reed

definition. The sharpness of a picture on the TV screen.

Delancey Street: The Crisis Within
US 1975 74m colour TVM
Paramount (Emmet Lavery Jnr)

A dramatized account of a San Francisco hostel for people in trouble.
Glum do-goodery which dramatically just doesn't take off despite obvious earnestness all round.

w Robert Foster *d* James Frawley

Walter McGinn, Carmine Caridi, Lou Gossett, Michael Conrad, Mark Hamill

Deliver Us from Evil*
US 1973 74m colour TVM
Warner/Playboy

Five men recover a fortune from a skyjacker and fight their own greed and each other.
Smartly made open-air fable with predictable outcome.

w Jack Sowards *d* Boris Sagal

George Kennedy, Jan-Michael Vincent, Bradford Dillman, Jack Weston, Charles Aidman

Della
US 1964 66m colour TVM
Four Star

An attorney visits a small town to negotiate land purchase with a wealthy lady recluse.
Peyton Place-style pilot for a projected series called *Royal Bay*, which didn't materialize.

d Robert Gist

Joan Crawford, Diane Baker, Paul Burke, Charles Bickford, Richard Carlson

The Delphi Bureau
US 1972 99m colour TVM
Warner

An agency of gifted people with total recall is responsible only to the President.
Ingenuous spy capers with the usual high gloss and nonsense plot. This pilot led to a series of eight one-hours, which was not a success.

w Sam Rolfe *d* Paul Wendkos

Laurence Luckinbill, Joanna Pettet, Celeste Holm, Bob Crane, Cameron Mitchell, Bradford Dillman, Dean Jagger

Delta Country USA
US 1977 96m colour TVM
Paramount/Leonard Goldberg

Problems of young people in a southern city.
Peyton Place all over again, not badly done.

w Thomas Rickman *d* Glen Jordan *m* Jack Elliott, Alyn Ferguson

Jim Antonio, Jeff Conaway, Joanna Miles, Peter Donat, Lola Albright, Robert Hayes, Ed Power

Delvecchio
US 1976 22 × 50m colour
NBC/Universal (William Sackheim, Lane Slate)

Stories of a tough cop with underworld connections.
Disappointing cop show headlining a new star who wasn't.

cr Sam Rolfe, Joseph Polizzi

Judd Hirsch

Demarest, William (1892–). Veteran American comedy character actor with long vaudeville and film career. TV series: *Tales of Wells Fargo, Love and Marriage, My Three Sons.*

demographics. The science of knowing what proportion of the total audience watches a given show and whether it appeals to certain age, sex and class groups.

Denis, Armand (1897–1971) **and Michaela** (*c* 1920–). Husband and wife explorers whose half-hour travel films were very popular in the fifties.

Denning, Richard (1914–) (Louis A. Denninger). Light American leading man of the forties; in TV played *Mr and Mrs North, The Flying Doctor* and *Michael Shayne* and later appeared occasionally in *90 Bristol Court* and as the governor in *Hawaii Five-O.*

The Dennis O'Keefe Show
US 1959 39 × 25m bw
CBS

Tribulations of a widowed columnist and his young son.
Forgettable sentimental comedy series.

Dennis O'Keefe, Ricky Kelman, Hope Emerson

Dennis the Menace*
GB title: *Just Dennis*
US 1959–63 146 × 25m bw
CBS/Columbia/Darriel

Adventures of a mischievous small boy in a toney suburb.
The American answer to William, from Hank Ketcham's comic strip. A generally amusing series, notable for young Dennis's uneasy relationship with the next-door neighbour, Mr Wilson.

Jay North, Joseph Kearns, Gale Gordon, Herbert Anderson, Gloria Henry

Denver, Bob (1935–). Eccentric American comedy actor whose style is a cross between Stan Laurel and Jerry Lewis. TV series: *Dobie Gillis*, *Gilligan's Island*, *The Good Guys*, *Dusty's Trail*.

Department S
GB 1970   28 × 50m   colour
ATV

Specialists investigate major international crimes for the government.
The British *Mission Impossible*, just about watchable.

Peter Wyngarde, Joel Fabiani, Rosemary Nichols

The Deputies
aka: *Law of the Land*
US 1976   98m   colour   TVM
Quinn Martin

Three young deputies and their elderly boss solve murders of local prostitutes.
Downbeat western detection, very dark, very slow and very boring. A failed pilot.

Jim Brown, Barbara Parkins

The Deputy*
US 1959–60   76 × 25m   bw
NBC/Top Gun

In the 1880s, a western marshal takes a reluctant deputy.
Modestly pleasing western series notable for Henry Fonda's comparatively few appearances as the marshal.

Henry Fonda, Allen Case

Deputy Dawg
US 1960   104 × 25m   colour
CBS/Terrytoons

A simple-minded sheriff maintains law and order in the old west.
Amusing canine cartoons (four to the half-hour).

voice Dayton Allan

Desilu. The studio formed in the early fifties by Desi Arnaz and Lucille Ball; later absorbed by Paramount.

Desilu Playhouse*
US 1958–9   54 × 50m   bw
CBS/Desilu

Generally pleasing anthology drama series with top stars.

The Desperate Miles*
US 1975   74m   colour   TVM
Universal/Joel Rogosin

To prove his independence, a disabled war veteran undertakes a 130-mile road trip by wheelchair.
Impressive or foolish according to one's point of view: well enough put together and acted.

w Joel Rogosin, Arthur Ross   *d* Daniel Haller

Tony Musante, Joanna Pettet, Jeanette Nolan, Lynn Loring, John Larch

Desperate Mission
US 1971   98m   colour   TVM
TCF/Ricardo Montalban

Episodes in the career of Joaquin Murieta.
Moderate western fare fictionalized from the exploits of a real-life outlaw.

w Jack Guss   *d* Earl Bellamy

Ricardo Montalban, Slim Pickens, Earl Holliman, Ina Balin, Rosie Greer

Destination America**
GB 1976   6 × 50m   colour
Thames

A rather overpowering but monumental series of documentaries covering the various ethnic groups who fled from Europe to make modern America.

Destry
US 1964   13 × 50m   bw
ABC/Universal

The new young sheriff of Bottleneck doesn't wear guns.
Thin imitation of the famous films.

John Gavin, Mari Blanchard

The Detectives*
US 1959–60   67 × 25m   bw
US 1961   30 × 50m   bw
ABC/Four Star

Captain Matt Holbrook gets his villains.
Clean, competent cop show.

Robert Taylor, Ursula Thiess (in half-hours), Tige Andrews, Adam West, Mark Goddard

Detour to Nowhere*
aka: *Banacek*
US 1971   98m   colour   TVM
Universal (George Eckstein)

A wealthy Polish Bostonian collects lost and valuable property for insurance companies . . . at a ten per cent finder's fee.
Overlong but fairly ingenious pilot about a gold heist in the desert with no getaway tracks. It made a rather boring addition to *Mystery Movie*.

w Anthony Wilson   *d* Jack Smight

George Peppard, Christine Belford, Ed Nelson

Devenish
GB 1977–8   13 × 25m   colour (VTR)
Granada (John G. Temple)

The other executives in a toy factory despise an irritating busybody.

Wholly unsympathetic comedy which doesn't begin to be funny despite a good cast.

w/cr Anthony Couch *d* Brian Mills

Dinsdale Landen, Terence Alexander, Geoffrey Bayldon, Geoffrey Chater, Veronica Roberts

The Devil and Miss Sarah*
US 1971 73m colour TVM
Universal (Stan Shpetner)

A man captures an outlaw and brings him to justice, but the outlaw – who may be the devil – turns the mind of the wife his way.
Oddball western semi-fantasy which drags more often than it sparkles.

w Calvin Clements *d* Michael Caffey

Gene Barry, James Drury, Janice Rule, Charles McGraw, Slim Pickens

The Devil's Crown***
GB 1978 13 × 50m colour (VTR)
BBC (Richard Beynon)

The history of the Plantagenets.
A strikingly written and played version in the modern vernacular, with deliberately artificial medieval-style sets.

w Ken Taylor *d* Alan Cooke *m* David Cain

BRIAN COX, Jane Lapotaire, Christopher Gable

The Devil's Daughter*
US 1972 74m colour TVM
Paramount (Edward J. Mikis)

When a girl turns 21, she finds that her dead mother had sold her soul to the devil.
Moderately creepy black magic mumbo jumbo sparked by its star performance.

w Colin Higgins *d* Jeannot Szwarc

SHELLEY WINTERS, Robert Foxworth, Belinda Montgomery, Joseph Cotten, Jonathan Frid, Martha Scott, Diane Ladd

Devine, Andy (1905–77). Husky-voiced American comedy character actor, the fat sidekick in many a western. TV series: *Wild Bill Hickok* (as Jingles).

Diagnosis Unknown
US 1960 39 × 25m bw
CBS

Cases of a New York pathologist.
Adequate medical mystery series.

Patrick O'Neal, Phyllis Newman, Carl Bellini, Chester Morris

Dial Hot Line
US 1970 98m colour TVM
Universal (William Sackheim)

A psychiatric social worker starts a clinic for those in desperate mental straits.
Ho-hum do-gooder which sparked a very short series, *Matt Lincoln.*

w Carol Sobieski *d* Jerry Thorpe

Vince Edwards, Chelsea Brown, Kim Hunter, June Harding

Dial 999
GB 1958 39 × 25m bw

Stories of Scotland Yard.
Good elementary police thrillers.

Robert Beatty

Diana
US 1973 13 × 25m colour
NBC/Talent Associates

A British divorcee finds her way in New York.
Disappointingly ordinary star comedy.

Diana Rigg, Richard B. Shull, David Sheiner, Barbara Barrie

'One marvels at American TV's capacity to reduce even the best to its level.' – Jack Edmund Nolan

Dick and the Duchess. British half-hour comedy series of the fifties starring Patrick O'Neal and Hazel Court.

Dick Tracy*
US 1950 130 × 5m colour
ABC/UPA

Cases of the famous comic strip detective with the jut jaw (created by Chester Gould in 1931).
Slick but rather curious cartoons in which the celebrated detective stays home and sends his assistants out on the cases.

†A 1950 live-action half-hour series had starred Ralf Byrd.

The Dick Van Dyke Show***
US 1961–5 158 × 25m bw
CBS/William Morris/Calvada (Carl Reiner)

The private life of a comedy scriptwriter.
Phenomenally successful series which was half farce, half warm observation of a young married couple and their friends, with echoes of vaudeville from the supporting cast. See Van Dyke, Dick.

cr CARL REINER

DICK VAN DYKE, MARY TYLER MOORE, MOREY AMSTERDAM, ROSE MARIE, RICHARD DEACON, CARL REINER

Dickens of London
GB 1977 10 × 50m colour (VTR)
Yorkshire TV (David Cunliffe)

The ageing Dickens reviews scenes from his life.
Elaborate but singularly unpersuasive series with the star also playing Dickens's father.

w Wolf Mankowitz *d* Marc Miller *m* Monty Norman

Roy Dotrice, Diana Coupland, Karen Dotrice, Richard Leech, Adrienne Burgess

The Dickie Henderson Show. British half-hour star comedy vehicle, popular on Rediffusion in the fifties. The star played himself, more or less, with June Laverick as his wife.

Diller, Barry (*c* 1937–). American executive who went from ABC (where he instigated the TV movie, more or less) to control of production at Paramount.

Dimbleby, Richard (1913–65). Archetypal British anchorman, especially associated with royal occasions and *Panorama*. His sons David and Jonathan carried on the tradition.

Dimmock, Peter (1920–). British sports commentator and executive who in the mid-seventies took up an appointment with the American ABC network.

Dinah. Half-hour morning talk show of the seventies, syndicated in the US five days a week, with Dinah Shore as hostess.

Dinner Party*. A format devised by ATV (GB) in the fifties: four eminent people were observed having dinner and discussing topics of the day.

The Dion Brothers
GB theatrical title: *The Gravy Train*
US 1974 96m colour TVM
Tomorrow (Roger Gimbel)

Two coal miners seek a quick fortune in the city as armed robbers.
Adequate modern gangster stuff.

w Bill Kerby, David Whitney (Terrence Malick) *d* Jack Starrett *m* Fred Karlin

Stacy Keach, Frederic Forrest, Margot Kidder, Barry Primus

director. The creative talent who directs the actors and the camera.

Dirty Sally
US 1974 13 × 25m colour
CBS/TCF (John Mantley)

In the old west, a young adventurer joins forces with a crusty old junk dealer.

BBC copyright

RICHARD DIMBLEBY lent a solid presence to the BBC's coverage of world events and royal occasions, and through the fifties and early sixties *Panorama* simply wouldn't have been the same without him.

Unsuccessful comedy western.

Jeanette Nolan, Dack Rambo

The Disappearance of Flight 412
US 1974   74m   colour   TVM
Cinemobile

Two air force jets disappear while chasing a UFO. Milk-and-water science fiction which adds up to very little.

w George Simpson, Neal Burger   d Jud Taylor

Glenn Ford, Bradford Dillman, Guy Stockwell, David Soul, Robert F. Lyons, Kent Smith

Disappearing World**. A series of documentaries of varying lengths made by Granada TV in the seventies: Brian Moser visited native tribes in remote parts of the world. The results were highly acclaimed.

Disney, Walt (1901–66). American animator and master showman whose organization from the mid-fifties provided a weekly Sunday evening show for the ABC network.

Divorce His, Divorce Hers
GB 1972   2 x 74m   colour   TVM
Harlech TV/John Heyman

Two films showing aspects of a divorce, one from the wife's viewpoint and one from the husbands'. Abysmally dull regurgitation of their own lives by the world's most boring showbiz couple.

w John Hopkins   d Waris Hussein   m Stanley Myers

Richard Burton, Elizabeth Taylor, Gabriele Ferzetti, Carrie Nye, Barry Foster, Rudolph Walker

Dixon of Dock Green**
GB 1955–76   250 approx. x 45m   bw/colour   (VTR)
BBC

Stories of an ageing cop in London's East End.
George Dixon was the policeman killed in the movie *The Blue Lamp*, but his creator revived him and he lasted 21 years, until the star playing him was 80. The early stories tended towards the domestic, but later Dixon became the station desk sergeant and action was the main element, looked after by the CID detectives.

cr Ted Willis

Jack Warner, Peter Byrne

DIXON OF DOCK GREEN, a BBC favourite for twenty years, featured Jack Warner as what had to be the oldest copper on the beat (eighty when he retired); but in many of the stories the burden of action fell on his son-in-law Andy, played by Peter Byrne.

Do Not Fold, Spindle or Mutilate**
US 1971   73m   colour   TVM
Aaron Spelling (Robert L. Jacks)

Four old biddies answer a computer dating service as one fictitious glamorous girl, but one of the applicants is a homicidal maniac.
Lively four-star comedy-thriller.

w John D. F. Black, *novel* Doris Miles Disney   d Ted Post

Myrna Loy, Helen Hayes, Sylvia Sidney, Mildred Natwick, Vince Edwards

Do You Take This Stranger?
US 1970   95m   colour   TVM
Universal/Roy Huggins

In order to inherit a million dollars, a desperate man must engineer a switch of identities.
Complex puzzle melodrama, good fun for addicts.

w Matthew Howard   d Richard Heffron

Gene Barry, Lloyd Bridges, Diane Baker, Joseph Cotten, Sidney Blackmer, Susan Oliver

Dobie Gillis
aka: *The Many Loves of Dobie Gillis*
US 1959–62   147 × 25m   bw
CBS/TCF

Troubles of a frustrated teenager.
Hackneyed college comedy from the stories by Max Shulman.

cr Max Shulman

Dwayne Hickman, Bob Denver, Frank Faylen, Tuesday Weld, Warren Beatty, Raymond Bailey

Doc
US 1975   ? × 25m   colour
CBS/Mary Tyler Moore

Anecdotes of a general practitioner in a poor New York district.
Mild ethnic comedy.

cr Ed Weinberger, Stan Daniels

Barnard Hughes, Elizabeth Wilson, Audra Lindley, David Ogden Stiers

Doc Elliot
US 1973   15 × 50m   colour
ABC/Lorimar

The life of a country practitioner in the south-west, making house calls in a camper.
Pleasant, modest, low-key country dramas.

James Franciscus, Neva Patterson, Noah Beery Jnr, Bo Hopkins

Dr Christian
US 1956   39 × 25m   bw
UA

Stories of a small-town practitioner.
Rather limp elaboration on the forties films and later radio series.

Macdonald Carey

Dr Cook's Garden*
US 1970   74m   colour   TVM
Paramount (Bob Markell)

A small-town doctor nurtures the healthy and weeds out the sick.
Macabre comedy melodrama which tries hard but does not quite come off.

w Arthur Wallace, *play* Ira Levin   d Ted Post

Bing Crosby, Frank Converse, Bethel Leslie, Blythe Danner

Doctor Dolittle
US 1970   17 × 22m   colour
NBC/TCF/De Patie–Freleng

The doctor who talks to animals has various adventures aboard the good ship Flounder.
Tolerable cartoon adventures.

Dr Finlay's Casebook**
GB 1959–66   150 approx × 50m   bw (VTR)
BBC

Stories of an old and a young doctor, not forgetting their canny housekeeper, in a small Scottish town in the twenties.
Highly atmospheric and character-filled series which absorbed a nation for many a Sunday evening, as social history as well as drama.

cr A. J. Cronin

Andrew Cruickshank, Bill Simpson, Barbara Mullen

Dr Hudson's Secret Journal
US 1955–6   78 × 25m   bw
Wesmor

Experiences of a brain surgeon.
Highly coloured medical hokum from a story by Lloyd C. Douglas.

John Howard

Doctor in the House*
GB 1970–3   90 × 25m   colour (VTR)
London Weekend

Riotous adventures of medical students.
Zany comedy following after the film series; this series was itself followed by *Doctor at Sea, Doctor at Large* and *Doctor on the Go.*

Barry Evans, Robin Nedwell, Ernest Clark, Geoffrey Davies

Dr Kildare**
US 1961–4   142 × 50m   bw
US 1965–6   58 × 25m   colour
NBC/MGM/Arena

A young intern gets guidance and inspiration from a crusty old doctor.
Highly successful medical series based on the forties films and the stories by Max Brand. The half-hour episodes were semi-serialized.

Richard Chamberlain, Raymond Massey

†See also *Young Dr Kildare*.

Dr Max
US 1974   74m   colour   TVM
CBS/James Goldstone

A small-town doctor neglects his family to look after his patients.
Modest domestic drama.

Lee J. Cobb, Robert Lipton, David Sheiner, Janet Ward

Dr Scorpion
US 1978   96m   colour   TVM
Universal/Stephen J. Cannell

An ex-CIA agent defeats a criminal mastermind.
Humourless carbon copy of *Doctor No*, a yawn to sit through.

w Stephen J. Cannell   *d* Richard Lang   *ph* Charles Correll   *m* Mike Post, Pete Carpenter

Nick Mancuso, Christine Lahti, Richard T. Herd, Sandra Kerns, Roscoe Lee Browne, Denny Miller

Dr Seuss. Pseudonym of Theodore Seuss Geisel (1904–), a highly successful American writer of illustrated stories for children which grown-ups also enjoy. Those transferred so far to TV, in half-hour special form, include *Horton Hears a Who*, *The Cat in the Hat*, *How the Grinch Spent Christmas*, *Dr Seuss on the Loose*, *The Hoober-Bloob Highway*. Animation has been by De Patie–Freleng.

Dr Simon Locke
Canada 1972   approx 45 × 25m   colour (16mm)
Chester Krumholz

Cases of a young intense doctor who joins an irascible old one in a small Canadian town.
Dr Kildare up north, all very cosy and predictable.

Sam Groom, Jack Albertson, Len Birman

†Dr Locke later moved to the city and became *Police Surgeon*.

Dr Who*. Highly coloured science fiction for older children, produced by the BBC in many hundreds of taped 25-minute segments since 1963. The leading character is a mystical gentleman (a 'Time Lord') who can travel through time and space in his 'Tardis' (which is disguised as a police box). His main opponents, a race of gravel-voiced robots called Daleks, became a household name. The series has been much criticized for its horrific monsters, but they always moved very slowly. The good doctor has been played by William Hartnell,

Jon Pertwee, Patrick Troughton and Tom Baker. Terry Nation was chief deviser of this odd entertainment, which has always been well mounted and accompanied by effective electronic music.

The Doctors. American soap opera which has played five times a week on NBC since 1964. James Pritchett, Lydia Bruce, Gerald Gordon.

The Doctors and the Nurses: see The Nurses

Doctors' Hospital
US 1975   12 × 50m   colour
NBC/Universal (Matthew Rapf, Jack Laird)

Problems of the staff and patients of a large metropolitan hospital.
Rather boring soap opera.

George Peppard, Zohra Lampert, Victor Campos

†See also pilot TV movie, *One of Our Own*.

Dodd, Ken (1927–). Rubber-faced, gap-toothed British comic from Knotty Ash (near Liverpool). Always in a variety format, he talks fast, sings quite well, employs a tickling-stick and created his own miniature chorus of Diddymen.

Dog and Cat**
US 1977   74m   colour   TVM
(Paramount) Lawrence Gordon (Largo) (Robert Singer)

When his partner is shot, a police detective reluctantly accepts a slightly kooky lady partner.
Amiable, slick, very entertaining pilot which pinches its plot from *The Maltese Falcon* but has a few extra tricks up its sleeve.

w Walter Hill   *d* Robert Kelljan   *m* Barry Devorzon

Lou Antonio, Kim Basinger, Richard Lynch, Charles Cioffi

†The resulting series disappointed and ran to only 7 × 50m episodes.

The Doll*
GB 1975   3 × 50m   colour (VTR)
BBC (Bill Sellars)

A publisher meets and helps a mysterious woman who later disappears . . .
Complex, well-paced and thoroughly enjoyable suspense mystery in the author's usual sub-Hitchcockian and entirely British vein.

w Francis Durbridge   *d* David Askey

John Fraser, Anouska Hempel, Geoffrey Whitehead, Derek Fowlds, Cyril Luckham, William Russell

Don Quixote: see The Adventures of Don Quixote

The Don Rickles Show
US 1968 × 25m colour (VTR)
ABC

A variety format starring the comedian, with Vic Mizzy's orchestra.

The Don Rickles Show
US 1971 13 × 25m colour
CBS/Sheldon Leonard

Stories of a suburbanite who is always behind the eight ball.
Fairly funny sitcom.

Don Rickles, Louise Sorel, Erin Moran, Joyce Van Patten, Robert Hogan, Edward Andrews

Donahue, Troy (1936–) (Merle Johnson). American juvenile lead of the fifties. TV series: *Surfside Six*, *Hawaiian Eye*.

Doniger, Walter (1917–). American writer–director. TV writing credits include *Bat Masterson*, *Maverick*, *The Survivors*, *Peyton Place*.

The Donna Reed Show
US 1958–65 275 × 25m bw
ABC/Screen Gems/Todon-Briskin

Standard star domestic comedy.
A long-runner, nimbly presented; it showed the ideal American house and family.

Donna Reed, Carl Betz, Shelley Fabares

Donny and Marie. A series of variety spectaculars with the toothiest hosts in the business, brother and sister Osmonds. Some of the guest numbers are inventively staged. A weekly one-hour series began in 1976 on ABC, produced by Sid and Marty Krofft.

Don't Be Afraid of the Dark*
US 1973 74m colour TVM
Lorimar/Allen Epstein

A young couple move into an old house and find supernatural creatures already in occupation.
Foolish but effective ghost story.

w Nigel McKeand *d* John Newland

Jim Hutton, Kim Darby, Barbara Anderson, William Demarest, Pedro Armendariz Jnr

Don't Call Me Charlie
US 1962 26 × 25m bw
NBC

In post-war Paris, an American private forms a friendship with his eccentric colonel.
Curious but unsuccessful comedy series.

Josh Prine, John Hubbard, Cully Richard, Linda Lawson

Don't Push, I'll Charge When I'm Ready
US 1969 97m colour TVM
Universal

Adventures of an Italian POW in the US.
Drawn-out farce over-exploiting Italian volubility.

w Al Ramus, John Shaner *d* Nathaniel Lande

Enzo Cerusico, Cesar Romero, Soupy Sales, Sue Lyon

The Doomsday Flight*
US 1966 97m colour TVM
Universal

A mad bomber is discovered on a jet plane between Los Angeles and New York.
Obvious but effective suspenser.

w Rod Serling *d* William Graham

Jack Lord, Edmond O'Brien, Katherine Crawford, Van Johnson, John Saxon

Doonican, Val (1932–). Easy-going Irish singer, the popular host of many British variety series in the sixties and seventies.

The Doris Day Show
US 1968–72 128 × 25m colour
CBS/Arwin (Terry Melcher)

A sitcom with four formats. To begin with the star played a country widow and mother, in the second she became a secretary in San Francisco, in the third she brought her children to the city, and in the fourth she was a bachelor news reporter.
None worked particularly well, but the intentions were amiable.

Doris Day, Denver Pyle, Billy de Wolfe, Edward Andrews, Patrick O'Neal, Kay Ballard, John Dehner

Dortort, David (1916–). American executive producer, notably of *Bonanza* and *High Chaparral*.

Dotrice, Roy (1923–). British character actor with a taste for senile impersonation which in 1969 won him a BAFTA award for his impression of John Aubrey in *Brief Lives*. Also notable in *Grand Babylon Hotel*, *Dickens of London*.

Double Deckers
GB 1970 17 × 25m colour
TCF (Roy Simpson)

Seven children use an old double-decker bus as their clubhouse and get into various scrapes.
Passable city version of the *William* books.

w Harry Booth, Glyn Jones *d* Harry Booth

Peter Firth, Bruce Clark, Brinsley Forde, Melvyn Hayes

Double Indemnity
US 1973   74m   colour   TVM
Universal (David Victor)

An insurance salesman helps a client to murder her husband.
A fair copy of the 1944 film without any of its character or effectiveness.

w from the original screenplay by Billy Wilder and Raymond Chandler and the novel by James M. Cain   d Jack Smight

Richard Crenna, Samantha Eggar, Lee J. Cobb, Robert Webber

The Double Life of Henry Phyfe
US 1965   17 × 25m   colour
ABC/Filmways

A meek clerk is plunged into espionage and intrigue.
Moderate, predictable comedy.

Red Buttons, Fred Clark

Double Your Money. British quiz based on *The 64,000 Dollar Question*: hosted by Hughie Green, it played for nearly 20 years from 1955.

Dougall, Robert (1913–). Dignified, popular British newsreader who on his retirement produced a book about TV, *In and Out of The Box*; also hosted *Stars on Sunday*, etc.

Douglas, Donna (1933–) (Doris Smith). American leading lady who scored as the dumb Ellie May in *The Beverly Hillbillies* but was not much heard from subsequently.

Douglas Fairbanks Jnr Presents: see Fairbanks, Douglas Jnr

Douglas, Jack (1927–). Tall, gangling British comedian who made an act out of nervous tics. Stooge to many other comedians; joined the *Carry On* team in the late sixties.

Douglas, Melvyn (1901–) (Melvyn Hesselberg). The immaculate American leading man of thirties and forties films and the impressive elder statesman of the American stage has played many guest roles on TV and appeared in a forgotten series called *Hollywood Offbeat*.

Douglas, Michael (1945–). American actor, son of Kirk Douglas; familiar as co-lead of *The Streets of San Francisco*.

Douglas, Mike (   ) (Michael Delaney Dowd Jnr). American linkman, host of a popular syndicated daytime talk show.

Downs, Hugh (1921–). American talk show host, on the *Today* programme in the mid-sixties.

Doyle, David (1925–). American character actor, seen to advantage in *Bridget Loves Bernie* and *Charlie's Angels*.

Dragnet**
aka: *Badge 714*
US 1951–8   300 approx. × 25m   bw
US 1967–9   98 × 25m   colour
NBC/MCA/Jack Webb

Stories of Los Angeles police sergeant Joe Friday.
Simple but revolutionary cop show recording the minutiae of investigation, conversation and characterization in stretches of apparently flat but hypnotic dialogue. ('8.22 a.m. We were on our way downtown ... All I want is the facts, ma'am.')

cr Jack Webb, Richard Breen

Jack Webb, Ben Alexander (later Harry Morgan)

Dragnet*
GB title: *The Big Dragnet*
US 1969   97m   colour   TVM
Universal/Jack Webb

Sgt Joe Friday investigates the murder of several models.
Enjoyable rehash of the old *Dragnet* formula.

w Richard L. Breen   d Jack Webb

Jack Webb, Harry Morgan, Vic Perrin, Virginia Gregg, Gene Evans

Drake, Charlie (1925–) (Charles Springall). Diminutive, roly-poly British comedian who scored a big hit in the fifties but subsequently grew tiresome.

A Dream for Christmas*
US 1973   100m   colour   TVM
Lorimar

A black parson moves from the Midwest to Los Angeles, and finds a whole new set of problems.
Pleasing family fare.

w John McGreevy   d Ralph Senensky

Hari Rhodes, Beah Richards, Lynn Hamilton, George Spell

The Dream Makers*
US 1975   74m   colour   TVM
MGM (Charles Robert McLain)

A college professor becomes a recording executive.
Unusual contemporary drama, not very exciting but convincingly done.

w Bill Svanoe   d Boris Sagal

James Franciscus, Diane Baker, John Astin, Kenny Rogers, Mickey Jones

DRAGNET. 'All we want is the facts.' Dogged cops Harry Morgan and Jack Webb look as though they don't even trust one another.

Dreier, Alex (1916–). Portly American news commentator who gave it up for a chance to become this generation's Sydney Greenstreet, and somehow muffed it.

Drive Hard, Drive Fast
US 1969 95m colour TVM
Universal (Jo Swerling Jnr)

A womanizing racing driver gets involved in a murder plot in Mexico City.
Unconvincing rigmarole padded out with local colour.

w Matthew Howard d Douglas Heyes

Brian Kelly, Joan Collins, Henry Silva, Joseph Campanella

Drury, James (1934–). Stalwart American leading man of the outdoor type. Series include *The Virginian*, *Firehouse*.

dry run. A dress rehearsal.

The Duchess of Duke Street*
GB 1976–7 31 × 50m colour (VTR)
BBC/Time–Life (John Hawkesworth)

The *Upstairs, Downstairs* team virtually changed channels en bloc to make this rather similar series about a working-class cook who becomes the no-nonsense owner of a fashionable London hotel. It was based on the true story of Rosa Lewis and the Cavendish hotel.
Carefully reconstructed period drama, slightly marred by its strident central character and her eccentric cohorts, but usually very watchable.

cr John Hawkesworth

Gemma Jones, Richard Vernon, Christopher Cazenove, John Cater, Victoria Plucknett, John Welsh

'A winning mixture of nostalgia and down-to-earth realism.' – *Sun*.

Duel*
US 1971 74 or 90m colour TVM
Universal (George Eckstein)

A car driver on the back roads of California is menaced by a petrol tanker.

Overlong (even longer for theatrical release) but brilliantly made TV movie which started its director off on a successful career. A simple suspenser, it pits one man against a huge anonymous threat as unexplained as the menace in *The Birds*.

w RICHARD MATHESON   *d* STEVEN SPIELBERG   *ph* JACK A. MARTA   *m* Billy Goldenberg

DENNIS WEAVER (the others are bit parts)

Duel, Pete (1940–71) (Peter Deuel). Promising young leading man of the sixties, a suicide victim. TV series: *Love on a Rooftop, Alias Smith and Jones*.

Duff, Howard (1917–). American leading man/character actor of the forties and fifties. Played many guest roles on TV and starred in three series: *Mr Adams and Eve, Dante, The Felony Squad*.

Duffy's Tavern
US 1954   × 25m   bw
NBC

A televersion of the radio programme about a bar–restaurant on New York's Third Avenue and the types who congregate therein.

Ed Gardner, Alan Reed, Patte Chapman, Jimmy Conlin

Duggan, Andrew (1923–). American character actor who played numerous second leads in the movies and became a TV star in *Bourbon Street Beat, Room for One More* and *Lancer*. 1979: Eisenhower in *Backstairs at the White House*.

Duke, Patty (1946–). American child star who grew up into a rather intense little actress of offbeat roles, married John Astin, and now calls herself Patty Duke Astin. Series: *The Patty Duke Show*.

The Dumplings
US 1976   8 × 25m   colour (VTR)
Norman Lear (Don Nicholl, Michael Ross, Bernie West)

Unsuccessful comedy series, based on a comic strip by Fred Lucky, about a couple who decide to run a restaurant.

James Coco, Geraldine Brooks

Duncan, Sandy (1946–). Gamine-like American star actress, usually in light comedy. Her series *The Sandy Duncan Show* (aka *Funny Face*) was not a success; more recently she played the title role in *Pinocchio*.

Dundee and the Culhane
US 1967   13 × 50m   colour
CBS (Sam Rolfe)

In the old west, a wandering anti-violence lawyer has an assistant who protects him.
A western with a twist which didn't quite work.

John Mills, Sean Garrison

Dunn, Clive (*c* 1923–). British character comedian who has been playing old men for 20 years. Became familiar in *Bootsie and Snudge* and had his biggest hit in *Dad's Army*.

Dunning, Ruth (1917–). Popular British character actress, at her peak in the sixties playing an assortment of middle-aged types.

Dunninger, Joseph (1896–). American mentalist who had several TV series in the fifties and sixties.

Durante, Jimmy (1893–). Classic American comedian who came late in life to TV but made a number of specials his own, and appeared regularly during the fifties in *All Star Revue, Colgate Comedy Hour, Texaco Star Theatre*, etc; his trademarks being his splendid nose or schnozzola or his sign-off line: 'Goodnight Mrs Calabash, wherever you are.'

Durbridge, Francis (1908–). British thriller writer who produced a number of splendid serials for the BBC: *Bat out of Hell, The World of Tim Frazer, The Doll*, etc.

The Dustbinmen. British half-hour comedy series about a gang of roughneck garbage collectors. Credited with starting the seventies trend towards crudity in British comedy. Created by Jack Rosenthal; with Brian Pringle, Trevor Bannister, Brian Wilde, Tim Wylton, Graham Haverfield.

Dusty's Trail
US 1973   26 × 25m   colour
Metromedia/Sherwood Schwartz

Five wagons on the way west are separated from their friends.
Alarmingly incompetent rehash of *Gilligan's Island*, sadly lacking in jokes, pace and timing, and not helped by cheeseparing production.

w/cr Sherwood and Elroy Schwartz

Bob Denver, Forrest Tucker, Lori Saunders, Ivor Francis, Jeannine Riley, Bill Cort

Dying Room Only*
US 1973   73m   colour   TVM
Lorimar

A woman's husband mysteriously disappears from the washroom of a roadside café.
Adequate suspenser.

w Richard Matheson   *d* Philip Leacock

Cloris Leachman, Ross Martin, Ned Beatty, Louise Latham

Dynasty*
US 1976   100m   colour   TVM
David Frost

Problems of an Ohio pioneer family who become rich between the 1820s and the 1880s.

Satisfying through-the-years family drama with pioneer background: a projected series did not go.

w Sidney Carroll, *novel* James A. Michener   *d* Lee Phillips

SARAH MILES, Stacy Keach, Harris Yulin, Harrison Ford, Tony Swartz

E

Earth II
US 1971 97m colour TVM
MGM/Wabe (William Reed Woodfield, Allan Balter)

A vast American space station is menaced by a Red Chinese nuclear weapon.
For its length probably the most expensive TV movie ever, scuttled by an entirely dull script and lack of humour.

w William Reed Woodfield, Allan Balter *d* Tom Gries *ph* Michel Hugo *m* Lalo Schifrin

Gary Lockwood, Scott Hylands, Hari Rhodes, Anthony Franciosa, Mariette Hartley, Gary Merrill, Inga Swenson, Lew Ayres

East Side West Side**
US 1963 26 × 50m bw
CBS/UA/Talent Associates

Problems of an urban social worker.
Solid drama series which tried to tackle issues of its day and was regarded as a milestone in series TV.

George C. Scott, Elizabeth Wilson

Ebsen, Buddy (1908–) (Christian Rudolf Ebsen). American eccentric dancer who developed into a well-liked character actor and comedian, especially in two phenomenally popular series, *The Beverly Hillbillies* and *Barnaby Jones*.

EBU. The European Broadcasting Union; a union of broadcasters founded in 1950.

The Ed Wynn Show
US 1958 15 × 25m bw
NBC/Screen Gems

Stories of a retired small-town judge and his orphan granddaughters.
Not quite this old vaudevillian's cup of tea.

Ed Wynn, Herb Vigran, Clarence Straight.

Edelman, Herb (1930–). American comedy character actor, in many guest roles, also series *The Good Guys*.

Edelman, Louis F. (19??–76). American independent producer whose hit series included *The Big Valley* and *Wyatt Earp*.

Edge of Night. American soap opera which has played on CBS and NBC five times a week since 1956. Features Ann Flood, Laurence Hugo, Donald May.

editor. 1. Creative technician who assembles pieces of film. 2. Creative producer of a current affairs series.

Edna the Inebriate Woman**
GB 1971 90m colour (16 mm)
BBC (Irene Shubik)

A vagrant woman gets all manner of help from the authorities but continues to go her own way.
Incisive drama-documentary.

w JEREMY SANDFORD *d* Ted Kotcheff

PATRICIA HAYES, Barbara Jefford, Pat Nye

Edvard Munch**
Norway/Sweden 1975 167m colour
Norsk Rikskringkasting/Sveriges Radio

The life and work of the Norwegian painter (1863–1944).
Punishingly long but often brilliant art film with most of the techniques expected of this film-maker.

w/d Peter Watkins *ph* Odd Geir Saether *a/d* Grethe Hajer

Geir Westby, Gro Fraas

Edward the Seventh****
US title: *The Royal Victorians*
GB 1976 13 × 50m colour (VTR)
ATV

The complete life of Queen Victoria's heir, with insights into the other royal personages involved.
A superb piece of historical re-creation and one of the milestones of TV drama, with research, writing, production and acting alike impeccable.

w various, from the biography by Philip Magnus

Timothy West, Annette Crosbie (Victoria), Robert Hardy (Albert), John Gielgud

The Edwardians*
GB 1972 8 × 50m colour (VTR)
BBC

Biographies of eight Edwardian figures: Conan Doyle, Lloyd George, Horatio Bottomley, E. Nesbit, Rolls and Royce, etc.

EDWARD THE SEVENTH. Here Annette Crosbie and Robert Hardy are Victoria and Albert to the life.

EDWARD THE SEVENTH. A remarkable performance by forty-year-old Timothy West was only one of the attractions of this plush and immensely enjoyable royal saga.

Edwards, Ralph (1913–). American ex-announcer who came to fame in the fifties as host of *This Is Your Life*.

Edwards, Vince (1928–) (Vincento Eduardo Zoine). Intense American leading man who on TV had his greatest success as *Ben Casey* and never found another series to match it, certainly not *Matt Lincoln*; but played many guest roles.

Egan, Richard (1921–). American leading man of the fifties who never quite fulfilled his promise. TV series: *Empire*, *Redigo*.

The Egg and I
US 1951   ? × 12m   bw
CBS

TV series following the fortunes of the owners of a chicken farm; from the book by Betty McDonald and the popular film.

Patricia Kirkland, Frank Craven, Grady Sutton

Eggar, Samantha (1939–). British leading lady of the sixties. TV series: *Anna and the King*. Also played Billie Burke in *Ziegfeld: The Man and his Women*.

Eight is Enough
US 1977–   × 50m   colour
Lorimar (Robert L. Jacks)

A middle-class widower with eight children seeks a new wife.
Modestly pleasing family comedy–drama which recovered remarkably when its leading lady died after two episodes.

cr William Bluin, from the book by Thomas Braden

Dick Van Patten, Diana Hyland (replaced by Betty Buckley)

84 Charing Cross Road*
GB 1975   75m   colour (VTR)
BBC (Mark Shivas)

An American lady corresponds with a London bookshop over twenty years, and her pen friend dies before her first visit.
Charming, bookish playlet from published letters.

w Hugh Whitemore, *book* Helene Hanff *d* Mark Cullingham

Anne Jackson, Frank Finlay

87th Precinct*
US 1961   30 × 50m   bw
NBC/Hubbell Robinson

Problems of hard-working police personnel in New York.

Likeable, crisply told cop stuff with domestic asides; the *Police Story* of its time, and less glum.

cr Ed McBain

Robert Lansing, Norman Fell, Gregory Walcott, Ron Harper, Gena Rowlands

Elam, Jack (1916–). Genial, evil-faced American character actor, in innumerable films and TV guest roles. TV series: *The Dakotas, Temple Houston, The Texas Wheelers*.

Eleanor and Franklin**
US 1976   2 × 100m   colour   TVM
Talent Associates

After Franklin Roosevelt's death his wife looks back on their years together.
Careful saga of a political marriage, well though not excitingly presented.

w James Costigan, *book* Joseph P. Nash   *d* Daniel Petrie

EDWARD HERRMANN, JANE ALEXANDER, Ed Flanders, Rosemary Murphy

Eleanor and Franklin: the White House Years*
US 1977   147m   colour   TVM
Talent Associates/David Susskind

A well-received sequel, though sitting through it was a bit of a slog.

w James Costigan   *d* Daniel Petrie   *ph* James Crabe   *m* John Barry

Jane Alexander, Edward Herrmann, Walter McGinn, Priscilla Pointer, Rosemary Murphy, Blair Brown, John Beal, Donald Moffat

The Electric Company. Children's Television Workshop's successor to *Sesame Street*, aimed at older children who have difficulty in reading.

Elephant Boy
GB   1974   26 × 25m   colour (16mm)
STV/Global

A native boy and his elephant on a Ceylon tea plantation have various adventures.
Mild and rather strained children's series with agreeable backgrounds.

The Elevator*
US 1974   74m   colour   TVM
Universal (William Frye)

A variety of people including an escaping thief are trapped in a high rise elevator.
Tolerable panic situation melodrama which does not quite thrill as it should.

w Bruce Shelly, David Ketchum, Rhoda Blecker   *d* Jerry Jameson

James Farentino, Myrna Loy, Teresa Wright, Roddy McDowall, Carol Lynley, Don Stroud, Craig Stevens

The Eleventh Hour*
US 1962–3   62 × 50m   bw
NBC/MGM/Arena

Stories of a psychiatrist's practice.
Downbeat, rather well-made dramas, often with endings a little too pat to be taken seriously.

Wendell Corey (later Ralph Bellamy), Jack Ging

Elizabeth R***
GB 1971   6 × 85m   colour (VTR)
BBC (Roderick Graham)

A splendid pageant of the Renaissance queen and her age.

'The Lion's Cub'
w John Hale   *d* Claude Whatham

'The Marriage Game'
w Rosemary Anne Sisson   *d* Herbert Wise

'Shadow in the Sun'
w Julian Mitchell   *d* Richard Martin

'Horrible Conspiracies'
w Hugh Whitemore   *d* Roderick Graham

'The Enterprise of England'
w John Prebble   *d* Donald McWhinnie

'Sweet England's Pride'
w Ian Rodgers   *d* Roderick Graham

GLENDA JACKSON

Ellery Queen
aka *Mystery Is My Business*
US 1954   32 × 25m   bw
Norvin/Arrow

Adventures of the elegant sleuth.
Moderate series which never quite captured the atmosphere.

Hugh Marlowe

Ellery Queen
US 1974   22 × 50m   colour
NBC/Universal/Fairmont-Foxcroft (Richard Levinson, William Link)

Well-mounted revival, carefully set in the forties and featuring a final confrontation of suspects in a locked room. Despite the who-done-it element, it lacked flair.

cr Richard Levinson, William Link   *m* Elmer Bernstein

Jim Hutton, David Wayne, John Hillerman

'An old-fashioned Valentine to the classic movie mystery.' – NBC promotion

Elliott, Denholm (1922–). Popular British character actor, often in light or tipsy roles.

Elwes, Polly (c 1925–). British TV hostess of comforting presence; married Peter Dimmock and virtually retired.

Ely, Ron (1938–) (Ronald Pierce). American athlete who became TV's *Tarzan*; also starred in *The Aquanauts*.

Emergency
US 1971 100m colour TVM
Universal/Jack Webb

Adventures of a paramedic unit supervised by the city hospital and fire departments.
Rather dull multi-storied ambulance-chasing action drama which spawned a five-year series.

w Harold Jack Bloom *d* Christian Nyby

Julie London, Rudolph Mantooth, Robert Fuller, Bobby Troup

Emergency!
US 1972–7 × 50m colour
NBC/Universal/Jack Webb (Ed Self, Robert A. Cinader)

Paramedics work out of the Los Angeles Fire Department.
'Action without violence', with four or five stories per hour; in other words, *Adam 12* writ large. Watchable in the sense that there is always something happening, but the acting and writing are flat and there is never anything to engage the mind. Which is presumably why it was a great success.

Julie London, Rudolph Mantooth, Kevin Tighe, Robert Fuller, Bobby Troup

Emergency Plus Four
US 1973–4 24 × 22m colour
Universal/Mark VII/Fred Calvert

A cartoon spin-off from *Emergency* in which the paramedics are assisted by four kids.
Doleful.

Emergency Ward Ten. British soap opera which ran twice a week from 1957 until the mid-sixties and proved a useful training ground for young actors. In 1960 a movie version, *Life in Emergency Ward Ten*, was released to little effect. In a sense the original TV series re-emerged in the seventies as *General Hospital*.

EMERGENCY WARD TEN. A twice-weekly serial of the fifties which launched many careers. Here are Charles Tingwell, Rosemary Miller, Frederick Bartram, Jill Browne, John Paul.

Emerson, Faye (1917–). American leading lady who after a modest Hollywood career became a popular TV host and panellist in the fifties.

Emery, Dick (1919–). Stocky British comedian with a bent for dressing up; highly popular in half-hour sketch shows in the early seventies, he lacked writers skilful enough to broaden his appeal.

Emmerdale Farm. British soap opera set in the Yorkshire dales and concentrating on a farming community: supplied twice weekly by YTV since 1972.

Emmy. See Academy of Television Arts and Sciences

Empire
GB title: *Big G*
US 1962 26 × 50m colour
NBC/Columbia (William Sackheim)

Action stories about the operation of the Garret family's huge ranch in New Mexico.
Handsome, efficient family saga on the style of *The Big Valley*, *Bonanza* and *Dallas*.

cr Frank Nugent *m* Johnny Green

Richard Egan, Anne Seymour, Terry Moore, Ryan O'Neal

'TV's first major dramatic series set in the real west of today.' – publicity

† When the show failed, there followed a short half-hour series about the Egan character, called *Redigo*.

English, Arthur (1913–). British 'wide boy' comedian of the forties who aged into a sympathetic TV actor in both plays and series.

An Englishman's Castle*
GB 1978 3 × 50m colour (VTR)
BBC (Innes Lloyd)

The plight of a TV writer trying to tell the truth in a Britain 30 years after the Nazis won World War II.
A low-key dramatic trilogy which provides civilized dramatic entertainment without really surprising in any way.

w Philip Mackie *d* Paul Ciappesoni

Kenneth More, Isla Blair, Anthony Bate

An Englishman's Journey: see Priestley, J. B.

Ensign O'Toole
US 1962 26 × 25m bw
NBC/Four Star/Lederer

Predicaments of a young naval officer and his shipmates.
Mindless service comedy, all very predictable but occasionally funny.

Dean Jones, Jay C. Flippen, Harvey Lembeck, Jack Albertson, Beau Bridges

The Entertainer*
US 1976 100m colour TVM
Robert Stigwood

A middle-aged vaudeville comedian considers his failure.
American TV adaptation of the famous play: it only springs into life when Ray Bolger's around.

w John Osborne *m* Marvin Hamlisch

Jack Lemmon, RAY BOLGER, Sada Thompson

The Entertainers*
GB 1965 50m bw (VTR)
Granada (Denis Mitchell)

A tour of pub entertainments which replaced music hall.
A vivid, smoky documentary which was temporarily banned by the IBA because a stripper twirled her tassels at the camera.

d Joe McGrath

The Epic That Never Was*
GB 1965 70m bw
BBC (Bill Duncalf)

Alexander Korda's 1937 film of *I, Claudius* was abandoned after two reels had been shot. This remarkable programme showed the remains and examined the reasons through interviews with the survivors, who included Merle Oberon, Josef Von Sternberg, Emlyn Williams and Flora Robson. Dirk Bogarde narrated.

w/d Bill Duncalf

Eric
US 1975 100m colour TVM
Lorimar

A teenage boy has an incurable disease.
One may suspect the motive and the point, but the thing is moderately well done.

w Nigel and Carol Ann McKeand, *memoir* Doris Lund *d* James Goldstone *m* Dave Grusin

John Savage, Patricia Neal, Claude Akins, Sian Barbara Allen, Nehemiah Persoff

The Errol Flynn Theatre: see Flynn, Errol

Escapade
US 1978 50m colour
Quinn Martin/Woodruff (Brian Clemens)

Two carefree spies pursue another who vanishes.
Unsuccessful pilot for an American version of *The Avengers*.

w Brian Clemens *d* Jerry London *ph* Jack Swain *m* Patrick Williams

Granville Van Dusen, Morgan Fairchild, Len Birman, Janice Lynde

'All that is understandable about this pilot is the reason it didn't sell.' – *Daily Variety*

Escape
US 1971   74m   colour   TVM
Paramount

An escapologist becomes a spy.
Silly comic strip adventures with entertainingly hare-brained action climaxes.

w Paul Playdon   *d* John Llewellyn Moxey

Christopher George, Avery Schreiber, Marlyn Mason, Gloria Grahame, William Wimdom, John Vernon, William Schallert

Escape
US 1973   × 25m   colour
Jack Webb

Anthology dramas about people caught in hair-raising situations, allegedly from real life.

narrator Jack Webb   *m* Frank Comstock

Escape from Bogen County
US 1977   96m   colour   TVM
Paramount–Moonlight–Aries (Frank von Zerneck, Robert Greenwald)

A corrupt state boss sends police after his runaway wife.
Rather tiresome melodrama about unpleasant people.

w Judith Parker, Christopher Knopf *d* Steve Stern *ph* Fred Jackman *m* Charles Bernstein

Jaclyn Smith, Mitch Ryan, Michael Parks, Henry Gibson, Pat Hingle

Escape to Mindanao
US 1968   95m   colour   TVM
Universal (Jack Leewood)

Two Americans escape from a Japanese POW camp.
Routine war action.

w Harold Livingston   *d* Don McDougall

George Maharis, Willi Coopman, Nehemiah Persoff, James Shigeta

Espionage*
GB 1963   24 × 50m   bw
ATV/NBC/Plautus

An anthology of spy stories, some of them partly true.
A somewhat gloomy but well-made series with excellent guest stars.

'The producer's overall thesis was that political intrigue degrades man, jeopardizes peace, and in the final analysis is ineffective. One quickly learned to expect a glum hour that would end in melancholia.' – Don Miller.

European Broadcasting Union: see EBU

Eurovision. Device by which members of the European Broadcasting Union can receive simultaneous telecasts of each other's programmes.

The Evacuees***
GB 1975   73m   colour (16mm)
BBC (Mark Shivas)

Two Jewish boys are evacuated to St Anne's at the start of World War II, but try to escape back to Manchester.
Moving and amusing nostalgic comedy, impeccably realized.

w JACK ROSENTHAL   *d* ALAN PARKER   *ph* Brian Tufano

Gary Carp, Steven Serember, Maureen Lipman, Margery Mason, Ray Mort

'Stunning to look at and easy to feel.' – *Daily Mirror*

Evans, Barry (1945–). British leading man who during a rather desultory career starred in two TV series, *Doctor in the House* and *Mind Your Language*.

Evans, Maurice (1904–). Welsh Shakespearian actor on Broadway; in the fifties he produced and starred in much Shakespeare for TV, and later acted in *Bewitched*.

Evening in Byzantium
US 1978   2 × 96m   colour   TVM
Universal (Glen Larson)

A film producer at the Cannes Festival ponders his business and sexual problems.
Mildly watchable novelization.

w Glen Larson, Michael Sloan, *novel* Irwin Shaw   *d* Jerry London

Glenn Ford, Gloria de Haven, Shirley Jones, Eddie Albert, Vince Edwards, Patrick MacNee, Erin Gray, Gregory Sierra, Harry Guardino, Simon Oakland

Everett, Chad (1937–) (Raymond Cramton). American leading man of the sixties whose main success was in the TV series *Medical Center*. Previously in *The Dakotas*.

Every Man Needs One
US 1972   74m   colour   TVM
Spelling–Goldberg

A swinging bachelor who steers clear of female attachments is forced to hire a woman assistant who takes him over.
Mild contemporary comedy.

w Carl Kleinschmitt   *d* Jerry Paris

Ken Berry, Connie Stevens, Henry Gibson, Louise Sorel

Everybody's Looking: see Tenafly

Everything Money Can't Buy
US 1976   13 × 25m   colour
Columbia (Austin and Irma Kalish)

An angel in a bowler hat enables frustrated people to achieve their dreams.

A troubled comedy series, once called *Heaven Sent* and finally shown as *Good Heavens*. A mixture of *Here Comes Mr Jordan* and *If I Had a Million*, it never worked with Jose Ferrer or Carl Reiner, largely because the stories were dim and the angel didn't have enough to do.

Evil Roy Slade*
US 1971   100m   colour   TVM
Universal (Jerry Belson, Gary Marshall)

The west's meanest outlaw reforms when he falls in love.
Overlong spoof, at its best better than *Blazing Saddles*.

w Jerry Belson, Gary Marshall   *d* Jerry Paris

John Astin, Mickey Rooney, Pamela Austin, Dick Shawn, Henry Gibson, Dom De Luise, Edie Adams, Milton Berle

Ewell, Tom (1909–) (S. Yewell Tompkins). Crumple-faced American comedy character actor who in the fifties had a brief spell as a Hollywood star. TV series include *The Tom Ewell Show, Baretta*.

The Execution of Private Slovik*
US 1973   120m   colour   TVM
Universal

During World War II an American soldier is executed for desertion.
Factual case history, earnestly but rather drearily retold.

w Richard Levinson, William Link, *book* William Bradford Huie   *d* Lamont Johnson

Martin Sheen, Ned Beatty, Gary Busey, Warren Kemmerling, Mariclare Costello

executive producer. In TV, usually the head of a department (comedy, light entertainment, etc.), but also the moneybags in charge of a particular production and sometimes (as with Jack Webb) the creative force of the enterprise.

Executive Suite
US 1976   19 × 50m   colour
MGM (Rita Lakin)

Boardroom and domestic problems of those who control a large corporation.
The pilot hour promised smart adult drama akin to the original movie, but compromise set in and the show was watered down to accommodate a youth element. As a serial it lacked cliffhangers, and was suddenly chopped

without an end to the story. A cautionary tale for those interested in American TV practice.

cr Arthur Bernard Lewis, Norman Felton, Stanley Rubin

Mitch Ryan, Sharon Acker, Stephen Elliott, Madlyn Rhos, Leigh McCloskey, Brenda Sykes, Percy Rodrigues

Exoman
US 1977   96m   colour   TVM
Universal

Permanently paralysed after an attack by gangsters, a professor devises a super suit which makes him mobile enough to exact revenge.
Tasteless gimmick pilot.

w Martin Caidin, Howard Rodman   *d* Richard Irving

David Ackroyd, Anna Schedeen, Harry Morgan

The Expert*
GB 1970–5   54 × 50m   colour (VTR)
BBC (Andrew Osborn)

Cases of a pathologist.
Police mystery stories with a dry medical flavour and a self-effacing performance from the star.

Marius Goring

The Explorers**
GB 1975   13 × 50m   colour
BBC (Michael Latham)

A series of documentary reconstructions of the lives of famous explorers, hosted by David Attenborough. The Amundsen episode, directed by David Cobham, won the BAFTA award for best documentary.

Exton, Clive (1930–). British playwright who in the fifties produced some memorable single plays (*No Fixed Abode, Soldier, The Trial of Dr Fancy*). Became a film scriptwriter, but gradually descended to routine efficiency.

The Eyes of Charles Sand*
US 1972   75m   colour   TVM
Warner (Hugh Benson)

A young man with second sight solves a bizarre murder mystery.
Old-fashioned horror comic, well camped up.

w Henry Farrell, Stanford Whitmore   *d* Reza S. Badiyi

Peter Haskell, Joan Bennett, Barbara Rush, Sharon Farrell, Bradford Dillman, Adam West

F

F Troop*
US 1965–6   65 × 25m   34 bw, 31 colour
ABC/Warner

Wacky goings-on at a fort in the old west.
Pratfall army comedy, smartly enough presented to
keep one laughing.

Forrest Tucker, Larry Storch, Ken Berry, Melody
Patterson, Edward Everett Horton (as an Indian)

Fabares, Shelley (1942–   ). American leading lady,
niece of Nanette Fabray. Series: *The Brian Keith
Show*.

Fabray, Nanette (1920–   ) (Nanette Fabares).
American comedienne, once a star of *Our Gang*. Many
variety appearances.

The Face of Fear*
US 1971   72m   colour   TVM
Quinn Martin

A young woman who has (she believes) a terminal illness arranges for her own murder. And then . . .
An old chestnut adequately warmed over.

w Edward Hume, *novel* Sally E. V. Cunningham   *d*
George McCowan

Elizabeth Ashley, Ricardo Montalban, Jack Warden,
Dane Clark

Face the Music. A long-running BBC2 musical quiz,
presided over by pianist Joseph Cooper.

Face to Face. A famous fifties series of interviews on
BBC by John Freeman, with portrait drawings by
Feliks Topolski. Freeman proved a relentless inquisitor
and on one famous occasion reduced Gilbert Harding to
tears.

faction. A neologism coined to describe the late seventies breed of TV movies purporting to give the factual
lives of famous people, but invariably straying pretty
far from the truth. Also called *docu-drama*.

Fade Out*
GB 1970   96m colour   TVM
HTV (Patrick Dromgoole, Harry Field)

A television news team is involved in a top level government scandal.
Efficient power play.

w Leon Griffiths, *play* David Watson   *d* John Nelson
Burton

Stanley Baker, George Sanders, Geoffrey Bayldon,
Ronald Hines, Ann Lynn, Francis Matthews, Faith
Brook

Fadiman, Clifton (1904–   ). American literary man-
of-all-trades who in the fifties became famous as the
host of TV's *Information Please*.

The Failing of Raymond*
US 1971   73m   colour   TVM
Universal (George Eckstein)

An embittered student seeks revenge against the middle-
aged lady teacher responsible for his not passing an
exam.
Fairly good suspenser.

w Adrian Spies   *d* George Eckstein

Jane Wyman, Dean Stockwell, Dana Andrews, Murray
Hamilton, Paul Henreid, Tim O'Connor

Fair Exchange
US 1962   14 × 50m   bw
US 1963   13 × 25m   bw
CBS/Desilu

An American and an Englishman exchange families for
a year.
Halting comedy series which never made its mark.

Eddie Foy Jnr, Victor Maddern, Lynn Loring, Judy
Carne

Fairbanks, Douglas Jnr (1909–   ). American leading light actor, son of Douglas Fairbanks. Between
1954 and 1956 he produced and occasionally starred in
at least 120 half-hour dramas of very variable quality.
Made England, they glutted the world's TV sets.

The Falcon: see The Adventures of the Falcon

Falk, Peter (1927–   ). Cast-eyed American character
actor who scored his greatest hit as the shabby but per-
ceptive detective *Columbo*, whose apparently diffident
and casual harassment of murder suspects became one
of the greatest bores of the seventies. Previously appeared in *The Trials of O'Brien*.

The Fall and Rise of Reginald Perrin
GB 1976–   20 approx × 25m   colour (VTR)
BBC (John Howard Davies)

Frustrations of a middle-aged suburbanite with a dead-end executive job.
A frenetic comedy series rather lacking in funny jokes and tending to overuse the ones it has.

w David Nobbs

Leonard Rossiter, Pauline Yates, John Barron

Fame is the Name of the Game*
US 1966   100m   colour   TVM
Universal

A magazine reporter on assignment discovers a girl's body and traps her murderer.
Ho-hum glossy melodrama which sparked off a three-season series of telefeatures about the magazine, *The Name of the Game*.

w Ranald MacDougall   *d* Stuart Rosenberg

Anthony Franciosa, Jill St John, Jack Klugman, George Macready, Lee Bowman, Nanette Fabray, Jay C. Flippen, Jack Warden

Family*
US 1976–   × 50m   colour
Spelling–Goldberg (Mike Nichols)

Problems of a middle-class Los Angeles family.
Impeccable production and nice manners make this look like the typical family of the commercials, but the show is well-meaning, the acting reliable and the stories usually plausible.

cr Jay Presson Allen   *m* John Rubinstein

James Broderick, Sada Thompson, Gary Frank, Kristy McNichol, John Rubinstein, Elayne Heilveil

The Family**
GB 1974   12 × 30m   colour (16mm)
BBC (Paul Weston)

A camera unit stays with the working-class Wilkins family of Reading for several months and gains a supposedly accurate portrayal of their behaviour.
A much criticized series, copying *An American Family*; it appeared to show up all the more vulgar elements in the family's life, though it must be admitted that Mrs Wilkins emerged as a telly star.

Family Affair*
US 1966–70   138 × 25m   colour
CBS/Universal/Don Fedderson (Edmund Hartmann)

A New York bachelor takes over the care of his nieces and nephew, much to the dismay of his English manservant.
Popular comedy with satisfactory style and performances.

cr Don Fedderson, Edmund Hartmann

Brian Keith, Sebastian Cabot, Anissa Jones, Johnnie Whittaker, Kathy Garver

A Family at War*
GB 1970–2   52 × 50m   colour (VTR)
Granada (Richard Doubleday)

Tribulations of a Liverpool working-class family during World War II.
Earnest, moderately realistic chronicle, sometimes so glum as to give the impression of *Cold Comfort Farm*.

w/cr John Finch   *d* June Howson

Margery Mason, Colin Douglas, Lesley Nunnerly, Shelagh Fraser, John McKelvey, Coral Atkins, Keith Drinkel, Colin Campbell, Barbara Flynn

Family Flight*
US 1972   73m   colour   TVM
Universal (Harve Bennett)

A light plane crashes in the desert and the family involved needs all its ingenuity to survive.
Taut, efficient action suspenser apparently inspired by *The Flight of the Phoenix*.

w Guerdon Trueblood   *d* Marvin Chomsky

Rod Taylor, Dina Merrill, Kristoffer Tabori, Janet Margolin, Gene Nelson

The Family Holvak
US 1976   13 × 50m   colour
NBC/Universal (Dean Hargrove, Roland Kibbee)

Stories of a poor backwoods minister in the thirties, from the novel *Ramey* by Jack Farris.
Rather dreary nostalgia, following on from the TV movie *The Greatest Gift*.

Glenn Ford, Julie Harris, Lance Kervin, Elizabeth Cheshire

The Family Kovack
US 1974   74m   colour   TVM
Warner/Playboy

A Chicago family bands together when the son is accused of bribing a city official.
Forgettable family drama distinguished by excellent location atmosphere, which was not enough to turn it into a series.

w Adrian Spies   *d* Ralph Senensky

James Sloyan, Sarah Cunningham, Andy Robinson, Richard Gilliland

The Family Nobody Wanted
US 1975   74m   colour   TVM
Universal (David Victor)

A minister and his wife adopt a very miscellaneous family of twelve, but find they are resented in a new parish.
Old-fashioned sentimentality, laid on with a trowel.

w Suzanne Clauser, *book* Helen Doss   *d* Ralph Senensky

Shirley Jones, James Olson, Woodrow Parfrey, Ann Doran

A FAMILY AT WAR. The Ashtons in their drab wartime living-room: you can smell the hide furniture.

The Family Rico
US 1972 73m colour TVM
CBS/George LeMaire

A crime syndicate leader is in trouble when his younger brother defects.
Shades of *On the Waterfront* and *The Brotherhood*, but actually from a Simenon novel previously filmed as *The Brothers Rico*. Enough is enough.

w David Karp *d* Paul Wendkos

Ben Gazzara, James Farentino, Sal Mineo, Jo Van Fleet, Dane Clark, Jack Carter, Leif Erickson, John Marley

The Famous Adventures of Mr Magoo*
US 1964 26 × 25m colour
NBG/UPA

Cartoon adaptations of literary classics.
A wheeze that works far better than might have been expected is to have Magoo 'play' characters in the stories, e.g. Frankenstein, Dr Watson, Dr Jekyll. The result, well animated, is an amusing series of pastiches.

The Fantastic Four
US 1967 19 × 25m colour
ABC/Hanna-Barbera

The passengers in a rocketship acquire fantastic powers when they pass through a radioactive belt.
Animated Marvel Comics adventures with a human torch, a stretcher, an invisible woman and a Thing.

Fantastic Journey
US 1977 74m colour TVM
Columbia/Bruce Lansbury

A small boatload of people, lost in a cloud in the Bermuda Triangle, find themselves on an island with different historical time zones, escaping from one weird adventure to the next.
Inept, cut-price science fiction nonsense which is boring when not laughable.

w/cr Merwin Gerard *d* Andrew V. McLaglen
m Robert Prince

Jared Martin, Katie Saylor, Ike Eisenmann, Roddy McDowall

† The resultant series, equally poor, ran to 13 × 50m episodes.

103

Fantastic Voyage
US 1967   17 x 22m   colour
TCF/Filmation

Scientists are miniaturized and injected into an ailing human body so that they can repair it from inside.
Adequate cartoon transcription of the movie.

Fantasy Island*
US 1977–   2 x 95m,   x 50m   colour
ABC/Spelling–Goldberg

For ten thousand dollars a weekend, the rich can go to a mysterious luxury island and have their wishes granted.
Despite two abysmally slow pilots, this mixture of *Outward Bound*, *Westworld*, *The Tempest* and *The Wizard of Oz* proved manna to the luxury-starved public.

Ricardo Montalban, Herve Villechaize

Far Out Space Nuts
US 1975   17 x 22m   colour
TCF/Sid and Marty Krofft

Two ground-crew men are accidentally propelled into outer space.
Resistible cartoon adventures.

Faraday and Company: see Mystery Movie and Say Hello to a Dead Man

Faraway Hill. Claimed as TV's first dramatic serial, this American half-hour effort of 1946 was actually a monologue for one woman (Flora Campbell) who, usually seen in close-up, spoke to a number of off-screen voices.

Farentino, James (1938–). Saturnine American leading man who appeared in many TV guest roles and the series *Cool Million* and *The Bold Ones*.

Farewell to Manzanar
US 1976   105m   colour   TVM
Universal/NBC/John Korty

During World War II, many Japanese-Americans are interned.
Solid, solemn, not very compulsive communal guilt-shedding by film-makers who weren't involved.

w Jeanne Wakatsuki Houston, James D. Houston, John Korty   d John Korty   m Paul Chihara

Yuki Shimoda, Nobu McCarthy, Mako, Pat Morita

The Farmer's Daughter*
US 1963–5   101 x 25m   bw (26 colour)
ABC/Columbia

A governess becomes influential in the home of a widowed congressman.
Reasonably intelligent sitcom after the movie.

Inger Stevens, William Windom, Cathleen Nesbitt

Farr, Jamie (*c* 1940–). Long-nosed American character comedian who was seen in *Chicago Teddy Bears* and (more memorably) as the transvestite Corporal Klinger in *M*A*S*H*.

Farrow, Mia (1945–). American leading lady of the seventies, daughter of John Farrow and Maureen O'Sullivan. She became famous as Alison in *Peyton Place* but appeared in no other series; single TV appearances include *Johnny Belinda*, *Goodbye Raggedy Ann*, *Peter Pan*.

Fast Friends
US 1978   96m   colour   TVM
Columbia/Green–Epstein/Sandra Harmon

A TV talk show host feuds with his head writer.
Moderate, forgettable semi-adult entertainment.

w Sandra Harmon   d Steven H. Stern

Dick Shawn, Carrie Snodgress

Fat Albert and the Cosby Kids
US 1971–4   54 x 22m   colour
CBS/Bill Cosby/Filmation

Adventures of a group of street kids.
Tolerable children's cartoon series enlivened by Bill Cosby's voices.

Father Brown*
GB 1974   26 x 50m   colour (VTR)
ATV (Ian Fordyce)

Adventures of G. K. Chesterton's thoughtful clerical detective.
Not at all a bad interpretation of this rather difficult material, but it didn't appeal to an audience eager for easy sensation.

w Hugh Leonard   d Robert Tronson

Kenneth More

Father Dear Father**
GB 1968–73   40 approx x 25m   colour (VTR)
Thames

A philanderer has trouble keeping his daughters under control.
Smart-paced farce, an excellent vehicle for a skilful star.

Patrick Cargill, Ursula Howells, Noel Dyson, Joyce Carey

† In 1977 Cargill appeared in seven more episodes made in Australia.

Father Knows Best*
US 1954–9   191 x 25m   bw
CBS/Columbia (Eugene B. Rodney)

The life of a typical American family.
As played, somewhere between the Hardys and the Joneses. And who can quarrel with success?

Robert Young, Jane Wyatt, Elinor Donahue, Billy Gray, Lauren Chapin

† In 1977 two taped 'reunion' programmes were made with all the members present.
†† The original sponsor dropped the show after the first 26 episodes, which shows what sponsors know.

The Father Knows Best Reunion
US 1977 74m colour (VTR)
Columbia (Renee Valente, Hugh Benson)

The Andersons celebrate their 35th wedding anniversary, and all the kids turn up.
Sentimental, obvious, and sure of a large audience.

w Paul West *d* Marc Daniels

Robert Young, Jane Wyatt, Elinor Donahue, Billy Gray, Lauren Chapin

† The title of the second special was *Father Knows Best: Home for Christmas.*

Father of the Bride*
US 1961 34 × 25m bw
MGM (Robert Maxwell)

When the daughter of a prosperous family decides to marry, it's her father who suffers most.
Smooth comedy from Edward Streeter's book and the subsequent film.

Leon Ames, Ruth Warrick, Myrna Fahey, Burt Metcalfe

Faulk, John Henry (*c* 1918–). American commentator whose firing by CBS in the fifties, because of alleged Communist affiliations, and his subsequent lawsuit, formed a *cause célèbre* of the time and were recapitulated in the 1975 TV movie *Fear on Trial.*

Fawcett-Majors, Farrah (*c* 1948–) (formerly Farrah Fawcett). American pin-up actress of the seventies who became a national celebrity during the first year of *Charlie's Angels.* When she refused to sign up for a second year, she discovered her true worth.

Fawlty Towers**
BBC 1975 6 × 30m colour (VTR)
BBC 1979 7 × 30m colour (VTR)
BBC (John Howard Davies)

Misadventures of a manic hotel proprietor.
Hilariously funny and original farce series with an inimitable if rather taxing performance from its star.

w John Cleese, Connie Booth

John Cleese, Connie Booth, Prunella Scales, Andrew Sachs

'Low comedy with fast movement.' – John Cleese
'Outrageously funny ... draws its humour from both the head and the bowels.' – *Sunday Telegraph*

† BAFTA award best comedy series.

Fay
US 1975 3 × 25m colour
NBC/Universal (Danny Thomas, Paul Junger Witt)

Adventures of a divorcee on the make.
Sophisticated comedy noted for the fastest cancellation in television history.

Lee Grant

The FBI*
US 1965–73 208 × 50m colour
Warner/Quinn Martin

Case histories, largely fictional, and usually dividing the time available between the crooks' efforts to get away and the G-men's efforts to catch them.
Often a routine series, but the routine was tried and tested, and few people switched off.

Efrem Zimbalist Jnr, Philip Abbott, William Reynolds

'Since the series artistically has been on the shoddy side, the FBI's close cooperation with the producer doesn't make the viewer think too highly of the FBI's acumen.' – Don Miller, 1965

The FBI versus Alvin Karpis, Public Enemy Number One
US 1974 100m colour TVM
Warner/Quinn Martin

J. Edgar Hoover personally joins in the chase for a most wanted criminal of the thirties.
Long and flatly told crime-busting epic, one of a short-lived series of telefeatures which followed the one-hour series *The FBI* which ran nine years. See also: *Attack on Terror.*

w Calvin Clements *d* Marvin Chomsky

Robert Foxworth, Eileen Heckart, Kay Lenz, David Wayne, Harris Yulin, Gary Lockwood, Anne Francis

Fear No Evil
US 1969 98m colour TVM
Universal

A scientist dies after buying an antique mirror: a supernatural expert probes its secret.
Overlong scary suspenser which failed to start a series even after a second pilot, *Ritual of Evil*, was tried.

w Richard Alan Simmons *d* Paul Wendkos

Louis Jourdan, Bradford Dillman, Marsha Hunt, Wilfrid Hyde White, Lynda Day, Carroll O'Connor

Fear on Trial**
US 1975 100m colour TVM
Alan Landsburg (Stanley Chase)

The story of John Henry Faulk, a radio commentator who was caught up in fifties blacklisting but finally won his suit alleging wrongful dismissal.
Fascinating re-creation of recent history with a powerhouse performance from Scott as Louis Nizer.

w David Rintels   *d* Lamont Johnson

GEORGE C. SCOTT, William Devane, Dorothy Tristan, William Redfield, David Susskind

Feather and Father
US 1976   74m   colour   TVM
Columbia (Larry White)

A smart lady lawyer solves cases with the help of her con man father and his underworld friends.
Dismal rehash of forties routines, a long way from Damon Runyon.

w Bill Driskill   *d* Buzz Kulik

Stefanie Powers, Harold Gould, John Forsythe, Frank Delfino, Bettye Ackerman, Jim Backus, Severn Darden

The Feather and Father Gang
US 1976   13 × 50m   colour
Columbia/Larry White

An unenterprising series following from the above, with the same talents.

Feldman, Marty (1933–).
Bug-eyed British comedian who began as a writer and showed great promise, but whose talent seemed to decline in inverse ratio to his international acceptance. Various TV series include *Marty* (BAFTA award 1969) and *The Gold Diggers.*

Felix the Cat.
The original silent Felix cartoons by Pat Sullivan, made in the early twenties, have all been on TV, but the versions most seen were made in colour in the fifties by King Features, in semi-serialized form.

The Felony Squad*
US 1966–8   73 × 25m   colour
ABC/TCF (Walter Grauman)

On- and off-duty lives of three cops: old, young and medium.
Efficient cop show with strong stories and sleek production.

Howard Duff, Ben Alexander, Dennis Cole

Female Artillery
US 1972   73m   colour   TVM
Universal (Winston Miller)

A western fugitive is protected from outlaws by a band of women who have been banished from a wagon train.
Failed mix of comedy and action.

w Bud Freeman   *d* Marvin Chomsky

Ida Lupino, Dennis Weaver, Sally Ann Howes, Nina Foch, Linda Evans, Lee Harcourt Montgomery, Albert Salmi

Sherlock Holmes: 14 movie classics starring Basil Rathbone   and Nigel Bruce ★★★★ Leo A. Gutman, Inc. (212) 682-5652

FEATURE FILMS. Although television proved willing to pay up to 20 million dollars each for the biggest block-busters, among the most popular feature films remained old black-and-whiters from the thirties and forties, including the Basil Rathbone/Sherlock Holmes films, twelve of which were made as cheap second features.

The Female Instinct: see The Snoop Sisters

The Feminist and the Fuzz*
US 1970 74m colour TVM
Columbia

A cop and a women's-libber end up sharing an apartment.
Brisk romantic comedy with San Francisco backgrounds.

w Jim Henderson   d Jerry Paris

David Hartman, Barbara Eden, Joanne Worley, Julie Newmar

Fenady, Andrew J. (1928–). American writer–producer whose series include *The Rebel, Branded, Hondo.*

The Fenn Street Gang: see Please Sir

Fennell, Albert (1920–). British independent producer, associated with *The Avengers* and *The Professionals.*

Fer de Lance*
GB theatrical title: *Death Dive*
US 1975 98m colour TVM
Leslie Stevens (Dominic Frontière)

A submarine full of scientists is stuck on the ocean bed and terrorized by poisonous snakes.
Smooth but unlikely thriller.

w Leslie Stevens   d Russ Mayberry

David Janssen, Hope Lange, Ivan Dixon, Jason Evers, Charles Robinson

Fernwood 2-Night*. American spoof talk show which lingered through the 1977 season after the demise of *Mary Hartman, Mary Hartman*, whose characters appeared in it. A rather uncomfortable entertainment.

Fibber McGee and Molly
US 1959 26 × 25m bw
NBC

Adventures of a suburban husband who gets himself into trouble by exaggeration.
Reliable sitcom based on the radio character.

Bob Sweeney, Cathy Lewis, Addison Richards, Hal Peary

Field, Sally (1946–). American juvenile actress of the sixties whose series include *The Flying Nun, Gidget, The Girl with Something Extra.*

The Fight Against Slavery**
GB 1974 6 × 50m colour (16mm)
BBC/Time–Life (Christopher Ralling)

A dramatized history of the freeing of black slaves within the British Empire.
A first-class BBC job which puts *Roots* several degrees in the shade.

John Castle, Dinsdale Landen, Terence Scully, David Collings, Ronald Pickup, Willie Jonah

'Something like a masterpiece.' – *Daily Telegraph*

Final Eye
US 1977 96m colour TVM
Paramount

A case for a private eye in the year 2001.
Lamebrained pilot for a series about the world's last practising private detective. A long way after Sherlock Holmes.

Susan George, Donald Pleasence, David Huddleston, Liam Sullivan

Finlay, Frank (1926–). British general purpose actor who has been very well exposed on TV, in single plays such as *The Last Days of Hitler* and *Count Dracula* and in serials such as *Casanova* and *Bouquet of Barbed Wire.*

Fire
US 1977 96m colour TVM
Warner/Irwin Allen/NBC

A forest fire threatens a mountain community.
Cheapjack semi-spectacular.

w Norman Katkov, Arthur Weiss   d Earl Bellamy   m Richard La Salle

Ernest Borgnine, Vera Miles, Patty Duke Astin, Alex Cord, Donna Mills, Lloyd Nolan, Neville Brand, Ty Hardin

Fireball Forward
US 1972 98m colour TVM
TCF

In World War II France, a general finds a spy in his division.
Adequate actioner with spy trimmings.

w Edmund North   d Marvin Chomsky

Ben Gazzara, Edie Albert, Ricardo Montalban, Dana Elcar, Anne Francis, Morgan Paull, L. Q. Jones

Fireball XL5
GB 1962 26 × 25m bw
ATV (Gerry Anderson)

Intergalactic adventures of Steve Zodiac and his crew.
Adequate puppet fantasies.

The Firechasers*
GB 1970 74m or 101m colour TVM
ITC (Julian Wintle)

An insurance investigator chases an arsonist.
Lumpy, disjointed, watchable adventures.

w Philip Levene *d* Sidney Hayers

Chad Everett, Keith Barron, Anjanette Comer, Joanne Dainton, Rupert Davies, Robert Flemyng, Roy Kinnear, John Loder, James Hayter

Firehouse
US 1973 74m colour TVM
Metromedia (Dick Berg)

Racist conflicts erupt in a city fire department during an arson outbreak.
Totally unsurprising action yarn which generated a shortlived series.

w Frank Cucci *d* Alex March

Richard Roundtree, Vince Edwards, Andrew Duggan, Richard Jaeckel

Firehouse
US 1974 13 × 25m colour (16mm)
ABC/Metromedia/Stonehenge (Dick Berg, John Ireland, Richard Collins)

The shortlived series which spun off from the TV movie had at least two adventures per half-hour and a somewhat changed cast.

James Drury, Richard Jaeckel, Michael Delano, Brad Davis, Bill Overton

The First Churchills**
GB 1969 13 × 45m bw (VTR)
BBC (Donald Wilson)

A saga of the family of the Duke of Marlborough. Excellent high-style period soap-opera.

w/d Donald Wilson

John Neville, Susan Hampshire, James Villiers

First Person Singular*
US 1953 ? × 25m bw
NBC

An anthology of stories using the subjective camera technique in which the camera becomes the eye of the protagonist. Developed by Fred Coe; results interesting but not very popular.

The First 36 Hours of Dr Durant
US 1975 74m colour TVM
Columbia (James H. Brown)

A young surgeon reports to a city hospital and learns the realities of his career.
Dr Kildare rides again. Adequate for insomniacs who don't mind watching operations.

FIREHOUSE. Professionals in action were always fun to watch, and *Firehouse* concentrated on the action. Bill Overton, James Drury, Brad Davis, Richard Jaeckel, Michael Delano.

w Stirling Silliphant   d Alexander Singer

Scott Hylands, Lawrence Pressman, Katherine Helmond, Karen Carlson

Fish
US 1977   × 25m   colour (VTR)
Columbia/Mimus (Danny Arnold)

A spin-off from *Barney Miller*; Fish retires from the police to look after underprivileged children.
Not too successful.

Abe Vigoda, Florence Stanley, Barry Gordon

The Fitzpatricks
US 1977   13 × 50m   colour
Warner (John Cutts)

Stories of a blue-collar family in Michigan.
Sentimental family series which proved a shade too icky to survive.

cr John Sacret Young

Bert Cramer, Mariclare Costello

Five Desperate Women
US 1971   73m   colour   TVM
Aaron Spelling

Five women on holiday find that one of two men on an island with them is a murderer.
Fair goosepimpler.

w Marc Norman, Walter Black   d Ted Post

Anjanette Comer, Joan Hackett, Denise Nichols, Stefanie Powers, Bradford Dillman, Robert Conrad, Julie Sommars

Five Fingers
US 1959   16 × 50m   bw
NBC/TCF

Adventures of a US intelligence agent.
Strained unpersuasive stories which had nothing to do with the film or, as alleged, with the book *Operation Cicero* by L. C. Moyzich.

David Hedison, Luciana Paluzzi

The 500 Pound Jerk
GB title: *The Strong Man*
US 1972   73m   colour   TVM
David Wolper (Stan Margulies)

A hillbilly giant is groomed as an Olympic weightlifter.
Mild satirical comedy.

w James B. Henderson   d William Cronick

James Franciscus, Alex Karras, Hope Lange, Howard Cosell, Victor Spinetti

Flight*
US 1958   39 × 25m   bw
NBC/McCadden

Stories of aviation from Kitty Hawk to Cape Canaveral.
Early docu-drama series, quite effectively presented.

Flight to Holocaust
US 1977   96m   colour   TVM
A. C. Lyles/First Artists/NBC

Professional troubleshooters are called to the 20th floor of a skyscraper, into which a plane has crashed.
Modest action pilot with fairly good stunt effects.

w Robert Heverly   d Bernie Kowalski   m Paul Williams

Patrick Wayne, Christopher Mitchum, Desi Arnaz Jnr, Fawne Harriman, Sid Caesar, Paul Williams, Lloyd Nolan, Rory Calhoun, Greg Morris

The Flintstones**
US 1960–5   166 × 25m   colour
NBC/Hanna–Barbera

In the Stone Age, ebullient Fred Flintstone gets himself and his neighbour Barney Rubble into frequent bouts of trouble.
Amusing cartoon series for all ages, the Stone Age gimmick fitting in well with what sound like old Burns and Allen scripts, lightly worked over. Semi-animation was of a higher standard than we have seen since, and there always seemed to be something inventive going on. Emulating Lucy, the Flintstones had a baby during the series, and became a national institution; but later spin-offs such as *Pebbles and Bam Bam* (animated, 1971) were less successful. The 'live' characters also appeared in many specials and ice shows.

Flipper*
US 1964–6   88 × 25m   colour
MGM/Ivan Tors

In a Florida marine preserve, a boy makes friends with a dolphin.
Good looking animal series: the plots may have been strained but Flipper was always a delight.

Brian Kelly, Luke Halpin

The Flying Doctor
Australia 1959   39 × 25m   bw
Crawford

Cases of a doctor serving remote bush areas.
Routine adventures, simply told.

Richard Denning, Peter Madden, Jill Adams, Alan White

Flying High
US 1978   96m   colour   TVM
CBS/Mark Carliner

Three girls from different backgrounds become airline stewardesses.

Pitifully thin time-passer which scored high enough ratings to warrant a series the following season.

w Marty Cohan, Dawn Aldredge d Peter Hunt ph William J. Jurgensen m David Shire

Kathryn Witt, Pat Klous, Connie Sellecca, Howard Platt, Jim Hutton

'No sex, no action, no conflict, no problems, no interest. It makes *Charlie's Angels* look like Shakespeare by comparison.' – *Daily Variety*

The Flying Nun

US 1967–9   82 × 25m   colour
ABC/Columbia/Harry Ackerman (Jon Epstein, William Sackheim)

A novice nun discovers that she can fly.
How this very small and silly idea was stretched out to 82 episodes is a mystery, but it was, and people watched it.

cr Harry Ackerman, Max Wylie, from the book *The Fifteenth Pelican* by Tere Ross

Sally Field, Alejandro Rey, Marge Redmond, Madeleine Sherwood

'Last year they took the wild route because ABC surveys indicated that's what the kids like. What the computers or somebody else forgot was that they would lose most of the other viewers. Those surveys, laid end to end, don't really mean a lot, but they do keep a lot of people off the unemployment rolls.' – Dave Kaufman, 1970

Flynn, Errol (1909–59). Tasmanian leading man who electrified Hollywood in the thirties. In the mid-fifties he lent his rather dissipated presence to a half-hour TV anthology called *The Errol Flynn Theatre*.

Follow the Sun

US 1961   30 × 50m   bw
ABC/TCF

Three freelance writers have fun in Honolulu.
Passable lightweight series of its time.

Barry Coe, Brett Halsey, Gary Lockwood, Gigi Perreau

Fonda, Henry (1905–). American leading actor, a star in Hollywood for 40 years. Always busy, he has also found time for TV series: *The Deputy*, *The Smith Family*.

Fontaine, Frank (1920–). American zany comedian who became a minor star on Jackie Gleason's show from 1962.

Footsteps

US 1972   74m   colour   TVM
Metromedia (Dick Berg)

A tough coach is hired to whip a small college football team into shape.
Minor sporting drama.

w Alvin Sargent, Robert E. Thompson, *novel* Hamilton Maule d Paul Wendkos

Richard Crenna, Joanna Pettet, Forrest Tucker, Clu Gulager, Mary Murphy

For the Love of Ada*

GB 1970–2   26 × 25m   colour (VTR)
Thames

Two 70-year-olds fall in love and marry.
Geriatric sitcom which really worked. The subsequent movie version didn't.

Irene Handl, Wilfred Pickles

Force Five

US 1975   74m   colour   TVM
Universal (Michael Gleason, David Levinson)

An undercover police unit is formed to control street crime.
Yet another elite force hopes and fails to make the grade as a series.

w Michael Gleason, David Levinson d Walter Grauman

Gerald Gordon, Nick Pryor, William Lucking, James Hampton, Roy Jenson, David Spielberg, Leif Erickson, Bradford Dillman

Ford, Glenn (1916–) (Gwyllyn Ford). Stocky, virile Canadian–American film star of the forties and fifties. His forays into TV include innumerable guest roles and some series: *Cade's County*, *The Family Holvak*, *Once an Eagle*, *Havoc*, *Evening in Byzantium*.

Ford, 'Tennessee' Ernie (1919–). American southern-style singer and presenter, popular throughout the fifties.

Foreign Exchange

GB 1969   72m   colour   TVM
Cohen–Sangster

A private eye is called back into the British Secret Service.
Espionage hokum which with *The Spy Killer* makes two failed pilots for the same non-series.

w Jimmy Sangster d Roy Baker

Robert Horton, Sebastian Cabot, Jill St John, Dudley Foster, Eric Pohlmann

Foreign Intrigue

US 1951–4   154 × 25m   bw
NBC/Sheldon Reynolds

Adventures of foreign correspondents in Europe.
Punchy little 'behind the headlines' melodramas.

Jerome Thor, James Daly, Gerald Mohr (at different times)

†Syndicated as *Cross Current*, *Dateline Europe*, *Overseas Adventure*.

The Forest Rangers
Canada 1965   104 × 25m   colour
ITC/ASP

Stories of a group of junior rangers in the Canadian Northwoods.
Flabbily shot outdoor adventure for kids.

Graydon Gould, Michael Zenon, Gordon Pinsent

Forever
US 1978   96m   colour   TVM
EMI (Marc Trabulus, Merrit Malloy)

Teenagers fall in and out of love in Northern California.
Yawnsville.

w A. J. Carothers, *novel* Judy Blume   *d* John Korty   *ph* Dave Meyers   *m* Fred Karlin

Stephanie Zimbalist, Dean Butler, John Friedrich, Beth Raines, Diana Scarwid

'The scenes have all the compulsion of shampoo tele-blurbs ... the ironies of youthful romance are drawn out into tedium.' – *Daily Variety*

The Forgotten Man*
US 1971   73m   colour   TVM
ABC Circle (Walter Grauman)

Five years after being reported missing, a soldier returns from Vietnam, finds his wife remarried, and becomes desperate.
Well-filmed and rather poignant melodrama.

w Mark Rodgers   *d* Walter Grauman

Dennis Weaver, Anne Francis, Lois Nettleton, Andrew Duggan, Percy Rodrigues

Forster, Robert (1942–). Sullen-looking American leading man of the seventies. TV series: *Banyon*, *Nakia*.

The Forsyte Saga***
GB 1968   26 × 50m   bw (VTR)
BBC/MGM (Donald Wilson)

The story of a family of London merchants from the 1870s to the 1920s, and especially the story of unsympathetic Soames and his disastrous marriage.
A solid success, this expensive serial drama played around the world and its influence was much felt, all the way to the novelizations of the mid-seventies. The first half was undoubtedly the best, but so it is in John Galsworthy's books.

adaptor Lennox Philips, others   *d* James Cellan Jones, David Giles

Eric Porter, Nyree Dawn Porter, Kenneth More, Susan Hampshire, John Welsh, Joseph O'Conor, Fay Compton, Margaret Tyzack, Lana Morris

Forsyth, Bruce (1921–). Jaunty British comedian who rose to fame in the fifties as compere of *Sunday Night at the London Palladium*, and consolidated his stardom in the seventies with *The Generation Game*.

Forsythe, John (1918–) (John Freund). Pleasing, soft-spoken, American leading man who never quite made it in films but has enjoyed residuals from several successful TV series: *Bachelor Father*, *The John Forsythe Show*, *To Rome with Love*. The voice of Charlie in *Charlie's Angels*.

The Forty Eight Hour Mile
US 1970   97m   colour   TVM
Universal

A private eye pursues a tense triangle situation which leads to murder.
OK who's-following-whom mystery.

d Gene Levitt

Darren McGavin, William Windom, Kathy Brown, Carrie Snodgress

45 Cranley Drive***
GB 1961   40m   bw (16mm)
Granada (Tim Hewat)

Pioneering docu-drama recapitulating the events leading to the arrest of the Portland spies, rather more effectively than the subsequent movie version.

d Mike Wooller

Foster and Laurie*
US 1975   100m   colour   TVM
Arthur Stolnitz

The true story of two New York cops, shot in the line of duty.
A well-intentioned tribute, but basically the same old mean streets cops and robbers.

w Albert Ruben, *book* Al Silverman   *d* John Llewellyn Moxey   *m* Lalo Schifrin

Perry King, Dorian Harewood, Talia Shire, Jonelle Allen

Foster, Jodie (1962–). American teenage actress of the seventies: made her first mark in the short-lived 1974 series *Paper Moon*, in which she took over the Tatum O'Neal role.

Foster, Julia (1942–). British leading actress, mainly on TV, often in slightly fey roles. Series include *Emergency Ward Ten*, *Moll Flanders*, *Wilde Alliance*.

JOHN FORSYTHE. Never a big hit in 'movie movies', he became a television star of the first magnitude in several long-running series and also TV movies such as *Cry Panic*.

The Fosters
GB 1976–7 22 approx. × 25m colour (VTR)
LWT

Misadventures of a black family in London.
A rather unattractive comedy series, vaguely borrowed from *The Jeffersons*.

Norman Benton, Isabelle Lucas

Four in One
US 1970 24 × 50m colour
MCA/Universal

A rotating series intended to break in four possible series, each running every fourth week. In fact only *McCloud* and *Night Gallery* went on to better things. The others were *San Francisco International*, with Lloyd Bridges, and *The Psychiatrist* with Roy Thinnes.

The Four Just Men*
GB 1959 39 × 25m bw
ATV

Four men agree to combat injustice throughout the world.
Not much to do with the Edgar Wallace book, but a convenient way of allowing four billed stars to work only every fourth week. Unfortunately the stories were disappointing and de Sica's English was a shade too fractured.

Jack Hawkins, Richard Conte, Dan Dailey, Vittorio de Sica

Four Star. An American television production company founded to utilize the talents of Dick Powell, Charles Boyer, Rosalind Russell and Joel McCrea. In fact the last two hardly contributed and David Niven was co-opted, with some assistance from Ida Lupino. The main drama output was channelled into *Four Star Playhouse*, which was highly regarded.

Fowley, Douglas (1911–). American character actor who spent 30 years playing gangsters in movies, then moved to TV and played grizzled old fellows in such series as *Gunsmoke* and *Pistols 'n' Petticoats*.

Foxx, Redd (1922–) (John Elroy Sanford). Black American character comedian who became a major star in *Sanford and Son* and subsequently starred in a weekly variety series.

Fractured Flickers
US 1961 26 × 25m bw
Jay Ward

Comedy series hosted by Hans Conried, featuring re-edited sequences from classic silent films with zany commentaries. Not likely to please film buffs.

Franciosa, Tony (1928–) (Anthony Papaleo). Beaming American leading man who is a bigger star on TV than in movies. Series include *Valentine's Day*, *The Name of the Game*, *Search*, *Rich Man*, *Poor Man*, *Wheels*.

Francis, Arlene (c 1908–) (Arlene Kazanjian). American character actress, a favourite TV panellist of the fifties.

Francis Gary Powers: The True Story of the U-2 Spy Incident*
US 1976 96m colour TVM
Charles Fries/NBC (Edward J. Montagne, John B. Bennett)

In May 1960 an American spy plane is shot down over the Soviet Union.
Acceptable dramatization of a true incident.

w Robert E. Thompson, *book Operation Overflight* by Francis Gary Powers *d* Delbert Mann *m* Gerald Fried

Lee Majors, Nehemiah Persoff, Noah Beery Jnr, William Daniels, Lew Ayres, Biff McGuire, Thayer David

Francis, Raymond (c 1909–). British character actor who had a long run of success as Superintendent Lockhart in Rediffusion's Scotland Yard series of the fifties: *Crime Sheet*, *Murder Bag*, *No Hiding Place*.

Franciscus, James (1934–). American leading man the sixties who didn't manage a big Hollywood career but proved adequate in several TV series: *Naked City*, *Mr Novak*, *Longstreet*, *Doc Elliott*, *Hunter*.

Frankenheimer, John (1930–). American director who scored his greatest successes in movies but had his roots in TV and went to Hollywood originally to film his successful TV production of *The Young Stranger*.

Frankenstein Jnr and the Impossibles
US/GB 1966–7 52 × 25m colour
Hanna–Barbera

Government agents and their 30-foot robot pose as a rock and roll group.
Witless cartoon series.

Frankenstein: The True Story
US/GB 1973 200m colour TVM
Universal (Hunt Stromberg Jnr)

It never was a true story anyway, this version doesn't stick to the book any more than the others, and at this length it is just an embarrassment, though good performances flicker through the tedium.

w Christopher Isherwood, Don Bachardy *d* Jack Smight

James Mason, Leonard Whiting, David McCallum, Michael Sarrazin, Jane Seymour, Nicola Pagett, John Gielgud, Margaret Leighton, Ralph Richardson, Michael Wilding, Tom Baker, Agnes Moorehead

Franklyn, William (1926–). Smooth British general purpose performer who has been seen as actor, revue host, panellist, and especially as the voice-over in innumerable commercials.

Fraser, Bill (1907–). Heavyweight British character actor who became a TV star in the fifties for his appearances as the bullying sergeant in *The Army Game* and *Bootsie and Snudge*. Also appeared in many plays.

Fraser, Ronald (1930–). Chubby British character actor much seen in films and TV. Series include *The Misfit*.

Frawley, William (1887–1966). Crumple-faced American character comedian who after hundreds of Hollywood roles became a TV star as Lucille Ball's long-suffering neighbour in *I Love Lucy* and went on to play Grandpa in *My Three Sons*.

Freedom Riders
US 1978 96m colour TVM
Columbia (Doug Benton)

An FBI undercover man infiltrates the Ku Klux Klan.
Reasonably interesting docu-drama.

w Lane Slate, Roger O. Hirson, *book My Undercover Years with the Ku Klux Klan* by Gary Thomas Rowe Jnr *d* Barry Shear

Don Meredith, James Wainwright, Albert Salmi, Clifton James, Edward Andrews, Slim Pickens, Maggie Blye, Michele Carey

Freeman, John (c 1913–). British TV personality, the relentless interrogator of *Face to Face*, who subsequently became British Ambassador to the US and chairman of London Weekend Television.

Freud, Clement (1924–). Lugubrious British TV personality who went on to become a Liberal MP.

Friendly, Ed (   ). American independent producer: *Little House on the Prairie*, *The Young Pioneers*, *Backstairs at the White House*, etc.

Friendly, Fred W. (1915–). Distinguished American journalist and commentator, long associated as producer with Edward R. Murrow and subsequently president of CBS News.

113

Friendly Persuasion
US 1975   100m   colour   TVM
International (Herbert B. Leonard)

At the outbreak of the Civil War a family of Quakers has to consider its position.
Modest remake of the 1956 movie in the hope of a series. The hope was forlorn.

w William P. Woods   *d* Joseph Sargent

Richard Kiley, Shirley Knight, Michael O'Keefe, Tracie Savage

Friends and Lovers
US 1974   13 × 25m   colour
MTM (Steve Pritzker)

Misadventures of a violinist in the Boston Symphony Orchestra.
Vehicle for a new comedy star with a style which was too subdued to succeed in the ratings.

Paul Sand, Michael Pataki, Penny Marshall

Fries, Chuck (*c* 1927–) (Charles M. Fries). American independent producer, mainly of TV movies. Series include *Spiderman*.

From Here to Eternity
US 1979   6 × 50m   colour
Columbia/Bennett–Kartleman (Buzz Kulik)

Life on a Marine base in Hawaii at the time of Pearl Harbor.
TV retread of a somewhat overrated movie: plenty of power, and frankness remarkable for TV, but not much style.

w Don McGuire, Harold Gast, *novel* James Jones   *d* Buzz Kulik   *ph* Jerry Finnermann   *m* Walter Scharf

William Devane, Natalie Wood, Roy Thinnes, Peter Boyle, Steve Railsback, Joe Pantoliano, Kim Basinger

† A 'one-hour' series followed.

Frontier Circus
US 1961   26 × 50m   bw
CBS/MCA/Calliope

A travelling circus has adventures out west.
Unusual family western which didn't quite make it.

Chill Wills, John Derek, Richard Jaeckel

Frost, David (1939–). Ubiquitous British tele-personality. Revue host of *That was the Week that Was*, interviewer of the rich and famous, compere and comedian in his own series, producer of an assortment of projects, relentless transatlantic commuter and finally rather a bore.

Frost Over England. Title of an occasional late sixties series in which David Frost, Ronnie Barker, Ronnie Corbett and John Cleese presented topical sketches. Winner at the 1967 Montreux Festival.

The Fugitive**
US 1963–6   120 × 50m   bw (30 colour)
ABC/Quinn Martin

A doctor is on the run from an avenging policeman for the murder of his wife, and persistently tries to track down the real villain, a one-armed man.
Ingenious variation on *Les Misérables*; most of the episodes were more like *Shane*, with a mysterious stranger coming into a new community each week, solving some of its problems and leaving. The format seized the imagination of a vast public, and the final episodes, which revealed all, emptied the streets all round the world. Generally speaking, the show was a professional job.

David Janssen, Barry Morse

Fuller, Robert (1934–). Easy-going American second lead, in series from *Wagon Train* and *Laramie* to *Emergency*.

The Funky Phantom*
US 1971   17 × 22m   colour
ABC/Hanna–Barbera

Three teenagers release the timid ghost of an old colonial, who helps them to chase other ghosts.
Fairly lively cartoon updating of *The Canterville Ghost*.

Funny Face
US 1971   13 × 25m   colour
Paramount

A college student does TV commercials on the side.
Extremely mild comedy; no relation to the movie.

Sandy Duncan

The Funny Side
US 1971   13 × 50m   colour (VTR)
NBC/Bill Persky, Sam Denoff

Comedy variety series hosted by Gene Kelly, with sketches showing attitudes to modern life as revealed by five couples, including one black, one old and one working-class.

Warren Berlinger, Pat Finley, Jenna McMahon, Dick Clair, Michael Lembeck, Cindy Williams, John Amos, Teresa Graves, Burt Mustin, Queenie Smith

Funt, Allen (1914–). American funster, who after working on army concealment techniques in World War II evolved and presented the format of *Candid Camera*.

Fury
aka *Brave Stallion*
US 1955–9   114 × 25m   bw
ITC

Adventures of a boy and his horse on a western ranch.
Innocuous action series for children.

Bobby Diamond, Peter Graves

Future Cop
aka: *Cleaver and Haven*
US 1976 96m colour TVM
Paramount/Culzean/Tovern (Gary Damsker, Anthony Wilson)

An old-fashioned cop is given a robot partner.
Uncertain mix of comedy, sentiment and action; it doesn't jell.

w Anthony Wilson, Allen Epstein *d* Jud Taylor

Ernest Borgnine, Michael Shannon, John Amos, John Larch

†Six one-hours followed, and in 1978 another movie (*The Cops and Robin*), but the producers were flogging a dead horse.

G

Galactica: see Battlestar Galactica

Gale is Dead**
GB 1969 50m colour (VTR)
BBC

A harrowing, pioneering documentary about the death of a young girl following drug addiction.

The Gale Storm Show
aka *Oh Susannah!*
US 1956–9 125 × 25m bw
Roach/ITC

Problems of a social director on a luxury liner.
The original of *Love Boat*, this seemed quite amusing at the time.

Gale Storm, Zasu Pitts, Roy Roberts, James Fairfax

The Gallant Men
US 1962 26 × 50m bw
Warner

Stories of war correspondents in World War II Italy.
Rather talky war adventures.

Robert McQueeney, William Reynolds

The Galloping Gourmet. This soubriquet was mysteriously adopted by Graham Kerr, whose rather ragged cooking shows were a big daytime hit in the sixties with ladies across the world.

Galloway, Don (1937–). American second lead, best remembered as aide to Raymond Burr in *Ironside*.

Galton, Ray (1930–). British scriptwriter who, with Alan Simpson, reached unique heights of comedy with *Hancock* and *Steptoe and Son*, after which the standard of invention and characterization seemed to fall somewhat alarmingly.

Gangsters
GB 1976–7 1 × 110m, × 50m colour (VTR)
BBC (David Rose)

Birmingham is Britain's Chicago, riddled with crime and vice, and in danger of being taken over by the yellow peril.
Curious melodramatic serial which was not much appreciated by viewers because it began as realism and rose, or degenerated, into spoof. Viewed as an update of *The Perils of Pauline*, parts of it weren't bad, but the attempt was somewhat foolhardy.

w Philip Martin *d* Alastair Reid

Maurice Colbourne, Elizabeth Cassidy, Ahmed Khalil, Zia Mohyeddin, Saeed Jaffrey, Chai Lee, Robert Lee

Garden, Graeme (1943–). British comedy performer, one of the Goodies.

Gardner, Ed (1904–) (Edward Poggenberg). American character actor, host and linkman of the radio series *Duffy's Tavern*, which came briefly to TV in the fifties.

Gargoyles*
US 1972 74m colour TVM
Tomorrow (Roger Gimbel)

An anthropologist and his daughter in Mexico are menaced by ancient legendary creatures.
Foolish but effective horror piece.

w Elinor and Stephen Karpf *d* B. W. L. Norton

Cornel Wilde, Jennifer Salt, Grayson Hall

Garland, Beverly (1926–) (Beverly Fessenden). American leading lady of the fifties who made a good impression in several series: *Decoy, The Bing Crosby Show, My Three Sons*.

Garland, Judy (1922–69) (Frances Gumm). Celebrated American singer, the story of whose tragic decline after a Hollywood star career is well known. Her chief contribution to TV is the CBS 50m series of 1964 (24 specials with guest stars), and the story of that was well told by Mel Tormé in his book *The Other Side of the Rainbow*.

Garland, Patrick (1936–). British producer–director, mainly on stage. His contributions to TV include *Famous Gossips, Brief Lives, The Snow Goose*.

Garner, James (1928–) (James Baumgarner). Easy-going American leading man who after a pretty good Hollywood career scored several hits in the TV series field: *Maverick, Nichols, The Rockford Files*.

Garnett, Tony (1936–). British drama producer and writer, noted for tackling uncommercial subjects.

Garrett, Betty (1919–). American light actress, widow of Larry Parks. She pleased in a few films then retired more or less until her appearance as a regular in *All in the Family*.

Garrison's Gorillas*
US 1967 26 × 50m colour
ABC/Selmur

During World War II, the US Army recruits convicts for use in dangerous missions behind enemy lines.
The producer had obviously seen *The Dirty Dozen*, but the point really is that this is an exciting, explosive series of war yarns, and why it wasn't renewed is one of the mysteries of TV.

Ron Harper, Cesare Danova, Brendon Boone, Christopher Cary

Garroway, Dave (1913–). American host and commentator, one of the famous telly men of the fifties and the originator of NBC's *Today* programme.

Gascoigne, Bamber (1935–). Intellectual British quizmaster, with *University Challenge* since 1962. In 1977 he wrote and presented a serious 13-hour study of *The Christians*.

The Gathering
US 1977 96m colour
Hanna–Barbera

A man who knows he has only a few months to live seeks reconciliation with his family.
Talky, sentimental, wholly artificial Christmas piece, with the invalid appearing perfectly healthy as usual.

w James Poe *d* Randal Kleiser *ph* Dennis Dalzell *m* John Barry

Ed Asner, Maureen Stapleton, Rebecca Balding, Bruce Davison, Sarah Cunningham

The Gathering Storm: see Walk With Destiny

Gavin, John (1928–). Tall, serious American leading man of the sixties. He was the lead in two unsuccessful TV series, *Convoy* and *Destry*.

Gazzara, Ben (1930–). Glowering American leading man who had a modest Hollywood career punctuated by TV series and movies – *Arrest and Trial*, *Run for your Life*.

Geer, Will (1902–78). American character actor who ran into trouble with the Un-American Activities Com-

BAMBER GASCOIGNE, perennial quizmaster of *University Challenge*, here discusses evolution with Noddy the Chimp for an episode of *The Christians*. No prizes for guessing which one is Bamber.

mittee but resurfaced in old age as a key character actor and star of *The Waltons*.

Geisel, Theodore: see Doctor Seuss

Geller, Bruce (1929–78). American producer. Series include *Mission Impossible* and *Mannix*, both of which he also created.

Gemini Man
US 1976   74m   colour   TVM
Universal

Recasting of the failed *Invisible Man* series; not much better.

w Leslie Stevens   *d* Alan Levi

Ben Murphy

The Gene Autry Show
US 1950–3   85 × 25m   bw
Flying A

The boss of the Melody Ranch is a stickler for range justice.
Anaemic western series with songs.

Gene Autry, Pat Buttram, Gail Davis, Champion the Wonder Horse

† Syndicated as *Gene Autry's Melody Ranch*.

General Hospital. This is the title of a soap opera in the US and in Britain.

The General's Day**
GB 1973   60m   colour (VTR)
BBC (Irene Shubik)

An elderly general woos a timid schoolmistress, but she finds that he has had sexual liaisons with his charlady.
A subtle, entertaining and moving play enshrining most of its author's preoccupations; most lovingly produced and acted.

w WILLIAM TREVOR   *d* John Gorrie

ALASTAIR SIM, Annette Crosbie, Dandy Nichols

'Wholly convincing, with a hundred lovely touches on the way.' – *The Times*

The Generation Game. An elaborately produced game show produced by BBC for a winter season every year through the seventies, with Bruce Forsyth replaced in 1978 by Larry Grayson. Each pair of contestants had to be related and of different generations, and their tasks involved acting out a wildly farcical sketch.

generic title. One which groups together a number of disparate programmes, e.g. 'Million Dollar Movie', 'Mystery Movie'. Also called 'umbrella title'.

Gentle Ben
US 1967–8   56 × 25m   colour
Ivan Tors (George Sherman)

A boy makes friends with a huge wild bear.
Agreeable family fare.

Dennis Weaver, Clint Howard

George and Mildred
GB 1976–   × 25m   colour (VTR)
Thames

Misadventures of the social climbing Mrs Roper and her layabout husband.
Quite funny but vaguely unsympathetic vehicle for the landlords of *A Man about the House*.

w Johnnie Mortimer, Brian Cooke

Yootha Joyce, Brian Murphy

The George Burns and Gracie Allen Show: see The Burns and Allen Show

George, Christopher (1929–). Dependable, tough-looking American leading actor, seen almost entirely on TV. Series include *The Rat Patrol*, *The Immortal*.

George of the Jungle
US 1967–8   51 × 25m   colour
ABC/Jay Ward

Adventures of an accident-prone Tarzan.
Moderately amusing cartoon series, including segments devoted to *Super Chicken* and *Tom Slick*.

The George Sanders Mystery Theatre
US 1957   13 × 25m   bw
NBC/Columbia

Stereotyped mystery playlets, hosted by the occasional star.

Gerber, David (*c* 1926–). American independent producer, recently in residence at Columbia. *Cade's County*, *Police Woman*, *Police Story*, etc.

Get Christie Love
US 1974   74m   colour   TVM
David Wolper

Adventures of a black undercover policewoman.
The mixture as before; it led to a one-season series.

w George Kirgo   *d* William Graham

Teresa Graves, Harry Guardino, Louise Sorel, Paul Stevens

† The series which followed consisted of 22 × 50m films, also produced by Wolper and starring Teresa Graves and Charles Cioffi.

Get Smart**
US 1965–9   138 × 25m   colour
Talent Associates/Heyday/NBC (Arne Sultan)

Adventures of a bumbling spy.
Highly amusing comedy spoof which managed to keep up its impetus until its final season.

cr Mel Brooks, Buck Henry

Don Adams, Barbara Feldon, Edward Platt

Get Some In
GB 1974–   × 25m   colour (VTR)
Thames (Michael Mills)

The exploits of national service RAF recruits in the fifties.
Variable comedy series.

w John Esmonde, Bob Larbey   *d* Michael Mills

Tony Selby

Getting Away from It All
US 1971   74m   colour   TVM
Palomar

Two middle-class, middle-aged couples sell up and seek the simple life.
Fairly amusing contemporary comedy.

d Lee Phillips

Barbara Feldon, Jim Backus, Larry Hagman

Getting Married
US 1978   96m   colour   TVM
Paramount/Moonlight (Frank Von Zerneck, Robert Greenwald)

A TV newsroom apprentice falls for the lady newscaster and after a strenuous campaign finally – and unconvincingly – wins her.
Silly comedy drama with annoying stereotyped characters and not enough plot to stay the course.

w John Hudock   *d* Steven Hilliard Stern   *ph* Howard Schwartz   *m* Craig Safan

Richard Thomas, Bess Armstrong, Dana Dietrich, Fabian, Van Johnson, Audra Lindley, Mark Harmon, Katherine Helmond

'A cute idea that spends a long time getting nowhere.' – *Daily Variety*

Getting Together
US 1971   15 × 25m   colour
Columbia (Bob Claver)

Two young songwriters who live in an antique store try to carve themselves a Hollywood career.
Ho-hum vehicle for ho-hum stars.

Bobby Sherman, Wes Stern, Pat Carroll, Jack Burns, Susan Beher

ghost. A double image on a TV set, usually caused by waves bouncing off a nearby tall building.

The Ghost and Mrs Muir*
US 1968–9   50 × 25m   colour
TCF (David Gerber)

A widow finds that her new house is haunted by the friendly ghost of a sea captain.
Pleasing fantasy comedy based on the 1947 film.

cr Jean Holloway   *p/d* Gene Reynolds   *m* Dave Grusin

Hope Lange, Edward Mulhare, Charles Nelson Reilly, Reta Shaw

Ghost Busters
US 1975   17 × 25m   colour (VTR)
Filmation (Norman Abbott)

Kong and Spencer, with a gorilla named Tracy, set up as ghost hunters and confront legendary monsters.
Cheapjack knockabout which makes Columbia two-reelers of the early thirties look like *Gone with the Wind*.

cr Mark Richards   *d* Norman Abbott

Forrest Tucker, Larry Storch, Bob Burns

The Ghost of Flight 401
US 1978   96m   colour   TVM
Paramount (Emmet Lavery)

When a passenger plane crashes, the ghost of the captain is subsequently seen on other planes in the area.
Flat transcription of an allegedly true story.

w Robert Malcolm Young, *book* John Fuller   *d* Steven Stern, Bob Rosenbaum

Ernest Borgnine, Gary Lockwood, Kim Basinger, Robert F. Lyons

Ghost Story
US 1972   24 × 50m   colour
Columbia (William Castle)

An anthology of modern ghost stories, mostly too long or too silly. The title was changed at mid-season to *Circle of Fear*.

host Sebastian Cabot

A Ghost Story for Christmas. The BBC's generic title for a series of adaptations which have appeared since 1971 within the octave of Christmas, all directed by Laurence Gordon Clark. Stories so far: 1971, *The Stalls of Barchester Cathedral* by M. R. James; 1972, *A Warning to the Curious* by M. R. James; 1973, *Lost Hearts* by M. R. James; 1974, *The Treasure of Abbot Thomas* by M. R. James; 1975, *The Ash Tree* by M. R. James; 1976, *The Signalman* by Charles Dickens.

The Ghosts of Motley Hall*
GB 197   × 25m   colour (VTR)
Granada

The ghosts of a stately home resent intruders.
Lively comedy with effective trick work and a host of amusing characterizations.

Freddie Jones, Arthur English, Sheila Steafel

119

Gibbsville (TV movie): see The Turning Point of Jim Malloy

Gibbsville**
US 1976   13 × 50m   colour
NBC/Columbia/David Gerber (John Furia Jnr)

Stories of a Pennsylvania mining town in the forties, based on John O'Hara's short stories and following on from the pilot film *The Turning Point of Jim Malloy*. The stories are seen through the eyes of two journalists.

cr Frank D. Gilroy

John Savage, Gig Young, Bill McGuire, Peggy McKay

'A series that makes the commonplace a most exciting place.' – promotion

Gideon's Way*
GB 1964   26 × 50m   bw
ATV (Robert S. Baker, Monty Berman)

Cases of a CID police inspector in London.
Standard cop show, efficient in all departments.

John Gregson, Alexander Davion, Daphne Anderson

Gidget
US 1965   32 × 25m   colour
ABC/Columbia

Exploits of a California teenage girl with a passion for surfing.
Moderate domestic comedy for and with the empty-headed.

Sally Field, Don Porter

Gidget Gets Married
US 1971   73m   colour   TVM
Columbia (E. W. Swackhamer)

She was bad enough as a teenager, but the cast helps.

w John McGreevey   *d* E. W. Swackhamer

Macdonald Carey, Paul Lynde, Don Ameche, Joan Bennett, Michael Burns, Monie Ellis

Gidget Grows Up
US 1969   74m   colour   TVM
Columbia (Jerome Courtland)

See above.

w John McGreevey   *d* James Sheldon

Karen Valentine, Robert Cummings, Edward Mulhare, Paul Lynde, Nina Foch, Warner Anderson

Gifford, Denis (1927–   ). British film buff and compiler of Thames's nostalgia series *Looks Familiar*.

Gilbert, James (*c* 1926–   ). British light entertainment producer whose outstanding shows have included *It's a Square World, Frost Over England, Not Only But Also, The Two Ronnies, Whatever Happened to the Likely Lads?, Last of the Summer Wine*.

Gilligan's Island*
US 1964–6   98 × 25m   bw (30 in colour)
CBS/Gladasaya/UA

Rich vacationers are marooned on an uninhabited island.
A surprisingly effective collection of old sight gags, mostly borrowed from Buster Keaton and Laurel and Hardy.

Jim Backus, Bob Denver, Natalie Schaefer, Alan Hale Jnr, Tina Louise

† A cartoon series, *The New Adventures of Gilligan*, was produced by Filmation in 1974, and a new live action pilot, *Return to Gilligan's Island*, appeared in 1978.

The Girl Called Hatter Fox
US 1977   96m   colour   TVM
CBS/EMI (Roger Gimbel/George Schaefer)

A doctor in New Mexico rehabilitates a rebellious Indian teenager.
Powerful scenes in *Miracle Worker* vein don't quite atone for an aimless and overlong script.

w Darryl Ponicsan, *book* Marilyn Harris   *d* George Schaefer   *ph* Howard Schwarz   *m* Fred Karlin

Ronny Cox, Joanelle Romero, Conchata Ferrell, Donald Hotten

'The world gave her hell! Now she's giving it back!' – publicity

The Girl from UNCLE
US 1966   29 × 50m   colour
NBC/MGM/Arena (Norman Felton)

Insipid follow-on from *The Man From UNCLE*, which wasn't all that strong in the first place.

Stefanie Powers, Noel Harrison, Leo G. Carroll

The Girl in the Empty Grave
US 1977   96m   colour   TVM
MGM/Richard O. Linke

Another case for the sheriff of Eagle Lake.
And another failed attempt to get *Winter Kill/Adams of Eagle Lake* into a series.

w Lane Slate   *d* Lou Antonio

Andy Griffith, Sharon Spellman, Hunter von Leer, Edward Winter

The Girl Most Likely To
US 1973   74m   colour   TVM
ABC Circle

An ugly college girl tries plastic surgery.
Rather tasteless comedy with obvious situations.

w Joan Rivers, Agnes Gallin, *novel* Joan Rivers   *d* Lee Phillips

Stockard Channing, Ed Asner, Warren Berlinger, Jim Backus, Joe Flynn

A Girl Named Sooner
US 1974 100m colour TVM
TCF

A hillbilly orphan girl inspires the devotion of an unhappy vet.
Slow-moving drama.

w Suzanne Clauser from her novel   d Delbert Mann

Cloris Leachman, Richard Crenna, Lee Remick, Don Murray, Susan Deer, Anne Francis

The Girl on the Late Late Show
US 1974 74m colour TVM
Columbia

A talk show executive tracks down a mysterious silent film star, and uncovers a guilty secret.
Patchy mystery drama with a muddled plot and too many stops for guest cameos.

w Mark Rodgers   d Gary Nelson

Don Murray, Laraine Stephens, Gloria Grahame, Walter Pidgeon, Yvonne de Carlo, Van Johnson, Cameron Mitchell, John Ireland

Girl on the Run
US 1958 77m bw TVM
Warner (William T. Orr, Roy Huggins)

A hired killer menaces a beautiful nightclub singer.
Pasted together episodes of *77 Sunset Strip*.

w Marion Hargrove   d Richard L. Bare

Efrem Zimbalist Jnr, Edd Byrnes, Erin O'Brien, Shepperd Strudwick, Barton MacLane, Vince Barnett

The Girl Who Came Gift-Wrapped
US 1974 74m colour TVM
Spelling–Goldberg

A publisher who has everything is given a beautiful girl for his birthday.
Empty-headed nonsense.

w Susan Silver   d Bruce Bilson

Richard Long, Karen Valentine, Louise Sorel, Reta Shaw, Dave Madden, Tom Bosley

The Girl With Something Extra
US 1973 22 × 25m colour
NBC/Columbia/Bob Claver (Larry Rosen)

A young wife has psychic powers.
Feeble offering by producers looking for another *Bewitched*.

cr Bernard Slade

Sally Field, John Davidson, Zohra Lampert, Jack Sheldon

The Girls of Huntington House*
US 1973 73m colour TVM
Lorimar (Robert L. Jacks)

Problems at a school for unwed mothers.
Well acted soaper.

w Blossom Elfman from her novel   d Alf Kjellin

Shirley Jones, Mercedes McCambridge, Sissy Spacek, William Windom

Glaser, Paul Michael (c 1945–). American general purpose actor who shot to fame as the first half of *Starsky and Hutch*.

The Glass House*
US 1972 73m colour TVM
Tomorrow

Tensions mount between the inmates of a state prison.
Good acting, routine plot.

w Tracy Keenan Wynn, *story* Truman Capote   d Tom Gries

Alan Alda, Vic Morrow, Clu Gulager, Billy Dee Williams, Dean Jagger, Kristoffer Tabori

The Glass Menagerie
US 1973 110m approx colour TVM
David Susskind

A reclusive girl in old New Orleans admits her first gentleman caller.
Tiresome revamp of the famous play, with the star miscast as the awful mum.

w Tennessee Williams   d Anthony Harvey

Katharine Hepburn, Sam Waterston, Michael Moriarty, Joanna Miles

Gleason, Jackie (1916–). Rotund American comic who after 1949 exposure in *Life with Riley* came to notice as star of *The Honeymooners*. Success subsequently went somewhat to his head, but after sundry Hollywood experiences he returned to TV as host of many variety specials.

Glencannon
GB 1958 39 × 25m bw
Gross-Krasne

Adventures of an old seafaring man.
Talkative, studio-bound comedies.

Thomas Mitchell

The Glittering Prizes**
GB 1976 6 × 75m colour (VTR)
BBC (Mark Shivas)

The lives of a group of people who met as undergraduates at Cambridge in the fifties.
A British equivalent of *The Group*, and almost as biting an indictment of its generation, with many scenes of great interest even though it comes to no especial conclusion.

w Frederic Raphael   d Waris Hussein, Robert Knights

TOM CONTI, Barbara Kellerman, Leonard Sachs, Angela Down, Malcolm Stoddart, Eric Porter, Dinsdale Landen

'The unmistakable feel of quality, as of rich cloth being taken between the fingers.' – *Daily Telegraph*

Glynis
US 1963   13 × 25m   bw
CBS/Desilu (Jess Oppenheimer)

A lawyer's wife writes detective stories.
Thin vehicle which didn't sustain.

Glynis Johns, Keith Andes

Go Ask Alice*
US 1973   74m   colour   TVM
Metromedia (Gerald I. Isenberg)

The diary of a teenage drug addict from a good family.
If we have to go through all this again, it's well done.

w Ellen Violett, from anonymous book   *d* John Korty

William Shatner, Julie Adams, Andy Griffith, Jamie Smith Jackson, Ruth Roman, Wendell Burton

Go Go Gophers
US 1968   24 × 25m   colour
CBS/Total TV/Leonardo

The adventures of two accident-prone Indians trying to keep the white man out of the west.
Uninspired cartoon series.

Go West Young Girl*
US 1978   74m   colour   TVM
Columbia/Harve Bennett, Harris Katleman (George Yanok)

In 1886 Arizona a newspaperwoman and an attractive widow are in search of Billy the Kid.
Amusing pilot for a comedy western.

w George Yanok   *d* Alan J. Levi   *ph* Gerald Perry Finnerman   *m* Jerrold Immel

Karen Valentine, Sandra Will, Michael Bell, Cal Bellini, David Dukes, Charles Frank, Stuart Whitman, Richard Jaeckel

Gobel, George (1919–). Diffident American comic who caused a mild flutter in the fifties but was subsequently little heard from.

God slot. In Britain, an offhand term for the 'Sunday break' or closed period, when religious or inspirational programmes must be shown.

The Godchild
US 1974   74m   colour   TVM
MGM/Mor/Alan Neuman

Three outlaws care for a baby whose mother has died.
Three Godfathers all over again; enough was enough.

w Ron Bishop   *d* John Badham

Jack Palance, Jack Warden, Keith Carradine, Ed Lauter, Jose Perez

Goddard, Willoughby (1932–). Corpulent British character actor. Series include *William Tell*, *The Mind of J. G. Reeder*.

The Godfather. When this film was transmitted on American TV in 1977 it was in a 10-hour version incorporating not only both released parts but an hour of footage previously edited out and now ploughed back by Francis Ford Coppola, who also spent months reshaping his massive TV movie to fit the requirements of commercial breaks.

Godfrey, Arthur (1903–). One of America's first TV personalities, usually as host or talent scout.

Goff, Ivan (1910–). Australian writer in Hollywood, often in partnership with Ben Roberts. Series include *The Rogues*, *Burke's Law*, *Charlie's Angels*.

Going My Way
US 1962   39 × 50m   bw
ABC/Universal

Father O'Malley comes to a difficult New York parish.
Amiable retread of a favourite movie.

Gene Kelly, Leo G. Carroll

Going Straight*
GB 1978   6 × 30m   colour (VTR)
BBC (Sydney Lotterby)

Fletcher gets out of jail but finds that life on the outside is hard.
Disappointing sequel to *Porridge*, with funny lines but too many old situations.

w Dick Clement, Ian La Frenais

Ronnie Barker, Richard Beckinsale, Patricia Brake

The Going Up of David Lev
US 1971   74m   colour   TVM (16mm)
Hallmark

A boy learns how his father, a Jewish American, died in the Six Day War.
Modest Israeli adventure drama

w Ernest Kinoy, Ephraim Kishon   *d* James F. Collier

Topol, Claire Bloom, Melvyn Douglas, Brandon Cruz

Gold, Jack (1930–). British director. *Stocker's Copper*, *Catholics*, *The Naked Civil Servant*, etc.

The Goldbergs. This comedy series about a Bronx Jewish family dates from the era of live TV, but in 1956

Gertrude Berg filmed 39 half-hours in which the family moved to the suburbs. Robert H. Harris played Jake.

The Golden Shot. A popular British quiz show which ran on ATV from 1967 to 1975: contestants earned the right to answer questions by shooting bolts at moving targets from an elaborate rifle machine. Bob Monkhouse was the most prevalent host.

Goldenrod*
US/Canada 1977 96m colour TVM
David Susskind/Film Funding (Lionel Chetwynd, Gerry Arbeid)

Problems of a rodeo hero in the 1950s.
Pleasingly made character drama on a rather boring subject.

w Lionel Chetwynd d Harvey Hart md Franklin Boyd novel Herbert Harker

Tony Lo Bianco, Gloria Carlin, Donald Pleasence

'It took his wife and sons to show him that there was more than one way to become a man.' – publicity

Goldenson, Leonard (1905–). American executive, chairman of ABC.

Goldie
aka: *The Betty Hutton Show*
US 1959 26 × 25m bw
William Morris

A manicurist becomes the sole heiress of a millionaire. Modestly pleasing comedy series.

Betty Hutton, Tom Conway, Gigi Perreau, Richard Miles, Joan Shawlee, Jean Carson, Gavin Muir

'Like an old Jane Withers movie.' – Don Miller

Goldie, Grace Wyndham (1901–). British executive with a primary interest in current affairs. In her long career at the BBC she fostered the talents of many young producers.

Gomer Pyle USMC
US 1964–8 150 × 25m colour (1st 30 bw)
CBS/Ashland

Troubles of a naïve recruit to the Marines.
Pratfall service comedy with a particularly gormless hero.

Jim Nabors, Frank Sutton

Goober and the Ghost Chasers
US 1973 17 × 22m colour
Hanna–Barbera

A cowardly dog helps his owners to chase ghosts.
Inept cartoon series with below-par animation, a curiously quick copy of *Scooby Doo*.

Good against Evil*
US 1977 74m colour
TCF (Ernie Frankel, Lin Bolen)

A baby girl is dedicated to Satan, and on her 21st birthday his emissary comes to fetch her.
A surprisingly close rip-off of *The Exorcist* (not to mention *The Devil's Daughter*), this pilot is well made and acted but didn't make a series.

w Jimmy Sangster d Paul Wendkos

Dan O'Herlihy, Dack Rambo, Elyssa Davalos, Richard Lynch, Peggy McCay

The Good Guys
US 1968 42 × 25m colour
CBS/Talent Associates (Leonard Stern/Jerry Davis)

A cab driver and a restaurateur have delusions of grandeur.
Mild ethnic comedy.

w Jay Sandrich, Hal Cooper

Bob Denver, Herb Edelman, Joyce Van Patten

Good Heavens: see Everything Money Can't Buy

A Good Human Story*
GB 1977 62m colour (16mm) TVM
Granada (Julian Amyes)

Three journalists follow up clues to a murder in a seaside resort out of season.
Sharply observed, cynical talk-piece with a slightly disappointing ending.

w David Nathan d Gordon Flemyng

Warren Clark, Michael Elphick, Kenneth Haigh

'The first telly drama to catch the truth about Fleet Street.' – *People*

The Good Life
US 1971 15 × 25m colour
NBC/Columbia/Lee Rich (Claudio Guzmen)

A suburban couple decide that the most comfortable life in these days of high taxes is as butler and housekeeper to a millionaire.
A good idea lacking the writing to sustain it.

cr Fred Freeman, Lawrence J. Cohen

Larry Hagman, Donna Mills, David Wayne, Hermione Baddeley

The Good Life***
GB 1974–8 30 approx. × 30m colour (VTR)
BBC

A young draughtsman and his wife decide on self-sufficiency, and to the stunned disbelief of their neighbours bring pigs into their suburban garden.
Likeable and funny sitcom series with well-rounded characters.

w Bob Larbey, John Esmonde

RICHARD BRIERS, FELICITY KENDAL, PAUL EDDINGTON, PENELOPE KEITH

'A happy and somewhat rare combination of intelligent writing and superb playing.' – *Daily Telegraph*

Good Morning World
US 1967 26 × 25m bw
CBS/Discus/Bill Persky, Sam Denoff

The love lives of two disc jockeys in a Los Angeles radio station.
Abortive comedy series.

Joby Baker, Ronnie Schell, Julie Parrish, Billy de Wolfe, Goldie Hawn

The Good Old Days*. British old-time music hall show which since the mid-fifties has been irregularly transmitted from the City Varieties Theatre, Leeds, where the audience voluntarily dresses up in fashions of the 1890s and the chairman, excelling in fantastic feats of vernacular verbosity, has invariably been Leonard Sachs. Produced by Barney Colehan.

Good Times
US 1973 13 × 25m colour (VTR)
Tandem (Norman Lear)

Misadventures of a black family living in a poor section of Chicago.
Fairly routine ethnic comedy spun off from *All In the Family*.

cr Eric Monte, Mike Evans

Esther Rolle, John Amos, Jimmie Walker, Janet Du Bois, Bernadette Stanis

Goodbye Raggedy Ann*
US 1971 73m colour TVM
Studio Center/Fielder Cook

A Hollywood starlet is driven to the point of suicide.
Well-made but rather obvious and unsympathetic mini-drama.

w Jack Sher d Fielder Cook

Mia Farrow, Hal Holbrook, John Colicos, Ed Flanders, Martin Sheen

The Goodies*
GB 1973–8 40 approx. × 30m colour (VTR)
BBC

Three goons get into trouble.
Anarchic farcical comedy, each episode starting at least

THE GOOD, THE BAD AND THE INDIFFERENT. A hunting parson, the Rev. Eric Wheeler, was only one of the anomalies turned up by this probing investigation into the fortunes of the Church of England.

as a spoof on some aspect of life but degenerating into a hopefully hilarious mess of sight gags, one-liners and elaborate visual trickery.

written by the performers Graeme Garden, Bill Oddie, Tim Brooke-Taylor

'We think in terms of a human animated cartoon which inevitably means that half the humour is technical.' – Tim Brooke-Taylor

† The series won two Silver Roses at Montreux.

Goodnight My Love**
US 1972 73m colour TVM
ABC Circle

Two private eyes – one a dwarf – are hired by a beautiful blonde to find her missing boy friend.
Successful spoof of a Chandler forties mystery, with good lines and excellent re-created Los Angeles settings.

w/d PETER HYAMS

RICHARD BOONE, MICHAEL DUNN, Barbara Bain, Victor Buono, Walter Burke

Goodson, Mark (1916–). Former American scriptwriter who with Bill Todman became the world's most prolific inventor of panel games.

Goodson–Todman Productions. A company set up in 1946 to market game show formats, which it did most successfully, with *What's My Line?*, *Beat the Clock*, *To Tell the Truth*, *The Price is Right* and *Family Feud*. Their entry into series production in the sixties was less successful, *The Richard Boone Show* being their most prestigious effort. Mark Goodson and William Todman were both radio performers.

Gordon, Gale (1905–) (Gaylord Aldrich). American comedy actor who after his vaudeville days was prominent in such series as *Junior Miss*, *Dennis the Menace* and *The Brothers* before becoming Lucille Ball's huffing, puffing boss or other nemesis.

Gordon, Noele (1922–). British character actress and linkwoman who has had a long, long run in the soap opera *Crossroads*.

Goring, Marius (1912–). British character actor who has been popular in all media but became most familiar on TV as the pathologist hero of *The Expert*.

The Governor and J. J.
US 1969 39 × 25m colour
CBS/Talent Associates (Leonard Stern, Arne Sultan, Reza Badiga)

A widowed governor is helped by his young daughter.
Mildly political comedy which didn't really appeal.

cr Leonard Stern

Dan Dailey, Julie Sommars, Neva Patterson

Grade, Lord (or Lord Lew Grade, as Americans call him) (1906–) (Lew Winogradsky). British impresario and executive who after years as a vaudeville dancer and an agent became Mr ATV in the fifties and set out to sell British shows to America, a policy which brought many failures but can count among its successes *The Saint*, *Danger Man*, *Thunderbirds*, *The Persuaders*, *The Julie Andrews Hour*, *Space 1999* and *The Muppets*. In the seventies he gradually abandoned TV for the production of international multi-star movies which met with varying success.

Graham, Virginia (1912–). American commentator, humorist and panellist (*Girl Talk*, *The Jack Paar Show*).

Granada TV. British independent TV company serving the Lancashire area, founded in 1955 by Sidney Bernstein. Somewhat more intellectual than the other ITV companies, it counts among its notable projects *World in Action*, *Disappearing World*, *Coronation Street*, *University Challenge*, *All Our Yesterdays*, *Country Matters*, *A Family at War*, *Cinema*, *Clapperboard* and *Laurence Olivier Presents*.

Grand Ole Opry. A variety show, popular in America in the fifties, exclusively devoted to country and western entertainers.

Grandstand. The BBC's Saturday afternoon programme of sport.

Grant, Lee (1929–) (Lyova Rosenthal). American character actress who had a moderate film career with several highlights. Her attempts at TV series have seldom got further than the pilot stage: *Fay* was cancelled after two episodes.

Graves, Peter (1925–) (Peter Aurness). American leading man, much seen on TV, seldom in movies. Series include *Fury*, *Whiplash*, *Court Martial*, *Mission Impossible*.

Graves, Teresa (c 1947–). Black American leading lady who starred in *Get Christie Love*. Also visible in *Laugh-In*.

Gray, Donald (1914–78) (Eldred Tidbury). South African leading man who lost an arm in the war and despite this handicap – or perhaps because of it – made a popular hero of *Saber of London* in the early sixties.

The Gray Ghost
US 1957 39 × 25m bw
Lindsley Parsons

Civil War stories of a rebel daredevil.
Moderate action stuff with a special appeal in the South.

Tod Andrews, Phil Chambers

Grayson, Larry (1926–). British comedian of the seventies, the first deliberately to suggest a gay persona; not otherwise remarkably talented, though his catchphrase 'Shut that door' and his stories of his friend Everard swept the land.

The Great American Beauty Contest
US 1972 73m colour TVM
Spelling–Goldberg (Everett Chambers)

A beauty contest is threatened by scandal.
Acceptable comedy drama.

w Stanford Whitmore *d* Robert Day

Eleanor Parker, Bob Cummings, Louis Jourdan, Barbi Benson, Farrah Fawcett, Tracy Reed

A Great American Tragedy*
GB title: *Man at the Crossroads*
US 1972 74m colour TVM
Metromedia (Gerald I. Isenberg)

A middle-aged executive loses his job and finds it hard to get another.
Convincing sketch of a familar situation.

w Caryl Ledner *d* J. Lee-Thompson

GEORGE KENNEDY, Vera Miles, William Windom, Kevin McCarthy, Natalie Trundy

Great Britons
GB 1978 6 × 60m colour (VTR)
BBC (Malcolm Brown)

Distinguished biographies of famous men and women are turned into television documentaries.
A pleasing idea rather disappointingly carried out.

Horatio Nelson by David Haworth
Thomas Cook and Son by John Pudney
Florence Nightingale by Philippa Stewart
Robert Burns by David Daiches
David Lloyd George by John Gregg
Marlborough by Corelli Barnett

Great Expectations*
GB 1975 116m colour TVM
ITC (Robert Fryer)

Dickens's novel about the growing up of young Pip and his adventures with Miss Havisham, Estella and a convict named Magwitch.
So-so version planned as a musical but with the music removed.

w Sherman Yellen *d* Joseph Hardy *ph* Freddie Young

Michael York, Sarah Miles, James Mason, Margaret Leighton, Robert Morley, Anthony Quayle, Rachel Roberts, Joss Ackland, Andrew Ray, Heather Sears

The Great Gildersleeve
US 1955 39 × 25m bw
Finkel and Rapf

Anecdotes of a pompous small-town bureaucrat.
Modest comedy for the easily pleased, from the long-running radio show, a spin-off from *Fibber McGee and Molly*.

Willard Waterman, Stephanie Griffin

The Great Houdinis*
US 1976 96m colour TVM
ABC Circle

The career of the great escapologist told in retrospect. Rather slow and gloomy to start, this curious biopic has enough guest cameos and restagings of famous tricks to hold the interest.

w/d Melville Shavelson *m* Peter Matz *technical advisor* Harry Blackstone Jnr

Paul Michael Glaser, Sally Struthers, Ruth Gordon, Vivian Vance, Adrienne Barbeau, Bill Bixby, Peter Cushing, Jack Carter, Nina Foch, Wilfrid Hyde White, Maureen O'Sullivan, Clive Revill

The Great Ice Rip-Off*
US 1974 74m colour TVM
ABC Circle/Dan Curtis

Four jewel thieves get away on an interstate bus.
Lively comedy-thriller.

w Andrew Peter Marin *d* Dan Curtis

Lee J. Cobb, Gig Young, Grayson Hall, Robert Walden

The Great Man's Whiskers
US 1971 96m colour TVM
Universal (Adrian Scott)

President-elect Abraham Lincoln agrees with a little girl's suggestion that he should grow a beard.
Whimsy based on fact, far too long for its substance.

w John Paxton, *play* Adrian Scott *d* Philip Leacock

Dennis Weaver, Dean Jones, Ann Sothern, John McGiver

The Great Movie Cowboys. An ingenious one-hour show evolved by NTA in the seventies. Old Republic second feature westerns were cut down to size and introduced by Roy Rogers.

The Great Niagara*
US 1974 74m colour TVM
Playboy

During the Depression, a river family helps guide those who challenge Niagara Falls.
Unusual, watchable open-air drama.

w Robert E. Thompson *d* William Hale

Richard Boone, Randy Quaid, Jennifer Salt, Michael Sacks, Burt Young

The Great Wallendas*
US 1978 96m colour TVM
NBC/Daniel Wilson

The story of a circus high-wire family.
Well-staged, unusual, but slightly disappointing account of a real family, the head of which was killed in a wire fall after the film was shown.

w Jan Hartman d Larry Elikann ph Robert Bailin m Joe Weber, Bill Soden

Lloyd Bridges, Britt Ekland, Taina Elg, John Van Dreelen, Ben Fuhrman, Bruce Ornstein

The Great War***
GB 1964 26 × 50m bw
BBC

An account of World War I, built from archive newsreels.
A magnificent effort and a historical monument, though a little over-extended.

p Tony Essex narrator Michael Redgrave

The Greatest Gift
US 1974 100m colour TVM
Universal

The life of a preacher in the midwest early in the century.
Slow, earnest, rather empty pilot for an unsuccessful series (The Family Holvak).

w Abby Mann d Boris Sagal

Glenn Ford, Julie Harris, Lance Kerwin

The Greatest Thing That Almost Happened
US 1977 96m colour TVM
CBS/Crestview (Charles Fries, Herbert Hirschman)

A high-school athlete is threatened by leukaemia.
Black variation on the medium's favourite theme.

w Peter Beagle, novel Don Robertson d Gilbert Moses ph Joe Wilcots m David Shire

Jimmie Walker, James Earl Jones, Deborah Allen

'From cheers to tears – a very special love story!' – publicity

Green Acres
US 1965–70 170 × 25m colour
CBS/Filmways (Paul Henning/Jay Sommers)

A city lawyer moves his luxury-loving wife out to a farm.
The Beverly Hillbillies in reverse: Ma and Pa Kettle style humour which amused America for five seasons.

cr Jay Sommers

Eddie Albert, Eva Gabor, Pat Buttram, Tom Lester, Alvy Moore

Green Eyes*
US 1976 96m colour TVM
Lorimar (David Seltzer, John Erman)

An American war veteran searches Vietnam for his illegitimate son.
Critically liked sentimental melodrama with production values above average.

w David Seltzer d John Erman m Fred Karlin

Paul Winfield, Rita Tushingham, Jonathan Lippe

The Green Hornet
US 1966 26 × 25m colour
ABC/TCF (William Dozier)

With the help of a karate expert, a masked crusader fights for justice.
Another form of Batman, from yet another comic strip and radio series. The punch didn't connect.

m Billy May

Van Williams, Bruce Lee, Walter Brooks, Lloyd Gough

Green, Hughie (1920–). Canadian/British juvenile actor, quizmaster (Double Your Money) and talent discoverer (Opportunity Knocks). His manner has been much mimicked.

Greene, Graham (1904–). Celebrated British novelist who finds life on the dour side. In 1976 Thames filmed many of his short stories in an anthology series called Shades of Greene.

Greene, Hugh Carleton (c 1902–). British executive, brother of Graham Greene and ex-director-general of BBC.

Greene, Lorne (1915–). Canadian character actor who, apart from a few films, devoted most of his career to TV and became one of its major stars. Series: Sailor of Fortune, Bonanza, Griff, Battlestar Galactica.

Gregson, John (1919–75). Scottish leading actor with a busy film career. TV series: Gideon's Way, Shirley's World, Dangerous Knowledge.

Griff*
aka: Man on the Outside
US 1974 102m colour TVM
Universal (David Victor)

When his private eye son is murdered, an ex-cop takes over the business and hunts down the murderer.
Smooth pilot for an unsuccessful series.

w Larry Cohen d Boris Sagal

Lorne Greene, James Olson, Lorraine Gary, Lee H. Montgomery

†The resulting ABC series added Ben Murphy as Griff's aide but was a poor production and was easily beaten by the very similar Barnaby Jones. It ran to 12 × 50m episodes.

Griffin and Phoenix: A Love Story
GB theatrical title: *Today is Forever*
US 1976   96m   colour   TVM
ABC Circle (Tony Thomas)

Two people dying of incurable diseases fall in love.
TV moviedom's favourite theme in a double helping.
Almost insufferable despite good production and performances.

w John Hill   *d* Daryl Duke   *m* George Aliceson
Tipton

Peter Falk, Jill Clayburgh, Dorothy Tristan, John
Lehne, George Chandler, Milton Parsons

Griffin, Merv (1925–   ). American talk show host
who has been widely syndicated since the early sixties.

Grindl*
US 1963   32 × 25m   bw
NBC/Columbia (David Swift)

A middle-aged maid gets a new job, and a new adventure, every week.
The star tended towards the eccentric and the stories
veered towards the macabre, which gave the show two
plusses, and several episodes still stand up as very funny
in their own right.

cr David Swift

Imogene Coca, James Milhollin

The Grove Family. A BBC twice-weekly serial of the
early fifties.

Grundy, Bill (1923–   ). British linkman, mainly for
Granada and Thames. Easily bored, he hit the headlines
in 1977 when he allowed a punk rock group to utter
four-letter words on a live teatime show.

Guardino, Harry (1925–   ). American second lead,
in many films and TV guest spots. Series: *The Reporter*,
Monty Nash, *The New Perry Mason*.

Guess Who's Sleeping in My Bed?
US 1973   74m   colour   TVM
ABC Circle/Mark Carliner

A man and his overwhelming family, including a large
dog, turn up to stay with his ex-wife.
Thin, fairly likeable comedy.

w Pamela Herbert Chais   *d* Theodore Flicker

Dean Jones, Barbara Eden, Kenneth Mars, Reta Shaw,
Suzanne Benton

Guestward Ho!
US 1960   38 × 25m   bw
ABC/Desilu

City slickers take over a dude ranch and are hindered
by a wily Indian.

Very moderate comedy.

Joanne Dru, Mark Miller, J. Carrol Naish

The Guiding Light. American soap opera, on CBS
five days a week from 1952, mostly in a 15-minute slot.
With Millette Alexander, Charita Bauer, Anthony
Call.

**Guilty or Innocent: The Sam Sheppard Murder
Case***
US 1975   156m   colour   TVM
Universal (Harve Bennett)

In 1954, a Cleveland doctor is convicted, then
acquitted, of murdering his wife: he later gives up his
practice and becomes a professional wrestler.
Pretty absorbing true-life stuff, but this is too long a
time to spend on a tale with no end: the doctor died
without revealing the truth.

w Harold Gast   *d* Robert Michael Lewis

George Peppard, William Windom, Nina Van Pallandt,
Walter McGinn, Barnard Hughes

Gulager, Clu (*c* 1929–   ). American character actor,
of Cherokee and Danish stock, mostly on TV and with
a tendency to imitate James Stewart. Series: *The Tall
Man* (as Billy the Kid), *The Virginian*, *Harry O*.

The Gun
US 1974   74m   colour   TVM
Universal (Richard Levinson, William Link)

A gun passes from hand to hand.
Shades of *Tales of Manhattan* . . . but the mini-stories
here are not very interesting.

w Richard Levinson, William Link   *d* John Badham

Steven Elliott, Pepe Serna, Edith Diaz, Mariclare
Costello, Jean Le Bouvier

The Gun and the Pulpit
US 1974   74m   colour   TVM
Danny Thomas

A gunslinger on the run masquerades as a preacher.
Hesitant variation on *The Left Hand of God*.

w William Bowers   *d* Daniel Petrie

Marjoe Gortner, Estelle Parsons, David Huddleston,
Slim Pickens

The Gun of Zangara*
US 1961   97m   bw   TVM
Desilu/Quinn Martin

An assassin's bullet marked for the President hits the
Mayor of Chicago.
Solidly entertaining *Untouchables* feature.

w William Spier

Robert Stack, Bruce Gordon, Joe Mantell, Anthony
George, Claude Akins

The Guns of Will Sonnett*
US 1967–8 50 × 25m colour
ABC/Spelling–Thomas

An old man takes his grandson on a long journey to find his gunfighter father.
Western saga ingeniously providing something for everybody, including a main theme not unlike *The Fugitive*.

Walter Brennan, Dack Rambo

Gunsmoke*
US 1955–60 156 × 25m bw
US 1961–75 356 × 50m colour
CBS (Charles Marquis Warren, Norman McDonnell, John Mantley)

Marshal Dillon keeps law and order in a small western town.
Phenomenally successful family western which in its later years came perilously close to soap opera.

James Arness, Amanda Blake, Milburn Stone, Ken Curtis, Glenn Strange and, in early years, Dennis Weaver

Gwynne, Fred (*c* 1924–   ). Long-faced, lugubrious American comedy actor, seen to advantage in *Car 54 Where Are You?* and as Herman the Frankenstein-monster-like father in *The Munsters*.

Gypsy Warriors
US 1978 50m colour
Universal (Stephen J. Cannell)

In World War II, two Yanks in occupied France enlist the aid of a trio of gypsies.
Tepid pilot which didn't sell.

w Stephen J. Cannell, Phil deGuere *d* Lou Antonio *ph* Enzo Martinelli *m* Mike Post, Pete Carpenter

James Whitmore Jnr, Tom Selleck, Joseph Ruskin, Lina Raymond, Michael Lane

H

Hadleigh*. British one-hour drama series (Yorkshire TV) about the problems of a landowner in keeping up his stately home. The rather languid Gerald Harper scored in the lead, and the scripts were generally interesting, intelligent and unusual. Several seasons were presented during the seventies.

Hadley, Reed (1911–74) (Reed Herring). American radio actor who starred in one of the earliest TV film series, *Racket Squad*.

Haggard, Piers (1939–). British director who has made a few films but seems principally to be a wizard in the electronic medium, notably with the series *Pennies from Heaven*.

Hagman, Larry (1930–). American comedy actor who pops up everywhere but never seems to pick the right series. *I Dream of Jeannie, Here We Go Again, The Good Life, Dallas*.

Haigh, Kenneth (1929–). Introspective British leading actor often seen in bullying roles; well cast as *Man at the Top*, and in *The Search for the Nile*.

Hale, Alan Jnr (1918–). American light character actor, as cheerfully burly as his father. TV series: *Casey Jones, Gilligan's Island*.

Hall, Monty (1923–). American quizmaster and host, latterly with the daily *Let's Make a Deal*.

Hallmark Hall of Fame. Generic title for an irregular series of drama specials sponsored by Hallmark Cards since 1952. Either the plays or the performers usually have something classical about them.

Halls of Ivy*
US 1955   39 × 25m   bw
TPA/ITC

Problems of a college president.
Charming, unusual comedy series carefully devised for its star.

Ronald Colman, Benita Hume

Hamill, Mark (*c* 1953–). American leading man who starred in *The Texas Wheelers* – and *Star Wars*!

Hampshire, Susan (1938–). Demure-seeming British leading lady best remembered on TV as Fleur in *The Forsyte Saga*, and later in *The Pallisers*.

Hancock, Tony (1924–68). Ebullient British comedian who found his niche as the seedy, argumentative, bumptious, self-important buffoon of *Hancock's Half Hour* on radio and TV. Some of the early sixties scripts, such as *The Train, The Bowmans, The Reunion Party, The Blood Donor* and *The Missing Page* are classics by any definition; but the star's tragedy was that he refused to take advice.

The Hancocks
US 1976   96m   colour   TVM
Warner (Jerry Thorpe, Philip Mandelker)

BBC copyright

TONY HANCOCK, always playing the unwilling underdog, provided a touch of the comic genius to his series of the fifties and sixties. Recordings of such sketches as *The Blood Donor* and *The Reunion Party* are still treasured by collectors, but the sharp comic edge obscured the comedian's personal tragedy.

Problems of a well-to-do family, especially a young wife who feels she must leave her husband and children for a while.

High-class soap, slow-moving and pretentious; the technical sheen and the good life depicted make it look like a feature-length commercial.

w Barbara Turner   d Jerry Thorpe

Joanna Pettet, Kim Hunter, Anne Archer, John Anderson, Lawrence Casey, Claudette Nevins, Robert Sampson, James Houghton

Handl, Irene (1902–). Cheerful, dumpy little British character actress, a popular favourite for many years. TV series: *For the Love of Ada, Maggie and Her.*

The Hands of Cormac Joyce
Australia 1972   74m   colour   TVM
Fielder Cook

A killer storm threatens a fishing community off the Irish coast.

Slow, folksy outdoor drama.

w Thomas Rickman, *novel* Leonard Wibberly d Fielder Cook

Stephen Boyd, Cyril Cusack, Colleen Dewhurst, Dominic Guard

The Hanged Man
US 1965   87m   colour   TVM
Universal (Ray Wagner)

A crook fakes his own death and goes undercover.
Complicated thieves-fall-out mystery set against a New Orleans mardi gras festival; a remake of the cinema film *Ride the Pink Horse.*

w Jack Laird, Stanford Whitmore d Don Siegel

Edmund O'Brien, Vera Miles, Gene Raymond, Robert Culp, J. Carrol Naish, Norman Fell, Archie Moore

The Hanged Man
US 1974   74m   colour   TVM
Bing Crosby Productions

A gunslinger is unjustly hanged, but recovers and becomes a mysterious avenger.
Doom-laden western comic strip which failed to take off as a series.

w Ken Trevey d Michael Coffey

Steve Forrest, Cameron Mitchell, Sharon Acker, Dean Jagger, Will Geer

Hank
US 1965   26 × 25m   colour
NBC/Warner

Adventures of an unregistered college student.
A series which didn't even please its intended young audience.

Dick Fallman, Linda Foster, Howard St John

Hanna–Barbera. A brand name that means cartoons, and especially those scores of indistinguishable yakkity-yak series which fill American TV screens on Saturday mornings. In fact William Hanna and Joe Barbera were the creators of Tom and Jerry, back at MGM in the thirties, and it was much later that they opened their TV factory with its economical system of semi-animation (which means that the characters had a very limited number of movements). The most striking products so far have been *The Flintstones, The Jetsons, Scooby Doo* and *Wait Till Your Father Gets Home.*

Happy
US 1960   26 × 25m   bw
NBC/Roncom

Parents discover that their six-month-old baby not only talks but knows more than they do.
Unfunny variation on *Mister Ed.*

Ronnie Burns, Yvonne Lime

Happy Days*
US 1974–   × 25m   colour
ABC/Paramount/Miller–Milkis (William S. Bickley)

Domestic crises of a small-town American family in the fifties.
A nostalgic series inspired by *American Graffiti*, this homely show was quickly taken over by the character of Fonzie, a braggart college friend of the young son, and this made it the top-rated comedy show of 1975 and 1976.

Henry Winkler, Ron Howard, Tom Bosley, Marion Ross, Anson Williams, Donny Most

Happy Ever After. Basic British sitcom of the seventies, with Terry Scott and June Whitfield as long-married getting into farcical scrapes. A perennial BBC favourite, written by John Chapman and Eric Merriman.

Harben, Philip (c 1906–70). Diminutive British cookery expert, ever-present on TV in the fifties and sixties.

Harbor Command
US 1957   39 × 25m   bw
UA

Stories of the harbour police.
Adequate action series.

Wendell Corey

Harbormaster
aka: *Adventure at Scott Island*
US 1957   26 × 25m   bw
CBS/United Artists

Stories of a New England crime chaser in a sailboat.
Adequate action series of its time.

Barry Sullivan, Paul Burke, Nina Wilcox, Murray Matheson

HARD TIMES. A north country fairground in Victorian days was rigged up in the car park of a TV studio for this atmospherically vivid production.

Hard Times**

GB 1977   4 × 50m   colour
Granada/WNET (Peter Eckersley)

A pompous northern industrialist takes an ex-circus girl as his ward.
Talkative televersion of a difficult Dickens novel, strengthened by good bravura acting and at the beginning some remarkable local colour in the Victorian factory town and circus setting.

w Arthur Hopcraft *d* John Irvin *design* Roy Stonehouse (BAFTA award)

Patrick Allen, Timothy West, Edward Fox, Alan Dobie, Ursula Howells, Jacqueline Tong

'One of the most impressive achievements of the year.'
– *Baltimore Sun*

Hardcase

US 1971   73m   colour   TVM
Matt Rapf

A western adventurer returns home to find his ranch sold and his wife run away with a Mexican.
Tolerable quest western.

w Harold Jack Bloom, Sam Rolfe   *d* John Llewellyn Moxey

Clint Walker, Stefanie Powers, Alex Karras, Pedro Armendariz Jnr

Hardin, Ty (1930–   ) (Orton Hungerford). American leading man who came from nowhere to be TV's *Bronco*, and subsequently had a very desultory film career. Australian series: *Riptide*.

Harding, Gilbert (1907–60). British panellist and talk show guest who became popular in the fifties as the rudest man on TV, though he usually talked good sense. His crumpling under intense personal interrogation by John Freeman in *Face to Face* is a famous piece of television.

The Hardy Boys

US 1969   17 × 25m   colour
TCF/Filmation

Adventures of two crime-solving teenagers who use a travelling rock group as a cover.
Animated Saturday morning filler.

The Hardy Boys/Nancy Drew Mysteries

US 1977–8   58 × 50m   colour
Universal (Glen. A Larson)

BBC copyright

GILBERT HARDING was intolerant, irascible and rude . . . and the British public loved him for it, especially when he got testy with the contestants on *What's My Line?*

Alternating stories from the books featuring famous teenage detective heroes.

For indulgent children. Miss Drew fares better than the awful Hardys; the films stray further and further from the books, and the contempt for the audience shows in appalling inattention to detail.

cr Glen A. Larson

Pamela Sue Martin, Shaun Cassidy, Parker Stevenson

†Only ten Nancy Drew episodes were made.

The Harness*

US 1971 97m colour TVM
Universal (William Sackheim)

A California farmer finds his toughness gone when his wife becomes ill.

Adequate character drama which outstays its welcome.

w Leon Tokatyan, Edward Hume, *story* John Steinbeck *d* Boris Sagal

Lorne Greene, Louise Latham, Julie Sommars, Murray Hamilton, Lee H. Montgomery

Harper, Gerald (1929–). Languid, aristocratic British leading man who came to the fore in *Adam*

Adamant and later personified the landowner *Hadleigh*.

Harper, Ron (1935–). Tough-looking American leading man, once understudy to Paul Newman. Series include *87th Precinct*, *Wendy and Me*, *The Jean Arthur Show*, *Garrison's Gorillas*.

Harper, Valerie ( ). American comedy actress who after several seasons in *The Mary Tyler Moore Show* became star of her own half-hour, *Rhoda*.

Harpers West One. British one-hour tape series of 1960, created by ATV and featuring the staff of a fictional department store.

Harpy

US 1969 100m colour TVM
CBS/Cinema Center 100 (Gerald Seth Sindell)

A divorced psychiatrist rehabilitates an Indian boy who jealously trains his pet eagle to kill anyone who comes between them.

A half-hour story stretched out to four times its natural length.

133

GERALD HARPER oozed aristocratic breeding at a time when it was in short supply, and became one of British television's most familiar figures; as for different reasons did Penelope Keith, seen with him here in *Hadleigh*.

w William Wood   *d* Gerald Seth Sindell   *ph* Robert B. Hauser   *m* David Shire

Hugh O'Brian, Elizabeth Ashley, Tom Nardini, Marilyn Mason

Harrigan and Son
US 1960   34 × 25m   bw
ABC/Desilu

A widowed lawyer conflicts with his son about how to run the business.
Watchable at the time, but no *Defenders*.

cr Cy Howard

Pat O'Brien, Roger Perry

Harris, Rolf (1930–). Bearded Australian entertainer, who won fame as much by sloshing around with pots of paint as by his songs, which however include *Tie Me Kangaroo Down, Sport* and *Nick A Teen and Al K Hall*. Many variety series.

Harry O
US 1974   75m   colour   TVM
Warner

An ex-cop private eye with a bullet in his back lives in a beach shack and takes on occasional cases.
Glum *policier* which took off as a series after the second pilot, *Smile Jenny You're Dead*.

w Howard Rodman   *d* Jerry Thorpe

David Janssen, Martin Sheen, Margot Kidder, Sal Mineo, Will Geer

† The resulting ABC series ran to approx 50 × 50m episodes, all of adequate production quality. Also starring Henry Darrow/Anthony Zerbe; executive producer: Jerry Thorpe; for Warner.

Harry's Girls
US 1963   15 × 25m   bw
NBC/MGM

A hoofer escorts girl dancers around Europe.
Disappointing comedy drawn from the films *Les Girls* and *Idiot's Delight*.

Larry Blyden

Hartman, David (1937–). Rather awkward-looking American character actor, the Donald Sutherland of TV. Series include *The Virginian, The Bold Ones, Lucas Tanner*.

Hartnell, William (1908–75). British character actor who was the first to establish two memorable figures: *Dr Who* and the sergeant in *The Army Game*.

Harty, Russell (1934–). British talk-show host of the seventies, notable for interrupting his guests at the wrong moment.

Harvest of Shame***
US 1960   50m   bw
CBS (Fred W. Friendly)

Classic documentary with a purpose, narrated by Edward R. Murrow and exposing the victimization of migrant agricultural workers in the Midwest; a latter-day *Grapes of Wrath* which proved the influence of TV in government circles.

The Hatfields and the McCoys
US 1975 74m colour TVM
Charles Fries

The story of the hillbilly feud which exploded because two young people wanted to marry.
Surprisingly botched retelling of a story which has so often been told before.

w/d Clyde Ware

Jack Palance, Steve Forrest, Richard Hatch, Karen Lamm

The Hathaways
US 1961 26 × 25m bw
ABC/Columbia (Ezra Stone)

A suburban family adopts three chimps.
Elementary family farce which had trouble lasting a season.

Jack Weston, Peggy Cass

Haunts of the Very Rich***
US 1972 73m colour TVM
Lillian Gallo

Holidaymakers at a lush tropical resort find that they may be dead and this may be hell.
Smooth, palatable, exciting updating of *Outward Bound*, only marred by an unnecessarily tricksy and confusing finish.

w William Wood *d* PAUL WENDKOS

LLOYD BRIDGES, Cloris Leachman, MOSES GUNN, Anne Francis, Ed Asner, Tony Bill, Robert Reed, Donna Mills

Hauser's Memory*
US 1970 96m colour TVM
Universal (Jack Laird)

A scientist receives another man's memory by chemical transfer.
Variation on *Donovan's Brain*, quite pacy and likeable.

w Adrian Spies, *novel* Curt Siodmak *d* Boris Sagal

David McCallum, Lilli Palmer, Susan Strasberg, Robert Webber, Leslie Nielsen, Helmut Kautner

Have Gun Will Travel**
US 1957–62 225 × 25m bw
GBS (Julian Claman)

A retired gunfighter hires himself out to right wrongs . . .
. . . and becomes the Philip Marlowe of the old west. A careful and effective mixture of western and detection, with the right star and clever little gimmicks. (The hero's name is Paladin and a chess knight is printed on his calling card.)

chief d Andrew McLaglen *m* Bernard Herrmann ballad theme sung by Johnny Western

Richard Boone

'For all his educated ways, Paladin is nothing but a hired gun who has made violence a business.' – Don Miller

Having Babies
US 1977 96m colour TVM
ABC/Paramount/Jozak (Lew Gallo)

Three couples experience the birth of a baby by 'natural' methods.
Heavy-going serious soap.

w Elizabeth Clark *d* Robert Day

Desi Arnaz Jnr, Adrienne Barbeau, Ronny Cox, Harry Guardino, Linda Purl, Jan Sterling, Jessica Walter, Karen Valentine, Abe Vigoda, Vicki Lawrence, Greg Mullavey

†Two more TV movies followed, then the format changed into a one-hour series, *Julie Farr MD*.

Havoc
aka: *When Havoc Struck*
GB 1977 13 × 22m colour
ITC

Glenn Ford narrates, with the help of the Sherman Grinberg film library, the stories of spectacular disasters. Modest international filler.

Hawaii Five-O**
US 1968 73m colour TVM
LEONARD FREEMAN

Adventures of a special investigation unit of the Hawaii state government.
Pilot for an immensely successful series.

d Leonard Freeman

Jack Lord, Nancy Kwan, Leslie Nielsen, Andrew Duggan, Lew Ayres, James Gregory

† The resulting series ran for more than 220 × 50m episodes. By denying its leading man any background characterization it was able to concentrate on the crime and its solution, and the exotic locations took away any bad smell of violence. The production team of Bill Finnegan and Bob Sweeney was replaced in the seventh season by Richard Newton and Philip Leacock.

Hawaiian Eye
US 1959–62 134 × 50m bw
ABC/Warner

Cases of a team of private investigators in Hawaii.
Elementary crime stories aimed at the youth audience, with lots of surfing when crime got dull.

Robert Conrad, Grant Williams, Connie Stevens, Troy Donahue, Poncie Ponce

'Afflicted with a severe case of the cutes . . . as for the cases, Peter Gunn could have solved them before the opening commercial.' – Don Miller

Hawk*

US 1966   17 × 50m   colour
ABC/Columbia/Hubbell Robinson (Robert Markell)

Stories of a Red Indian police detective in New York. His racial origins didn't make much noticeable difference to the stories, but the shows were pretty crisp and cancellation was a surprise.

cr Alan Sloane

Burt Reynolds

Hawkesworth, John (1920–). British producer associated with nostalgic shows such as *Upstairs, Downstairs* and *The Duchess of Duke Street*. He also wrote many scripts for these and for *Blackmail, The Gold Robbers, Crimes of Passion*, etc.

Hawkeye and the Last of the Mohicans

Canada 1956   39 × 25m   bw
CBC/Normandie

Stories based on Fenimore Cooper's hero and his faithful Indian Chingachgook.
Modest schoolboy adventure.

John Hart, Lon Chaney Jnr

Hawkins on Murder*

aka: *Death and the Maiden*
US 1973   74m   colour   TVM
MGM (Norman Felton)

A famous homespun lawyer defends an heiress of a triple killing.
Careful, unexciting star pilot which ran to a short series of 74m follow-ups under the titles shown below.

w David Karp   *d* Jud Taylor

James Stewart, Bonnie Bedelia, Strother Martin, Kate Reid, Robert Webber
Sequels:
DIE, DARLING DIE (*d* Paul Wendkos)
MURDER IN MOVIELAND (*d* Jud Taylor)
A LIFE FOR A LIFE (*d* Jud Taylor)
BLOOD FEUD (*d* Paul Wendkos)
MURDER IN THE SLAVE TRADE (*d* Paul Wendkos)
MURDER ON THE 13TH FLOOR (*d* Jud Taylor)

Hayes, Patricia (*c* 1915–). Diminutive British character actress who after years of stooging in comedy shows came into her own in the title role of *Edna the Inebriate Woman*.

Hayes, Peter Lind (*c* 1908–). Easy-going American comedy actor who with his wife Mary Healy was a staple of early TV variety shows.

Haynes, Arthur (*c* 1919–70). British comedian who starred in several series during the sixties, usually playing a fishy character with a warm heart.

PATRICIA HAYES spent years as a comedy foil before being recognized as a serious actress. Here she is seen in *The Portland Millions*, an episode of *Victorian Scandals*.

Haynes, Lloyd (*c* 1937–). Black American actor who starred in *Room 222*.

Hazel

US 1961–5   154 × 25m   bw
NBC/Columbia/Harry Ackerman (James Fonda)

Comedy series about a suburban household in which the maid is really boss.

Adequate domestic situations constructed for a likeable star.

cr William Cowley, Peggy Chantler, from a *Saturday Evening Post* cartoon character by Ted Key

SHIRLEY BOOTH, Don Defore, Whitney Blake

Hazell*
GB 1978   10 × 50m   colour (VTR)
Thames (June Roberts)

Adventures of an ex-cop turned private eye in London's rougher districts.
Abrasive and generally likeable if slightly muddled attempt to translate Chandler's Marlowe to another setting. Not a complete success, and too violent, but good TV entertainment.

w various, from the books by Gordon Williams and Terry Venables

Nicholas Ball, Roddy McMillan

He and She*
US 1967   26 × 25m   colour
Talent Associates (Arne Sultan)

Adventures of a serious young cartoonist and his slightly daffy wife.
Modern urban comedy with an agreeable dash of sophistication.

Richard Benjamin, Paula Prentiss, Jack Cassidy

The Headmaster*
US 1970   14 × 25m   colour
ADA/Aaron Ruben

Problems for the headmaster of a private school
Pleasing but commercially unsuccessful star comedy.

Andy Griffith

The Healers
US 1974   100m   colour   TVM
Warner

Life in a medical research hospital.
Boring, rather pretentious pap.

w John Furia Jnr, Howard Dimsdale   d Tom Gries

John Forsythe, Pat Harrington, John McIntire, Beverly Garland, Anthony Zerbe

Heat of Anger*
aka: *Fitzgerald and Pride*
US 1971   74m   colour   TVM
Metromedia (Dick Berg)

A lady attorney and her young assistant defend a murderer.
Competent courtroom pilot which didn't make it.

w Fay Kanin   d Don Taylor

SUSAN HAYWARD, James Stacy, Lee J. Cobb, Fritz Weaver, Bettye Ackerman

Heatwave**
US 1974   74m   Technicolor   TVM
Universal (Harve Bennett)

An energy crisis topped by a heat wave incapacitates the city and sends people scurrying for the mountains.
Uncomfortably convincing and well-observed social melodrama.

w Peter Allan Fields, Mark Weingart   d Jerry Jamison

Bonnie Bedelia, Ben Murphy, Lew Ayres, Lionel Johnston, Naomi Stevens, David Huddleston

Hec Ramsey: see Mystery Movie

Hedison, David (1926–) (Ara Heditsian). Handy American leading man of the second rank. TV series: *Five Fingers, Voyage to the Bottom of the Sea.*

Hedley, Jack (1930–). Pleasant, diffident British leading man who scored a hit in *The World of Tim Frazer* but oddly never had another series to himself.

Hee Haw
US 1969–74   95 × 50m   colour (VTR)
Youngstreet/CBS

Lowbrow comedy variety show, a kind of hick version of *Laugh-In*.

The Heist*
GB title: *Suspected Person*
aka: *The Caper*
US 1973   73m   colour   TVM
Paramount (Edward J. Milkis)

An armoured car guard is framed for the robbery of his vehicle.
Competent routine crime melodrama.

w Lionel E. Siegel   d Don McDougall

Christopher George, Elizabeth Ashley, Howard Duff, Norman Fell, Cliff Osmond

Helen – A Woman of Today*
GB 1973   13 × 50m   colour (VTR)
LWT

Middlebrow serial about the problems of a married woman; not quite so good as the previous entry from the same stable, *A Man of our Times.*

Help! It's The Hair Bear Bunch
US 1972   16 × 22m   colour
Hanna–Barbera

Animals try to improve living conditions at the zoo.
Unmemorable semi-animated cartoon series.

Helter Skelter*
US 1976 2 × 100m colour TVM
Lorimar (Tom Gries)

A fictionalized account of the Manson Murders.
Extremely powerful, *In Cold Blood* type treatment of a
case which is certainly not entertaining and should
possibly have been left in the newspaper files. The narrative is somewhat confusing, assuming too much prior
knowledge.

w J. P. Miller *d* Tom Gries

Henderson, Dickie (1922–). British comedian, son
of another; tremendously popular in the fifties as star of
a domestic comedy series, *The Dickie Henderson Show*;
in the sixties made progressively less regular variety
appearances, concentrating on dancing; made a comeback in 1977.

Henderson, Florence (1937–). American operatic
singer who found herself also in demand as a light actress and mother of *The Brady Bunch*.

Hendry, Ian (1931–). British character lead, in innumerable plays and in guest parts in series.

Hennesey*
US 1959–61 96 × 25m bw
CBS/Hennesey Co/Jackie Cooper

Comedy adventures of a naval doctor at the San Diego
base.
Lively service comedy which gave good value.

cr Don McGuire *m* Sonny Burke

Jackie Cooper, Roscoe Karns, Abby Dalton, James
Komack

Henning, Doug (*c* 1947–). American magician,
noted for his slim, youthful appearance (absolutely nothing concealed about his person); also for his careful
re-creations of elaborate classical illusions. Mainly seen
in his own variety specials.

Henning, Paul (1911–). American radio comedy
writer who made a big hit in TV as creator of *The Bob
Cummings Show*, *The Beverly Hillbillies*, *Petticoat
Junction* and *Green Acres*.

Henry, Buck (1930–) (B. Zuckerman). American
multi-talent whose chief service to TV has been as
creator of *Get Smart* (with Mel Brooks), *Captain Nice*
and *Quark*.

Henson, Jim (1936–). American puppeteer, creator
of *The Muppets* (which derived from his *Sesame Street*
inventions).

Hepton, Bernard (1925–). British character actor,
a man of many faces. Series include *Colditz*, *Sadie It's
Cold Outside*, *Secret Army*.

The Herculoids
US 1967 26 × 25m colour
Hanna–Barbera

On a distant planet, mythical animals protect their king
against monsters from other galaxies.
Cartoon series sadly lacking the imagination of its premise.

Here Come the Brides
US 1968–9 52 × 50m colour
ABC/Columbia (Paul Claver)

When Seattle was a village, its menfolk imported a
boatload of brides from the east.
Pastiche of *Seven Brides for Seven Brothers* which falls
somewhere between comedy, adventure and *Peyton
Place*.

Robert Brown, David Soul, Bobby Sherman, Joan
Blondell, Mark Lenard

Here We Go Again*
US 1971 13 × 25m colour
ABC/Metromedia (Lew Gallo, Steve Pritzker)

Newlyweds are plagued by the constant intrusion of
their former, over-friendly, spouses.
Fairly rare attempt for TV at sophisticated comedy of
the Powell–Loy kind. It didn't last because of strong
opposition, but it did try.

cr Bob Kaufman

Larry Hagman, Diane Baker, Dick Gautier, Nita
Talbot

Here's Lucy*
US 1968–73 144 × 25m colour
CBS/Lucille Ball Productions (Gary Morton)

Last of the Lucy half-hour series, this one finds her as a
widow working in an employment agency; but the gags
are much as before.

LUCILLE BALL, GALE GORDON, Lucie Arnaz

† See also *I Love Lucy* and *The Lucy Show*.

The Hero
US 1966 16 × 25m colour
NBC/Talent Associates

A western star is scared of horses.
A thin premise makes a thin comedy.

Richard Mulligan, Mariette Hartley

Hewat, Tim (*c* 1930–). Australian current affairs
producer who, in Britain in the fifties and sixties, made
his mark with *Searchlight* and *World in Action*, TV's
equivalent of the best kind of penny press.

Hey I'm Alive*
US 1975 74m colour TVM
Charles Fries (Lawrence Schiller)

The true account of two people who survived a light
plane crash in the frozen Yukon.

A good start, but it gets a bit gruelling and repetitive.

w Rita Lakin, *book* Helen Klauben   *d* Larry Schiller

Ed Asner, Sally Struthers

Hey Jeannie*
US 1956   32 × 25m   bw
Four Star/Tartan

A Scots girl in New York helps a taxi cab driver.
Simple-minded but pleasing comedy series, a good showcase for a star who subsequently retired from the scene.

JEANNIE CARSON, Allen Jenkins, Jane Dulo

Hey Landlord
US 1966   31 × 25m   colour
Mirisch–Rich/UA

An aimless young man inherits a New York brown stone and has trouble keeping it in order.
Forgettable comedy series.

Will Hutchins, Sandy Baron, Michael Constantine, Pamela Rodgers

Heyes, Douglas (1923–). American writer–director. In TV, wrote and directed pilots for *The Outsider*, *The Bearcats*.

Hickman, Dwayne (1934–). American juvenile lead of the forties, TV's *Dobie Gillis*.

High Chaparral*
US 1967–71   98 × 50m   colour
NBC/David Dortort/ (James Schmerer)

The life of a rich Arizona rancher and his sons in the 1870s.
Bonanza under another name, but a good western series with excellent location work.

cr David Dortort

Leif Erickson, Cameron Mitchell, Mark Slade, Linda Cristal, Henry Darrow, Frank Silvera

High Risk*
US 1976   74m   colour   TVM
MGM/Danny Thomas (Robert E. Relyea)

A group of professionals with special skills take on impossible missions at a half million dollars a time.
Polished, predictable, highly derivative entertainment.

w Robert Carrington   *d* Sam O'Steen

Victor Buono, Don Stroud, Joe Sirola, Joanna Cameron, Ronne Troup, Wolf Roth

High Tor. Claimed as the first telefilm, this 1955 American production took 12 days to shoot. In the Maxwell Anderson fantasy Bing Crosby starred as the dentist who refuses to sell his land on the Hudson and is visited by ghosts from America's past. Julie Andrews and Nancy Olson co-starred.

Highway Patrol**
US 1955–8   156 × 25m   bw
Ziv

Stories of the California mobile cops.
An efficient series which had the whole world answering 'Ten four' for agreement.

BRODERICK CRAWFORD

Hijack
US 1973   74m   colour   TVM
Spelling–Goldberg

A truck driver with a secret cargo has to frustrate several hijack attempts along his route.
Rather sluggish action melodrama.

w James D. Buchanan, Ronald Austin   *d* Leonard Horn

David Janssen, Lee Purcell, Keenan Wynn, Jeanette Nolan, Tom Tully

Hiken, Nat (   ). Outstanding American comedy writer who created Sergeant Bilko and *Car 54 Where Are You?*

Hill, Benny (1925–). Rotund British comedian who writes the scripts for his own variety specials, which consist of rude rhymes and burlesque-type sketches, which he gets away with because of his ability to charm his audience as a naughty boy. His impersonations are usually his best effects.

Hillerman, John (*c* 1934–). American comedy character actor, often of neat and prissy types. On form in *The Betty White Show*.

Hiram Holliday: see The Adventures of Hiram Holliday

Hirsch, Judd (*c* 1940–). American leading actor of the rough diamond type, seen on TV in *The Law*, *Delvecchio*, and *Taxi*.

Hirschman, Herbert (*c* 1919–). American producer, sometimes writer, with credits stretching back from *Perry Mason* and *The Defenders* through *The Men from Shiloh* to *Planet of the Apes*.

Hit Lady*
US 1974   74m   colour   TVM
Spelling–Goldberg

A glamorous lady artist is really a professional killer.
Ludicrously unlikely murder melodrama with predictable twists and glossy presentation.

w Yvette Mimieux   *d* Tracy Keenan Wynn

Yvette Mimieux, Dack Rambo, Joseph Campanella, Clu Gulager, Keenan Wynn

BENNY HILL has obviously just seen a voluptuous girl go past: that's the level of humour in his ever-popular comedy-variety series.

Hitchcock, Alfred (1899–). See Alfred Hitchcock Presents

Hobley, MacDonald (*c* 1915–). British announcer and light actor, one of TV's earliest personalities.

Hogan's Heroes**
US 1965–70   168 × 25m   colour
CBS/Bing Crosby Productions (Edward H. Feldman)

American prisoners raise Cain in a German camp during World War II.
Based unofficially on *Stalag 17*, this is a rather tactless farce which comes off, chiefly because the Germans are likeable idiots. The level of plot invention is quite high, considering the constrained settings.

Bob Crane, Werner Klemperer, John Banner, Robert Clary, Richard Dawson, Ivan Dixon

Holiday Lodge
US 1961   13 × 25m   bw
J & M/Universal

Two incompetents are social directors at a summer resort.
A disappointing Hollywood excursion for Canada's favourite comics.

Johnny Wayne, Frank Shuster

Holliman, Earl (1928–). American actor who graduated from weak roles to toughies. TV series include *Hotel de Paree, The Wide Country, Police Woman.*

Holloway, Stanley (1890–). British comedy character actor and music hall performer who has tried almost everything through a long career. TV series: *Our Man Higgins, Thingummyjig.*

Hollywood and the Stars*
US 1963   31 × 25m   bw
Wolper/UA (Jack Haley Jnr)

Compilations of old movie scenes, introduced by Joseph Cotten. Those dealing with a theme (gangsters, monsters) are best.

ALFRED HITCHCOCK. The great director became a TV personality with his gag intros for his own series...

... but he still took his directing very seriously.

Hollywood Off Beat
US 1953   13 × 25m   bw
Marion Parsonnet

Dire private eye yarns wasting an excellent star.

Melvyn Douglas

Hollywood Palace. A regular feature of the late fifties and early sixties, this American hour-long series recreated an old-time vaudeville bill, and most of the world's big stars appeared in it.

Hollywood Squares. An elaborate quiz show in which nine celebrities have to answer the questions, and contestants guess whether they are right, with scores like noughts and crosses (tic tac toe). Popular throughout the seventies, in Britain as *Celebrity Squares*.

Holm, Celeste (1919–   ). American character actress. TV series: *Nancy*.

Holm, Ian (1932–   ). British character actor with an air of toughness. Series include *The Sweeney*.

Holmes and Yo Yo
US 1975   13 × 25m   colour
NBC/Universal (Leonard Stern, Jackie Cooper)

An experienced cop finds his new partner is a robot.
Flat comedy in the wake of *Six Million Dollar Man*. See also *Future Cop*, an attempt to take the same subject seriously.

John Shuck, Richard B. Shull

Holocaust**
US 1978   9 × 50m   colour
NBC/Herb Brodkin, Robert Berger

The story of a Jewish family under the Nazis.
Predictably harrowing, but gripping and well-written though less than marvellously made piece of fictionalized history. It caused controversy wherever it was shown.

w Gerald Green   *d* Marvin Chomsky

Joseph Bottoms, David Warner, Michael Moriarty, Meryl Streep, Fritz Weaver, Rosemary Harris, Tovah Feldshuh, George Rose, Tom Bell, Marius Goring, Ian Holm, Robert Stephens

Home***
GB 1972   90m   colour (VTR)
BBC

The reminiscences of two old men in a home for the elderly.
A feast of brilliant acting, primarily, and a record of a theatrical event; but the play itself may emerge as a classic.

w DAVID STOREY   *d* LINDSAY ANDERSON

JOHN GIELGUD, RALPH RICHARDSON, Dandy Nichols, Mona Washbourne

Home for the Holidays*
US 1972   74m   colour   TVM
Spelling–Goldberg (Paul Junger Witt)

Four daughters go home for Christmas and murders ensue.
Surprisingly grisly whodunnit, quite exciting once it gets going.

w Joseph Stefano   *d* John Llewellyn Moxey

Walter Brennan, Eleanor Parker, Jessica Walter, Julie Harris, Sally Field, Jill Haworth

A Home of Our Own
US 1976   100m   colour   TVM
Quinn Martin

The true story of Father William Wasson, a Catholic priest who provided homes for Mexican orphans.
Well-meaning, uninteresting do-goodery.

d Robert Day

Jason Miller, Pancho Cordova, Pedro Armendariz Jnr

Home to Stay*
US 1978   74m   colour
David Susskind (Fred Brogger)

An Illinois farmer ponders whether to send his half-senile father into a rest home.
Poignant and well-acted domestic drama on a subject usually pushed under the carpet.

w Suzanne Clauser, *novel* Janet Majerus   *d* Delbert Mann   *ph* Reg Morris   *m* Hagood Hardy

Henry Fonda, Michael McGuire, Kristen Vigard, Frances Hyland

The Homecoming*
US 1971   100m   colour   TVM
Lorimar (Robert L. Jacks)

Life for a poor country family in 1933.
Christmas sentimentality, slow-moving but well-detailed, this was the springboard for the highly successful series *The Waltons*, which surfaced the following year with a different cast.

w Earl Hamner Jnr, from his novel   *d* Fielder Cook

Patricia Neal, Richard Thomas, Andrew Duggan, William Windom

† The original material had also been used as a cinema film, *Spencer's Mountain*.

Homeward Borne
US 1957   82m   bw   TVM
Columbia/Playhouse 90

A pilot back from the war feels unwanted because his wife has adopted an orphan.
Woman's magazine stuff, capably presented.

novel Ruth Chatterton   *d* Arthur Hiller

Linda Darnell, Richard Kiley, Keith Andes, Richard Eyer

Homicide. An Australian one-hour police series, by Crawford Productions. As live, tape or film it worked with its intended market for a period of nearly 10 years from 1967.

Hondo
US 1967   17 × 50m   colour
ABC/Batjac/Fenady/MGM

Adventures of a cavalry scout during the Indian wars. Rather ho-hum western, competent at best.

Ralph Taeger, Noah Beery Jnr, Kathie Browne, Michael Pate

Honey West
US 1965   30 × 25m   bw
ABC/Four Star

Cases of a lady detective who is also a judo expert. Moderately amusing idea, pinched from *The Avengers*; less than moderate execution.

Anne Francis, John Ericson, Irene Hervey

Honeymoon with a Stranger*
US 1969   74m   colour   TVM
TCF (Robert L. Jacks)

Some days after marrying an American woman, a wealthy European vanishes. Then an impostor arrives, claiming his rights . . .
This well-worn story started as an episode of *The Whistler*, was filmed as *Chase a Crooked Shadow*, became a play, *Trap for a Lonely Man* and a TV movie, *One of My Wives is Missing*. It always works.

w David Harmon, Henry Slesar   *d* John Peyser

Janet Leigh, Rossano Brazzi, Cesare Danova, Barbara Rush

The Honeymooners***
US 1949–54   × 25m   bw (VTR)
ABC

Misadventures of a blundering bus driver, his wife and their married friends.
Simple-minded but classic TV comedy series: the male leads became national figures.

JAMES GLEASON, ART CARNEY, AUDREY MEADOWS, Joyce Randolph

† The first three of the cast, with Jane Kean, got together for a 25th anniversary special in 1976.
†† The sketches were originally seen on *Cavalcade of Stars*, with Pert Kelton as Alice, to whom Gleason always said admiringly at the close: 'Baby, you're the greatest!'

Hong Kong
US 1960   26 × 50m   bw
ABC/TCF

An American correspondent helps the British fight crime in the orient.

Fairly efficient but unremarkable studio-set adventures.

cr Robert Buckner

Rod Taylor, Lloyd Bochner

Hong Kong Phooey
US 1974   16 × 22m   colour
Hanna–Barbera

A meek janitor has a double life as a disaster-prone super-detective.
Acceptable Batman-spoofing cartoon.

Honky Tonk*
US 1974   74m colour   TVM
MGM

A con man meets his match in old Nevada.
Acceptable spin-off from the Clark Gable movie: it didn't make a series though.

d Don Taylor

Richard Crenna, Margot Kidder, Will Geer, Stella Stevens

Honor Thy Father*
US 1972   100m   colour   TVM
Metromedia (Charles Fries)

The everyday life of a New York Mafia family.
A mini-*Godfather*, watered down from a popular novel.

w Lewis John Carlino, *novel* Gay Falese   *d* Paul Wendkos

Raf Vallone, Richard Castellano, Brenda Vaccaro, Joe Bologna

Hopalong Cassidy
US 1951   52 × 26m   bw
William Boyd

Adventures of the black-garbed cowboy.
Tightly-paced little westerns, made to order when Hopalong's old movies caused a TV sensation.

William Boyd

Hope, Bob (1903–) (Leslie Townes Hope). American wisecracking comedian, star of radio, movies and TV. His TV appearances have normally been in the form of one-hour specials, of countless number, but he has also guested in almost everyone else's shows, including *The Muppets*.

Hopkins, Anthony (1941–). Stocky British actor in the Burton mould; he seemed for a while to be concentrating on TV and has appeared in such major projects as *War and Peace* (BAFTA award 1972), *QB VII*, *The Lindbergh Kidnapping Case*, *Victory at Entebbe*.

Hopkins, John (1931–). British TV playwright whose most-acclaimed dramas include *Talking to a Stranger, Fathers and Families.*

Horizon. Umbrella title for a long-running BBC series of documentaries on scientific research and advance. (The brief is taken very loosely.) BAFTA award best factual programme 1972, 1974. Outstanding recent items have included *The Great Wine Revolution* and *The Case of the Ancient Astronauts,* the latter a debunking of the theories of Erich Von Daniken.

Horizon 2002*
GB 1977 55m colour (VTR)
BBC

An elaborate spoof showing what *Horizon* might be like 25 years on, when it surveys the (mythical) scientific advances which have happened in the meantime.

Horror at 37,000 Feet*
US 1972 73m colour TVM
Anthony Wilson

An evil power is set loose in a transatlantic jet from stones of an old English abbey which are being shipped to America.
Enjoyably arrant nonsense.

d David Lowell Rich

Buddy Ebsen, Chuck Connors, Tammy Grimes, France Nuyen, Lynn Loring, William Shatner, Roy Thinnes, Paul Winfield

Horton, Robert (1924–) (Mead Howard Horton). American leading man of the fifties. Made a big hit in *Wagon Train* but his only subsequent series was *A Man Called Shenandoah,* which was not a success.

Hospital**
GB 1977 9 × 45m colour (16mm)
BBC (Roger Mills)

Cinéma vérité documentaries showing, quite brilliantly, aspects of life in a big general hospital (in Bolton). Riveting and disturbing.

w/d Tim King

'Nerve-twistingly brilliant.' – *Daily Telegraph*
'It isn't possible to make a better documentary.' – *Guardian*

† BAFTA award 1977, best documentary (*Casualty* episode).

The Hostage Heart
US 1977 96m colour
MGM/Andrew Fenady

Terrorists plan to infiltrate a hospital and hold up a delicate operation.
Good opportunities in a familiar suspense vein are thrown away by a boring script.

w Andrew J. Fenady, Charles Sailor, Eric Kalder, *novel* Gerald Green *d* Bernard McEveety *ph* Matthew F. Leonetti *m* Fred Karlin

Bradford Dillman, Loretta Swit, Vic Morrow, Sharon Acker, George DiCenzo, Cameron Mitchell, Paul Shanar, Belinda J. Montgomery

'All the elements – murder, doctors, terrorism, open-heart surgery, police, the FBI and a chase – have been dumped in the mixer to prove that mechanical suspense and plastic characters won't deliver a rewarding meller.' – *Daily Variety*

Hot off the Wire: see The Jim Backus Show

Hot*l Baltimore
US 1975 13 × 25m colour (VTR)
TAT/Norman Lear (Ron Clark, Gene Marcione)

Peculiar characters converge in the lobby of a downbeat Manhattan hotel.
Unsuccessful attempt at a different kind of comedy: the critics latched on but the public didn't.

play Lanford Williams

Conchita Ferrell, James Cromwell, Al Freeman Jnr, Richard Masur

Hotel de Paree
US 1959 33 × 25m bw
CBS (Bill Self)

The Sundance Kid, a reformed character, hides out with his girlfriend at a frontier hotel.
Light western with some small claim to originality.

Earl Holliman, Jeanette Nolan

hotelvision. A system pioneered in the early seventies by which hotel guests for a fee could see new movies on their TV set. It quickly descended to pornography and became an embarrassment.

The Hound of the Baskervilles
US 1972 73m colour TVM
Universal (Stanley Kallis)

Sherlock Holmes investigates a spectral hound which roams Dartmoor.
Risible version with stolid acting and the most inappropriate sets.

w Robert E. Thompson from the novel by Sir Arthur Conan Doyle *d* Barry Crane

Stewart Granger, William Shatner, Bernard Fox, John Williams, Anthony Zerbe, Jane Merrow

The Houndcats*
US 1972 26 × 25m colour
NBC/De Patie–Freleng

Cat and dog agents combat evil.
Lively cartoon spoof of *Mission Impossible.*

m Doug Goodwin

The House on Greenapple Road*
US 1970 113m colour TVM
Quinn Martin

A suburban wife has apparently been savagely murdered . . . or has she?
Efficient and generally holding but awesomely long murder mystery, a premature pilot for the *Dan August* series which later emerged with a different lead.

w George Eckstein, *novel* Harold R. Daniels *d* Robert Day

Christopher George, Janet Leigh, Julie Harris, Tim O'Connor, Walter Pidgeon, Barry Sullivan

The House that Wouldn't Die*
US 1970 72m colour TVM
Aaron Spelling

The owner of a Georgetown house feels threatened by an evil spirit and tries to exorcize it.
Single-minded and adequately chilling ghost story.

w Henry Farrell *d* John Llewellyn Moxey

BARBARA STANWYCK, Richard Egan, Michael Anderson Jnr, Mabel Albertson

Houston, We've Got a Problem
US 1974 74m colour TVM
Universal (Harve Bennett)

A reconstruction of the Apollo 13 mission of 1970.
A rather unnecessary fictionalization of facts which speak for themselves.

w Richard Nelson *d* Lawrence Doheny

Robert Culp, Clu Gulager, Gary Collins, Sandra Dee, Ed Nelson

How Awful about Allan*
US 1970 72m colour TVM
Aaron Spelling

A blind young man in his elder sister's care is tormented by strange voices . . .
Artful mystery chiller in the vein of the author's sagas about Baby Jane and Sweet Charlotte.

w Henry Farrell *d* Curtis Harrington

Anthony Perkins, Julie Harris, Joan Hackett

How Green Was My Valley*
GB 1976 6 × 50m colour (VTR)
BBC/TCF (Martin Lisemore)

The life of the Morgan family in a Welsh mining valley between the wars.
Solidly professional transcription of a semi-classic novel.

w Elaine Morgan, *novel* Richard Llewellyn *d* Ronald Wilson

Stanley Baker, SIÂN PHILLIPS, Huw Justin, Rhys Powys

How I Spent My Summer Vacation
GB theatrical title: *Deadly Roulette*
US 1967 96m colour TVM
Universal (Jack Laird)

A young man accepts an invitation to a summer cruise aboard a millionaire's yacht, and finds himself among members of a crime syndicate.
Puffed-out and tediously flashy comedy adventure which soon wears out its welcome except as a tour round lush backgrounds.

w Gene Kearney *d* William Hale

Robert Wagner, Peter Lawford, Lola Albright, Walter Pidgeon, Jill St John, Michael Ansara

How the West Was Won: The MacAhans
US 1976 120m colour
NBC/MGM (John Mantley)

A heavyweight but slow starting pilot about a family moving west in the 1870s.

How the West Was Won*
US 1977 3 × 96m (1st season), 10 × 96m (2nd season) 11 × 96m (3rd season) colour
NBC/MGM/John Mantley

Episodes in the life of the wandering MacAhan family. Expensive but stretched-out series following at some distance from the above pilot. Story line desultory but individual scenes well mounted.

d Bernard and Vincent McEveety, others

James Arness, Bruce Boxleitner, Eva Marie Saint/ Fionnula Flanagan. Guest stars include Christopher Lee, Lloyd Bridges, Ricardo Montalban, Horst Buchholz, Brian Keith, Cameron Mitchell, Mel Ferrer

How to Break Up a Happy Divorce
US 1976 74m colour TVM
Charles Fries/NBC

A divorcee tries to get her husband back.
Modestly sophisticated comedy.

w Gerald Gardner, Dee Caruso *d* Jerry Paris *m* Nelson Riddle

Barbara Eden, Hal Linden, Peter Bonerz, Marcia Rodd, Harold Gould

How to Impeach a President*
GB 1974 60m colour (VTR)
BBC (Tam Fry)

A modern treatment of the impeachment of Andrew Jackson, with interruptions from modern interviewers and TV techniques.
A documentary reconstruction produced at the time of the possible impeachment of Richard Nixon. Interesting in its own right, for its clever techniques, and as a precursor of the 1977–8 spate of docu-dramas presenting more questionable interpretations of climaxes in the lives of historical figures.

w John Lloyd   *d* Alvin Rakoff

Walter Klavun, Robert MacNeil

'Packed with excitement, excellent oratory, and best of all it really happened.' – *Daily Mirror*

How to Steal an Airplane
aka: *Only One Day Left before Tomorrow*
US 1970   100m   colour   TVM
Universal (Roy Huggins)

Two adventurers pose as tourists in a Latin American country to repossess a Lear jet stolen by the dictator's irresponsible son.
Modest, unremarkable adventure.

w Robert Foster, Philip de Guere Jnr   *d* Leslie H. Martinson

Pete Duel, Clinton Greyn, Claudine Longet, Sal Mineo, Julie Sommars

Howard, John (1913–) (John Cox). American juvenile lead of the late thirties; retired from acting after early TV series *The Adventures of Sea Hawk*, *Dr Hudson's Secret Journal*.

Howard, Ken (1944–). Giant-size American leading man with Broadway and Hollywood credentials. Series: *Adam's Rib*, *Manhunter*.

Howard, Ron (1953–). Fresh-faced American juvenile lead, former child actor. Series include *The Andy Griffith Show*, *The Smith Family*, *Happy Days*.

Howard, Ronald (1918–). British light character actor, son of Leslie Howard. TV series: *Sherlock Holmes*, *Cowboy in Africa*.

Howarth, Jack (1897–). British character actor familiar as Albert Tatlock in *Coronation Street*.

Howdy Doody. American studio show for children hosted by a rather crude cowboy marionette. Immensely popular throughout its run (1947–60).

Howerd, Frankie (1921–) (Francis Howard). British eccentric comedian whose inimitable stumbling style is full of oohs and ahs and other curious exclamations. Many taped variety and sitcom series from the mid-fifties.

A Howling in the Woods*
US 1971   96m   colour   TVM
Universal

In a creepy house by Lake Tahoe, a girl is menaced by what appears to be a spectral dog, and a murder secret is unearthed.
Enjoyable spinechiller with not quite enough plot for its length.

w Richard de Roy   *d* Daniel Petrie

Larry Hagman, Vera Miles, Barbara Eden, John Rubenstein

H. R. Pufnstuf*
US 1969   17 × 22m   colour
NBC/Sid and Marty Krofft

A boy finds a magic flute and sails away to a fantasy land threatened by a wicked witch.
Elaborate variation on *The Wizard of Oz*, peopled by talking things in elaborate costumes. Commendably high production standards.

Jack Wild

†A feature version was made, to rather less effect.

Hubley, John (1914–77). American animator, a founder member of UPA. Many specials for TV including *Everybody Rides the Carousel*.

Huckleberry Finn
US 1974   75m   colour   TVM
ABC Circle (Steven North)

Rough-edged TV version of Mark Twain's juvenile classic about adventures on the Mississippi.

w Jean Holloway   *d* Robert Totten

Ronny Howard, Jack Elam, Merle Haggard, Donny Most, Sarah Selby, Jean Howard, Clint Howard, Royal Dano

Huckleberry Hound. A rather boring cartoon character with elements of Mickey Mouse. Introduced by Hanna–Barbera in 1958, he shared 195 half-hour shows with Pixie and Dixie and Hokey Wolf.

Hudson, Rock (1925–) (Roy Scherer). American beefcake leading man of the fifties who proved willing to try anything. In TV this led him to *McMillan and Wife* in which, with or without moustache (or wife) he proved fairly adept at the old Thin Man type of mystery comedy.

Hudson's Bay
Canada 1959   39 × 25m   bw
North Star

Adventures of a trapper in the Canadian northlands.
Dull, flimsy adventure yarns partly redeemed by location shooting.

cr/d Sidney J. Furie

Barry Nelson, George Tobias

Huggins, Roy (1914–). American independent producer. TV series include *The Fugitive*, *Run for Your Life*.

Hull, Rod (*c* 1939–). Australian comedian whose right arm manipulates the neck and beak of a silent but highly aggressive emu. Very popular in Britain in the seventies.

The Human Jungle*
GB 1963   × 50m   bw
Parkyn–Wintle/ABC

Stories from a psychiatrist's case book.
Lively melodramas with a whiff of *The Seventh Veil.*

Herbert Lom

Humperdinck, Engelbert (*c* 1934–) (Gerry Dorsey). British pop singer who hit the heights at home in the sixties and around the world in the seventies. TV appearances mainly in specials.

The Hunted Lady
US 1977   97m   colour   TVM
Quinn Martin (William Robert Yates)

A policewoman is framed for murder by the syndicate.

w William Robert Yates   *d* Richard Lang   *ph* Paul Lohmann

Donna Mills, Robert Reed, Lawrence Casey, Will Sampson, Andrew Duggan

Hunter
US 1977   7 × 50m   colour
Lorimar (Christopher Morgan)

Adventures of a ruthless spy.
Smooth but intrinsically fifth-rate James Bondery.

cr William Blinn

James Franciscus, Ralph Bellamy

Hunter, Tab (1931–) (Andrew Arthur Kelm). American teenage rave of the early fifties; starred in *The Tab Hunter Show.*

Hunters Are for Killing*
US 1970   100m   colour   TVM
Cinema Center (Hugh Benson)

An ex-con finds himself in danger from his own family and his girl friend's father.
Complex suspenser which passes the time.

w Charles Kuenstle   *d* Bernard Girard   *ph* Jerry Finnermann   *m* Jerry Fielding

Burt Reynolds, Melvyn Douglas, Martin Balsam, Suzanne Pleshette, Larry Storch

Hunters of the Reef
US 1978   96m   colour   TVM
Paramount/Writers Company (Stanley Kallis)

Marine salvagers in Florida are menaced by sharks.
Boring outdoor movie with predictable elements.

w Eric Bercovici   *d* Alex Singer   *ph* Andrew Laszlo   *m* Richard Makowitz

Michael Parks, Mary Louise Weller, William Windom

'Excitement is kept to a minimum.' – *Daily Variety*

Huntley, Chet (1911–74). American news reporter and linkman, for many years an essential half of NBC's *Huntley–Brinkley Report.*

Hurricane
US 1974   74m   colour   TVM
Metromedia

Several people are caught up in a Gulf Coast hurricane.
Piffling multi-drama making far too obvious use of news footage at the expense of personal involvement.

w Jack Turley   *d* Jerry Jameson

Larry Hagman, Martin Milner, Jessica Walter, Barry Sullivan, Michael Learned, Will Geer

Hurt, John (1940–). British character actor who tends to play neurotics and eccentrics, and gave a notable performance as Quentin Crisp in *The Naked Civil Servant* (BAFTA award 1975).

Husbands, Wives and Lovers
US 1978   13 × 50m   colour (VTR)
TCF (Hal Dresner)

Misdemeanours and attempted misdemeanours of a group of young married suburbanites.
Relentlessly 'funny' comedy series showing the lighter side of *No Down Payment* but not doing it very convincingly. The original pilot was called *Husbands and Wives.*

cr Joan Rivers, Hal Dresner   *w* Harry Cauley and others   *d* Marc Daniels and others   *m* Ken and Mitzi Welch

Ron Rifkin, Jesse Willis, Eddie Barth, Lynne Marie Stewart, Mark Lonow, Randee Heller, Charles Siebert, Claudette Nevins, Tom Miller, Stephen Pearlman, Cynthia Harris

'Coarse and unfunny.' – *Daily Variety*

Hustling*
US 1975   96m   colour   TVM
Filmways/Lillian Gallo

A woman reporter tries to write the truth about New York prostitution.
Grainy, gritty, true-life semi-documentary. The fuzzy sound recording makes fiction or fact preferable to this well-meant compromise, but it tries hard.

w Fay Kanin, *book* Gail Sheehy   *d* Joseph Sargent

Lee Remick, JILL CLAYBURGH, Monte Markham, Alex Rocco

Hutchins, Will (1932–). Slow-speaking American actor who played the lead in *Sugarfoot* and was subsequently seen in *Blondie* and *Hey Landlord.*

Hutton, Betty (1921–) (Betty Jane Thornburg). Vivacious American leading lady of the forties whose star waned rather quickly. Her only TV series was *Goldie.*

I

I Am the Law
US 1952   26 × 25m   bw
Cosman

Cases of a city police inspector.
Routine cop show.

George Raft

IBA. The Independent Broadcasting Authority, a state-devised body which in GB controls commercial television and radio.

I, Claudius**
GB 1976   13 × 50m   colour (VTR)
BBC (Martin Lisemore)

The life and times of the eccentric Roman emperor.
A highly entertaining black comedy (when it isn't being too bloodthirsty), this celebrated series has some patches of splendid writing and acting, though the make-up at times verges on the ludicrous.

w Jack Pulman, *novels* Robert Graves

DEREK JACOBI (BAFTA award 1976), SIÂN PHILLIPS, Brian Blessed, George Baker, Stratford Johns, John Hurt

I Deal in Danger
US 1966   89m   colour   TVM
TCF

In World War II, a member of the Nazi High Command is really an American spy.
Tall tale put together from bits of the series *The Blue Light*.

w Larry Cohen   *d* Walter Grauman

Robert Goulet, Christine Carere, Donald Harron, Horst Frank, Werner Peters

I Didn't Know You Cared
GB 1975   approx 25 × 30m   colour (VTR)
BBC (Bernard Thompson)

Episodes in the lives of a phlegmatic Yorkshire family who usually look on the black side but have a laugh about it.
Uneasy example of the northern penchant for funereal comedy.

w Peter Tinniswood, from his books

Robin Bailey, John Comer, Liz Smith, Anita Carey, Stephen Rea, Vanda Godsell, Gretchen Franklin, Deirdre Costello

'A rich ribald slice of Yorkshire pudding.' – *Daily Mail*

I Dream of Jeannie*
US 1965–70   139 × 25m   colour (30 bw)
NBC/Columbia/Sidney Sheldon (Claudio Guzman)

An astronaut finds himself the master of a glamorous genie.
Amusing light comedy, pleasantly played; devised by the studio to extend the success of *Bewitched*.

cr Sidney Sheldon

Larry Hagman, Barbara Eden, Hayden Rorke

†An animated version, *Jeannie*, was made in 1973 by Hanna–Barbera.

I Heard the Owl Call My Name*
US/Canada 1973   74m   colour   TVM
Tomorrow

A sickly young priest is sent to a remote Canadian Indian village and dies there.
Scenic, moving, slightly pointless personal saga.

w Gerald de Pego, *book* Margaret Craven   *d* Daryl Duke

Tom Courtenay, Dean Jagger

I Led Three Lives
US 1953–5   117 × 25m   bw
UA

Or, I was a Communist for the FBI.
Dated cold war flagwaver.

Richard Carlson

I Love a Mystery
US 1967   98m   colour   TVM
Universal (Frank Price)

Three super-detectives seek a missing billionaire.
Woefully unfunny transfer to film of a spoof radio serial.

w Leslie Stevens, *serial* Carlton E. Morse   *d* Leslie Stevens

Ida Lupino, Les Crane, David Hartman, Jack Weston, Don Knotts

I Love Lucy****
US 1951–5   179 × 25m   bw
Desilu/CBS

A band leader and his dizzy wife are indulged by their neighbours.

Classic TV comedy series which not only had the highest possible standard for script and performance quality but pioneered independent production as well as the three-camera quick-film system. Still irresistibly funny.

LUCILLE BALL, DESI ARNAZ, WILLIAM FRAWLEY, VIVIAN VANCE

† Frawley and Vance were hired when Gale Gordon and Bea Benaderet proved unavailable.

I Love You . . . Goodbye

US 1974 74m colour TVM
Tomorrow

A suburban housewife leaves her family in an attempt to fulfil herself.
Mildly interesting character study.

w Diana Gould d Sam O'Steen

Hope Lange, Earl Holliman, Michael Murphy, Patricia Smith

I Married Joan*

US 1952–6   × 25m bw
Volcano/NBC

Another dizzy wife comedy, her husband this time a long-suffering judge.
Funny but not marvellous.

Joan Davis, Jim Backus

I Spy

US 1955 39 × 25m bw
Reah

Adequate anthology of spy stories, ancient and modern.

host Raymond Massey

I Spy**

US 1965–7 82 × 50m colour
Sheldon Leonard/NBC

Two US spies travel around the world as tennis players. Light-hearted suspense stories, very adequately played and produced. Notable as the first co-starring of black with white on TV.

ROBERT CULP, BILL COSBY

I Want to Keep My Baby

US 1976 96m colour TVM
CBS (Joanna Lee)

A pregnant teenager makes a decision.
Competent exploitation piece.

w Joanna Lee d Jerry Thorpe m George Aliceson Tipton

Mariel Hemingway, Susan Anspach, Jack Rader, Vince Begatta

I Will Fight No More Forever*

US 1975 101m colour TVM
Stan Margulies

The story of Indian chief Joseph who in 1877 led his people on a 1600-mile trek rather than live on a reservation.
Earnest historical account, a shade thin for its length.

w Jeb Rosebrook, Theodore Strauss d Richard Heffron

James Whitmore, Ned Romero, Sam Elliott

idiot board. Caption card held up out of camera range to assist star's failing memory.

If Tomorrow Comes

US 1971 74m colour TVM
Aaron Spelling (Richard Newton)

Before Pearl Harbor, an American girl marries a Japanese . . .
Predictable tearjerker.

w Lew Hunter d George McCowan

Patty Duke, Frank Liu, James Whitmore, Anne Baxter, Pat Hingle

If You Had a Million: see The Millionaire

I'm Dickens He's Fenster*

US 1962 32 × 25m bw
Heyday (Leonard Stern)/ABC

Misadventures of two incompetent carpenters.
A deliberate attempt to revive slapstick, this was sometimes amusing but fell a long way short of Laurel and Hardy.

John Astin, Marty Ingels

The Immortal*

US 1969 74m colour TVM
Paramount (Lou Morheim)

Our hero has a rare blood type which gives immunity not only to disease but to ageing . . .
Superman rides again. Some fun, but the subsequent series was shortlived.

w Robert Specht d Joseph Sargent

Chris George, Barry Sullivan, Jessica Walter, Ralph Bellamy, Carol Lynley

The Impatient Heart

US 1971 95m colour TVM
Universal (William Sackheim)

A lady social worker tries to turn every relationship into a case.
Romantic comedy-drama: strictly for ladies.

w Alvin Sargent d John Badham

Carrie Snodgress, Michael Brandon, Michael Constantine, Marian Hailey

The Imposter

US 1974 75m colour TVM
Warner

An actor hires himself out to the security force as an impersonator of famous people.
Tiresome idea, tiresome pilot; no series ensued.

w John Sevorg, Ken August d Edward Abrams

Paul Hecht, Nancy Kelly, Ed Asner, Meredith Baxter, John Vernon

In Name Only

US 1969 75m colour TVM
Columbia (E. W. Swackhamer)

Marriage brokers discover that ceremonies they performed in the past were not legal, and set out to make them so.
A well-worn theme, lamely tackled.

w Bernard Slade d E. W. Swackhamer

Michael Callan, Ann Prentiss, Paul Ford, Eve Arden, Elsa Lanchester, Ruth Buzzi, Chris Connelly

In Old San Francisco: see Barbary Coast

In Search of America*

US 1970 72m colour TVM
Four Star

A family sets out to see the country by van, and to make its own mind up on contemporary values.
Naïve, patchy, sometimes agreeable semi-documentary.

d Paul Bogart

Carl Betz, Vera Miles, Jeff Bridges, Ruth McDevitt, Howard Duff, Kim Hunter, Sal Mineo

In Tandem*

aka: Movin' On
US 1974 74m colour TVM
Metromedia/D'Antoni-Weiss

A pair of truckers help an orange farmer save his land.
Tense, well-characterized pilot with reminiscences of Thieves' Highway and The Wages of Fear; the resultant series ran two seasons, under the title Movin' On.

w Bob Collins, Herb Meadow d Bernard Kowalski

CLAUDE AKINS, FRANK CONVERSE, Richard Angarola, Ann Coleman

In the Matter of Karen Ann Quinlan*

US 1977 96m colour TVM
Warren V. Bush (Hal Sitowitz)

Parents fight for the right to remove a life support machine from their comatose and incurable daughter.
Painful and not especially complete or enlightening rehash of a case which was already only too familiar from newspaper headlines. A solid stripe against docudrama, despite earnest performances.

w Hal Sitowitz d Hal Jordan ph Arch Dalzell m Bill Conti

Brian Keith, Piper Laurie, David Huffman, David Spielberg, Biff McGuire, Stephanie Zimbalist, Louise Latham, Bert Freed

'At times, extremely moving . . . other times, it seems to be heading down avenues it never actually approaches.'
– Daily Variety

In This House of Brede*

GB 1975 105m colour TVM
Tomorrow

A widowed businesswoman becomes a nun.
Sincere, simplified Nun's Story: good watching.

w James Costigan, novel Rumer Godden d George Schaefer

Diana Rigg, Judi Bowker, Pamela Brown, Gwen Watford

Inch High, Private Eye

US 1973 13 × 25m colour
Hanna–Barbera/NBC

Adventures of the world's smallest detective.
Very moderate cartoon series.

Incident in San Francisco

US 1970 98m colour TVM
Quinn Martin

A man tries to help in a street brawl and finds himself accused of murder: he is saved by a crusading journalist.
Efficient but rather tedious melodrama.

w Robert Dozier, novel Incident at 125th Street by J. E. Brown d Don Medford

Richard Kiley, Chris Connelly, Dean Jagger, Leslie Nielsen, Phyllis Thaxter, Ruth Roman, John Marley

Incident on a Dark Street

aka: The Guardians, Incident in a Dark Alley
US 1972 98m colour TVM
TCF

The US attorney's office makes a stab at organized crime.
Routine crime-fighting melodrama.

w David Gerber d Buzz Kulik

James Olson, Richard Castellano, William Shatner, David Canary, Gilbert Roland

The Incredible Hulk*

US 1978 2 × 93m × 50m colour
MCA/Universal (Glen A. Larson)

A scientist studying human strength takes an overdose and when he gets angry turns into a jolly green giant.
Jekyll-and-Hyde comic strip hokum, played tongue-in-cheek by a producer who has clearly seen all the old Frankenstein movies.

Bill Bixby, Lou Ferrigno

THE INCREDIBLE HULK took its comic strip origins seriously, and managed to interest most sections of the public in its Jekyll-and-Hyde shenanigans. Here's Bill Bixby with his *alter ego* Lou Ferrigno. Between them they got through a lot of shirts, but curiously never managed to split a pair of pants.

† This began life as one of a series of *Marvel Superheroes* pilots but the first episode was so successful (in ratings terms) that it quickly became a series.

The Incredible Machine*
US 1975 50m colour
National Geographic/Wolper (Irwin Rosten)

New techniques enable the camera to see the inner workings of the human body.
A remarkable documentary.

w/d Irwin Rosten *narrator* E. G. Marshall

Independent Broadcasting Authority: see IBA

Indict and Convict*
US 1974 100m colour TVM
Universal (David Victor)

The attorney-general's office investigates a murder which may have been committed by a public official.

Reasonably absorbing courtroom drama with attention to detail.

w Winston Miller *d* Boris Sagal

George Grizzard, Reni Santoni, William Shatner, Susan Howard, Eli Wallach, Myrna Loy, Harry Guardino

Information Please. American panel game of the early fifties in which viewers sent in questions in an attempt to stump the experts – usually Franklin P. Adams, Oscar Levant and John Kiernan, with Clifton Fadiman as moderator.

inherited audience. The one that remains with a programme from the previous show on the same channel, from being too idle to switch over.

The Initiation of Sarah
US 1978 96m colour TVM
Stonehenge/Charles Fries (Jay Benson)

A college girl finds her sorority riddled with strange goings-on, which unleash her own psychic powers.

151

Rather coy *Carrie* derivative with a few spooky moments.

w Don Ingalls, Carol Saraceno, Kenette Geller *d* Robert Day *ph* Ric Waite *m* Johnny Harris

Kay Lenz, Shelley Winters, Kathryn Crosby, Morgan Brittany, Morgan Fairchild, Tony Bill, Tisa Farrow

'An innocent coed, a secret sorority, its bizarre rites of womanhood ... suddenly, a quiet college campus is plunged into an endless night of terror!' – publicity

Inman, John (1936–   ). British comic actor, smart, smiling and effeminate, who soared to fame in *Are You Being Served?* but floundered a little when given his own series *Odd Man In*.

International Detective
US/GB 1959   39 × 25m   bw
Delry/A. Edward Sutherland/ABP

Stories of an international detective agency.
Quite a lively crime filler with a fake *March of Time* atmosphere.

Arthur Fleming

The Interns
US 1970   24 × 50m   colour
CBS/Columbia (Bob Claver)

Stories of young doctors in a city hospital, following on from two feature films, *The Interns* and *The New Interns*.
A flop show in which nothing went right.

cr William Blinn

Broderick Crawford, Stephen Brooks, Chris Stone, Hal Frederick, Mike Farrell

Interpol Calling
GB 1959   39 × 25m   bw
ATV/Rank/Wrather

Stories of the organization which chases criminals around the world.
Adequate potboilers.

Charles Korvin

The Interrupted Journey*
aka: *The UFO Incident*
US 1975   100m   colour   TVM
Universal

A black man and his wife claim to have seen a flying saucer and to have been invited aboard.
Overlong fictionalization of an incident reported in a book by John G. Fuller: quite amusing.

d Richard A. Colla

James Earl Jones, Estelle Parsons

THE INTERNATIONAL POP PROMS were a 1976 idea of Granada's light entertainment supremo Johnny Hamp. The ambitious and expensive musical programmes were received without much comment by an increasingly blasé public.

The Intruders
US 1967 95m colour TVM
Universal (Bert Granet)

Western townsfolk look to their reluctant marshal for defence against approaching gunmen.
High Noon style minor western: nothing surprising.

w Dean Riesner *d* William Graham

Edmond O'Brien, Don Murray, John Saxon, Anne Francis

The Invaders*
US 1966–7 43 × 50m colour
ABC/Quinn Martin

An architect is on the run from alien invaders, who want to shut his mouth . . . and no one else will believe him.
Ingenious variation on *The Fugitive* from the same producer, extremely well produced and quite imaginative, with villains who crumble into coloured dust when damaged.

Roy Thinnes, Kent Smith

† There was some uproar when the show was unexpectedly cancelled without a final episode: it just stopped. (The same fate befell *Planet of the Apes*, *Executive Suite*, and a score of other series in which the hero was left in considerable trouble.)

The Invasion of Johnson County
aka: *Brahmin*
US 1976 98m colour TVM
Universal (Roy Huggins)

A Bostonian con man in Wyoming prevents a private army from routing small-time ranchers.
What begins like a promising reprise of *Maverick* turns into a very limp outdoor drama, protracted way beyond its dramatic possibilities.

w Nicholas E. Baehr *d* Jerry Jameson

Bill Bixby, Bo Hopkins, John Hillerman, Billy Green Bush, Alan Fudge

The Invisible Man
GB 1958 39 × 25m bw
ATV (Ralph Smart)

A scientist uses his power of invisibility to solve crimes.
Smooth hokum. The name of the actor playing the invisible man was never revealed.

The Invisible Man*
US 1975 74m colour TVM
Universal (Harve Bennett, Steven Boshco)

Quite a good updating of the theme; just occasionally it even catches the flavour of the original novel. The tricks are good, but the resultant series didn't work.

w Steven Bochco *d* Robert Michael Lewis

David McCallum, Jackie Cooper, Henry Darrow, Melinda Fee

† This revised version led to a disappointingly brief series of 13 × 50m. The following season it was tried again as *The Gemini Man*.

Iron Horse*
US 1966–7 47 × 50m colour
ABC/Columbia (Matthew Rapf, Fred Freiburger)

The building of railroads through the west in the 1870s, as seen by the fighting president of the BPS & D.
Adequate western series.

Dale Robertson, Gary Collins, Ellen McRae, Bob Random

Ironside*
GB title: *A Man Called Ironside*
US 1967 97m colour TVM
Universal (Collier Young)

San Francisco's chief of detectives is crippled for life after a shooting, but traps his attacker.
Fair pilot for a series that ran eight years and was usually watchable though seldom stimulating.

w Don M. Mankiewicz, Collier Young *d* James Goldstone

RAYMOND BURR, Don Galloway, Barbara Anderson, Donald Mitchell, Geraldine Brooks, Wally Cox, Kim Darby

† The series which followed was phenomenally successful and ran to 177 × 50m and 8 × 96m episodes. It co-starred Barbara Anderson and Don Galloway. Creator: Collier Young; executive producer: Cy Chermak/Joel Rogosin, for Harbour Productions/Universal/NBC.

Is There Anybody There?
Australia 1976 74m colour TVM
Paramount/Gemini (David Hannay)

Two women are locked in a penthouse for the weekend with a murderer.
Mildly watchable, uninspired psycho-thriller.

w Bruce A. Wishart *d* Peter Maxwell *ph* Russell Boyd

George Lazenby, Wendy Hughes, Tina Grenville, Charles Tingwell

Isaacs, Jeremy (1931–). British producer with special interest in current affairs; especially noted for *The World at War*. Programme controller of Thames TV 1974–8.

Island of Adventure: see The Swiss Family Robinson

The Islanders
US 1960 24 × 50m bw
ABC/MGM

Two adventurers own a seaplane.
Happy-go-lucky Pacific idyll.

cr Richard L. Bare

William Reynolds, James Philbrook, Diane Brewster

Isn't It Shocking?*
US 1973 73m colour TVM
ABC Circle

In a sleepy New England town, someone is killing off the senior citizens.
Unusual black comedy. It doesn't quite work, but at least it's different.

w Lane Slate, Ron Bernstein, Howard Roseman *d* John Badham

Alan Alda, Ruth Gordon, Louise Lasser, Edmond O'Brien, Lloyd Nolan, Will Geer

Istanbul Express
US 1968 94m colour TVM
Universal (Richard Irving)

Secret information is due to be exchanged on the train from Paris to Istanbul.
Underdeveloped and rather tedious spy caper.

w Richard Levinson, William Link *d* Richard Irving

Gene Barry, John Saxon, Mary Ann Mobley, Jack Kruschen, John Marley, Moustache, Senta Berger

It Ain't Half Hot, Mum**
GB 1973–7 30 approx. × 30m colour (VTR)
BBC

In World War II India, a platoon of British soldiers is busy organizing a concert party.
Efficiently nostalgic army farce with a preponderance of gay jokes.

Michael Bates, Windsor Davies, Don Estelle, Melvyn Hayes

It Couldn't Happen to a Nicer Guy
US 1974 74m colour TVM
Jozak (Arne Sultan)

A real estate agent is raped at gunpoint by a mysterious woman.
And it doesn't get any better after that. Silly, tasteless comedy.

w Arne Sultan, Earl Barrett *d* Cy Howard

Paul Sorvino, Michael Learned, Adam Arkin, Ed Barth

It Happened at Lake Wood Manor
US 1977 96m colour TVM
Alan Landsburg (Peter Nelson)

Resort guests are threatened by a plague of ants.
Mild horror filler.

w Guerdon Trueblood, Peter Nelson *d* Robert Scheerer

Suzanne Somers, Robert Foxworth, Lynda Day George, Gerald Gordon, Myrna Loy

'Pleasure seekers trapped by a deadly menace from the depths of the earth.' – publicity

It Happened One Christmas
US 1977 126m colour TVM
Universal

When she contemplates suicide as a failure, a loan company operator is visited by her guardian angel who shows her how important her life has been.
Workaday rehash of *It's a Wonderful Life* which gives no clue as to why anyone thought it was a good idea.

w Lionel Chetwynd *d* Donald Wrye

Marlo Thomas, Wayne Rogers, Orson Welles, Cloris Leachman, Barney Martin, Ceil Cabot, Richard Dysart

It Takes a Thief*
US 1965–9 65 × 50m colour
ABC/MCA/Universal (Jack Arnold)

A master thief is paroled if he will do his thing for the government's behalf among the international jet set.
Some comedy, some suspense, but mostly fantasy, which was found in this case to be quite a saleable commodity.

cr Collier Young

Robert Wagner, Malachi Throne, Fred Astaire in some episodes

ITA. What the IBA was until the seventies: the Independent Television Authority.

ITCA. A central company which services the ITV companies: the Independent Television Companies' Association. Its function is largely secretarial.

ITN. Independent Television News, a production company which provides the daily news bulletins and is jointly financed by the ITV companies.

It's a Great Life
US 1954–5 78 × 25m bw
Raydic/NBC

Two young men try to make it in Hollywood.
Palatable happy-go-lucky 'realistic' comedy.

James Dunn, Michael O'Shea, William Bishop, Frances Bavier

It's a Man's World
US 1962 19 × 50m bw
Revue/NBC

Four young fellows live in a houseboat on the Ohio river.
An unsuccessful attempt to do something different. It was too understated for public acceptance.

cr Peter Tewksbury

Glenn Corbett, Ted Bessell, Sandy Boone, Michael Burns

It's a Square World*. British live/tape comedy series of the fifties and sixties, reprised to less effect in the seventies; built round its star Michael Bentine, who gives crazy illustrated lectures in which anything can happen, e.g. models and diagrams come to life. A pointer towards *Monty Python*.

It's About Time
US 1966   26 × 25m   colour
Redwood/Gladasaya/UA

Two astronauts find themselves in a timewarp and land in the Stone Age.
Woeful attempt to make a live-action Flintstones: a promising cast has egg on its face.

cr Sherwood Schwartz

Imogene Coca, Joe E. Ross, Frank Aletter, Jack Mullaney, Mike Mazurki

It's Good to be Alive*
US 1974   100m   colour   TVM
Metromedia

The story of baseball player Roy Campanella, paralysed after an auto accident.

Another 'inspiring' real life case of the miseries; sympathetically done, but not exactly riveting.

w Steven Gethers   *d* Michael Landon

Paul Winfield, Ruby Dee, Lou Gossett, Julian Burton

ITV. An unofficial abbreviation for Independent (i.e. commercial) Television and all its companies; often confused with ATV, which is simply one of the companies.

ITV, This is Your Life*
GB 1976   135m   colour (VTR)
ITV

A handy retrospective of ITV's first 21 years, featuring most of the outstanding personalities connected with it.

I've Got a Secret. Highly successful American (Goodson–Todman) panel show of the fifties, a variation on *What's My Line?* in which the panel had to wrest from the contestant a 'secret' which had already been divulged to the viewers. Garry Moore was the regular host.

J

Jabberjaw
US 1977   17 × 21m   colour
Hanna–Barbera (Iwao Takamoto)

A lovable shark helps four underwater teenagers.
Very mild Saturday morning cartoon fare.

cr Joe Ruby, Ken Spears

The Jackson Five
US 1971–2   23 × 22m   colour
ABC/Rankin–Bass

Misadventures of a rock group.
Hasty cartoon cash-in on a popular group of the time.

Jackson, Glenda (1937–). Leading British actress who became internationally popular through her TV performance as *Elizabeth R*.

Jackson, Gordon (1923–).British character actor who after a lifetime in films playing everything from callow youths to spies, became an international star as Hudson the butler in *Upstairs, Downstairs*, and followed this with *The Professionals*.

Jackson, Kate (*c* 1950–). American leading lady of the seventies, in two highly successful series: *The Rookies, Charlie's Angels*.

Jacobi, Derek (1939–). British character actor who distinguished himself in the title role of *I, Claudius* (BAFTA award 1976) and subsequently played Mac-Lean in *Burgess, Philby and MacLean*.

Jacobs, David (*c* 1925–). Genial British host, anchorman and disc jockey, in constant employment since the early fifties.

Jacques, Hattie (1924–). Giant-size British comedy character actress, much on TV with Eric Sykes (as his sister).

Jaffe, Sam (1897–). Eccentric-looking American character actor whose big TV hit was as Dr Zorba in *Ben Casey*.

James at 15
US 1977   13 × 50m   colour
TCF (Martin Manulis)

The sexual awakening of an American teenager.
A well-made series which clearly would not be everybody's cup of tea.

Lance Kerwin, Lynn Carlin, Linden Chiles

James, Sid (1913–76). Crumple-faced South African comic actor who became a great favourite in GB and a staple of the 'Carry On' comedies. Series include *Taxi, Hancock's Half Hour, Citizen James, Bless This House*.

Jamie
US 1954   × 25m   bw
ABC

After the death of his parents, a young boy goes to live with his grandfather.
Sentimental comedy which worked at the time.

Brandon de Wilde, Ernest Truex, Kathleen Nolan, Polly Rowles, Alice Pearce

Jane Eyre*
GB 1971   108m   colour   TVM
Omnibus (Frederick H. Brogger)

A much-abused Victorian governess falls for her moody master.
Over-bright teleplay with a strong Rochester and not much else.

w Jack Pulman, *novel* Charlotte Brontë *d* Delbert Mann *ph* Paul Beeson *m* John Williams *ad* Alex Vetchinsky

GEORGE C. SCOTT, Susannah York, Jack Hawkins, Nyree Dawn Porter, Ian Bannen, Kenneth Griffith, Peter Copley, Rachel Kempson, Jean Marsh, Constance Cummings

The Jane Wyman Theatre
US 1956–60   163 × 25m   bw
ABC/Lewman

Variable anthology series hosted by the star.

Janssen, David (1930–) (David Meyer). Popular if rather glum American leading man who had only moderate success in feature films but has been one of the staples of TV, both in movies and series: *Richard Diamond, The Fugitive, O'Hara US Treasury, Harry O*.

Japan has two TV channels, both supported by licence fees and operated by NHK, a government-controlled organization. There are 30 million sets in use.

Jarrett
US 1973   74m   colour   TVM
Columbia (David Gerber)

An adventurer combats a wily villain for the possession
of rare scrolls.
Foolish comic strip capers with a star far too old for
this kind of thing.

w Richard Maibaum   d Barry Shear

Glenn Ford, Anthony Quayle, Forrest Tucker, Laraine
Stephens, Richard Anderson

Jason King
GB 1971   26 × 50m   colour
ATV

A famous thriller writer lends his sleuthing services to
the government.
Moderate spin-off from *Department S*, with the leading
man a shade too effete.

Peter Wyngarde

Jason, Rick (1929–   ). Smooth, slick American leading man, star of TV series *The Case of the Dangerous
Robin* and *Combat*.

The Jean Arthur Show
US 1966   12 × 25m   colour
CBS/Universal

Cases of mother-and-son lawyers.
Unsuccessful comedy–drama series with an uncomfortable star.

Jean Arthur, Ron Harper, Leonard Stone, Richard
Conte

Jefferson Drum
US 1958   26 × 25m   bw
Columbia/Goodson–Todman

A newspaper editor fights corruption in an 1850s
mining town.
Acceptable semi-western with no surprises.

Jeff Richards, Eugene Martin, Cyril Delevanti, Robert
Stevenson

The Jeffersons
US 1975   13 × 25m   colour (VTR)
CBS/Norman Lear (Don Nicholl, Michael Ross,
Bernie West)

The black neighbours from *All in the Family* move to
Manhattan's upper east side.
Ethnic spin-off which didn't appeal, perhaps because it
was too reminiscent of *The Beverly Hillbillies*.

cr Don Nicholl, Michael Ross, Bernie West

Mike Evans, Isabel Sanford, Sherman Hemsley, Roxie
Roker

Jennie, Lady Randolph Churchill****
GB 1975   7 × 50m   colour (VTR)
Thames/Stella Richman (Andrew Brown)

The life of American Jennie Jerome, mother of Sir
Winston Churchill.
Immaculately detailed period biography with precisely
the right weight in every department.

w JULIAN MITCHELL   d JAMES CELLAN JONES

LEE REMICK, RONALD PICKUP, Cyril Luckham, Rachel
Kempson, Dan O'Herlihy, Barbara Parkins, Warren
Clarke, Christopher Cazenove

'Constant enchantment.' – *Daily Express*

Jericho
aka: *Code Name Jericho*
US 1966   16 × 50m   colour
CBS/MGM (Norman Felton)

In World War II, an allied spy team works behind
enemy lines.
Rather flat adventure fare.

John Leyton, Marino Mase, Don Francks

Jesus of Nazareth****
GB 1977   2 × 150m   colour
ITC/RAI (Vincenzo Labella)

The life of Jesus.
A star-packed spectacular, often sensational to look at;
providing parts for many famous actors, it deliberately
plays down the supernatural, but becomes a more gripping and emotional experience than any of the big-
screen treatments of the subject.

w Anthony Burgess, Suso Cecchi d'Amico, Franco
Zeffirelli   d FRANCO ZEFFIRELLI   m Maurice Jarre

ROBERT POWELL (Jesus), Anne Bancroft (Mary
Magdalene), Laurence Olivier (Nicodemus), Ralph
Richardson (Simeon), James Mason (Joseph of
Arimathea), Anthony Quinn (Caiaphas), Peter Ustinov
(Herod), Rod Steiger (Pilate), Christopher Plummer
(Herod Antipas); and Ernest Borgnine, Claudia
Cardinale, Valentina Cortese, James Farentino, James
Earl Jones, Michael York, Stacy Keach, Ian MacShane,
Donald Pleasence, Fernando Rey, Olivia Hussey, Cyril
Cusack

Jet Jackson, Flying Commando: see Captain
Midnight

The Jetsons*
US 1962   24 × 25m   colour
ABC/Hanna–Barbera

Problems of a 21st-century suburban family.
A kind of reverse sequel to the successful *Flintstones*,
this was an amusing cartoon series which somehow
didn't hit the spot with the public.

voices Penny Singleton, Daws Butler, George
O'Hanlon, Janet Waldo

JENNIE. The christening of Winston Churchill finds Ronald Pickup as Randolph, Lee Remick as Jennie, Rachel Kempson as the Duchess of Marlborough, Cyril Luckham as the Duke, John Westbrook as Blandford, Barbara Laurenson as Bertha and Virginia Denham as Rosamond.

Jigsaw*
US 1972 98m colour TVM
Universal (Stanley Kallis)

A disgraced policeman seeks the missing witness who can save him from a murder charge.
Sufficiently engrossing plot and some fine desert chases keep the pot boiling.

w Robert E. Thompson *d* William Graham

James Wainwright, Vera Miles, Andrew Duggan, Edmond O'Brien, Marsha Hunt, Irene Dailey, Richard Kiley

† A series of 50m episodes about the Missing Persons Bureau was begun, but only eight were made, all starring James Wainwright.

Jigsaw John
US 1976 13 × 50m colour
MGM/NBC (Ronald Austin, James Buchanan)

The adventures of a police detective whose real name was 'Jigsaw' John St John.
Tolerable police series.

cr Al Martinez

Jack Warden, Alan Feinstein, Pippa Scott

† A 74m pilot film, *They Only Come Out at Night*, was aired the previous November.

The Jim Backus Show
aka: *Hot Off the Wire*
US 1960 39 × 25m bw
NBC/Ray Singer, Dick Chevillat

Adventures of a newspaper editor and owner perpetually striving to stave off bankruptcy.
Adequate comedy series for syndication.

Jim Backus, Nita Talbot, Bob Watson

Jim Bowie: see The Adventures of Jim Bowie

The Jimmy Stewart Show*
US 1971 24 × 25m colour
NBC/Warner (Hal Kanter)

Domestic problems of a small-town anthropology professor.
Slightly disappointing but generally pleasing comedy vehicle, perhaps too perfectly tailored for its star.

cr Hal Kanter *m* Van Alexander

James Stewart, Julie Adams, John McGiver

Jim's Inn. The most popular and long-lived of the British advertising magazines, this ran from 1957 until the IBA banned the genre in the mid-sixties. Jimmy Hanley chatted to the regulars in his pub about new products on the market. Nobody loved it but the public.

Joe Forrester
US 1975 13 × 50m colour
NBC/Columbia (David Gerber)

Stories of the policeman on the beat in a rough area.
A spin-off from the TV movie *The Return of Joe Forrester*, this unexciting show debuted during the same season as *The Blue Knight*, which had the same subject and was only slightly better.

Lloyd Bridges, Pat Crowley, Eddie Egan

Joe 90*
GB 1968 30 × 25m colour
ATV (Gerry Anderson)

A boy helps his father in advanced science.
Smooth, entertaining puppet series.

The Joey Bishop Show
US 1961 26 × 25m bw
NBC/Danny Thomas/Bellmar

Domestic problems of a public relations man.
Adequate star comedy vehicle.

m Earle Hagen

Joey Bishop, Marlo Thomas, Madge Blake, Warren Berlinger

† Another attempt was made in 1962–4 (97 episodes – 70 in colour); in this case the star was a nightclub comedian, and supporting players included Abby Dalton, Corbett Monica, Joe Besser and Mary Treen.

The John Forsythe Show
US 1965 30 × 25m colour
NBC/Universal

Trials of the headmaster of a privately owned girls' school.
Unsurprising star comedy.

John Forsythe, Guy Marks, Elsa Lanchester, Ann B. Davis

Johnny Go Home**
GB 1975   75m colour
Yorkshire

A documentary investigating the plight of runaway boys in London.
Well-researched thought piece which provoked a national outcry. BAFTA award for best documentary.

Johnny Midnight
US 1958 39 × 25m bw
MCA/Revue/Jack Chertok

A Manhattan actor turns detective and roams the Times Square area.
Predictable mysteries with a shade more flair than most.

Edmond O'Brien

JOHNNY GO HOME movingly investigated the plight of the runaway boy in the big city, and turned up an underworld as horrifying as that in *Oliver Twist*. This is Tommy Wylie from Glasgow.

Johnny Ringo
US 1958   38 × 25m   bw
CBS/Four Star (Aaron Spelling)

A gunfighter turns sheriff of a lawless Arizona town.
Good routine western.

Don Durant

Johnny Staccato**
aka: *Staccato*
US 1959   27 × 25m   bw
NBC/MCA/Universal

A jazz pianist in a Greenwich Village club turns detective.
Moodily-shot and performed mysteries with a good
music score: a cut above the average crime series.

John Cassavetes, Eduardo Ciannelli

Johnny, We Hardly Knew Ye
US 1977   96m   colour   TVM
Talent Associates/Jamel (David Susskind)

The early political background of John F. Kennedy.
Moderately compelling biopic; hard tack for the un-
initiated.

w Lionel Chetwynd *d* Gilbert Cates *m* Garry
Sherman

Paul Rudd, William Prince, Burgess Meredith, Shirley
Rich

Johns, Stratford (1925–). Burly South African
actor who scored in Britain as Inspector Barlow in the
Z Cars series. As so often, his career floundered when
he escaped from this typecasting, and *Barlow at Large*
was much less popular.

Johnson, Celia (1908–). Celebrated British stage
and film actress. TV includes *Mrs Palfrey at the Clare-
mont*, a play which won her a BAFTA award in 1973;
also *The Dame of Sark*.

Jones, Dean (1933–). Busy American perennial
leading man. TV series: *Ensign O'Toole, The Chicago
Teddy Bears*.

Jones, Freddie (1927–). British character actor,
often enjoyably over the top, who came to the medium
in middle age and made a big hit as Claudius in *The
Caesars*. Most recent series: *The Ghosts of Motley
Hall*.

Jones, Gemma (1942–). British character actress
who became famous as *The Duchess of Duke Street*.

Jones, Henry (1912–). American character actor.
Series: *Channing, Phyllis*.

Jones, Peter (1920–). British comedy character
actor, a familiar face since 1950 but best known as the
harassed boss in *The Rag Trade*.

Jones, Shirley (1934–). American leading lady,
singer and actress. She has appeared in many TV guest
roles, but her sole series is *The Partridge Family*.

Jones, Tom (1940–) (Thomas Woodward). Virile-
looking Welsh pop singer who became an even bigger
hit in America than at home. His 1970 series of specials
for ATV was oddly unsuccessful in ratings terms.

Jonny Quest*
US 1964   26 × 25m   colour
Hanna–Barbera

The young son of a famous scientist helps him in secret
intelligence work.
Successful attempt at limited animation: the drawings
have the look of a newspaper comic strip.

Jordan, Richard (1938–). American leading man
who became noted on TV in *The Captains and the
Kings*.

Jory, Victor (1902–). Reliable American character
actor who has very often played saturnine villains. TV
series: *Manhunt*

Josie and the Pussycats
US 1970–3   104 × 22m   colour
CBS/Hanna–Barbera

Adventures of an all-girl rock group.
Middling cartoon series for Saturday morning.

†In 1972 the series was revived as *Josie and the
Pussycats in Outer Space*, which was self-explanatory
and stupid.

Journey from Darkness
US 1975   74m   colour   TVM
Columbia/Bob Banner

A blind student fights to enter medical school.
Another true weepie, more moving than dramatic.

w Peggy Chantler Dick *d* James Goldstone

Mark Singer, Kay Lenz, Wendell Burton, William
Windom, Joseph Campanella, Jack Warden

Journey to the Center of the Earth
US 1967   17 × 25m   colour
ABC/TCF/Filmation (Lou Scheimer)

Adventures below ground of Professor Lindenbrook
and his companions.
Pretty fair cartoon rendering of the Jules Verne adventure.

Journey to the Unknown*
GB 1968   17 × 50m   colour
TCF/Hammer (Joan Harrison)

An anthology of weird stories. Quality very variable,
but usually something of interest. No host, which killed
it.

m Harry Robinson *story editor* John Gould

Joyce, Yootha (1927–). Angular British character actress who gained unexpected popularity as the landlady in *A Man About the House*, which led to co-star billing in *George and Mildred*.

Jubilee*
GB 1977   13 × 50m   colour (VTR)
BBC (Pieter Rogers)

Separate plays trace the changing attitudes over the 25 years of the reign of Elizabeth II.
An interesting concept with several good plays, but none proved very memorable or very popular.

d Peter Moffatt, Paul Ciapessoni, Valerie Hanson, Ruth Caleb

Judd for the Defense*
US 1967–8   50 × 25m   colour
ABC/TCF (Paul Monash)

Cases of a big-time lawyer.
Good solid courtroom series with an agreeable touch of the flamboyant.

Carl Betz, Stephen Young

The Judge and Jake Wyler
US 1972   100m   colour   TVM
Universal (Richard Levinson, William Link)

An eccentric lady judge, retired for health reasons, employs an ex-con as her 'legs' to solve murder cases.
Another comical pair of investigators, and this time their heart plainly isn't in it: they must have seen the script.

w David Shaw, Richard Levinson, William Link   *d* Gil Melle

Bette Davis, Doug McClure, Eric Braeden

Judge Horton and the Scottsboro Boys
US 1976   98m   colour (VTR)
Tomorrow Entertainment (Paul Leaf)

A reconstruction of the 1931 court case in which nine black men in Alabama were accused of raping two white women.
A conscientious dramatic special which fails to shed fresh light on the subject.

w John McGreevey   *d* Fielder Cook

Arthur Hill, Vera Miles, Lewis J. Stadlen

Judge Roy Bean: see The Adventures of Judge Roy Bean

Judgment: The Court Martial of Lt William Calley*
US 1975   100m   colour (VTR)
Stanley Kramer/David Wolper

A reconstruction of the trial of the Vietnam war veteran accused of leaving civilians to die.
Well-intentioned and very adequately made docudrama.

w Henry Denker   *d* Stanley Kramer

Tony Musante, Richard Basehart, Bo Hopkins, Bill Lucking

Juke Box Jury. A popular panel show of the fifties in which guests were asked to judge new records, sometimes not knowing that the recording artist was behind a screen. It was to some extent superseded in the seventies by *New Faces*.

Julia*
US 1968–70   86 × 25m   colour
NBC/Savannah/Hanncar/TCF (Hal Kanter)

A young Negro widow has a six-year-old son, an apartment in an integrated block and a job as a nurse.
Much-discussed, and quite successful comedy; the first to have an attractive black female lead on equal terms with whites, it veered between the slick and the sentimental.

cr Hal Kanter

Diahann Carroll, Lloyd Nolan, Marc Copage

The Julie Andrews Hour*
GB/US 1972   26 × 50m   colour (VTR)
ABC/ITC (Nick Vanoff)

The star's best TV outlet, a series of stylish and varied musical hours with top guest stars: also Rich Little, Alice Ghostley, and Nelson Riddle and his Orchestra.

The June Allyson Show
US 1959–60   57 × 25m   bw
CBS/Four Star

Variable anthology series in which the hostess sometimes starred.

Jungle Jim
US 1955   26 × 25m   bw
Columbia

Adventures of a white hunter and his son in the African jungle.
As if the old features weren't bad enough, here came a crappy series in the same mould . . .

Johnny Weissmuller, Martin Huston

Junior Miss. A 1953 American half-hour domestic comedy about a college girl (Barbara Whiting) and her temperamental father (Gale Gordon).

Just Dennis: see Dennis the Menace

Just Me and You
US 1978   96m   colour   TVM
EMI/Roger Gimbel (William S. Gilmore Jnr)

A girl answers an ad to drive across America with a man she doesn't know.
An interesting starting point, but the plot wears out of

steam and the heroine is too neurotic to be sympathetic.

w Louise Lasser *d* John Erman *ph* Gayne Rescher *m* Fred Karlin

Louise Lasser, Charles Grodin, Julie Borvasso, Mark Syers

'Unfortunately the couple is not mismatched – both parties are abominable.' – Judith Crist

Just William*
GB 1976–7   26 × 15m   colour (VTR)
London Weekend/Stella Richman

The adventures of Richmal Crompton's awful but imaginative child, very pleasingly done with authentic series settings.

Adrian Dannatt, Diana Dors (as Mrs Bott), Hugh Cross (as Mr Brown; in a previous film version he played William's brother Robert)

Justice*
GB 1972–3   26 approx. × 50m   colour (VTR)
Yorkshire (Jacky Stoller)

Cases of a lady barrister.
A solid vehicle for a star.

MARGARET LOCKWOOD, Anthony Valentine, John Stone

K

Kansas City Massacre*
US 1975 100m colour TVM
Dan Curtis

Melvin Purvis, the midwestern G-man who captured Dillinger, is ambushed when he transports a prisoner by train.
Pretty good gangster thriller, violent by TV standards.

w/d Dan Curtis

Dale Robertson, Bo Hopkins

Kanter, Hal (1918–). American writer–producer. TV series created by him include *The George Gobel Show, Valentine's Day, Julia, The Jimmy Stewart Show.*

Karen
US 1975 13 × 25m colour
ABC/TCF (Gene Reynolds, Larry Gelbart)

Problems of a citizens' action group in Washington DC.
Curious comedy vehicle for a much trumpeted new star. Both failed.

Karen Valentine, Charles Lane

†A previous short-lived series named *Karen* was part of *90 Bristol Court.*

Karlin, Miriam (1925–) (Miriam Samuels). British character actress, best remembered as the strike-prone Paddy in *The Rag Trade.*

Karloff, Boris (1887–1969) (William Pratt). British character actor, a tall, cadaverous but kindly gentleman forever associated with horror films. TV series include *Colonel March of Scotland Yard, Thriller.*

Kate
GB 1970–1 39 approx × 50m colour (VTR)
Yorkshire TV

Private problems of the writer of a woman's page.
Moderately popular drama series.

Phyllis Calvert, Penelope Keith

Kate Bliss and the Tickertape Kid*
US 1978 96m colour TVM
Aaron Spelling (Richard E. Lyons)

A lady detective goes out west in disguise as a women's wear salesman.
Lively period comedy.

w William Bowers, John Zodorow *d* Burt Kennedy *ph* Lamar Boren *m* Jeff Alexander

Suzanne Pleshette, Don Meredith, Tony Randall, Harry Morgan, Burgess Meredith, David Huddleston, Gene Evans

'Full of high spirits.' – *Daily Variety*

Kate MacShane
US 1975 100m colour TVM
Paramount (E. Jack Neuman)

A lady lawyer with an Irish family defends a socialite on a murder charge.
Tiresomely talkative and restless courtroom pilot with a highly unconvincing dénouement.

w E. Jack Neuman *d* Marvin Chomsky

Anne Meara, Sean McClory, Christine Belford, Charles Cioffi, Larry Gates

†A short-lived series (13 × 50m) followed, with E. Jack Neuman in charge.

Katherine*
US 1975 96m colour TVM
Jozak (Gerald I. Isenberg)

A young heiress becomes a terrorist.
Quite a well-composed moral tale of the sixties.

wd JEREMY KAGAN *ph* Frank Stanley

Sissy Spacek, Art Carney, Henry Winkler, Julie Kavner, Jane Wyatt, Hector Elias

Kaye, Danny (1913–) (David Daniel Kaminsky). Master American comedian and entertainer whose one-hour series in 1966 had a little too much quality for popular success. His other stabs at TV have been modest, including *Peter Pan* (as Captain Hook) and *Pinocchio* (as Gepetto, among others).

Kaz. New American 50m show for the 1978 season, with Ron Leibman as a 'streetwise' lawyer who has learned his trade in prison and goes to work for a smoothie played by Patrick O'Neal.

Keach, Stacy (1941–). American character actor, in all media. He starred in an unsuccessful TV series, *Caribe.*

Kearns, Joseph (1907–62). Grouchy American character actor best remembered as the long-suffering neighbour in *Dennis the Menace.*

Kee, Robert (*c* 1926–). British TV reporter, associated with *Panorama*, *This Week* and election coverage. BAFTA: Richard Dimbleby Award 1975.

Keefer
US 1978 74m colour TVM
Columbia/David Gerber (James H. Brown)

In 1942, a Lisbon café owner is also an allied spy. Shades of *Casablanca*, shot down by a dullsville script.

w Bill Driscoll, Simon Muntner *d* Barry Shear *ph* Gerald Perry Finnerman *m* Duane Tatro

William Conrad, Jeremy Kemp, Michael O'Hare, Cathy Lee Crosby, Marcel Hillaire, Kate Woodville.

The Keegans
US 1975 74m colour TVM
Universal (George Eckstein)

Problems of an Irish family living near Boston. Predictable to the last drop of blarney, this cosy family drama suddenly turns into a murder plot.

w Dean Riesner *d* John Badham

Adam Roarke, Judd Hirsch, Joan Leslie, Spencer Milligan, Paul Shenar

Keen, Geoffrey (1918–). Incisive British character actor whose best series role was in *The Trouble Shooters*.

Keith, Brian (1921–) (Robert Keith Jnr). Burly, adaptable American character actor whose TV series have included *Crusader*, *The Westerner*, *Family Affair*, *Archer* and *The Little People* (re-titled *The Brian Keith Show*).

Keith, Penelope (*c* 1941–). British comedy character actress with a strong line in toffee-nosed virgins. She achieved sudden popularity in the mid-seventies as a result of work in such series as *Kate* and *The Good Life*.

Kelly, Chris (*c* 1940–). Gentle-voiced British linkman, commentator and host, familiar from *Clapperboard* and *Wish You Were Here*.

Kelly, Gene (1912–). Outstanding American singer and dancer. TV work includes the series *Going My Way* and numerous specials including *Jack and the Beanstalk* and a tribute to him called *An American in Pasadena*.

Kemp-Welch, Joan (1906–). Outstanding British director, especially of the early TV plays of Harold Pinter. Former actress.

Kendal, Felicity (1946–). British leading lady often in fey or mischievous roles; most famous for *The Good Life*.

Kendall, Kenneth (1924–). Distinguished-looking British BBC newsreader.

Kennedy, Arthur (1914–). Distinguished American character actor. His only TV series was the ill-fated *Nakia*.

Kennedy, George (1925–). Imposing but rather bland American character actor who began by playing villains. TV series: *Sarge*, *The Blue Knight*.

Kentucky Jones
US 1964 26 × 25m bw
NBC (Buzz Kulik)

Stories of a vet and horse trainer who adopts a small oriental boy.
Forgettable sentiment.

cr Albert Beich, William Wright

Dennis Weaver, Rickey Der, Harry Morgan

Kerr, Graham (1934–). Genial British entertainer and occasional cook who in the late sixties made himself a darling of the ladies in *The Galloping Gourmet*; subsequently retired in search of truth.

Key West
US 1972 91m colour TVM
Warner (Anthony S. Martin)

Documents incriminating a US senator are sought by crooks and agents on the Florida keys.
Ho-hum hokum.

w Anthony S. Martin *d* Philip Leacock

Stephen Boyd, Woody Strode, Sheree North, Earl Hindman, Tiffany Bolling, William Prince

Khan
US 1975 4 × 50m colour
CBS/Laurence Heath (James Heinz)

Cases of a Chinese private detective in San Francisco. Disastrous attempt to revive the Charlie Chan syndrome. There's even a number one son.

Khigh Dhiegh, Irene Yah-Ling Sun, Evan Kim

Kilgallen, Dorothy (1913–65). American columnist who became a TV celebrity as a *What's My Line?* panellist in the fifties.

Kill Me If You Can
US 1977 98m colour TVM
Columbia (Peter Katz)

A reconstruction of Caryl Chessman's finally unsuccessful attempts to stave off execution as the 'red light' killer.
Tasteless and exploitative docu-drama with the star in a false nose and much lingering over the gas chamber scenes.

w John Gay *d* Buzz Kulik

Alan Alda, Talia Shire, Barnard Hughes, John Hillerman

Killdozer

US 1974 74m colour TVM
Universal (Herbert F. Solow)

A bulldozer affected by a strange meteorite murderously attacks a construction crew on a remote site. And they can't run fast enough to get out of its way. Silly nonsense.

w Theodore Sturgeon, Ed MacKillop *d* Jerry London

Clint Walker, James Wainwright, Carl Betz, Neville Brand

The Killer Bees*

US 1974 74m colour TVM
RSO

The elderly matriarch of a strange family is obsessed by bees and can use them to kill.
Flabby, over-talkative suspenser with a couple of good sequences; mainly notable for the reappearance of its star.

w Joyce and John William Corrington *d* Curtis Harrington

GLORIA SWANSON, Edward Albert, Kate Jackson, Roger Davis, Craig Stevens

Killer by Night*

US 1971 100m colour TVM
Cinema Center 100 (Fred Engel)

A doctor seeks a diphtheria carrier, a cop seeks a killer . . . and they're both looking for the same man.
Didn't this use to be *Panic in the Streets*? Well enough done again, anyway.

w David P. Harmon *d* Bernard McEveety *ph* Robert B. Hauser *m* Quincy Jones

Robert Wagner, Diane Baker, Greg Morris, Theodore Bikel, Robert Lansing, Mercedes McCambridge, Pedro Armendariz Jnr

Killer on Board

US 1977 96m colour TVM
Lorimar (Sandor Stern)

A Pacific cruise is menaced by a mysterious disease.
Cliché-strewn suspenser without much suspense.

w Sandor Stern *d* Philip Leacock *ph* William H. Cronjager *m* Earl Hagen

Claude Akins, Patty Duke Astin, Frank Converse, William Daniels, George Hamilton, Murray Hamilton, Beatrice Straight

'500 desperate people trapped at sea and dying – one at a time!' – *publicity*

The Killer Who Wouldn't Die

aka: *Ohanian*
US 1976 96m colour TVM
Paramount (Ivan Goff, Ben Roberts)

An ex-detective takes to his boat when his wife is killed in mistake for himself, but finds himself harbouring a hired killer and avenging the death of a friend.
Lame crime pilot with the star using his own name and his own boat; it's all a mite too relaxed to make suspenseful melodrama.

w Cliff Gould *d* William Hale *m* George Garvarantz

Mike Connors, Samantha Eggar, Patrick O'Neal, Clu Gulager, Grégoire Aslan, Robert Hooks, Robert Colbert, James Shigeta, Mariette Hartley

The Killers*

US 1964 95m colour TVM
U-I (Don Siegel)

Zesty, brutal remake of the 1946 movie, intended for TV, but released theatrically because of its violence.

w Gene L. Coon *d* Don Siegel *ph* Richard L. Rawlings *m* Johnny Williams

John Cassavetes, Lee Marvin, Clu Gulager, Angie Dickinson, Ronald Reagan, Claude Akins

Killiam, Paul (1916–   ). American producer who specializes in restoring silent films and packaging them into such series as *Silents Please* and *Movie Museum*.

A Killing Affair

US 1977 96m colour TVM
Columbia/David Gerber (James H. Brown)

A woman police detective falls in love with her black partner.
Heavy-going cop drama in which the action is relegated to the sidelines and the limelight reserved for some realistic – and boring – bed scenes.

w E. Arthur Kean *d* Richard Sarafian *ph* Al Francis *m* Richard Shores

Elizabeth Montgomery, O. J. Simpson, Dean Stockwell, Dolph Sweet, Todd Bridges, Todd Sussman

'An affair of overkill.' – *Daily Variety*

The Killing Stone

US 1978 96m colour TVM
NBC/Universal (Michael Landon)

An innocent man is released after eleven years in prison, is funded by a publisher and becomes a private eye.
Proficient pilot which didn't take.

w/d Michael Landon *ph* Ted Voigtlander *m* David Rose

Gil Gerard, J. D. Cannon, Jim Davis, Nehemiah Persoff, Corinne Michaels, Matthew Laborteaux

Kilvert's Diary*
GB 1977   26 × 15m   colour (VTR)
BBC

Incidents from the diary of a 19th-century country cleric.
Delightful series, just the right length, re-creating middle-class life of its time. The kind of production that only the BBC would do.

King
US 1978   3 × 96m   colour
NBC/Filmways/Abby Mann (Paul Maslansky)

The life and times of Martin Luther King.
Protracted treatment of an over-familiar subject, with reverence largely replacing characterization.

w/d Abby Mann ph Michael Chapman m Billy Goldenberg

Paul Winfield, Cicely Tyson, Ossie Davis, Al Freeman Jnr, Steven Hill, Clu Gulager, Roscoe Lee Browne, Cliff de Young

The King and Odie: see King Leonardo and his Short Subjects

King, Dave (1929–). British cockney comedian who was big in the fifties and even succeeded in America, then had a long period out of fashion before he returned in the mid-seventies as a character actor.

The King Family. An American singing family who were popular in the sixties. As a rule the show was limited to William King and seven children, but on occasions it swelled to as many as 36 family members.

King Kong
US 1966–8   78 × 25m   colour
Videocraft

On a Javanese island, the son of a research scientist befriends a 60-foot gorilla, and they combat the evil Dr Who.
Bland cartoon rehash of a horror classic. Also included in each half-hour is a segment of *Tom of T. H. U. M. B.*, about a dwarf spy.

King Leonardo and his Short Subjects
aka: *The King and Odie*
US 1960–2   39 × 25m   colour
Leonardo TV

An African lion and his assistant Odie Calognie combat the evil influence of Itchy Brother and Biggy Rat.
Childish cartoon series.

King of Diamonds
US 1961   38 × 25m   bw
Ziv/UA

Adventures of a security chief for the diamond industry.
Ham-fisted thick-ear.

Broderick Crawford, Ray Hamilton

King's Row. One of the rotating segments of *Warner Brothers Present* in 1959 was a one-hour series derived from the famous film of a small town's dark secrets, the hero having now become a psychiatrist. Jack Kelly was Paris; Nan Leslie, Randy; Robert Horton, Drake; and Victor Jory played a revived Dr Tower.

Kingston: Confidential
US 1977   13 × 50m   colour
Universal/RB/Groverton/NBC (David Victor)

Adventures of a senior investigative reporter for a group of newspapers and TV stations.
Abortive series with an addled star; it never got off the ground.

cr David Victor, Raymond Burr, Dick Nelson, Guy Della Cioppa

Raymond Burr, Nancy Olson

Kit Carson: see The Adventures of Kit Carson

Klemperer, Werner (1919–). German–American character actor, facially typecast to play a monocled Nazi, which he did superbly, with comic emphasis, in *Hogan's Heroes*.

Klondike
US 1960   18 × 25m   bw
NBC

Gold rush adventures.
Efficiently made adventure series which didn't jell.

James Coburn, Ralph Taeger, Mari Blanchard, Joi Lansing

Klugman, Jack (1922–). Amiable, worried-looking American character actor, usually in slouchy comedy parts, who apart from films has had his fair share of TV series: *Harris Against the World*, *The Odd Couple*, *Quincy*.

Kneale, Nigel (1922–). Manx writer whose most notable contributions to TV include the *Quatermass* series, *The Year of the Sex Olympics*, *The Road*.

Knight Errant
GB 1957–60   × 50m   bw (VTR)
Granada

Stories of a debonair adventurer for hire.
Lighter-than-air time filler which pleased in its day.

cr Philip Mackie

John Turner, Kay Callard, Richard Carpenter

Knight, Ted (c 1925–) (Tadewurz Wladzui Konopka). American character actor who scored as the braggart announcer in *The Mary Tyler Moore Show* and in 1978 began a rather unrewarding *Ted Knight Show*, a spin-off from *Busting Loose* in which he played the head of an escort agency.

Knotts, Don (1924–). Sour-faced American character comedian who has appeared in several slapstick films and is a frequent TV performer. Series: *The Andy Griffith Show*.

Kodiak
US 1974   13 × 25m   colour
ABC/Kodiak Productions (Stan Shpetner)

Adventures of the Alaska State Patrol.
Acceptable action filler in an unfamiliar landscape.

cr Stan Shpetner, Anthony Laurence

Clint Walker, Abner Biberman, Maggie Blye

Kojak*
US 1973–7   110 × 50m   colour
CBS/Universal (Matthew Rapf)

Cases of a bald-headed New York cop with a penchant for lollipops and fancy waistcoats.
Variable crime series which at its best gave an accurate picture of New York's seamier side and made a star and a so-called singer out of a character actor who had been busy playing villains.

cr Abby Mann

Telly Savalas, George Savalas, Dan Frazer, Kevin Dobson

† See also *The Marcus Nelson Murders*, which served as pilot.

Kolchak: The Night Stalker
aka: *The Night Stalker*
US 1975   22 × 50m   colour
MCA/Universal

A crime reporter has a penchant for getting mixed up with all kinds of monsters.
Self-consciously absurd comedy-horror spin-off from the high-rating TV movies *The Night Strangler* and *The Night Stalker*. The humour is thin, and the series ran out of monsters after half a dozen episodes.

cr Dan Curtis

Darren McGavin

Kona Coast
US 1968   93m   colour   TVM
Warner/Richard Boone

The South Seas skipper of a fishing boat avenges his daughter's death from drugs.
Listless thick-ear which never made a series.

w Gil Ralston, *novel* John D. MacDonald   *d* Lamont Johnson

Richard Boone, Vera Miles, Joan Blondell, Kent Smith

Kossoff, David (1919–). Amiable, soft-spoken British character actor whose most successful appearances on TV were in the series *The Larkins* and *A Little Big Business* and as a Bible reader for all occasions.

KONTAKION. Even commercial television feels the need to score brownie points occasionally, and this ballet by the London Contemporary Dance Theatre was Thames TV's contribution for Easter 1973. William Louther stars.

Kovacs, Ernie (1919–62). Big, burly, cigar-smoking American comedian whose shows of the fifties had an agreeable touch of satire. He is credited with the remark: 'Television is a medium, so called because it is neither rare nor well done.'

Kreskin: see The Amazing World of Kreskin

Krofft, Sid (–   ) **and Marty** (–   ). American puppeteers and comic costume designers, whose series for children have included *H. R. Pufnstuf* and *Lidsville.*

Kukla, Fran and Ollie. A puppet show for children which ran on NBC from 1947 until the mid-fifties. Fran was Fran Allison, the only live performer seen on the show. Puppeteer and creator was Burr Tillstrom.

Kulp, Nancy (*c* 1927–   ). Angular American comedy actress who became internationally popular as the banker's secretary in *The Beverly Hillbillies.*

Kung Fu***
US 1971   75m   colour   TVM
ABC/Warner (Jerry Thorpe)

In the 1870s a half-American buddhist monk flees to America with a price on his head.
Curious, likeable mixture of Oriental wisdom, western action and martial arts, impeccably photographed and fascinating to watch.

w Ed Spielman, Howard Friedlander   *d* Jerry Thorpe

David Carradine, Barry Sullivan, Keye Luke, Albert Salmi, Wayne Maunder

† The series which followed ran three years (72 × 50m) and because of its star and its style became an immense success in a world in which a more violent form of karate had been popularized by Bruce Lee. By the end of the second season, however, the plots had worn very thin and the style, still remarkable for a TV series, was all that was left. Produced by Alex Beaton and Herman Miller for Jerry Thorpe and Warners; created by Ed Spielman.

L

La Frenais, Ian (*c* 1938–). British comedy writer, usually in tandem with Dick Clement.

La Rosa, Julius (1930–). American tenor who was a TV hit in the early fifties on *The Arthur Godfrey Show*.

Lacy and the Mississippi Queen
US 1978 96m colour TVM
Paramount/Lawrence Gordon (Lew Gallo)

Sisters who hardly knew each other wander through the old West avenging their father's murder.
Abysmal pilot for a show which could have been moderately entertaining. Slack handling prevents any reaction but boredom.

w Kathy Donnel, Madeleine DiMaggio-Wagner *d* Robert Butler *ph* Ted Voigtlander *m* Barry Devorzon

Kathleen Lloyd, Debra Feuer, Jack Elam, Edward Andrews, James Keach

Lafferty, Perry (1922–). American executive producer, with CBS for many years. Series include *Hawaii Five O*, *Big Hawaii*.

Laine, Frankie (1913–) (Frank Paul Lo Vecchio). American pop singer of the fifties, much on TV as variety star and theme singer of *Rawhide*.

Lambert, Verity (1935–). British executive producer. Among programmes she has developed are *Dr Who*, *Adam Adamant*, *Somerset Maugham Stories* (BAFTA award 1969), *Shoulder to Shoulder*, *Budgie*, *Hazell*.

Lancelot Link, Secret Chimp
US 1970–1 52 × 25m colour
ABC/Sandler–Burns

A chimpanzee spy working for APE (Agency to Prevent Evil) counters the machinations of CHUMP (Criminal Headquarters for Underground Master Plan).
Live action series for children with chimpanzees playing the roles with the aid of dubbed human voices. Different, anyway.

Lancer
US 1968–9 51 × 50m colour
CBS/TCF (Alan Armer)

A ranching family fights for survival in the San Joaquin Valley in the 1870s.
An attempt at another *Bonanza*, and rather a dull one.

cr Samuel A. Peeples, Dean Riesner *m* Jerome Moross

Andrew Duggan, James Stacy, Wayne Maunder, Elizabeth Baur

Land of the Giants*
US 1968–9 51 × 50m colour
ABC/TCF/Irwin Allen (Bruce Fowler)

A rocketship crashes on a planet ruled by giants.
Ingenious mixture of *Planet of the Apes* and *Dr Cyclops*. Very good trick photography and special sets are its chief recommendations.

cr Irwin Allen *m* John Williams *ad* Jack Martin Smith, Rodger E. Maus *special effects* L. B. Abbott, Art Cruickshank, Emil Kosa Jnr

Gary Conway, Steve Matheson, Kurt Kasznar, Don Marshall, Deanna Lund

Land of the Lost
US 1974 17 × 22m colour
NBC/Hanna–Barbera

A forest ranger and his children are caught in a time vortex and find themselves in a country populated by prehistoric monsters.
Curious attempt at a live action *Valley of the Dinosaurs*. Predictably, the monsters are not too convincing.

Wesley Eure, Kathy Coleman, Spencer Milligan

Landau, Ely (1920–). American executive, creator of NTA, film producer and guiding light of the American Film Theatre.

Landau, Martin (1933–). Sensitive-looking, rather glum American character actor who had leading roles in *Mission Impossible* and *Space 1999*.

Landon, Michael (1937–) (Michael Orowitz). American TV actor who became famous as Little Jo in *Bonanza*: later concentrated on writing and producing TV movies, also *Little House on the Prairie*.

Lange, Hope (1931–). Gentle-spoken American leading lady. TV series include *The Ghost and Mrs Muir*, *The New Dick Van Dyke Show*.

Lanigan's Rabbi
US 1976   98m   colour   TVM
Universal/Heyday (Leonard B. Stern)

A rabbi with a penchant for detection helps the local police chief solve a murder.
Initially pleasant but overlong and finally undistinguished pilot for a *Mystery Movie* segment. See *Mystery Movie* for subsequent titles.

w Don M. Mankiewicz, Gordon Cotler, *novel Friday the Rabbi Slept Late* by Harry Kemelman   *d* Lou Antonio   *ph* Andrew Jackson   *m* Leonard Rosenman

Stuart Margolin, Art Carney, Janet Margolin, Janis Paige

Lansing, Robert (1929–) (Robert H. Broom).
American leading man, mostly on TV. Series: *87th Precinct, Twelve O'Clock High, The Man Who Never Was.*

Lapotaire, Jane (1944–). British leading actress who played *Madame Curie.*

Laramie*
US 1959–62   124 × 50m   64 bw, 60 colour
NBC/Revue

Two friends own a trading station in Wyoming after the Civil War.
Passers-by each week meant a long guest list and a wide range of stories. A good family western series.

John Smith, Robert Fuller, Spring Byington

Laredo
US 1966–7   56 × 50m   colour
NBC/Universal

Adventures of three Texas Rangers.
Unsubtle and rather charmless western series.

Neville Brand, William Smith, Peter Brown, Phil Carey

Large, Eddie: see Little, Syd and Large, Eddie

The Larkins*. British half-hour tape comedy of the fifties, about a cockney couple who keep a country pub. With David Kossoff, Peggy Mount.

Larry
US 1974   74m   colour   TVM
Tomorrow

A normally intelligent man of 26 has been considered mentally retarded and hospitalized since infancy. Interesting case history based on fact.

w David Seltzer   *d* William A. Graham

Frederic Forrest, Tyne Daly, Michael McGuire, Robert Walden

Lasser, Louise (*c* 1942–). American comic character actress who scored a hit as the lead of *Mary Hartman, Mary Hartman.*

Lassie
US 1964–70   186 × 25m   colour
Jack Wrather

A collie dog owned by a farmer protects him and his family.
Innocuous family fare. 15 × 50m episodes were also made, and several were combined to make movies.

Tommy Rettig, George Cleveland; then Jon Provost, Cloris Leachman; then Jon Provost, Hugh Reilly, June Lockhart; then Robert Bray

Lassie: The New Beginning
US 1978   96m   colour   TVM
Jack Wrather/Tom McDermott

When grandmother dies, Lassie accompanies the children on their way to a new home, but gets separated from them.
Rather muddled attempt to launch a new series; it gets by on the dog rather than any astuteness in plotting or characterization.

w Jack Miller   *d* Don Chaffey   *ph* Charles F. Wheeler   *m* Jerrold Immel

Jeanette Nolan, John McIntire, John Reilly, Lee Bryant, Gene Evans, David Wayne

Lassie's Rescue Rangers
US 1973–4   48 × 22m   colour
Filmation

Lassie commands an all-animal rescue crew in the Rocky Mountains.
Clean but otherwise unremarkable cartoon series.

The Last Angry Man
US 1974   74m   colour   TVM
Columbia

The last cases of an old doctor in New York's poor quarters.
Unnecessary TV remake of the 1959 film. Quite flat.

w Gerald Green   *d* Jerrold Freedman

Pat Hingle, Lynn Carlin, Tracy Bogart, Michael Margotta, Andrew Duggan, Sorrell Booke

The Last Child*
US 1971   73m   colour   TVM
Aaron Spelling (William Allyn)

A future government denies married couples the right to more than one child; one family tries to escape.
Orwellian fantasy, rather better than *Zero Population Growth* which it resembles.

w Peter S. Fischer   *d* John Llewellyn Moxey

Michael Cole, Janet Margolin, Van Heflin, Harry Guardino, Ed Asner

The Last Day*
US 1975   100m   colour   TVM
Paramount/A. C. Lyles

A retired gunman brings out his weapons to defend his town against the Dalton gang.
Trickily made western which would have played better straight but has some nice conceits and performances.

w Jim Byrnes, Steve Fisher   *d* Vincent McEveety

Richard Widmark, Robert Conrad, Barbara Rush, Loretta Swit, Tim Matheson, Christopher Connelly, Richard Jaeckel

Last Hours before Morning*
US 1975   74m   colour   TVM
MGM/Charles Fries

A hotel house detective is involved in a murder.
Chandleresque murder mystery, quite effectively done; it didn't go as a series.

w Robert Garland, George Yanok   *d* Joseph Hardy

Ed Lauter, Rhonda Fleming, Robert Alda, Kaz Garas, Peter Donat, Don Porter

The Last Hurrah
US 1977   96m   colour   TVM
Columbia (Terry Becker)

An old politician has one last fling.
Competent but unnecessary retread of a semi-classic film.

w Carroll O'Connor, *novel* Edwin O'Connor *d* Vincent Sherman *ph* Gerald Perry Finnerman *m* Peter Matz

Carroll O'Connor, Mariette Hartley, Patrick Wayne, Jack Carter, Burgess Meredith, Robert Brown

The Last of the Belles*
US 1974   98m   colour   TVM
Robert Buzz Burger

How F. Scott Fitzgerald met his wife Zelda.
Odd, underplayed romantic piece, quite out of the normal run.

d George Schaefer

Richard Chamberlain, Blythe Danner, Susan Sarandon

Last of the Good Guys*
US 1978   96m   colour   TVM
Columbia (Jay Daniel)

A young cop starts an elaborate con game to ensure that the family of his dead buddy gets a pension.
Livelier than usual TV movie fodder.

w John D. Hess, Theodore J. Flicker, Clark Howard *d* Theodore J. Flicker *ph* Emmett Bergholz *m* Dana Kaproff

Robert Culp, Dennis Dugan, Richard Narita, Ji Tu Cumbuka, Larry Hagman, Marlyn Mason, Jonathan Harris

The Last of the Powerseekers*
US 1969   101m   colour   TVM
Universal

Complications and sudden deaths ensue when a banker accuses his son-in-law of embezzlement.
Ingenious stretch-out of several episodes from the unsuccessful Harold Robbins series *The Survivors*; most of the glamorous sequences are included, and the new plot hangs together remarkably well.

w/d Walter Doniger, Joseph Leytes, Paul Henreid

Lana Turner, George Hamilton, Ralph Bellamy, Kevin McCarthy, Louis Hayward, Diana Muldaur, Jan-Michael Vincent

Last of the Summer Wine*
GB 1974–8   approx 30 × 30m   colour (VTR)
BBC

Three old school friends in a Yorkshire village find themselves elderly and unemployed, so spend their days enjoying life.
Pleasing and unusual regional comedy.

w Roy Clarke

Michael Bates, Bill Owen, Peter Sallis

'A new, mellow and gorgeous comedy series.' – *Guardian*

The Last Survivors
US 1975   74m   colour   TVM
Columbia/Bob Banner

After a sea disaster, an officer must decide which passengers shall remain in an overcrowded lifeboat.
Bathtub remake of the cinema film *Seven Waves Away*. Not as good (or even worse).

w Douglas Day Stewart   *d* Lee H. Katzin

Martin Sheen, Diane Baker, Tom Bosley, Christopher George, Bruce Davison, Anne Francis, Percy Rodrigues, Anne Seymour, Bethel Leslie

† The theme was borrowed in both cases from the 1937 film *Souls at Sea*.

Laugh-In
US 1967–72   approx 130 × 50m   colour (VTR)
NBC/George Schlatter

Wildfire vaudeville series with injections of satire and many running gags: a mix of *Hellzapoppin*, *That Was the Week that Was* and *Monty Python's Flying Circus*. Catchphrases to emerge included 'Sock it to me', 'Here come de judge' and 'Very interesting ... but stupid'. Light entertainment all round the world was influenced by it, and famous people, including presidents, queued to be sent up on it, but a revival in 1977 produced hardly a ripple of interest.

Dan Rowan, Dick Martin, Goldie Hawn, Ruth Buzzi, Lili Tomlin, Joanne Worley, Teresa Graves, Arte Johnson, Judy Carne

171

LAURENCE OLIVIER PRESENTS *Cat on a Hot Tin Roof*. An ambitious Anglo-American co-production of the seventies was the Granada/NBC version of Tennessee Williams's play, with Natalie Wood, Laurence Olivier and Robert Wagner.

laugh track. Fake laughter added electronically to a comedy show which has been recorded without an audience. One of the banes of TV.

Laurel and Hardy. A five-minute cartoon series developed by Larry Harmon was syndicated in the US in 1966, with voices by John McGeorge and Larry Harmon. It did not match the originals, whose comedies have been playing on TV around the world since 1948.

Laurence Olivier Presents**
GB 1977   colour (VTR)
Granada

A series of plays of various lengths, allegedly selected by Olivier as the best of their years and usually featuring him as star or director. Made at the rate of three per year, the first six were not especially imposing, the American ones being co-productions with NBC.

The Collection by Harold Pinter: Alan Bates, Olivier
Cat on a Hot Tin Roof by Tennessee Williams: Olivier, Robert Wagner, Natalie Wood
Hobson's Choice by Harold Brighouse: Donald Pleasence
Saturday Sunday Monday by Eduardo de Filippo: Joan Plowright, Frank Finlay, Olivier

Come Back Little Sheba by William Inge: Olivier, Joanne Woodward
Daphne Laureola by James Bridie: Joan Plowright, Olivier, Arthur Lowe

Laurenson, James (1935–). New Zealand actor who made his greatest mark on TV as the Aborigine detective in *Boney*, made in Australia.

Laurie, John (1897–). Fruity Scottish actor, a staple of British films for 30 years. On TV, best remembered as the doom-laden undertaker in *Dad's Army*.

Lavender, Ian (*c* 1948–). British juvenile actor who played the shy Private Pike in *Dad's Army*.

Laverne and Shirley
US 1976–   × 25m   colour
Paramount/Miller–Miklis/Henderson (Garry Marshall)

The adventures of two girls working in a Milwaukee brewery in the late fifties.
Smileable spin-off from *Happy Days*.

cr Garry Marshall, Lowell Ganz, Mark Rothman   *m* Charles Fox

Penny Marshall, Cindy Williams

LAVERNE AND SHIRLEY. This spin-off from *Happy Days*, with Penny Marshall and Cindy Williams, continued the success of Garry Marshall's nostalgic youth-oriented comedies. This one concerned two bottle washers in a Milwaukee brewery of the fifties.

The Law**

US 1974   120m   colour   TVM
Universal

The work of a public defender in a murder trial.
Harsh, sometimes quite brilliant drama documentary which goes on too long.

w Joel Oliansky   *d* John Badham

Judd Hirsch, John Beck, Bonnie Franklin, Sam Wanamaker

The Law and Mr Jones

US 1960–1   45 × 25m   bw
ABC/Four Star/Saxon

An honest lawyer helps the poor and needy.
Obvious but quite appealing family drama.

cr Sy Gomberg

James Whitmore, Janet De Gore

Law and Order*

US 1976   144m approx   colour   TVM

Paramount/PA (E. Jack Neuman)

An Irish Catholic New York cop has troubles stemming from the past as well as the present.
Heavy going if well-detailed crime chronicle with a confusing technique which means that the star always seems either too old or too young.

w E. Jack Neuman, *novel* Dorothy Uhnak   *d* Marvin Chomsky   *ph* Jack Marquette

Darren McGavin, Suzanne Pleshette, Will Geer, Art Hindle, Keir Dullea, Robert Reed, James Olson, Teri Garr, Biff McGuire, Jeanette Nolan

The Law of the Plainsman

US 1959   30 × 25m   bw
NBC/Four Star/Cardiff

In 1885, an Apache is Marshal of part of New Mexico.
Adequate western.

Michael Ansara

Lawbreaker
aka: *Lee Marvin Presents Lawbreaker*
US 1963   32 × 25m   bw
UA/Rapier/Maurice Unger

Dramatizations of actual criminal cases.
Efficient latter-day *Crime Does Not Pay*.

host Lee Marvin

Lawford, Peter (1923–   ). British leading man of
the forties, in Hollywood since childhood. TV series:
Dear Phoebe, The Thin Man.

The Lawgiver: see Moses

The Lawless Years*
US 1959–60   52 × 25m   bw
Jack Chertok/NBC

A New York cop battles lawlessness in the twenties.
Another network's answer to *The Untouchables*. Not
bad, but not very factual.

James Gregory

Lawman
US 1958–61   156 × 25m   bw
Warner

Cases of the Marshal of Laramie.
Absolutely standard TV western, and very entertaining
in its time.

John Russell, Peter Brown, Peggie Castle

Lawson, Sarah (1928–   ). Fresh-looking British
leading lady of the fifties; by 1978 she had graduated
to prison governess in *Within these Walls*.

Le Mesurier, John (1912–   ). Diffident-seeming
British character actor, a familiar face since the mid-
fifties. Acclaimed for his performance in *Traitor*; better
known as Sergeant Wilson in *Dad's Army*.

Le Vien, Jack (1918–   ). American documentary
producer who persuaded Winston Churchill to give his
consent to the series *The Valiant Years*, and a few
specials, then made them very efficiently.

Leachman, Cloris (1928–   ). Angular but appealing
American character actress willing to try her hand at
anything. Series include *Lassie, The Mary Tyler Moore
Show, Phyllis.*

Lear, Norman (1928–   ). American writer and
comedy producer who in the seventies scored enormous
hits with a series of taped half-hour comedies, mostly
on ethnic themes and always extending the borders of
the permissible. *All in the Family, Maude, Sanford and
Son, Mary Hartman, Mary Hartman*, etc. Less successful were *Good Times, The Jeffersons, One Day at a Time,
The Dumplings, Hot*l Baltimore, All's Fair* and *The
Nancy Walker Show.*

Learned, Michael (*c* 1937–   ). American character
actress who became a star as Mom in *The Waltons*.

Leave it to Beaver
US 1957–62   234 × 25m   bw
CBS/Revue

Domestic sitcom with emphasis on two mischievous
small boys.
Small-town America as the clichés would have it – and
extremely popular.

Jerry Mathers

Leave it to Charlie*
GB 1978   × 25m   colour (VTR)
Granada (Eric Prytherch)

Adventures of an accident-prone young insurance agent
in Bolton.
Cheerful character comedy with a genuine Lancashire
feel, occasionally stymied by rather thin plots.

cr H. V. Kershaw   *d* Eric Prytherch   *m* Derek Hilton

David Roper, Peter Sallis, Jean Heywood, Gwen
Cherrill

Leave Yesterday Behind
US 1978   96m   colour   TVM
ABC Circle (Paul Harrison)

A young paraplegic retires bitterly from the world, but
a young girl shows him he can still find love.
Yawnworthy if pretty-looking love story, its very
obvious plot line dragged out interminably.

w Paul Harrison   *d* Richard Michaels   *ph* Ric
Waite   *m* Fred Karlin

John Ritter, Carrie Fisher, Buddy Ebsen, Ed Nelson,
Carmen Zapata, Robert Urich

'A 78 disc love song played at 33 rpm.' – *Daily Variety*

Lee   Marvin   Presents   Lawbreaker: see
Lawbreaker

The Legend of Custer: see Custer

The Legend of Jesse James*
US 1965   26 × 25m   bw
TCF (David Weisbart)

The famous outlaw is presented as a kind of western
Robin Hood.
Quite a slick and attractive series which didn't sustain.

cr Samuel A. Peeples

Chris Jones, Allen Case, Ann Doran

The Legend of Lizzie Borden*
US 1975   100m   colour   TVM
Paramount (George LeMaire)

An account of the Fall River murders of 1892, when the
daughter of the house was suspected of having forty
whacks at each of her parents . . .

A decently made film which takes a long time to produce no fresh evidence, and goes a bit overboard on the axe murders.

w William Bast   *d* Paul Wendkos

Elizabeth Montgomery, Fritz Weaver, Katherine Helmond, Ed Flanders, Don Porter, Fionnuala Flanagan, John Beal

The Legend of Valentino
US 1975   100m   colour   TVM
Spelling–Goldberg

The alleged life and loves of the silent screen's sex idol.
A foolish fantasy which scarcely touches truth at all.

w/d Melville Shavelson   *ph* Arch Dalzell

Franco Nero, Suzanne Pleshette, Yvette Mimieux, Judd Hirsch, Lesley Warren, Milton Berle, Harold J. Stone

Legs. A 1978 one-hour pilot for a show about showgirls in Las Vegas. It was previously a failure as *Mrs Blansky's Beauties*; the title was eventually changed to *Who's Minding the Kids?* The producer so keen on his project is Garry Marshall.

Leonard, Sheldon (1907–) (Sheldon Bershad). American character actor who turned to producing TV shows and made quite a success of it: *I Spy, My Friend Tony, Big Eddie* (also acted).

Lester, Dick (1932–). American film director in Britain; started his rise to fame in TV, especially with the *Goon Shows* of the fifties.

Let's Make a Deal. Long-running game show, on NBC several times a week from 1963, in which compere Monty Hall dares successful contestants to risk their winnings for even more loot. For some obscure reason he also encourages the contestants to dress in weird clothes. America loves it.

Let's Switch
US 1975   74m   colour   TVM
Universal (Bruce Johnson)

A woman's magazine editor and her old friend, a suburban housewife, decide to change places.
Smooth, predictable comedy.

w Peter Lefcourt, Chubby Williams, Sid Arthur, Ruth Brooks Flippen   *d* Alan Rafkin   *m* Harry Geller

Barbara Eden, Barbara Feldon, George Furth, Richard Schaal, Pat Harrington, Joyce Van Patten

The Letters*
US 1972   73m   colour   TVM
Spelling–Goldberg

Three important letters are delayed a year in delivery.
Multi-mini-drama, all quite watchable in its predictable way.

w Ellis Marcus, Hal Sitowitz, James G. Hirsch   *d* Gene Nelson, Paul Krasny

Barbara Stanwyck, John Forsythe, Dina Merrill, Ida Lupino, Leslie Nielsen, Ben Murphy, Jane Powell

Letters from Three Lovers
US 1973   74m   colour   TVM
Spelling–Goldberg

More delayed letters have dramatic consequences.
Success means a reprise.

w Ann Marcus, Jerome Kass   *d* John Erman

Barry Sullivan, June Allyson, Ken Berry, Juliet Mills, Martin Sheen, Belinda Montgomery, Robert Sterling

Levene, Philip (–). British writer, especially associated with *The Avengers*, to which he contributed most of the macabre stories.

Levenson, Sam (1911–). American ex-schoolmaster who in the fifties was a popular talker, compere and light comedian.

Lewis, Jerry: see Martin, Dean and Lewis, Jerry

Lewis, Robert Q. (1921–). American TV personality of the fifties, usually as host or panellist.

Lewis, Shari (*c* 1927–). Canadian ventriloquist and puppeteer whose most memorable creation is 'Lamb Chop'.

Liberace (1919–) (Wladziu Valentino Liberace). American pianist and entertainer, all glitter and extravagance. Derided in the fifties, he showed his tenacity and in the mid-seventies was still a big star of specials and cabaret.

library film. Another phrase for stock shot: one not made at the time of the production, but taken from a shelf.

Lidsville
US 1971   17 × 25m   colour (VTR)
ABC/Sid and Marty Krofft

A boy is lost in a fantasy land where all the characters are hats.
Ingenious but limited modern fairy tale.

The Lieutenant
US 1963   29 × 50m   bw
NBC/Arena/MGM

Stories of a young officer in the peacetime Marines.
Very ho-hum.

Gary Lockwood, Robert Vaughn

Lt Schuster's Wife*
US 1972   73m   colour   TVM
Universal (Steven Bochco)

When a policeman is killed and slandered, his widow goes into action.
Adequate, well-paced pilot which didn't get anywhere.

w Bernie Kukoff, Steven Bochco   d David Lowell Rich

Lee Grant, Jack Warden, Don Galloway, Paul Burke, Eartha Kitt, Nehemiah Persoff, Murray Matheson

The Life and Assassination of the Kingfish*
US 1977   96m   colour   TVM
Tomorrow Entertainment (Paul Leaf)/NBC

The career and sudden death in 1937 of aggressive senator Huey Long.
Not an improvement on *All the King's Men*, but as a TV movie fairly commendable.

w/d Robert Collins

ED ASNER, Nicholas Pryor, Diane Kagan, Fred Cook

The Life and Death of Picture Post*
GB 1977   60m   colour
BBC (John Ormond)

The rise and fall of an influential picture magazine which was begun in 1938 and at its height during World War II.
Fascinating journalism which collects together, before it's too late, all those involved, including Stefan Lorant, Tom Hopkinson, Fyfe Robertson and James Cameron.

w John Ormond   narrator Rene Cutforth

The Life and Legend of Wyatt Earp**
US 1955–60   226 × 25m   bw
Louis F. Edelmann/Wyatt Earp Enterprises

Stories of the Marshal of Tombstone.
A very good western series with something to please almost everybody.

Hugh O'Brian

The Life and Times of Grizzly Adams*
US 1976–7   34 × 50m   colour (16mm)
NBC/Sunn Classic

THE LIFE AND TIMES OF LORD MOUNTBATTEN. Prominent public figures were brought a little closer into general focus by documentaries such as this fine series, broadcast in 1969.

A man escapes to the mountains after an unjust accusation of murder, and lives there with an old prospector and a pet bear. '
Family fare made to order and computer-controlled by a Mormon company. High-class moving wallpaper with neither animal nor human getting hurt.

Dan Haggerty, Denver Pyle

Life at Stake
GB 1978   8 × 50m   colour (VTR)
BBC (Frank Cox)

Drama-documentaries reconstructing kidnappings, disasters and other terrorist incidents of recent years.
Well made but somewhat unnecessary series.

Life Goes to the Movies*
US 1977   150m approx.   colour
TCF/Time–Life (Jack Haley Jnr)

The story of America between 1936 and 1972 as shown in the movies.
A spectacularly well-edited compilation which gives the genuine flavour of Hollywood's golden age.

w Richard Schickel   *d* Mel Stuart

Life Goes to War*
aka: *The Movies Go to War*
US 1977   96m   colour (VTR)
TCF/Time–Life

A companion piece to the above with more emphasis on newsreels of World War II and the activities of the movie stars of that period.

The Life of Riley. A half-hour American comedy series which had a season in 1949 with Jackie Gleason and Rosemary de Camp as the not-too-bright suburban riveter and his wife. It came back in 1953, and played five seasons, with William Bendix and Marjorie Reynolds.

Life With Father*
US 1954   26 × 25m   bw
CBS/McCadden

Life in an upper-middle-class New York household at the turn of the century.
Amiable period comedy which manages a better atmosphere than the expensive film version.

Leon Ames, Lurene Tuttle

Life With Luigi
US 1952   39 × 25m   bw
CBS

Problems of an Italian antique dealer in Chicago.
Adequate comedy series from a radio show.

J. Carrol Naish/Vito Scotti, Alan Reed/Thomas Gomez, Jody Gilbert/Muriel Landers, Sig Ruman

The Likely Lads***
GB 1965–9   × 30m   bw/colour (VTR)
BBC

Escapades of two disaster-prone young men in Northumberland.
The funny side of *Saturday Night and Sunday Morning*, this comedy series made its mark through clever writing and acting.

cr/w Ian La Frenais, Dick Clement

Rodney Bewes, James Bolam

† In 1973 came a final series of 26, *Whatever Happened to the Likely Lads?* This took up the story several years later, when Bolam returns from the army to find Bewes married to his girl.
†† An unrepresentative feature film version was released in 1976.

limbo. When applied to scenery, this means no scenery at all, just an illuminated cyclorama suggesting illimitable distance, or black velvet curtains.

The Lindbergh Kidnapping Case*
US 1976   156m   colour   TVM
Columbia

The 1934 trial of Bruno Hauptmann for the kidnapping and murder of the Lindbergh baby.
Lethargic semi-documentary of a famous trial. The film has nothing new to say, and expounds the facts without flair.

w J. P. Miller   *d* Leonard Horn

ANTHONY HOPKINS, Cliff de Young, Sian Barbara Allen, Walter Pidgeon, Joseph Cotten, Martin Balsam, Keenan Wynn, Laurence Luckinbill

The Line-up*
US 1959   18 × 50m   bw
Marjeff

One-hour version of *San Francisco Beat*, snappily made on the actual locations.
An excellent cop show.

Warner Anderson

Linkletter, Art (1912–). American talk show host of the fifties, concentrating in his *House Party* series on drawing out ordinary people from the audience to voice their opinions.

Lisa Bright and Dark
US 1972   74m   colour   TVM
Hallmark

A mentally disturbed teenaged girl has days when she becomes dangerous.
Cheerless case history, rather well acted.

w John Neufeld, from his novel   *d* Jeannot Szwarc   *m* Rod McKuen

Kay Lenz, Anne Baxter, John Forsythe, Debralee Scott

Lisemore, Martin (1940–77). British TV director whose most notable achievements were *The Pallisers* and *I, Claudius*.

A Little Big Business
GB 1964   × 25m   bw (VTR)
Granada

A young man is taught the furniture business by his father.
Amusing, slightly offbeat, sitcom.

David Kossoff, Francis Matthews

A Little Game*
US 1971   73m   colour   TVM
Universal (George Eckstein)

A man suspects that his 11-year-old stepson may be homicidal.
Quite a chilling little melodrama.

w Carol Sobieski, *novel* Fielden Farrington   *d* Paul Wendkos

Ed Nelson, Diane Baker, Katy Jurado, Howard Duff

Little House on the Prairie*
US 1974–   × 50m   colour
NBC/Ed Friendly (Michael Landon)

The struggles of a family of homesteaders to survive on the American plains a hundred years ago, as seen through the eyes of the children.
Rather prettified but attractively made and played version of the books by Laura Ingalls Wilder.

Michael Landon, Melissa Gilbert

The Little People: see The Brian Keith Show

Little Rascals. The TV name for the old *Our Gang* comedies, made by Hal Roach between the mid-twenties and the mid-forties, and still going strong.

Little, Syd (1942–) **and Large, Eddie** (1942–). British lowbrow comedians and impressionists in the Abbott and Costello mould, popular in the late seventies after an introduction in *Who Do You Do?*

The Littlest Hobo
Canada 1963   57 × 25m   bw
McGowan/Canamac

Adventures of a wandering Alsatian dog.
Curiously titled, otherwise adequate children's series.

Live Again, Die Again*
US 1974   74m   colour   TVM
Universal (David Victor)

A woman kept frozen for forty years is revived and cured; returning home, she finds that someone is trying to kill her.
Nuthouse melodrama which early abandons its crionics

theme and subjects the audience to every trick in the book: colour filters, distorted sound, surrealist montages, the lot. Unfortunately the plot is not strong enough to stand up to it.

w Joseph Stefano   *d* Richard A. Colla

Donna Mills, Walter Pidgeon, Vera Miles, Geraldine Page, Cliff Potts, Mike Farrell

The Liver Birds*. British (BBC) half-hour tape comedy by Lew Schwartz, Myra Taylor and Carla Lane; it ran sporadically from 1969 until 1978. The distaff side of *The Likely Lads*, it originally starred Polly James and Nerys Hughes, but there were several changes of cast and approach.

The Lives of Jenny Dolan*
US 1975   100m   colour   TVM
Paramount/Ross Hunter

A lady journalist investigates four puzzling deaths which prove to be connected.
Sleek, ambitious soaper which doesn't really work.

w Richard Alan Simmons, James Lee   *d* Jerry Jameson

Shirley Jones, Stephen Boyd, John Gavin, Dana Wynter, Stephen McNally, James Darren, David Hedison, Farley Granger, Lynn Carlin, George Grizzard, Ian MacShane, Pernell Roberts, Percy Rodrigues

Livingstone, Mary (c 1903–) (Sadye Marks). American comedienne, widow of Jack Benny; she appeared in most of his radio and TV shows.

The Lloyd Bridges Show*
US 1962   34 × 25m   bw
CBS/Four Star/Loring–Caron

Adventures of a roving international journalist.
Virtually an anthology series, and a good one, in which the star not only hosts in one guise but plays a leading part in another.

Loach, Ken (1936–). Socially conscious British director, often working with producer Tony Garnett. *Up the Junction, Cathy Come Home, Days of Hope, The Price of Coal*, etc. BAFTA award 1967.

Lock, Stock and Barrel
US 1970   96m   colour   TVM
Universal

A runaway couple encounter savage animals, vengeful parents and natural hazards.
Slow starting adventure comedy featuring the couple later seen married in *Hitched*.

w Richard Alan Simmons   *d* Jerry Thorpe

Belinda Montgomery, Tim Matheson, Jack Albertson, Neville Brand, Burgess Meredith, Felicia Farr, John Beck, Robert Emhardt

Lock Up
US 1959–60 78 × 25m bw
United Artists

A lawyer helps the wrongly accused.
Adequate courtroom series.

Macdonald Carey

Lockhart, June (1925–   ). American actress, daughter of Gene Lockhart. TV series: *Lassie*.

Lockwood, Gary (1937–   ) (John Gary Yusolfsky). American leading man. TV series: *Follow the Sun, The Lieutenant*.

Lockwood, Margaret (1916–   ) (Margaret Day). British film star who turned to the stage and TV when roles on the big screen became hard to find. Series: *The Flying Swan, Justice*.

Locusts*
US 1974 74m colour TVM
Paramount

A discharged World War II pilot comes home in dejection but finds himself fighting a locust plague.
Very moderate personal drama gives way to very moderate special effects.

w Robert Malcolm Young d Richard T. Heffron

Ben Johnson, Ron Howard, Lisa Gerritsen, Katherine Helmond

The Log of the Black Pearl
US 1975 100m colour TVM
Universal/Jack Webb

A stockbroker inherits a ship and a clue to sunken treasure
Rather like a modernized Treasure Island, but not as good.

w Harold Jack Bloom d Andrew McLaglen

Jack Kruschen, Glenn Corbett, Ralph Bellamy, John Alderson, Anne Archer, Kiel Martin

Logan's Run
US 1977 74m colour TVM
MGM

Two fugitives from a city of the future, in which one must die at the age of 30, meet various strange civilizations in the outside world.
Intriguing if rather plodding pilot which uses some of the more spectacular footage from its feature film original.

w William F. Nolan, Saul David d Robert Day

Gregory Harrison, Heather Menzies, Donald Moffat

† The resulting series ran only 13 × 50m episodes.

logo. An image or motif designed to implant a company, a film or a series in the public mind; e.g. MGM's lion, Fox's searchlights.

London Belongs to Me
GB 1977 7 × 50m colour (VTR)
Thames (Paul Knight)

Various problems are faced by inhabitants of a dreary London lodging house before World War II.
Slightly disappointing, overstretched televersion of a solid novel which also made an excellent film.

w Hugh Leonard, *novel* Norman Collins d Raymond Menmuir

Derek Farr, Patricia Hayes, Peter Jeffrey, Fiona Gray, Madge Ryan

London Weekend Television. The ITV (commercial) company holding since 1968 the London franchise for Friday (from 7 pm) and the whole of Saturday and Sunday.

The Lone Ranger
US 1952–6 182 × 25m bw (39 colour)
Jack Wrather

A mysterious masked rider fights for justice.
Pleasantly made comic strip western for children.

Clayton Moore (occasionally John Hart), Jay Silverheels

† A series of Lone Ranger cartoons (26 × 25m) was made in 1966.

The Lone Wolf
aka: *Streets of Danger*
US 1953 39 × 25m bw
Gross–Krasne

Stories of a gentleman rogue who fights crime.
An old reliable of the cinema failed to excite on TV.

Louis Hayward

The Loneliest Runner
US 1976   74m colour TVM
NBC (Michael Landon)

Problems of a teenage bed-wetter.
An incredible subject, but by the end a rather touching little drama.

w/d Michael Landon

Michael Landon, Lance Kerwin, Brian Keith

The Lonely Profession*
US 1969 96m colour TVM
Universal (Jo Swerling Jnr)

A private eye's client is murdered.
Acceptable sub-Chandler goings on.

w/d Douglas Heyes

Harry Guardino, Dean Jagger, Troy Donahue, Joseph Cotten, Fernando Lamas, Dina Merrill

The Loner
US 1965   26 × 25m   bw
CBS/Greenway/Interlaken/TCF

An ex-soldier tries to find himself after the Civil War.
Shane-styled western; atmosphere rather rarefied.

cr Rod Serling

Lloyd Bridges

The Long Hot Summer*
US 1965   26 × 50m   bw
ABC/TCF (Frank Glicksman)

Small-town troubles centre round a blustering local
tycoon and his family.
Vaguely based on William Faulkner stories, but more
clearly on the film of the same title, this domestic drama
had a little more strength than *Peyton Place* but was
handicapped by an intractable star and petered out
when he was replaced.

cr Dean Riesner

Edmond O'Brien (later Dan O'Herlihy), Nancy
Malone, Roy Thinnes, Ruth Roman

Long John Silver: see The Adventures of Long John
Silver

Long, Richard (1927–74). Easy-going American lead-
ing man who proved an attractive series figure: *77
Sunset Strip*, *Bourbon Street Beat*, *The Big Valley*,
Nanny and the Professor.

The Long Search**
GB 1977   13 × 50m   colour (16mm)
BBC/RM (Munich)/Time–Life (Peter Montagnon)

Ronald Eyre travels around the world finding out what
people's religions mean to them in modern life.
A solidly watchable, intelligent series in which only a
few of the episodes would have been better at half the
length.

'Has all the makings of a milestone.' – *Observer*

The Longest Hundred Miles
US 1967   93m   colour   TVM
Universal

An American soldier in the Philippines leads a civilian
flight away from the Japanese invasion.
Routine war adventure.

w Winston Miller   *d* Don Weis

Doug McClure, Katharine Ross, Ricardo Montalban

The Longest Night*
US 1972   74m   colour   TVM
Universal (William Frye)

A girl is kidnapped and buried alive in a coffin with a
limited life support system.
Suspenseful crime melodrama based on an actual case.

w Merwin Gerard   *d* Jack Smight

David Janssen, James Farentino, Phyllis Thaxter, Skye
Aubrey, Charles McGraw, John Kerr

Longstreet
US 1970   74m   colour   TVM
Paramount (Joseph Sargent)

A New Orleans criminal insurance investigator is
blinded in a chase but carries on.
Shades of Edward Arnold in *Eyes in the Night*. This
very moderate mystery led to a one-season series.

w Stirling Silliphant   *d* Joseph Sargent

James Franciscus, Bradford Dillman, John McIntire,
Jeanette Nolan

† The resulting series ran to 24 × 50m episodes.

Look What Happened to Rosemary's Baby
US 1968   96m   colour   TVM
Paramount/Culzean (Anthony Wilson)

A sequel to the 1968 film, with many of the same characters watching the devilish child grow up.
Rather unattractive supernatural thriller.

w Anthony Wilson   *d* Sam O'Steen   *m* Charles
Bernstein

Stephen McHattie, Ruth Gordon, Ray Milland, Patty
Duke, Broderick Crawford, George Maharis, Tina
Louise, Donna Mills, Lloyd Haynes

Looks Familiar. An easy-going nostalgia programme
devised for Thames TV by Denis Gifford in the mid-
seventies. Denis Norden chairs a panel of three 'experts' who identify clips of film of thirties and forties
bandleaders, singers and film stars. The score is quite
irrelevant: the gossip's the thing. (The series was originally a radio show called *Sounds Familiar*.) Producer,
David Clark.

Loose Change
US 1978   3 × 96m   colour
Universal (Jules Irving)

Three girls graduate from Berkeley in 1962 and we
follow their subsequent lives.
Weary rehash of all the modern clichés – free love, student protest, politics, abortion – without much thought
for professionalism or entertainment.

w Corinne Jacker, Charles E. Israel, Jennifer Miller,
book Sara Davidson   *d* Jules Irving   *ph* John
Elsenbach, Harry Wolfe   *m* Don Costa

Cristina Raines, Laurie Heineman, Season Hubley,
Theodore Bikel, David Wayne, Stephen Macht,
Michael Tolan, Gregg Henry, Ben Masters, Kate Reid,
June Lockhart

Lord, Jack (1922–   ) (John Joseph Ryan). Durable
American leading man, in series *Stony Burke* and the
long-running *Hawaii Five O*.

Lord Peter Wimsey. Ian Carmichael impersonated Dorothy L. Sayers' aristocratic detective of the twenties in three pleasing BBC serials in the early seventies.

The Loretta Young Show*
US 1953–60   255 × 25m   bw
NBC

Anthology dramas with introductions and occasional appearances by the star.
Superior series of its time.

Lorimar. Independent production company headed by Lee Rich. Its first major success was *The Waltons*.

Lost Flight
US 1969   105m   colour   TVM
Universal

After a plane crash in an island jungle, the passengers learn to survive.
Memories of *Five Came Back*, and of another ill-fated series called *The New People*. This one did not take – it wasn't very good – but the seventies brought yet more pilots on the theme.

w Dean Riesner   *d* Leonard Horn

Lloyd Bridges, Anne Francis, Bobby Van, Ralph Meeker, Andrew Prine, Linden Chiles

Lost in Space
US 1965–7   83 × 50m   colour
CBS/Irwin Allen/TCF

A family of the future is shipwrecked on an unknown planet.
Cheerfully studio-bound adventure, mainly for kids: too much talk for grown-ups.

Mark Goddard, Jonathan Harris, Marta Kristen, Billy Mumy

The Lost Saucer
US 1975   16 × 22m   colour (VTR)
TCF/Sid and Marty Krofft

Two androids in a flying saucer collect two earth children and they all have adventures in space.
Rather heavy-footed fantasy for children, with good set design.

Ruth Buzzi, Jim Nabors

Lotterby, Sidney (–   ). British BBC producer mainly associated with comedy, his most generally acclaimed hit being *Porridge*.

Lou Grant*
US 1977–   × 50m   colour
Mary Tyler Moore

Dramas in a news editor's office.
A skilfully made and written if occasionally rather

earnest vehicle for a middle-aged star from *The Mary Tyler Moore Show*.

Ed Asner

Louis Armstrong, Chicago Style*
US 1975   74m   colour   TVM
Charles Fries/Dick Berg

The famous musician struggles for his fame and fights the mob.
Presumably true anecdotes, quite well made and entertaining.

w James Lee   *d* Lee Phillips

Ben Vereen, Red Buttons, Janet McLachlan, Margaret Avery

A Love Affair: The Eleanor and Lou Gehrig Story*
US 1977   96m   colour   TVM
Charles Fries

The private life of a baseball star who died of lateral sclerosis.
Superior in production and craftsmanship, this docudrama contains nothing surprising.

w Blanche Hanalis, *book* My Luke and I by Eleanor Gehrig   *d* Fielder Cook   *m* Michel Hugo   *md* Eddy Lawrence Manson

Blythe Danner, Edward Herrmann, Patricia Neal, Ramon Bieri, Lainie Kazan, Jane Wyatt, Gerald J. O'Loughlin, Georgia Engel

†The same story was told in the 1942 Gary Cooper film *The Pride of the Yankees*.

Love American Style*
US 1969   74m   colour   TVM
ABC/Paramount

Four comedy sketches on the theme of love: a successful series resulted.

w various   *d* Charles Rondeau, Marc Daniels, Gary Marshall, Hy Averback

Don Porter, Marjorie Lord, Michael Callan, Penny Fuller, Greg Morris, Darryl Hickman, Robert Reed, Jeannine Riley

'We can do for situation comedies what *Laugh-in* did for variety shows.' – Arnold Margolin

†The series ran four seasons (112 × 50m). Creators: Douglas S. Cramer, Tom Miller; executive producers: Arnold Margolin, Jim Parker; for Paramount.

Love among the Ruins**
US 1974   100m   colour   TVM
ABC Circle

An elderly actress turns to a former lover for legal counsel in a breach of promise case.
Splendid people are forced to overact because this high class taradiddle goes on too long and makes their char-

acters unconvincing. Still, it's a delight to have something so civilized.

w James Costigan, *novel* Angela Thirkell d George Cukor

KATHARINE HEPBURN, LAURENCE OLIVIER, Richard Pearson, Colin Blakely, Joan Sims, Leigh Lawson, Gwen Nelson, Robert Harris

Love and Marriage*
US 1959   26 × 25m   bw
NBC/Louis F. Edelman

Frustrations of a Tin Pan Alley music publisher.
Unusual comedy format with more than usual amusement.

William Demarest, Stubby Kaye, Kay Armen

The Love Boat*
US 1977–   × 50m   colour
Spelling–Goldberg

Comedies and dramas about passengers on a pleasure boat cruise.
A hoary format scores more hits than misses. (The 50m series was prefaced by three experimental pilots, two at 96m and one at 74m.)

Gavin McLeod

'Everything I've tried to forget about the movies is recaptured in this ABC hour.' – Robert MacKenzie, *TV Guide*

Love, Hate, Love
US 1970   72m   colour   TVM
Aaron Spelling

Newlyweds are violently harassed by the girl's ex-suitor.
Rather unpleasant melodrama.

d George McCowan

Ryan O'Neal, Lesley Warren, Peter Haskell

Love is Not Enough
US 1978   96m   colour   TVM
Universal (Stanley C. Robertson)

A black widower moves himself and his children from Detroit to a new way of life in Los Angeles.
Sentimental wallow for those who like that sort of thing.

w Arthur Ross   d Ivan Dixon

Bernie Casey

† A short run of one-hour episodes followed.

Love on a Rooftop
US 1966   26 × 25m   colour
ABC/Columbia/Harry Ackerman (E. W. Swackhamer)

Newlyweds live in a top-floor flat in San Francisco.
Ordinary comedy.

cr Bernard Slade

Pete Duel, Judy Carne

Love Story
US 1973   13 × 50m   colour
Paramount/NBC (George Schaefer)

An anthology of romances, usually two to an hour, this failed to repeat the success of the movie after which it was named.

† The title had previously been used by Britain's ATV for a long-running and occasionally distinguished series of tape hours.

Love That Bob: see Cummings, Robert

Love Thy Neighbour*. A tape comedy created in 1971 for Thames TV by Vince Powell and Harry Driver, about a working-class bigot with black neighbours. The cast (Jack Smethurst, Kate Williams, Rudolph Walker, Nina Baden-Semper) made it work, though it never rose above the obvious. An American attempt in 1973 to repeat its success closed after 12 episodes.

† A feature film version was released in 1973.

The Love War*
aka: *The Sixth Column*
US 1969   74m   colour   TVM
Spelling–Thomas

Killers attacking each other in a small California town are actually aliens from another planet fighting for control of Earth.
Smooth, inventive, good-looking science fiction with plenty of suspense.

w David Kidd, Guerdon Trueblood d GEORGE McCOWAN

Lloyd Bridges, Angie Dickinson, Harry Basch, Byron Foulger

Lovejoy, Frank (1912–62). Tough-looking American actor. TV series: *Meet McGraw.*

The Lovers*. A tape comedy about a working-class courtship created in 1970 for Granada TV by Jack Rosenthal, this was distinguished by funny lines delivered in a highly stylized and artificial way. It made stars of Paula Wilcox and Richard Beckinsale.

† A feature film version was released in 1973.

Love's Dark Ride
US 1978   96m   colour   TVM
NBC/Mark VII (Joseph M. Taritaro)

When a designer is accidentally blinded he turns against his friends.
Dislikeable and pathetic romantic melodrama with a predictable happy ending.

LOVE THY NEIGHBOUR. Race hatred was made funny by this lowbrow comedy series in which even the bigot was essentially good-natured. Jack Smethurst, Kate Williams, Nina Baden-Semper and Rudolph Walker have smiles all round.

w Ann Beckett, Kane O'Connor, Dennis Nemec *d* Delbert Mann *ph* Robert Wyckoff *m* Tom Sullivan, John D'Andrea, Michael Lloyd

Cliff Potts, Carrie Snodgress, Jane Seymour, Granville Van Dusen, Shelly Novack, Tom Sullivan

'Viewers were probably hard put to stay awake.' – *Daily Variety*

Lowe, Arthur (1914–). Portly, self-important British character actor who after a career in bit parts became a TV star as Mr Swindley in *Coronation Street*. Subsequent series built around him included *Pardon the Expression* and *Turn Out the Lights*, but he really came into his own as the memorable Captain Mainwaring in *Dad's Army*, and later as the star of *Bless Me, Father* and *Potter*.

Lowry, Judith (1890–1976). American small-part character actress who became famous in extreme old age as the game old lady in *Phyllis*.

Lucan
US 1977   74m   colour
ABC/MGM/Barry Lowen

A boy brought up with wolves helps people in distress while trying to find his parents.
A surly hero with only moderately special powers seems unlikely for TV, but the idea, stemming from the real-life case recounted in Truffaut's *The Wild Child*, had been tried once before in *Stalk the Wild Child*. *Lucan* led to a series of 11 × 50m.

Kevin Brophy

Luckinbill, Laurence (1934–). American leading man. Series include *The Delphi Bureau*, *The Secret Storm*.

The Lucy Show*
US 1962–8   156 × 25m   colour (30 bw)
CBS/Desilu (Gary Morton)

The middle section of Lucy's TV career, in which she played a gallant widow with Vivian Vance as her friend (for three seasons) and Gale Gordon as her boss. See also *I Love Lucy* and *Here's Lucy*.

Lumet, Sidney (1924–). American director who before his successful film career triumphed on TV with *You Are Here*, *Omnibus*, *Mama*, etc.

Lumley, Joanna (1946–). Pert British leading lady who shot to fame as Purdey in *The New Avengers*.

Lupino, Ida (1914–). British actress in Hollywood who towards the end of her film career turned director and handled many TV episodes; also appeared in the series *Mr Adams and Eve*.

Lynde, Paul (1926–). American character comedian with mournful face and funny voice. TV series: *The Paul Lynde Show*, *Temperatures Rising*.

Lynn, Dame Vera (1921–). British sentimental singer, World War II's 'sweetheart of the forces'. She still presents occasional musical hours.

M

M Squad*
US 1957–9   117 × 25m   bw
NBC/MCA/Latimer/Universal

Stories of a plainclothes detective in the Chicago police.
Good standard cop show, cleanly produced.

Lee Marvin

MacArthur, James (1937–). American second lead who has been content to appear as just that in *Hawaii Five-O* for 10 years.

McCallum, David (1933–). Engaging British actor in Hollywood who scored a TV hit as Kuryakin in *The Man from UNCLE* and a lesser one in *Colditz* and as *The Invisible Man*.

McCloud: see Mystery Movie and Who Killed Miss USA

McClure, Doug (1935–). Virile American action lead who grew up hopping from one series to another (*Checkmate, Overland Trail, The Virginian, Search*, etc.) before moving over to movies.

McCord, Kent (1942–) (Kent McWhirter). American leading man who made his big impact with *Adam 12* but hasn't been around much since.

McCoy: see Mystery Movie and The Big Rip-Off

McDowall, Roddy (1928–). British actor in America, former child star, who pops up in films and TV guest spots. He also played the leading ape in the series *Planet of the Apes*.

McEachin, James (1931–). Black American actor who played the title role in *Tenafly*. He also appeared in *The Alpha Caper* and many other telefilms.

McGavin, Darren (1922–). Diligent, reliable American TV leading man and character actor. Series include *Mike Hammer, Riverboat, The Outsider, The Night Stalker, Kolchak*.

McGiver, John (1913–75). Owlish American character actor who was always welcomed by the public, whether in films or in TV series such as *Many Happy Returns, The Jimmy Stewart Show*.

McGoohan, Patrick (1928–). Quirky Anglo-American leading actor who became a household word in *Danger Man*, went over the top in *The Prisoner*, and made a brief comeback ten years later in *Rafferty*.

McHale's Navy
US 1962–5   138 × 25m   bw
ABC/MCA/Sto–Rev/Universal

The wacky antics of a PT crew in the World War II Pacific.
Routine service goings-on à la Hollywood, and highly popular.

Ernest Borgnine, Joe Flynn, Tim Conway

Machinegunner
GB 1976   74m   colour   TVM
Harlech TV (Patrick Dromgoole)

A Bristol debt collector uncovers a crime ring.
Misleadingly titled but thoroughly predictable crime caper.

w Bob Parker, Dave Martin   d Patrick Dromgoole

Leonard Rossiter, Nina Baden-Semper, Kate O'Mara. Colin Welland

McKay, Gardner (1932–). American leading man, star of *Adventures in Paradise*; not much heard from since.

McKeever and the Colonel
US 1962   26 × 25m   bw
ABC/Four Star

A military school cadet is in constant hot water.
Forgettable comedy.

Scott Lane, Allyn Joslyn

McKenzie's Raiders
US 1958   39 × 25m   bw
United Artists

Stories of the independently-commanded outfit which brought law and order to the southwest.
Passable western.

Richard Carlson

Mackie, Philip (c 1918–). British writer, always of civilized entertainments. *Saki, The Victorians, Maupassant, Paris 1900, The Caesars, The Organization, Napoleon and Love, Good Girl, Raffles, The Naked Civil*

PATRICK McGOOHAN. A versatile and commanding actor who never quite achieved the expected stardom; he is seen here in one of Granada's fifties adaptations of modern classics: *All My Sons*, with Betta St John and Albert Dekker.

Servant, *An Englishman's Castle*, etc. Winner of many prizes; also occasional producer.

The McLean Stevenson Show
US 1976   13 × 25m   colour (VTR)
M and M (Monty Hall)

Domestic problems of the owner of a hardware store. Archetypal star domestic comedy.

McLean Stevenson, Barbara Stuart, Ayn Ruymen

McMahon, Ed (1923–   ). American character actor, Johnny Carson's announcer and feed on the *Tonight* show.

MacMahon, Horace (1907–71). American character actor with a prizefighter's face. He spent many years playing gangsters in movies, then on TV became a household word in *Naked City*, and retired after his next, *Mr Broadway*.

McMillan (and Wife): see Mystery Movie and Once Upon a Dead Man

MacMurray, Fred (1907–   ). American leading man of Hollywood's golden age. He came to TV in the long-running series *My Three Sons* and has done occasional guest spots.

McNaughton's Daughter
US 1976   96m   colour   TVM
Universal/David Victor (David J. O'Connell)

The daughter of a successful defence lawyer wants to follow in father's footsteps.
Ho-hum courtroom melodrama which spun off three one-hour episodes and collapsed.

w Ken Trevey   *d* Jerry London

Susan Clark, Ralph Bellamy, Vera Miles, Louise Latham, Mike Farrell

MacNee, Patrick (1922–   ). Elegant British leading man who created the character of the suave John Steed in *The Avengers*, borrowing most of it from Ralph Richardson in the cinema film *Q Planes*.

McQueen, Steve (1930–). Tough American leading man who before his film fame starred in a TV series, *Wanted Dead or Alive*.

Macy, Bill (1922–). American character actor, nationally famous as the husband of *Maude*.

Mad Bull
US 1977 96m colour TVM
Filmways (Richard M. Rosenbloom)

A tough wrestler falls in love and helps to catch a dangerous fanatic.
Muddled comedy–melodrama which takes an age to get into its stride.

w Vernon Zimmerman *d* Walter Doniger, Len Steckler *ph* Jacques Marquette

Alex Karras, Susan Anspach, Nicholas Colasanto, Danny Dayton, Elisha Cook Jnr

Madame Sin*
GB 1971 73m colour TVM
ITC (Lou Morheim)

A former CIA agent is brainwashed by a ray gun and forced to work for a female mastermind operating out of a Scottish castle.
High camp for star fans: not much fun for anyone else.

w Barry Oringer, David Green *d* David Greene *ph* Tony Richmond *m* Michael Gibbs

Bette Davis, Robert Wagner, Denholm Elliott, Gordon Jackson, Dudley Sutton, Catherine Schell

† An 88m cinema version was also released.

Madigan: see Mystery Movie and Brock's Last Case

Madison, Guy (1922–) (Robert Moseley). Lean American leading man who became TV's *Wild Bill Hickok*, then vanished in a flurry of Italian westerns.

The Magic Carpet*
US 1971 97m colour TVM
Universal (Ranald MacDougall)

A pretty American student in Rome becomes a tourist guide.
A pleasant tour of Italy, with some nonsense going on in the foreground.

w Ranald MacDougall *d* William A. Graham

Susan St James, Robert Pratt, Nanette Fabray, Jim Backus, Wally Cox

The Magician*
US 1973 73m colour TVM
Paramount

A professional magician uses his trickery to outsmart kidnappers.

Polished nonsense which led to a one-season series of the same ilk (24 × 50m).

w Laurence Heath *d* Marvin Chomsky

BILL BIXBY, Kim Hunter, Barry Sullivan, Elizabeth Ashley, Signe Hasso, Joan Caulfield, Keene Curtis

Magilla Gorilla
US 1964–5 58 × 25m colour
Hanna–Barbera

A mischievous gorilla causes havoc in the pet shop.
Quite a lively cartoon series, from the firm's better days. Also included each week: a segment featuring *Ricochet Rabbit*, a western spoof.

The Magnificent Magical Magnet of Santa Mesa
US 1977 74m colour TVM
Columbia/David Gerber

A young scientist invents a magnet which can solve the world's energy crisis.
Footling slapstick farce with a few obvious laughs.

w Gerald Gardner *d* Hy Averback

Michael Burns, Susan Blanchard, Harry Morgan, Tom Poston, Keene Curtis

The Magnificent Thief*
aka: *A Thief Is a Thief Is a Thief; It Takes a Thief*
US 1967 100m colour TVM
Universal (Frank Price)

A master thief is promised parole if he becomes a US agent.
Smooth, silly pilot for a long-running series (*It Takes a Thief*).

w Roland Kibbee, Leslie Stevens *d* Leslie Stevens

Robert Wagner, Senta Berger, John Saxon, Susan St James, Malachi Throne

Magpie. British twice-weekly magazine programme for children, produced by Thames Television.

Maharis, George (1928–). Smooth American leading man who has had a fairly successful career in both films and TV. Series: *Route 66*, *The Most Deadly Game*, *Rich Man, Poor Man*.

Mahoney, Jock (1919–) (Jacques O'Mahoney). Stalwart American leading man, a former Tarzan. Series include *The Range Rider*, *Yancy Derringer*.

Maigret*. A superb series of 50m tape dramas produced by the BBC in the late fifties, with Rupert Davies as Simenon's pipe-smoking Parisian sleuth who gets results from studying character rather than clues. Producer: Andrew Osborn.

Majors, Lee (*c* 1940–). Beefcake American leading man. Series include *The Big Valley*, *The Men from Shiloh*, *Owen Marshall*, *Six Million Dollar Man*.

Make a Wish*
US 1971–5 96 × 22m colour (VTR)
ABC News and Public Affairs/Lester Cooper

Informational series for children, the instruction being applied with a gentler hand than in *Sesame Street*, but equally effectively.

w/d Lester Cooper *host and songwriter* Tom Chapin

Make Room for Daddy*
US 1953–5 and 1957–63 199 × 26m bw
ABC/T & L

A nightclub entertainer has family trouble.
Efficient long-running star comedy, later known as *The Danny Thomas Show*. It was followed in 1970 by 26 hours of *Make Room for Granddaddy*, in colour, but this was not a success.

Danny Thomas, Marjorie Lord (Jean Hagen first three seasons)

Malden, Karl (1913–) (Mladen Sekulovich). Intense American character actor who after years of second leads in Hollywood was promoted by TV to the top rank in *Streets of San Francisco*.

Malibu Run: see The Aquanauts

Mallory
aka: *Circumstantial Evidence*
US 1976 96m colour TVM
Universal (William Sackheim)

A once successful lawyer now operates under a cloud of suspicion since he was jailed (unjustly, of course) for perjury.
Failed pilot featuring the star in a curly wig, which tends to distract from an efficient story.

w Joel Oliansky *d* Boris Sagal *m* James di Pasquale

Raymond Burr, Mark Hamill, Robert Loggia

Malone, Dorothy (1930–). American leading actress who did pretty well in Hollywood, and even better in TV (as the star of *Peyton Place*) until her career suddenly seemed to peter out.

Mama. Live half-hour comedy show on CBS for eight seasons (1949–56), with Peggy Wood as the head of a Swedish–American family; based on the film *I Remember Mama*, and the book *Mama's Bank Account* by Kathryn Forbes; with Judson Laire, Dick Van Patten, Rosemary Rice.

The Man*
US 1971 100m colour TVM
Lorimar/ABC Circle

The US gets its first black president.
Solid mini-screen adaptation of a successful novel.

w Rod Serling, *novel* Irving Wallace *d* Joseph Sargent

James Earl Jones, Martin Balsam, Burgess Meredith, William Windom, Barbara Rush, Lew Ayres, Anne Seymour

A Man About the House*
GB 1973–6 39 × 25m colour (VTR)
Thames

Two girls share their flat with a man because he is an expert on cookery.
Very slightly daring farce which became much more so when translated to American TV as *Three's Company*. The dumb landlord and his wife were sufficiently popular to qualify for a series of their own, *George and Mildred*.

w JOHNNIE MORTIMER, BRIAN COOKE

RICHARD O'SULLIVAN, PAULA WILCOX, SALLY THOMSETT, YOOTHA JOYCE, BRIAN MURPHY

Man Alive. Long-running BBC series, the umbrella title covering films and discussions on the predicament of man in today's world.

The Man and the Challenge
US 1959 36 × 25m bw
United Artists (Ivan Tors)

A scientist tests problems of human survival.
Unusual semi-documentary series with the accent on space training.

George Nader

The Man and the City
US 1971 13 × 50m colour
ABC/MCA/Universal

Problems of the widowed mayor of a southwestern city.
A carefully made series, following the pilot *The City*, which despite a powerful star never got off the ground.

Anthony Quinn, Mike Farrell, Mala Powers

Man at the Top*
GB 1971–3 approx 39 × 50m colour (VTR)
Thames (Jacqueline Davis)

Further adventures of Joe Lampton, the aggressive hero of the cinema film *Room at the Top*.
Plain-spoken Monday night adult entertainment which led to yet another film, this time based on the series.

w Tom Brennand, Roy Bottomley, after John Braine

Kenneth Haigh, Zena Walker

The Man Behind the Badge
US 1954 38 × 25m bw
Buckeye

True-life police stories, hosted by Charles Bickford. Predictable formula stuff.

A Man Called Ironside: see Ironside

A Man Called Shenandoah*
US 1965 34 × 25m bw
ABC/MGM

After the Civil War, an amnesia victim seeks his true identity.
Fairly stylish, sombre western which didn't take.

Robert Horton

The Man Called X
US 1955 39 × 25m bw
UA

Hokum crime series.

Barry Sullivan

Man From Atlantis
US 1977 3 × 96m, 1 × 74m, 13 × 50m colour
NBC/Taft H–B/Herb Solow

An amnesiac with webbed hands is found washed up on the beach and because of his undersea skills is coopted by the US Navy.
A hokum idea which was initially handled with some charm and imagination, but lost its minimal style in translation to a one-hour series.

Patrick Duffy, Belinda J. Montgomery

The Man From Black Hawk
US 1959 37 × 25m bw
Columbia/Stuart–Oliver

Cases of an insurance investigator in the old west.
Standard crime series, watchable in its day.

Robert Rockwell

Man From Interpol
GB 1959 39 × 25m bw
Danzigers

Adventures of a Scotland Yard special agent.
Like an old Monogram second feature, but shorter.

Richard Wyler

The Man From UNCLE*
US 1964–7 99 × 50m colour
NBC/MGM

Adventures of Napoleon Solo, Ilya Kuryakin and Mr Waverly, leading lights of an international spy organization on the right side.
Sometimes amusing, sometimes silly imitation of James Bond with its tongue firmly planted in its cheek.

cr Norman Felton, Sam Rolfe (with 'guidance' from Ian Fleming)

Robert Vaughn, David McCallum, Leo G. Carroll
'The weekly perils of Solo and Co have been damned by most critics with the faint praise that they're good clean fun. I don't think they're much fun, and I'm certain they aren't good. I also have doubts about their cleanliness.' – Don Miller, 1965

† See also *The Girl from UNCLE*. (The letters stand for 'United Network Command for Law and Enforcement'.)

The Man Hunter
US 1969 98m colour TVM
Universal (Don Roth)

A banker hires an African white hunter to track down and kill the murderer of his son.
Watchable action/chase nonsense.

w Meyer Dolinsky, *novel* Wade Miller *d* Don Taylor

Roy Thinnes, Sandra Dee, Albert Salmi, Sorrell Booke, David Brian

Man in a Suitcase*
GB 1967 30 × 50m colour
ATV

Adventures of a bounty-hunting secret agent.
Competent espionage thick-ear.

Richard Bradford

The Man in the Iron Mask*
US/GB 1977 96m colour TVM
Norman Rosemont/ITC

The half-brother of Louis XIV is imprisoned for years in the Bastille and rescued by D'Artagnan.
Modest swashbuckler which despite effort all round can hardly compete with the 1939 film.

w William Bast *d* Mike Newell *m* Allyn Ferguson

Richard Chamberlain, Patrick McGoohan, Louis Jourdan, Jenny Agutter, Ian Holm, Ralph Richardson, Vivien Merchant, Brenda Bruce, Esmond Knight

Man of Many Faces: see Toma

A Man of Our Times*
GB 1968 13 × 50m bw (VTR)
London Weekend

Worries of a middle-aged executive, with problems at home and at work.
Excellent drama series.

George Cole

Man of the World
GB 1962 20 × 50m bw
ATV

Adventures of a roving photographer.
Very moderate, glossy actioner.

Craig Stevens

MAN IN A SUITCASE. Like all good British series which wanted to sell abroad, this one had an American hero, Richard Bradford; who hasn't been much heard from since.

Man on a String
US 1971   73m   colour   TVM
Columbia

An ex-policeman goes undercover with the mob.
So routine you don't even need to watch it.

w Ben Maddow   *d* Joseph Sargent

Christopher George, Joel Grey, William Schallert, Jack Warden

Man on the Outside: see Griff

The Man Who Could Talk to Kids
US 1973   73m   colour   TVM
Tomorrow

A frustrated child finds one adult with whom he can express himself.
Tedious taradiddle, well-meaning but dull.

w Douglas Day Stewart   *d* Donald Wrye

Peter Boyle, Robert Reed, Scott Jacoby, Collin Wilcox-Horne

The Man Who Died Twice*
US 1970   100m   colour   TVM
Cinema Center 100 (Steve Shagan)

An American artist in Spain finds it convenient to sham dead, which leads to complications.
Slightly unusual, location-shot drama which keeps the interest.

w Jackson Gillis   *d* Joseph Sargent   *ph* Gabriel Torres   *m* John Parker

Stuart Whitman, Brigitte Fossey, Jeremy Slate, Bernard Lee, Severn Darden

The Man Who Never Was
US 1966   18 × 25m   colour
ABC/TCF (John Newland)

An unpleasant German is impersonated by his double, a US agent.
Cheeky melodrama inspired less by the film of the same name than by the old Chevalier vehicle *Folies Bergère*.

cr John Newland, Teddi Sherman, Judith and Julian Plowden

Robert Lansing, Dana Wynter

Man with a Camera
US 1958   29 × 28m   bw
MCW (Lewis and Sharpe)

A freelance photographer gets involved in mysteries.
Punchy melodramas somewhat enlivened by an emerging star.

Charles Bronson

The Man with the Power
US 1977   96m   colour   TVM
Universal

A man whose father hailed from another planet has the power to perform amazing feats through eye concentration, and rescues a kidnapped princess.
Lead-footed fantasy pilot.

w Allan Balter   *d* Nick Sgarro

Bob Neill, Persis Khambatta, Tim O'Connor, Vic Morrow

The Man without a Country*

US 1973   73m   colour   TVM
Norman Rosemont

In the 18th century a young man damns his country and is sentenced never to set foot on it again.
Well-acted presentation of an American fable which in the end seems rather foolish.

w Sidney Carroll, *story* Edward Everett Hale   d Delbert Mann

Cliff Robertson, Beau Bridges, Peter Strauss, Robert Ryan, Patricia Elliott, Walter Abel

Mandrake the Magician

US 1954   × 25m   bw

Young Mandrake, who learned his secrets by ancient Tibetan tradition, crusades against evil with his servant Lothar.
Enthusiastic comic strip hokum.

Coe Norton, Woody Strode

Mandrake the Magician

US 1978   96m   colour   TVM
Universal (Rick Husky)

Mandrake operates as an undercover agent for the government.
Inept and styleless updating: miscasting plus a snail's pace produce boredom.

w Rick Husky

Anthony Herrara, Simone Griffith, Ji-Tu Cumbaka

Maneater

US 1973   74m   colour   TVM
Universal (Robert F. O'Neill)

Holidaymakers are trapped in a wild animal quarry whose mad owner releases tigers to stalk and kill them.
The Hounds of Zaroff ride again, but not very excitingly.

w Vince Edwards, Marcus Demian, Jimmy Sangster   d Vince Edwards

Richard Basehart, Ben Gazzara, Sheree North, Kip Niven

Maneaters are Loose!

US 1978   96m   colour   TVM
CBS/Mona/Finnegan (Robert D. Wood, William Finnegan)

A small town is menaced by escaped tigers.
Choppy, cliché-ridden suspenser which doesn't thrill but does irritate.

w Robert W. Lenski, *book Maneater* by Ted Willis   d Timothy Galfas   ph Hugh Gagnier   m Gerald Fried

Tom Skerritt, Steve Forrest, G. D. Spradlin, Harry Morgan, Frank Marth, Diana Muldaur

Manhunt

US 1959–60   78 × 25m   bw
Columbia (Jerry Briskin)

Stories of the San Diego Police Department.
Crime on location, quite efficient.

Victor Jory

Manhunter*

US 1974   74m   colour   TVM
Quinn Martin

In 1933, when his fiancée is killed by public enemies, an ex-marine becomes a travelling G-man dedicated to their capture.
Dour pilot with a good period feel and a hulking Superman hero; the one-season series which followed was surprisingly dull.

w Sam Rolfe   d Walter Grauman

Ken Howard, Gary Lockwood, Tim O'Connor, James Olson, Stefanie Powers

Mann, Abby (1927–). Prolific playwright of American TV's 'golden age', noted for *Judgment at Nuremberg*, *The Marcus Nelson Murders*, *King* and many others.

Mann, Delbert (1920–). American TV director who gained a huge reputation with such plays as *Marty*, *Middle of the Night* and *The Bachelor Party*. His subsequent career in Hollywood was less inspired.

Mannix*

US 1967–74   192 × 50m   colour
CBS/Paramount/Bruce Geller (Ivan Goff, Ben Roberts)

Cases of a private investigator.
Well-made, action-filled crime show.

cr Richard Levinson, William Link

Michael Connors, Gail Fisher

Mantooth, Rudolph (1945–). American leading man, half-Seminole, who leaped to stardom in *Emergency*.

Many Happy Returns

US 1964   26 × 25m   bw
CBS/MGM/Lindabob

Business and domestic trials of the complaints manager of a department store.
Engaging but unsuccessful star vehicle.

John McGiver, Elinor Donahue, Mark Goddard

MANNIX. A long-running private eye show which made Mike Connors a very rich man. Here he's seen with guest star Eddie Egan, ex-cop and the original Popeye of *The French Connection*.

The Many Loves of Arthur
US 1978 50m colour
MTM (Philip Barry)

A gentle vet and an insecure stewardess fall in love after being hurt by past romances.
Pleasant but not outstanding two-character comedy which failed to sell a series.

w Gerald DiPego *d* Bill Bixby *ph* Chuck Arnold *m* Paul Williams

Richard Masur, Silvana Gallardo, Constance McCashin, Robert Ridgely

The Many Loves of Dobie Gillis: see Dobie Gillis

The Marcus Nelson Murders*
US 1973 148m colour TVM
Universal (Abby Mann)

A New York detective tries to help a black youth wrongly arrested for the murder of two women.
Dour, unrecognizable pilot for *Kojak*: the series was much more escapist in tone than this grimly accurate exploration of New York ghettoes.

w Abby Mann, from files on record *d* Joseph Sargent

Telly Savalas, Marjoe Gortner, Gene Woodbury, Jose Ferrer, Ned Beatty

Marcus Welby MD
aka: *A Matter of Humanities*
US 1968 98m colour TVM
Universal (David Victor)

An elderly small-town doctor with heart trouble takes on a young assistant and together they help a small boy who can't speak or write.
Dullish pilot for long-running series. The star subsequently got a better haircut.

w Don M. Mankiewicz *d* David Lowell Rich

Robert Young, James Brolin, Anne Baxter, Pete Duel, Susan Strasberg, Lew Ayres

†The resulting series ran nine seasons; 172 × 50m episodes, created and produced by David Victor. Syndication title: *Robert Young Family Doctor*.

Margie
US 1961   26 × 25m   bw
TCF

Scrapes of a twenties college girl.
Mild comedy, loosely based on the movie.

Cynthia Pepper, Penny Parker

Marie Curie**
GB 1977   5 × 50m   colour (VTR)
BBC/Time–Life/Polytel (Peter Goodchild)

The life of Marie Curie, discoverer of radium.
A harsher attitude than usual, based on fresh research,
but a complete picture, impeccably produced.

w ELAINE MORGAN, *book* Robert Reid   *d* John Glenister

JANE LAPOTAIRE, Nigel Hawthorne, Penelope Lee,
William Sleigh

'An exceptional piece of work.' – *Observer*

† BAFTA award 1977, best series.

Marine Boy
US–Japan 1966   78 × 25m   colour
Seven Arts

Adventures of a young agent for Ocean Patrol, an international undersea defence organization.
Stereotyped cartoon adventures.

The Mark of Zorro
US 1974   74m   colour   TVM
TCF

Much-filmed adventure story about a Robin Hood of
old California.
Modestly competent TV version.

w Brian Taggert   d Don McDougall

Frank Langella, Ricardo Montalban, Gilbert Roland,
Louise Sorel, Yvonne de Carlo, Robert Middleton

Mark Saber. Two separate crime series of the fifties
featured this rather characterless character. In the
American version he was a police inspector played by
Tom Conway. In the British, played by Donald Gray,
he was a one-armed private eye. In both cases he was
inept, and so were his films.

Markham*
US 1959–60   60 × 25m   bw
Markham/Universal

Adventures of a globe-trotting investigator.
Fairly polished cops-and-robbers.

Ray Milland

Markham, Monte (1935–). American leading man
who appears fairly exclusively on TV but never made a
real hit. Series: *The Second Hundred Years, Mr Deeds
Goes to Town, The New Perry Mason.*

Marlowe, Hugh (1914–) (Hugh Hipple).
American second lead of the fifties. TV series: *Ellery
Queen.*

Marriage: Year One
US 1970   100m   colour   TVM
Universal/Norman Felton (Stephen Karpf)

Problems of lovers who marry while still at college.
The kind of problems most adult viewers at least can do
without.

Sally Field, Robert Pratt, William Windom, Agnes
Moorehead, Neville Brand

Marsh, Jean (1938–). British general purpose actress who scored a great personal hit, especially in the
US, as Rose the maid in *Upstairs, Downstairs.*

Marshall, E. G. (1910–) (Everett G. Marshall).
Distinguished American character actor. TV work includes *The Defenders* and *The Bold Ones* (series) and an
excellent impersonation of Truman in *Collision Course.*

Martin, Dean (1917–) (Dino Crocetti) **and
Lewis, Jerry** (1926–) (Joseph Levitch). The
American comedy team made their name on TV, in the
Colgate Comedy Hour between 1950 and 1952. Later,
as singles, Martin did better than Lewis with his long-
running series of specials.

Martin Kane, Private Eye
aka: *The New Adventures of Martin Kane*
US 1957   39 × 25m   bw
Ziv

Stories of an American private eye in London.
Fairly flatulent working over of a radio character, with
the same star.

William Gargan

Martin, Millicent (1934–). British songstress who
came to the fore in *That Was the Week that Was* and
later had her own series *From a Bird's Eye View.*

Marvin, Lee (1924–). Leading American heavy
who briefly became a somewhat improbable star. TV
series: *M Squad, Lawbreaker.*

Marx, Groucho (1890–1977) (Julius Marx).
American comedian, the leading zany of the Marx
Brothers, who in later life became a TV personality,
allegedly conducting a quiz show, but in fact mostly
insulting his guests with off-the-cuff quips. See *You Bet
Your Life.*

Mary Hartman, Mary Hartman*
US 1976   325 × 25m   colour (VTR)
Tandem/Norman Lear (Viva Knight)

Semi-spoof soap opera, its appeal a little hard to de-
termine for any but hardened daytime viewers, about a

LEE MARVIN, a small-scale cinema villain, became a star of television series like *M Squad*, then had the good fortune to go back to the big money of the big screen as a most unlikely superstar.

suburban community where the most awful things happen. Its producer sold it direct to syndicated stations, and for half a season it was a fashionable late-night attraction, but its appeal soon waned and production became uneconomic. It pointed the way for the more concentrated *Soap* which arrived the following year; its own unsuccessful sequels included *Forever Fernwood* and *Fernwood 2 Nite*.

cr Gail Parent, Ann Marcus, Jerry Adelman, Daniel Gregory Browne

Louise Lasser, Victor Kilian, Greg Mullavey, Graham Jarvis, Mary Kay Place

'We are simply taking a look at our life and times through another kind of prism. Of course, the prism may appear to have been fashioned by a drunken lens maker in a darkly wooded German forest.' – Norman Lear

Mary Jane Harper Cried Last Night
US 1977 96m colour TVM
Paramount/Christiana (Joanna Lee)

A neurotic wife takes to beating her infant daughter. Resistable case history.

w Joanna Lee *d* Allen Reisner *ph* Gayne Rescher *m* Billy Goldenburg

Susan Dey, Bernie Casey, Tricia O'Neill, John Vernon, Kevin McCarthy

'The most vicious crime in America is being committed by those who love their victims most.' – publicity

The Mary Tyler Moore Show***
US 1970–4 120 × 25m colour
CBS/Mary Tyler Moore

A bachelor girl works in the news room of a Minneapolis TV station.
Simple, efficient comedy show, filmed on two sets with three cameras, which worked by filling its heroine's two lives, at home and at work, with funny people saying funny things. It led to three direct spin-offs, *Rhoda*, *Phyllis* and *Lou Grant*.

cr/executive p JAMES L. BROOKS, ALLAN BURNS

MARY TYLER MOORE, CLORIS LEACHMAN, VALERIE HARPER, ED ASNER, TED KNIGHT, GAVIN MCLEOD, GEORGIA ENGEL, BETTY WHITE

Mary White*

US 1977 96m colour TVM
Radnitz/Mettel (Robert B. Radnitz)

Friends remember the 16-year-old daughter of William Allen White, who died in 1921 after a riding accident.
A well-engineered compound of nostalgia and emotion, not too true to the facts.

w Caryl Ledner *d* Jud Taylor *ph* Bill Butler *m* Leonard Rosenman

Ed Flanders, Fionnula Flanagan, Tim Matheson, Donald Moffatt, Diana Douglas

M*A*S*H****

US 1972– × 25m colour
CBS/TCF (GENE REYNOLDS, LARRY GELBART)

Frustrations, mainly medical and sexual, of a mobile army surgical unit in Korea.
Bitter, hilarious and occasionally tragic comedy about carrying on with a wisecrack in the most impossible conditions. Its success as a concept is greater than that of the film from which it stemmed, and the effect of that success on TV comedy is incalculable.

ALAN ALDA, MCLEAN STEVENSON, LORETTA SWIT, LARRY LINVILLE, JAMIE FARR, William Christopher, Wayne Rogers, GARY BURGHOF, (later) HARRY MORGAN

The Mask

US 1954 14 × 50m bw (live)
ABC

Cases of brother defence attorneys.
Cited as TV's first live one-hour mystery series, and who's arguing?

Gary Merrill, William Prince

The Mask of Sheba

US 1970 100m colour TVM
MGM

Experts from the Foundation of Man fly to Ethiopia to seek a previous expedition and a priceless heirloom.
Inept adventure hokum which never seems to get going.

w Sam Rolfe *d* David Lowell Rich

Eric Braeden, Stephen Young, Inger Stevens, Joseph Wiseman, Walter Pidgeon, William Marshall

Massacre at Sand Creek

US 1956 74m bw TVM
Columbia/Playhouse 90

An Indian-hating colonel leads his troops unnecessarily into battle.
Adequate mini-western.

d Arthur Hiller

Everett Sloane, John Derek, Gene Evans, H. M. Wynant

Massey, Raymond (1896–). Popular Canadian actor whose long career included two TV series, *I Spy* and *Dr Kildare*.

Mastermind. A relentlessly highbrow BBC quiz of the seventies, in which successful contestants must have more than one special subject as well as wide general knowledge. The questions are at university level and the atmosphere extremely tense. Bill Wright produces, with Magnus Magnusson as questionmaster, and the series achieves remarkably high ratings.

Matt Helm

US 1975 74m colour TVM
Columbia

An ex-CIA agent becomes a Los Angeles private eye.
Unrecognizable from the movie series starring Dean Martin, and as routine as can be.

w Sam Rolfe *d* Buzz Kulik

Tony Franciosa, James Shigeta, Patrick MacNee, Laraine Stephens

† The series ran 13 × 50m episodes. Developed by Sam Rolfe; music by Morton Stevens; producers Charles FitzSimons, Ken Pettus.

Matt Lincoln

US 1970 16 × 50m colour
NBC/MCA/Universal/Vince Edwards

A psychiatrist goes to the people who really need him: the poor.
Rather dreary drama series with a social conscience.

Vince Edwards

† See also *Dial Hot Line* (pilot).

A Matter of Humanities: see Marcus Welby MD

A Matter of Wife and Death

aka: *Shamus*
US 1975 74m colour TVM
Columbia

Adventures of another tough private eye.
Boring.

w Don Ingalls *d* Marvin Chomsky

Rod Taylor, Tom Drake, Anita Gillette, Joe Santos

Maude***

US 1972–7 140 approx. × 25m colour (VTR)
CBS/Tandem (Norman Lear, Bud Yorkin)

A middle-class woman in Tuckahoe NY can't cope as well as she thinks.
Realistic social comedy which spun itself off from *All in the Family* and proved at least an equal success. In its

later seasons it began to tackle serious subjects such as abortion and rape, always with an eye for character nuances and an ear for a funny line. The leading character became an American classic.

BEATRICE ARTHUR, BILL MACY, ADRIENNE BARBEAU, Conrad Bain, Hermione Baddeley

Maunder, Wayne (1942–). American leading man who surfaced in *Custer* and *Lancer*, then disappeared.

Maupassant**
GB 1960   13 × 50m   bw (VTR)
Granada (Philip Mackie)

Short stories by Guy de Maupassant, usually two or three to the hour with a framing link.
At the time an original television style, with high gloss and entertainment value.

cr PHILIP MACKIE   *d* Silvio Narizzano

Gwen Watford, Derek Francis, Thorley Walters

'A cracking pace and a great sense of period.' – *Guardian*

Maverick**
US 1957–61   138 × 50m   bw
ABC/Warners

One of the family of cowboy heroes Warners created at this time, Maverick was a cowardly good-looking gambler who got out of trouble by the skin of his teeth, and the scripts had more humour than the usual western action. (One show turned Sheridan's *The Rivals* into a western.) When Bret Maverick wasn't available, his brother or his cousin took over.

JAMES GARNER (Bret); Jack Kelly (Bart); Roger Moore (Beau)

† James Garner also appeared occasionally as Pappy Beauregard.

Maya
US 1967   18 × 50m   colour
NBC/MGM/King Brothers

An American boy in modern India searches for his white hunter father.
Uncompelling series from a feature film original. Nice scenery and elephants.

Jay North, Sajid Khan

Maybe I'll Come Home in the Spring
US 1970   74m   colour   TVM
Metromedia (Charles Fries)

A teenage runaway comes back home and tries to see her parents' point of view.
Well detailed domestic drama, just a wee bit over earnest.

w Bruce Feldman   *d* Russ Metty

Eleanor Parker, Jackie Cooper, Lane Bradbury, Sally Field, David Carradine

Mayberry RFD
US 1968–70   78 × 25m   colour
CBS/Paramount/RFD   (Richard O. Linke, Andy Griffith)

Doings of a small town and its councillors.
Small beer.

cr Bob Ross

Ken Berry, George Lindsay, Arlene Golonka, Paul Hartman, Jack Dodson

Mayday at 40,000 Feet
US 1976   96m   colour   TVM
Warner/Andrew J. Fenady

A convict under escort goes berserk on a transcontinental plane.
Boring, overstretched suspenser.

w Austin Ferguson, Dick Nelson, Andrew J. Fenady   *d* Robert Butler

David Janssen, Don Meredith, Christopher George, Ray Milland, Lynda Day George, Broderick Crawford, Maggie Blye, Tom Drake, Jane Powell

Maynard, Bill (*c* 1928–). Oversize British comic actor who usually plays bluff, hearty characters. Series: *Oh No It's Selwyn Froggitt, Trinity Tales*.

Mayor of the Town
US 1954   39 × 25m   bw
Rawlings–Grant, Gross–Krasne

Small-town dramas linked by the benevolent mayor.
Mildly satisfactory tales with a moral.

Thomas Mitchell

Mc: see under Mac

MCA. Music Corporation of America, a talent agency founded in the twenties by Jules Stein. It later acquired Universal Studios, Decca Records and Revue Productions, and when prodded by the government gave up the talent business entirely. It is now known chiefly as a TV distributor for Universal products.

Me and the Chimp
US 1971   13 × 25m   colour
CBS/Paramount

A family adopts a chimp.
See *The Hathaways*. Simple-minded would be a charitable way of describing the level of humour.

Ted Bessell

Meadows, Audrey (1929–) (Audrey Cotter). American comedy actress who made few appearances subsequent to her celebrated star role as Jackie Gleason's wife in *The Honeymooners*.

Meadows, Jayne (1925–) (Jane Cotter). American actress and TV personality, wife of Steve Allen, familiar in *I've Got a Secret* and *Masquerade Party*.

Medic**
US 1954–5   59 × 25m   bw
NBC

Filmed in hospitals, this docu-drama series told suspense stories about diseases to illustrate medicine's latest advances.
Clinical, well-told stories related in a manner which then touched a new note of authenticity.

Richard Boone (as narrator)

Medical Center
GB title: *Calling Doctor Gannon*
US 1969–75   170 approx. × 50m   colour
CBS/MGM/Alfra (Frank Glicksman, Al C. Ward)

Stories of a young surgeon in a university hospital.
Long-running drama series which tinged on the sensational but usually gave good value for money.

cr Frank Glicksman, Al C. Ward

Chad Everett, James Daly

†See *Operation Heartbeat* (pilot).

Medical Story**
US 1975   100m   colour   TVM
NBC/Columbia (David Gerber)

An idealistic intern has some successes but loses his most valued patient.
Sharply made, hard-hitting and realistic hospital drama, pilot for a short-lived series.

w Abby Mann,   *d* Gary Nelson

Beau Bridges, Jose Ferrer, Harriet Karr, Shirley Knight, Carl Reiner, Claude Akins

†The subsequent series consisted of 13 × 50m episodes, all of high production quality but depressing content.

Meet Corliss Archer
US 1954   39 × 25m   bw
United Artists

Scrapes of a scatty teenage girl, from the play and film *Kiss and Tell*.
Witless pre-Gidget Gidgetry.

Ann Baker, Bobby Ellis

Meet McGraw
US 1957   39 × 25m   bw
MM/Sharpe–Lewis

A private eye wages a one-man crusade against crime.
Adequate mystery series.

Frank Lovejoy

Meet Mr McNutley
US 1953   39 × 25m   bw
CBS

Problems of a drama professor at a girls' college.
Acceptable star froth.

Ray Milland, Phyllis Avery, Minerva Urecal, Gordon Jones

Meeting at Potsdam*
aka: *Truman at Potsdam*
US 1976   74m   colour (VTR)
David Susskind/PBS

A recreation of the 1945 international conference which brought World War II to an end.
Solid drama-documentary marred by an unsatisfactory imitation of Churchill.

w Sidney Carroll   *d* George Schaefer

Ed Flanders (Truman), Jose Ferrer (Stalin), John Houseman (Churchill), Alexander Knox (Stimson), Barry Morse (Byrnes)

Melvin Purvis G-Man*
GB theatrical title: *The Legend of Machine Gun Kelly*
US 1974   74m   colour   TVM
AIP/Dan Curtis

In 1933, a midwestern G-man captures Machine Gun Kelly.
Adequate gangster thriller which didn't make a series.
See also *Kansas City Massacre*.

w John Milius, William F. Nolan   *d* Dan Curtis   *ph* Jacques Marquette   *m* Richard Cobert

Dale Robertson, Margaret Blye, Harris Yulin, Dick Sargent, David Canary

The Men. Umbrella title for an American series of one-hour action thrillers: *Assignment Vienna*, *The Delphi Bureau* and *Jigsaw*.

Men at Law
aka: *Storefront Lawyers*
US 1971   10 × 50m   colour
CBS/Leonard Freeman

Young lawyers join a big old-fashioned firm.
Mixed-up series which made two format changes, then quietly died.

Gerald S. O'Loughlin, Robert Foxworth, David Arkin, Sheila Larkin

The Men from Shiloh
US 1970   24 × 74m   colour
MCA/Universal

New name given to the last season of *The Virginian* after several cast changes.

Stewart Granger, James Drury, Doug McClure, Lee Majors

Men of Anapolis
US 1957 39 × 25m bw
United Artists

Stories of the US naval academy.
Predictable uplifters and flagwavers.

Men of the Dragon**
US 1974 74m colour TVM
David Wolper (Stan Margulies)

A young American in Hong Kong combats a sinister
organization to get back his kidnapped sister.
It's well-staged action all the way in this Kung Fu
penny dreadful. Great fun.

w Denne Bart Petitclerc d Harry Falk m Elmer
Bernstein

Jared Martin, Joseph Wiseman, Katie Saylor, Robert
Ito

Men into Space
US 1959 28 × 25m bw
United Artists

The USAF prepares for space exploration.
Docu-dramas, informative but repetitive.

William Lundigan

Mercer, David (1928–). British TV playwright. *A
Suitable Case for Treatment, For Tea on Sunday, The
Parachute, Let's Murder Vivaldi, The Arcata Promise,
Huggy Bear, Shooting the Chandelier*, etc.

Merchant, Vivien (1929–) (Ada Thompson).
British character actress especially associated with the
plays of Harold Pinter, to whom she was married
during the sixties and early seventies.

Meriwether, Lee (*c* 1939–). American leading
lady, former Miss America, in series *Time Tunnel,
Batman* (as Batwoman), *Barnaby Jones*.

Mervyn, William (1912–76). Portly British character
actor who played many lords and bishops. Starred in
several TV series including *Mr Rose, All Gas and
Gaiters, Saki, The Liars*.

Message to My Daughter
US 1973 74m colour TVM
Metromedia/Gerald Isenberg

A girl learns much about herself and her stepfather
while listening to tapes recorded by her mother, now
dead.
Icky and unconvincing weepie.

w Rita Lakin d Robert Michael Lewis

Bonnie Bedelia, Martin Sheen, Kitty Wynn, Neva
Patterson

Metro–Goldwyn–Mayer. The giant Hollywood film
studio has made its share of TV series, but they have
been somewhat half-hearted when compared with its
great days of movie-making.

Metromedia. American broadcasting network which
in the seventies went into TV production (briefly) and
distribution.

Miami Undercover
US 1961 38 × 25m bw
Schenk–Koch

An investigator works with the police to keep Miami
crime-free.
Old warmed-over hokum in a glamorous setting.

Lee Bowman, Rocky Graziano

Michael Shayne
US 1960 32 × 50m bw
ABC/Four Star

Cases of Brett Halliday's happy-go-lucky detective.
Adequate mystery filler.

Richard Denning

Michell, Keith (1926–). Australian leading actor in
Britain, whose fame got a lift when he played the king
in *The Six Wives of Henry VIII*.

Michelmore, Cliff (1919–). Cheerful, avuncular
British anchorman, quizmaster and general TV personality who found his niche in the fifties with *Tonight*.
Subsequently quizmaster and host in a variety of programmes.

Mickey
US 1964 17 × 25m bw
ABC/Selmur

A family man inherits a luxury California hotel.
Not a bad comedy series, but it didn't collect ratings.

Mickey Rooney, Sammee Tong, Emmaline Henry

Mickey Mouse Club. A Walt Disney format of the
fifties, revived in the seventies, consisting largely of clips
from old Disney material plus a newly shot serial,
linked by groups of kids marching around and singing
the club's theme tune. Regular members were known as
Mouseketeers. Jimmy Dodd and Roy Williams led the
revels.

Mickey Spillane's Mike Hammer
US 1957–8 78 × 25m bw
MCA/Revue

Adventures of a tough private eye.
And they did seem tough in those days, even though
humour had been injected to sweeten the pill. Generally
an entertaining series.

Darren McGavin

Microbes and Men*
GB 1974   6 × 50m   colour (VTR)
BBC (Peter Goodchild)

Stories of the elimination of various diseases by dedicated scientists.
Like visiting the Warner biopics of the thirties all over again. Riveting stuff.

w Martin Worth, John Wiles, Bruce Norman

Arthur Lowe, Robert Lang

The Mighty Continent*
GB 1975   13 × 50m   colour (VTR)
BBC/SDR Stuttgart/Time–Life (Peter Morley)

A history of Europe in the 20th century.
Solid schoolbook extension at sixth-form level.

w John Terraine

The Mighty Hercules. An American five-minute cartoon series syndicated in 1960, based pretty loosely on the Greek legends.

Mighty Mouse. A cartoon spoof of Superman which ran in the fifties, usually in six-minute segments but sometimes built up into half-hours.

Miles, Michael (1919–71). Quizmaster in Britain, popular from 1955 in the appalling *Take Your Pick*.

Miles to Go before I Sleep*
US 1974   75m   colour   TVM
Tomorrow

A lonely elderly man fulfils himself by helping teenage delinquents.
Yes, very worthy, and well acted, but not exactly compelling.

w Judith Parker, Bill Svanoe   d Fielder Cook

Martin Balsam, Mackenzie Philips, Kitty Wynn, Elizabeth Wilson

Milland, Ray (1905–) (Reginald Truscott-Jones). Welsh-born leading man of the American cinema. He turned into a fairly considerable actor, and became a TV star in two series, *Markham* and *Meet Mr McNutley*. In his seventies he was to be found playing guest roles in several major projects such as *Rich Man, Poor Man*.

Miller, Joan (c 1910–). British TV presenter, an early (1936) host of *Picture Page*.

Miller, Mitch (1911–). American oboeist and impresario who became a household word in the fifties with his pop music show *Sing Along with Mitch*.

Milligan, Spike (1918–). Zany British comedian, an acquired taste, who pops up in all media. Series include *Idiot's Weekly, A Show Called Fred, Milligan at Large, Q5, Curry and Chips, Oh In Colour, Q6, Q7*, etc.

The Million Dollar Ripoff
US 1976   74m   colour   TVM
Charles Fries/NBC (Edward J. Montagne)

A gang plans to rob the payroll of a big city transport system.
Fair sub-Rififi caper melodrama.

w William Devane, John Pleshette   d Alexander Singer

Freddie Prinze, Allen Garfield, Brooke Mills, Joanna de Varona

The Millionaire
aka: *If You Had a Million*
US 1954–9   188 × 25m   bw
CBS (Don Fedderson)

The secretary of an eccentric multi-millionaire presents one million dollars, tax free, to a different needy person each week.
Wholly American fantasy comedy with the obvious moral that money isn't everything; based on the 1932 movie *If I Had a Million*.

Marvin Miller

Mills, Annette (1894–1955). Gentle-mannered British personality who in the fifties presented a puppet called Muffin the Mule.

Milner, Martin (1927–). American actor who aged rather quickly from callow youths to character roles. TV series: *The Trouble with Father, The Life of Riley, Route 66, Adam 12*.

Milton the Monster
US 1965–6   26 × 25m   colour
ABC/Hal Seeger

Adventures of the world's most lovable monster, who lives on Horrible Hill in Transylvania.
Adequate Saturday morning cartoon filler, also featuring a segment on *Fearless Fly*.

The Mind of J. G. Reeder
GB 1971   16 × 50m   colour (VTR)
Thames

A clerk in the office of the Director of Public Prosecutions has a nose for unravelling mysteries.
Pleasant but unmemorable re-creations of Edgar Wallace's twenties crime stories.

Hugh Burden, Willoughby Goddard

Miner, Worthington (1900–). American TV producer of the fifties: *The Goldbergs, Medic, Studio One*.

ANNETTE MILLS with MUFFIN THE MULE who seems fairly elementary as modern marionettes go; the Muppets certainly wouldn't give him house room. But he was a big attraction of live British television in the fifties.

mini-series. A term given in the mid-seventies to serializations of famous novels, which tended to appear in four to six episodes of various lengths, often scheduled on successive nights.

Minstrel Man*
US 1976   98m   colour   TVM
Tomorrow/First   Artists   (Mitchell   Brower,   Bob Lovenheim)

A dramatized account of the 19th-century minstrel shows.
Unusual, well-produced musical period piece.

w Richard and Esther Shapiro   *d* William A. Graham

Glynn Turman, Ted Ross, Stanley Clay, Saundra Sharp

Miracle on 34th Street
US 1973   100m   colour   TVM
TCF

A department store Santa Claus claims to be the real thing.
Dull TV remake of the 1947 film with too much footage and inadequate talent.

w Jeb Rosebrook   *d* Fielder Cook

Sebastian Cabot, Roddy McDowall, Jane Alexander, David Hartman, Jim Backus, Suzanne Davidson

Miss Jones and Son*
GB 1977–   × 25m   colour (VTR)
Thames

An unmarried mother looks after her child and greets life with a smiling face.
Smart comedy which caused a few raised eyebrows but won a large following.

cr Peter Waring

Paula Wilcox

The Missiles of October***
US 1974   150m   colour (VTR)
Viacom (Irv Wilson, Buzz Berger, Herb Brodkin)

President Kennedy deals with the Cuban missile crisis of 1962.
Gripping political drama which began the mid-seventies fashion for 'factions' or reconstructions with actors of real-life events.

w STANLEY R. GREENBERG   *d* ANTHONY PAGE

WILLIAM DEVANE, Martin Sheen, Howard da Silva, Ralph Bellamy, John Dehner, Andrew Duggan

The Missing Are Deadly
US 1974   74m   colour   TVM
Allen Epstein

A mischievous youth steals a rat from a laboratory and nearly starts a plague.
Obvious, uninteresting suspenser.

w Kathryn and Michael Michaelian   *d* Don MacDougall

Ed Nelson, Leonard Nimoy, Jose Ferrer, Marjorie Lord

Mission Impossible*
US 1966–72   171 × 50m   colour
CBS/Paramount/Bruce Geller (Stanley Kallis, Bruce Lansbury)

A special unit of spies and saboteurs is trained to attempt the impossible.
Clean-limbed adventure series with a good deal of silent action and teamwork, prefaced by instructions irresistibly delivered on a self-destructing record. (The phone would have been simpler and safer.)

cr BRUCE GELLER

Steven Hill, Martin Landau, Barbara Bain; later Peter Graves, Greg Morris, Leonard Nimoy, Peter Lupus, Lesley Warren, Lynda Day George

Mission Magic
US 1973   26 × 22m   colour
Filmation

Miss Tickle and her students enter fantasy land through a magic blackboard.
Bland cartoon adventures.

Mr Adams and Eve*
US 1956–7   66 × 25m   bw
CBS/Bridget

The disagreements of a couple of married movie stars. Borrowed from the cinema film *Simon and Laura*, but in itself no worse for that.
A moderately astringent comedy for its time.

Ida Lupino, Howard Duff

MISSION IMPOSSIBLE starred the dogged Peter Graves (right) as the leader of an undercover spy team with special skills. He plays here with guest stars Robert Goulet and Dewey Martin.

Mr and Mrs Bo Jo Jones*
US 1971   74m   colour   TVM
TCF (Lester Linsk)

A young couple have to get married, and do well despite parental interference.
Convincing, well-scripted domestic drama.

w William Wood, *novel* Ann Head   *d* Robert Day

Desi Arnaz Jnr, Chris Norris, Susan Strasberg, Dan Dailey, Tom Bosley, Dina Merrill, Lynn Carlin

Mr and Mrs North
US 1953–4   57 × 25m   bw
NBC/Bernard L. Schubert

A young wife constantly stumbles across murders.
Thin Man imitation, quite passable.

Barbara Britton, Richard Denning

Mr Broadway*
US 1964   13 × 50m   bw
CBS/Talent Associates

Adventures of a New York public relations man.
Sophisticated drama series with a good local flavour; but somehow it seemed to be neither fish, flesh nor good red herring.

cr Garson Kanin

Craig Stevens, Horace McMahon

Mr Deeds Goes to Town
US 1969   17 × 25m   colour
ABC/Columbia (Harry Ackerman, Bob Sweeney)

A country cousin finds himself heir to a 50-million-dollar city enterprise.
Carbon copy of the old movie without the old flair.

cr Harry Ackerman, Bernie Slade

Monte Markham, Pat Harrington

Mr District Attorney
US 1954–5   78 × 25m   bw
United Artists

Stories from a DA's case book.
Slick courtroom stuff.

David Brian

Mister Ed*
US 1960–5   143 × 25m   bw
CBS/Filmways (Al Simon)

A suburbanite has a horse which talks only to him.
Televersion of the *Francis* movies, rather restricted in setting but often quite amusing.

Alan Young, Connie Hines, Leon Ames, Florence McMichael

† Larry Keating and Edna Skinner played the neighbours in the first 78 films.

Mr Inside, Mr Outside*
US 1973   74m   colour   TVM
Metromedia/Phil D'Antoni

One of a pair of cops goes undercover to trap diamond smugglers.
Adequate location *policier*.

w Jerry Coppersmith   *d* Alex March

Hal Linden, Tony Lo Bianco, Phil Bruns, Paul Benjamin

Mr Jerico*
GB 1969   85m   colour   TVM
ITC (Julian Wintle)

Adventures of a con man.
Pleasant chase-and-caper yarn.

w Philip Levene   *d* Sidney Hayers

Patrick MacNee, Connie Stevens, Herbert Lom, Marty Allen

Mr Lucky
US 1959   34 × 25m   bw
Spartan/Sharpe–Lewis (Jack Arnold)

Adventures of the owner of a gambling ship (loosely based on a 1943 Cary Grant film).
Very moderate comedy-drama series.

supervisor Blake Edwards   *m* Henry Mancini

John Vivyan, Ross Martin

Mr Magoo. A myopic cartoon character created by UPA in the late forties and voiced by Jim Backus. The adventurous old codger who never knew whether he was talking to a cop or a phone box later appeared in everything from five-minute episodes to features and half-hour series; most notable was *The Famous Adventures of Mr Magoo*.

Mr Novak
US 1963–4   60 × 50m   bw
MGM

Experiences of a young schoolteacher.
Goodish American drama which didn't travel.

James Franciscus, Dean Jagger (later Burgess Meredith)

Mr Peepers*
US 1952–4   105 approx. × 25m   bw
NBC

Adventures of a shy but dependable science teacher.
Likeable comedies which are still fondly remembered in the US.

Wally Cox, Tony Randall, Marion Lorne, Georgiana Johnson, Pat Benoit, Ernest Truex, Norma Crane

Mr Roberts
US 1965   30 × 25m   colour
NBC/Warner

Adventures of a young naval lieutenant on board ship in wartime.
Watered-down version of the movie and stage play.

Roger Smith, George Harmon, Steve Ives, Richard X. Slattery

Mr Rogers' Neighbourhood. American public TV chat show for and about children and their attitudes to the serious matters of life and death. Fred Rogers, the host, was a Presbyterian minister. It ran from 1968 to 1974.

Mr Rose*
GB 1967–70   30 approx. × 50m   bw (VTR)
Granada (Philip Mackie)

A retired Scotland Yard inspector continues to solve murder cases.
Influential great detective format with two young legmen: a direct predecessor of *Ironside*, but with aspirations to sophistication.

cr Philip Mackie   *d* Michael Cox, David Cunliffe

William Mervyn, Donald Webster, Gillian Lewis

Mr Smith Goes to Washington
US 1963   13 × 25m   colour
ABC/Screen Gems

Adventures of an honest country politician in the Capitol.
Thin transcription of the famous movie.

Fess Parker, Sandra Warner, Red Foley

Mr T and Tina
US 1976   13 × 25m   colour
James Komack

A Japanese inventor in Chicago hires a Nebraska governess for his children.
Anna and the King played for farce: too eager to please.

cr James Komack, Stan Cutler, George Tibbles

Pat Morita, Susan Blanchard

Mr Terrific
US 1967   13 × 25m   colour
CBS

A mild scientist turns into an all-powerful giant when he swallows a certain pill.
Comedy variation on the Jekyll/Hyde formula, rather ineptly done.

Stephen Strimpell, Dick Gautier, John McGiver

Mrs G. Goes to College
US 1961   26 × 25m   bw
CBS/Four Star/JAHFA

An elderly widow becomes a college freshman.

Curious to say the least, but the stars seemed to enjoy it.

Gertrude Berg, Cedric Hardwicke

Mrs Sundance
US 1973   74m   colour   TVM
TCF

The widow of the outlaw tries to go straight and becomes a schoolmistress, then finds she isn't a widow at all.
Disappointing western considering the possibilities: it takes too long to get going.

w Christopher Knopf   *d* Marvin Chomsky

Elizabeth Montgomery, Robert Foxworth, L. Q. Jones, Lurene Tuttle, Dean Smith, Arthur Hunnicutt

Mrs Thursday. A 1966 one-hour series contrived by Ted Willis as a vehicle for favourite character actress Kathleen Harrison, who retired shortly afterwards. She played an elderly lady who comes into a fortune.

Mitchell, Cameron (1918–). (Cameron Mizell). Burly American character actor who has turned his hand to every kind of part. TV series: *The Beachcomber*, *High Chaparral*.

Mitchell, Denis (*c* 1920–). British documentarist.

Mitchell, Leslie (1905–). Veteran British commentator and compere, still going strong in the late seventies as presenter of *Those Wonderful TV Times*, a Tyne Tees nostalgia offering.

Mitchell, Thomas (1892–1962). Outstanding Irish–American character actor who in his later days tackled TV series: *Mayor of the Town*, *O. Henry Playhouse*, *Glencannon*.

Mitchell, Warren (1926–). British character actor who after years of being unnoticed shot to national fame as the bald-headed bigot Alf Garnett in *Till Death Us Do Part*, the forerunner of *All in the Family*. Since the show ended Mitchell has been too identified with the character to find success in other fields.

Mitzi and One Hundred Guys*
US 1975   50m   colour (VTR)
CBS/Green Isle (Mort Green)

A streamlined variety special, extremely well-drilled, in which by clever cut-ins the star appeared to be dancing with a 'million-dollar chorus' including Bob Hope, Bill Bixby, Andy Griffith, Ross Hunter, Dean Jones, Leonard Nimoy and William Shatner.

w Jerry Mayer   *d* Tony Charmoli

Mitzi Gaynor, Jack Albertson, Michael Landon

203

Mixed Blessings
GB 1978   × 25m   colour (VTR)
LWT (Derrick Goodwin)

A university student wants to marry a black girl and both sets of parents disapprove.
Vulgar comedy turning up every cliché in the book.

w Sid Green   *d* Derrick Goodwin

Christopher Blake, Muriel Odunton, Joan Sanderson, Sylvia Kay, George Waring, Carmen Munro

Mobile Two
US 1975   74m   colour   TVM
Universal/Jack Webb (Mike Mesehoff)

Adventures of a TV news reporter.
Tolerable pilot.

w David Moessinger, James M. Miller   *d* David Moessinger

Jackie Cooper, Julie Gregg, Jack Hogan, Edd Byrnes

†A shortlived one-hour series followed under the title *Mobile One*, with the same two stars under producer William Bowers. It ran to 13 × 50m episodes.

Moby Dick and the Mighty Mightor
US 1967   26 × 25m   colour
Hanna–Barbera

Double-header cartoon series featuring a whale who protects shipwrecked children and a meek and mild boy who changes into a crusading giant.
Uninspired Saturday morning fillers.

The Mod Squad
US 1968–72   124 × 25m   colour
ABC/Thomas/Spelling (Harve Bennett, Tony Barrett)

Reformed hippies help the Los Angeles Police Department.
Fairly slick adventures but boring people.

cr Aaron Spelling, Buddy Ruskin, Sammy Hess

Peggy Lipton, Michael Cole, Clarence Williams III, Tige Andrews

Mona McCluskey
US 1965   26 × 25m   bw
United Artists/NBC (George Burns)

A glamorous film star tries to lead a double life as an ordinary housewife.
Dud vehicle for a bright star.

Juliet Prowse

Money to Burn
US 1973   74m   colour   TVM
Universal (Harve Bennett)

A crooked couple work out a counterfeiting caper even though the husband is in prison.
Initially ingenious crime comedy which suddenly peters out.

w Gerald di Pego   *d* Robert Michael Lewis

E. G. Marshall, Mildred Natwick, Cleavon Little, Alejandro Rey, David Doyle, Charles McGraw

Mongo's Back in Town*
US 1971   73m   colour   TVM
Bob Banner

A professional killer is hired by his brother to kill a rival.
Tough, competent gangster thriller.

w Herman Miller, *novel* E. Richard Johnson   *d* Marvin Chomsky

Telly Savalas, Sally Field, Anne Francis, Martin Sheen, Joe Don Baker, Charles Cioffi, Ned Glass

Monitor. Famous BBC arts magazine which ran through the fifties and early sixties, introduced by Huw Wheldon.

The Monk
US 1969   74m   colour   TVM
Spelling–Thomas

A private eye guards an envelope, but it is stolen and his client killed.
Adequate mystery with San Francisco backgrounds.

w Tony Barrett   *d* George McCowan

George Maharis, Janet Leigh, Jack Soo, Raymond St Jacques, Jack Albertson, Carl Betz, Rick Jason

The Monkees**
US 1966–7   28 × 25m   colour
NBC/Columbia

Four musical friends have mad adventures.
Ingenious and deliberate re-creation of the Beatles in American terms, complete with Dick Lester-style tricks, zany humour and speeded-up photography. The series culminated in a way-out motion picture called *Head*.

David Jones, Peter Tork, Mickey Dolenz, Mike Nesmith

'A combination of uninhibited young talents, visual innovation and infectious music.' – promotion

Monkhouse, Bob (1928–). British comedian and host of game shows such as *The Golden Shot* and *Celebrity Squares*.

The Monroes*
US 1966   26 × 50m   colour
ABC/TCF/Qualis (Frederick Brogger)

Orphaned children in the old West struggle to hang on to their parents' homestead.
Spirited western drama with admirable scenery.

ph Monroe Askins, Jack Marta

Michael Anderson Jnr, Barbara Hershey, Keith and Kevin Schultz, Tammy Locke, James Brolin, Ben Johnson

The Montefuscos
US 1975   13 × 25m   colour (VTR)
NBC/Persky–Denoff

Three generations of an Italian–American family live in Connecticut.
Witless shouting match which soon outstayed its welcome.

cr Bill Persky, Sam Denoff

Joe Sirola, Naomi Stevens, Ron Carey

Montgomery, Belinda J. (c 1949–). American leading lady: *Man from Atlantis*, etc.

Montgomery, Elizabeth (1933–). American leading lady (daughter of Robert Montgomery) who starred for many seasons in *Bewitched*.

Montgomery, George (1916–) (George Montgomery Letz). American leading man who after a moderately successful career in films made a western TV series: *Cimarron City*.

Montgomery, Robert (1904–) (Henry Montgomery Jnr). Smooth, elegant American leading man of the thirties who before retiring from show business to politics hosted in 1950–6 a one-hour anthology series, *Robert Montgomery Presents*.

Monty Nash
US 1971   14 × 25m   colour
Four Star/Almada

Cases of a travelling State investigator.
Predictable thick-ear.

Harry Guardino

Monty Python's Flying Circus***
GB 1969–74   approx. 45 × 30m   colour (VTR)
BBC (Ian MacNaughton)

Zany variety show written and performed by an ex-Cambridge group which never shirks from incomprehensibility or bad taste, and often prefers to have the beginning of the show at the end, but frequently reaches heights of inspired lunacy. Its sketches always end abruptly or *segue* into others without reaching a curtain line.

JOHN CLEESE, GRAHAM CHAPMAN, ERIC IDLE, MICHAEL PALIN, TERRY GILLIAM, TERRY JONES

Moon of the Wolf*
US 1972   74m   colour   TVM
Filmways (Everett Chambers)

A southern town is terrorized by a werewolf.
Horror hokum which looks pretty silly in modern dress, but packs a scare or two.

w Alvin Sapinsley   d Daniel Petrie

David Janssen, Barbara Rush, Bradford Dillman, John Beradino

Moore, Dudley (1935–). British pianist and light entertainer, one of the original 'Beyond the Fringe' team; usually seen on TV with Peter Cook in *Not Only But Also*.

Moore, Garry (1915–) (Thomas Morfit). American comedian and linkman popular in the fifties, especially as host of *I've Got a Secret*.

Moore, Mary Tyler (1936–). Cute American leading lady who started her TV career in *Steve Canyon*, proceeded to be a sexy unseen voice in *Richard Diamond*, scored a big hit in *The Dick Van Dyke Show* and her own smash long-runner *The Mary Tyler Moore Show*. She subsequently preferred to withdraw her apple pie personality from the tube and become head, with her husband Grant Tinker, of MTM Productions.

Moore, Roger (1928–). British leading man who had a long TV career in *Ivanhoe*, *The Alaskans*, *Maverick*, *The Saint* and *The Persuaders* before becoming the cinema's James Bond.

Moorehead, Agnes (1906–74). Sharp-featured American character actress with long film career. TV series: *Bewitched*.

More, Kenneth (1914–). Jaunty British leading actor whose career has been largely confined to stage and movies, though he makes occasional TV appearances and starred with effect in *The Forsyte Saga*, *Father Brown* and *An Englishman's Castle*.

More O'Ferrall, George (c 1906–). British director who had some early success in TV.

Morecambe, Eric (1926–) (Eric Bartholomew). British comedian, the bespectacled half of Morecambe and Wise, top comic team of British TV in the sixties and seventies. Owes much to Laurel and Hardy and Abbott and Costello, but has his own inimitable range of expressions. See also Wise, Ernie.

Morell, André (1909–79) (André Mesritz). English character actor, a fine speaker; many appearances include Tiberius in *The Caesars*.

Moriarty, Michael (1941–). American actor whose best TV role has been as the Nazi in *Holocaust*.

Morgan, Henry or Harry (1915–) (Harry Bratsburg). Reliable American character actor who apart from innumerable movies and TV guest shots has appeared in a number of series: *Kentucky Jones*, *Dragnet*, *December Bride*, *Pete and Gladys*, *Oh Those Bells*, *The Richard Boone Show*, *The DA*, *M*A*S*H*.

Morley, Peter (c 1926–). British documentary producer. BAFTA award 1964 (with Cyril Bennett) for *This Week*.

The Morning After*
US 1974 74m colour TVM
David Wolper (Lawrence Turman, Stan Margulies)

A businessman becomes an alcoholic.
An actor's piece which doesn't really convince.

w Richard Matheson d Richard Heffron m Pete Carpenter, John Lennon

DICK VAN DYKE, Lynn Carlin, Don Porter, Jewel Blanch

Morris, Johnny (c 1916–). Cheerful, avuncular British TV personality who in his friendly, jokey style has conducted travel series and children's animal documentaries since the early fifties.

Morse, Barry (1919–). British light actor who made his main career in Canadian theatre. TV series: *The Fugitive* (as the relentless Lt Gerard), *Zoo Gang*, *The Adventurer*, *Space 1999*.

Mosel, Tad (–). American TV playwright of the fifties, one of the 'golden greats'.

Moses*
aka: *The Lawgiver*
GB/Italy 1976 6 × 50m colour
ATV/RAI (Vincenzo Labella)

The life of Moses.
Sober biblical account, filmed in Israel and rather slow; an unexpected popular success.

w Anthony Burgess, Vittorio Bonicelli d Gianfranco DeBosio

Burt Lancaster, Anthony Quayle, Ingrid Thulin, Irene Papas, Laurent Terzieff

The Most Deadly Game
US 1970 12 × 50m colour
ABC/Aaron Spelling (Joan Harrison)

A sophisticated team solves unsolvable crimes.
Polished detective story nonsense.

cr David Fine, Mort Friedkin

Ralph Bellamy, Yvette Mimieux, George Maharis

Most Wanted*
US 1976 74m colour TVM
Quinn Martin

An elite force is formed and tackles the capture of a maniac who rapes and murders nuns.
What starts as a serious police drama becomes totally conventional and eventually hilariously inept.

w Larry Heath d Walter Grauman

Robert Stack, Sheree North

† The series which followed consisted of 22 × 50m episodes.

The Mothers-in-Law*
US 1957–8 56 × 25m colour
NBC/Desi Arnaz

Two neighbouring suburban families are linked through their offsprings' marriage.
Mildly amusing domestic vehicle for two contrasting stars.

Eve Arden, Kaye Ballard, Herbert Rudley, Richard Deacon

Mount, Peggy (1916–). British comedy character actress, a gargantuan presence with a stentorian voice. Series: *The Larkins, George and the Dragon, You're Only Young Twice*.

The Mouse Factory*
US 1972 24 × 22m colour (16mm)
Walt Disney

Guest stars 'signing on' at the Disney studio theme-link such items as cars, houses and ghosts with footage from old Disney movies.
An ingenious bringing together of some classic scenes; only the commentary is resistible.

Mousey*
GB theatrical title: *Cat and Mouse*
GB 1973 74m colour TVM
RSO (Beryl Vertue, Aida Young)

An unhinged schoolteacher taunts his ex-wife with murder threats.
Unusual psychological thriller.

w John Peacock d Daniel Petrie ph Jack Hildyard m Ron Grainer

Kirk Douglas, Jean Seberg, John Vernon, Sam Wanamaker, James Bradford, Bessie Love

The Movie Maker**
US 1967 91m colour TVM
Universal (Harry Tatelman)

The last of the old-time movie tycoons finds his life and his career falling apart.
Sympathetic portrait of a Louis B. Mayer or Darryl F. Zanuck type.

w Rod Serling, Steven Bochco d Josef Leytes

ROD STEIGER, Robert Culp, James Dunn, Sally Kellerman, Anna Lee

The Movie Murderer*
US 1970 99m colour TVM
Universal (Jack Laird)

An insurance investigator traps an arsonist who tries to destroy the negative of a movie in which he was filmed.
Lively suspense thriller with good performances.

w Stanford Whitmore d Boris Sagal

Arthur Kennedy, Tom Selleck, Warren Oates, Jeff Corey, Nita Talbot, Robert Webber, Severn Darden

Movie of the Week. Name given by the American ABC network in 1969–74 to its weekly slot for newly produced TV movies. *Movie of the Weekend* followed. Both slots took 74m films.

The Movies Go to War: see Life Goes to War

Movin' On*
US 1974–5   48 × 50m   colour
NBC/D'Antoni–Weltz (Joe Gantman)

Adventures of two gypsy truckers, following on from the TV movie *In Tandem*.
A comfortable, friendly series sometimes let down by silly stories but benefiting from two likeable stars.

m Don Ellis

Claude Akins, Frank Converse

Mower, Patrick (1940–). British general purpose actor, almost entirely on TV: *Haunted, Callan, Special Branch, Target.*

Moxey, John Llewellyn (1930–). British film director who went to Hollywood and turned out innumerable TV movies of no especial merit.

Muggeridge, Malcolm (1904–). British TV personality, philosopher and pontificator, former editor of *Punch*; a familiar figure in the sixties and seventies.

Muir, Frank (1919–). British humorist and TV personality, originally a radio comedy writer with Denis Norden. Pops up in panel games like *Call My Bluff* and gives a touch of easy-going old-English wit; delights in puns.

Muldaur, Diana (1943–). Gracious American leading lady, a frequent guest star. Series: *Hec Ramsey, McCloud, Born Free.*

Mullen, Barbara (1914–79). Irish character actress who after a solid film career made a big hit as Janet, the all-knowing housekeeper in *Dr Finlay's Casebook.*

Mulligan Stew
US 1977   74m   colour   TVM
Paramount/Christiana (Joanna Lee)

The parents of five children adopt four orphans. Relentlessly cute family comedy after the style of *Yours Mine and Ours* and *Room for One More.*

w Joanna Lee   *d* Noel Black

Elinor Donahue, Lawrence Pressman, Johnny Whitaker, Alex Karras

† A series of 13 × 50m episodes followed.

Munster Go Home*
US 1966   96m   colour   TVM
Universal (Joe Connelly, Bob Mosher)

The family of monsters who want to be just the same as anyone else inherit a British manor house.

MOVIN' ON. Two freelance truck drivers were the all-American heroes in this likeable drama series with its catchy theme tune – and Claude Akins and Frank Converse became nationally known.

Not a pilot, as it came *after* the popular comedy show: the funny folk are a little less amusing in colour.

w George Tibbles, Joe Connelly, Bob Masher   *d* Earl Bellamy

Fred Gwynne, Yvonne de Carlo, Al Lewis, Butch Patrick, Debbie Watson, Hermione Gingold, Terry Thomas

The Munsters**
US 1964–5   70 × 25m   bw
CBS/MCA/Universal (Joe Connelly)

A suburban family consists of the Frankenstein monster, a couple of vampires and a wolf-boy. They think other people are odd.
Slightly cruder than *The Addams Family*, which came out the same season, this amiable horror spoof got by on winning characterizations and a catchy music theme. In a comical way it also had a message.

cr Joe Connelly, Bob Mosher

FRED GWYNNE, Yvonne de Carlo, Al Lewis

The Muppet Show****
GB 1976–   × 25m   colour (VTR)
ATV/Henson Associates (Jim Henson, Jon Stone)

Puppets put on a weekly variety show.
The puppets vary from glove puppets to men dressed up, and have an agreeable madness in their design. The format comes from *Hellzapoppin*, the jokes and the songs are old and good, and characters such as Kermit the Frog, Fozzie Bear and aged hecklers Statler and Waldorf are already part of TV history. The Muppets graduated from *Sesame Street* through *The Julie Andrews Hour* to become stars in their own right. A human guest star appears each week to be sabotaged.

cr Frank Oz, Jim Henson

'The Muppets make you smile even when the scriptwriters don't . . . Jim Henson and his puppeteers invest their little characters with love, which is the same as making them live.' – Robert MacKenzie, *TV Guide*

Murder at the Mardi Gras
US 1977   96m   colour   TVM
Paramount/Jozak/Richard Nader

A Philadelphia cashier wins a ticket to New Orleans and finds her life in danger.
Glum, overstretched whodunnit without even the usual roster of guest stars.

w Stanley Ralph Ross   *d* Ken Annakin   *ph* Roland Smith   *m* Peter Matz

Barbi Benton, Didi Conn, Bill Daily, David Groh, Gregg Henry, Harry Morgan, Joyce Van Patten, David Wayne, Ron Silver, LaVerne Hooker

'Anyone expecting a taut, slick mystery telefilm better not look.' – *Daily Variety*

Murder at the World Series
US 1977   96m   colour   TVM
ABC Circle (Cy Chermak)

Various people are drawn into a kidnapping plot during a football game.
Dreary multi-star time-filler.

w Cy Chermak   *d* Andrew V. McLaglen   *m* John Cacavas

Janet Leigh, Lynda Day George, Karen Valentine, Murray Hamilton, Gerald S. O'Loughlin, Michael Parks, Hugh O'Brian, Nancy Kelly, Joseph Wiseman, Bruce Boxleitner

'Out for revenge he stalks his victims . . . in a stadium packed with 45,000 screaming fans.' – publicity

Murder in Peyton Place
US 1977   96m   colour   TVM
TCF/Peter Katz

A recap of events in America's most famous small town, and new trouble in which two of its most celebrated characters are done in.
Curious up-date of the successful soap opera of the sixties, not too badly done.

w Richard DeRoy   *d* Robert Hartford-Davis, Bruce Kessler   *ph* Gert Andersen   *m* Laurence Rosenthal (theme by Franz Waxman)

Dorothy Malone, Ed Nelson, Tim O'Connor, Christopher Connelly, Joyce Jillson, David Hedison, Stella Stevens, James Booth, Kaz Garas

Murder on Flight 502*
US 1975   100m   colour   TVM
Spelling–Goldberg (David Chasman)

Murder on a jet airliner: will the killer strike again?
Watchable old-fashioned suspenser.

w David P. Harmon   *d* George McCowan

Ralph Bellamy, Polly Bergen, Theodore Bikel, Sonny Bono, Dane Clark, Laraine Day, Fernando Lamas, George Maharis, Hugh O'Brian, Molly Picon, Walter Pidgeon, Robert Stack

Murder Once Removed*
US 1971   74m   colour   TVM
Metromedia (Bob Markell)

A doctor finds his wife is unfaithful and plans the 'perfect' murder.
Carefully plotted, very watchable will-he-get-away-with-it suspenser.

w Irving Gaynor Neiman   *d* Charles Dulsin

John Forsythe, Richard Kiley, Barbara Bain, Joseph Campanella, Wendell Corey

Murder One: see The DA: Murder One

Murder by Natural Causes*
US 1978   96m   colour   TVM

True Life
An adulterous wife tries to kill her husband. Lively homicidal suspenser.

w Richard Levinson, William Link   d Robert Day

Hal Holbrook, Katherine Ross, Barry Bostwick

Murder or Mercy?
US 1974   74m   colour   TVM
Quinn Martin

An attorney emerges from retirement to defend a man who killed his terminally ill wife.
Good acting in a human drama which isn't especially dramatic.

w Douglas Day Stewart   d Harvey Hart

Melvyn Douglas, Bradford Dillman, Denver Pyle, Mildred Dunnock, David Birney, Don Porter, Robert Webber, Kent Smith

Murdock's Gang
US 1973   84m   colour   TVM
Don Fedderson

After serving a prison term, a flamboyant attorney becomes a private eye with a staff of ex-cons.
Unpersuasive time-passer.

w Edmund H. North   d Charles Dubin

Alex Dreier, Janet Leigh, Murray Hamilton, William Daniels, Harold Gould, Don Knight

Murphy, Brian (1933–). British character actor who played the landlord in *A Man About the House* and went on to star as the same obtuse character in *George and Mildred*.

Murray, Arthur (1895–) (Arthur Murray Teichman). American dancing instructor ('Arthur Murray taught me dancing in a hurry') who in the fifties hosted, with his wife, TV's *Arthur Murray Dance Party*.

Murray, Ken (1903–) (Don Court). American comedian, an inveterate Hollywood party-goer whose home movies have bolstered up many a TV show.

Murrow, Ed (1908–65). American current affairs reporter, never separated from his cigarette, noted for hard-hitting current affairs shows like *See It Now* (which started the downfall of Senator McCarthy) and personality link-ups like *Small World* and *Person to Person*. Famous too were his broadcasts from London during the Blitz, and he by-lined many controversial documentaries including *Harvest of Shame*.

Musante, Tony (1941–). American leading actor often cast as a hoodlum but with an interesting range. Series: *Toma*.

Music by Jerome Kern*
GB 1977   60m   colour (VTR)
BBC/ABC Australia/CBC Canada (Kenneth Corden)

A slickly produced recap of the songs of Jerome Kern, styled on the lines of *Side by Side by Sondheim* but set in a TV studio with some dexterous camera movement.

w Arthur Schwartz, Benny Green   *choreo* Gillian Gregory   d Ron Isted   *musical arrangements* Dennis Wilson

ARTHUR SCHWARTZ, David Kernan, Elizabeth Seal, Julia McKenzie, Teddy Green

My Father's House*
US 1975   96m   colour   TVM
Filmways

A high pressure executive has a heart attack and recalls family life with his father who suffered a similar fate.
Watchable but somewhat padded and elementary personal drama.

w David Sontag, David Seltzer, *novel* Philip Kunhardt Jnr   d Alex Segal

Robert Preston, Cliff Robertson, Rosemary Forsyth, Eileen Brennan

My Favorite Husband
US 1953–4   approx 78 × 25m   bw
CBS

A young banker has a scatterbrained wife.
Stereotyped domestic comedy.

Joan Caulfield/Vanessa Brown, Barry Nelson, Bob Sweeney, Alexandra Talton

My Favorite Martian
US 1963–5   107 × 25m   bw (32 colour)
CBS/Jack Chertok

A stranded Martian adopts a young newspaperman as his nephew and nobody else can see him.
Moderately amusing adaptation of the *Mister Ed* format.

Ray Walston, Bill Bixby, Pamela Britton

† A half-hour cartoon version was subsequently made by Filmation under the title *My Favorite Martians*.

My Friend Flicka
US 1956   39 × 25m   colour
CBS/TCF

The small son of a Midwestern family loves his horse.
Archetypal family show from the film and book by Mary O'Hara. Technical accomplishment modest, popularity wide.

Johnny Washbrook, Gene Evans, Anita Louise

My Friend Irma
US 1952–3   70 approx. × 25m   bw
CBS

Two New York secretaries share an apartment, and one is beautiful but dumb.
Inept comedy, mainly remembered because the film version introduced Martin and Lewis to the big screen.

Marie Wilson, Cathy Lewis/Mary Shipp, Sid Tomack, Hal March, Sig Arno, Donald MacBride

My Friend Tony
US 1968 16 × 50m colour
NBC/Sheldon Leonard

A criminology professor is helped by a young Italian swinger.
Forgettable mystery series: the elements didn't jell.

James Whitmore, Enzo Cerusico

My Hero
aka: *The Robert Cummings Show*
US 1952 33 × 25m bw
NBC/Sharpe–Lewis

Domestic problems of a happy-go-lucky real estate agent.
Mild comedy which started the TV bigtime for its star.

Robert Cummings, John Litel, Julie Bishop

My Little Margie
US 1952–4 126 × 25m bw
CBS/Hal Roach Jnr/Roland Reed

A slightly hare-brained 21-year-old hinders rather than helps her widowed father.
Family relationships through rose-tinted spectacles. Credited as the first series to be 'stripped', i.e. played five days a week at the same time.

Charles Farrell, Gale Storm

My Living Doll
US 1964 26 × 25m bw
CBS/Jack Chertok

A psychiatrist gets custody of a glamorous female robot.
Daffy comedy with some laughs, but too restricted to be a long-runner.

Robert Cummings, Julie Newmar, Doris Dowling, Jack Mullaney

My Mother the Car
US 1965 30 × 25m colour
NBC/United Artists/Cottage Industries/NBC

A suburbanite buys an old car which turns out to be the reincarnation of his dead mother, who continues to domineer him.
Thought at the time to mark the outer limits of TV idiocy, this comedy has long been surpassed and now seems merely inept.

Jerry Van Dyke, the voice of Ann Sothern

My Partner the Ghost: see Randall and Hopkirk (Deceased)

My Sister Eileen*
US 1960 26 × 25m bw
CBS/Columbia/Harry Ackerman (Dick Wesson)

Two Midwestern sisters arrive in New York and set up housekeeping in a basement flat in Greenwich Village. Friendly, zany comedy with agreeably mixed characters and a definite plus in its star.

ELAINE STRITCH, Shirley Bonne, Leon Belasco

My Son Reuben
GB 1974 13 × 25m colour (VTR)
Thames

The love/hate relationship of an overprotective Jewish mother and her errant son who runs a dry cleanery.
Modest, obvious comedy.

w Vince Powell

Bernard Spear, Lila Kaye

My Sweet Charlie*
US 1970 96m colour TVM
Universal (Bob Banner)

In a deserted beach house a young girl and a black man hide out from society for different reasons.
Well made but slow and pretentious character drama.

w Richard Levinson, William Link, *novel* David Westheimer *d* Lamont Johnson

Patty Duke, Al Freeman Jnr, Ford Rainey

My Three Sons*
US 1960–71 369 × 25m bw
ABC/Don Fedderson (Edmund Hartmann)

A widower watches his children grow up.
Simple, effective domestic comedy which dragged on rather longer than anyone intended.

cr Peter Tewksbury

Fred MacMurray, William Frawley (later William Demarest), Beverly Garland, Stanley Livingston, Tim Considine

My World and Welcome to It**
US 1969 26 × 25m colour
NBC/Sheldon Leonard (Danny Arnold)

A cartoonist sees his home life in terms of his drawings.
Ingenious and friendly domestic comedy drawn from James Thurber material, with interpolated cartoons an added plus. It was, of course, too good for the public.

cr Mel Shavelson

William Windom, Joan Hotchkis, Liza Gerritsen, Harold J. Stone

'Deserves an A for effort.' – Jack Edmund Nolan

Mystery Is My Business: see Ellery Queen (1954)

Mystery Movie. In 1971 Universal began making films for this NBC slot which required either 74 or 97 minutes. Most of the films were too long at either length for their plots, and few were genuine mysteries, but some of the detective characters became household words. They included the shabby police detective COLUMBO, who usually got his man by annoying him; MCCLOUD, a policeman who treated New York City like the open west where he came from; MCMILLAN AND WIFE, a Thin Man-like pair who banteringly saved San Francisco from violent crime. These heroes were played respectively by Peter Falk, Dennis Weaver, Rock Hudson and Susan St James. Less successful, and shorter-lived, were the New York cop MADIGAN (Richard Widmark); the private eyes FARADAY AND COMPANY (Dan Dailey, James Naughton); the elderly thriller writers THE SNOOP SISTERS (Helen Hayes, Mildred Natwick); the western detective HEC RAMSAY (Richard Boone); the black detective TENAFLY (James McEachin); the con man MCCOY (Tony Curtis); the man-for-millionaire-hire in COOL MILLION (James Farentino). A moderate success was the expensive loot finder BANACEK (George Peppard).

The films were as follows (74m unless otherwise stated). The series ended with the 1977 season.

Columbo (see *Prescription Murder*)

RANSOM FOR A DEAD MAN
MURDER BY THE BOOK
DEAD WEIGHT
SHORT FUSE
BLUEPRINT FOR MURDER
SUITABLE FOR FRAMING
LADY IN WAITING
DEATH LENDS A HAND
DAGGER OF THE MIND (96m)
DOUBLE SHOCK
ETUDE IN BLACK (97m)
THE GREENHOUSE JUNGLE
THE MOST CRUCIAL GAME
THE MOST DANGEROUS MATCH
REQUIEM FOR A FALLING STAR
A STITCH IN CRIME
ANY OLD PORT IN A STORM (96m)
CANDIDATE FOR A CRIME (96m)
DOUBLE EXPOSURE
LOVELY BUT LETHAL
MIND OVER MAYHEM
PUBLISH OR PERISH
SWAN SONG (97m)
A FRIEND IN NEED (97m)
AN EXERCISE IN FATALITY (97m)
NEGATIVE REACTION (96m)
BY DAWN'S EARLY LIGHT (96m)
PLAYBACK
A DEADLY STATE OF MIND
TROUBLED WATERS (97m)
FORGOTTEN LADY (97m)
A MATTER OF HONOUR
A CASE OF IMMUNITY
IDENTITY CRISIS (98m)
LAST SALUTE TO THE COMMODORE
NOW YOU SEE HIM (89m)

McMillan and Wife (see *Once Upon a Dead Man*)

EASY SUNDAY MURDER CASE
MURDER BY THE BARREL
HUSBANDS, WIVES AND KILLERS
THE FACE OF MURDER
DEATH IS A SEVEN-POINT FAVOURITE
TILL DEATH US DO PART
AN ELEMENTARY CASE OF MURDER
BLUES FOR SALLY M
COP OF THE YEAR
THE FINE ART OF STAYING ALIVE
NIGHT OF THE WIZARD
NO HEARTS, NO FLOWERS
TERROR TIMES TWO
TWO DOLLARS ON TROUBLE TO WIN
CROSS AND DOUBLE CROSS (96m)
DEATH OF A MONSTER, BIRTH OF A LEGEND
THE DEVIL YOU SAY
FREE FALL TO TERROR
THE MAN WITHOUT A FACE (96m)
REUNION IN TERROR
DOWNSHIFT TO DANGER (97m)
GAME OF SURVIVAL (97m)
BURIED ALIVE (97m)
GUILT BY ASSOCIATION (98m)
NIGHT TRAIN TO L.A. (97m)
LOVE, HONOUR AND SWINDLE (96m)
DEADLY INHERITANCE (97m)
REQUIEM FOR A BRIDE (97m)
AFTERSHOCK (97m)
SECRETS FOR SALE (97m)
GREED (97m)
POINT OF LAW (97m)
THE DEADLY CURE (98m)

McCloud (see *Who Killed Miss USA?*)

ENCOUNTER WITH ARIES
FIFTH MAN IN A STRING QUARTET
SOMEBODY'S OUT TO GET JENNIE
TOP OF THE WORLD, MA
DISPOSAL MAN
A LITTLE PLOT AT TRANQUIL VALLEY
THE BAREFOOT STEWARDESS CAPER (96m)
THE MILLION DOLLAR ROUND-UP (96m)
THE NEW MEXICAN CONNECTION
THE PARK AVENUE RUSTLERS
SHOWDOWN AT THE END OF THE WORLD
BUTCH CASSIDY RIDES AGAIN (96m)
THE COLORADO CATTLE CAPER
THE SOLID GOLD SWINGERS (98m)
COWBOY IN PARADISE (97m)
THIS MUST BE THE ALAMO (96m)
THE 42ND STREET CAVALRY (96m)
THE GANG THAT STOLE MANHATTAN (96m)
THE CONCRETE JUNGLE CAPER (96m)
THE BAREFOOT GIRLS OF BLEECKER STREET (99m)
SHIVAREE ON DELANCY STREET (98m)
THE LADY ON THE RUN (97m)
RETURN TO THE ALAMO
SHARKS (98m)
PARK AVENUE PIRATES (97m)
THREE GUNS FOR NEW YORK (98m)
SHOWDOWN AT TIMES SQUARE (97m)
FIRE! (99m)

OUR MAN IN THE HAREM (98m)
THE DAY NEW YORK TURNED BLUE (98m)
NIGHT OF THE SHARK (98m)

Madigan (see *Brock's Last Case*)
THE MANHATTAN BEAT
THE MIDTOWN BEAT
THE LISBON BEAT
THE LONDON BEAT
THE NAPLES BEAT
THE PARK AVENUE BEAT

Banacek (see *Detour to Nowhere*)
THE GREATEST COLLECTION OF THEM ALL
LET'S HEAR IT FOR A LIVING LEGEND
A MILLION THE HARD WAY
NO SIGN OF THE CROSS
PROJECT PHOENIX
TO STEAL A KING
THE TWO MILLION CLAMS OF CAP'N JACK
TEN THOUSAND DOLLARS A PAGE
A HORSE OF A SLIGHTLY DIFFERENT COLOR
IF MAX IS SO SMART, WHY DOESN'T HE TELL US WHERE HE IS?
ROCKET TO OBLIVION
FLY ME — IF YOU CAN FIND ME
NO STONE UNTURNED
NOW YOU SEE IT, NOW YOU DON'T
THE THREE MILLION DOLLAR PIRACY
THE VANISHING CHALICE

Hec Ramsey (see *The Century Turns*)
THE MYSTERY OF CHALK HILL (96m)
THE MYSTERY OF THE YELLOW ROSE (96m)
THE GREEN FEATHER MYSTERY
HANGMAN'S WAGES
DEAD HEAT (95m)
THE DETROIT CONNECTION
A HARD ROAD TO VENGEANCE (98m)
SCAR TISSUE (97m)
ONLY BIRDS AND FOOLS (96m)

Cool Million (see *Cool Million*)
THE ABDUCTION OF BAYARD BARNES
ASSAULT ON GAVALONI

HUNT FOR A LONELY GIRL
MILLION DOLLAR MISUNDERSTANDING

Faraday and Company (see *Say Hello to a Dead Man*)

FIRE AND ICE
A MATTER OF MAGIC
A WHEELBARROW FULL OF TROUBLE

The Snoop Sisters (see *The Snoop Sisters* aka: *The Female Instinct*)

CORPSE AND ROBBERS
A BLACK DAY FOR BLUEBEARD
FEAR IS A FREE THROW
THE DEVIL MADE ME DO IT

McCoy (see *The Big Rip-Off*)

BLESS THE BIG FISH
DOUBLE TAKE (96m)
IN AGAIN OUT AGAIN (98m)
NEW DOLLAR DAY

Amy Prentiss

THE DESPERATE WORLD OF JANE DOE (96m)
PROFILE IN EVIL
BAPTISM OF FIRE (99m)

Tenafly (see *Tenafly*)

THE CASH AND CARRY CAPER
JOYRIDE TO NOWHERE
MAN RUNNING
THE WINDOW THAT WASN'T

See also: Quincy

The Mystery of Loch Ness**
GB 1976 50m colour (16mm)
BBC (Peter Dale, Hugh Burnett)

An open-minded account of the evidence for and against a monster in Loch Ness.
Excellent documentary with clear statements.

w/commentator Hugh Burnett

N

Nabors, Jim (c 1932–). Moonfaced American comic actor, former opera singer; a hit as the foolish Gomer Pyle in *The Andy Griffith Show*, later on his own in *Gomer Pyle USMC*.

Nader, George (1921–). American leading man who after a modest success in the fifties disappeared from view, but not before making TV series: *Ellery Queen, Shannon, The Man and the Challenge*.

Naked City***
US 1958–62   39 × 25m, 99 × 50m   bw
ABC/Columbia/Herbert B. Leonard

Cases of an old and a young cop on the New York force.
First-rate location-shot crime-in-the-streets series with strong stories, excellent guest stars, and a tendency to crazy titles. A milestone in TV production.

cr Stirling Silliphant

25m: John McIntire, James Franciscus
50m: Horace MacMahon, Paul Burke, Nancy Malone, Harry Bellaver

The Naked Civil Servant***
GB 1975   80m   colour (16mm)
Thames

The life of acknowledged homosexual Quentin Crisp. Brilliant documentary drama using captions and other Brechtian alienation effects. It created a new career for its elderly hero, who became a TV celebrity, and it won many awards.

w PHILIP MACKIE   *d* JACK GOLD

JOHN HURT

Nakia
US 1974   15 × 50m   colour
ABC/Columbia/David Gerber (Charles Larson)

An Indian becomes deputy sheriff of a New Mexico town.
Self-consciously socially conscious modern western which didn't take. Filmed near Albuquerque.

Robert Forster, Arthur Kennedy, Gloria de Haven, Taylor Lacher

The Name of the Game. This series of 74-minute movies which sprang from *Fame Is the Name of the Game* (qv) ran three seasons (1968–70). The films were watchable but almost always over-padded, better on the crime themes than the social concern. Gene Barry played the managing editor of *Fame* magazine, with Robert Stack looking after crime and Tony Franciosa current affairs; they usually appeared on a rotating basis. Susan St James was Barry's secretary. Executive producer: Richard Irving; producers: George Eckstein (Stack), Dean Hargrove (Barry), Gene L. Coon (Franciosa). For NBC.
The titles were as follows:
ORDEAL (RS, Farley Granger, Martha Hyer, Jessica Walter)
WITNESS (GB, RS, Victor Jory, Joan Hackett)
THE BOBBY CURRIER STORY (RS, Brandon de Wilde, Julie Harris)
THE FEAR OF HIGH PLACES (GB, TF, Zsa Zsa Gabor, Jeanne Crain, John Payne)
THE TAKER (GB, TF, Bradford Dillman, Laraine Day, Estelle Winwood)
THE INQUIRY (RS, Barry Sullivan, Jack Kelly, Gia Scala)
SHINE ON, SHINE ON, JESSE GIL (TF, Darren McGavin, Juliet Prowse)
NIGHTMARE (RS, Martin Balsam, Troy Donahue)
THE WHITE BIRCH (GB, Boris Karloff, Lilia Skala, Roddy McDowall)
AN AGENT FOR THE PLAINTIFF (GB, Honor Blackman, Maurice Evans)
THE PROTECTOR (GB, Robert Young, Anne Baxter, Ralph Meeker)
HIGH ON A RAINBOW (RS, June Allyson, Broderick Crawford, Van Johnson)
LOLA IN LIPSTICK (GB, Ed Begley, Dana Wynter, William Windom)
INCIDENT IN BERLIN (GB, Kevin McCarthy, Dane Clark, Geraldine Brooks)
THE SUNTAN MOB (RS, Suzanne Pleshette, Wilfrid Hyde White)
COLLECTORS' EDITION (TF, John Saxon, Senta Berger, Nina Foch, Paul Lukas)
THE REVOLUTIONARY (GB, Harry Guardino, Simon Oakland)
THE THIRD CHOICE (GB, Shirley Jones, Ossie Davis)
SWINGERS ONLY (RS, Robert Lansing, Ann Blyth, Jack Klugman)
LOVE-IN AT GROUND ZERO (GB, Keenan Wynn, Tisha Sterling)
PINEAPPLE ROSE (GB, Mel Tormé, Susan Strasberg)
THE BLACK ANSWER (TF, Abby Lincoln, Ivan Dixon)
THE INCOMPARABLE CONNIE WALKER (TF, GB, Ivan Dixon, Dina Merrill)
A WRATH OF ANGELS (RS, Ricardo Montalban, Edward Andrews)
KEEP THE DOCTOR AWAY (TF, Robert Goulet, Vera Miles)

THE NAKED CIVIL SERVANT was a bombshell for all kinds of reasons. Here the real Quentin Crisp (left) teaches John Hurt how to play him . . .

... and here is Hurt as he looked on the screen.

BREAKOUT TO A FAST BUCK (RS, Barry Nelson, Arthur O'Connell)

GIVE TILL IT HURTS (RS, Diane Baker, Dennis Weaver)

THE GARDEN (RS, Richard Kiley, Anne Francis, Brenda Scott)

CHAINS OF COMMAND (RS, Sidney Blackmer, Dorothy Lamour, Pernell Roberts)

THE CIVILIZED MEN (RS, Jack Kelly, Rod Cameron, Jill St John)

THE EMISSARY (GB, Craig Stevens, Charles Boyer)

THE TAKEOVER (GB, Anne Baxter, David Sheiner, Michael Ansara)

BRASS RING (RS, Celeste Holm, Van Johnson)

MAN OF THE PEOPLE (GB, Fernando Lamas, Vera Miles, Robert Alda)

A HARD CASE OF THE BLUES (RS, Keenan Wynn, Sal Mineo, Russ Tamblyn)

THE POWER (RS, William Conrad, Broderick Crawford, Gene Raymond)

THE SKIN GAME (RS, Rossano Brazzi, Suzanne Pleshette)

GOODBYE HARRY (GB, Darren McGavin, Dane Clark)

LADY ON THE ROCKS (GB, Janice Rule, Nigel Davenport, James R. Justice)

THE TRADITION (GB, Ina Balin, Nico Minardos)

THE PRISONER WITHIN (TF, Steve Forrest, Ron Hayes)

HIGH CARD (GB, John Colicos, Gene Raymond, Barry Sullivan)

THE PERFECT IMAGE (GB, Ida Lupino, Hal Holbrook, Clu Gulager)

BLIND MAN'S BLUFF (TF, Broderick Crawford, Jack Klugman)

ISLAND OF GOLD AND PRECIOUS STONES (TF, Lee Meriwether, Henry Jones)

LAURIE MARIE (TF, Mark Richman, Antoinette Bower)

THE OTHER KIND OF A SPY (TF, Ed Begley, Leslie Nielsen, Joseph Campanella)

THE KING OF DENMARK (TF, Joseph Cotten, Margaret Leighton, Noel Harrison)

ECHO OF A NIGHTMARE (RS, Ricardo Montalban, Arthur Hill)

ONE OF THE GIRLS IN RESEARCH (GB, Brenda Vaccaro, Will Geer)

TAROT (GB, William Shatner, Luther Adler, Jose Ferrer)

JENNY WILDE IS DROWNING (TF, Pamela Franklin, Frank Gorshin)

AQUARIUS DESCENDING (GB, William Smithers, Arthur Hill, Hermione Gingold)

THE TIME IS NOW (GB, Jack Klugman, Yaphet Kotto, Roscoe Lee Browne)

A LOVE TO REMEMBER (GB, Lee Grant, Ray Milland, J. D. Cannon)

THE WAR MERCHANTS (RS, Robert Wagner, Scott Brady)

THE BROKEN PUZZLE (GB, Chuck Connors, Pat Crowley, Alex Dreier)

BATTLE AT GANNON'S BRIDGE (RS, Darren McGavin, Jan Murray, Joan Blondell)

WHY I BLEW UP DAKOTA (RS, Jose Ferrer, Carolyn Jones, Clu Gulager)

THE GLORY SHOUTER (RS, William Shatner, Dina Merrill, Howard Duff)

SO LONG, BABY, AND AMEN (RS, Julie Harris, James Gregory)

ALL THE OLD FAMILIAR FACES (GB, Burgess Meredith, Michael Constantine)

THE SAVAGE EYE (RS, Pete Duel, Jim Hutton, Marianne Hill)

CYNTHIA IS ALIVE AND LIVING IN AVALON (GB, Robert Culp, Mickey Rooney, Barbara Feldon)

LITTLE BEAR DIED RUNNING (Robert Culp, Steve Forrest)

THE ENEMY BEFORE US (TF, Orson Welles, Martin Balsam, Katina Paxinou)

A SISTER FROM NAPOLI (Peter Falk, Geraldine Page, Tom Ewell, Kurt Kasznar)

BEWARE OF THE WATCHDOG (RS, Richard Kiley, Pernell Roberts, Diana Muldaur)

LA 2017 (GB, Barry Sullivan, Edmond O'Brien, Paul Stewart)

THE MAN WHO KILLED A GHOST (Robert Wagner, Janet Leigh, David Hartman)

APPOINTMENT IN PALERMO (GB, Brenda Vaccaro, Harry Guardino)

A CAPITOL AFFAIR (GB, Suzanne Pleshette, Larry Hagman, Mercedes McCambridge)

THE SHOWDOWN (GB, Warren Oates, Albert Salmi, Jack Albertson)

SEEK AND DESTROY (RS, Leif Erickson, John Vernon, John McGiver)

I LOVE YOU, BILLY BAKER (two parts) (TF, Sammy Davis Jnr, Joey Bishop)

Nancy
US 1970   17 × 25m   colour
NBC/Columbia (Sidney Sheldon)

What it's like to be the 21-year-old daughter of the President.
Whimsical comedy which never gained much attention.

cr Sidney Sheldon

Rennie Jarrett, Celeste Holm, Robert F. Simon, John Fink

The Nancy Walker Show
US 1976   13 × 25m   colour
Norman Lear/TAT (Rod Parker)

A talent agent has trouble with her family.
Ho-hum star filler.

cr Norman Lear, Rod Parker

Nancy Walker, William Daniels, Ken Olfson, Beverly Archer, William Schallert

The Nanette Fabray Show: see Yes, Yes, Nanette

Nanny and the Professor*
US 1969–71   54 × 25m   colour
ABC/TCF (David Gerber)

A widower with three children is helped by a nanny with apparently magical powers.
Second-rate *Mary Poppins* with occasional ingratiating charm.

cr A. J. Carothers

Richard Long, Juliet Mills

Napoleon and Love
GB 1974   9 × 50m   colour (VTR)
Thames

Stories of the women in Napoleon's life.
An ambitious series which strangely failed to appeal.

w Philip Mackie

Ian Holm

NARAL. A British ITV trade term meaning Nett Advertising Revenue After Levy, figures which affect the proportional payments of the various independent companies for any programme.

Narizzano, Silvio (c 1927–). Canadian director in Britain. TV highlights include *Death of a Salesman* and *Oscar Wilde on Trial*.

Nashville 99
US 1977   4 × 50m   colour
TCF/Ernie Frankel (Richard Newton)

A Nashville police lieutenant is also a farmer when he finds time for it.

Muddled action series with a sentimental side. Four episodes were made as a try-out and that was it.

d Andrew V. McLaglen

Claude Akins, Lucille Benson, Jeannine Riley, Jerry Reed

National Broadcasting Company: see NBC

The National Dream*
Canada 1975   6 × 50m   colour (16mm)
CBC/BBC

The story of the building of the Canadian Pacific Railroad, as described in Pierre Berton's book.

National Educational Television: see NET

National Velvet
US 1960–1   58 × 25m   bw
NBC/MGM

A girl brought up with horses dreams of winning the Grand National.
Well-made, thinly scripted stories for well-brought-up children; from the movie and Enid Bagnold's book.

Lori Martin

Nationwide. BBC magazine programme which has run five days a week at 6pm through the seventies, and maintains a generally light-hearted tone, with contributions from the regions as well as London.

Naughton, James (1945–). American leading man. Series: *Faraday and Company*, *Planet of the Apes*.

Navy Log
US 1955–7   102 × 25m   bw
CBS/Sam Gallu

Anthology of stories about the navy, with guest stars.
Competent flagwaver.

NBC. National Broadcasting Company, one of America's three major networks; an offshoot of RCA, its progress has been dogged and competent rather than sparkling, and its innovations have often been further developed by competitors. It introduced early-morning and late-night talk shows, TV movies, press conferences, two-man newscasts, mini-series and longform series such as *Mystery Movie*.

Nearest and Dearest
GB 1968–72   47 × 25m   colour (VTR)
Granada

When the aged owner of a Lancashire pickle factory dies, the ne'er-do-well son returns to help his maiden sister.
Archetypal north country farce borrowed from Stanley Price's *The Dear Departed* and later itself plagiarized for the John Inman series *Odd Man In*. Undoubted

lavatory humour, its vulgarity had a certain vigour. An American version was attempted under the title *Thicker than Water*.

Hylda Baker, Jimmy Jewel, Joe Baldwin

The Nearly Man*
GB 1974   53m   colour (16mm)
Granada (Peter Eckersley)

An erstwhile socialist intellectual MP finds himself on the rocks in middle age.
Vivid, fairly absorbing character drama.

w Arthur Hopcraft   *d* John Irvin

TONY BRITTON, Ann Firbank, Michael Elphick, Wilfred Pickles

'It unmercifully strips the superficial glint from the life of a politician.' – *Daily Express*

† Broadcasting Guild award, best play.
†† A series of 7 × 50m plays followed.

Nedwell, Robin (1946–). British comedy actor seen in LWT's 'Doctor' series.

Needles and Pins
US 1973   14 × 25m   colour
NBC/Columbia/David Gerber (Herb Wallerstein)

An American *Rag Trade*, set in a dress manufacturer's workroom in New York's garment district.
A little more realistic than most American comedies, so not to the public taste.

cr Adele and Burt Styler   *m* Marvin Hamlisch

Norman Fell, Deirdre Lenihan, Louis Nye, Bernie Kopell, Sandra Dee

Negus, Arthur (1903–). Genial British commentator on antiques in programmes of the sixties and seventies: *Going for a Song*, *Antiques Roadshow*, etc

Nelson, Ed (1928–). American general purpose actor who came to the fore as Mr Rossi in *Peyton Place* and was subsequently starred in *The Silent Force*.

Nelson, Ozzie (1906–75). Unassuming American bandleader who with his wife Harriet Hilliard and their children starred for nearly 20 years in the archetypal domestic series *The Adventures of Ozzie and Harriet*. He subsequently made a small comeback in *Ozzie's Girls*.

The Neon Ceiling*
US 1971   97m   colour   TVM
Universal (William Sackheim)

A runaway wife and her daughter take temporary refuge in a desert shack with a colourful dropout.
Talkative but ingratiating and very well acted three character drama.

w Carol Sobieski, Henri Simoun   *d* Frank Pierson

GIG YOUNG, LEE GRANT, Denise Nickerson

NET. National Educational Television: the company which supplies programmes for America's public broadcasting channel.

network. In America, one of the major broadcasting organizations which commissions and broadcasts programmes in prime time through its chain of affiliated stations. In Britain, usually refers to the ITV (commercial) channel, where a programme is said to be networked if all the stations (i.e. the entire country) are taking it.

Nevada Smith
US 1975   74m   colour   TVM
MGM/Martin Rackin

Thin pilot with the hero a wandering, sometimes revengeful, do-gooder.

w John Michael Hayes, Martin Rackin   *d* Gordon Douglas

Cliff Potts, Lorne Greene

Never Mind the Quality, Feel the Width
GB 1967–9   27 × 25m   colour   (VTR)
Thames

Manny Cohen and Patrick Kelly run a tailoring business in London's east end.
Friendly farce comedy with all the expected ethnic jokes.

w Vince Powell, Harry Driver

Joe Lynch, John Bluthal

The New Adventures of Batman
US 1977   16 × 22m   colour
Filmation (Don Christensen)

A cartoon version using the voices of Adam West and Burt Ward.

The New Adventures of Charlie Chan
GB 1957   39 × 25m   bw
Vision/ITC

Rather scruffy cases for the oriental detective, with a star plainly unhappy in the role.

J. Carrol Naish

The New Adventures of Gilligan
US 1974   17 × 22m   colour
Filmation

A cartoon version using the voices of the *Gilligan's Island* stars.

The New Adventures of Huck Finn*
US 1968   20 × 25m   colour
NBC/Hanna–Barbera

Not much to do with Mark Twain, more about three kids who go through caves to various fantasy lands, but an ingenious blending of live actors and cartoon backgrounds.

Michael Shea, Ted Cassidy

The New Adventures of Martin Kane: see Martin Kane, Private Eye

The New Adventures of Perry Mason
US 1973   13 × 50m   colour
CBS/Cornwall Jackson/TCF

The old sleuthing and courtroom format simply didn't work with even a touch of realism added, and different actors (perhaps because they were *better* actors) were resented. See *Perry Mason*.

Monte Markham, Harry Guardino, Sharon Acker, Dane Clark

The New Andy Griffith Show
US 1972   10 × 25m   colour
CBS/Ada

Problems for the mayor of a small town in North Carolina.
A format which didn't work for a star who needed one that did.

Andy Griffith, Lee Ann Meriweather, Marty McCall

The New Breed
US 1961   36 × 50m   bw
Quinn Martin/Selmur/ABC

Activities of a select squad of the Los Angeles Police.
Competent, forgettable cop show.

Leslie Nielsen, John Beradino, Greg Roman, John Clark

The New Daughters of Joshua Cabe
US 1976   74m   colour   TVM
Spelling–Goldberg

Josh is unjustly imprisoned on a murder charge and his three 'daughters' evolve an escape plan.
Tired time-filler.

w Paul Savage   *d* Bruce Bilson

John McIntire, Jeanette Nolan, Jack Elam, Liberty Williams, Renne Jarrett, Lezlie Dalton

†See also *The Daughters of Joshua Cabe*.

The New Dick Van Dyke Show
US 1971–3   72 × 25m   colour
Cave Creek (Dick Van Dyke)

Our hero is now an Arizona disc jockey who enjoys the simple life. (The third season moved him to Hollywood but did not repair falling ratings.)

A sequel that failed to equal its predecessor. Perhaps the supporting cast wasn't right; or perhaps the star was just a little too old. See *The Dick Van Dyke Show*.

Dick Van Dyke, Hope Lange, Barbara Rush, Dick Van Patten, Henry Darrow, Richard Dawson, Chita Rivera, Marty Brill, Fannie Flagg

New Faces
GB 1973–8   100 approx. × 55m   colour (VTR)
ATV

Long-running talent scout show in which new professional acts are judged by a panel of showbiz personalities.

host Derek Hobson

The New Healers
aka: *The Paramedics, The Storm*
US 1972   74m   colour   TVM
Paramount

Three ex-armed-forces medical students help the doctor of a rural area and are accepted after a flood.
Predictable, watchable medico-action drama which didn't make a series.

w Stirling Silliphant   *d* Bernard L. Kowalski

Leif Erickson, Kate Johnson, Robert Foxworth, Jonathan Lippe, Burgess Meredith, William Windom

The New Land*
US 1974   15 × 50m   colour
ABC/Warner/William Blinn (Philip Leacock)

Scandinavian immigrants scrape a living in 1850s Minnesota.
Earnest outdoor dramas inspired by the Swedish film.

Scott Thomas, Bonnie Bedelia, Kurt Russell, Donald Moffat

The New Original Wonder Woman
US 1975   74m   colour   TVM
Warner/Douglas S. Cramer

See *Wonder Woman*. More nonsense adventures, slightly more firmly strung together with a World War II backdrop.

w Stanley Ralph Ross   *d* Leonard Horn

Lynda Carter, Cloris Leachman, Lyle Waggoner, Red Buttons, Stella Stevens, Kenneth Mars, John Randolph

The New People
US 1969   17 × 50m   colour
ABC/Spelling–Thomas/Rod Serling (Harold Gast)

Survivors of a plane crash make a new life on a deserted island where an abandoned town once housed atom test personnel.
Idealistic youth hokum, vaguely political and rather dull. The idea has been tried several times before.

cr Aaron Spelling, Larry Gordon

Richard Kiley, Tiffany Bolling, Lee Jay Lambert, Kevin Michaels, Brenda Sykes, David Moses

The New Phil Silvers Show
US 1963   30 × 25m   bw
Gladasaya/United Artists (Rod Amateau)

Ruses of a conniving factory foreman.
Eagerly awaited sequel to *Bilko*, with none of the old spark.

Phil Silvers, Herbie Faye, Elena Verdugo

The New Temperatures Rising: see Temperatures Rising

New York Confidential
US 1958   39 × 25m   bw
ITC

Stories of an adventurous newspaper columnist.
Walter Winchell, more or less; but even the real Winchell couldn't make it on TV.

Lee Tracy

Newhart, Bob (1929–). American comedian who usually plays the underdog. *The Bob Newhart Show* ran 144 episodes from 1972, with the star as a psychiatrist and Suzanne Pleshette as his wife; produced by MTM for CBS.

Newland, John (*c* 1916–). American actor and director best remembered as the cold-eyed host of *One Step Beyond*.

Newman, Barry (1940–). American general purpose actor who starred in the movie *The Lawyer*, then in the same role did a TV pilot *Night Games* and finally ran two seasons with it as *Petrocelli*.

Newman, Sydney (*c* 1915–). Canadian drama producer who made an impact in England from 1958 as producer of 'Armchair Theatre'; later appointed Canadian Film Commissioner and Chairman of the National Film Board.

Nichols*
US 1971   26 × 50m   colour
NBC/Warner/Cherokee (Meta Rosenberg)

Stories of the motorcycling sheriff of a small western town in 1915.

NEWS. A picture which sums up the dangers of getting it to us.

Easy-going semi-western littered up with too many cute characters and ideas (such as killing off the hero and bringing back his 'tougher' twin brother).

James Garner, Neva Patterson, Margot Kidder, Stuart Margolin, John Beck

Nichols, Dandy (1907–). British character actress who became a national character as Alf Garnett's wife Else in *Till Death Us Do Part*.

Nichols, Mike (1931–) (Michael Igor Peschkowsky). American film director who began as a TV cabaret turn and later was executive producer of the series *Family*.

Nichols, Peter (1927–). British dramatist who began in TV (*Promenade, Ben Spray, The Gorge, Hearts and Flowers, The Common*, etc.).

Nielsen, Leslie (1925–). Tall Canadian actor often seen as villain or weakling. A frequent guest star; series include *The Bold Ones, The New Breed, Bracken's World*.

Nielsens. American Nielsen ratings supplied by the A. C. Nielsen Company. In each area a statistical sample of homes is supplied with an audimeter which records what channel, if any, is being watched during each minute. This information is converted into graph form and a rating and share of audience produced for each programme.

Night Chase
US 1970   100m   colour   TVM
Cinema Center 100 (Collier Young)

A wealthy businessman on the run from police is nearly trapped in Los Angeles.
Overlong chase melodrama with attractive locations.

w Marvin A. Gluck   *d* Jack Starret   *ph* Fred J. Koene-kamp   *m* Laurence Rosenthal

David Janssen, Yaphet Kotto, Victoria Vetri, Elisha Cook Jnr, Joe de Santis

Night Cries
US 1977   96m   colour   TVM
Charles Fries

A woman is tormented by cries which seem to be those of her own dead baby.
Watchable suspense melodrama.

w Brian Taggert   *d* Richard Lang

Susan St James, William Conrad, Michael Parks, Dolores Dorn, Cathleen Nesbitt, Diana Douglas

Night Gallery*
US 1969   98m   colour   TVM
Universal (William Sackheim)

Three short stories of the supernatural, introduced by

Rod Serling through paintings.
Not a bad package: the first is the best.

w Rod Serling   *d* Boris Sagal, Steven Spielberg, Barry Shear

Ossie Davis, George Macready, Roddy McDowall, Joan Crawford, Barry Sullivan, Richard Kiley, Sam Jaffe

†The one-hour series which followed kept the same format and ran to 28 episodes, followed by about 50 half-hours. It repeated most of the plots from *Twilight Zone*.

Night Moves
US 1974   74m   colour   TVM
Paramount (Thomas L. Miller, Edward J. Milkis)

A small-town lawyer defends a socialite on a murder charge.
The pilot for the series *Petrocelli*; routine competence in all departments.

w E. Jack Neman   *d* Don Taylor

Barry Newman, Susan Howard, Albert Salmi, Stefanie Powers, Anjanette Comer, Ralph Meeker, Henry Darrow

Night of Terror*
US 1972   73m   colour   TVM
Paramount (Edward J. Milkis)

A young woman is terrorized by an unknown assailant. Nothing new, but plenty of suspense and inventive use of locations.

d Jeannot Szwarc

Donna Mills, Eddie Egan, Martin Balsam, Chuck Connors, Agnes Moorehead

Night Slaves*
US 1970   74m   colour   TVM
Bing Crosby Productions (Everett Chambers)

In a small peaceful hotel, a man wakes up to find that his wife has been abducted by alien forces which have taken over the town.
Unexpected, intriguing sci-fi.

w Everett Chambers, Robert Specht   *d* Ted Post

James Franciscus, Lee Grant, Leslie Nielsen, Tisha Sterling, Andrew Prine

The Night Stalker*
US 1971   73m   colour   TVM
Aaron Spelling

A vampire stalks Las Vegas.
Horror comic with a sense of humour. (See also below.)

w Richard Matheson   *d* John Llewellyn Moxey

Darren McGavin, Carol Lynley, Simon Oakland, Claude Akins, Charles McGraw, Barry Atwater, Elisha Cook Jnr, Kent Smith

The Night Strangler*
US 1972   74m   colour   TVM
Aaron Spelling/Dan Curtis

The reporter who tracked down the night stalker turns his attention to Seattle and a multi-murderer 120 years old.
More horror nonsense, rather less effective than before, but highly watchable. The two films led to a monster series called *Kolchak: The Night Stalker* (which made no sense); a more stylish pilot had been tried in *The Norliss Tapes*.

w Richard Matheson   *d* Dan Curtis

Darren McGavin, Jo Ann Pflug, Simon Oakland, Scott Brady, Margaret Hamilton, Wally Cox, John Carradine

Night Terror
US 1977   74m   colour   TVM
Charles Fries/NBC

A woman has to flee for her life because she has witnessed a murder.
Old-hat screamer, very roughly assembled.

w Carl Gabler, Richard De Neut   *d* E. W. Swackhamer

Valerie Harper, Richard Romanus, Michael Tolan, Beatrice Manley

The Night that Panicked America*
US 1975   100m   colour   TVM
Paramount (Anthony Wilson, Joseph Sargent)

An account of Orson Welles's 1938 broadcast of *The War of the Worlds* and the effect it had on the nation.
The studio re-creation is excellent, but the film bogs down when it deals with the domestic dramas, which are totally predictable.

w Nicholas Meyer, Anthony Wilson   *d* Joseph Sargent

Vic Morrow, Cliff de Young, Michael Constantine, Paul Shenar, Walter McGinn, Meredith Baxter, Tom Bosley, Will Geer

The Night They Took Miss Beautiful
US 1977   96m   colour   TVM
Don Kirshner (George Lefferts)

A plane with five beauty contestants is hi-jacked.
Tediously incompetent caper story.

w George Lefferts   *d* Robert Michael Lewis

Phil Silvers, Gary Collins, Chuck Connors, Henry Gibson, Peter Haskell, Sheree North, Stella Stevens, Gregory Sierra

Nightingale's Boys*
GB 1975   7 × 50m   colour (VTR)
Granada (Brian Armstrong)

A schoolmaster on the brink of retirement meets again members of his most remarkable class.
Rather disappointing drama series, the plays being too

different in tone for any kind of unity in the *Carnet de bal* style.

cr Arthur Hopcraft   *w* Arthur Hopcraft, Jack Rosenthal, C. P. Taylor, Colin Spencer, John Finch, Alexander Baron   *d* Richard Everett, Les Chatfield, Peter Plummer, Roger Tucker, June Howson

Derek Farr

Nightmare*
US 1973   75m   colour   TVM
Mark Carliner

A man in a Manhattan apartment witnesses a murder and becomes the quarry of the killers.
The old old story, excitingly filmed but foolish in detail.

w David Wiltse   *d* William Hale

Richard Crenna, Patty Duke, Vic Morrow

Nightmare in Badham County
US 1976   96m   colour   TVM
ABC Circle/Douglas S. Cramer

Two innocent college girls escape from a women's prison farm.
Predictable melodrama.

w Jo Heims   *d* John Llewellyn Moxey   *m* Charles Bernstein

Deborah Raffin, Lynne Moody, Chuck Connors, Fionnula Flanagan, Tina Louise, Robert Reed, Ralph Bellamy

Nightmare in Chicago
US 1964   80m   colour   TVM
Universal

A hunted killer finds himself trapped by police road blocks and commits more violence in an attempt to escape from the city.
Rough, occasionally vivid police story which eventually becomes tiresome to watch.

w David Moessinger   *d* Robert Altman

Robert Ridgeley, Charles McGraw, Philip Abbott

Nimmo, Derek (1931–   ). British comic actor, adept at the bashful curate type which he played to perfection in *All Gas and Gaiters*, *Oh Brother* and *Oh Father*. Also 'Bertie' in *The World of Wooster*.

Nimoy, Leonard (1931–   ). American general purpose actor, a rave in *Star Trek* as the point-eared outer space denizen Mr Spock. Also appeared in *Mission Impossible*.

1990
GB 1977   16 × 50m   colour (VTR)
BBC (Prudence Fitzgerald)

In the last decade of the 20th century in Britain the concept of common good is replacing the rights of the individual.

LEONARD NIMOY. An actor who had to wear pointed ears to get noticed . . . as the famous Mr Spock in *Star Trek*. Since when, alas, he has been little heard from. The lady with him in this episode is Jane Wyatt.

Not a bad effort, but *1984* said it all much more succinctly.

cr Wilfred Greatorex *w* Wilfred Greatorex, Edmund Ward, Arden Winch

Edward Woodward, Robert Lang, Yvonne Mitchell, Lisa Harrow, Clive Swift, Tony Doyle, Barbara Kellerman, Paul Hardwick

'The right mixture of honest suspense with growing paranoia.' – *Variety*

90 Bristol Court

US 1964 13 × 74m bw
NBC

A trio of unrelated comedies all set in the same apartment block: *Harris Against the World*, *Karen* and *Tom Dick and Mary*. They quickly failed.

Nixon, David (1919–78). Bland bald British magician with a deceptively nervous manner; had his own occasional series from the early fifties, and was also a favourite panellist.

Nixon, Richard (1913–). The deposed American president's interviews with David Frost caused an international sensation in the spring of 1977.

No Hiding Place*

GB 1959–66 170 approx. × 50m bw (VTR)
Associated Rediffusion (Ray Dicks)

Favourite, straightforward Scotland Yard mystery series, with Raymond Francis as Superintendent Lockhart and Eric Lander as his assistant. Clean if not very clever.

No, Honestly. A comedy format presented by LWT in 1974, from scripts by Charlotte Bingham. Much in the manner of Burns and Allen, John Alderton and Pauline Collins, as patient husband and scatty wife, topped and tailed a comedy sketch by speaking directly to the audience. They were later replaced by Donal Donnelly and Liza Goddard, and the title was changed to *Yes, Honestly*. In all cases production was by Humphrey Barclay.

No Place to Run

US 1972 73m colour TVM
Spelling–Goldberg

An old man flees to Canada with his orphan grandson of whom he can't get legal custody.
Patchy action drama with weepy interludes.

w James G. Hirsch *d* Delbert Mann

Herschel Bernardi, Larry Hagman, Stefanie Powers, Neville Brand, Scott Jacoby

1984, a milestone in BBC television drama, caused a sensation on its first transmission in 1954 and retained much of its impact when revived in 1977. Yvonne Mitchell, Peter Cushing, André Morell.

No Time for Sergeants
US 1964   34 × 25m   bw
Warner

A hillbilly is recruited to the Air Force.
Or, see *Gomer Pyle*. Obvious service humour.

Sammy Jackson, Harry Hickox, Kevin O'Neal, Andy Clyde

No Trams to Lime Street**
GB 1959   50m   bw (VTR)
ABC (Sydney Newman)

Three sailors have a night out in Liverpool.
One of the most famous Armchair Theatre plays, in the Paddy Chayefsky *Bachelor Party* style.

w ALUN OWEN   *d* Ted Kotcheff

Billie Whitelaw, Jack Hedley, Alfred Lynch, Tom Bell

† Revived by the BBC in 1965 and 1970.

Noah's Ark
US 1956   23 × 25m   bw
MCA/Universal/Jack Webb

Experiences of a vet.
Very obvious animal series.

Paul Burke, May Wynn

Noble, Peter (*c* 1920–   ).
British show business personality, scriptwriter and occasional actor; author of, among other publications, *The Negro in Film* and *The Fabulous Orson Welles*. Editor of *Screen International* and *The British Film and Television Year Book*.

Norden, Denis (*c* 1924–   ).
British comedy scriptwriter (formerly with Frank Muir), panellist, wit and interlocutor of Thames's nostalgia programme *Looks Familiar*.

The Norliss Tapes**
US 1973   74m   colour   TVM
Metromedia/Dan Curtis

A supernatural investigator looks into the case of a woman whose diabolist husband has risen from the dead a ravening monster.
Smoothly made, fast-paced and genuinely frightening horror movie, an example of what can be done on a low budget.

w William F. Nolan   *d* DAN CURTIS

Roy Thinnes, Angie Dickinson, Claude Akins, Hurd Hatfield

223

THE NORMAN CONQUESTS. The splendid cast of Alan Ayckbourn's funny three-parter. Richard Briers, Tom Conti, Penelope Wilton, David Troughton, Penelope Keith.

The Norman Conquests**

GB 1977   3 × 100m (approx.)   colour (VTR)
Thames/WNET

Three plays showing the same awful family weekend from different angles.
Civilized, funny plays by Alan Ayckbourn, given precisely the right TV treatment, unspectacular and unhurried but just right. A rare treat.

d Herbert Wise

RICHARD BRIERS, PENELOPE KEITH, TOM CONTI, David Troughton, Penelope Wilton

North, Jay (1952–   ). American child actor who played *Dennis the Menace*; grew up a little and appeared in *Maya*; then left the industry.

Northwest Passage

US 1957   26 × 25m   colour
NBC/MGM

Rogers' Rangers fight the French–Indian wars.
North-western based on the movie rather than the book. The low budget shows.

Keith Larsen, Buddy Ebsen, Don Burnett

Not for Hire

US 1959   39 × 25m   bw
NBC

Cases of a Honolulu cop.
Average thick-ear.

Ralph Meeker

Not in Front of the Children. British half-hour domestic comedy series of the sixties, from Thames TV, starring Wendy Craig. From it were derived *And Mother Makes Three*, etc.

Not So Much a Programme, More a Way of Life: see That Was the Week that Was

Now You See It, Now You Don't

aka: *Midnight Oil*
US 1967   96m   colour   TVM
Universal (Roland Kibbee)

An art appraiser plans to sell a fake Rembrandt to a Middle Eastern prince.
Woebegone, overlong comedy with much mugging from the star.

w Roland Kibbee   *d* Don Weis

Jonathan Winters, Luciana Paluzzi, Steve Allen, Jayne Meadows, Jack Weston

Nowhere to Hide
US 1977 74m colour TVM
Mark Carliner/Viacom

A marshal is assigned to protect a former syndicate hit man.
Pretty fair action suspenser.

w Edward Anhalt *d* Jack Starrett

Lee Van Cleef, Russell Johnson, Tony Musante, Charlie Robinson, Edward Anhalt, Lelia Goldoni

Nowhere to Run*
US 1978 96m colour TVM
MTM/NBC (Jim Byrnes)

An accountant plans to make a killing at Las Vegas so that he can afford to ditch his nagging wife.
Elaborate but slow-starting suspenser with a good tense finale.

w Jim Byrnes, *novel* Charles Einstein *d* Richard Lang *ph* Chuck Arnold *m* Jerrold Immel

David Janssen, Stefanie Powers, Allen Garfield, Linda Evans, Neva Patterson, John Randolph

'A slick, wryly amusing coincidence stretcher.' – *Daily Variety*

The Nurses*
aka: *The Doctors and the Nurses*
US 1962–4 103 × 50m bw
CBS/Plautus

What goes on in a large hospital.
Slickly made soap opera which doesn't always pull its punches.

Shirl Conway, Zina Bethune, Michael Tolan, Joseph Campanella

NYPD (New York Police Department)*
US 1967–8 49 × 25m colour (16mm)
ABC/Talent Associates (Danny Melnick)

Cases of New York's 27th precinct.
Vivid, rough-looking street cases dressed up as fiction, with plenty of screaming tyres.

cr Albert Ruben

Frank Converse, Robert Hooks, Jack Warden

O

The O. Henry Playhouse
US 1956 39 × 25m bw
Gross–Krasne

Anthology of short stories about old New York, introduced by Thomas Mitchell.
Not at all bad.

O'Brian, Hugh (1925–) (Hugh Krampke).
Adequate, unsmiling American leading man who after a good start in TV made little headway in movies; series include *The Life and Legend of Wyatt Earp*, *It's a Man's World*, *Search*.

O'Brien, Edmond (1915–). Irish–American character actor who grew from a slim youth to a fat slob but was always eminently watchable. TV series: *Johnny Midnight*, *Sam Benedict*, *The Long Hot Summer*.

Occasional Wife
US 1966 30 × 25m colour
NBC/Columbia/Harry Ackerman (Robert Claver)

A bachelor executive hires a wife when he needs one for social occasions.
Mildly amusing comedy.

cr Fred Freeman, Lawrence J. Cohen

Michael Callan, Patricia Harty

O'Connor, Carroll (1922–). American general purpose actor who after 10 years of secondary film roles became a national figure as Archie Bunker in *All in the Family*.

O'Connor, Des (c 1935–). British comedian and singer who graduated from a holiday camp.

O'Connor, Donald (1925–). Sprightly American child actor and later song-and-dance man. When musicals died he became popular in TV as a talk show host.

The Odd Couple**
US 1970–4 90 × 25m colour
ABC/Paramount (Garry Marshall, Sheldon Keller)

Two divorced men share an apartment and get on each other's nerves.
Successful extension of the Neil Simon play: skilful writing and playing keep the laughs flowing free.

Tony Randall, Jack Klugman, Al Molinaro, Penny Marshall, Janis Hansen, Elinor Donahue

The Oddball Couple
US 1975   × 22m colour
De Patie–Freleng

A messy dog shares premises with a neat cat.
Anthropomorphic cartoon version of the stage and film success.

voices Paul Winchell, Frank Nelson

Oddie, Bill (1941–). British comedy writer and actor, since 1970 one of *The Goodies*.

O'Farrell, George More: see More O'Farrell, George

Ogilvy, Ian (1943–). British light leading man who stars in *The Return of the Saint*.

Oh No It's Selwyn Froggitt
GB 1976–   × 25m colour (VTR)
Yorkshire (Ronnie Baxter)

Adventures of an accident-prone handyman with an irritatingly cheerful disposition.
Slightly unusual but generally resistible star comedy.

w Alan Plater

Bill Maynard

Oh Susanna!: see The Gale Storm Show

Oh Those Bells! *
US 1962 13 × 25m bw
CBS

Adventures of the custodians of a Hollywood prop shop.
Zany, amusing vehicle for under-used stars.

THE WIERE BROTHERS, Henry Morgan

O'Hara US Treasury
aka: *Operation Cobra*
US 1971 98m colour TVM
Universal/Jack Webb

Suddenly widowed by an accident, a deputy sheriff from the midwest becomes a customs agent and cracks a narcotics ring.
Semi-documentary thick ear which led to a moderately successful series.

THE ODD COUPLE. An unexpected smash success, this comedy proved that you *can* get big audiences on television for witty lines and good acting. Jack Klugman and Tony Randall were the ill-assorted protagonists.

w James E. Moser   *d* Jack Webb

David Janssen, Lana Wood, Jerome Thor, Gary Crosby, William Conrad

† The series which followed consisted of 52 × 50m episodes.

Oil Strike North
GB 1976   13 × 50m   colour (VTR)
BBC/TCF (Gerard Glaister)

Lives of men who work on an offshore oil rig.
Tolerably well-made drama series which just didn't catch on.

Nigel Davenport, Barbara Shelley, Michael Witney, Angela Douglas, Callum Mill

OK Crackerby
US 1965   17 × 25m   bw
ABC/United Artists/Beresford

A self-made millionaire wants his children to break into society.

Careful but unfunny star comedy.

cr Abe Burrows, Cleveland Amory

Burl Ives, Hal Buckley

The Old Grey Whistle Test. Mysterious title for BBC2's long-running token pop music show.

The Old Man Who Cried Wolf*
US 1970   74m   colour   TVM
Aaron Spelling

An old man sees his friend beaten to death but the police don't believe him: only the killer does.
Modestly effective, predictable suspenser.

w Luther Davis   *d* Walter Grauman

EDWARD G. ROBINSON, Martin Balsam, Diane Baker, Ruth Roman, Percy Rodrigues

Oliver, Stephen (–   ) (Stephen John Walzig). American juvenile lead who appeared in series *Bracken's World, Peyton Place.*

227

LAURENCE OLIVIER. His plays for Granada, on the eve of his seventieth birthday, found him in versatile form, whether as an old Italian in *Saturday, Sunday, Monday* . . . or as a drunken American in *Come Back Little Sheba*. The overall effect of the season, however, was disappointing.

Olivier, Sir Laurence (Lord Olivier) (1907–). Distinguished British actor whose occasional TV ventures include *John Gabriel Borkman, The Moon and Sixpence, The Power and the Glory, Uncle Vanya, David Copperfield, Long Day's Journey into Night, The Merchant of Venice, Love Among the Ruins*. In 1976 in association with Granada TV he began *Laurence Olivier Presents* (qv).

Omnibus. A cultural hour transmitted on ABC from 1951 to 1956, produced by Robert Saudek and introduced by Alistair Cooke: the equivalent of BBC's *Monitor*.

On the Buses. British half-hour comedy series tending towards the cheerfully crude and vulgar, about a bus conductor, his mum, his homely sister and idle brother-in-law, his driver friend and their dim-witted inspector. Some fun on the comic postcard level. More than 60 episodes were produced between 1968 and 1975.

Reg Varney, Cicely Courtneidge (later Doris Hare), Anna Karen, Michael Robbins, Bob Grant, Stephen Lewis

On the Move. A BBC ten-minute series of the mid-seventies, entertainingly instructing adults who can't read or write. BAFTA award 1976, best special programme of the year; producer David Hargreaves.

On the Rocks
US 1976   13 × 25m   colour (VTR)
Metromedia/John Rich

The schemes of inmates of a minimum security prison. Unsuccessful transposition to America of the British hit *Porridge*.

w Dick Clement, Ian La Frenais   *d* John Rich

Jose Perez, Mel Stewart, Hal Williams, Rick Hurst, Bobby Sandler, Tom Poston

On Trial*
GB 1962   10 × 50m   bw (VTR)
Granada (Peter Wildeblood)

Courtroom recreations of the trials of Casement, Wilde, Dilke, Stead, Cowper, Byng, Joseph Wall, Horatio Bottomley, the Tichbourne claimant and the Edward VII baccarat scandal.
Absorbing 'faction' TV.

Once an Eagle
US 1977   9 × 50m   colour
NBC/Universal (William Sackheim, Peter Fischer)

The lives of two friends intertwine through two world wars.
Lumbering mini-series from the doorstop novel by Anton Myrer. Something of a slog, with a few lively segments.

ON THE BUSES. A cheerful group of people who in the series were seldom speaking to each other. Michael Robbins, Bob Grant, Anna Karen, Reg Varney, Doris Hare, Stephen Lewis.

w Peter Fischer *d* E. W. Swackhamer, Richard Michaels

Sam Elliott, Cliff Potts, Darleen Carr, Glenn Ford, Clu Gulager, Lynda Day George, Amy Irving

Once Upon a Brothers Grimm
US 1977 100m approx. colour (VTR)
Vidtronics/Bernard Rothman, Jack Wohl

The Brothers Grimm, stranded in a forest, become involved with the problems of some of their own creations.
Bland, studio-bound family special which seldom rouses itself out of lethargy.

w Jean Holloway *d* Norman Campbell *m* Mitch Leigh *ly* Sammy Cahn *choreo* Ron Field

Dean Jones, Paul Sand, Ruth Buzzi, Chita Rivera, Cleavon Little, Arte Johnson, Clive Revill, Teri Garr

Once Upon a Dead Man**
US 1971 100m colour TVM
Universal (Leonard B. Stern)

San Francisco's police chief and his zany wife uncover an art racket.
Easily digestible, hard-to-follow mystery climaxing in a cycle chase. Pilot for the *McMillan and Wife* series.

w Leonard B. Stern, Chester Krumholtz *d* Leonard B. Stern

Rock Hudson, Susan St James, Jack Albertson, René Auberjonois, Kurt Kazsnar, Jonathan Harris, Herb Edelman, John Schuck, James Wainwright

† See Mystery Movie.

One Day at a Time
US 1975 × 25m colour (VTR)
Norman Lear/TAT (Dick Pensfield, Perry Grant)

A newly divorced woman has two teenage daughters.
Modestly pleasing comedy series.

cr Whitney Blake, Allan Mannings *d* Herbert Kenwith

Bonnie Franklin, Mackenzie Phillips

229

One of My Wives Is Missing**
US 1975 97m colour TVM
Spelling–Goldberg (Barney Rosenzweig)

A man arrives at a holiday resort and reports to the police that his wife has vanished. A woman he has never seen before then turns up claiming to be his wife . . .
Satisfying what's-it-all-abouter which plays pretty fair and deals suspicion like a pack of cards. The plot is borrowed from *Chase a Crooked Shadow* and other sources.

w Peter Stone, *play Trap for a Lonely Man* by Robert Thomas *d* Glen Jordan

James Franciscus, Jack Klugman, Elizabeth Ashley, Joel Fabiani

One of Our Own
US 1975 98m colour TVM
Universal (Matthew Rapf, Jack Laird)

The chief of a large hospital faces numerous crises.
Predictable pilot for the unsuccessful series *Doctors' Hospital*.

w Jack Laird *d* Richard Sarafian

George Peppard, Oscar Homolka, William Daniels, Louise Sorel, Strother Martin, Zohra Lampert, Albert Paulsen

One Step Beyond**
US 1958–60 94 × 25m bw
ABC/Collier Young (Merwin Gerard)

Unexplained real-life experiences which tend towards the supernatural.
Simply-staged occult adventures which did a good deal for TV production by its use of limbo sets and having its narrator walk in and out of the action.

cr MERWIN GERARD *host* JOHN NEWLAND

†In 1978 the format was revived for prime access time under the title *The Next Step Beyond*, but the old style was not evident.

The Onedin Line*
GB 1974–8 50 × 50m colour (VTR)
BBC

The saga of a Liverpool shipping family.
19th-century open-air adventure mixes with boardroom and bedroom drama: an irresistible combination for Sunday nights.

cr Cyril Abraham

Peter Gilmore, Howard Lang, Jessica Benton, Brian Rawlinson, Mary Webster, Jill Gascoine

†Exterior locations: Exeter and Dartmouth.

The Only Way Out Is Dead
aka: *The Man Who Wanted to Live Forever*
Canada 1970 100m colour TVM
Palomar

A man determined to live forever selects other people's organs for his future use.
A talky rather than gruesome, but still rather tasteless suspenser.

w Henry Denker *d* John Trent

Burl Ives, Sandy Dennis, Stuart Whitman, Ron Hartman, Robert Goodier

Only with Married Men*
US 1974 74m colour TVM
Spelling–Goldberg

A sexy girl who only wants to date married men meets a sly bachelor who pretends to be married so as not to get involved.
Brash, bright sex comedy which sustains well for most of its length.

w Jerry Davis *d* Jerry Paris

David Birney, Michele Lee, John Astin, Judy Carne, Dom De Luise

Ooh La La!*
GB 1973 6 × 50m colour (VTR)
BBC (Douglas Argent)

Six adaptations of Feydeau farces, impeccably presented with a star who was made for them.

adaptors Caryl Brahms, Ned Sherrin

PATRICK CARGILL

Open Door. BBC2's late night access programme, open to any minority groups who prove they can stage an interesting and fair programme.

open-ended programme. One which does not have to finish at a specific time, or can be programmed to its full length instead of being cut to fit another network junction.

The Open University. A series of college standard courses made to fit TV series presented during daytime by the BBC and sponsored by the government. More than 50,000 people take advantage of this scheme.

Operation Cobra: see O'Hara US Treasury

Operation Heartbeat*
aka: *UMC*
US 1969 100m colour TVM
MGM (A. C. Ward)

Life at a university medical centre.
Competent pilot for the long-running series *Medical Center*.

w A. C. Ward *d* Boris Sagal

Richard Bradford, James Daly, Edward G. Robinson, Maurice Evans, Kevin McCarthy, William Windom, Kim Stanley, J. D. Cannon

Operation Petticoat
US 1977   96m   colour   TVM
Universal (Leonard Stern)

Life on an antique submarine during the Pacific War.
Tedious rehash of an old movie which wasn't particularly inspired to begin with.

w Leonard Stern   *d* John Astin

John Astin, Richard Gilliland, Jackie Cooper, Craig Cassidy

† A half-hour series followed. In the second season the leads changed to Randolph Mantooth and Robert Hagan.

Operation Prime Time: see Best Sellers

Operation Runaway: No Prince for My Cinderella
US 1978   96m   colour   TVM
Quinn Martin (William Robert Yates)

A lawyer tracks down missing teenagers.
Dreary pilot which unaccountably sold a series. It didn't last long.

w William Robert Yates   *d* William Wiard   *ph* William W. Spencer   *m* Richard Markowitz

Robert Reed, James Olson, Terri Nunn, Karen Machon

'Robert Reed's job is to track down runaway teenagers. And he's pretty good at it. Unfortunately the show provides no compelling reason for wanting them back.'
– *Daily Variety*

Oppenheimer, Jess (1918–). American comedy writer: *I Love Lucy, Angel, Glynis,* (creator) *The Debbie Reynolds Show.*

Opportunity Knocks. A British talent scout show which ran on a weekly basis for most of each year from 1956 to 1977. Hughie Green presided and was much imitated for his smarmy introductions. About a score of the finalists achieved significant careers.

Orchard, Julian (1930–). British character comedian, frequently seen as beaming, effeminate foil to stars.

Ordeal*
US 1973   74m   colour   TVM
TCF

An injured businessman is left for dead in the desert by his wife and her lover.
Remake of *Inferno*, considerably less effective.

w Francis Cockrell, Leon Tokatyan   *d* Lee H. Katzin

Arthur Hill, Diana Muldaur, James Stacy, Michael Ansara, Macdonald Carey

The Oregon Trail
US 1975   100m   Technicolor   TVM
Universal

A pioneer family heads west.
Talky mini-western pilot, making lavish use of clips from older and better movies, but with a certain integrity of purpose.

w Michael Gleason   *d* Boris Sagal

Rod Taylor, Blair Brown, Douglas Fowley, Andrew Stevens

† The series which followed more than a year later was poorly conceived and produced, and limped along for 13 × 50m episodes, not all of which were played. Rod Taylor again starred, but the presentation was perfunctory in the extreme.

Orkin, Harvey (–1975). American scriptwriter, notably for Phil Silvers.

Orson Welles Great Mysteries
GB 1973   26 × 25m   colour (VTR)
Anglia (John Jacobs)

Anthology of strange stories, hosted by a cloaked Orson Welles (who does not appear in any of them). Some quite good playlets, some very bad ones, and too much variation in the level to allow an effective series.

Osborn, Andrew (1912–). British producer (former actor): *Maigret, Dr Finlay's Casebook,* etc. Subsequently BBC's head of series.

Oscar: see Academy Awards Telecast

The Osmonds
US 1972–3   26 × 22m   colour
ABC/Rankin–Bass/Halas & Batchelor

The Osmonds rock group are appointed goodwill ambassadors by the United States Music Committee.
Passable cartoon series with music.

OSS
GB 1958   26 × 25m   bw
ITC/Buckeye

Exploits of the Office of Strategic Services during World War II.
Adequate espionage series.

Ron Randell, Lionel Murton

O'Sullivan, Richard (1944–). British leading light actor, former child star. Series: *A Man About the House, Doctor in Charge, Robin's Nest.*

The Other Side of Hell*
US 1978   150m   colour   TVM
NBC/James T. Aubrey, Ronald Lyon

A man who has attempted suicide is committed to a hospital for the criminally insane.

Quite a powerful and compassionate study of the state of modern therapy, with several strong performances.

w Leon Tokatyan d Jan Kadar ph Adam Holender m Leonard Rosenman

Alan Arkin, Roger E. Mosley, Morgan Woodward, Seamon Glass, Leonard Stone

Our Man at St Mark's. Early sixties British half-hour comedy from Rediffusion, its hero being a likeable young British vicar, played by Donald Sinden/Leslie Phillips, with Joan Hickson as the housekeeper. The British answer to *Going My Way*.

Our Man Higgins*
US 1962   34 × 25m   bw
ABC/Columbia

An American suburban family inherits a British butler. Adequate, predictable star vehicle with its star in very good form.

cr Paul Harrison, from the radio series *It's Higgins, Sir*

STANLEY HOLLOWAY, Frank Maxwell, Audrey Totter

Our Miss Brooks*
US 1952–6   127 × 25m   bw
Desilu

Misadventures of a high-school teacher.
Lively star vehicle.

Eve Arden, Gale Gordon, Robert Rockwell, Richard Crenna

Our Town*
US 1977   96m   colour (VTR)
Hartwest (Saul Jaffe)

A new production, carefully styled for TV, of Thornton Wilder's no-scenery play about life in a New Hampshire town at the turn of the century.

d George Schafer p/d Roy Christopher

Hal Holbrook, Glynnis O'Connor, Robby Benson, Ronny Cox, Barbara Bel Geddes, Ned Beatty, Sada Thompson, Don Beddoe

The Outcasts*
US 1968   26 × 50m   colour
ABC/Columbia (Jon Epstein)

After the Civil War, a white and a black man pair up as bounty hunters.
Good tough western.

Don Murray, Otis Young

The Outer Limits***
US 1963–4   49 × 50m   bw
United Artists/Daystar (Leslie Stevens, Joseph Stefano)

Anthology of science fiction thrillers.
A mainly stylish collection over which cultists still en-

thuse, discussing such episodes as *It Crawled Out of the Woodwork*, *Galaxy Being*, *Corpus Earthling*, *Behold Eck*, *The Hundred Days of the Dragon*, *The Zanti Misfits*, *The Soldier* and *Demon with a Glass Hand*. In between these high spots lay quite a bit of junk, but the main title disarmed criticism.

cr LESLIE STEVENS

Outlaws*
US 1960–1   50 × 50m   bw
NBC

In the old West, two lawmen go after the remaining badmen.
Pretty satisfying action series which at the time was criticized for its violence.

Bruce Yarnell, Don Collier, Barton MacLane

Outrage**
US 1973   74m   colour   TVM
ABC Circle/Michael Green

A well-to-do businessman is harassed at home by marauding teenagers and finds himself powerless to do anything about it.
Based on a true case of a man who finally took the law into his own hands, this is a chilling and well-observed piece of unpleasantness.

w William Wood d Richard Heffron

Robert Culp, Marlyn Mason, Beah Richards, Thomas Leopold

The Outsider*
US 1968   26 × 50m   colour
CBS/Universal/Public Arts (Roy Huggins)

Cases of a Los Angeles private eye.
Philip Marlowe in all but name, with the right cynical flavour; pilot film was *The Lonely Profession*.

cr Roy Huggins

Darren McGavin

The Over the Hill Gang*
US 1969   74m   colour   TVM
Spelling–Thomas

Retired – really retired – Texas Rangers bring law and order to a corrupt town.
Mildly amusing comedy western full of old faces.

w Jameson Brewer d Jean Yarborough

Pat O'Brien, Walter Brennan, Chill Wills, Edgar Buchanan, Jack Elam, Andy Devine, Gypsy Rose Lee, Rick Nelson, Edward Andrews

The Over the Hill Gang Rides Again
US 1970   74m   colour   TVM
Spelling–Thomas

Three retired Texas Rangers rescue a drunken friend and make him a marshal.
More of the above, not exactly inspired.

w Richard Carr   *d* George McCowan

Walter Brennan, Fred Astaire, Edgar Buchanan, Chill Wills, Andy Devine

Overland Trail
US 1960   17 × 50m   bw
MCA/Stagecoach/Revue

Adventures of a stagecoach driver and his young assistant.
Adequate western.

William Bendix, Doug McClure

Owen Marshall: Counselor at Law
US 1971   100m   colour   TVM
Universal (Douglas Benton)

A California lawyer defends a young man accused of rape and murder.
Comfortable, over-prolonged courtroom stuff which turned into a series.

w Jerry McNeely   *d* Buzz Kulik

Arthur Hill, Vera Miles, Joseph Campanella, William Shatner, Bruce Davison

† The series ran to 69 × 50m episodes.

Ozzie and Harriet: see The Adventures of Ozzie and Harriet

Ozzie's Girls
US 1973   24 × 25m   colour (VTR)
Filmways

The Nelsons rent out their sons' bedrooms to two college girls.
Lukewarm comedy for ageing fans, following what seemed like a lifetime of *Ozzie and Harriet* and their family.

Ozzie Nelson, Harriet Nelson

P

Paar, Jack (1918–). American talk show host who made *Tonight* popular on NBC between 1957 and 1962. After that, showbiz saw little of him.

Page, Patti (1927–) (Clara Ann Fowler). American band singer who had her own TV series in the middle and late fifties.

Pagett, Nicola (*c* 1946–). British leading lady. *Upstairs, Downstairs, Napoleon and Love, Anna Karenina*, etc.

Palin, Michael (1943–). British comic actor and writer, one of *Monty Python's Flying Circus*, and the creator of *Ripping Yarns*.

The Pallisers*
GB 1975   26 × 50m   colour (VTR)
BBC (Martin Lisemore)

The saga of a Victorian semi-noble family with political leanings.
Elaborate, expensive serial which didn't quite catch the public fancy.

w Simon Raven *novels* Anthony Trollope   *d* Hugh David, Ronald Wilson

Susan Hampshire, Roland Culver, Philip Latham, Fabia Drake, Carole Mortimer, Sonia Dresdel, Sarah Badel, Gary Watson

Palmer, Tony (*c* 1935–). British writer–director with special interest in pop music. *How It Is* (series), *The World of Hugh Hefner, The World of Miss World, All You Need Is Love* (series on history of pop music), etc.

Panache*
US 1976   76m   colour   TVM
Warner

Adventures of a 'second team' of the king's musketeers in 17th-century France.
A mark for trying, but both acting and production are very laboured.

w Duke Vincent   *d* Gary Nelson

René Auberjonois, David Healy, Charles Seibert

Panic!
US 1957   31 × 25m   bw
McCadden/NBC (Al Simon)

Anthology about people in jeopardy situations. The most memorable had James Mason and his family

marooned for the weekend on the top floor of an office skyscraper.

cr Al Simon

Panic in Echo Park
US 1977   74m   colour   TVM
Edgar J. Scherick

Problems of a doctor in a minority community. Heavy-going failed pilot.

w Dalene Young   *d* John Llewellyn Moxey

Dorian Harewood, Catlin Adams, Robin Gammell

Panic on the 5.22*
US 1974   74m   colour   TVM
Quinn Martin

Wealthy train passengers are terrorized by three incompetent hoodlums who are exasperated at finding credit cards instead of money.
Smooth, odd little suspenser which goes on too long and submerges in cliché philosophy. Some smart moments, though.

w Eugene Price   *d* Harvey Hart

Lynda Day George, Laurence Luckinbill, Ina Balin, Andrew Duggan, Bernie Casey, Linden Chiles, Dana Elcar, Eduard Franz, Reni Santoni

Panorama. The BBC's Monday night current affairs hour, which has been going almost as long as the BBC has and was once hosted by Richard Dimbleby. Over the years it has gained the reputation of being rather earnest and dull, and the BBC seems content to leave it that way, low viewing figures and all.

The Paper Chase*
US 1978   × 50m   colour
TCF (Robert C. Thompson)

Problems of a group of older students at law school.
Pleasing but uncommercial rewrite of the feature film, with John Houseman reprising his ferocious professor.

w James Bridges   *d* Joseph Hardy

JOHN HOUSEMAN, James Stephens, Tom Fitzsimmons, Katherine Dunfee Clarke, Robert Ginty, James Keane

Paper Man*
US 1971   74m   colour   TVM
TCF (Tony Wilson)

Anthology about people in jeopardy situations. The most memorable had James Mason and his family

Complicated melodrama which finally loses the interest after a very smart beginning.

w James D. Buchanan, Ronald Austin *d* Walter Grauman

Dean Stockwell, Stefanie Powers, James Stacy, James Olson, Elliott Street

Paper Moon*
US 1974   13 × 25m   colour
ABC/Paramount/The Directors' Company

A bible-selling con man and a smart little girl team up in the farm belt during the thirties.
A fair copy of the movie; some said it was better. But it didn't please.

Christopher Connelly, Jodie Foster

Paris, Jerry (1925–). American actor turned director, most successfully with *The Dick Van Dyke Show* and *Happy Days*.

Paris Precinct
US 1953–5   26 × 25m   bw
Etoile

French Sûreté inspectors clean up crime in Paris.
Cop show modelled on New York patterns.

Louis Jourdan, Claude Dauphin

Paris 7000
US 1969   10 × 50m   colour
ABC/Universal

An American attached to the embassy staff helps visiting countrymen in Paris.
Inept hokum hurriedly conceived to use up the star's contract when *The Survivors* was cancelled.

George Hamilton, Gene Raymond, Jacques Aubuchon

Parker, Alan (1944–). British director, now into films, but with TV experience. *No Hard Feelings, The Evacuees* (BAFTA award, 1975).

Parker, Eleanor (1922–). American star actress who when movies failed her made occasional forays into TV, the most successful of which was the series *Bracken's World*.

Parker, Fess (1925–). American leading man of the fifties. TV series: *Daniel Boone, Mr Smith Goes to Washington*.

Parker, Willard (1912–) (Worster van Eps). American leading man of a few forties films. TV series: *Tales of the Texas Rangers*.

Parkinson, Michael (1931–). Yorkshire reporter turned talk show host. His ability to get the best guests is offset by his constant references to 'my show'.

Parks, Bert (1915–). American compere and quizmaster of the fifties; later became associated with the Miss America pageant.

Parsons, Nicholas (1928–). British light actor and quizmaster; once a stooge for the comedian Arthur Haynes, in the seventies he became inseparable from *Sale of the Century*.

The Partners
US 1971   20 × 25m   colour
NBC/Universal/Don Lee/NBC

A black and a white cop find themselves in as much trouble as the criminals.
Integrated comedy chase show which quickly ran out of steam.

cr Don Adams

Don Adams, Rupert Crosse

Partners in Crime
US 1973   74m   colour   TVM
Universal (Jon Epstein)

A retired lady judge and a reformed crook set up a detective agency.
A recast version of *The Judge and Jake Wyler* with a plot about an amnesiac robber who can't find his own loot. Still no takers.

w David Shaw   *d* Jack Smight, Jon Epstein

Lee Grant, Lou Antonio, Harry Guardino, Richard Jaeckel, Bob Cummings, Lorraine Gary, Charles Drake

The Partridge Family*
US 1970–3   96 × 25m   colour
ABC/Columbia (Bob Claver, Larry Rosen)

Five singing kids tour with their widowed mother.
Amiable comedy with music which became a teenage rave when David Cassidy soared to stardom.

cr Bernard Slade

Shirley Jones, DAVID CASSIDY, Susan Dey, Danny Bonaduce, Dave Madden

Passage West*
GB 1975   2 × 50m   colour (16mm)
BBC/National Film Board of Canada (Philip Donnellan)

A study of the great British emigration across the Atlantic, told through two cases, one today and one a hundred years ago.
Solidly engrossing documentary stuff.

m John Faulkner

Patterson, Neva (1925–). American character actress. TV series: *The Governor and J. J., Nichols*.

The Patty Duke Show
US 1963–5   104 × 25m   bw
ABC/Chrislaw (William Asher)

A New York high school girl welcomes her identical European cousin for a visit.
Predictable family capers.

cr Sidney Sheldon   *m* Sid Ramm, Harry Geller

Patty Duke, William Schallert, Jean Byron

Paul, John (1921–). British actor who became a national figure as *Probation Officer*, but when that show finished was little heard from.

The Paul Lynde Show
US 1972   26 × 25m   colour
ABC/Columbia (Harry Ackerman, William Asher)

Domestic problems of an attorney.
Flustered generation gap comedy tailored for its star.

cr Sam Clark, Ron Bobrick, from stage play *Howie*

Paul Lynde, Elizabeth Allen, John Calvin, Herb Voland

The Paul Sand Show *
US 1974   13 × 25m   colour
CBS/MTM

Adventures of a bachelor bass player with the Boston Symphony Orchestra.
Slightly unusual and quite likeable situation comedy.

Paul Sand

pay TV. A system, in the experimental stage in the seventies, which would enable viewers to receive more expensive entertainment of their choice – movies, special events – by putting money in the slot.

Peabody Awards. Merit awards made annually to radio/television people and stations; awarded since 1940 in honour of George Foster Peabody, a New York banker.

Peacock, Michael (1929–). British executive who for a shortish period in the sixties and seventies was controller of BBC1, managing director of London Weekend Television, and president of network production for Warner TV in Burbank.

peak time. Usually thought of in the UK as between 7.30 and 10.30pm and in the US (which calls it prime time) as between 8 and 11pm. The half-hour between 7.30 and 8pm is known in the US as prime access time. The need to define it at all is because in peak or prime time, when most people are supposed to be watching, maximum rates can be charged.

Peckinpah, Sam (1926–). American director with a taste for violence. In his earlier days he created and sometimes directed such TV series as *The Rifleman*, *Klondike* and *The Westerner*.

Peck's Bad Girl
US 1959   39 × 25m   bw
ABC

Misadventures of a 12-year-old girl.
Absolutely unsurprising suburban comedy.

Patty McCormack, Wendell Corey, Marsha Hunt

penetration. The extent to which TV is capable of being watched in specified areas; put a simpler way, the percentage of people having TV sets.

Pennies from Heaven **
GB 1978   6 × 75m   colour (VTR)
BBC (Kenith Trodd)

In the mid-thirties, a frustrated song salesman tells himself that everything will be all right, but it isn't.
A unique concept, not entirely satisfactory but impeccably assembled, in which the more depressing the story gets (and it ends with the hero's execution and rebirth), the more frequently the leading characters break into song and dance, or rather mouth to recordings of the time. Undeniably overlong and repetitive, it is superbly acted and directed, and the musical sequences, though their purpose remains slightly mysterious, often equal in delight those of many a major film musical.

w Dennis Potter   *d* PIERS HAGGARD   *choreo* TUDOR DAVIES

BOB HOSKINS, Gemma Craven, Cheryl Campbell, Kenneth Colley, Freddie Jones, Hywel Bennett, Ronald Fraser, Dave King

'It helps us to look at our own world with an alert and sardonic eye. And there is no reason why we should not hum a tune and tap our feet as we do so.' – BBC publicity
'Sparkling, brave, clever and caring.' – *Daily Mail*

People. Based on *People* magazine, this is a half-hour magazine format created for the 1978 season by Time–Life, with stylish segments corresponding to the feature pages of a modern illustrated magazine.

The People *
US 1971   74m   colour   TVM
Metromedia

A young teacher takes a job in a remote town and finds that her employers and pupils are aliens from another planet.
Quiet, understated science fiction with plenty of charm but not enough get-up-and-go.

w James M. Miller   *d* John Korty

Kim Darby, Dan O'Herlihy, William Shatner, Diane Varsi

People Like Us*
GB 1978 13 × 50m colour (VTR)
LWT (Tony Wharmby, James Brabazon)

Life in a suburban avenue during the twenties.
All décor (very good) and no dramatic substance, or at least no characters one cares about.

w James Saunders and others *novel The Avenue* by R. F. Delderfield m Wilfred Josephs

Barbara Shelley, Jim Norton

The People's Choice
US 1956–8 104 × 25m bw
Norden Productions

A politically ambitious young man loves the mayor's daughter.
Wholly American comedy which went down well with the voters.

Jackie Cooper, Patricia Breslin

Peppard, George (1929–). American leading man who came to TV with moderate success as *Banacek*.

Perfect Gentlemen
US 1978 96m colour TVM
Paramount/Bud Austin (Jackie Cooper)

Four women whose husbands are in jail decide to steal back a large bribe to a go-between.
Slow-starting comedy which disappoints despite its star cast.

w Nora Ephron d Jackie Cooper ph William K. Jurgensen m Dominic Frontiere

Lauren Bacall, Ruth Gordon, Sandy Dennis, Lisa Pelikan, Robert Alda, Stephen Pearlman

'Intrinsically a caper telefilm, show doesn't get hopping till the second hour, and then only fitfully.' – *Daily Variety*

Perilous Voyage
US 1969 97m colour TVM
Universal (Jack Laird)

A revolutionary hijacks a ship and its cargo of machine guns.
Highly-coloured adventure story with plenty of action but not much sense.

w Oscar Millard, Sid Stebel, Robert Weverka d William Graham

William Shatner, Lee Grant, Michael Parks, Michael Tolan, Frank Silvera, Louise Sorel

The Perils of Pauline*
US 1967 98m colour TVM
Universal (Herbert B. Leonard)

An orphan girl has international adventures but finally marries the richest man in the world.

Sometimes engaging burlesque of the silent serial, afflicted by an attack of the cutesy-poos.

w Albert Beich d Herbert B. Leonard, Joseph Shelley ph Jack Marta m Vic Mizzy

Pat Boone, Pamela Austin, Terry-Thomas, Edward Everett Horton, Kurt Kasznar, Leon Askin

The Perils of Penelope Pitstop
US 1969–70 17 × 22m colour
Hanna–Barbera

A lady racing driver travels round the world combating her evil rival the Hooded Claw.
Acceptable cartoon humour.

voices Janet Waldo, Paul Lynde, Mel Blanc

Perry Mason***
US 1957–65 245 × 50m bw (last episode in colour)
CBS/Paisano (Gail Patrick Jackson)

Cases of a defence lawyer who, aided by a smart secretary and a friendly detective, always proves his client innocent and someone else guilty. From stories by Erle Stanley Gardner.
Totally formalized and immensely popular, this cleanly made show was a worldwide success and its characters welcome in almost everybody's living-room, especially the DA who never won. Its mystery plots were complex but generally capable of being followed, and watching the show gave something of the satisfaction gained by crossword addicts.

Raymond Burr, Barbara Hale, William Talman, William Hopper, Ray Collins

†In the last episode, *The Case of the Final Fadeout*, guest stars included Erle Stanley Gardner as the judge.
††In *The Case of the Constant Doyle*, when Burr was ill, Bette Davis played a lawyer friend who also won her case.

Person to Person. Long-distance interview series created by and featuring Ed Murrow. It ran successfully through the late fifties.

The Persuaders*
GB 1971 24 × 50m colour
ITC

Two wealthy adventurers fight corruption all over the world.
Not much more serious than the 'Road' films, this series conveyed plenty of fun and its American failure was a mystery.

Roger Moore, Tony Curtis

Persuasion*
GB 1969 5 × 50m colour (VTR)
Granada (Howard Baker)

Anne Elliott rejects the man she loves but later wins him back.

THE PERSUADERS. Tony Curtis with a gun, Roger Moore with a glass . . . all that's needed is women and song, and the series provided plenty of the former at least.

Diligent adaptation of Jane Austen's last romantic novel, filmed in Dorset and Somerset.

w Julian Mitchell   *d* Howard Baker

Ann Firbank, Bryan Marshall

Pete and Gladys
US 1960–1   70 × 25m   bw
CBS

Archetypal domestic comedy, a spin-off from *December Bride*.

Harry Morgan, Cara Williams, Verna Felton

Pete Kelly's Blues
US 1959   13 × 25m   bw
NBC/Universal/Jack Webb

Adventures of a trumpet player in Kansas City in the twenties.
An unsuccessful, moody reprise of an unsuccessful, moody movie.

William Reynolds, Connie Boswell

Peter Gunn*
US 1958–60   114 × 25m   bw
Spartan (Blake Edwards)

Cases of a big city private eye.
Amusing tongue-in-cheek semi-spoof of the genre, with performances and production in key and from the star a fine impersonation of Cary Grant. A movie, *Gunn*, was subsequently made.

cr BLAKE EDWARDS   *m* Henry Mancini

CRAIG STEVENS, LOLA ALBRIGHT, Herschel Bernardi

Peter Loves Mary
US 1960   32 × 25m   bw
NBC/Four Star

The private lives of a show business couple.
Standard domestic farce.

Peter Lind Hayes, Mary Healy

Peter Lundy and the Medicine Hat Stallion
US 1977   96m   colour   TVM
NBC/Ed Friendly

A Pony Express rider recalls his youth in Nebraska.
Overlong pilot which caused no enthusiasm.

w Jack Turley, *novel* Marguerite Henry   *d* Michael O'Herlihy   *ph* Robert L. Morrison   *m* Morton Stevens

Leif Garrett, Mitch Ryan, John Anderson

Peter Pan. The legendary TV production of the J. M. Barrie classic was the one originally presented live in 1955 by NBC, directed by Michael Kidd, with Mary Martin and Cyril Ritchard. Taped the following year, it was repeated many times.

Peter Pan
GB 1976   96m   colour (VTR)
ITC (Gary Smith)

THE PERSUADERS. An element of spoofing was what mainly commended this series: the principals were clearly enjoying themselves, and so here is guest star Gladys Cooper.

A stagey version, lacking in inspiration throughout.

adaptors Andrew Birkin, Jack Burns · *d* Dwight Hemion *songs* Leslie Bricusse, Tony Newley

Mia Farrow, Danny Kaye

Peter Potamus
US 1964 42 × 25m colour
Hanna–Barbera

Adventures of a globe-trotting purple hippo and his monkey assistant So-So. Other segments introduce

Breezely and Sneezely, a polar bear and a seal; and Yippy, Yappy and Yahooey, three dogs.

Petrocelli
US 1974 48 × 50m colour
NBC/Paramount (Thomas L. Miller, Edward J. Milkis)

A lawyer of Italian origin practises in a southwestern cattle town.

Courtroom series drawn from the TV movie *Night Moves*, which was itself derived from the theatrical movie *The Lawyer*. Quite efficient, not very likeable. Filmed in Tucson.

cr Sidney J. Furie, Harold Buchman, E. Jack Neuman

Barry Newman, Susan Howard, Albert Salmi

Petticoat Junction*
US 1963–9 148 × 25m colour
Filmways (Al Simon/Charles Stewart)

Misadventures in a rural hotel and the train which serves it.
Studio-bound farce, quite nimbly presented by an engaging cast.

cr Paul Henning

Bea Benaderet, Edgar Buchanan, Linda Kaye, Douglass Dumbrille, Charles Lane, Rufe Davis, Smiley Burnette, Meredith McRae, Lori Saunders (June Lockhart replaced Bea Benaderet who died during fifth season)

Pettifer, Julian (1935–). British roving reporter: *Panorama*, *24 Hours*, etc. BAFTA award 1969 for his coverage of the Vietnam war.

Peyton Place***
US 1964–8 514 × 25m colour (1st two seasons bw)
ABC/TCF (Paul Monash)

Twice-weekly serial revealing the dark secrets of a small town.
Initially at least a superior piece of dramaturgy, cleverly directed, photographed and cast. The inevitable lapse came well before the end, with the departure of the first set of characters.

cr PAUL MONASH from the novel by Grace Metalious

DOROTHY MALONE, Ed Nelson, MIA FARROW, Christopher Connelly, George Macready, Dan Duryea, BARBARA PARKINS, RYAN O'NEAL, TIM O'CONNOR

† An unsuccessful – and dreadful – daytime soap opera, *Return to Peyton Place*, occupied the 1972 season. A telemovie, *Murder in Peyton Place*, appeared in 1977.

The Phantom of Hollywood*
US 1974 74m colour TVM
MGM

When a film studio's back lot is bulldozed, mysterious deaths are caused by a masked figure.
Cheeky transplanting of *The Phantom of the Opera*; unfortunately the script isn't quite up to it.

w George Schenck *d* Gene Levitt

Jack Cassidy, Peter Lawford, Skye Aubrey, Jackie Coogan, Broderick Crawford, Peter Haskell, John Ireland

The Phil Silvers Show: see You'll Never Get Rich

Philby, Burgess and MacLean*
GB 1977 78m colour (16mm)
Granada (Jeremy Wallington)

A dramatized reconstruction of how the famous trio of Foreign Office officials became red spies and absconded to Moscow.
A fascinating piece of character drawing which touches a few nerves.

w Ian Curteis *d* Gordon Flemyng

DEREK JACOBI, Anthony Bate, Michael Culver, Elizabeth Seal, Arthur Lowe

'Ninety spellbinding minutes of insight and revelation.' – *Sunday Express*

Philpott, Trevor (1927–). Familiar British documentarist with the common touch, on BBC in occasional series about the British way of life.

Phoenix, Patricia (1924–). British character actress, *Coronation Street*'s Elsie Tanner.

Phyllis*
US 1975–6 39 × 25m colour
Mary Tyler Moore (Ed Weinberger, Stan Daniels)

Phyllis, a character from *The Mary Tyler Moore Show*, is always behind the eight ball. When her husband dies, she goes to live in San Francisco with her unsympathetic in-laws.
Initially an amusing comedy full of cranky people, this had worn out its welcome by the end of its first season.

cr Ed Weinberger, Stan Daniels

Cloris Leachman, Henry Jones, Barbara Colby

The Phyllis Diller Show: see The Pruitts of Southampton

Pickles, Vivian (1933–). British character actress who has made occasional hit appearances, notably as Isadora Duncan.

Pickles, Wilfred (1904–78). Yorkshire compere and comedian at his height in the forties; came back in the sixties as a character actor and was prominent in *For the Love of Ada* and *The Nearly Man*.

Pickup, Ronald (*c* 1940–). British stage actor who was notable on TV as Randolph Churchill in *Jennie*.

The Picnic
GB 1975 30m colour (16mm)
BBC (Terry Hughes)

Silent comedy about the disasters which befall a crusty general and his family when they picnic by a river.
Disappointing, rather ill-timed pratfall farce, like Jacques Tati on an off day.

w David Huggett, Larry Keith

Ronnie Barker, Ronnie Corbett, Madge Hindle, Barbara New, Patricia Brake

The Picture of Dorian Gray
GB 1976 100m colour (VTR)
BBC

A lethargic adaptation of Oscar Wilde's famous story about an evil young Victorian who stays young while his portrait gets older and more raddled. Distinguished by Gielgud as Henry Wotton, but let down by Firth's impossibly pansy and broad-accented Dorian.

adaptor John Osborne *d* John Gorrie

JOHN GIELGUD, Peter Firth, Jeremy Brett

The Pigeon
US 1969 70m colour TVM
Spelling–Thomas

A black private eye tries to protect a family from the Mafia.
Unoriginal detection caper.

w Edward Lask *d* Earl Bellamy

Sammy Davis Jnr, Dorothy Malone, Ricardo Montalban, Pat Boone, Roy Glenn Snr, Victoria Vetri

Pilger, John (*c* 1940–). Australian investigative journalist in Britain.

pilot. A film made in order to test a format and its public reaction. At one time the pilot simply became the first episode, but in the seventies for economic reasons it became normal to make a two-hour pilot even for a half-hour comedy. This resulted in some exceptionally boring pilots which squandered promising ideas.

Pine Canyon is Burning
US 1977 74m colour TVM
Universal

A fireman leaves the city to begin a one-man country rescue operation.
Busted pilot, spun off from *Emergency*. Very routine.

w R. A. Cinader *d* Chris Nyby III

Kent McCord, Diana Muldaur, Dick Bakalyan, Andrew Duggan

The Pink Panther. A cartoon character from the title sequence of the film of the same name. *The Pink Panther Show* was a series of half-hours composed of the theatrical cartoons by De Patie–Freleng featuring the Panther and accident-prone Inspector Clouseau.

Pinky and Perky. Two puppet pigs, very popular on British TV in the fifties and early sixties.

Pinocchio*
US 1976 74m colour (VTR)
Vidtronics/Bernard Rothman, Jack Wohl

Musical version of the Collodi story of a puppet who becomes human.
Rather stiff at the joints, this old fashioned TV studio production nevertheless finds the stars in good form.

w Herbert Baker *d* Ron Field, Sidney Smith *songs* Billy Barnes

Danny Kaye (as Gepetto, Stroganoff and Collodi), Sandy Duncan, Flip Wilson, Clive Revill, Gary Morgan

Pinter, Harold (1930–). British playwright whose dialogue falls splendidly on the ear but whose meaning is often impenetrable. Work specifically written for TV includes *A Night Out, Tea Party, The Lover*.

Pioneer Woman*
US 1973 74m colour TVM
Filmways

Even after her husband is killed, a western-bound woman sets up house with her family.
Earnest sodbusting epic which unfortunately never made a series: it's convincingly done.

w Suzanne Clouser *d* Buzz Kulik

Joanna Pettet, David Janssen, William Shatner, Lance Le Gault

Pistols 'n' Petticoats
US 1966 26 × 25m colour
CBS/Universal

Adventures of the long-suffering family of two rootin' tootin' hillbilly women.
Dismal farce which unhappily ended the career of its star.

Ann Sheridan, Ruth McDevitt, Douglas Fowley

The Plane Makers*
GB 1963 × 50m bw (VTR)
ATV

Drama series about management and union disputes in an aircraft factory.
A solid series which gradually spotlighted the performance of Patrick Wymark as John Wilder. After two seasons the centre of interest moved entirely to the board room and the title was changed to *The Power Game*.

cr WILFRED GREATOREX

PATRICK WYMARK, Barbara Murray, Jack Watling, Reginald Marsh

Planet of the Apes**
US 1974 14 × 50m colour
CBS/TCF (Herbert Hirschman)

Two astronauts lost in a time warp land on a planet where the apes are masters.
Clever retread of a powerful movie in a format somewhere between *The Fugitive* and *Gulliver's Travels*. Unfortunately it was badly scheduled, and the usual

public indifference to quality merchandise caused a sudden cancellation, so that the astronauts are never rescued.

Ron Harper, James Naughton, Roddy McDowall, Booth Colman, Mark Lenard

† A cartoon series, *Return to the Planet of the Apes*, was made in 1975 by De Patie–Freleng.

Playhouse 90. Ambitious for its time (1958), this CBS season of '90-minute' film dramas supplied by Columbia marked the real beginning of the TV movie. Producer: Hubbell Robinson.

Playmates**
US 1972 74m colour TVM
Lillian Gallo

Two divorced men from different backgrounds become friends when taking their kids to the park. Later each begins to date the other's ex-wife.
Amusing modern comedy, smartly scripted and edited.

w Richard Baer *d* Theodore J. Flicker

Alan Alda, Doug McClure, Connie Stevens, Barbara Feldon

Please Don't Eat the Daisies
US 1965–6 58 × 25m colour
NBC/MGM

Comedy of a suburban family, including a wife who writes and a shaggy dog. From the book (and film) by Jean Kerr.
Unexceptionable and unexceptional.

Pat Crowley, Mark Miller

Please Sir*
GB 1968 40 approx. × 25m colour (VTR)
London Weekend

A young schoolmaster has trouble with a rough mixed class.
Watchable sitcom depicting the lighter side of *The Blackboard Jungle* and *To Sir with Love*; borrowed in the US by the makers of *Welcome Back Kotter*. The staff room scenes were the most amusing. When the star departed the kids continued as *The Fenn Street Gang*.

JOHN ALDERTON, Erik Chitty, Joan Sanderson, DERYCK GUYLER

PLEASE SIR. John Alderton refuses to be browbeaten by his unruly class.

Pleasure at Her Majesty's*
GB 1976   100m   colour (16mm)
Amnesty (Roger Graef)

A charity stage show, with peeps backstage.
A bit of a shambles, but useful as a record of some of
the best sketches of the *Beyond the Fringe* and *Monty
Python* teams, not to mention Barry Humphries and the
Goodies.

Alan Bennett, John Bird, Eleanor Bron, Tim Brooke-
Taylor, Graham Chapman, John Cleese, Peter Cook,
Graeme Garden, Barry Humphries, Jonathan Miller,
Bill Oddie, Michael Palin

Pleshette, Suzanne (1937–). American leading
lady, familiar in many movies and on TV in the long-
running *Bob Newhart Show*.

Plimpton, George (1927–). American investigative reporter who in the early seventies appeared in
several specials showing him getting right inside the
activity concerned: a professional footballer, a bit part
player in a John Wayne western, an auto racer, etc.
Generally more foolhardy than valiant.

Poldark
GB 1976–7   29 × 50m   colour (VTR)
London Films/BBC (Tony Coburn, Richard Beynon,
Morris Barry)

A serial adaptation of Winston Graham's novels about
the adventures of a squire in 18th-century Cornwall.
Moderately popular period tushery, as well done as
need be.

w Jack Pulman, Paul Wheeler, Peter Draper, Jack
Russell, Alexander Baron, John Wiles, Martin
Worth   *d* Christopher Barry, Paul Annett, Kenneth
Ives, Philip Dudley, Roger Jenkins

Robin Ellis, Angharad Rees, Jill Townsend, Eileen
Way, Judy Geeson, Ralph Bates

Police Five: see Taylor, Shaw

Police Story**
US 1975   × 50m   colour
NBC/Columbia/David Gerber (Stanley Kallis)

Anthology of serious dramas showing the human and
social side of police work.
At its best, a compelling series, but the lack of a continuing thread made it easy to miss. In 1977 it was reduced to 8 × 95m episodes a season, which gave more
room for dramatic development.

Police Surgeon
Canada 1972–3   52 × 25m   colour (16mm)
CIV–Colgate (Wilton Schiller)

Dr Simon Locke (q.v.) moves into the big city.
Tolerable series with the doc encountering more criminals than Mike Hammer.

Sam Groom, Len Birman, Larry D. Mann

† *Police Surgeon* was also the title of an ABC (GB) bw
tape series out of which grew *The Avengers*.

Police Woman*
US 1975–   × 50m   colour
NBC/Columbia/David Gerber (Douglas Benton)

A more hokey extension of *Police Story*, spun off from
an episode entitled *Dangerous Games*. The star is
decorative but doesn't do much except get herself into
rather foolish and repetitive jeopardy situations.
Production values high, though.

Angie Dickinson, Earl Holliman, Charles Dierkop, Ed
Bernard

Police Woman Decoy: see Decoy

Pony Express
US 1959   39 × 25m   bw
NBC

Exploits of the pony express riders.
Quite acceptable youth western.

Grant Sullivan

Poor Devil
US 1972   73m   colour   TVM
Paramount

An aide of Satan fails to persuade a book-keeper to sign
one of his contracts.
Grimly unfunny heavenly pantomime with all
concerned ill at ease.

w Arne Sultan, Earl Barrett, Richard Baer   *d* Robert
Scheerer

Sammy Davis Jnr, Christopher Lee, Jack Klugman

Popeye. The original 234 Max Fleischer cartoons of
the spinach-eating sailorman were gobbled up by TV,
and King Features Syndicate in 1961 made 220 new
ones running five minutes each, but without the old
spark. 17 half hour shows followed in 1978.

Popi
US 1976   13 × 25m   colour
ITP/Allied Artists (Herbert B. Leonard)

Adventures of a lower-class Puerto Rican New
Yorker.
Dismal ethnic comedy drama.

cr Tina and Lester Pine, from the film of the same
name   *m* George Del Barrio

Hector Elizondo, Edith Diaz, Anthony Perez

The Poppy Is Also a Flower
GB title: *Danger Grows Wild*
US 1966   105m   colour   TVM
Comet/Euan Lloyd/TelsUN

United Nations agents destroy a narcotics ring.
All-star do-goodery sponsored by the United Nations;
not much of a film.

POLITICS. British programme companies were either inclined or persuaded to take political matters with great seriousness. Here Mike Scott prepares a carefully chosen cross-section of voters to comment on the aims of the parties.

w Jo Eisinger, *theme* Ian Fleming   *d* Terence Young

Yul Brynner, Omar Sharif, Trevor Howard, Angie Dickinson, Rita Hayworth, E. G. Marshall, Gilbert Roland, Anthony Quayle, Eli Wallach, Stephen Boyd, Jack Hawkins, Marcello Mastroianni

Porridge***
GB 1974–7   30 approx. × 30m   colour (VTR)
BBC (Sidney Lotterby)

An old lag in prison knows all the angles.
Hilarious, sometimes thoughtful comedy of prison life, undoubtedly one of Britain's top sitcoms, largely because of its brilliant but unselfish star but partly because of the best comedy dialogue since *Steptoe and Son*.

cr/w IAN LA FRENAIS, DICK CLEMENT

RONNIE BARKER, RICHARD BECKINSALE, FULTON MCKAY, BRIAN WILDE

† In 1978 began *Going Straight*, a sequel showing Fletcher's attempt to adapt himself to his old home life.

Porter, Don (1912–). American second lead of the forties who grew into a useful character actor via TV

roles in the series *Private Secretary*, *Our Miss Brooks*, *The Ann Sothern Show* and *Gidget*.

Porter, Eric (1928–). Gaunt British character actor whose finest hour was as Soames in *The Forsyte Saga*.

Porter, Nyree Dawn (1940–). Attractive New Zealand leading lady who landed a plum role as Irene in *The Forsyte Saga*. Also appeared in *The Protectors*.

Portrait*
GB 1978   6 × 25m   colour (16mm)
BBC (Michael Begg)

Six people are painted by famous artists, and chat about their feelings as the portrait goes through its various stages.
A simple but effective idea, though the degree of interest must vary widely with the subject.

Robert Morley painted by David Poole, Chris Bonnington by Alexander Goodie, Twiggy by Peter Blake, Eric D. Morley by Michael Noakes, the Earl of Lichfield by Lorne McKean, Ted Willis by Jim Mendoza

† In each case the model's fee was the portrait!

The Possessed
US 1977 74m colour TVM
Warner/NBC (Philip Mandelker)

A defrocked minister fights the devil in a girls' school.
Gloomy screamer, yet another attempt to bring *The Exorcist* to TV. (See *Spectre*.]

w John Sacret Young *d* Jerry Thorpe *m* Leonard Rosenman

Potter, Dennis (*c* 1934–). British TV playwright, noted for one-off plays and series on controversial themes: *Stand Up, Stand Up, Nigel Barton, Son of Man, Brimstone and Treacle, Pennies from Heaven, Joe's Ark, Blue Remembered Hills*, etc.

Potts, Cliff (*c* 1942–). Tough-looking American leading man. Series: *Once an Eagle, Big Hawaii.*

Powder Keg*
US 1970 93m colour TVM
Filmways

In the 1914 southwest, two car-driving troubleshooters agree to get back a hijacked train from Mexico.
Ambitious pilot which flags between the action highlights. The resulting series, *Bearcats*, was shortlived.

w/d Douglas Heyes

Rod Taylor, Dennis Cole, Michael Ansara, Fernando Lamas, Tisha Sterling, John McIntire, Luciana Paluzzi, Reni Santoni

Powell, Dick (1904–63). American leading man and singer of Hollywood in the thirties; in the forties he proved himself an actor and then, with David Niven and Charles Boyer, founded Four Star Television (there was no fourth) which in the fifties was quite a driving force of the industry. Before the camera, he hosted *Dick Powell Theatre*, which won many awards, and *Zane Grey Theatre.*

Powell, Vince (19 –). British scriptwriter, often with Harry Driver.

The Power Game. An ATV monochrome VTR series of the mid-sixties which followed its predecessor *The Plane Makers* into the boardroom and made a star of Patrick Wymark as John Wilder, the power-hungry executive whom everybody loved to hate. Also much involved were Barbara Murray and Jack Watling. Wilfred Greatorex created both series.

The Practice
US 1976–7 30 × 25m colour
NBC/MGM/Danny Thomas (Paul Junger Witt)

Conflict arises between an old New York doctor and his son who shares the same practice.
Reasonably lively Jewish comedy series.

story consultant James Ritz *m* David Shire

Danny Thomas, David Spielberg

Pray for the Wildcats*
US 1974 100m colour TVM
ABC/Tony Wilson

Four business associates take a motor cycle trip into a remote region, but they end up fighting natural obstacles and each other.
A timid version of the cinema film *Deliverance:* not bad on its level.

w Jack Turley *d* Robert Michael Lewis

Andy Griffith, Marjoe Gortner, Robert Reed, William Shatner, Angie Dickinson, Janet Margolin, Lorraine Gary

Prescription Murder**
US 1967 99m colour TVM
Universal (Richard Irving)

A smoothie doctor murders his wife, but a dim-looking police lieutenant is on his trail.
Actually the first *Columbo* (see *Mystery Movie*) made four years before the series proper began. One of the best, with the formula intact.

w Richard Levinson, William Link, from their play *d* Richard Irving

Peter Falk, Gene Barry, Katharine Justice, Nina Foch, William Windom

presentation. The department in a TV company responsible for getting the programme on to the air, supervising announcements, making timings, checking prints, meeting network junctions, etc.

The President's Mistress*
US 1978 96m colour TVM
Stephen Friedman/Kings Road/Richard Bright (Herbert Hirschman)

The American president's secret mistress is suspected by the CIA of being a Russian spy.
Intriguing suspenser set in high places.

w Tom Lazarus, *novel* Patrick Anderson *d* John Llewellyn Moxey *ph* Robert Morrison *m* Lalo Schifrin

Beau Bridges, Joel Fabiani, Larry Hagman, Karen Grassle, Don Porter, Thalmus Rasulala, Gail Strickland

'A swift, attention-getting telefilm with good suspense and sharp twists.' – *Daily Variety*

The President's Plane Is Missing*
US 1971 94m colour TVM
ABC Circle

Air Force One disappears with the President aboard . . .

245

Rather mild political suspenser which disappoints despite a strong cast.

w Mark Carliner, Ernest Kinoy   *d* Daryl Duke

Buddy Ebsen, Peter Graves, Arthur Kennedy, Rip Torn, Raymond Massey, Tod Andrews, Mercedes McCambridge, Joseph Campanella

Pretty Boy Floyd
US 1974   74m   colour   TVM
Universal (Jo Swerling Jnr)

The hunt for a 1930s public enemy.
Routine law-and-gangster stuff.

w/d Clyde Ware

Martin Sheen, Michael Parks, Kim Darby, Ellen Corby

The Price Is Right. American game show, showing since the late fifties, sometimes on several nights a week. Contestants are involved in guessing the value of various items of merchandise, sometimes via complex games, and the remarkable thing about the show is the amount of hysteria generated.

Pride of the Family
US 1953   40 × 25m   bw
MCA/Revue

Misadventures of a family in which the husband can't do anything right.
Primitive sitcom.

Paul Hartman, Fay Wray, Natalie Wood

The Priest Killer*
US 1971   100m   colour   TVM
Universal

San Francisco's law forces combine to catch a madman who murders Catholic priests.
Oddball cop show in which Ironside meets Sarge, and between them they get their man. Originally intended as two episodes of *Ironside*.

w Robert Van Scoyk, Joel Oliansky   *d* Richard A. Colla

Raymond Burr, George Kennedy, Don Galloway, Louise Jeffries, Don Mitchell, Anthony Zerbe

Priestley, J. B. (1894–). British writer of renown who has been seen infrequently on TV unless as an occasional pundit or tubthumper for his own new books. In 1977 however he trudged through the midlands and north, revisiting old haunts for a disappointing series of three half-hours called *An Englishman's Journey* (BBC; producer George Green).

The Prime of Miss Jean Brodie*
GB 1978   7 × 50m   colour
Scottish TV

Adaptation of Muriel Spark's novel about a headstrong spinster schoolteacher in thirties Edinburgh.

Better frissons than the film, but too extended.

Geraldine McEwan

prime time: see peak time

Primus
US 1971   26 × 25m   colour
Metromedia/Ivan Tors

An undersea expert fights crime as well as sharks.
An updated *Sea Hunt*, quite good to look at.

Robert Brown, Will Kuluva

The Prince of Central Park*
US 1977   74m   colour   TVM
Lorimar (Harvey Hart)

Two children make a Shangri-La of the big city park.
Rather unusual, well-made little idyll.

w Jeb Rosebrook *novel* Evan H. Rhodes   *d* Harvey Hart   *m* Arthur B. Rubenstein

Ruth Gordon, T. J. Hargrave, Lisa Richard, Brooke Shields

Prinze, Freddie (1953–76). Puerto Rican light actor, a suicide victim during the run of his big hit *Chico and the Man*.

The Prison*
GB 1975   78m   colour   TVM
Thames/Euston Films

A businessman is told that his wife has killed her sister out of jealousy.
Tortuous suspenser, quite neatly packaged.

w Geoffrey Gilbert *novel* Georges Simenon   *d* David Wickes

James Laurenson, Ann Curthoys, James Maxwell, Kenneth Griffith, André Morell, Philip Madoc, George Murcell

'A first-class all-location job.' – *Daily Express*

The Prisoner**
GB 1967   17 × 50m   colour
ATV (Patrick McGoohan)

An ex-secret agent is captured and brainwashed in a curious Shangri-La civilization from which he finds he can never escape.
Downright peculiar, sometimes fascinating, often irritating and trendy melodrama in which the episodes, though well made and acted, tended towards repetition. The much-awaited final episode explained nothing and fell apart almost completely, the intention apparently being to make a statement about Vietnam.

Patrick McGoohan

† Revived in 1976, the show turned into a minor cult, and Portmeirion, the private Welsh village in which it was filmed, again attracted unwelcome hordes of tourists.

THE PRISONER. Typical goings-on from this over-the-top spy series which its star, who increasingly took control, apparently thought made some kind of comment about Vietnam. In charge: Leo McKern. Enthroned: Patrick McGoohan.

Private Secretary*
aka: *Susie*
US 1952–3   104 × 25m   bw
ITC/Ann Sothern

The secretary in a talent agency has more power than the boss.
Amusing sitcom with stars working well in tandem.

Ann Sothern, Don Porter

† See *The Ann Sothern Show.*

Prix Italia. An international merit prize established in 1948 by RAI. The competition is held each year in an Italian city and programmes can be submitted under many headings.

Prix Jeunesse. An international merit prize established for excellence in the production of TV programmes for children awarded every other year in Munich by a foundation sponsored by the EBU and UNESCO.

Probation Officer. A successful British one-hour series of the late fifties, which made stars of John Paul and David Davies, who failed to stay the course. A Rediffusion production with many courtroom scenes.

Probe*
aka: *Search*
US 1972   97m   colour   TVM
Warner (Leslie Stevens)

CIA agents are monitored by implanted radio devices.
Childlike James Bond stuff which works very well because it has a sense of humour and the bigger than usual budget is well spent. The resultant series, however, fell apart because of rotating leads.

w/d RUSSELL MAYBERRY

Hugh O'Brian, John Gielgud, Angel Tompkins, Elke Sommer, Burgess Meredith, Lilia Skala, Kent Smith

The Profane Comedy
aka: *Set This Town on Fire*
US 1969   96m   colour   TVM
Universal (Roy Huggins)

A convict is pardoned and announces that he will run for Lieutenant Governor.
Hard-to-like, awkwardly paced and obscurely narrated melodrama.

w John Thomas James   *d* David Lowell Rich

Chuck Connors, Carl Betz, Lynda Day George, John Anderson, Jeff Corey

Professional Foul*
GB 1977   80m   colour (VTR)
BBC (Mark Shivas)

An academic in Prague for a conference is asked by a former student to smuggle a manuscript out to the free world.
Undoubtedly superior but only patchily engrossing tragi-comedy from a fashionable playwright who suffers from verbal diarrhoea.

w Tom Stoppard   *d* Michael Lindsay-Hogg

PETER BARKWORTH

'Funny, engrossing and suspenseful.' – *Daily Telegraph*
'A serious response by a writer of comedies to Amnesty's Prisoner of Conscience Year.' – Mark Shivas

The Professionals
GB 1978   × 50m   colour
LWT/Avengers (Albert Fennell, Brian Clemens)

An elite squad of MI5 deals with dangerous cases.
Derivative thick-ear which turned out not to be the *Sweeney* of the spy world.

Gordon Jackson, Martin Shaw, Lewis Collins

Project UFO
US 1978   23 × 50m   colour
Jack Webb

Investigations into flying saucer sightings.
The trouble is too much build-up for what must strictly speaking be a letdown, and the terse Webb style doesn't help in this case: three stories could have been got into each hour.

William Jordan, Caskey Swain

Promise Him Anything
US 1975   74m   colour   TVM
Seven Arts (Stanley Rubin)

Having suggested on her computer dating card that 'anything goes', a girl is taken to court when she doesn't produce.
The comedy doesn't produce either.

w David Freeman   *d* Edward Parone

Eddie Albert, Meg Foster, Frederic Forrest, William Schallert, Tom Ewell

The Protectors
GB 1971   26 × 25m   colour (16mm)
ATV

International assignments for top private detectives.
Routine hokum, competently presented.

Nyree Dawn Porter, Robert Vaughn, Tony Anholt

Provine, Dorothy (1937–   ). American leading lady who was scarcely noticed in *The Alaskans* but made

PUBLIC EYE. Alfred Burke as the down-at-heel detective (a far cry from Raymond Chandler) faces a client played by Ronald Lewis.

a hit as the singer in *The Roaring Twenties*. It subsequently emerged that she couldn't really sing.

The Pruitts of Southampton
aka: *The Phyllis Diller Show*
US 1966   30 × 25m   colour
ABC/Filmways

Stories from a novel by Patrick Dennis about the eccentric old pillar of Long Island society who protects her family's reputation.
Unfortunately the character and the actress meet in head-on collision, and the result is uneasy farce.

Phyllis Diller, Reginald Gardiner, Grady Sutton, John McGiver, Richard Deacon, Gypsy Rose Lee

The Psychiatrist: God Bless the Children
US 1970   97m   colour   TVM
Universal (Edgar Small, Norman Felton)

A psychoanalyst helps a small town fight a school drug epidemic.
Ho-hum social conscience stuff.

w Jerrold Freedman   *d* Daryl Duke

Roy Thinnes, Pete Duel, Luther Adler, Katherine Justice

Public Defender
US 1953–4   59 × 25m   bw
Hal Roach

Stories of the counsel appointed to give free legal aid to the poor.
Modest courtroom dramas.

Reed Hadley

Public Eye**
GB 1969–73   33 × 50m   21 colour, 12 bw
Thames

Cases of a down-at-heel private eye.
Moderately realistic detective dramas with a likeable hero who even goes to jail at the end of the series.

Alfred Burke

DR MAGNUS PYKE faces a giant image of himself in *Don't Ask Me*. His popularity at the age of sixty-eight is an illustration of the public's love of a 'character' and also its awe of wisdom when brought down to the level of the common man.

Pueblo**
US 1973   100m   colour   TVM (videotape)
Titus (Herb Brodkin)

An American ship is seized by the North Koreans.
Dramatic documentary, very powerfully made.

Hal Holbrook, Andrew Duggan, Richard Mulligan,
George Grizzard, Gary Merrill, Mary Fickett

Punch and Jody
US 1974   74m   colour   TVM
Metromedia

An executive leaves his wife and joins the circus as a
clown. 15 years later his daughter comes looking for
him.
Drippy drama, awash in sentimentality and self-pity.

w John McGreevey   *d* Barry Shear

Glenn Ford, Pam Griffin, Ruth Roman, Kathleen
Widdoes

The Pursuers
GB 1963   39 × 25m   bw
Jack Gross

Scotland Yard stories, involving the use of police dogs.
Very moderate mysteries.

Louis Hayward

Pyke, Dr Magnus (1910–   ). British TV personality
of the seventies, a scientist who on *Don't Ask Me* and
other shows displayed a propensity for talking very fast
and waving his arms around, thus making himself
famous as an easy target for impressionists. He was
soon doing commercials.

Q

QB VII*
US 1974   315m   colour
Columbia/Douglas Cramer

An American author in a novel accuses a Jewish doctor of war crimes; the doctor sues.
Thinly disguised fact from the book by Leon Uris; as drama rather overstretched and patchily directed and acted, the fact being more remarkable than the fiction. Its interest is as the first of the very long TV novelizations of the seventies: it was played in two 'three-hour' segments and its qualified success led to *Rich Man, Poor Man* and *Best Sellers*.

d Tom Gries

Anthony Hopkins, Ben Gazzara, Juliet Mills, Leslie Caron, Edith Evans, Jack Hawkins, Lee Remick, John Gielgud, Dan O'Herlihy

Quarantined
US 1970   74m   colour   TVM
Paramount

A case of cholera hits a hospital just as a kidney donor is needed.
Medical suspenser, not very interesting.

w Norman Katkov   *d* Leo Penn

John Dehner, Gary Collins, Sharon Farrell, Wally Cox, Sam Jaffe

Quark
US 1978   50m   colour
Columbia/David Gerber (Bruce Johnson)

Adventures of a garbage collector in outer space.
Woefully unfunny opening episode for a shortlived half-hour series (eight of them made it).

cr Buck Henry   *w* Steve Zacharias   *d* Hy Averback
ph Gerry P. Finnerman   *m* Perry Botkin Jnr

Richard Benjamin, Conrad Janis, Hans Conried, Henry Silva, Tim Thomerson, Richard Kelton, Douglas Fowley

The Quatermass Experiment***
GB 1953   6 × 30m   bw (VTR)
BBC

Professor Quatermass's space ship returns from its test flight with one surviving crew member who gradually turns to a loathsome putrescence.
Highly effective serial chiller of its day: it kept the whole of Britain glued to its sets.

w NIGEL KNEALE   *d* RUDOLF CARTIER

Reginald Tate, Isabel Dean, Duncan Lamont, Paul Whitsun-Jones, Ian Colin

† Within a few years Kneale produced two further six-parters: *Quatermass II* (aliens take over a food processing plant) and *Quatermass and the Pit* (the evil influence of aliens who landed on earth five million years ago is felt when a pit is dug). All three were later filmed.

The Queen and I
US 1968   13 × 25m   colour
CBS/Ed Feldman

Fun on a pleasure cruiser.
Tepid comedy.

Billy de Wolfe

Queen for a Day.
American daytime show, a big hit between 1955 and 1964 after 10 years of similar success on radio. Five contestants competed to tell sob stories about why they needed a particular expensive item, and audience applause decided which of them should win. The nadir of American TV.

Queen of the Stardust Ballroom**
US 1975   109m   colour   TVM
Robert Christianson, Rick Rosenberg

A middle-aged Bronx widow finds a new interest in life – the local dance hall.
Charming, well-written, homely drama reminiscent of *Marty*.

w Jerome Cass   *d* Sam O'Steen

Maureen Stapleton, Charles Durning, Michael Brandon, Michael Strong

Quentin Dergens MP*
Canada 1966   20 approx. × 50m   colour (VTR)
Ronald Weyman/CBC

Problems of a Canadian MP.
Solidly interesting series which might have been expected to do more for its star's career.

cr George Robertson

Gordon Pinsent

The Quest*
US 1976   100m   colour   TVM
Columbia/David Gerber (Christopher Morgan)

Two brothers seek their sister who years ago was abducted by Indians.

Expensive but glum pilot.

w Tracy Keenan Wynn   *d* Lee H. Katzin

Kurt Russell, Tim Matheson, Brian Keith, Neville Brand, Cameron Mitchell, Keenan Wynn, Will Hutchins

†The resulting series flopped through being too dour and violent: it lasted 13 × 50m episodes. Producers: Mark Rodgers, James H. Brown.

A Question of Guilt
US 1978   96m   colour   TVM
Lorimar (Peter Katz)

A loose woman is accused of murdering her two children, and public opinion and a prejudiced cop almost convict her.
Heavy-going socially conscious melodrama: they don't bother to tell us who did kill the kids.

w Jack and Mary Willis   *d* Robert Butler   *ph* Ric Waite   *m* Artie Kane

Tuesday Weld, Ron Leibman, Peter Masterson, Alex Rocco, Viveca Lindfors, Lana Wood

'It strains credulity too often to be believable.' – *Daily Variety*

The Questor Tapes
US 1973   100m   colour   TVM
Universal

A superstrong robot is partly human but has no emotions.
A rather boring bit of science fiction which was elbowed out of the series stakes by *Six Million Dollar Man*.

w Gene Roddenberry, Gene L. Coon   *d* Richard A. Colla

Robert Foxworth, Mike Farrell, John Vernon, Lew Ayres, Dana Wynter, James Shigeta

Quick Draw McGraw*
US 1959–62   135 × 25m   colour
Hanna–Barbera

A dim-witted horse tries to maintain law and order in the old west.
The cartoon series which followed the phenomenally successful *Huckleberry Hound*. Superior by TV standards. Also involved: *Snagglepuss*, a trouble-prone lion with a Bert Lahr voice; *Snooper and Blabber*, another cat and mouse team; *Augie Doggie and Doggie Daddy*, a generation gap comedy.

Quiller
GB 1975   13 × 50m   colour (VTR)
BBC/TCF (Peter Graham Scott)

A top level government agent sometimes has doubts about his superiors.
Po-faced spy stuff, full of the clichés of the genre.

Michael Jayston, Moray Watson, Sinead Cusack

Quincy*
US 1976–   × 50m   colour
Universal/Glen A. Larson

A medical examiner in the coroner's office can't resist poking his nose in and finding cases of murder.
Despite the number of corpses about, this is a lighthearted series and its star often triumphs over necessarily unconvincing scripts.

cr Glen A. Larson, Lou Shaw

JACK KLUGMAN, Robert Ito, Garry Walberg

†The series began as part of *Mystery Movie*, with four 96m episodes. See also: *A Star is Dead*.

Quinn, Anthony (1915–). Virile, dominating Mexican–American character actor with a long career in films. His one TV series, *The Man and the City*, was unsuccessful.

The Quinns
US 1977   74m   colour   TVM
Daniel Wilson

Life with a family of New York Irish who have been firefighters for four generations.
Tolerable failed pilot.

w Sidney Carroll   *d* Daniel Petrie   *m* John Scott

Barry Bostwick, Susan Browning, Liam Dunn, Pat Elliott, Geraldine Fitzgerald

quiz game scandal. In 1959 quiz shows were competing with each other to give the highest prizes, and in the US contestants like Charles Van Doren were national celebrities from remaining unbeaten champions on shows like *Twenty One* and *The 64,000 Dollar Question*. It was then revealed that Van Doren and others had been briefed with answers to the tougher questions, and the entire nation felt cheated. The House of Representatives was brought in, heads rolled, the networks promised to take greater responsibility for their shows. Among the long-term results were a shift away from sponsorship of complete programmes towards time-buying, and the replacement of quiz and game shows by filmed series.

quota. Most countries are obliged to fill a quota of home-produced material. In GB this is as high as 86 per cent for ITV, which means that only 14 per cent can be bought in. The BBC operates a similar, but vaguer, control.

Racket Squad
US 1951–3 98 × 25m bw
Hal Roach

The police expose corruption.
Formulary cop show.

Reed Hadley

Rafferty*
US 1977 13 × 50m colour
Warner

Cases of an eccentric but concerned doctor in a general hospital.
It turned out more like the Patrick McGoohan Show, with the star giving a richly hammy performance. But the writing and production were good, and the public's lack of interest was surprising.

Patrick McGoohan

Raffles*
GB 1975 78m colour (VTR)
Yorkshire TV

An adaptation of the E. W. Hornung stories about a turn of the century gentleman cracksman.
Stylish but slightly disappointing new version of an old yarn, let down by the look of the thing, with too many hot colour tones.

w Philip Mackie d Christopher Hodson

Anthony Valentine

† A series of 13 × 50m episodes followed.

The Rag Trade. A British comedy half-hour which began on BBC in the 1950s and was revived, rather surprisingly, twenty years later with Peter Jones and Miriam Karlin from the original cast. Set in a dressmakers' workroom, showing how the girls take advantage of their long-suffering boss, it had grown cruder in the interim. Missing from the revised version were Sheila Hancock and Reg Varney; added were Anna Karen and Christopher Beeny. Creators: Ronald Wolfe, Ronald Chesney.

Raid on Entebbe*
US 1977 150m colour TVM
Edgar J. Sherick/TCF/NBC

How the Israeli commandos rescued a planeload of hostages from Uganda.
Probably the best treatment of this subject. (The others: *Victory at Entebbe* and the Israeli movie *Operation Thunderbolt*.)

w Barry Beckerman d Irvin Kershner m David Shire

Charles Bronson, Peter Finch, Yaphet Kotto, Jack Warden, Martin Balsam, Horst Buchholz, Eddie Constantine, Robert Loggia, John Saxon, Sylvia Sidney

The Raiders
US 1964 75m colour TVM
Universal

Bushwhacked cattle drivers get some famous westerners to help them.
Mildly fanciful western.

w Gene L. Coon d Herschel Daugherty

Robert Culp, Brian Keith, Judi Meredith, Alfred Ryder, Simon Oakland

Ramar of the Jungle
US 1952–3 52 × 25m bw
Jon Hall

Adventures of a doctor in Africa.
Correction: on somebody's back lot. Jungle Jim Rides Again.

Jon Hall

Rambo, Dack (1941–) (Norman Rambo). Personable American leading man. Series: *The Guns of Will Sonnett*, *Dirty Sally*.

Randall and Hopkirk (Deceased)
US title: *My Partner the Ghost*
GB 1972 26 × 50m colour
ATV

A private detective, killed on a case, comes back as a ghost but is invisible except to his partner.
Mister Ed meets *Here Comes Mr Jordan*: fair fun once you accept the premise, but it would have been better at half the length.

Kenneth Cope, Mike Pratt, Annette Andre

Randall, Joan and Leslie. Husband-and-wife team popular in the early days of British TV, as panellists, advertising announcers and actors in their own serial soap opera.

Randall, Tony (1924–). American character comedian, long a familiar figure in films. TV series: *Mr Peepers*, *The Odd Couple*, *The Tony Randall Show*.

The Range Rider
US 1951–2 76 × 25m bw
Flying A (Gene Autry)

A mysterious do-gooder rides the range.
Standard kids' western, not unlike *The Lone Ranger*.

Jock Mahoney, Dick Jones

The Rangers
aka: *Sierra*
US 1974 74m colour TVM
Universal/Jack Webb (Edwin Self)

Problems of rangers in Yosemite National Park.
Typical Webb multi-drama in which the more exciting
rescue bits look fake. The resulting series, *Sierra*, was a
dead loss.

w Robert A. Cinader, Michael Donovan, Preston
Wood *d* Chris Nyby Jnr

James G. Richardson, Colby Chester, Jim B. Smith,
Laurence Delaney

Rango
US 1966 17 × 25m colour
Spelling–Thomas

Misadventures of a bumbling Texas Ranger.
Spoof which didn't quite work.

Tim Conway, Guy Marks, Norman Alden

Rankin–Bass Productions. Arthur Rankin Jnr and
Jules Bass formed an animation company in the late
fifties and have had considerable success, some of the
work being done in Japan. Series include *The Jackson
Five* and *The Osmonds*; specials, *Frosty the Snowman*
and the perennial *Rudolph the Red-Nosed Reindeer*.
They vary between cartoon and puppetry, and despite
their proficiency have never achieved a house style in
the same way as UPA.

Ransom for Alice
US 1977 96m colour TVM
Universal

Deputy marshals search for a young girl on the Seattle
waterfront of the 1880s.
A failed pilot of no particular interest.

w Jim Byrnes *d* David Lowell Rich

Gil Gerard, Yvette Mimieux, Gene Barry, Barnard
Hughes, Harris Yulin

Rantzen, Esther (1940–). Toothy and toothsome
British anchorlady who started as assistant to Bernard
Braden and succeeded him as host of a light-hearted
consumer programme *That's Life*. Also hosted *The Big
Time*, in which ordinary folk achieved their wildest
dreams.

Rapf, Matthew (1920–). American writer of many
series episodes; also producer of *Kojak*.

The Rat Catchers*
GB 1961–3 39 × 50m bw (VTR)
Associated Rediffusion

Activities of a group of government spymasters.
Fairly absorbing melodramas which cast a commendably cold eye on the spy game after the excessive
glamour of James Bond.

Gerald Flood, Glyn Owen, Philip Stone

The Rat Patrol
US 1966–7 58 × 25m colour
ABC/United Artists/Mirisch–Rich

Allied commandos harass the Nazis in North Africa
during World War II.
A moderately competent production which caused all
hell to break loose in GB because of the British Army's
apparently minuscule contribution to the success of the
operations; not since Flynn conquered Burma was there
such an uproar.

Christopher George, Gary Raymond, Lawrence Casey,
Justin Tarr

ratings. The star which TV programmers steer by. By
a variety of methods, broadcasters discover to their own
satisfaction how many people watched each particular
show, and the rating is the proportion of TV sets tuned
in out of those available in that area. As some of these
may not be in use, a secondary figure, the share, is also
given: this represents the proportion of those actually
watching TV who tuned in to this particular show.

Rattigan, Sir Terence (1912–77). British dramatist
whose material was always civilized, competent and
middle-class. His TV plays include *The Final Test*.

Rawhide**
US 1958–65 144 × 50m bw
CBS

Adventures on a cattle drive.
Dour western series with a memorable theme tune and
imitable characters and catchphrases ('Git 'em up ...
move 'em out!'). The trail stopped so frequently for
miscellaneous dramas that it was a wonder the cattle
ever arrived at their destination.

singer Frankie Laine

ERIC FLEMING, CLINT EASTWOOD, PAUL BRINEGAR

The Ray Bolger Show
aka: *Where's Raymond?*
US 1955 39 × 25m bw
ABC

The romantic and comic adventures of a song and
dance man.
Amiable star vehicle.

Ray Bolger, Margie Millar, Richard Erdman, Charles
Smith

The Ray Milland Show
US 1954   39 × 25m   bw
CBS/MCA/Revue

Problems of a drama professor at a co-ed college.
Time-filling star froth, the only difference from the previous season's *Meet Mr McNutley* being that that was
set at a girls' college.

Ray Milland, Phyllis Avery, Lloyd Corrigan

Ray, Robin (*c* 1934–). British linkman and quizmaster, son of Ted Ray; has a special interest in
music.

Raye, Martha (1916–) (Maggie O'Reed). Rubber-
faced, wide-mouthed American slapstick comedienne
who had a youthful career in the movies and later came
to TV, primarily in 1955–6 in *The Martha Raye Show*
but later in *The Bugaloos* and *McMillan*.

Ready When You Are, Mr McGill**
GB 1976   50m   colour (VTR)
Granada (Michael Dunlop)

An actor who has always been an extra gets two lines to
speak and can't manage them.
Plain funny comedy, many of the jokes being at the
expense of TV.

w JACK ROSENTHAL   *d* MIKE NEWELL

Joe Black, Barbara Moore-Black, Diana Davies, Jack
Shepherd

The Real McCoys*
US 1957–62   224 × 25m   bw
CBS/Brennan–Westgate

Misadventures of a hillbilly family in rural California.
Some people said this show set back TV's development
by ten years . . . until *The Beverly Hillbillies* came along.
It was efficiently written and it made people laugh.

Walter Brennan, Richard Crenna, Kathy Nolan

The Real West**
US 1961   50m   bw
NBC (Donald Hyatt)

An outstanding edition of the Project 20 series which
tried to sum up the truth behind the fiction of the wild
west, this memorable documentary also marked host
Gary Cooper's last appearance before the cameras.

w Philip Reisman Jnr

The Rebel
US 1959–60   76 × 25m   bw
Goodson–Todman

Johnny Yuma, a Confederate soldier, settles in the west
after the Civil War.
Reasonably thoughtful western.

Nick Adams

Red Alert*
US 1977   96m   colour   TVM
Paramount (Barry Goldberg)

Things go dangerously wrong on an atomic plant.
Excellent suspenser.

w Sandor Stern, *novel Paradigm Red* by Harold
King   *d* William Hale

William Devane, Michael Brandon, Adrienne Barbeau,
Ralph Waite

The Red Badge of Courage*
US 1974   74m   colour   TVM
TCF/Norman Rosemont

During the American Civil War, a shy youth gets his
first taste of battle.
Adequate, uninspired TV remake of the MGM feature
film of 1950.

w John Gay   *d* Charles B. Fitzsimons   *novel* Stephen
Crane

Richard Thomas, Michael Brandon, Wendell Burton,
Warren Berlinger, Charles Aidman

The Red Pony*
US 1973   100m   colour   TVM
Universal/Omnibus (Frederick Brogger)

When his pony dies after an illness a farmer's son loses
faith in his father.
Well-meaning, overlong and dullish TV remake of the
1949 cinema film.

w Robert Totten, Ron Bishop   *d* Robert Totten

Henry Fonda, Maureen O'Hara, Ben Johnson, Clint
Howard

Redcap*
GB 1964–6   30 approx. × 50m   bw (VTR)
Thames

Stories of the military police.
Brisk yarns of characters in action, as cold and crisp as
one would expect.

John Thaw

Redigo
US 1963   15 × 25m   colour
NBC/Columbia/Wilrich

Problems of a modern rancher.
Misguided half-hour series left over when *Empire* was
cancelled.

Richard Egan

Reed, Robert (1932–). American leading man, one
of the busiest in TV. Apart from innumerable guest
appearances, he has been in two of the most successful
series, *The Defenders* and *The Brady Bunch*.

Reflections of Murder
US 1974 96m colour TVM
ABC Circle (Aaron Rosenberg)

At a remote boys' school, the headmaster's wife and mistress plot to murder him.
Dismal remake of *Les Diaboliques*, totally without pace or atmosphere.

w Carol Sobieski   *d* John Badham

Sam Waterston, Joan Hackett, Tuesday Weld, Lucille Benson

Regan*
GB 1974 78m colour (16mm) TVM
Thames/Euston Films (Ted Childs)

A Flying Squad detective breaks all the rules in his hunt for the killer of a young policeman.
Solidly watchable pilot for *The Sweeney*.

w Ian Kennedy Martin   *d* Tom Clegg

John Thaw, Dennis Waterman, Lee Montague, Garfield Morgan, David Daker, Janet Key, Maureen Lipman

'Spanking direction and excellent deadpan acting.' – *Guardian*

The Regiment*
GB 1972–3 26 × 50m colour (VTR)
BBC (Anthony Coburn)

Stories from the officers' mess in the days of the Raj.
Elegant little melodramas which usually entertain, and always look good.

w Jack Ronder, Robert Holmes, others

Malcolm McDowell, Christopher Cazenove

Rehearsal for Armageddon: see Ring of Passion

Reiner, Carl (1922–). American actor, writer, jack of all trades, associated above all with Sid Caesar and Dick Van Dyke. Starred in series *Heaven Help Us*.

Reiner, Rob (1945–). American actor who played the idle son-in-law in *All in the Family*. Also produced and starred in *Free Country*.

Reith, John (Lord Reith) (1889–1970). British administrator, the first controller of BBC radio and imposer of the BBC's 'Auntie' image. He failed to come to grips with TV, but his influence was felt until the sixties.

Relentless
US 1978 74m colour TVM
CBS (Fredric Baum)

Bank robbers are hampered by a snowstorm which grounds their getaway airplane.
Efficient, routine chase and caper film.

w Sam H. Rolfe, *novel* Brian Garfield   *d* Lee H. Katzin   *ph* Jack Whitman   *m* John Cacavas

Will Sampson, Monte Markham, John Hillerman, Marianna Hill

'The plot's whiskers have turned white despite the contemporary trappings.' – *Daily Variety*

The Reluctant Heroes
aka: *The Egghead on Hill 656*
US 1972 73m colour TVM
Aaron Spelling

A knowledge of history helps a lieutenant on foot patrol during the Korean War.
Thin war comedy, a long way before *M*A*S*H*.

w Herman Hoffman, Ernie Frankel   *d* Robert Day

Ken Berry, Cameron Mitchell, Warren Oates, Jim Hutton, Ralph Meeker

Remember When*
US 1973 96m colour TVM
Danny Thomas

Problems of a Connecticut family in wartime.
Rather untidily assembled nostalgia with a warmly sentimental core.

w Herman Raucher   *d* Buzz Kulik

Jack Warden, Nan Martin, William Schallert

Remick, Lee (1935–). American leading actress, in international films and TV. Best-known on the small screen for *Jennie* (BAFTA award 1974), *Wheels*, and *Ike*.

Renaldo, Duncan (1904–) (Renault Renaldo Duncan). American leading man; TV's Cisco Kid.

The Reporter*
US 1964 13 × 50m bw
CBS/Richelieu (Keefe Braselle)

Investigations of a columnist for the New York Globe.
Smooth, very adequate comedy–drama entertainment.

cr Jerome Weidman

Harry Guardino, Gary Merrill, George O'Hanlon

re-runs. It used to be an infallible rule that the American TV season lasted 39 weeks, from September to May, and was followed by 13 selected re-runs. As costs rose, the number of new programmes dwindled to the present 22/25, and re-runs consequently increased, though a show may be pre-empted at any time of the year for special programming. Once the network has finished with a show, it can of course start a new life in syndication – if there are enough episodes to make it usable as a strip.

Rescue 8
US 1958–9   73 × 25m   bw
Columbia/Wilbert (Herbert B. Leonard)

Exploits of a two-man emergency rescue team.
Adequate location action filler.

Jim Davis, Lang Jeffries

residuals. Sums of money which must be paid to artists, musicians, etc. if and when a show is played in another territory.

The Restless Gun
US 1958–9   77 × 25m   bw
MCA/Revue/Window

Adventures of a trouble shooter in the old west.
Standard half-hour western series.

John Payne

The Return of Captain Nemo
US 1978   3 × 50m   colour
Warner/Irwin Allen

Captain Nemo is melted out from an ice cupboard and saves the modern world.
Flatulent seafaring hokum with too much dialogue and not enough humour.

w Norman Katkov, Preston Wood, Lamar Boren   d Alex March   ph Paul Rader   m Richard La Salle   a/d Eugene Lourie

Jose Ferrer, Burgess Meredith, Burr de Benning, Tom Hallick, Warren Stevens

'Both situation and dialogue are pitched strictly at the kidvid audience.' – Daily Variety

The Return of Joe Forrester*
US 1975   74m   colour   TVM
Columbia

Problems of a cop on the beat.
Adequate pilot for an adequate series, Joe Forrester, relying heavily on its star.

w Mark Rodgers   d Virgil W. Vogel

Lloyd Bridges, Pat Crowley, Jim Backus, Dane Clark, Charles Drake, Dean Stockwell, Della Reese, Janis Paige, Edie Adams, Tom Drake, Eddie Egan, Hari Rhodes

The Return of the Gunfighter
aka: As I Rode Down from Laredo
US 1967   98m   colour   TVM
MGM

An ex-gunslinger avenges the deaths of a Mexican girl's parents.
Sluggish low-budget western.

w Robert Buckner   d James Neilson

Robert Taylor, Chad Everett, Ana Martin, Lyle Bettger, Michael Pate

The Return of the World's Greatest Detective
aka: Alias Sherlock Holmes
US 1976   74m   colour   TVM
Universal (Roland Kibbee, Dean Hargrove)

A motor cycle cop has an accident and recovers believing himself to be Sherlock Holmes.
Inept spoof apparently inspired by They Might Be Giants, and originally intended to become a series within Mystery Movie. No way.

w Roland Kibbee, Dean Hargrove   d Dean Hargrove   ph William Mendenhall   m Dick de Benedictus

Larry Hagman, Jenny O'Hara, Nicholas Colasanto, Woodrow Parfrey, Ivor Francis

Return to Peyton Place
US 1972   50 × 22m   colour (VTR)
NBC/TCF (George Paris)

Incredibly inept daytime soap opera sequel to the famous twice-weekly peak-time serial.

d Allen Pultz, Frank Pacelli

Bettye Ackerman, Frank Ferguson, Katherine Glass, Julie Parrish, Warren Stevens, Guy Stockwell

Revenge!
US 1971   73m   colour   TVM
Aaron Spelling (Mark Carliner)

A man is lured and locked up in a cellar by a crazy woman who thinks he has wronged her.
Heavy-going melodrama with the star well over the top.

w Joseph Stefano, novel Elizabeth Davis   d Jud Taylor

Shelley Winters, Bradford Dillman, Carol Rossen, Stuart Whitman

Revenge for a Rape
US 1977   96m   colour   TVM
Albert S. Ruddy (Alan P. Horowitz)

When his wife is raped, a man takes the law into his own hands.
Death Wish all over again. One is enough.

w Yabo Yablonsky   d Timothy Galfas   m Jerrold Immel

Mike Connors, Robert Reed, Tracy Brooks Swope, Deanna Lund

Rex Harrison Presents Three Stories of Love
aka: Three Faces of Love
US 1974   100m   colour   TVM
Universal

Three stories ranging from uninteresting to inept.
Epicac by Kurt Vonnegut, Kiss Me Again Stranger by Daphne du Maurier, The Fortunate Painter by Somerset Maugham. Harrison doesn't help.

w Liam O'Brien, Arthur Dales, John T. Kelley *d* John Badham, Arnold Laven, Jeannot Szwarc

Julie Sommars, Bill Bixby, Roscoe Lee Browne, Lorne Greene, Leonard Nimoy, Juliet Mills, Agnes Moorehead

Reynolds, Burt (1936–). American leading man with an insolent grin. After years of TV apprenticeship he rather surprisingly became a major movie star; his best remembered TV series are *Riverboat*, *Gunsmoke* (three seasons as an Indian), *Hawk* and *Dan August*.

Reynolds, Sheldon (1923–). American international reporter who turned producer with *Foreign Intrigue* and *Sherlock Holmes*.

Reynolds, William (*c* 1929–). American all-purpose actor. Series: *Pete Kelly's Blues*, *The Islanders*, *The Gallant Men*, *The FBI*.

The Rhinemann Exchange
US 1977   2 × 96m, 1 × 50m   colour
Universal

At the outbreak of World War II, an escape specialist is sent to Argentina on a dangerous espionage mission. Adequate capsule version of a bestseller.

novel Robert Ludlum   *d* Burt Kennedy

Jeremy Kemp, Stephen Collins, Lauren Hutton, Pedro Armendariz Jnr, Claude Akins, René Auberjonois, Vince Edwards, Larry Hagman, John Huston, Roddy McDowall

Rhoda**
US 1974–8   110 approx. × 25m   colour
Mary Tyler Moore

Adventures of a slightly kooky girl in New York.
Well written and characterized comedy, spun off from *The Mary Tyler Moore Show* and enriched by its new Jewish milieu. During the first two seasons Rhoda got married and divorced.

cr/executive p James L. Brooks, Allan Burns

VALERIE HARPER, Nancy Walker, Harold Gould

Rhodes, Hari (or Harry) (1932–). Handsome black American actor. Series: *The Bold Ones*.

rhubarb. What crowd actors are always supposed to mutter over and over again when they have no lines.

Rich, Lee ( ). Independent producer, head of Lorimar Productions (*The Waltons*, *Helter Skelter*, etc.). He was formerly a partner in Mirisch–Rich Productions.

RICH MAN, POOR MAN. Peter Strauss, Susan Blakely and Nick Nolte as the trio of destiny . . .

The cinematic equivalent of a good read, this pioneering mini-series was well produced and acted, and kept its melodramatic excesses within check. It was an enormous and somewhat unexpected hit, and novelizations were in. See *Best Sellers*.

w Dean Riesner, *novel* Irwin Shaw

PETER STRAUSS, NICK NOLTE, Susan Blakely, Dorothy McGuire, Ed Asner, Ray Milland, Craig Stevens, William Smith

'Glossy melodrama, with the suds occasionally armpit deep.' – Alvin H. Marill

Rich Man, Poor Man: Book Two*
US 1976   22 × 50m   colour
NBC/Universal (Frank Price)

The fortunes in industry of the surviving brother Rudy from *Rich Man, Poor Man*, and his relationships with his stepson and nephew.
A totally artificial extension of a smash success, this lengthy serial gave the impression of being made up as it went along, and of not knowing when to stop. (In fact the hero was killed off at the actor's own request.) All that can be said in its favour is that it filled a slot just about adequately.

Peter Strauss, Gregg Henry, James Carroll Jordan, Susan Sullivan

The Richard Boone Show**
US 1963   25 × 50m   bw
NBC/Classic/Goodson–Todman

An anthology of original and somewhat ambitious dramas, performed by a repertory and hosted by the star.

... and William Smith as the man who made the world shiver.

Rich Man, Poor Man***
US 1976   12 × 50m (or 6 × 95m)   colour
NBC/Universal (Frank Price)

The fortunes of two sons of an immigrant baker, from the end of World War II to the seventies.

RICH MAN, POOR MAN: BOOK TWO. Peter Strauss, sole survivor from Book One, now has troubles with another generation, represented by James Carroll Jordan and Gregg Henry.

A smoothly carpentered concept which failed to catch the public fancy. Contributors included Rod Serling, Clifford Odets, Robert Dozier.

consultant Clifford Odets

RICHARD BOONE, Warren Stevens, Bethel Leslie, Lloyd Bochner, Robert Blake, Guy Stockwell, Harry Morgan, Jeanette Nolan, Ford Rainey

'A serious effort to raise the standards of television drama.' – Don Miller

Richard Diamond*
US 1959–60   51 × 25m   bw
Four Star

Cases of a smart young city detective.
Streamlined wisecracking crime series.

David Janssen, Mary Tyler Moore

Richard the Lionheart
GB 1962   39 × 25m   bw
Danziger

Uneasy period adventures which seemed to be aimed at neither children nor adults.

Dermot Walsh

Richie Brockelman, Private Eye
US 1977   1 × 74m (and 4 × 50m)   colour
Universal (Steven J. Cannell)

Cases of an earnest 22-year-old private eye who is ridiculed by his family and friends.
Mildly amusing mini-series based on a character from *The Rockford Files*.

w Steven J. Cannell, Steven Bochco   *d* Hy Averback

Dennis Dugan, Suzanne Pleshette, Lloyd Bochner, Norman Fell

Richman, Stella (1925–   ). British executive producer. *Jennie, Clayhanger, Just William*, etc.

Ridley, Arnold (1895–   ). British playwright, author of *The Ghost Train*, who in old age became a TV star as Private Godfrey in *Dad's Army*.

Riesner, Dean (*c* 1930–   ). American screenwriter, mostly for TV: *Rich Man, Poor Man*, was the peak of his achievement.

The Rifleman*
US 1957–61   168 × 25m   bw
ABC/Four Star/Sussex

Problems of a widowed rancher and his young son.
Good family western.

Chuck Connors, Johnny Crawford

Rigg, Diana (1938–   ). Intelligent British leading lady of stage and screen. On TV, created Emma Peel in *The Avengers* and after many years of trying had an American series to herself; but *Diana* was a failure, as was *The Diana Rigg Show* on BBC.

Rin Tin Tin: see The Adventures of Rin Tin Tin

Ring of Passion
aka: *Rehearsal for Armageddon*
US 1978   96m   colour   TVM
TCF

Political shadows of the Max Schmeling–Joe Louis fight in New York in the thirties.
Good: overall feeling strong, detail sometimes naïve.

w Larry Forrester   *d* Robert Michael Lewis, Stephen Macht, Bernie Casey, Allen Garfield

Rintels, David W. (*c* 1935–   ). American writer responsible for *Fear on Trial* and *Washington Behind Closed Doors*.

Ripcord
US 1961–2   76 × 25m   bw
Rapier/United Artists (Ivan Tors)

Two unusual detectives are trained skydivers.
The ultimate in eccentric ideas becomes hokum.

Larry Pennell, Ken Curtis

Rising Damp**
GB 1974–8   28 × 25m   colour (VTR)
Yorkshire (Ronnie Baxter)

In a run-down apartment building, tenants tease the mean and sneaky landlord.
Virtually a single-set comedy series in which laughs constantly rise from the grime because of funny scripts and great ensemble acting.

w ERIC CHAPPELL

LEONARD ROSSITER, DON WARRINGTON, RICHARD BECKINSALE, FRANCES DE LA TOUR

Ritual of Evil
US 1969   98m   colour   TVM
Universal (David Levinson)

A psychiatrist who is also a supernatural investigator loses one of his patients to a witchcraft ritual.
An interesting theme is spun out and becomes nonsense.

w Robert Presnell Jnr   *d* Robert Day

Louis Jourdan, Anne Baxter, Diana Hyland, John McMartin, Belinda Montgomery

The Rivals of Sherlock Holmes*
GB 1972–3   26 × 50m   colour (VTR)
Thames

An anthology of stories about Victorian detectives.
Variable but generally interesting selection from anthologies published by Hugh Carleton Greene.

RISING DAMP. The awful Rigsby (Leonard Rossiter), flanked by Don Warrington and Frances de la Tour, surprises guests Deborah Watling and Alun Lewis.

River of Gold
US 1970 74m colour TVM
Aaron Spelling

Two American divers in Mexico become involved in the undersea search for a relic.
Below average adventure hokum.

w Salvatore C. Puedes *d* David Friedkin

Dack Rambo, Roger Davis, Ray Milland, Suzanne Pleshette, Melissa Newman

River of Mystery
US 1969 96m colour TVM
Universal (Steve Shagan)

Two oil wildcatters in Brazil are lured into helping rebels.
Jungle thick-ear: quite unremarkable.

w Albert Ruben *d* Paul Stanley

Vic Morrow, Claude Akins, Niall MacGinnis, Edmond O'Brien, Nico Minardos, Louise Sorel

Riverboat*
US 1959–60 44 × 50m bw
NBC/Revue/Meladre

Adventures on a Mississippi steamboat in the 1840s.
The setting made for a refreshingly different series, though most of the writing was pure corn.

Darren McGavin, Burt Reynolds

Riviera Police
GB 1964 26 × 50m bw (VTR)
Associated Rediffusion

Rumour has it that the title, which says it all, was offered in a spirit of humour and snapped up seriously by a programme controller who shall be nameless.

William Franklyn

The Road Runner. Character featuring in a series of
Warner cartoons, an imperturbable bird who always escapes from the clutches of Wile E. Coyote.

The Road West*
US 1966 26 × 50m colour
NBC/Universal

A widower with three children joins a wagon train in the 1850s and settles on the prairies.
Adequate sodbusting saga. The first two episodes were

joined together and released theatrically as *This Rugged Land*.

Barry Sullivan, Andrew Prine, Brenda Scott, Kelly Corcoran

The Roaring Twenties*
US 1960–1   45 × 50m   bw
ABC/Warner

Two reporters during prohibition find most of their best stories coming out of one night club.
Ho-hum series given a special sparkle by its use of (a) a famous backlot and (b) the catchiest songs of the period.

Rex Reason, Donald May, Dorothy Provine

The Robert Cummings Show: see My Hero

Robert Montgomery Presents*
US 1950–6   150 approx. × 25   bw

Anthology dramas hosted by the star, who occasionally performs.
A series of generally high standards.

Roberts, Ben (*c* 1914–   ). American screenwriter, often with Ivan Goff.

Robertson, Cliff (1925–   ). Sober-looking American leading actor who is occasionally seen on TV (*Washington Behind Closed Doors*) and in 1953 played the title role in *Rod Brown of the Rocket Rangers*.

Robertson, Dale (1923–   ). American western star, former schoolmaster. TV series: *Tales of Wells Fargo*, *The Iron Horse*.

Robertson, Fyfe (1903–   ). British reporter, an emaciated bearded Scot who has been a familiar TV figure since the early fifties.

Robinson, Hubbell (1905–   ). American executive producer who oversaw CBS drama in the fifties.

Robinson, Robert (*c* 1925–   ). Witty, somewhat acidulous British commentator and game show host, noted for programmes as diverse as *Points of View*, *Ask the Family*, *Call My Bluff*.

Rock Follies*
GB 1976–7   9 × 50m   colour (VTR)
Thames (Andrew Brown)

Three girls on a seedy tour aspire to be the world's greatest rock group.
Pithy modern drama with Busby Berkeley-style fantasy sequences, an interesting contrast with *Pennies from Heaven* though less meaningful.

ROCK FOLLIES. The backstage goings-on were relentlessly modern, but the fantastically staged numbers had more than a touch of the Busby Berkeleys. Rula Lenska, Julie Covington, Charlotte Cornwell.

w Howard Schuman *d* BRIAN FARNHAM, JON SCOFFIELD *m* Andrew Mackay

Charlotte Cornwell, Julie Covington, Rula Lenska

†BAFTA 1977: best drama series.

Rocket Robin Hood
Canada 1967 52 × 25m colour
Trillium Productions

In AD 2000 New Sherwood Forest is a floating aster-oid.
Undistinguished cartoon capers.

The Rockford Files*
US 1974 74m colour TVM
Universal/Cherokee/Public Arts (Meta Rosenberg)

An ex-con private eye investigates 'closed' cases and helps a young woman to find out whether her father was murdered.
Lively pilot for a moderately successful series, shot in Los Angeles and the desert and maintaining a nice sense of humour.

w Stephen J. Cannell *d* Richard Heffron

James Garner, Lindsay Wagner, Noah Beery Jnr, William Smith

†The resulting series was still running in 1979. Crea-tors: Roy Huggins, Stephen J. Cannell; producer: Roy Huggins; for Universal/Cherokee/Public Arts.

Rocky and his Friends**
US 1959–60 158 × 25m colour
Jay Ward

A cartoon ragbag with some splendid items. Rocky the flying squirrel appears in a serial with his dim-witted moose friend Bullwinkle (the real star of the show), combating the machinations of Boris Badenov. Other segments include *Fractured Fairy Tales*, narrated by Edward Everett Horton; *Dudley Do-Right*, a simple-minded mountie; *Aesop's Fables*; and *Peabody's Improbable History*. Throughout is evident a distinct vein of wit.

Rocky Jones Space Ranger
US 1953 39 × 25m bw
Roland Reed

An interplanetary adventurer has an atomic space ship.
Kiddie fare, not a patch on Flash Gordon.

Richard Crane, Sally Mansfield

Roddenberry, Gene. American producer, creator of *Star Trek*, after which he didn't seem able to manage another hit.

Roger and Harry
US 1977 74m colour TVM
Columbia/Bruce Lansbury (Anthony Spinner)

Our two heroes offer a service: they recover missing objects, including people.
Highly derivative failed pilot.

w Alvin Sapinsley *d* Jack Starrett *m* Jack Elliott, Allyn Ferguson

John Davidson, Barry Primus, Susan Sullivan, Richard Lynch, Carole Mallory, Harris Yulin, Biff McGuire

Rogers, Wayne (*c* 1939–). American leading man whose series include *M*A*S*H* and *City of Angels*.

Rogue Male*
GB 1976 96m colour (16mm) TVM
BBC/TCF (Mark Shivas)

Before World War II, a British aristocrat whose fiancée has been murdered by the Nazis sets out to shoot Hitler, narrowly misses, and is hounded back to England by the SS.
Deliberately cold-blooded film of a cold-blooded book (previously filmed by Fritz Lang as *Man Hunt*). Sequences impress, but the whole thing becomes rather silly and unpleasant.

w Frederic Raphael *novel* Geoffrey Household *d* Clive Donner

Peter O'Toole, Alastair Sim, John Standing, Harold Pinter

The Rogues**
US 1964 29 × 50m bw
NBC/Four Star (Collier Young)

Adventures of a family of upper-class con men, who always do the right thing in the end.
Jet-set Robin Hoods, they are seen in all the best places and headquartered in foggy London. An amusing and skilful series, too light in touch to catch the public fancy.

cr Collier Young

Gig Young, Charles Boyer, David Niven, Gladys Cooper, Robert Coote

Roll, Freddy, Roll
US 1975 74m colour TVM
Persky–Denoff

In order to win a place in the Guinness Book of Records, a mild-mannered computer programmer lives for seven days on roller skates.
Slow-starting but finally quite hilarious comedy.

w Bill Persky, Sam Denoff *d* Bill Persky

Tim Conway, Jan Murray, Henry Jones, Scott Brady, Ruta Lee

Roll on Four O'Clock*
GB 1971 57m colour (16mm)
Granada (Kenith Trodd)

The plight of a sensitive boy in a tough school.
A serious theme played effectively for comedy.

w Collin Welland   *d* Roy Battersby

Colin Welland, Clive Swift, George A. Cooper

† *Sun* award, best play.

Rolling Man*
US 1972   73m   colour   TVM
Aaron Spelling

An ex-con tries to find his sons who have been farmed
out to foster homes.
Efficient, slightly unusual melodrama.

w Steve and Elinor Karpf   *d* Peter Hyams

Dennis Weaver, Don Stroud, Agnes Moorehead, Donna
Mills, Jimmy Dean, Sheree North

Rollout
US 1973   13 × 25m   colour
CBS/TCF (Gene Reynolds, Larry Gelbart)

Exploits of the Red Ball Express, suppliers of resources
to the fighting men at the front in World War II.
Curiously unsuccessful black comedy which attempted
to extend the success of *M*A*S*H*.

Stu Gilliam, Billy Hicks, Mel Stewart, Ed Begley Jnr

Roman Grey
aka: *The Art of Crime*
US 1975   74m   colour   TVM
Universal (Richard Irving)

A New York gypsy antique dealer tries to save a friend
on a murder charge.
Uninspired and rather desperate pilot which didn't go.

w Martin Smith, Bill Davidson   *d* Richard Irving

Ron Leibman, Jose Ferrer, David Hedison, Jill
Clayburgh, Eugene Roche

Romance**
GB 1977   6 × 50m   colour (VTR)
Thames (Peter Duguid)

Adaptations of six romantic novels, mostly bestsellers,
from Victorian times to the present.
The treatments are variable, but the high style applied
to such famous but unread books as *Moths* by Ouida
(writer Hugh Whitemore, director Waris Hussein) and
Three Weeks by Elinor Glyn (writer Gerald Savory,
director Waris Hussein, star Elizabeth Shepherd) make
them TV classics, and Ethel M. Dell's curious *The
Black Knight* was made by adaptor John Kershaw and
director Peter Hammond to seem much more interesting than it probably is.

Romper Room. American format which was sold
continuously around the world from 1953. The aim was
to entertain and instruct the very young, and to this end
props, toys, scripts and even a teacher were supplied so
that the local station could make the programme.

The Rookies*
US 1971   73m   colour   TVM
Aaron Spelling

Recruits adjust to police life in a big city.
Semi-documentary cop show, tersely narrated.

w William Blinn   *d* Jud Taylor

Darren McGavin, Cameron Mitchell, Paul Burke

† The resulting series ran to 68 × 50m films over four
seasons. Gerald S. O'Loughlin was added to the regular cast of George Stanford Brown, Sam Melville,
Bruce Fairbairn and Kate Jackson. Producers: Hal
Sitowitz, Rick Husky.

Room for One More
US 1961   26 × 25m   bw
ABC/Warner

The parents of four children adopt two more.
Winsome televersion of a barely tolerable film.

Andrew Duggan, Peggy McCay

Room 222*
US 1969–72   113 × 25m   colour
ABC/TCF (Gene Reynolds)

The history teacher at Walt Whitman High is a Negro.
Character comedy borrowed from *To Sir with Love* and
vaguely mirroring social progress. Everybody is very
nice indeed to each other.

cr James Brooks, Gene Reynolds

Lloyd Haynes, Michael Constantine, Karen Valentine,
Denise Nicholas

Roots**
US 1977   12 × 50m   colour
ABC/David Wolper (Stan Margulies)

The saga of a black family from the capturing of an
African slave to the time of the Civil War.
Scene for scene this heavily socially conscious epic was
not too compelling, but America needed it as a kind of
expiation, and when it played on eight consecutive
nights during a week of blizzards the ratings were un-
precedented and it immediately became a TV landmark.
As a British executive said rather cynically, its success
may have been due to the fact that one third of America
was snowed up, another third is black and the rest
watch ABC anyway.

w William Blinn, Ernest Kinoy, James Lee, M. Charles
Cohen, from Alex Haley's book   *d* David Greene,
John Erman, Marvin J. Chomsky, Gilbert Moses   *ph*
Stevan Larner, Joseph Wilcots   *m* Quincy Jones,
Gerald Fried

Ed Asner, Chuck Connors, Carolyn Jones, O. J.
Simpson, Ralph Waite, Lou Gossett, Lorne Greene,
Robert Reed, LeVar Burton, BEN VEREEN, Lynda Day
George, Vic Morrow, Raymond St Jacques, Sandy
Duncan, John Amos, Leslie Uggams, MacDonald
Carey, George Hamilton, Ian MacShane, Richard
Roundtree, Lloyd Bridges, Doug McClure, Burl Ives

†Haley's claim that the book told the story of his own ancestors was challenged after detailed research by international news reporters.

Rose, Reginald (1921–). American TV playwright, one of the props of the 'golden age' of the fifties. His contributions included *Twelve Angry Men*, *Thunder on Sycamore Street* and *A Man is Ten Feet Tall*. He also created *The Defenders*.

Rosemont, Norman (*c* 1930–). American producer, usually of music specials or semi-classic one-offs (*The Man without a Country*, *The Man in the Iron Mask*).

Rosenthal, Jack (1931–). Much-lauded British dramatist with a special flair for comedy. *The Lovers* (series), *The Dustbinmen* (series), *Another Sunday and Sweet F.A.*, *Mr Ellis Versus the People*, *The Evacuees*, *Sadie It's Cold Outside* (series), *Ready When You Are, Mr McGill*, *Barmitzvah Boy*, *Spend Spend Spend*, etc.

Ross, Joe E. (1905–). American nightclub comedian with a frenzied manner. Series include *Car 54 Where Are You?*, *It's About Time*.

Rossetti and Ryan
aka: *Men Who Love Women*
US 1977   96m   colour   TVM
Universal (Leonard B. Stern)

Two elegant lawyers, one an ex-cop, solve a murder case.
Fated attempt to put Starsky and Hutch in the courtroom: too much chat and not enough plot.

w Don Mankiewicz, Gordon Cotler   *d* John Astin

Tony Roberts, Squire Fridell, Bill Dana, Patty Duke, Jane Elliot, Susan Anspach

†A subsequent 50m series ran to eight episodes.

Rossiter, Leonard (1927–). British character actor who can play serious or comic; in the latter vein he admirably conveys frustration and envy. Series: *Rising Damp*, *The Fall and Rise of Reginald Perrin*, *The Losers*.

rotating series. A scheduling pattern in which three series are rotated so that each appears every third week. This was tried out in the US with *The Men* (unsuccessfully) and *Mystery Movie* (successfully). In the UK, the BBC have occasionally tried it, but it seems to weaken the appeal of all the series involved.

Rough Riders
US 1958   39 × 25m   bw
United Artists

After the Civil War two Union officers journey west to find a new life.

Kent Taylor, Jan Merlin, Peter Whitney

The Rounders
US 1966   17 × 25m   colour
ABC/MGM (Ed Adamson)

Adventures of two idle, woman-chasing modern cowboys.
The soporific atmosphere got through to the audience.

Ron Hayes, Patrick Wayne, Chill Wills

Route 66**
US 1960–3   116 × 50m   bw
CBS/Columbia/Herbert B. Leonard

Two youthful wanderers travel across America in search of adventure.
A precursor of *Easy Rider*, this well-made show bor-. rowed its plots from well-known movies. (The first, *Black November*, was *Bad Day at Black Rock*.) Towards the end it got a little sentimental and even eccentric, as in the unsatisfactory *Lizard's Leg and Owlet's Wing* which brought together, and wasted, Boris Karloff, Peter Lorre, Lon Chaney Jnr and Martita Hunt.

George Maharis, Martin Milner

†The idea was frequently borrowed by other series, e.g. 1978's *The American Girls*.

The Roy Rogers Show
US 1951–6   100 × 25m   bw
CBS/Roy Rogers

A rancher in Mineral City is also the owner of a diner. Light modern western allowing the star to do his thing.

Roy Rogers, Dale Evans, Pat Brady, Harry Lauter

Royal Family***
GB 1969   110m   colour
BBC (Richard Cawston)

An informal look at the private life of Queen Elizabeth II.
A charming, easy and fresh documentary which managed not to put a foot wrong and was mainly responsible for bringing the monarchy down from its pedestal.

Royal Heritage**
GB 1977   9 × 50m   colour (16mm)
BBC (Michael Gill, Ann Turner)

A tour of the royal collection of paintings, antiques and ancient buildings.
Slightly reverent but undeniably impressive walk through fabled halls overflowing with history and artistic richness.

w Huw Wheldon, J. H. Plumb   *narrator* Huw Wheldon   *d* David Heycock   *ph* Kenneth MacMillan

'Worthy to stand beside *Civilization* and *America*.' – *Financial Times*

'The BBC's jubilee export number, nimbly and enthusiastically presented.' – *The Times*

The Royal Victorians: see Edward the Seventh

Royce
US 1976   50m   colour
MTM (William F. Phillips)

A new sheriff settles in Arizona in the 1870s.
Sleek pilot, but westerns were not in favour.

w Jim Byrnes   d Andrew V. McLaglen   m Jerrold
Immel

Robert Forster, Maybeth Hurt, Michael Parks

Rudolph the Red-Nosed Reindeer*
US 1964   48m   colour
Videocraft (Arthur Rankin Jnr, Jules Bass)

A reindeer with a red nose is derided by his friends but
becomes the leader of Santa Claus's troupe.
Puppet fantasy which while not outstanding in itself did
give us a universally known song and became an
American annual event.

w Romeo Muller   d Larry Roemer   narrator Burl
Ives

Ruff 'n' Reddy
US 1957–9   156 × 25m   colour
Hanna–Barbera

Ruff the Cat and Reddy the Dog fight the forces of
evil.
Routine cartoon capers.

The Ruggles
US 1950   13 × 25m   bw
ABC

Archetypal domestic comedy.

Charles Ruggles, Erin O'Brien Moore, Margaret
Kerry

Rumour*
GB 1974   76m   colour (16mm)   TVM
Thames (Mike Hodges)

A Fleet Street columnist is given a tip about a cabinet
minister being blackmailed, but finds he is being used to
start a non-existent scandal.
Complex but exciting thriller, shot entirely on location.

w/d MIKE HODGES

Michael Coles, Ronald Clarke, Mark Baxter, Joyce
Blair

Rumpole of the Bailey*
GB 1978–9   13 × 50m   colour (VTR)
Thames

A down-at-heel barrister usually manages to be on the
right scent.
Sharply written comedy-dramas which proved rather
too literary for the public taste.

w John Mortimer

LEO MCKERN

† The character had been introduced in a 1976 BBC
play, also by John Mortimer.

Run a Crooked Mile
GB 1969   100m   colour   TVM
Universal (Ian Lewis)

An amnesiac is manipulated by a mysterious group of
businessmen on whose secret he has accidentally stum-
bled.
Absurd sub-Hitchcock hokum with the hero disbelieved
by everybody until . . .

w Trevor Wallace   d Gene Levitt

Louis Jourdan, Mary Tyler Moore, Wilfrid Hyde
White, Stanley Holloway, Alexander Knox, Laurence
Naismith

Run Buddy Run
US 1966   16 × 25m   colour
CBS/Talent Associates

The underworld is after a frightened book-keeper who
has overheard secret information.
A comic *Fugitive*, and quite a good one, but spoofs are
seldom popular.

Bernie Kopell, Jack Sheldon, Bruce Gordon, Malcolm
Atterbury

Run for Your Life*
US 1965–7   85 × 50m   colour
NBC/Universal/Roy Huggins

When told he has two years to live, a middle-aged man
decides to seek rewarding adventures.
It's really *The Fugitive* all over again, and they let him
off the hook at the end. Good popular drama.

cr Roy Huggins

Ben Gazzara

† Although the hero was given only two years to live,
the show ran three seasons.

Run Joe Run
US 1974   26 × 25m   colour
NBC/TCF/D'Angelo (William P. D'Angelo)

A German shepherd dog is on the run, accused unjustly
of attacking his master.
A doggy *Fugitive*, or Rin Tin Tin rides again. Purely for
kids.

Arch Whiting, Chad States

Run Simon Run
US 1970   74m   colour   TVM
Universal

An ex-con Indian seeks revenge against the real murderer of his mother.
Tedious but good-looking open-air melodrama which
shifts from suspense to racial discussions.

w Lionel E. Siegel   *d* George McGowan

Burt Reynolds, Inger Stevens, James Best, Royal Dano

Runaway*
US 1973   74m   colour   TVM
Universal (Harve Bennett)

A ski train carrying holidaymakers down a mountain has no brakes.
Modestly effective mini-disaster movie, quite watchable.

w Gerald di Pego   *d* David Lowell Rich

Ben Murphy, Ben Johnson, Vera Miles, Martin Milner, Ed Nelson, Darleen Carr, Lee Harcourt Montgomery

The Runaway Barge
aka: *The Rivermen*
US 1975   75m   colour   TVM
Lorimar

Three men earning a living on a Mississippi boat become involved in a kidnapping.
Slow starting, heavily accented adventure which didn't make a series.

w Sanford Whitmore   *m* Nelson Riddle   *d* Boris Sagal

Bo Hopkins, Tim Matheson, Jim Davis, Nick Nolte, James Best, Clifton James

The Runaways
US 1975   74m   colour   TVM
Lorimar

A teenage boy and a leopard meet in the wilderness: both have run away from insoluble problems . . .

Silly-serious extravaganza which looks good but dramatically makes little impact.

novel Victor Canning   *d* Harry Harris

Dorothy McGuire, Van Williams, John Randolph, Neva Patterson, Josh Albee

Russell, Ken (1927–). British director, the *enfant terrible* of the big screen who makes amazing extravaganzas out of serious subjects. His TV work, however, has mainly been sharper, wiser and occasionally tinged with genius, presumably because in this medium he is not tempted by big budgets. TV films include *Elgar*, *Bartok*, *Debussy*, *Rousseau*, *Isadora*, *Dante's Inferno*, *A Song of Summer* (Delius), *Richard Wagner*, *Clouds of Glory*.

Russell, Kurt (1947–). American leading man, long familiar as a Disney juvenile. TV series: *The Travels of Jamie McPheeters*, *The New Land*, *The Quest*. A hit in 1979 as *Elvis*.

Ryan, Irene (1903–73) (Irene Riorden). Diminutive comedy character actress who after a lifetime in minor film roles became a national institution as Granny in *The Beverly Hillbillies*.

Ryan, Mitch (1928–). Stalwart American character actor who has had series leads in *Dark Shadows*, *Chase* and *Executive Suite*.

Ryan's Hope. ABC soap opera (born 1975) dealing with the young hopefuls of New York; with Bernard Barrow, Helen Gallagher, Michael Hawkins, Frank Latimore.

S

Saber of London: see Mark Saber

Sabrina (c 1931–) (Norma Sykes). British glamour girl, amply endowed; introduced as figure of fun by Arthur Askey in the fifties.

Sackheim, William (1919–). American executive producer, in charge of development at Universal. Series include *The Flying Nun*, *Night Gallery*. Former writer with widespread credits.

Sailor**
GB 1976   13 × 50m   colour
BBC (John Purdie)

A documentary look at today's navy.
Appealing, well-shot series. The episode entitled *The Rescue* won a BAFTA award.

Sailor of Fortune
GB 1956   26 × 50m   bw

A seafaring wanderer helps people in trouble.
The studio sets killed this one, but its star went on to better things.

Lorne Greene, Rupert Davies

The Saint**
GB 1963–8   114 × 50m   43 colour, 71 bw
ATV

Stories of Simon Templar, the Robin Hood of crime, from the books by Leslie Charteris.
On the whole the most satisfactory incarnation of this durable fantasy figure, with the right kind of light-weight star.

Roger Moore

† 1978 brought *The Return of the Saint* with Ian Ogilvy, from the same stable.

St James, Susan (1946–) (Susan Miller). American leading lady of the slightly kooky kind; made

THE SAINT. A rather shoddy sort of glamour pervaded this series, but the stories were usually good. Here Erica Rogers flirts with Roger Moore.

an impression as the second half of *McMillan and Wife*. Also in *The Name of the Game*.

Saints and Sinners*
US 1962   18 × 50m   bw
Four Star/Hondo

Human stories uncovered by the reporters of a city newspaper.
Once again a better-than-average series bites the dust.

Nick Adams, John Larkin

Saki**
GB 1962   13 × 50m   bw (VTR)
Granada (Philip Mackie)

An elegant compendium of the witty stories of H. H. Munro. (*w* Philip Mackie; *d* Gordon Flemyng); with Martita Hunt, Fenella Fielding, William Mervyn, Richard Vernon

Sale of the Century. A popular GB quiz show from Anglia TV, with three contestants answering increasingly difficult questions and using their scores to buy discounted goods. Nicholas Parsons as host.

Sales, Soupy (1926–) (Milton Hines). American comedian, usually seen performing corny jokes and slapstick in children's time.

Salomon, Henry Jnr (–1957). American documentary producer, noted for *Victory at Sea* and several NBC *White Papers* including *The Twisted Cross*.

Salty
US 1974   26 × 25m   colour
Salty Co/TCF (Kobi Jaeger)

Adventures of an intelligent sea lion and his young owner.
Infallible kids' stuff.

Mark Slade, Julius Harris, Johnny Doran

Sam**
GB 1973–5   39 × 50m   colour (VTR)
Granada (Michael Cox)

How a boy grew up among the poor of a Pennine mining town.
Ambitious drama serial which tended to wear out its welcome; as Sam grew up, interest shifted from him to his redoubtable grandfather, and towards the end it all smacked of *Cold Comfort Farm*.

w/cr JOHN FINCH

Barbara Ewing, Ray Smith, MICHAEL GOODLIFFE, James Hazeldine, John Price, Althea Charlton

Sam
US 1978   7 × 25m   colour
Jack Webb (Leonard B. Kaufman)

Cases of a police dog.
Four incidents to a segment: the principle didn't work so well as with *Adam 12*.

cr Jack Webb, Dan Noble

Mark Harmon, Len Wayland

SAM. Michael Goodliffe as Dad (later Grandad) was the hit of the show, Althea Charlton abetted him nobly.

Sam Benedict**
US 1962   28 × 50m   bw
MGM

Cases of an adventurous lawyer and his assistant.
Smooth, superior courtroom drama with action interludes. Unbelievable, but palatable.

cr E. Jack Neuman

Edmond O'Brien, Richard Rust

Samson and Goliath
US 1967   × 25m   colour
Hanna–Barbera

Whenever a boy utters magic words, he is turned into a
superman and his dog into a lion.
Derivative cartoon series.

San Francisco Beat*
aka: *The Line-Up*, qv for 50m series
US 1954–8   183 × 25m   bw
Desilu

An old and a young cop combat crime on the streets.
Who said *Streets of San Francisco* was a new idea?
This pacy cop show preceded it by nearly 20 years.

Warner Anderson, Tom Tully

San Francisco International Airport**
US 1970   96m   colour   TVM
Universal (Frank Price)

A day's problems for the manager of a big airport.
No mad bomber, otherwise a mini-*Airport* and quite
slick and entertaining.

w William Read Woodfield, Allan Balter   *d* John
Llewellyn Moxey

Pernell Roberts, Clu Gulager, Beth Brickell, Van
Johnson, Nancy Malone, David Hartman, Cliff Potts,
Tab Hunter

† A subsequent series of 6 × 50m episodes was aired as
part of *Four In One*.

San Pedro Beach Bums
US 1977   1 × 74m, 11 × 50m   colour
Spelling–Cramer (E. Duke Vincent)

Adventures of a noisy harbour gang whose hearts are in
the right place.
Or, The Bowery Boys Go Boating. Noised as the start
of a sensational new trend, it performed the remarkable
feat of underestimating the taste of the American
public, and submerged.

w E. Duke Vincent   *d* (pilot) Barry Shear

Chris Murney, Jeffrey Druce, John Mark Robinson,
Stuart Pankin, Barry McCullough

Sand, Paul (*c* 1943–   ). Amiable American character
comedian who was tried out in his own TV series
Friends and Lovers.

The Sandy Duncan Show
US 1972   13 × 25m   colour
Paramount/Jefferson–Sultan

Misadventures of a student teacher at UCLA.
A threadbare format which was tried out when *Funny
Face* didn't work. This one didn't either.

Sandy Duncan, Tom Bosley, Marian Mercer

Sanford and Son**
US 1972–6   approx 90 × 25m   colour (VTR)
NBC/Bud Yorkin, Norman Lear/NBC (Saul Turteltaub,
Bernie Orenstein)

Father and son run a junk yard in Los Angeles.
Black version of *Steptoe and Son*, a great American success which in this form didn't travel.

Redd Foxx, Desmond Wilson

† A 1977 spin-off called *Sanford Arms* failed to work.

Sara
US 1975   13 × 50m   colour
MCA/Universal (George Eckstein)

The life of a spinster schoolteacher in a burgeoning
town in the old west. From a novel by Marian
Cockrell.
Too quiet a show to suit the western background; these
stories could have happened anywhere.

Brenda Vaccaro, Bert Kramer, Albert Stratton

Sara T: Portrait of a Teenage Alcoholic*
US 1975   100m   colour   TVM
Universal (David Levinson)

A case history of a schoolgirl alcoholic.
Sensationalized documentary drama, the most popular
TV movie of its year in America.

w Richard and Esther Shapiro   *d* Richard Donner

Linda Blair, Verna Bloom, William Daniels, Larry
Hagman

Sarge. See also *The Badge or the Cross*, *The Priest
Killer*. The series, which had started in *Four In One*, ran
to 13 × 50m episodes.

Sargent, Dick (*c* 1937–   ). American light leading
man. TV series: *One Happy Family*, *Broadside*,
Bewitched.

Sarnoff, David (1891–1971). American executive,
founder of the NBC network, president of the RCA
corporations; also the radio operator who first heard
the distress signals of the *Titanic* when it sank in 1912.

Satan's School for Girls
US 1973   74m   colour   TVM
Spelling–Goldberg

A schoolmistress fights the devil for control of a girls'
school.

Lunatic farrago which might have been more suspensefully narrated and produced.

w Arthur A. Ross *d* David Lowell Rich

Roy Thinnes, Kate Jackson, Pamela Franklin, Jo Van Fleet, Lloyd Bochner

Satan's Triangle*
US 1975 74m colour TVM
James Rokos–Danny Thomas

Dead bodies are found in a drifting boat in the Bermuda mystery area.
Good-looking hocus pocus which doesn't make much dramatic sense.

w William Read Woodfield *d* Sutton Roley

Kim Novak, Doug McClure, Alejandro Rey, Jim Davis, Ed Louter

satellite. An orbiting space station which, unmanned, picks up and relays television information from continent to continent. Satellites have been in use since 1960.

Savage*
US 1972 74m colour TVM
Universal (Paul Mason)

Adventures of the hard-hitting front man of a news commentary team.
Smooth topical melodrama which didn't run to a series.

w Mark Rodgers, William Link, Richard Levinson *d* Steven Spielberg

Martin Landau, Barbara Bain, Will Geer, Barry Sullivan, Louise Latham, Pat Hingle, Susan Howard

The Savage Bees
US 1976 96m colour TVM
Alan Landsburg/Don Kirshner/NBC

Killer bees invade New Orleans during the Mardi Gras.
Satisfactory stunt thriller, not outstanding but certainly better than the very similar, much heralded theatrical movie *The Swarm*.

w Guerdon Trueblood *d* Bruce Geller *m* Walter Murphy

Ben Johnson, Michael Parks, Paul Hecht, Horst Buchholz, Gretchen Corbett

Savages*
US 1974 74m colour TVM
Spelling–Goldberg

An unarmed youth in the desert flees from a deranged hunter.
Adventure suspense, not badly done.

w William Wood, *novel Death Watch* by Robb White *d* Lee H. Katzin

Andy Griffith, Sam Bottoms, Noah Beery Jnr, James Best, Randy Boone

Savalas, Telly (1924–) (Aristotle Savalas). Bald, beaming Greek-American character actor who achieved instant stardom as *Kojak*.

Savile, Jimmy (*c* 1930–). Long-haired, platinum-blond British disc jockey and TV personality; an acquired taste.

Saville, Philip (*c* 1930–). British TV director with innumerable top shows to his credit. A few of the most memorable: *A Night Out, Prisoner and Escort, The Rainbirds, Secrets, Gangsters* (pilot), *Count Dracula*.

Savory, Gerald (1904–). British dramatist, most famous for *George and Margaret*. Later became head of drama for Granada, then BBC. 1977: wrote *Count Dracula*.

Say Goodbye, Maggie Cole*
US 1972 73m colour TVM
Spelling–Goldberg

A widow returns to medical practice in a tough slum area.
Efficient woman's tearjerker.

w Sandor Stern *d* Jud Taylor

Susan Hayward, Darren McGavin, Michael Constantine, Dane Clark, Beverly Garland

Say Hello to a Dead Man*
US 1972 73m colour TVM
Universal

Escaping from 15 years in a South American jungle prison, a private eye returns to his old practice (which is being run by his son) and finds it difficult to adjust.
A silly premise at least provides some good jokes and chases. Pilot for *Faraday and Company* (see *Mystery Movie*).

d Gary Nelson

Dan Dailey, James Naughton, Sharon Glass, Craig Stevens, Geraldine Brooks, David Wayne, Howard Duff

Scalplock
US 1967 100m colour TVM
Columbia

A gambler wins a railroad.
Western pilot for *The Iron Horse* series. Prolonged but watchable.

w Stephen Kandel *d* James Goldstone

Dale Robertson, Robert Random, Diana Hyland

Scenes from a Marriage**
Sweden 1973 6 × 50m colour
Swedish TV (Ingmar Bergman)

A dissolving marriage is shown in a series of dialogues.

TELLY SAVALAS as Kojak. The bald, elegant, lolly-sucking cop once more gets his man.

Powerful drama of the intimate kind TV does best.

w/d Ingmar Bergman   *ph* Sven Nykvist

Liv Ullmann, Erland Josephson, Bibi Andersson, Gunnel Lindblom

Schuck, John (1941–   ). Lumpy, bewildered-looking American character actor who scored in comic roles in *McMillan and Wife* and *Holmes and Yoyo*. 1979 series: *Bewitched.*

Schwartz, Sherwood (   ). American producer and creator of comedy formats which are all basically the same: *Gilligan's Island, The Brady Bunch, Dusty's Trail.*

Scooby Doo, Where are You?*
US 1969–71   72 × 22m   colour
Hanna–Barbera

Four teenage ghost-hunters are hindered by their cowardly dog.
Another cartoon variation on a familiar theme (*The Funky Phantom, Goober and the Ghost Chasers*) but this one certainly provokes laughs and proved the most popular.

The Scorpio Letters
US 1967   98m   colour   TVM
MGM

British government agencies compete to smash a black-mailing ring
Ho-hum spy hokum.

w Adrian Spies, Jo Eisinger   *d* Richard Thorpe

Alex Cord, Shirley Eaton, Laurence Naismith

Scott Free
US 1977   74m   colour   TVM
Universal (Meta Rosenberg)

A Las Vegas gambler has contacts which enable him to solve difficult cases.
Busted pilot. Its fate is unsurprising in view of its un-attractive presentation.

w Stephen J. Cannell   *d* William Wiard

Michael Brandon, Susan Saint James, Robert Loggia, Michael Lerner

Scott, George C. (1926–   ). Leading American character actor. TV work includes a series, *East Side West Side*; guest appearances in many others, including *The Road West* and *The Virginian*; and specials such as *The Andersonville Trial* and *Fear on Trial*.

Scott, Michael (1931–). British linkman, long with Granada, especially on *Cinema*. Also producer of current affairs programmes: *Nuts and Bolts of the Economy*, etc.

Scott, Peter Graham (1923–). British producer/director: *The Trouble Shooters* (also created), *The Onedin Line* (also created), *Quiller*, *The Doombolt Chase*, etc.

Scott, Terry (*c* 1933–). Tubby British character comedian. Series include *Hugh and I, Scott On, Son of the Bride, Happy Ever After*.

Scream of the Wolf*
aka: *The Hunter*
US 1974   74m   colour   TVM
Metromedia–Dan Curtis

What appears to be a mad killer animal is actually a werewolf.
Adequately scary piece with not much sense in its script.

w Richard Matheson   *d* Dan Curtis

Clint Walker, Peter Graves, Jo Ann Pflug, Phil Carey

Scream, Pretty Peggy*
US 1973   74m   colour   TVM
Universal (Lou Morheim)

A girl student takes a summer job in a sinister house, and chooses the wrong allies.
Fairly obvious but well presented Grand Guignol.

w Jimmy Sangster, Arthur Hoffe   *d* Gordon Hessler

Bette Davis, Ted Bessell, Sian Barbara Allen, Charles Drake

The Screaming Woman*
US 1971   73m   colour   TVM
Universal (William Frye)

A woman recently ill thinks there is a woman buried somewhere in the grounds of her house. And there is.
Predictable suspenser with a nice cast.

w Merwin Gerard, *story* Ray Bradbury   *d* Jack Smight

Olivia de Havilland, Yvonne de Carlo, Rock Hudson, Maxwell Reed, Denis O'Dea, Michael Goodliffe, Bryan Forbes, Ivor Barnard, Arthur Wontner

Screen Directors' Playhouse*
US 1955   39 × 25m   bw
Eastman Kodak

Anthology dramas directed by Hollywood's top talents.
None of these playlets compares with the directors' top Hollywood product, but glimmerings of style can be seen. Among those represented are John Ford (with John Wayne starring), Leo McCarey, H. C. Potter, Norman Z. McLeod, Tay Garnett, Fred Zinnemann, George Waggner, William A. Seiter, George Marshall (with Buster Keaton starring) and John Brahm.

Screen Gems. Columbia's TV subsidiary; in the seventies it was renamed Columbia Pictures Television.

Screen Test. A 1975 format pioneered (unsuccessfully) by Universal for syndication. Don Addams showed film clips and then persuaded members of the audience to act them out.

Sea Hawk: see The Adventures of the Sea Hawk

Sea Hunt*
US 1957–60   155 × 25m   bw
Ziv

An ex-navy frogman hires himself out for underwater adventure.
Simple, well-made, popular show. The wonder is how they managed to find 155 underwater stories.

Lloyd Bridges

Sea Song
GB 1974   78m   colour   TVM
Thames (Peter Hammond)

A young tycoon on a single-handed ocean race discovers a stowaway in the shape of an attractive journalist.
A quite agreeable comedy adventure which doesn't add up to much but looks good while it's on.

w Guy Slater   *d* Peter Hammond

Tom Bell, Kika Markham

Search
US 1972   24 × 50m   colour
Warner/Leslie Stevens

World Securities has agents primed for international protection of the wealthy.
A poor variation on a much zippier pilot called *Probe*. The fact that each star was seen every third week didn't help.

Hugh O'Brian, Doug McClure, Tony Franciosa, Angel Tompkins

The Search for Green Eyes
US 1976   100m   colour   TVM
Lorimar

A black soldier goes back to Vietnam to seek his native wife and child.
Documentary style tearjerker with lots to say about the tragedy of war.

d John Erman

Paul Winfield, Rita Tushingham

Search for the Gods*
US 1975 100m colour TVM
Warner/Douglas S. Cramer

A rare medallion sends three adventurers seeking evidence of ancient visitors to earth.
Overstretched action hokum with pleasing moments.

w Herman Miller, Ken Pettus *d* Jud Taylor

Kurt Russell, Stephen McHattie, Ralph Bellamy, Victoria Racimo, Raymond St Jacques

The Search for the Nile**
GB 1971 6 × 60m colour (16mm)
BBC/Time–Life (Charles Ralling)

Dramatized historical documentaries of a very high standard, showing how explorers traced the source of the Nile.

w Derek Marlowe, Michael Hastings

Kenneth Haigh, John Quentin, Norman Rossington, Michael Gough

Search for Tomorrow. American soap opera, on CBS since 1951. Small-town goings-on starring Mary Stuart, Larry Haines, Carl Low.

Searchlight. Hard-hitting British documentary series created for Granada by Tim Hewat in the fifties before *World in Action* took over.

Seaway*
Canada 1965 30 × 50m bw (2 colour)
ASP/CBS/ATV

Special police guard the St Lawrence seaway.
An efficient, well-made series which somehow didn't excite.

Stephen Young, Austin Willis

Second Chance
US 1971 74m colour TVM
Metromedia

A stockbroker buys a Nevada ghost town and decks it out as a new community for people like himself.
Sluggish comedy drama.

w Michael Morris *d* Peter Tewkesbury

Brian Keith, Elizabeth Ashley, Juliet Prowse, Rosie Greer, Pat Carroll, William Windom

The Second Hundred Years
US 1967 26 × 25m colour
Columbia

A prospector is thawed out after 70 years in an Alaskan glacier, and finds himself a military secret.
Goofy comedy which proved too complicated despite enthusiasm all round.

Monte Markham, Arthur O'Connell, Frank Maxwell

Secret Agent: see Danger Man

The Secret Life of John Chapman
US 1977 74m colour TVM
Paramount/Jozak (Gerald W. Abrams)

A respected college president decides to work as a common labourer.
Unconvincing story of a seeker after truth. Rather boring, too.

w John R. Coleman, from his novel *Blue Collar Journal* *d* David Lowell Rich

Ralph Waite, Susan Anspach, Elayne Heilveil, Brad Davis, Pat Hingle

The Secret Lives of Waldo Kitty*
US 1975 17 × 22m colour
Filmation

When his lady friend is threatened by a bulldog, a tomcat has dreams of being a hero.
The derivation is obvious, the technique is slightly innovative, as the animals are real until the fantasy starts – in animation.

d Don Christensen *animation director* Rudy Larriva

The Secret Night Caller*
US 1975 74m colour TVM
Charles Fries/Penthouse

An otherwise respectable man has a compulsion to make obscene phone calls ...
Fairly interesting psycho-drama.

w Robert Presnell Jnr *d* Jerry Jameson

Robert Reed, Hope Lange, Michael Constantine, Sylvia Sidney, Elaine Giftos

Secrets
US 1977 96m colour TVM
Paramount/Jozak (Gerald W. Abrams)

A woman who has always done exactly as she pleased finds herself unsatisfied.
Woman's magazine stuff, adequately presented.

w Joanne Crawford *d* Paul Wendkos

Susan Blakely, Roy Thinnes, Joanne Linville, John Randolph

See How She Runs*
US 1978 96m colour TVM
CLN (George Englund)

A 40-year-old teacher, downtrodden by her family, decides to do something for herself – become a long-distance runner.
A telefilm of some quality which could nevertheless have been compressed into a single hour. It exhausts its welcome before half-time.

w Marvin A. Gluck *d* Richard Heffron *ph* Ron Lantore *m* Jimmy Haskell

Joanne Woodward, John Considine, Barnard Hughes, Lissy Newman

See How They Run*
US 1965 100m colour TVM
Universal (Jack Laird)

The children of a spy are menaced by neo-Nazis and helped by a G-man.
Lively chase adventure with good use of New York locations.

w Michael Blankfort d David Lowell Rich

John Forsythe, Senta Berger, Franchot Tone, Jane Wyatt, Leslie Nielsen

See It Now. CBS half-hour documentary series which handled controversial news matters, including the witch hunts of the fifties; it is credited with starting the downfall of McCarthy. It ran from 1951 to 1958 and was created and produced by Fred W. Friendly and Edward R. Murrow; the latter also introduced it.

See the Man Run*
US 1971 73m colour TVM
Universal (Stan Shpetner)

An actor devises a means of easy money but finds himself in the middle of a kidnap plot.
Ingenious suspenser which starts well and keeps its end up.

w Mann Rubin d Corey Allen

Robert Culp, Angie Dickinson, June Allyson, Eddie Albert, Charles Cioffi

Self, William (1921–). American producer and executive, head of Twentieth Century–Fox Television 1959–74.

semi-animation. General term for a number of processes which reduce cost by reducing the number of drawings necessary and producing a stylized but aesthetically unappealing effect: e.g. in conversation, the mouth will open and close repeatedly while the rest of the figure remains static.

Send in the Girls
GB 1978 7 × 50m colour (VTR)
Granada (June Wyndham-Davies)

Stories of girls on a sales promotion team.
Virtually an anthology of variable and highly resistible comedies and dramas.

Annie Ross, Anna Carteret, Diana Davies, Floella Benjamin

Senior Year
US 1974 74m colour TVM
Universal

Family and college problems in 1955.
Inspired by *American Graffiti*, this became a tedious but brief series called *Sons and Daughters*.

w M. Charles Cohen d Richard Donner

Gary Frank, Glynnis O'Connor, Scott Columby, Barry Livingston

A Sensitive, Passionate Man*
US 1977 96m colour TVM
Factor–Newland

An aerospace scientist loses his job and takes to drink.
Polished restatement of a familiar theme.

w Rita Lakin, *novel* Barbara Mahoney d John Newland

David Janssen, Angie Dickinson

Sentimental Agent
GB 1966 13 × 50m bw
ATV

An import–export agent finds himself rooting out criminals.
Flimsily-premised adventure series with a personable star.

Carlos Thompson, Clemence Bettany, John Turner

Sergeant Preston of the Yukon
US 1955-7 78 × 25m bw
Wrather

A Mountie and his dog enforce law and order in the wilds.
Acceptable *Boy's Own Paper* stuff.

Richard Simmons

Sergeant Ryker
US 1963 85m colour TVM
Universal (Frank Telford)

In Korea, army lawyers prepare the trial of a sergeant accused of being a traitor.
Muddled courtroom drama which began life as two episodes of the anthology series *Crisis* and also served as pilot for a one-hour series *Counsellors at War*, also known as *Court Martial*.

w Seeleg Lester, William D. Gordon d Buzz Kulik

Lee Marvin, Bradford Dillman, Peter Graves, Vera Miles, Lloyd Nolan, Murray Hamilton, Norman Fell

Serling, Rod (1924–75). American playwright who created *Twilight Zone* and its alter ego *Night Gallery*; also wrote in the mid-fifties such classic TV plays as *Patterns*, *The Rack*, *Requiem for a Heavyweight* and *The Velvet Alley*.

Serpico
aka: *The Deadly Game*
US 1976 98m colour TVM
Paramount/Emmet Lavery

A New York cop exposes corruption in the force: a true story which made a popular cinema film.
This is a TV remake/pilot, dour in mood and hard to follow: for New Yorkers who enjoy having their noses rubbed in the dirt.

w Robert Collins

David Birney, Tom Atkins

†The resulting series lasted half a season: 15 × 50 episodes.

Sesame Street********. One-hour series aimed at under-privileged city children learning to read and write. Produced by Joan Ganz Cooney through her Children's Television Workshop for PBS, it used every kind of cartoon and puppet trick, aped commercial techniques and brought in *Hellzapoppin*-type gags. By any standard superior TV and great entertainment for all ages, its Muppet creatures, the brainchild of Jim Henson, eventually had a successful series of their own. Hundreds of episodes were produced from 1969. Characters included Big Bird, Cookie Monster and Kermit T. Frog.

Sevareid, Eric (1912–). American news commentator, with CBS from 1939, and notable for his coverage of World War II in Europe.

Seven in Darkness
US 1969 74m colour TVM
Paramount

A chartered plane crashes in a mountainous region, and all the survivors are blind.
For connoisseurs of unlikely situations.

w John W. Bloch, *novel Against Heaven's Hand* by Leonard Bishop *d* Michael Caffey

Milton Berle, Dina Merrill, Sean Garrison, Arthur O'Connell, Alejandro Rey, Lesley Ann Warren

Seven Up. A Granada documentary of 1963 which selected seven children from various backgrounds and analysed their chances. At the appropriate times further programmes were made under the titles *Seven Plus Seven* and *Twenty One*, showing whether or not the children had achieved their ambitions. Michael Apted was researcher on the first programme and director of the others.

Seventh Avenue*
US 1977 3 × 96m colour
NBC/Universal (Franklin Barton, Richard Irving)

A young Jew makes it big, but loses his integrity, in New York's garment district in the thirties and forties.
One of the best of the early *Best Sellers* (it came fourth), but not the most popular.

w Lawrence Heath, *novel* Norman Bogner *d* Richard Irving

Steven Keats, Dori Brenner, Kristoffer Tabori, Jane Seymour, Alan King, Anne Archer, Eli Wallach, Jack Gilford

79 Park Avenue
US 1977 3 × 93m colour
MCA/Universal

The progress of a young New York whore and her involvement in a sensational murder case.
Dismally made backlot epic; the tawdry look suits its subject.

w Richard de Roy, *novel* Harold Robbins *d* Paul Wendkos

Lesley Ann Warren, Raymond Burr, Polly Bergen, Michael Constantine, Peter Marshall, Albert Salmi, Jack Weston

77 Sunset Strip*
US 1958–63 205 × 50m bw
Warner

A firm of private eyes operates from offices on Sunset Strip.
Long-running crime and glamour series which seems tatty now but hit the spot at the time.

Efrem Zimbalist Jnr, Roger Smith, Edd Byrnes, Louis Quinn

'Like most Warner TV films, they abound with corner-cutting, uninspired direction and distressing scripts.' – Don Miller

77th Bengal Lancers
US 1956 26 × 50m bw
Columbia/Herbert B. Leonard

Stiff-upper-lip capers in turn-of-the-century India. Not too bad apart from the Yank accents.

Phil Carey, Warren Stevens

Sex and the Married Woman
US 1978 96m colour TVM
Universal/NBC (George J. Santoro, Jack Arnold)

An authoress becomes famous when she publishes a dissertation on the sexual mores of 50 American women, but her own marriage founders.
Obvious marital comedy, sloppily constructed and very padded out, but with a few good lines.

w Michael Norell *d* Jack Arnold

Joanna Pettet, Barry Newman, Keenan Wynn, Dick Gautier, Fannie Flagg, Nita Talbot, Jayne Meadows

The Sex Symbol
US 1974 98m or 110m colour TVM
Columbia/Douglas S. Cramer

The private life of a Hollywood glamour queen.
Obsessively silly exposé obviously patterned after Marilyn Monroe.

w Alvah Bessie, from his novel *The Symbol* *d* David Lowell Rich *ph* J. J. Jones *m* Jeff Alexander

Connie Stevens, Shelley Winters, Don Murray, William Smith, James Olson, Nehemiah Persoff, Jack Carter

The Sextet*
GB 1972 8 × 50m colour (VTR)
BBC (Roderick Graham)

An attempt to create a TV repertory company. The actors were excellent but some of the dramas rather less.

Michele Dotrice, Ruth Dunning, Denholm Elliott, Richard Vernon, Dennis Waterman, Billie Whitelaw

'How about some sex and violence for poor ol' granny?'

SEX AND VIOLENCE. The truth in this cartoon is that however much our guardians of public morals castigate television for bringing down standards, the public makes no complaint at all.

SFTA. The Society of Film and Television Arts, a British institution now combined with the British Film Academy in BAFTA, the British Academy of Film and Television Arts.

Shades of Greene*
GB 1975   13 × 50m   colour (VTR)
Thames (Alan Cooke)

A very careful, but not entirely successful, attempt to dramatize Graham Greene's short stories, some of which defy TV interpretation. Top names, including Paul Scofield and John Gielgud, were employed, and sometimes there was more than one story to the hour. The entire enterprise was caviare to the general.

Shadow in the Streets*
US 1975   74m   colour   TVM
Playboy

A tough ex-convict becomes a parole agent.
Routine socially conscious melodrama, well put together.

w John D. F. Black   *d* Richard Donner

Tony Lo Bianco, Sheree North, Dana Andrews, Ed Lauter, Jesse Welles

Shadow over Elveron*
US 1968   100m   colour   TVM
Universal (Jack Laird)

An evil midwestern sheriff commits murder and is unmasked by the new young doctor.
Heavy melodrama on familiar lines, with the cinema films *Hot Spot* and *The Tattered Dress* for models.

w Chester Krumholz, *novel* Michael Kingsley   *d* James Goldstone

Leslie Nielsen, James Franciscus, Shirley Knight, Franchot Tone, James Dunn, Don Ameche

Shadow Squad. An early (1957) half-hour British tape series from Associated Rediffusion about a couple of private eyes; with Peter Williams and Rex Garner.

277

Shaft*
US 1974   7 × 74m   colour
MGM

A toned-down televersion of the film series about a black private eye. Skilfully made, but addicts seemed to miss the violence.

Richard Roundtree

Shane*
US 1966   17 × 50m   colour
Paramount/Titus (Herb Brodkin)

TV series in the shadow of a famous cinema western about a frontier family.

David Carradine

Shannon
US 1961   36 × 25m   bw
Columbia/Robert Sparks (Jerry Briskin)

Cases of an insurance investigator who covers ten states in a car laden with gimmicks.
It seemed quite stylish at the time.

cr John Hawkins

George Nader, Regis Toomey

'Action will predominate, with room for human interest, humor, pathos. The stories will be good for family audiences in that they will concentrate on people in trouble, not trouble in people.' – promotion

Sharon: Portrait of a Mistress
US 1977   96m   colour   TVM
Paramount/Moonlight (Frank von Zerneck)

In San Francisco a rich man's mistress is driven into paranoia by her position.
Watchable character study.

w Nancy Greenwald   d Robert Greenwald   ph Fred Jackman   m Roger Kellaway

Trish Van Devere, Patrick O'Neal, Janet Margolin, Sam Groom, Gloria de Haven, Mel Ferrer, Salome Jens

Shatner, William (1931–). Canadian leading actor who has displayed some integrity in hundreds of guest roles. Series: For the People, Star Trek, Barbary Coast.

Shazam!
US 1974   24 × 22m   colour (16mm)
Filmation/Warner

A radio announcer when he utters the magic word transforms himself into the all-powerful Captain Marvel.
Shoddy live-action retread of a hoary theme.

Michael Gray, John Davey, Les Tremayne

†Not to be confused with Shazzan! a 1967 Hanna–Barbera series of 26 × 22m cartoons: here a magic ring transports children to the Arabian Nights.

She Cried Murder*
US 1973   74m   colour   TVM
Universal (William Frye)

A model witnesses a murder, and the policeman who comes to investigate is the murderer.
A ripe chestnut, nicely shot on New York locations.

w Merwin Gerard   d Herschel Daugherty

Telly Savalas, Lynda Day George, Mike Farrell

She Lives
US 1973   74m   colour   TVM
ABC Circle

College newlyweds find that the wife is dying of a rare disease.
Dreary copy of Love Story.

w Paul Neimark   d Stuart Hagmann

Season Hubley, Desi Arnaz Jnr

She Waits*
US 1971   74m   colour   TVM
Metromedia

A bride is possessed by the evil spirit of her husband's first wife.
Obvious ghost story with a few frissons and a good cast.

w Arthur Wallace   d Delbert Mann

Dorothy McGuire, Patty Duke, David McCallum, Lew Ayres, Beulah Bondi

Sheen, Fulton (1895–). American Catholic bishop who became a leading TV personality with his fifties series Life is Worth Living.

Sheena Queen of the Jungle
US 1955   26 × 25m   bw
Nassour

Adventures from the comic strip about a female Tarzan.
Hilarious hokum with a splendidly Amazonian lead.

Irish McCalla, Christian Drake

Shell Game*
US 1975   74m   colour   TVM
TCF

A con man fleeces the crooked head of a charity fund.
Pleasant comedy suspenser on the lines of It Takes a Thief.

w Harold Jack Bloom   d Glenn Jordan

John Davidson, Tommy Atkins, Marie O'Brien, Jack Kehoe, Joan Van Ark

Shepherd, Jack (1940–). Gloomy-eyed but versatile British leading actor, notable in The Girls of Slender Means, Ready When You Are Mr McGill, Bill Brand, Count Dracula.

JACK SHEPHERD. A prototype of the star character of the seventies: not happy, not handsome, not successful, but blazing with his own kind of idealism. He is seen here as *Bill Brand*.

The Sheriff*
US 1970 74m colour TVM
Columbia (Jon Epstein)

A black sheriff gets into race trouble on a rape case. Routine adequately-made melodrama.

w Arnold Perl   *d* David Lowell Rich

Ossie Davis, Ruby Dee

Sherlock Holmes (1955): see The Adventures of Sherlock Holmes

Sherlock Holmes
GB 1967   26 × 50m   bw (VTR)
BBC

A careful series with a miscast star. Faithful to the original stories, but some needed too much padding out to fill the hour.

Peter Cushing, Nigel Stock

Sherlock Holmes in New York
US 1976   96m   colour   TVM
TCF/NBC (Nancy Malone, John Cutts)

Sherlock Holmes crosses the Atlantic to rescue Irene Adler from the clutches of Moriarty.
An appealing prospect, but the script and production prove boring and almost every actor is miscast.

w Alvin Sapinsley   *d* Boris Sagal   *m* Richard Rodney Bennett

Roger Moore, Patrick MacNee, John Huston, Charlotte Rampling, David Huddleston, Signe Hasso, Gig Young, Leon Ames, John Abbott, Jackie Coogan

Sherrin, Ned (1931–). British producer, associated chiefly with *That Was the Week that Was*; also debater and general teleman.

Shirley Temple Storybook: see Temple, Shirley

Shirley's World
GB 1971   17 × 25m   colour
ATV (Sheldon Leonard)

Assignments of a photo journalist.
Unpleasing comedy drama series with a star ill-at-ease.

cr Sheldon Leonard

Shirley Maclaine, John Gregson

Shirts/Skins*
US 1973   74m   colour   TVM
MGM

Six young businessmen turn themselves into competing teams on a crazy bet.
Spasmodically funny, erratically scripted comedy.

d William Graham

René Auberjonois, Bill Bixby, Leonard Frey, Doug McClure, McLean Stevenson, Robert Walden, Loretta Swit

Shore, Dinah (1917–) (Frances Rose Shore).
American popular songstress who in mid-career turned talk show hostess and through most of the seventies had her daily half-hour aimed mainly at women.

Short Walk to Daylight*
US 1972   73m   colour   TVM
Universal (Edward J. Montagne)

Eight people are trapped in the New York subway by an earthquake.

Unfortunately most of the excitement is at the beginning, but at least it's a good idea.

w Philip H. Reisman Jnr, Steven Bochco, Gerald di Pego   *d* Barry Shear

James Brolin, Don Mitchell, James McEachin, Abby Lincoln, Brooke Bundy

Shotgun Slade
US 1959–60   78 × 25m   bw
MCA/Revue/Shotgun (Frank Gruber)

Cases of a private detective in the old west.
Cheerful hokum, put together with some spirit.

m Gerald Fried

Scott Brady

Shoulder to Shoulder*
GB 1974   6 × 50m   colour (VTR)
BBC/Warner

The story of the suffragettes.
Rather perfunctory dramatizations of the lives of six women who led the movement; careful but not exactly compelling.

w Ken Taylor and others

Siân Phillips, Angela Down, Pamela Quinn

Shull, Richard B. (1929–). American comedy character actor. Series: *Diana, Holmes and Yo Yo*.

Sidekicks
US 1974   75m   colour   TVM
Warner/Cherokee

A black and a white con man get in and out of scrapes in the old west.
Rather dreary action comedy based on the cinema film *The Skin Game*. No go as a series.

w William Bowers   *d* Burt Kennedy

Lou Gossett, Larry Hagman, Blythe Danner, Jack Elam

Siege*
US 1978   96m   colour   TVM
Titus (Herbert Brodkin)

Senior citizens in a New York apartment house are terrified by hoodlums.
Fairly holding if unnecessary melodrama which almost sustains its length.

w Conrad Bromberg   *d* Richard Pearce   *ph* Alan Metzger   *m* Charles Gross

Martin Balsam, Sylvia Sidney, Dorian Harewood, James Sutorius

Sierra
US 1974   13 × 50m   colour
MCA/Universal/Jack Webb (Robert A. Cinader)

Cases for the rangers in Yosemite National Park (where Universal, by a strange coincidence, had just bought up the concessions).

Singularly inept attempt to do *Adam 12* in the open air, with badly matching stock footage; a short issue from the TV movie *The Rangers*.

James G. Richardson, Ernest Thompson, Mike Warren, Jack Hogan

Sigmund and the Sea Monsters
US 1973–4   24 × 22m   colour
Sid and Marty Krofft

Two boys who live near the California beach befriend a sea monster but keep his presence a secret.
Modest live-action fantasy.

w Si Rose, John Fenton Murray, Jack Raymond, Fred Fox, Seaman Jacobs   *d* Bob Lally

Bill Barty, Johnny Whittaker, Scott Kolden

The Silence*
US 1975   74m   colour   TVM
Palomar

For violating West Point's honour code, a cadet is shunned by his associates.
Mildly interesting story based on fact.

d Joseph Hardy

Richard Thomas, Gunnel Lindblom, Jorgen Lindstrom

The Silent Force
US 1970   15 × 25m   colour
Aaron Spelling

Undercover specialists work for the government.
Mission even more impossible. It failed.

cr Luther Davis

Ed Nelson, Percy Rodrigues, Lynda Day

The Silent Gun*
US 1969   74m   colour   TVM
Paramount (Bruce Lansbury)

A former gunfighter who has shunned weapons is appointed sheriff of his home town.
Adequate minor western.

w Clyde Ware   *d* Michael Caffey

Lloyd Bridges, John Beck, Ed Begley, Edd Byrnes, Pernell Roberts, Susan Howard

Silent Night, Lonely Night*
US 1969   98m   colour   TVM
Universal (Jack Farren)

Two lonely people with problems fall in love at Christmas in a small New England inn.
Acceptable rueful love story.

w John Vlahos, *play* Robert Anderson   *d* Daniel Petrie

Lloyd Bridges, Shirley Jones, Carrie Snodgress, Lynn Carlin

The Silent Service
US 1957–8   78 × 25m   bw
Twin Dolphins/NBC

Re-creations of true-life submarine adventures.
Adequate docu-drama making ample use of stock footage.

host Rear-Admiral Thomas M. Dykers

Silents Please*
US 1962–3   40 × 25m   bw
Paul Killiam/Gregstan

Potted versions of silent film classics, with informative commentary.
A service to American cinema, and a very entertaining job of work. Apart from compilation episodes, films compressed into 25m include *Tempest, Don Juan* (two parts), *The Hunchback of Notre Dame, Son of the Sheik, Lilac Time, The Black Pirate, Blood and Sand, Dr Jekyll and Mr Hyde* (1921), *The Thief of Bagdad, The Eagle, Nosferatu, The General, The Sea Beast* and *Intolerance*.

Silliphant, Stirling (1918–). American TV writer responsible for some of the best episodes of *Naked City, Route 66* and *Longstreet*. Now works primarily in movies.

Silverman, Fred (1938–). American executive who during the seventies was head of programming for CBS, ABC and NBC respectively.

Silvers, Phil (1912–) (Philip Silver). American burlesque and nightclub comedian who after a moderate success in films became one of the top TV stars of the fifties in *You'll Never Get Rich*, in which he created the character of conniving Sergeant Bilko and which was promptly rechristened *The Phil Silvers Show*. After a respite, *The New Phil Silvers Show* cast him as a factory foreman, but failed to take. He has subsequently made guest appearances.

Simard, Rene (1960–). French–Canadian pop singer who became something of a national star in a half-hour series of zany comedy items interlaced with music.

Simpson, Alan (1929–). British scriptwriter who with Ray Galton created *Hancock* and *Steptoe and Son*.

Simpson, Bill (1931–). Scottish actor known almost entirely as Dr Finlay in *Dr Finlay's Casebook*.

Sinden, Donald (1923–). Versatile British stage, screen and TV actor. Series include *Our Man at St Mark's, The Organization, Two's Company*.

Sing Along With Mitch. Cheerful series of one-hour pop song shows produced by NBC in the early sixties. Mitch was Mitch Miller, who conducted a strong team of vocalists.

'Shall we see what Mr. Fred Silverman has in store for us?'

FRED SILVERMAN. The real joke of this cartoon is the suggestion that a nation can be swayed by the commercial jockeyings of a network scheduler, however important the media think his moves are. In fact, ninety-five per cent of Americans probably still don't know who he is.

Sir Francis Drake
GB 1962   26 × 25m   bw
ATV

Adventures of Queen Elizabeth's master mariner. Tolerable cloak and sword stuff.

Terence Morgan, Jean Kent

Sir Lancelot: see The Adventures of Sir Lancelot

Sirota's Court
US 1976   8 × 25m   colour (VTR)
Universal/NBC/Peter Engel

The comic cases which are seen in a night court. Mildly exasperating comedy with everybody trying too hard.

Michael Constantine

sitcom. TV jargon for situation comedy.

Six-Five Special. A British BBC pop music series of the fifties.

The Six Million Dollar Man*
US 1972   74m   colour   TVM
Universal (Richard Irving)

An astronaut injured in a crash is remade with powerful artificial limbs and becomes a superhuman, bionic spy. A slow starter for an immensely popular science fiction series which injected love interest by later spinning off *The Bionic Woman*. Two other 74m starters were made before the show settled down into a one-hour slot; *Wine, Women and War* and *The Solid Gold Kidnapping*.

w Henri Simoun, *novel Cyborg* by Martin Caiden   d Richard Irving

Lee Majors, Darren McGavin, Martin Balsam, Barbara Anderson

† The resulting series reached its sixth season, with a virtually unchanged format, before cancellation in 1978.

The Six Wives of Henry VIII**
GB 1970   6 × 50m   colour
BBC/Mark Shivas (Ronald Travers)

Historical pageant and character study, one play per wife. Its star made a brave try but was not quite up to the older Henry. Scripts and production were however in the BBC's best style, and the project was popular in the US. It was also compressed into a disappointingly flat film, *Henry VIII and his Six Wives*.

w Jean Morris, Beverly Cross, Rosemary Anne Sisson

KEITH MICHELL, Annette Crosbie, Barbara Leigh-Hunt, Patrick Troughton, Elvi Hale, Angela Pleasence, Sheila Burrell

The Sixth Sense
US 1971   25 × 50m   colour
MCA/Universal

A professor investigates ESP and psychic phenomena. Rather too dry and scientific semi-occult chiller series with a few authentic jolts.

Gary Collins

Skelton, Red (1910–) (Richard Skelton). Durable American comic from the burlesque school; a big name in TV specials of the fifties and sixties, till excess drove him from the scene.

Ski Lift to Death
US 1978   96m   colour   TVM
Paramount/Jozak (Richard Briggs, Bruce J. Sallan)

Four groups of people at Lake Louise are trapped in a ski lift.
Routine, meandering suspenser of which only the last 20 minutes are worth watching.

w Laurence Heath   *d* William Wiard   *ph* Ozzie Smith   *m* Barry DeVorzon

Deborah Raffin, Charles Frank, Howard Duff, Don Galloway, Gail Strickland, Clu Gulager, Don Johnson

'Anyone expecting a neat murder mystery better not bother.' – *Daily Variety*

Skippy the Bush Kangaroo
Australia 1966–8   91 × 25m   colour
Norfolk International

A game ranger makes an unusual pet.
Enjoyable children's series with a prepossessing star.

Skippy, Gary Pankhurst, Ed Devereaux

Sky Heist*
US 1975   100m   colour   TVM
Warner/Jack Webb

Holidaymakers rescued by the Aero Bureau of the Los Angeles County Sheriff's office turn out to be criminals with a major robbery in hand.
Exciting but overlong caper yarn intended as a pilot for a helicopter series.

w William F. Nolan, Rick Rosner   *d* Lee H. Katzin

Don Meredith, Joseph Campanella, Larry Wilcox, Ken Swofford, Stefanie Powers, Frank Gorshin, Shelley Fabares

Sky King
US 1953–4   72 × 25m   bw
Jack Chertok

A modern ranch owner keeps law and order from his private plane.
Acceptable hokum series of its time.

Kirby Grant, Gloria Winters

Skyhawks
US 1969   17 × 25m   colour
Pantomime/Ken Snyder

Assignments of a daredevil air transport and rescue service.
Cleancut cartoon adventures.

Skyway to Death*
US 1974   74m   colour   TVM
Universal (Lou Morheim)

A mountain cable car gets stuck with passengers aboard.
Routine disaster/suspense adventure, dullish when everyone talks, okay when the action begins.

w David Spector   *d* Gordon Hessler

Bobby Sherman, Stefanie Powers, John Astin, Joseph Campanella, Ross Martin

Slade, Bernard (   ). American scriptwriter, creator of *The Flying Nun*, who went on to write the smash play *Same Time Next Year*.

Slater, John (1916–75). British character actor, often of cockney roles. Series: *Johnny You're Wanted*, *Z Cars*.

Slattery's People*
US 1964   36 × 50m   bw
Bing Crosby Productions (Matthew Rapf)

Cases of a state investigator.
Well-mounted political dramas which suffered the fate common on American TV with programmes of quality.

cr James Moser

Richard Crenna, Alejandro Rey, Francine York, Kathie Browne

Slay Ride*
US 1972   97m   colour   TVM
TCF

A New Mexico sheriff clears an Indian of a murder charge.
Competent outdoor murder mystery originally shown as two episodes of *Cade's County*.

w Anthony Silson, Rick Husky   *d* Marvin Chomsky

Glenn Ford, Edgar Buchanan, Victor Campos, Peter Ford, Tony Bill

Small Miracle*
US 1973 74m colour TVM
Hallmark

Remake of the film *Never Take No for an Answer*, about a small boy who takes his sick donkey to the Pope. Effective in its modestly sentimental way.

w John Patrick, Arthur Dales, *novel* Paul Gallico *d* Jeannot Szwarc *m* Ernest Gold

Marco della Cava, Vittorio de Sica, Raf Vallone

Small World. American talk show, on CBS in the fifties. The creation of Ed Murrow, who by means of international link-ups was able to discuss matters of the moment with three famous guests in their own homes in different parts of the world.

Smash-up on Interstate Five
US 1976 96m colour TVM
Filmways (Roger Lewis)

After a freeway pile-up, we see how some of those involved came to be there.
Once you've seen the crash, there's no point in waiting: it's *The Bridge of San Luis Rey* all over again, and that was better written.

w Eugene Price, Robert Presnell Jnr, *novel Expressway* by Elleston Trevor *d* John Llewellyn Moxey *m* Bill Conti

Robert Conrad, Buddy Ebsen, Vera Miles, David Groh, Harriet Nelson, Sue Lyon, Scott Jacoby, Donna Mills, Herb Edelman, Terry Moore

Smile Jenny, You're Dead*
US 1974 90m colour TVM
Warner

A private eye protects a cover girl from murder.
Second pilot for *Harry O*; smoothly made.

w Howard Rodman *d* Jerry Thorpe

David Janssen, Andrea Marcovicci, Jodie Foster, Zalman King, Clu Gulager

The Smith Family*
US 1971–2 39 × 25m colour
ABC/Don Fedderson

The domestic and professional life of a city policeman. As demonstrated by these stars, it's all too hygienic to be true, but the show, a curious attempt to present a family who looked as though they'd stepped right out of a commercial, was always mildly watchable.

cr Edmund Hartmann

Henry Fonda, Janet Blair, Darleen Carr, Ronny Howard, Michael-James Wixted, John Carter, Charles McGraw

Smith, Howard K. (1914–). American news correspondent, with CBS and ABC.

Smith, Jaclyn (*c* 1950–). American leading lady of the late seventies, one of *Charlie's Angels*.

Smith, John (1931–) (Robert Van Orden). Mild-mannered American second lead. TV series: *Cimarron City*, *Laramie*.

Smith, Kate (1909–). Amply proportioned American popular singer who had her own radio shows, followed by much TV in the fifties.

The Smothers Brothers: Tom (*c* 1932–) **and Dick** (*c* 1934–). This rather self-effacing comic duo with musical talent built themselves up to be a national American institution before suddenly fading from popularity and view. In 1965 they had a half-hour comedy series in which one played an apprentice angel coming back to earth to seek his brother's help; for the two following seasons they had a variety hour series. A 1975 attempted comeback was notably unsuccessful.

The Smugglers
US 1968 100m colour TVM
Universal (Norman Lloyd)

American ladies on holiday in Europe are pawns for an international smuggling ring.
Lively adventure comedy.

w Alfred Hayes, *novel* Elizabeth Hely *d* Norman Lloyd

Shirley Booth, Gayle Hunnicutt, Michael J. Pollard, Kurt Kasznar, Carol Lynley, David Opatoshu

Snatched*
US 1972 73m colour TVM
Spelling–Goldberg

The wives of three wealthy businessmen are kidnapped for ransom.
Slick, tough action melodrama.

d Sutton Roley

Howard Duff, Leslie Nielsen, Sheree North, Barbara Parkins, Robert Reed, John Saxon

The Snoop Sisters
aka: *The Female Instinct*
US 1972 96m colour TVM
Universal (Douglas Benton)

Two elderly lady mystery writers annoy their policeman nephew by investigating the death of a film star.
A promising format didn't really work despite the talent applied. See *Mystery Movie* for subsequent episodes.

w Leonard B. Stern, Hugh Wheeler *d* Leonard B. Stern

Helen Hayes, Mildred Natwick, Art Carney, Paulette Goddard (in a minuscule role), Craig Stevens, Bill Dana

Snoopy: see Charlie Brown

The Snow Goose*
GB 1971   50m   colour
MCA/Universal/BBC

At the time of Dunkirk, a wounded goose in the Essex marshes brings together an orphan girl and a crippled artist.
Sufficiently moving and capable version of Paul Gallico's carefully sentimental story.

Richard Harris, Jenny Agutter

Snowbeast
US 1977   96m   colour   TVM
Douglas Cramer

A ski resort is terrorized by a half-human, half-animal creature.
The yeti comes to Colorado. Overstretched chiller.

w Joseph Stefano   *d* Herb Wallerstein

Bo Svenson, Clint Walker, Yvette Mimieux, Sylvia Sidney, Robert Logan

Snyder, Tom (*c* 1939–). American anchorman, host of NBC's late night show *Tomorrow*.

So Soon to Die
US 1957   74m   bw   TVM
Columbia/Playhouse 90

An unemployed actor is employed to kill a girl, but falls for his prey.
Obvious, old-hat melodrama.

d John Brahm

Richard Basehart, Anne Bancroft, Sebastian Cabot, Torin Thatcher

Soap*
US 1977–   × 25m   colour (VTR)
(Columbia) Witt–Thomas–Harris (Paul Junger Witt, Tony Thomas)

The families of two sisters, one rich and one poor: both have lots of secrets.
Controversial black comedy series, supposedly a spoof of soap operas but actually a light satire of all kinds of trends in today's entertainment, including homosexuality, religion, sex and the Mafia. Sample remark of mother to gay son whom she finds trying on her clothes: 'I've told you a hundred times, that dress fastens at the back . . .'

cr/w SUSAN HARRIS

Richard Mulligan, Cathryn Damon, Robert Mandan, Katherine Helmond, Diana Canova, Billy Crystal, Robert Guillaume, Arthur Peterson, Robert Urich, Jennifer Salt, Ted Wass

'Some of the jokes have nothing going for them but bad taste, which isn't always enough. Is it funny? Yes, it is, mostly, and I guess that constitutes redeeming social value.' – Robert MacKenzie, *TV Guide*

Softly Softly*
GB 1966–76   × 50m   colour (VTR)
BBC

Perennially popular stories of a mythical Midlands police force.
Originally a spin-off from *Z Cars*, to follow the fortunes of Inspector Barlow, its cast suffered several changes and in its latter years the title became, rather clumsily, *Softy, Softly: Task Force*. Frank Windsor was on hand more or less throughout, as were Norman Bowler and Terence Rigby. Elwyn Jones was prominent among the writers, as were Robert Barr, Keith Dewhurst and Alan Plater.

'You can only sit rooted to your seat in joyful and generally fulfilled expectation.' – *Daily Express*

Soldiers of Fortune
US 1955–6   52 × 25m   bw
MCA/Revue

Two international adventurers offer themselves for hire.
Okay action series.

John Russell, Chick Chandler

The Sole Survivor*
US 1969   100m   colour   TVM
Cinema Center

A brigadier general helps to investigate the crash 17 years earlier of a plane which he navigated, and the ghosts of the dead watch helplessly.
Interesting but overstretched supernatural melodrama.

w Guerdon Trueblood   *d* Paul Stanley   *ph* James Crabe   *m* Paul Glass

Vince Edwards, William Shatner, Richard Basehart, Lou Antonio, Patrick Wayne

The Solid Gold Kidnapping: see The Six Million Dollar Man

Some May Live
GB/US 1966   100m   colour   TVM
(RKO) Foundation Pictures (Philip N. Krasne)

A woman army intelligence agent in Saigon passes classified information to her husband, a communist.
Boring political espionage adventure.

w David T. Chantler   *d* Vernon Sewell   *ph* Ray Parslow   *m* Cyril Ornadel

Joseph Cotten, Martha Hyer, Peter Cushing, John Ronane

Some Mothers Do 'Ave 'Em*
GB 1974–9   30 approx. × 30m plus specials   colour (VTR)
BBC (Michael Mills)

Adventures before and after marriage of the world's worst accident-prone misfit.
The star's curiously effeminate characterization proved

much to the public taste, and some of the stunts were magnificently conceived. Otherwise the series was necessarily repetitive and quickly began to wear out its welcome.

w Raymond Allen

MICHAEL CRAWFORD, Michele Dotrice

Someone I Touched*
US 1975 74m colour TVM
Charles Fries

A woman and her husband come to terms with each other when they find they have venereal disease.
Adequate 'outspoken' social melodrama.

w James Henderson   d Lou Antonio

Cloris Leachman, James Olson, Glynnis O'Connor, Andy Robinson, Allyn Ann McLerie, Kenneth Mars

Something Evil*
US 1971 73m colour TVM
Bedford Productions

A young couple and family move into a haunted farmhouse.
Flashy supernatural thriller with not enough plot.

w Robert Clouse   d Steven Spielberg

Sandy Dennis, Darren McGavin, Ralph Bellamy

Something for a Lonely Man
US 1968 98m colour TVM
Universal (Richard E. Lyons)

An old steam-engine brings prosperity to a western town.
Mildly enjoyable family western.

w John Fante, Frank Fenton   d Don Taylor

Dan Blocker, Susan Clark, John Dehner, Warren Oates, Don Stroud

Something for Joey
US 1977 96m colour TVM
MTM (Jerry McNeely)

A sportsman tries his best to please and stimulate his young brother.
Smooth sentimental drama

w Jerry McNeely   d Lou Antonio   m David Shire

Geraldine Page, Gerald S. O'Loughlin, Marc Singer, Jeff Lynas, Linda Kelsey

The Songwriters (GB 1978). A BBC series of 7 × 50m documentaries tracing the life and songs of outstanding British composers of this century, including Leslie Stuart, Lionel Monckton, Noël Coward, Lennon and McCartney. Pleasingly produced and written (on a modest budget) by Tony Staveacre.

Sons and Daughters
US 1974 13 × 50m colour
MCA/Universal/Barney Rosenzweig

Stories of small-town high-school students in the fifties.
Lame imitation of *American Graffiti*. See also *Senior Year* (pilot).

Gary Frank, Glynnis O'Connor

Sooty. A glove puppet manipulated by Harry H. Corbett; popular in Britain throughout TV's post-war decades, and one of the medium's first stars.

Sothern, Ann (1909–) (Harriet Lake). Pert, wise-cracking American leading lady of movies in the thirties and forties; in the fifties made a big name for herself as star of *Private Secretary* and *The Ann Sothern Show*.

The Sound of Anger
US 1968 100m colour TVM
Universal (Roy Huggins)

A team of lawyers defend teenage lovers accused of murdering the girl's father.
Moderate pilot for the series *The Bold Ones*. It achieves its purpose.

w Dick Nelson   d Michael Ritchie

Burl Ives, James Farentino, Dorothy Provine

The Sound of Laughter*
GB 1975 100m colour (VTR)
BBC

Reminiscences of early radio comedians and writers.
Rather a disappointing programme, but immensely valuable historically as a record of what was said.

Arthur Askey, Richard Murdoch, Maurice Denham, Deryck Guyler, Frankie Howerd, Barry Cryer

Sounder
US 1976 74m colour TVM
ABC Circle

Problems of a poor black family in the thirties.
Adventures of the Sounder family: a TV pilot that didn't take.

d William Graham

Ebony Wright, Harold Sylvester, Daryl Young

South Riding*
GB 1974 13 × 50m colour (VTR)
Yorkshire (James Ormerod)

An adaptation of Winifred Holtby's book about a mythical Yorkshire community in the mid-thirties.
Produced with standard efficiency, it met with moderate success. BAFTA judged it best series of the year.

w Stan Barstow

Dorothy Tutin, Hermione Baddeley, Nigel Davenport

Soviet Union. TV in Russia is entirely state-controlled, and although there is a reasonable mix of enter-

SOUTH RIDING's star, Dorothy Tutin – an under-used actress.

tainment programmes, everything is made to toe the party line. The bigger cities may have several channels, remote rural areas only one.

Space Ghost
US 1966–7   20 × 25m   colour
Hanna–Barbera

Exploits of an interplanetary crime fighter who can render himself invisible.
Very ordinary cartoon frolics.

Space 1999*
GB 1975–6   48 × 50m   colour
ATV/Gerry Anderson

A space station breaks away, travels through the universe and encounters alien civilizations.
Star Trek in all but name; an ambitious and sometimes imaginative production, handicapped by a lack of pace and humour and two very doleful leads.

Martin Landau,   Barbara   Bain,   Barry Morse, Catherine Schell

special. A term which in TV was originally applied to variety entertainments but came to mean any kind of non-fictional one-shot.

Special Branch
GB 1969–73   approx 50 × 50m   colour
Thames/Euston Films

Cases of Scotland Yard's security department.
Practised, competent cop show which made no great waves.

George Sewell, Patrick Mower

Special Olympics
aka: *A Special Kind of Love*
US 1978   96m   colour   TVM
EMI (Merritt Malloy, Marc Trabulus)

A widowed truck driver has three teenage sons, one of whom is mentally retarded.
Slow, heavy-going family drama which ends in a fine burst of love and sentimentality but takes a hell of a while to get there.

w John Sacret Young   *d* Lee Phillips   *ph* Matthew F. Leonetti   *m* Peter Matz

SPECIAL BRANCH. The arms of the law pictured here are Roger Rowland and George Sewell.

Charles Durning, Irene Tedrow, George Parry, Marc Winningham, Philip Brown

'Worthy causes don't necessarily make worthy drama.' – *Daily Variety*
'Against all odds – a retarded boy's courage unites his family in a special moment of joy!' – publicity

The Specialists
US 1974 74m colour TVM
Universal (Robert A. Cinader)

US public health experts trace an epidemic.
Lacklustre pilot.

w Preston Wood, R. A. Cinader *d* Richard Quine

Robert York, Jack Hogan, Maureen Reagan, Kyle Anderson, Tom Scott

Spectre
GB/US 1977 96m colour TVM
TCF/Gene Roddenberry

A criminologist specializes in the occult and exposes a coven of aristocratic devil worshippers in London.
Hilariously inept *Exorcist* rip-off with a starry cast all at sea. Special nude scenes were shot for a theatrical version which was never released.

d Clive Donner

Robert Culp, Gig Young, Gordon Jackson, James Villiers, Ann Lynn

Speed Buggy
US 1973–4 48 × 22m colour
Hanna–Barbera

Adventures of three teenagers in a car with personality.
Made to order cartoon series.

Speed, Doris (*c* 1905–). British character actress who since 1960 has played the redoubtable Annie Walker in *Coronation Street*.

Speight, Johnny (1921–). British writer, a former milkman with not much style but a sharp ear for the vernacular. Creator of Alf Garnett in *Till Death Us Do Part*.

The Spell
US 1977 74m colour TVM
Charles Fries (David Manson)

An overweight adolescent is possessed by the devil.
The author of *The Exorcist* should sue. Otherwise a fair spinetingler.

w Brian Taggert *d* Lee Philips *m* Gerald Fried

Lee Grant, James Olson, Susan Myers, Barbara Bostock, Lelia Goldoni

Spelling, Aaron (*c* 1918–). American producer who has made a small corner in empty-headed glamorous entertainments harking back to the old Hollywood, from *Burke's Law* to *Charlie's Angels* and *The Love Boat*.

Spencer's Pilots
US 1976   13 × 50m   colour
Sweeney/Finnegan (Larry Rosen)

Adventures of pilots for hire based at a small Midwestern airfield.
Despite an expensive first episode about barnstormers, this fated venture had the tired air of an old Monogram B feature.

cr Alvin Sapinsley   *m* Morton Stevens

Christopher Stone, Todd Susman, Gene Evans

Spend, Spend, Spend**
GB 1977   90m   colour (16mm)
BBC (Graeme MacDonald)

The story of a woman who won £152,000 on the football pools and spent it all, her husbands all dying of drugs and car accidents.
An obvious moral tale about vulgar people. Brilliantly made, it also has the merit of being true.

w JACK ROSENTHAL, from book by Vivian Nicholson   *d* JOHN GOLDSCHMIDT   *ph* Phil Meheux

Susan Littler, John Duttine, Helen Beck, Joe Belcher

'Working-class adrenalin in agonizing quantity . . . a heartbreaking piece.' – *Sunday Times*
'Beautifully organized . . . very funny.' – *Sunday Telegraph*

† BAFTA award 1977, best play.

Spiderman
aka: *The Amazing Spiderman*
US 1978   74m   colour   TVM
Charles Fries (Edward J. Montagne)

A scientist infected by a spider finds he can scale walls and spin webs.
A comic strip notion humanized without much flair, humour or variation on the single idea. Strictly for kids.

w Alvin Boretz   *d* E. W. Swackhamer

Nicholas Hammond

† A series of 13 × 50m episodes ensued.

Spiderman*
Canada 1967–8   52 × 22m   colour (16mm)
Grantray–Lawrence Animation

Cartoon version of the comic strip, quite stylishly done.

spin-off. An episode which introduces new characters and situations that are the projected starting-point for a different series. Also, the resulting series.

Spy Force
Australia 1970–1   42 × 50m   colour (16mm)
Paramount/Roger Mirams

Army Intelligence tracks the Japs during World War II.
Spy stuff from an unfamiliar angle, but a show which bites off rather more than its budget can chew and is often uncomfortably violent.

The Spy Killer
GB 1969   74m   colour   TVM
Cohen–Sangster

An ex-secret agent is blackmailed into looking for a mysterious notebook.
Companion piece to *Foreign Exchange*; no better.

w Jimmy Sangster   *d* Roy Baker

Robert Horton, Sebastian Cabot, Jill St John, Eleanor Summerfield, Barbara Shelley

Spycatcher. British (BBC) half-hour show of the fifties, written by Robert Barr, featuring Bernard Archard as Lt-Col Oreste Pinto, one of Army Intelligence's chief interrogators of suspected spies. Most of the shows consisted of a single across-the-table duologue, and were both tense and convincing, though not always quite true to fact.

The Squirrels
GB 1974–6   40 approx. × 25m   colour (VTR)
ATV (Shaun O'Riordan)

Misadventures of the workers in a small office.
Middling comedy series.

w Eric Chappell   *d* Shaun O'Riordan

Bernard Hepton, Ken Jones, Patsy Rowlands

SST: Disaster in the Sky
aka: *SST: Death Flight*
US 1977   96m   colour   TVM
ABC Circle (Ron Roth)

Sabotage threatens a supersonic airliner with an explosion if it lands.
Fairly watchable all-star jeopardy melodrama.

w Robert L. Joseph, Meyer Dolinsky   *d* David Lowell Rich   *m* John Cacavas

Robert Reed, Peter Graves, Doug McClure, Lorne Greene, George Maharis, Martin Milner, Brock Peters, Tina Louise, Susan Strasberg, Burgess Meredith, Bert Convy, Misty Rowe

Staccato: see Johnny Staccato

Stack, Robert (1919–) (Robert Modini). Cold-eyed American leading man who after an indifferent Hollywood career became a TV superstar when he played Eliot Ness in *The Untouchables*. His later series (*The Name of the Game, Most Wanted*) failed to achieve the same impact.

ROBERT STACK. The leader of *The Untouchables* is not only handy with a gun . . .

. . . but very athletic with it.

Stacy, James (*c* 1941–). American leading man who after appearing in *Lancer* was seriously injured in a car crash.

Stanley
US 1956   26 × 25m   bw
NBC

Stories of the bumbling proprietor of a hotel news stand.
Forgotten routine comedy.

Buddy Hackett, Carol Burnett

Stanton, Frank (   ). American executive, president of CBS 1946–72; a politician rather than a programmer.

Stapleton, Jean (1923–). American character actress who scored a hit as the long-suffering Edith in *All in the Family*.

A Star is Dead*
aka: *Quincy*
US 1976   74m   colour   TVM
Universal (Lou Shaw)

A pathologist investigates the death of a young actress.
Pilot for a *Mystery Movie* character: brisk, amusing and efficient but not exciting.

w Lou Shaw, Michael Kozoll   *d* Noel Black

Jack Klugman, Donna Mills, Robert Foxworth, June Lockhart, William Daniels

Star Maidens
GB 1975   13 × 25m   colour
Global/Scottish

Astronauts are marooned on a planet ruled by women. Humourless hokum whose only chance was to play for laughs.

Dawn Addams

Star Trek*
US 1966–8   79 × 50m   colour
Paramount/Norway/NBC (Gene Roddenberry)

An American space ship of the future reconnoitres the universe.
And finds monsters and mysteries at each stop. A highly successful space fiction concept, with simple but streamlined sets, imaginative dialogue, and a few parlour tricks such as a dematerialization process and an interplanetary crew member with big ears. The show became a cult: a movie version was made in 1979.

cr GENE RODDENBERRY

WILLIAM SHATNER, LEONARD NIMOY, De Forrest Kelley

† 17 episodes of a half-hour cartoon version were produced in 1973 by Filmation.

The Starlost
Canada 1973   16 × 50m   colour (VTR)
Glen–Warren/TCF

The last survivors of earth travel through space looking for a new home.
Confused, inept sci-fi which never grips the imagination.

cr Douglas Trumbull

Keir Dullea

The Stars Look Down*
GB 1975   13 × 50m   colour (VTR)
Granada (Howard Baker)

Hard times for Northumbrian miners in the thirties. Rather deliberately woebegone adaptation of a best-seller, with undeniably impressive sequences.

w Alan Plater, *novel* A. J. Cronin

Avril Elgar, Norman Jones, James Bate, Rod Cuthbertson

Stars on Sunday. An ingenious semi-religious concept devised by Yorkshire TV in 1969; it has run almost continuously thereafter as part of the Sunday religious break. Well-known stars respond to listeners' requests for popular semi-religious songs; the sets are determinedly archaic, the atmosphere is reliably comforting, and the linkman is always a personality well-loved by the public. The production costs are kept down by recording several songs from each star on the same day and then intercutting.

Starsky and Hutch*
US 1975   75m   colour   TVM
Spelling–Goldberg

Two undercover cops are subject to murder attempts, and want to find out why.
Rough-and-tumble cop show with lots of car chases; it led to a successful series.

w WILLIAM BLINN   *d* Barry Shear

DAVID SOUL, PAUL MICHAEL GLASER, Buddy Lester, Richard Lynch

STARSKY AND HUTCH. These rough-and-tumble young cops – played by Paul Michael Glaser and David Soul – were immensely popular with young audiences until the television censor cut down the action and made them sentimental.

†The resultant series was at press time in its fifth season, its success stemming from the personalities of its stars rather than the writing or production. The anti-violence campaign resulted in a strong injection of romance and sentimentality from the third season on.

State Trooper
US 1957–9   104 × 25m   bw
MCA/Revue

Stories of the Nevada State Police.
Adequate cop filler.

Rod Cameron

Steele, Tommy (1936–) (Thomas Hicks). British cockney entertainer whose TV appearances have been limited to the occasional special.

A Step Out of Line*
US 1970   100m   colour   TVM
Cinema Center 100 (Steve Shagan)

Korean War buddies use their skills in a daring civilian robbery.
Okay crime comedy.

w Steve Shagan, S. S. Schweizer   d Bernard McEveety
ph James Crabe   m Jerry Goldsmith

Vic Morrow, Peter Falk, Peter Lawford, Jo Ann Pflug, Lynn Carlin, Tom Bosley, John Randolph

Steptoe and Son****
GB 1964–73   approx 40 × 30m   bw, later colour (VTR)
BBC

The love–hate relationship between a frustrated rag-and-bone man and his exasperating old dad.
All kinds of barriers were broken by this earthy comedy series, each episode of which was at one time a national event and which was redrafted by the Americans as *Sanford and Son*. The standard fell off towards the end, but a dozen classical duologues remain.

w RAY GALTON, ALAN SIMPSON

HARRY H. CORBETT, WILFRID BRAMBELL

Stern, Leonard (c 1930–). American independent producer who has been mainly associated with light-hearted crime series: *The Governor and J.J., Faraday and Company, McMillan and Wife, Rossetti and Ryan*.

Steve Canyon
US 1958–9   39 × 25m   bw
Pegasus/NBC

Stories of an Air Force pilot on special assignment.
Juvenile hokum.

Dean Fredericks

Stevens, Connie (1938–) (Concetta Ingolia). American leading lady of the sixties. Starred in TV series *Hawaiian Eye*.

Stevens, Craig (1918–) (Gail Shekles). Mature American leading man of the fifties, later in character roles. His biggest success was on TV, where he seemed to impersonate Cary Grant. Series: *Peter Gunn, Man of the World, Mr Broadway, Rich Man, Poor Man*.

Stevens, Leslie (1924–). American independent writer–producer. Series: *The Outer Limits, Stony Burke, Search, The Invisible Man, Galactica*.

Stevenson, McLean (c 1932–). Tall, gangling American comedy actor who came into the limelight as Colonel Blake in *M*A*S*H* (a show which rather cheekily killed him off when he decided to leave). Also: *The Doris Day Show, The McLean Stevenson Show* (a simple-minded domestic comedy which ran 13 weeks in 1977), *Hello Larry*.

Stewart, Ed (1941–). British disc jockey, known as 'Stewpot'.

Stewart, James (1908–). American star actor, one of the great names in movies of the thirties, forties and fifties. Made two TV series, neither particularly success-ful: *The Jimmy Stewart Show* and *Hawkins on Murder*.

Sticking Together
US 1978   74m   colour   TVM
Viacom/William Blinn, Jerry Thorpe

A family of orphans in Hawaii persuade a conman to impersonate their Uncle Willy.
An attack of the cutes, well presented for those who can stomach that kind of thing.

w William Blinn   d Jerry Thorpe   ph Chuck Arnold
m John Rubenstein

Clu Gulager, Sean Roche, Lori Walsh, Sean Marshall

Stingray*
GB 1965   39 × 25m   colour
ATV/Gerry Anderson

Adventures of a super submarine of the future.
Superior puppet adventure series.

Stocker's Copper*
GB 1971   85m   colour (16mm)
BBC (Graeme McDonald)

Cornwall 1913. A policeman becomes friendly with one of the strikers he is supervising.
A raw political play whose power in this production is undeniable.

w Tom Clarke   d Jack Gold

Bryan Marshall, Jane Lapotaire, Gareth Thomas

Stone, Milburn (1904–). American character actor who after playing a hundred shady types in movies became a fixture as 'Doc' in *Gunsmoke*.

Stony Burke
US 1962 32 × 50m bw
United Artists/Daystar

Experiences of a rodeo rider.
Well-made series which fell somewhere between action and drama and hadn't really enough going for it.

cr Leslie Stevens

Jack Lord, Bruce Dern, Warren Oates

Stoppard, Tom (1937–). Intellectual, tongue-twisting, paronomasiac British playwright whose first TV success was *Professional Foul*.

Storch, Larry (1923–). American entertainer who started with Jackie Gleason and went on to *F Troop* as well as cabaret acts.

Storefront Lawyers: see Men at Law

Storm, Gale (1922–) (Josephine Cottle). American leading lady of a few forties films. In the fif-ties she rather surprisingly became a TV star in series *Oh Susanna!* (*The Gale Storm Show*) and *My Little Margie*.

A Story of David
GB 1960 99m colour TVM
William Goetz/Scoton/Mardeb (George Pitcher)

David's trouble with King Saul.
Competent biblical mini-epic.

w Gerry Day, Terrence Maple *d* Bob McNaught *ph* Arthur Ibbetson *m* Kenneth V. Jones

Jeff Chandler, Basil Sydney, David Knight, Barbara Shelley, Richard O'Sullivan, Donald Pleasence

The Story of David
US 1976 200m colour TVM
Columbia/Milburg Theatrical (Mildred Freed Alburg)

David's life from his battle with Goliath to the end of his reign.
Ho-hum religious biopic, overlong and sententious.

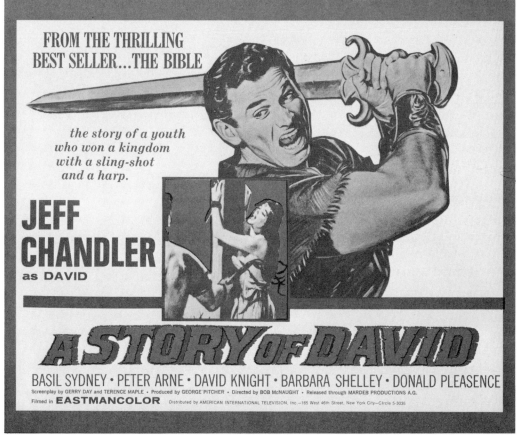

A STORY OF DAVID. Theatrical release for this TV movie produced one of the most irresistibly absurd publicity tag-lines of all time.

w Ernest Kinoy   *d* Alex Segal, David Lowell Rich   *m* Laurence Rosenthal

Timothy Bottoms, Keith Michell, Anthony Quayle, Jane Seymour, Susan Hampshire, Norman Rodway, Brian Blessed, Barry Morse

The Story of Jacob and Joseph

US 1974   100m   colour   TVM
Columbia/Milburg Theatrical (Mildred Freed Alburg)

Another biblical biopic, rather patchy and obliquely narrated.

w Ernest Kinoy   *d* Michael Cacoyannis   *m* Mikis Theodorakis

Keith Michell, Tony Lo Bianco, Colleen Dewhurst, Herschel Bernardi, Harry Andrews, Alan Bates (narrator)

'Probably the feature film most faithful to the Bible as a source.' – Jack Edmund Nolan

The Storyteller*

US 1977   96m   colour   TVM
Universal   Fairmount-Foxcraft (Richard Levinson, William Link)

A TV scriptwriter is troubled when a mother charges that his play caused her son's death.
Extended seminar on TV violence and its effects, surprising from this source. A thoughtful piece, well made.

w William Link, Richard Levinson   *d* Bob Markowitz   *ph* Terry K. Meade   *m* David Shire

Martin Balsam, Patty Duke Astin, Doris Roberts, James Daly, David Spielberg, Rose Gregorio

'Courageous, impressive . . . a valiant try.' – *Daily Variety*

Stowaway to the Moon

US 1974   100m   colour   TVM
TCF (John Cutts)

An 11-year-old boy stows away on a space flight.
Prolonged juvenile adventure.

w William R. Shelton, Jon Boothe   *d* Andrew V. McLaglen

Lloyd Bridges, Michael Link, John Carradine, Pete Conrad, Jeremy Slate

The Strange and Deadly Occurrence*

US 1975   74m   colour   TVM
Alpine/Charles Fries

A couple feel that their brand new house is haunted.
Stylish but rather strained suspenser with a lame ending.

w Sandor Stern   *d* John Llewellyn Moxey

Robert Stack, Vera Miles, L. Q. Jones, Herb Edelman, Margaret Willock

Strange Homecoming

US 1974   74m   colour   TVM
Alpine/Charles Fries

A burglar and murderer goes home for the first time in years and his family think him charming.
Anyone seen *Shadow of a Doubt* lately? It was better.

w Eric Bercovici   *d* Lee H. Katzin

Robert Culp, Glen Campbell, Barbara Anderson, Whitney Blake

Strange New World

US 1975   100m   colour   TVM
Warner

Three scientists return to earth after 200 years in a time capsule and find things very changed: women rule.
Third attempt at a new space fiction format. The other pilots were *Genesis II* and *Planet Earth*, and after this one they gave up.

w Al Ramrus, Ronald F. Graham, Walon Green   *d* Robert Butler

John Saxon, Kathleen Miller, Keene Curtis, James Olson, Martine Beswick

The Strange Possession of Mrs Oliver

US 1977   74m   colour   TVM
Columbia (Stan Shpetner)

A woman is possessed by the personality of someone long dead.
Adequate creepy thriller.

w Richard Matheson   *d* Gordon Hessler

Karen Black, George Hamilton, Robert F. Lyons, Lucille Benson

The Strange Report

GB 1968   13 × 50m   colour
ATV

A criminologist and his young aides outsmart the police.
Good conventional mystery series.

Anthony Quayle, Kaz Garas, Annake Wills

The Stranger*

US 1972   98m   colour   TVM
Bing Crosby Productions (Alan A. Armer)

An astronaut crashes on another planet and becomes a fugitive from the authorities.
Lively chase pilot which just didn't catch on.

w Gerald Sanford   *d* Lee H. Katzin

Glenn Corbett, Cameron Mitchell, Lew Ayres, Sharon Acker, Dean Jagger, Tim O'Connor, George Coulouris

Stranger on the Run*

US 1967   97m   colour   TVM
Universal (Richard E. Lyons)

A tramp arrives in a western town and becomes a murder suspect.
Routine western with the usual messages about goodwill towards men.

w Dean Riesner, *story* Reginald Rose *d* Don Siegel

Henry Fonda, Michael Parks, Anne Baxter, Dan Duryea, Sal Mineo

The Stranger Who Looks Like Me
US 1974 74m colour TVM
Filmways

An adopted girl searches for her real mother.
Efficient tearjerker.

w Gerald di Pego *d* Larry Peerce

Meredith Baxter, Beau Bridges, Whitney Blake, Walter Brooke, Neva Patterson

The Stranger Within*
US 1974 74m colour TVM
Lorimar

A pregnant mother is bizarrely controlled by her own unborn child.
The start of the monstrous baby cycle (*The Devil within Her*, *It's Alive*, *I Don't Want to Be Born*, etc). More subtle than most.

w Richard Matheson *d* Lee Philips

Barbara Eden, George Grizzard, Joyce Van Patten, David Doyle, Nehemiah Persoff

Strangers (GB 1978). A tough Granada police hour about tensions when Scotland Yard men are invited to join a northern police force as undercover men. Produced by Richard Everitt, with John Ronane heading the cast. Two seasons of 13 were made.

The Strangers in 7A*
US 1972 75m colour TVM
Palomar/Mark Carliner

The superintendent of an apartment building becomes a hostage in a robbery plot.
Adequate suspenser.

w Eric Roth, *novel* Fielden Farrington *d* Paul Wendkos

Andy Griffith, Ida Lupino, Michael Brandon, Suzanne Hildur

Strategy of Terror
US 1967 90m colour TVM
Universal

A New York police officer thwarts a plot to murder a UN leader.
Adequate chase thriller, originally a two-parter in the *Crisis* anthology.

w Robert L. Joseph *d* Jack Smight

Hugh O'Brian, Barbara Rush, Neil Hamilton, Harry Townes

The Strauss Family**
GB 1973 1 × 73, 12 × 50m colour (VTR)
ATV (Cecil Clarke, David Reid)

The private lives of the father-and-son composers.
Superior, expensively-staged biography with music; in TV's best middlebrow tradition.

w Anthony Skene, David Reid, David Butler

Eric Woolfe, Stuart Wilson, Tony Anholt, Anne Stallybrass, Lynn Farleigh

Strauss, Peter (1942–). Gentle, conventional American leading man who after a few film roles became a national figure as Rudy Jordache in *Rich Man, Poor Man* (Books One and Two).

Street Killing*
US 1976 74m colour TVM
ABC Circle (Richard Rosenbloom)

A public prosecutor connects a street mugging to a Napoleon of crime.
Tense, slightly unusual crime melodrama.

w Bill Driskill *d* Harvey Hart *ph* David M. Walsh *m* J. J. Johnson

Andy Griffith, Bradford Dillman, Harry Guardino, Robert Loggia, Don Gordon

Streets of Danger: see The Lone Wolf

The Streets of San Francisco**
US 1972 98m colour TVM
Warner/Quinn Martin

An old and a young police detective discover who murdered a young girl.
Highly efficient pilot for long-running location series.

w Edward Hume, *novel Poor Poor Ophelia* by Carolyn Weston *d* Walter Grauman

Karl Malden, Michael Douglas, Robert Wagner, Kim Darby

'Sometimes a fairish script, more often pointless chasing about San Francisco's hills.' – Jack Edmund Nolan

†The resulting series ran five seasons (120 × 50m episodes) and became an absolutely reliable action-packed crime entertainment. In the last season Michael Douglas was replaced by Richard Hatch.

Strike Force*
US 1975 75m colour TVM
D'Antoni–Weitz

An elite police force is set up to counter organized crime.
Rough, tough, realistic cop show which didn't take.

w Roger Hirson *d* Barry Shear

Cliff Gorman, Donald Blakely, Richard Gere, Edward Grover

THE STRAUSS FAMILY. This well-staged mini-series was more effective than either of the big-screen extravaganzas on this subject, and the music was beautifully recorded. Christopher Benjamin, Eric Woolfe (Johann) and Anne Stallybrass.

stripping. Playing a series five days a week at the same time.

Stritch, Elaine (1922–). Lanky, rasp-voiced, American comedienne and singer, an under-used talent. Series: *My Sister Eileen, Two's Company*.

Struthers, Sally (1947–). Pint-sized, hoarse-voiced American actress who made a big hit as the daughter in *All in the Family*.

Studs Lonigan*
US 1979   3 × 96m   colour
Lorimar (Harry R. Sherman)

An Irish–American grows up in Chicago in the 1920s. Solid transcription of a famous novel.

w Reginald Rose, *novel* James T. Farrell   *d* James Goldstone
Harry Hamlin, Colleen Dewhurst, Charles Durning

stunting. Cancelling regular weekly programmes in favour of special events.

Subterfuge
GB 1968   92m   colour   TVM
Intertel/Commonwealth United

An American agent runs into trouble in London. Second-rate espionage thick-ear.

d Peter Graham Scott

Gene Barry, Joan Collins, Michael Rennie, Suzanna Leigh, Richard Todd

Suddenly Single*
US 1971   73m   colour   TVM
Chris–Rose

A newly divorced man joins a California singles community.
Reasonably amusing contemporary comedy.

w Elinor and Stephen Karpf   *d* Jud Taylor

Hal Holbrook, Agnes Moorehead, Barbara Rush, Harvey Korman, Margot Kidder, Michael Constantine

Sugarfoot
US 1957–60   69 × 50m   bw
Warner

A young western wanderer helps people in trouble. Passable western which filled a need but is barely remembered.

cr Michael Fessier

Will Hutchins

ELAINE STRITCH in this shot appears to have a double-jointed thumb to go with her corncrake voice and immense singing talent. One more American whom the British have taken to their hearts.

Sugden, Mollie (1924–). North-country British character comedienne who usually plays a posh-talking but vulgar working-class lady. Series: *The Liver Birds, Are You Being Served?*.

Sullivan, Barry (1912–) (Patrick Barry). Reliable American leading man of the forties, later character actor. A frequent TV guest star. Series: *The Man Called X, The Tall Man, Adventures at Scott Island, The Road West, The Immortal*.

Sullivan, Ed (1902–74). American linkman, former columnist. His *Ed Sullivan Show*, on CBS from 1948, was the medium's best showcase for vaudeville talent.

Sullivan, Susan (*c* 1939–). Elegant American leading lady of the seventies: star of *Julie Farr MD*.

Sullivan's Empire
US 1967 90m colour TVM
Universal

Three sons seek their missing father in the South American jungle.
Watchable adventure hokum.

w Frank Chase *d* Harvey Hart, Thomas Carr

Martin Milner, Linden Chiles, Don Quine, Clu Gulager, Karen Jensen

A Summer Without Boys*
US 1973 74m colour TVM
Playboy

At a holiday resort during World War II, a woman becomes involved with a younger man and her daughter resents it.
Adequate woman's picture.

w Rita Lakin *d* Jeannot Szwarc

Barbara Bain, Michael Moriarty, Kay Lenz, Mildred Dunnock

Sunday Night at the London Palladium. A live one-hour variety show from the stage of the world's most famous variety theatre, this ATV presentation was a weekly event from 1954 until 1965 and included the most famous names in show business as well as a 'Beat the Clock' game interlude. Comperes included Tommy Trinder, Bruce Forsyth, Norman Vaughan and Jim Dale. The show was revived in the early seventies but for no good reason seemed less popular, though the format was identical; perhaps the talent was missing.

Sunset Across the Bay*
GB 1975 70m colour (16mm)
BBC (Innes Lloyd)

A manual worker retires and he and his wife go to live at Morecambe.
Sensitive but rather painful tragi-comedy of old age and death.

w Alan Bennett *d* Stephen Frears *ph* Brian Tufano

Harry Markham, Gabrielle Daye, Bob Peck, Albert Modley, Betty Alberge, Madge Hindle

'A moving work, modest on the surface, richer and deeper in memory.' – *Daily Mail*

Sunshine*
US 1973 121m colour TVM
Universal

A young wife finds she is dying of cancer.
Unbearably icky sudser which was popular among teenagers.

w Carol Sobieski *d* Joseph Sargent *ph* Bill Butler *m* John Denver

Cliff de Young, Brenda Vaccaro, Christina Raines

† A short-lived series ensued (13 × 25m) starring Cliff de Young as the sadly coping widower (producer: George Eckstein; director: John Badham). There was also a second TV movie, *Sunshine Christmas*, and a theatrical feature of 1976, *My Sweet Lady*, which was made up from fragments of the series.

The Sunshine Boys
US 1978 50m colour
Ray Stark/MGM/NBC (Michael Levee)

Two long-retired vaudeville comics are still squabbling with each other.

SUNDAY NIGHT AT THE LONDON PALLADIUM. A variety show which worked in the days when there were still stars: live from London's West End, it was a national family event in the fifties. The middle section was occupied by a game called *Beat the Clock*, over which a startlingly young-looking Bruce Forsyth is here presiding. A slicked-up version of the same format was launched by Thames in the seventies as *London Night Out*.

Interesting attempt to make a television series of the hit play and film. The pilot didn't jell.

w Neil Simon   *d* Robert Moore

Red Buttons, Lionel Stander

The Sunshine Patriot*

US 1968   98m   colour   TVM
Universal (Joel Rogosin)

A Russian secret agent takes the place of his double, an American businessman.
Adequate espionage suspenser.

w Gustave Field, Joel Rogosin, John Kneubuhl   *d* Joseph Sargent

Cliff Robertson, Dina Merrill, Wilfrid Hyde White, Lilia Skala, Antoinette Bower, Donald Sutherland, Luther Adler

The Super

US 1972   13 × 25m   colour (VTR)
ABC/Metromedia

Problems for the janitor of a semi-derelict New York apartment building.
Unattractive comedy series which didn't last.

Richard Castellano, Margaret Castellano

Super Friends

US 1973–4   26 × 45m   colour
Warner/Filmation

Adventures of a group of friends with special powers: Superman, Batman and Robin, Aquaman, Wonder Woman.
Enough is too much, especially of a semi-animated cartoon.

Superdome*

US 1978   96m   colour   TVM
ABC Circle (William Frye)

A security guard is murdered during a big football game in New Orleans.
Pretty suspenseful, well-written telemovie which passes the time without exhausting the patience.

w Barry Oringer   *d* Jerry Jameson   *ph* Matthew F. Leonetti   *m* John Cacavas

David Janssen, Jane Wyatt, Edie Adams, Clifton Davis, Peter Haskell, Ken Howard, Susan Howard, Van Johnson, Donna Mills, Ed Nelson, Vonetta McGee

Superman

US 1952–6   104 × 25m   52 colour, 52 bw
National Periodical Publications

The all-powerful hero from the planet Krypton masquerades as mild-mannered reporter Clark Kent.

Fairly ragged, watchable kiddie show from the comic strip.

George Reeves, Noel Neill

Surfside Six
US 1960–1   74 × 50m   bw
Warner

Three detectives live on a houseboat at Miami Beach. Very moderate mystery series aimed at teenagers.

Troy Donahue, Lee Patterson, Van Williams, Diane McBain

Survival. Half-hour wild-life film series which has been produced by Anglia TV at the rate of 13 or more episodes per year since the fifties. There have also been a number of one-hour specials including *The Flight of the Snow Goose*, *Tiger, Tiger* and *Gorilla*.

The Survivors*
US 1969   15 × 50m   colour
MCA/Universal (William Frye, Gordon Oliver, Walter Doniger)

Embezzlement and murder are just a couple of the things that happen in a millionaire's family.

An ill-starred attempt at a novel for TV by Harold Robbins. Chief fault was that the characters were rich but not interesting, and the Riviera story which was shot as a pilot was not used until the series folded and portions of it were used, with much dramatic contrivance, as a wrap-up. A TV movie called *Last of the Powerseekers* was also extracted from the general muddle, which was compounded by dissensions among staff and cast.

cr Harold Robbins   *story editors* John Wilder, Michael Gleason

Lana Turner, George Hamilton, Kevin McCarthy, Ralph Bellamy, Rossano Brazzi

Susie: see Private Secretary

Suspect*
GB 1974   76m   colour (16mm)
Thames (Mike Hodges)

A crime is committed in a remote village, and the life of a family is affected.

THE SURVIVORS starred Lana Turner, one of the big screen names who didn't make it in TV series. (Others: James Stewart, Anthony Quinn, Richard Widmark, Bette Davis.) Here, backed by George Hamilton, she fails to dominate the scene in this series.

S.W.A.T. was criticized in some quarters for its violence, but everyone knew that viewers only turned on to see the cops go into action. Steve Forrest (pointing) shows his men the best way to a happy ending.

Detailed, circumstantial police suspenser, well above average.

w/d Mike Hodges

Rachel Kempson, Michael Coles, George Sewell

Suspicion*
US 1957   21 × 50m   bw
MCA/Revue/Alfred Hitchcock

An anthology of suspense stories. (Hitchcock was not involved except as executive producer.)
A mixed bag, but the level of technical accomplishment was quite high.

Bette Davis, Ida Lupino, Nancy Kelly, etc.

Susskind, David (1920–). American independent producer and entrepreneur, usually involved with worthwhile material. Series include *East Side West Side*, *Get Smart*, and shows for *Kraft Theater* and *Play of the Week*. He also acted as moderator in a discussion programme, *The David Susskind Show*.

Swallow, Norman (1921–). British executive producer, often in tandem with Denis Mitchell; with BBC and Granada. BAFTA 1977: Desmond Davis Award.

S.W.A.T.*
US 1975–6   34 × 50m   colour
Spelling–Goldberg (Robert Hammer)

For tough cases the police call in a special weapons and tactical team.
Cop show much criticized for its toughness; it was cancelled because of the anti-violence lobby. It did however manage some rousing action sequences, though its situations were repetitive.

cr Robert Hamner

Steve Forrest, Robert Urich, Rod Perry, James Coleman, Mark Shera

† The pilot was a 96m episode of *The Rookies* called *S.W.A.T.* Two other 96m episodes were made, *Deadly Tide* and *Running Man*.

Swayze, John Cameron (*c* 1913–). American radio and TV newscaster of the forties and fifties: he always began with 'And a good evening to you' and closed with 'Glad we could get together.'

The Sweeney**
GB 1974–8   52 × 50m   colour
Thames/Euston Films

Cases of Scotland Yard's Flying Squad.
Rough, tough crime-in-the-streets cop melodrama, with

THE SWEENEY drew its title from cockney rhyming slang. Sweeney Todd, Flying Squad, get it? What viewers got was a cop tougher than the criminals, several of whom got beaten up in most episodes. Here John Thaw and Dennis Waterman put in a bit of practice before going after the real thing.

much bad language, low life and violence, not to mention a villain-hating hero. Despite some unnecessarily impenetrable plots, a thoroughly professional job.

JOHN THAW, DENNIS WATERMAN, Garfield Morgan

† The pilot for the series was a TV movie called *Regan*.

Sweeney, Bob (   ). American comic actor who played Fibber McGee and was one of *The Brothers*. Later he turned producer: *Hawaii Five O*, *The Andros Targets*.

Sweet Hostage
US 1977 96m colour TVM
Brut (Richard E. Lyons, Sidney D. Balkin)

A girl finds life in New Mexico less restful than she had hoped.
Overlong suspenser.

w Edward Hume, *novel Welcome to Xanadu* by Nathanial Benchley *d* Lee Phillips *ph* Richard C. Glouner *m* Luchi de Jesus

Linda Blair, Martin Sheen, Jeanne Cooper

Sweet Sweet Rachel*
US 1971 73m colour TVM
Stan Shpetner

An ESP expert tries to find out how a beautiful woman is being driven mad.
Reasonably chilling semi-supernatural thriller.

w Anthony Lawrence *d* Sutton Roley

Alex Dreier, Stefanie Powers, Pat Hingle, Louise Latham, Brenda Scott

Swift, David (1919–). American producer who at one point had a high reputation for the creation of comedy series: *Mr Peepers*, *Grindl*, *Camp Runamuck*.

The Swiss Family Robinson
GB title: *Island of Adventure*
US 1975 74m colour TVM
TCF/Irwin Allen

A family has to fend for itself when shipwrecked on a desert island.
Abysmal remake heralding a likewise series.

w Ken Trevey *d* Harry Harris

Martin Milner, Cameron Mitchell, Pat Delaney, Michael Wixted, John Vernon

† The series ran to 24 × 50m episodes.

Swit, Loretta (1948–). American character actress with comedic bent, a sensation as Hot Lips Houlihan in *M*A*S*H*.

301

Switch**
US 1975   74m   colour   TVM
Universal (Glen A. Larson)

A con man and an ex-cop are partners in an investigation agency and pull the wool over the eyes of a conniving police officer.
Fast moving, funny, not very comprehensible pilot based on the appeal of *The Sting*. Unfortunately the resultant series (66 × 50m) was tolerated rather than popular.

w Glen A. Larson   *d* Robert Day

Robert Wagner, Eddie Albert, Charles Durning, Sharon Glass

Sword of Freedom
GB 1957   39 × 25m   bw
ATV/Sapphire

Adventures of a 15th-century Italian Robin Hood. Tolerable costume hokum.

Edmund Purdom

Sword of Justice
US 1978   96m   colour   TVM
Universal (Glen Larson)

A playboy is framed on an embezzlement charge which has also caused the death of his parents. On his release from jail, having acquired special criminal skills, he sets about avenging himself on those responsible.
Doleful pilot which unaccountably resulted in a series order. Our hero will of course use his doubtful skills to help the oppressed.

Dack Rambo, Alexander Courtney, Bert Rosario

'In the tradition of such literary classics as *The Scarlet Pimpernel* and *The Count of Monte Cristo*, action and adventure combine with human emotion and sophisticated humour.' – publicity

†The series was cancelled after 13 × 50m episodes.

Sybil*
US 1976   2 × 96m   colour
Lorimar/NBC (Jacqueline Babbin)

The investigation of a girl with sixteen different personalities.
Docu-drama which goes thirteen better than *The Three Faces of Eve*. Conscientious but a little long.

w Stewart Stern, *book* Flora Rheta Schreiber   *d* Daniel Petrie   *m* Leonard Rosenman

Joanne Woodward, Sally Field, Brad Davis, Martine Bartlett, Charles Lane, William Prince

Sykes, Eric (1923–). British comedian and writer, who since the fifties has had regular series on BBC, with Hattie Jacques as his sister, Richard Wattis (early shows) as a neighbour, and (latterly) Deryck Guyler as a friendly policeman. They have always been funny in an amateurish way.

Sylvester, Victor (1902–78). British orchestra leader who ran the BBC's Dancing Club for many post-war years. Famous for his measured tempo: 'slow, slow, quick quick slow'.

syndication. What happens to shows after the networks have finished with them: they are sold to local stations, either singly or in groups.

Szysznyk
US 1977   6 × 25m   colour
Paramount/Four's Company (Jerry Weintraub)

An ex-Marine becomes a playground supervisor.
Dullsville sentimental comedy series. The title didn't help.

cr Jim Mulligan, Ron Landry

Ned Beatty, Olivia Cole, Susan Lanier

T

The Tab Hunter Show
US 1960   32 × 25m   bw
NBC/Famous Artists (Norman Tokar)

Romantic misadventures of the playboy artist of a popular comic strip.
Tolerable comedy filler series.

Tab Hunter, Richard Erdman, Jerome Cowan

Tabitha
US 1977   13 × 25m   colour
Columbia (Robert Stambler)

The daughter of the witch of *Bewitched* grows up and works in a television station.
Awful, youth-oriented sequel.

Lisa Hartman, Robert Urich, Mel Stewart

Taeger, Ralph (*c* 1929–   ). Standard American leading man. Series: *Acapulco, Klondike, Hondo*.

Tail Gunner Joe*
US 1977   150m   colour   TVM
Universal/NBC (George Eckstein)

The career of Senator Joe McCarthy.
Some absorbing material is a little too fancily presented in flashback, but the show gets marks for trying.

w Lane Slate   *d* Jud Taylor   *m/d* Billy May

Peter Boyle, Burgess Meredith, Patricia Neal, John Forsythe, Heather Menzies, Ned Beatty, Charles Cioffi, Andrew Duggan, Jean Stapleton, Henry Jones

Take Your Pick. An extremely tatty quiz show inflicted on the British for nearly 20 years from 1955 by Associated Rediffusion. Winners had the choice of opening a mystery box which would contain anything from a fortune to a dried prune. Michael Miles was the jokester in charge.

Tales of India*
GB 1978   6 × 40m   colour (VTR)
BBC (Stephen Peet)

Interviews with survivors from the time of the Raj.
Invaluable social history, though it is surprising how little photographic and newsreel material is available.

d/narrator Christopher Cook

Tales of the Texas Rangers
US 1955–6   52 × 25m   bw
Columbia

Present-day yarns, from a radio series. Not too bad, but no better than it needed to be.

Willard Parker, Harry Lester

Tales of the Unexpected
GB title: *Twist in the Tale*
US 1977   1 × 96m, 7 × 50m   colour
Quinn Martin

An unsuccessful anthology of thrillers with twist endings.

Tales of the Unexpected
GB 1979   × 25m   colour   VTR
Anglia (John Woolf)

Sardonic stories written and introduced by Roald Dahl.
Good sophisticated entertainment.

Tales of the Vikings
US 1960   39 × 25m   bw
United Artists/Brynaprod (Stanley Margulies)

Self-explanatory action item, rather risible.

Jerome Courtland, Buddy Baer

Tales of Wells Fargo*
US 1957–61   167 × 25m, 34 × 50m   bw
MCA/Universal/Overland

Stories of the stagecoach line during California's gold rush days.
Fairly rousing western adventures which showed the west not as it was but as we like to think of it.

Dale Robertson

The Tall Man*
US 1960–1   75 × 25m   bw
MCA/Universal

Sheriff Pat Garrett is helped by Billy the Kid.
An extraordinary perversion of history, but quite a slick entertainment.

Barry Sullivan, Clu Gulager

Tallahassee 7000
US 1959   26 × 25m   bw
Columbia

Cases of a Florida sheriff.
The star carries it, but some of the plots are weak.

Walter Matthau

Tarbuck, Jimmy (1940–). British north country comedian, cheerful but not very clever. Popular in the sixties, subsequently often used as quizmaster.

Target
US 1951   38 × 25m   bw
United Artists

Suspense anthology, vaguely centred on people of determination.

Adolphe Menjou (host and occasional star)

Target
GB 1977–8   22 × 50m   colour (16mm)
BBC (Philip Hinchcliffe)

Cases of a regional crime squad.
Tough police thriller series, in direct opposition to *The Sweeney* but without the saving grace of humour.

Patrick Mower, Philip Madoc, Brendan Price, Vivien Heilbronn

†Much criticized for its violence, the first series was curtailed. The last 13 were more restrained.

Target Risk
US 1975   74m   colour   TVM
Universal

Bonded couriers combat thieves and blackmailers.
Abysmal crime pilot marking a desperate shortage of style and ideas.

w Don Carlos Dunaway   *d* Robert Scheerer

Bo Svenson, Meredith Baxter, John P. Ryan, Robert Coote, Lee Paul

Target the Corruptors*
US 1961   34 × 50m   bw
Four Star/Velie–Burrows–Ackerman

An investigative reporter reveals corruption in high places. Based on articles by Lester Velie.
Well-made gangster exposé with a remarkable amount of acting talent in the guest spots.

Stephen McNally, Robert Harland

Tarzan*
US 1966–7   57 × 50m   colour
Banner (Sy Weintraub)

Tarzan returns to his jungle and helps the oppressed.
Neatly made jungle adventures, a little lacking in humour.

Ron Ely

A Tattered Web**
US 1971   74m   colour   TVM
Metromedia (Bob Markell)

A police detective protects himself by taking the law into his own hands.
Complex, satisfying crime melodrama with a twist or two.

w Art Wallace   *d* Paul Wendkos

Lloyd Bridges, Broderick Crawford, Murray Hamilton, Ann Helm

Taxi. New half-hourly comedy series for the 1978 season, about the adventures of a New York cab-driver.

Taylor, A. J. P. (1906–). British academician and historian who during the fifties, sixties and seventies was a familiar sight on TV giving lectures, usually without visual aids.

Taylor, Kent (1907–) (Louis Weiss). American leading man of the thirties; when roles grew few in Hollywood, he played in *Rough Riders* and *Boston Blackie* on TV.

Taylor, Rod (1929–) (Robert Taylor). Australian leading man in Hollywood; TV series between film roles include *Hong Kong, Bearcats, The Oregon Trail.*

Taylor, Shaw (1924–). British linkman and host who from the mid-sixties has been engaged in devising and presenting *Police Five*, a brief weekly programme in which the police ask for the public's help in solving crimes.

teaser. A trailer that whets the appetite without giving full details.

telecine. The apparatus which projects a film programme and converts it into electronic signals for transmission.

telefilm. What would now be called a TV movie.

telementary. A rather unnecessary neologism describing a documentary made for TV.

teleplay. A word used in the fifties and sixties as script credit on TV fiction. It grew into disuse.

telethon. A live discussion programme during which members of the public may ring in with their opinions.

Telethon
US 1978   96m   colour   TVM
ABC Circle (Robert Lovenheim)

Serious problems face several of the people involved in a charity-fund-raising broadcast from Las Vegas.
Moderate multi-story entertainment relying chiefly on the tawdry glitter of its setting.

w Roger Wilton   *d* David Lowell Rich   *ph* Jacques Marquette   *m* Peter Matz

Lloyd Bridges, Janet Leigh, Polly Bergen, Red Buttons, Edd Byrnes, Dick Clark, John Marley, Kent McCord, Jill St John

Temperatures Rising
US 1972 24 × 25m colour
Columbia/Harry Ackerman (William Asher)

The lighter side of hospital life . . .
. . . seemed to be inconceivable to both writers and cast.

James Whitmore, Cleavon Little, Joan Van Ark, Nancy Fox, David Bailey, Reva Rose

†The following season, 22 more episodes were made without Whitmore, under the title *The New Temperatures Rising*. Paul Lynde starred.

Temple Houston
US 1963 26 × 50m bw
Warner

A lawyer travels the old west.
Tolerable semi-western, rather too low key.

Jeffrey Hunter, Jack Elam

Temple, Shirley (1928–). American child film star, the multi-talented sensation of the thirties. Her main contribution to TV was a series of 14 × 50m fairy tales called *Shirley Temple Storybook*, produced in 1960 by William Asher. She starred in every third show.

Tenafly*
aka: *Everybody's Looking*
US 1972 74m colour TVM
Universal/Levinson–Link (Jon Epstein)

A black private eye with domestic problems solves the murder of the wife of a talk show host.
Adequate pilot for what became a one-season addition to *Mystery Movie*.

w Richard Levinson, William Link *d* Richard A. Colla

James McEachin, Mel Ferrer, Ed Nelson, John Ericson

Terraces
US 1977 74m colour TVM
Charles Fries

Crises in the lives of three women in a high-rise apartment block.
Tepid cross-cut domestic dramas.

w Lila Garrett, George Kirgo *d* Lila Garrett

Julie Newmar, Lloyd Bochner, Bill Gerber, Eliza Garrett, Kim McDonough, James Phipps

Terror in the Sky*
US 1971 74m colour TVM
Paramount (Matthew Rapf)

All the crew of a jet liner are stricken with food poisoning and the plane has to be brought down by a passenger.
Competent remake of the cinema film *Zero Hour*.

From the radio play and novel *Flight into Danger* by Arthur Hailey *d* Bernard Kowalski

Leif Erickson, Doug McClure, Roddy McDowall, Keenan Wynn, Lois Nettleton, Kenneth Tobey

Terror on the Beach
US 1973 74m colour TVM
TCF

A family outing is ruined by violence from beach bums.
Unsurprising melodrama.

w Bill Svanoe *d* Paul Wendkos

Dennis Weaver, Estelle Parsons, Susan Dey, Kristoffer Tabori, Scott Hylands

Testimony of Two Men
US 1977 3 × 96m colour
MCA/Universal

The fortunes of two doctors in a small town after the Civil War.
Uneasy costume drama, no *Gone with the Wind* but rising at the end to a fine pitch of frenzy. The actors work hard rather than effectively, and the low budget shows in the limited camera set-ups.

w William Hanley, James Miller, *novel* Taylor Caldwell *d* Larry Yust, Leo Penn

Steve Forrest, Margaret O'Brien, Barbara Parkins, David Birney, Ralph Bellamy, Theodore Bikel, Tom Bosley, J. D. Cannon, Ray Milland, Linda Purl, William Shatner, Inga Swenson

†This 'novelization' was the first production of *Operation Prime Time*, a project involving a collection of local stations in a bid to provide major entertainment material in competition with the networks. It worked pretty well.

The Texan
US 1958–9 78 × 25m bw
Rorvic/Desilu

A cowboy wanders through the old west.
Easy-going adventure series, quite proficient of its kind.

Rory Calhoun

The Texas Wheelers
US 1974 13 × 25m colour (VTR)
Mary Tyler Moore (Dale McRaven, Chris Hayward)

Misadventures of a family of idle Texans.
The idea was too negative; the series folded.

cr Dale McRaven

Gary Busey, Jack Elam, Mark Hamill, Tony Becker

Thaddeus Rose and Eddie
US 1978 96m colour TVM
CBS (Don Paulson, Rod Sheldon)

Two Texas bachelors decide to try their luck in the world outside.

Amiable, ambling comedy which despite good elements doesn't hold the attention.

w William T. Wittliff d Jack Starrett ph Robert Jessup m Charles Bernstein

Johnny Cash, Diane Ladd, Bo Hopkins, June Carter Cash

Thames Television. The British ITV company formed in 1968 from an amalgamation of ABC and Associated Rediffusion. It operates the weekday franchise in London.

That Certain Summer**
US 1972 74m colour TVM
Universal (Harve Bennett)

A teenager discovers that his father is a homosexual. Much acclaimed drama: TV comes of age, etc. Actually it takes a while to get started, but the acting is fine.

w Richard Levinson, William Link d Lamont Johnson

HAL HOLBROOK, Hope Lange, Scott Jacoby, Martin Sheen, Joe Don Baker, Marlyn Mason, James McEachin

That Girl*
US 1966–70 136 × 25m colour
Daisy (Bill Persky, Sam Denoff)

A midwestern girl arrives in New York determined to be an actress.
Predictable but likeable and refreshing comedy.

Marlo Thomas, Ted Bessell, Rosemary De Camp, Lew Parker

That Was the Week that Was***. A late-Saturday-night satire show which burst upon the nation in 1963 and changed the face of British – and later American – viewing. Suddenly we had so much satire that nothing and no one was sacred; then equally suddenly the boom ended and satire has scarcely been heard of since. *TW3*, as it was familiarly known, was produced by Ned Sherrin and encouraged by Donald Baverstock. It made a star of a very nervous young David Frost and established reputations for Millicent Martin, David Kernan, Bernard Levin, William Rushton and others. Presented before an audience, it took the form of a very rough-edged revue, with lots of barriers broken, especially rude words and abuse for the then Home Secretary, Henry Brooke and more amiable spoofing of the then Premier, Harold Macmillan. It was aimed at readers of the posh Sundays, and most viewers didn't understand what the fuss was about.

† Subsequent versions (much the same, really) were *Not So Much a Programme, More a Way of Life* and *BBC3*.

That's Hollywood*
US 1977 26 × 22m colour (VTR)
TCF (Jack Haley Jnr)

Themed compilations of clips from the TCF library.
A bit restricted in scope, and saddled with a blah commentary, this series nevertheless reminded us of many first-class scenes from the past. Unfortunately it was made on VTR, with loss of film transfer quality.

† Episodes include *The Great Detective, Here Come the Clowns, Masters of Disaster, The Song and Dance Men.*

That's Life. Light-hearted British consumer guidance show compered by Esther Rantzen, with Glyn Worsnip, Kieran Prendeville and Cyril Fletcher. Its investigations are made amusing rather than tragic. A BBC production, it has attracted large audiences since 1975. In the 1978–9 season Paul Heiney and Chris Serle replaced Worsnip and Prendeville.

That's My Mama
US 1974 24 × 25m colour (VTR)
Columbia/Allan Blye, Chris Bearde

Problems of a Negro barber in Washington, especially when his mother interferes in his life.
Unappealing black comedy with too much shouting.

cr Dan T. Bradley, Allan Rice

Clifton Davis, Theresa Merritt, Theodore Wilson, Lynne Moody

Thaw, John (1942–). Tough, unsmiling British leading actor, in series *Redcap, The Sweeney.*

T. H. E. Cat
US 1966 26 × 25m bw
NBC (Boris Sagal)

A super-bodyguard prefers jobs in which he can fight crime.
A rather pretentious suspense series with nothing to be pretentious about. The initials are for Thomas Hewitt Edward, and the Cat suggests that the hero might have been a cat burglar and is adept at hair-raising climbs.

Robert Loggia, R. G. Armstrong

Then Came Bronson
US 1968 95m colour TVM
MGM

Adventures of a drop-out who is motorcycling around America.
Slow-moving, amiable pilot for a one-season series.

w Denne Bart Petitclerc d William A. Graham

Michael Parks, Bonnie Bedelia, Sheree North, Akim Tamiroff, Gary Merrill

† The series lasted 26 × 50m episodes.

'It's a romantic adventure, a romance not in the sense of boy–girl, but in terms of his love with life.' – Robert Justman

They Call It Murder
US 1971 97m colour TVM
TCF/Parsons (Walter Grauman)

The District Attorney investigates a swimming pool murder.
Smooth pilot which got nowhere, featuring Erle Stanley Gardner's DA character.

w Sam Rolfe   *d* Walter Grauman

Jim Hutton, Lloyd Bochner, Jessica Walter, Carmen Matthews, Leslie Nielsen, Nita Talbot, Robert J. Wilke, Ed Asner

They Only Come Out at Night: see Jigsaw John

Thicker than Water. Shortlived 1973 American version of *Nearest and Dearest* with Julie Harris and Richard Long.

Thief*
US 1971   74m   colour   TVM
Metromedia (Dick Berg)

A smooth jewel thief outsmarts himself.
What seems to start as a light comedy later goes sour; a curious mixture.

w John D. F. Black   *d* William Graham

Richard Crenna, Angie Dickinson, Cameron Mitchell

A Thief Is a Thief Is a Thief: see The Magnificent Thief

The Thin Man*
US 1957–8   78 × 25m   bw
MGM

Nick and Nora Charles, sophisticated New York sleuths, and their dog Asta solve a crime or two while having a good time.
A passable light entertainment which seemed rather better than the later *Thin Man* movies though certainly not up to the first.

Peter Lawford, Phyllis Kirk

'The films started the vogue for comedy–mysteries distinguished by wit, pace and incisive cutting. The TV series lacks all these.' – Don Miller

Things in Their Season
US 1974   75m   colour   TVM
Tomorrow

A Wisconsin farm woman learns that she has leukaemia at a time when the family has other problems.
Another undramatic dying fall. *Dark Victory* has a lot to answer for.

w John Gay   *d* James Goldstone

Patricia Neal, Ed Flanders, Marc Singer, Meg Foster

Thinnes, Roy (1938–   ). Virile American action lead. Series: *The Long Hot Summer, The Invaders, The Psychiatrist, From Here to Eternity*.

Third Girl from the Left*
US 1973   73m   colour   TVM
Playboy

An ageing nightclub chorus girl tries to improve her lot.
Smart but not very interesting comedy drama.

w Dory Previn   *d* Peter Medak

Tony Curtis, Kim Novak, Michael Brandon

This is Noël Coward*
GB 1972   96m   colour (16mm)
Charles Castle

A valuable record of the life and career of Noël Coward, with film clips and interviews. The script also produced a book called *Noël*. Those appearing include Coward himself, John Gielgud, Maurice Chevalier, Richard Burton, David Niven, Lilli Palmer, Brian Aherne, Yul Brynner, Danny LaRue, Earl Mountbatten, John Mills, Gladys Cooper, Edith Evans, Hermione Gingold, Anna Neagle, Cecil Beaton, Sybil Thorndike, Joyce Grenfell, Celia Johnson. The wealth of original material makes the programme a valuable historical record despite the disappointing quality of the processing.

w/d Charles Castle   *ph* Dick Bush   *cartoons* Osbert Lancaster

This Is the West That Was
US 1974   74m   colour   TVM
Universal (Roy Huggins, Jo Swerling Jnr)

Wild Bill Hickok, Calamity Jane and Buffalo Bill fight each other and the baddies.
Lame western spoof.

w Sam H. Rolfe, Jo Swerling Jnr   *d* Fielder Cook

Ben Murphy, Kim Darby, Matt Clark, Jane Alexander, Tony Franciosa, Stuart Margolin

This Is Your Life. A half-hour 'live' show popular in America and Britain since the fifties, in which a celebrity is surprised by a party of his friends who recount his life story. Ralph Edwards has been the American host, Eamonn Andrews the British; and since it became the practice to record the show, embarrassment has been avoided. *This Is Your Life* has become the epitome of popular TV.

This Man Dawson
US 1959   39 × 25m   bw
United Artists

A law enforcement agency works on government missions.
Routine hokum.

Keith Andes

This Week. Thames TV's (previously Rediffusion's) weekly current affairs half-hour which has been an ITV staple since the network began in 1955. BAFTA award 1969. In 1978 it changed its title to *TV Eye*.

307

THIS WEEK is one of the programmes which have brought the problems of the third world to the drawing-rooms of the affluent. This rich but horrifying picture is from a story about famine in Ethiopia.

Thomas, Danny (1914–) (Amos Jacobs). American nightclub comedian whose most successful career was in TV, with the long-running *Danny Thomas Show* (*Make Room for Daddy*) and later *Make Room for Granddaddy*.

Thomas, Howard (1909–). British executive, former radio producer (creator of *The Brains Trust*) and director of the fortunes of ABC Television; after its merger with Thames he became chairman of the joint company. Autobiography 1977: *With An Independent Air*.

Thomas, Lowell (1892–). American journalist (with Lawrence in Arabia) and radio commentator; came to TV primarily as host of a travel series, *High Adventure*.

Thomas, Marlo (*c* 1934–). American leading lady, daughter of Danny Thomas. Series: *That Girl*.

Thomas, Richard (1951–). American juvenile lead, the popular John Boy of *The Waltons*.

Thornton, Frank (1921–). British comedy actor, usually of snooty types, e.g. Captain Peacock in *Are You Being Served?*

Thorpe, Jerry (*c* 1930–). American independent producer/director, son of Richard Thorpe. Series: *The Untouchables, Kung Fu, Chicago Teddy Bears, Harry O*.

Three Days in Szczecin*
GB 1976 90m colour (VTR)
Granada (Leslie Woodhead)

A reconstruction of a strike which halted a Polish ship-yard in 1971.
Quite well done, if it had to be done at all. The viewers seemed to think we have quite enough strikes of our own.

w Boleslaw Sulik   *d* Leslie Woodhead

Leslie Sands

Three for the Road
US 1975 74m colour TVM
Mary Tyler Moore

A photographer widower travels across America on jobs, with his two sons, in a camper.

Acceptable family fare which led to a shortlived series.

w Jerry McNeely *d* Boris Sagal *m* David Shire

Alex Rocco, Vincent Van Patten, Leif Garrett, Julie Sommars

†The series ran 13 × 50m episodes. Producer: Jerry McNeely; music: David Shire and James Di Pasquale; with Alex Rocco, Vincent Van Patten, Leif Garrett.

The Three Hostages*
GB 1977 85m colour (16mm)
BBC (Mark Shivas)

Richard Hannay reluctantly takes on the job of exposing a crime syndicate which has taken three significant hostages.

Well conceived and intriguing but in the event a disappointing entertainment which lacks pace and humour.

w John Prebble, *novel* John Buchan *d* Clive Donner

Barry Foster, John Castle, Diana Quick, Peter Blythe

The Three Thousand Mile Chase
US 1977 96m colour TVM
NBC/Universal (Roy Huggins)

A professional courier and an importer are chased across country by gangsters.

Another attempt (see *Target Risk*) to get a series out of the courier business. This one was competent, but nothing happened.

w Philip DeGuere Jnr *d* Russ Mayberry

Cliff De Young, Blair Brown, Glenn Ford, David Spielberg, Priscilla Pointer

Three's a Crowd
US 1969 74m colour TVM
Columbia

Erroneously thinking his first wife dead in a plane crash, a businessman remarries . . .

The cinema film *My Favourite Wife* revamped; each time to less effect.

w Buck Henry *d* James Frawley

Larry Hagman, E. J. Peaker, Jessica Walter, Norman Fell, Harvey Korman

Three's Company*
US 1977–   × 25m colour (VTR)
ABC/NRW/TTC

A young man moves in to share a flat with two girls.

Sexy American version of the British *A Man About the House*; it became a phenomenal success in the American ratings.

w various *d* Bill Hobin *m* Joe Raposo

John Ritter, Joyce de Witt, Suzanne Somers, Audra Lindley, Norman Fell

Thriller**
US 1960–1 67 × 50m bw
MCA/Revue/Hubbell Robinson (William Frye)

An anthology of horror stories, hosted by Boris Karloff, who also stars in several.

A patchy series, but the best items had a genuine chill, e.g. *The Incredible Dr Markesan*, *Pigeons from Hell*, *The Hungry Glass*.

Thunderbirds***
GB 1966 32 × 50m colour
ATV/Gerry Anderson

Men and women with special skills help to combat world criminals.

Like the later Muppets, this is a children's series, i.e. a puppet spoof of the James Bond syndrome, which has genuine sophistication, gaiety and adult appeal.

Tic Tac Dough. American quiz game of the fifties (British title *Criss Cross Quiz*). Contestants used their correct or incorrect answers to play noughts and crosses on an electronic board.

Tightrope*
US 1957 37 × 25m bw
Columbia

An undercover police officer joins the mob.

Sharply made but unavoidably repetitive gangster suspense series.

cr Russel Rouse, Clarence Greene

Michael Connors

Till Death Us Do Part****
GB 1964–74 50 approx. × 30m bw, later colour (VTR)
BBC

A loud-mouthed working-class bigot gets himself and his family into hot water.

A comedy series which seldom strayed from a tiny set and was often poorly plotted yet changed the face of TV by means of what it said and how it said it. Alf Garnett was held up as a monster yet he voiced opinions which many people secretly held, so people had a sneaking sympathy for him when he got into trouble. He and his long-suffering wife Else were magnificent comic creations in the Dickensian mould, superbly acted; and the series, with its frequent tirades about race and religion and royalty, could hardly fail to make the headlines or to change the face of TV comedy. The Americans picked up the format rather carefully, but it became a roaring success for them as *All in the Family*.

cr/w JOHNNY SPEIGHT

WARREN MITCHELL, DANDY NICHOLS, Una Stubbs, Anthony Booth

A Time for Love
US 1973 100m colour TVM
Paramount (Stirling Silliphant)

Two love stories of different types.

A format which didn't jell, even after the success of *Love Story*. No takers.

w Stirling Silliphant *d* George Schaefer, Joseph Sargent

Jack Cassidy, Bonnie Bedelia, John Davidson, Lauren Hutton, Christopher Mitchum

The Time Travelers
US 1976 74m colour TVM
ABC/TCF/Irwin Allen

Scientists go back in time and rescue a girl from the Chicago fire.
Scruffily-made fantasy with great chunks of tinted footage from *In Old Chicago*.

w Jackson Gillis, *story* Irwin Allen and Rod Serling *d* Alex Singer *a/d* Eugene Lourie

Sam Groom, Tom Hallick, Richard Basehart, Trish Stewart

Time Tunnel*
US 1966 30 × 50m colour
TCF/Irwin Allen

Scientists build a time tunnel and get caught in the fourth dimension.
A well-contrived piece of juvenile science fiction which deserves a nod for sheer audacity as our heroes each week get caught up in chunks of old Fox movies. The episode called *Ghost of Nero* is a lulu.

cr Irwin Allen

James Darren, Robert Colbert, Lee Meriwether

†In 1976 Fox made an ill-advised effort to revive the project with a TV movie called *The Time Travelers* in which an attempt was made to prevent the Chicago fire.

Tingwell, Charles (1917–). Bland Australian actor; in England during the fifties, he became a familiar face in *Emergency Ward Ten*. Also appeared in *Homicide*.

Tinker, Grant (1926–). American executive, husband of Mary Tyler Moore and in charge of her production company.

To All My Friends on Shore
US 1971 74m colour TVM
Bill Cosby

A black businessman discovers his young son has a fatal illness.
One wonders how dying has suddenly acquired such an appeal. This one is such a star weepie that it's hard to be sympathetic.

w Allan Sloane *d* Gilbert Cates

Bill Cosby, Gloria Foster, Dennis Hines

To Kill a Cop*
GB title: *Streets of Fear*
US 1978 2 × 96m colour TVM
Columbia/David Gerber

A black terrorist begins a wave of cop killings.
Above average crime melodrama.

w Ernest Tidyman, *novel* Robert Daley *d* Gary Nelson

Joe Don Baker, Lou Gossett, Patrick O'Neal, Desi Arnaz Jnr, Christine Belford, Scott Brady, Eddie Egan, Alan Fudge, Eartha Kitt

To Rome With Love
US 1969–70 48 × 25m colour
MCA/Universal/Don Fedderson (Edmund Hartmann)

A widowed college professor takes his family to live in Rome.
Rather uneasy attempt at a realistic sitcom shot on location.

John Forsythe, Kay Medford (first season), Walter Brennan (second season), Peggy Mondo, Vito Scotti

Tobias, George (1901–). American character actor. TV series: *Hudson's Bay*, *Adventures in Paradise*, *Bewitched*.

Today. NBC's easy-going morning news and chat show, which airs each weekday between 7am and 9am.

Todd, Bob (1922–). Beaming, balding, gurgling British comic actor who was a popular stooge to Benny Hill and others but failed in his own series *In For A Penny*.

The Tom and Jerry Show
US 1975 17 × 22m colour
Hanna–Barbera

Debased version of the classic cartoon characters: poor drawing, no violence, bad jokes. The original cartoons, thankfully, remain in circulation.

The Tom Ewell Show*
US 1960 26 × 25m bw
Four Star/Ewell/Carroll/Martin

Misadventures of a real estate agent whose home has 'wall-to-wall women'.
Friendly, competent and amusing domestic sitcom.

TOM EWELL, Marilyn Erskine, MABEL ALBERTSON

Tom Sawyer
US 1975 74m colour TVM

Adventures of a trouble-prone small boy in a town on the banks of the Mississippi.
A plain, even homely, version of the famous tale by Mark Twain.

w Jean Holloway *d* James Neilson

Buddy Ebsen, Jane Wyatt, Vic Morrow, John McGiver, Josh Albee, Jeff Tyler

Toma*

GB title: *Man of Many Faces*
US 1972 74m colour TVM
Universal (Earl A. Glick, Trevor Wallace)

Adventures of an undercover cop with a penchant for disguise.
Effective police melodrama with plenty of action sequences.

w Edward Hume, Gerald di Pego *d* Richard T. Heffron

Tony Musante, Susan Strasberg, Simon Oakland, Nick Colasanto, Abe Vigoda, Dave Toma

†There followed a series of 24 × 50m episodes (producers: Roy Huggins, Jo Swerling, Stephen Connell), after which the star resigned and the project was redesigned as *Baretta*.

Tombstone Territory*

US 1957–9 91 × 25m bw
Ziv

A sheriff and an editor combine to tame 'the town too tough to die'.

Absolutely standard western, quite pleasantly made.

Pat Conway, Richard Eastham

Tomorrow's World*. A 25m BBC studio series which every season from 1957 presented instances of advanced scientific gadgets which would eventually aid the public. For more than 20 years Raymond Baxter was the linkman.

Tonight. This title has been used for many magazine programmes, notably the BBC's light-hearted early evening one of the fifties, with Cliff Michelmore, and its more sober late evening version of the seventies. In America since 1954 it has heralded a late-night chat show, first with Steve Allen, then with Jack Paar, and from 1961 with Johnny Carson.

The Tony Randall Show

US 1976–7 44 × 25m colour
Mary Tyler Moore

The professional and home life of a widowed judge.

TOO LONG A WINTER. Real-life characters are meat and drink to TV, for the whole show is usually in their faces. This Yorkshire documentary by Barry Cockcroft featured Hannah Hauxwell, a moorland recluse who was later persuaded to visit London for an award, and didn't much care for it.

Nothing new, and the star seemed a little uneasy in this extreme contrast from his Felix in *The Odd Couple*.

cr Tom Patchett, Jay Tarses

Tony Randall, Allyn McLerie

Too Many Thieves
US 1966 95m colour TVM
Filmways/Mayo (Richard Alan Simmons)

A New York attorney helps ransom a priceless Middle Eastern treasure stolen from its shrine.
Would-be-funny rigmarole that outstays its welcome, adapted from episodes of a TV series *The Trials of O'Brien*.

w George Bellak *d* Abner Biberman

Peter Falk, Britt Ekland, Elaine Stritch, David Carradine, Nehemiah Persoff, Joanna Barnes, Pierre Olaf, George Coulouris, Ludwig Donath

Toomey, Regis (1902–). Familiar Irish–American character actor, in Hollywood from the early thirties. TV series: *Hey Mulligan*, *Richard Diamond*, *Shannon*, *Dante*, *Burke's Law*.

Top Cat*
GB title: *Boss Cat*
US 1961–2 30 × 25m colour
Hanna–Barbera

Life among the alley cats of New York City.
An amusing take-off of Sergeant Bilko, with draughtsmanship from the company's better days.

Top of the Pops. A long-running weekly BBC pop show in which the current top 20 discs are charted and a selection is sung.

Top Secret
US 1978 96m colour TVM
NBC/Sheldon Leonard/Jemmin

An art dealer is really a superspy doing work the CIA won't touch.
Dreary, witless spy capers against exotic backgrounds.

w David Levinson *d* Paul Leaf *ph* Gabor Pogany
m Ted Macero, Stu Gardner

Bill Cosby, Tracy Reed, Sheldon Leonard, Gloria Foster

Topper*
US 1953–4 78 × 25m bw
Bernard L. Schubert

A respectable banker has ghostly friends.
Reasonable fair copy of the movies: it seemed the height of sophistication when it came out.

Leo G. Carroll, Robert Sterling, Anne Jeffreys

Tors, Ivan (1916–). Hungarian–American independent producer whose series have usually involved animals or scientific gadgetry: *The Man and the Challenge*, *Sea Hunt*, *Ripcord*, *Flipper*, *Daktari*, *Primus*, etc.

Totter, Audrey (1918–). Sharp-edged American leading lady of the forties. Later in TV series: *Cimarron City*, *Our Man Higgins*.

Trackdown
US 1957–8 71 × 25m bw
Four Star

Adventures of an 1870s Texas Ranger.
Adequate action western.

Robert Culp

The Trackers
US 1971 73m colour TVM
Aaron Spelling

A posse depends on a black man to find a murderer.
Unremarkable western.

w Gerald Gaiser *d* Earl Bellamy

Sammy Davis Jnr, Ernest Borgnine, Julie Adams, Jim Davis, Connie Kreski, Arthur Hunnicutt

Trapped**
GB theatrical title: *Doberman Patrol*
US 1973 74m colour TVM
Universal (Richard Irving, Gary L. Messenger)

Department store doors close on a man who has been mugged, and he finds himself at the mercy of vicious guard dogs.
Rather silly but suspenseful melodrama.

w/d Frank de Felitta

James Brolin, Susan Clark, Earl Holliman

Trapped beneath the Sea
US 1974 100m colour TVM
ABC Circle

Four men are running out of oxygen at the bottom of the sea in a mini-sub.
Predictable, well-managed suspense.

w Stanford Whitmore *d* William Graham

Lee J. Cobb, Martin Balsam, Joshua Bryant, Paul Michael Glaser

The Travels of Jamie McPheeters*
US 1963 26 × 50m bw
MGM

A young boy's experiences on an 1840s wagon train.
Carefully mounted re-creation of frontier days; emphasis on character rather than action prevented popularity.

From the novel by Robert Lewis Taylor

Kurt Russell, Dan O'Herlihy, Charles Bronson

Travis Logan DA
US 1970 100m colour TVM
Quinn Martin

A DA upsets a murderer's careful plans.
Adequate courtroom job.

d Paul Wendkos

Vic Morrow, Hal Holbrook, Brenda Vaccaro, George
Grizzard

A Tree Grows in Brooklyn
US 1974 74m colour TVM
TCF

A thoughtful young girl grows up in the New York
slums at the turn of the century, and watches her ne'er-
do-well Irish father die of drink.
Unaffecting remake of the famous film, all too brightly
coloured.

w Blanche Hanalis, novel Betty Smith d Joseph
Hardy

Cliff Robertson, Diane Baker, Nancy Malone, James
Olson, Pamela Ferdin, Michael-James Wixted

The Trial of Chaplain Jensen*
US 1975 74m colour TVM
TCF

A naval chaplain is courtmartialled for adultery.
True-life courtroom drama, discreetly scripted.

w Loring Mandel, book Andrew Jensen d Robert
Day

James Franciscus, Joanna Miles, Charles Durning,
Lynda Day George

The Trial of Lee Harvey Oswald*
US 1978 2 × 96m colour TVM
Charles Fries (Richard Freed)

The film supposes that Oswald was never shot by Ruby
and that his trial proceeded.
Rather flashy and dramatically suspect fantasy which
plays about with facts and despite excellent cameos
doesn't really succeed as entertainment.

w Robert E. Thompson, play Amram Ducovny, Leon
Friedman d David Greene ph Villis Lopenieks m
Fred Karlin

Ben Gazzara, Lorne Greene, Frances Lee McCain,
Lawrence Pressman, John Pleshette, Marisa Pavan, Mo
Malone

Trial Run
US 1969 98m colour TVM
Universal (Jack Laird)

An ambitious lawyer overreaches himself.
Overlong courtroom drama.

w Chester Krumholz d William Graham

James Franciscus, Leslie Nielsen, Janice Rule, Diane
Baker

The Trials of O'Brien*
US 1965 20 × 50m bw
Filmways (Richard Alan Simmons)

A flamboyant defence lawyer seems always to get into
trouble.
Amusing light mystery series.

Peter Falk

The Tribe
US 1974 74m colour TVM
Universal (George Eckstein)

Problems of cro-magnon man.
Some Universal executive must have had a brainstorm:
the result isn't highbrow, it's paralysingly boring.

w Lane Slate d Richard A. Colla

Victor French, Warren Vanders, Henry Wilcoxon,
Adriana Shaw

Tribes*
GB theatrical title: The Soldier Who Declared Peace
US 1970 74m colour TVM
TCF/Marvin Schwarz

A hippie is called up and has a varying relationship
with his drill sergeant.
Mildly amusing contemporary comedy.

w Tracy Keenan Wynn, Marvin Schwarz d Joseph
Sargent ph Russell Metty

Darren McGavin, Jan-Michael Vincent, Earl
Holliman

Trilogy of Terror
US 1975 74m colour TVM
ABC Circle/Dan Curtis

Women have the problems in three strange stories.
Grab-bag of hauntings and neuroses; not exactly compulsive.

w William Nolan, Richard Matheson d Dan Curtis

Karen Black (in four roles), Robert Burton, John
Karlin, George Gaynes

Trinder, Tommy (1909–). Cheerful British cockney
comedian whose prime TV work was as the first host of
Sunday Night at the London Palladium.

Trinity Tales*
GB 1975 6 × 50m colour (VTR)
BBC (David Rose)

Six supporters on their way to a cup final tell tall
stories.
A cheeky updating of Chaucer with moments of charm
but an overall inability to keep up the pace. Half the
length would have been twice as good.

w Alan Plater d Tristan de Vere Cole

Bill Maynard, Francis Matthews, Colin Farrell, Susan
Littler, Paul Copley

Trouble Comes to Town
US 1972   73m   colour   TVM
ABC Circle (Everett Chambers)

Racial problems erupt in a small southern town. Obvious social melodrama.

w David Westheimer   *d* Daniel Petrie

Lloyd Bridges, Pat Hingle, Hari Rhodes, Janet McLachlan, Sheree North

Trouble Shooters
US 1959   26 × 25m   bw
Meridian

Adventures of construction gangs on difficult jobs. Poor action series: scope too limited.

Keenan Wynn, Bob Mathias

The Trouble With Father
US 1953–5   126 × 25m   bw
Hal Roach Jnr/Roland Reed

The family life of a high school principal. Predictable star sitcom.

Stuart Erwin, June Collyer

True*
US 1962   33 × 25m   bw
Jack Webb

Stories from the files of *True Magazine*. Adequate anthology: the stories, one suspected, were not *quite* true.

host Jack Webb

True Grit: A Further Adventure
US 1978   96m   colour   TVM
Paramount (Sandor Stern)

Rooster Cogburn and Mattie Ross continue on their way to Monterey. Uninspired sequel to a western which was overpraised to begin with. Understandably, no series resulted.

w Sandor Stern   *d* Richard Heffron   *ph* Steve Larner *m* Earle Hagen

Ben Johnson, Lisa Pelikan, Lee Meriwether, James Stephens

'Charitably, a mistake ... a ponderous tale, it's told ploddingly.' – *Daily Variety*

Tucker, Forrest (1919–). Burly American character actor, ex-vaudevillian. TV series: *Crunch and Des*, *F Troop*, *Dusty's Trail*.

Tugboat Annie: see The Adventures of Tugboat Annie

Tully
GB 1974   78m   colour (16mm)   TVM
Thames/Euston Films (James Gatward)

A high-powered insurance investigator chases a gang leader across the world. Routine pilot for a series which didn't happen.

w Ian Stuart Black   *d* James Gatward

Anthony Valentine, Barbara Neilsen, Kevin Miles

Turn of Fate*
US 1957   38 × 25m   bw
Four Star

An anthology from the halcyon period of this company, when the stars were really working.

Charles Boyer, David Niven, June Allyson, Robert Ryan, Jane Powell

The Turning Point of Jim Malloy**
aka: *Gibbsville*
US 1975   74m   colour   TVM
Columbia

A troublesome youth settles down as reporter on his hometown paper, in 1940s Pennsylvania. Thoroughly competent blend of *Peyton Place* and *King's Row*, with fast pace, excellent acting, and most of the old Hollywood skills in evidence. A series resulted in 1976, but disappointed.

w/d FRANK D. GILROY, *novel* John O'Hara

JOHN SAVAGE, GIG YOUNG, Biff McGuire, Kathleen Quinlan, Janis Paige

TV Hour of Stars: see The Twentieth Century-Fox Hour

Twelve O'Clock High*
US 1964–5   78 × 50m   bw (last 17 in colour)
Quinn Martin/TCF

Pressure problems for officers commanding USAF squadrons in Britain during World War II. A fair copy of the movie, but the long run brought many irrelevant episodes.

Robert Lansing (first 31 films), Paul Burke (after that)

The Twentieth Century-Fox Hour
aka: *TV Hour of Stars*
US 1955   49 × 50m   bw
TCF

Allegedly an anthology of mini-features, this in fact contained many thirties second features chopped down to length. New productions largely consisted of hasty retreads of successful Fox movies such as *Portrait for Murder* (*Laura*), *City in Flames* (*In Old Chicago*), *The Hefferan Family* (*Chicken Every Sunday*), *Lynch Mob* (*The Ox Bow Incident*), *Meet Mr Kringle* (*Miracle on 34th Street*), *Death Paints a Legacy* (*Christopher Bean*), *Operation Cicero* (*Five Fingers*). The stock footage was more entertaining than the new shooting.

Twenty-One. A quiz show popular in America and Britain in the fifties, vaguely based on blackjack and involving rival contestants in sealed booths. A major scandal was unleashed when it was revealed that in order to maintain suspense some contestants had been told the answers beforehand.

21 Beacon Street
US 1959   34 × 25m   bw
Filmways

A private eye has two young assistants.
Absolutely routine detection hokum.

Dennis Morgan, Brian Kelly, Jim Mahoney

21 Hours at Munich
US 1976   96m   colour   TVM
ABC/Filmways/Moonlight (Edward S. Feldman)

A reconstruction of the attack on Israeli athletes at the 1972 Olympic games.
Rather less thrilling, and much less thought-provoking, than the real thing.

w Edward Hume, Howard Fast   *d* William A. Graham

William Holden, Franco Nero, Richard Basehart, Shirley Knight, Anthony Quayle, Noel Willman

26 Men
US 1957–8   78 × 25m   bw
Russell Hayden/NBC

True stories of the Arizona Rangers around 1900.
Adequate western adventures.

Tris Coffin, Kelo Henderson

Twice in a Lifetime
US 1974   74m   colour   TVM
Martin Rackin

A retired navy cook in San Pedro operates his own salvage tugboat.
Easy-going family comedy-drama.

w Martin Rackin   *d* Herschel Daugherty

Ernest Borgnine, Della Reese, Arte Johnson, Slim Pickens, Herb Jeffries, Vito Scotti

Twilight Zone****
US 1959–63   134 × 25m, 17 × 50m   bw
Cayuga/CBS

Stories of space, time and the imagination.
Despite a good deal of repetition, this was a series with real mood, skill and intelligence, the kind of pacy imaginative entertainment which TV has in the seventies forgotten how to do. The series borrowed fearlessly from such writers as H. G. Wells and John Collier, and was probably most at home in dealing with time warps. Two typical, and excellent, episodes are *Where is Everybody*, in which an astronaut imagines he is the only person on earth (he is spending a week in a space test capsule) and *A Hundred Yards Over the Rim*, in which Cliff Robertson, as a covered wagonner stranded in the desert, comes across a modern roadside café and takes back some aspirin to cure his daughter's fever. The one-hour episodes didn't work, whereas *The Outer Limits*, a series similar in intent, was more at home with the extra length.

cr/w/host ROD SERLING

Two Faces West
US 1960   39 × 25m   bw
Columbia

A doctor and an irresponsible cowboy are twin brothers.
Acceptable western series which didn't really know what to do with its gimmick.

Charles Bateman

The Two-Five
US 1978   74m   colour   TVM
Universal (R. A. Cinader)

Two New York cops are accident-prone.
Failed attempt at a softened *Freebie and the Bean*.

w R. A. Cinader, Joseph Polizzi   *d* Bruce Kessler   *ph* Frank B. Beascoechea   *m* Peter Matz

Don Johnson, Joe Bennett, George Murdock, John Crawford

Two for the Money*
US 1971   73m   colour   TVM
Aaron Spelling

Two policemen become private detectives and hunt down a mass murderer.
Adequate failed pilot.

w Howard Rodman   *d* Bernard L. Kowalski

Robert Hooks, Stephen Brooks, Walter Brennan, Neville Brand, Catherine Burns, Mercedes McCambridge

Two on a Bench
US 1971   73m   colour   TVM
Universal/Link–Levinson

One of two eccentrics is known to be a spy, so the CIA brings them together and watches.
Muddled comedy.

w Richard Levinson, William Link   *d* Jerry Paris

Patty Duke, Ted Bessell, Andrew Duggan, John Astin, Alice Ghostley

The Two Ronnies. Little Ronnie Corbett and big Ronnie Barker took this title for a series of BBC comedy variety shows in the seventies, after being teamed in various shows by David Frost. Their trick was to endear themselves to the respectable middle-class and then get away with an immense amount of smut; but they are highly accomplished, professional and intelligent performers and several of their sketches are classics, while their fake news items, borrowed from Frost and contributed by many hands, have so far filled two paperback books.

Two's Company**
GB 1976–   × 25m   colour (VTR)
London Weekend

An American authoress in London takes on a very British butler.
Patchily written but generally delightful comedy vehicle for two splendid personalities who, when the author lets them, splendidly convey an acerbic love–hate relationship.

cr/w Bill McIlwraith

ELAINE STRITCH, DONALD SINDEN

The Tycoon
US 1964   32 × 25m   colour
Danny Thomas (Charles Isaacs)

An old corporation chairman can dominate his business but not his family.
Competent but forgettable star comedy vehicle.

Walter Brennan, Jerome Cowan, Van Williams, Janet Lake

Tyzack, Margaret (1933–). British character actress. TV work includes *The First Churchills*, *The Forsyte Saga* (BAFTA best actress 1969), *I, Claudius*.

U

UFO*
GB 1970 26 × 50m colour
ATV/Gerry Anderson

In the 1980s, SHADO is a defence organization against alien invaders.
Lively, well produced, rather humourless science fiction adventures, too early to catch the public fancy.

Ed Bishop, George Sewell

The Ugliest Girl in Town
US 1968 20 × 25m colour
Columbia/Harry Ackerman

For rather complex reasons (none of which hold water), a Hollywood talent agent must pose as a female model in order to join his fiancée in London.
A bottom-of-the-barrel fiasco.

cr Robert Kaufman

Peter Kastner, Patricia Brake, Gary Marshal, Jenny Till

'*The Ugliest Girl in Town* actually began at 3 o'clock one morning when one of Hollywood's most talented and original writers was lying awake thinking, "What if Twiggy is really a boy?" ' – promotion

umbrella title. One billed to hold together otherwise disparate units; e.g. *Million Dollar Movie, The Big Event, World Première.*

UMC: see Operation Heartbeat

The Underground Man
aka: *Archer*
US 1974 100m colour TVM
Paramount (Philip L. Parslow)

A private eye seeks a missing husband and father-in-law.
Dull adaptation of a John Ross Macdonald novel. A series, *Archer*, ensued but was quickly scuttled.

w Douglas Heyes *d* Paul Wendkos

Peter Graves, Celeste Holm, Sharon Farrell, Jim Hutton, Jack Klugman, Kay Lenz, Vera Miles, Judith Anderson

Union Pacific*
US 1958 39 × 25m bw
NBC

Adventures of a railway construction boss in the 1880s.
Good action series.

Jeff Morrow

University Challenge. British general knowledge quiz, produced by Granada since 1962, with Bamber Gascoigne as sole question master presiding over university teams. Based on the American *College Bowl*, with an extremely high level of erudition required.

The Untouchables***
US 1959–62 114 × 50m bw
Desilu/QUINN MARTIN

An élite squad of the Chicago police tracks down the criminals of the prohibition era.
Much criticized for its violence, this well-made series now seems rather tame. Its music, its commentary and its star all helped to keep the world tuned in for four seasons, and of all TV series it has had the best re-run life.

commentary WALTER WINCHELL

ROBERT STACK, NEVILLE BRAND (as Al Capone), BRUCE GORDON (as Frank Nitti); Jerry Paris, Abel Fernandez, Steve London, Nick Georgiade, Anthony George, Paul Picerni (the Untouchables)

Unwed Father
US 1974 74m colour TVM
David Wolper (Lawrence Turman, Stan Margulies)

A teenager wants custody of his illegitimate child.
What will they think of next? Something more entertaining, one hopes.

w W. Hermanos, Carol McKeand *d* Jeremy Kagan

Joe Bottoms, Kay Lenz, Joseph Campanella, Beverly Garland, Kim Hunter

Up Pompeii*. A BBC comedy series of the early seventies, plainly borrowed from *A Funny Thing Happened on the Way to the Forum*. Frankie Howerd, the host, was a Roman slave who masterminded his owner's household and commented intermittently on the farcical action. It was vulgar but funny; the film versions which followed, including *Up the Front* and *Up the Chastity Belt*, were merely crass.

317

UPSTAIRS, DOWNSTAIRS. One of the western world's most popular family groups: American audiences who saw the series on public broadcasting were ecstatic about it, and Jean Marsh (centre, back row) became a national figure.

Upstairs, Downstairs****
GB 1970–5 75 × 50m colour (VTR)
London Weekend (JOHN HAWKESWORTH)

In a London house between 1900 and 1930, the lives of masters and servants intermingle.

A simple but very clever concept which was aided by astute casting and a highly professional sheen in all departments, this highly agreeable series was a national institution in Britain and a surprising success (via PBS) in America.

cr Jean Marsh, Eileen Atkins

GORDON JACKSON (Hudson), ANGELA BADDELEY (Mrs Bridges), JEAN MARSH (Rose), DAVID LANGTON (Mr Bellamy), SIMON WILLIAMS (James Bellamy); and intermittently NICOLA PAGETT, John Alderton, Pauline Collins, Raymond Huntley, Christopher Beeny, Lesley-Anne Down

Urich, Robert (*c* 1944–). American leading man of the seventies. TV: *Bob and Carol and Ted and Alice*, *SWAT*, *Vegas*.

V

Valentine, Karen (c 1948–). American leading lady, a pert Debbie Reynolds type who hasn't quite hit the ultimate heights. Series: *Room 222, Karen*.

Valentine's Day
US 1964   34 × 25m   bw
TCF/Savannah–Yorktan

The love life of a bachelor editor.
Very moderate, rather tiresome New York comedy.

cr Hal Kanter

Tony Franciosa, Jack Soo, Janet Waldo, Patsy Kelly

The Valiant Years***
GB/US 1960   26 × 25m   bw
Columbia/JACK LE VIEN

Documentary series recalling World War II through newsreel footage and Churchill's own words (from his memoirs).
An excellent job of work and a valuable demonstration of how history can be popularized through TV.

narrator Richard Burton

Valley of Mystery
US 1967   90m   colour   TVM
Universal

Survivors of a plane crash fight for survival in a South American jungle.
Or, *Five Came Back* and back and back and back . . .
This version isn't even entertaining.

w Dick Nelson, Lowell Barrington   *d* Josef Leytes

Richard Egan, Peter Graves, Joby Baker, Lois Nettleton, Harry Guardino, Julie Adams, Fernando Lamas

Valley of the Dinosaurs*
US 1974   16 × 22m   colour
Hanna–Barbera (Iwao Takomoto)

Boating on the Colorado river, a family is swept away into a lost prehistoric valley.
Nicely styled cartoon series with good sense of prehistory.

Van Der Valk*
GB 1972   13 × 50m   colour (VTR)
Thames

Cases of a Dutch police inspector.
Likeable cops and robbers with a 'different' background, from the novels by Nicholas Freling. The filmed series of 13, which followed in 1977, was a disappointment, the stories seeming very thin.

Barry Foster

Van Dyke, Dick (1925–). American comic actor who had an enormous personal success in *The Dick Van Dyke Show* during the years when he played opposite Mary Tyler Moore, but failed to make the same grade a few years later in *The New Dick Van Dyke Show*. Meanwhile he had temporarily established for himself a niche as film actor and star of specials, but his appeal in these fields also waned.

Van Dyke, Jerry (c 1922–). American comic actor, brother of Dick; never in the same class, he did star in two series, *My Mother the Car* and *Accidental Family*.

Vance, Vivian (c 1903–). American comedy actress whose greatest hour came when she played the wisecracking neighbour in *I Love Lucy*.

Vanished**
US 1970   2 × 98m   colour   TVM
Universal

The President's top adviser goes missing and is revealed as a homosexual.
Reasonably absorbing, well acted and sharply written political melodrama on the lines of *Seven Days in May*.

w Dean Riesner, *novel* Fletcher Knebel   *d* Buzz Kulik

Richard Widmark, Robert Young, James Farentino, Skye Aubrey, Tom Bosley, Stephen McNally, Sheree North, Larry Hagman, Murray Hamilton, Arthur Hill, Robert Hooks, E. G. Marshall, Eleanor Parker, William Shatner

† Important as the forerunner of the 'Best Sellers' mini-series fashion, generally thought to have begun with *Rich Man Poor Man*.

Varney, Reg (1922–). British cockney comedian who was popular on TV in *The Rag Trade* and *On the Buses*, but fared less well when he left both in the hope of being a star of films and specials.

Vaughan, Norman (c 1928–). British stand-up comic with a nervous manner; popular from 1962 when he took over as compere of *Sunday Night at the London Palladium*, but his career subsequently faltered.

Vaughn, Robert (1932–   ). Serious-faced American actor who despite his dramatic ambitions is best known as star of *The Lieutenant, The Man from UNCLE* and *The Protectors*. Also played the Haldeman figure in *Washington Behind Closed Doors*.

Vegas*
US 1978   74m   colour   TVM
Aaron Spelling (E. Duke Vincent)

A private eye in Las Vegas solves a murder case.
Brisk, bright, old-fashioned mystery à la Chandler, with good local colour.

w Michael Mann   d Richard Lang   ph Arch Dalzell   m Dominic Frontiere

Robert Urich, Tony Curtis, June Allyson, Edd Byrnes, Red Buttons, Jack Kelly, Will Sampson, Greg Morris

† A series of 50m episodes resulted.

Verdugo, Elena (1926–   ). American character actress. TV series: *Meet Millie, The New Phil Silvers Show, Marcus Welby MD.*

Vernon, Richard (c 1907–   ). Dignified British actor of the old school, most at home in plays by Lonsdale or Maugham. His many TV series include *The Men in Room 17, The Liars, The Duchess of Duke Street.*

A Very Missing Person
aka: *Hildegarde Withers*
US 1972   73m   colour   TVM
Universal (Edward J. Montagne)

A lady sleuth and her policeman friend follow the disappearance of a young woman.
A bad stab at recasting the old Hildegarde Withers films.

w Philip Reisman   d Russell Mayberry

Eve Arden, James Gregory, Julie Newmar, Skye Aubrey

The Victim*
aka: *The Storm*
US 1972   73m   colour   TVM
Universal (William Frye)

A girl visits her sister during a storm, and finds a dead body and a lurking killer.
A very adequate *Psycho*-ish chiller using all the old tricks.

w Merwin Gerard   d Herschel Daugherty

Elizabeth Montgomery, George Maharis, Sue Ann Langdon, Eileen Heckart

Victorian Scandals
GB 1976   7 × 50m   colour (VTR)
Granada (Michael Cox)

Seven plays about headline-making incidents of the Victorian era.

Oblique narrative prevented these dramatizations of fact from being compelling drama.

Victory at Entebbe
US 1976   150m   colour (VTR)   TVM
David Wolper (Robert Guenette)

How the Israelis rescued a planeful of hostages held by terrorists at Entebbe.
Instant all-star re-creation of a famous event. At best competent, at worst fatuous.

w Ernest Kinoy   d Marvin J. Chomsky   ph James Kilgore   m Charles Fox

Helmut Berger, Theodore Bikel, Linda Blair, Kirk Douglas, Richard Dreyfuss, Julius Harris, Helen Hayes, Anthony Hopkins, Burt Lancaster, Christian Marquand, Elizabeth Taylor, Jessica Walter, Harris Yulin

'It succeeds only in diminishing what it sets out to glorify.' – *Monthly Film Bulletin*

Victory at Sea*
US 1952   1 × 75m, 20 × 50m   bw
NBC (Project 20)

The battle for sea power during World War II.
Absorbing documentary series put together from newsreel footage. A major achievement of its time.

Vigoda, Abe (c 1919–   ). Gaunt American character actor who after small film roles (e.g. *The Godfather*) became well known in the TV series *Barney Miller* and starred in *Fish*.

Village Hall*
GB 1975   14 × 50m   colour (VTR)
Granada (Michael Dunlop)

An anthology of plays all set in the same village hall, which is put to various uses.
A bright idea produced generally bright comedy-dramas, including contributions by Jack Rosenthal, Willis Hall and Kenneth Cope.

The Virginia Hill Story*
US 1974   74m   colour   TVM
RSO (Aaron Rosenberg)

After the 1947 killing of gangster Bugsy Siegel, his girl friend testifies before the Kefauver Commission.
Well-written crime exposé with good performances.

w Joel Schumacher, Juleen Compton   d Joel Schumacher

Dyan Cannon, Harvey Keitel, Alan Garfield, Robby Benson

The Virginian*. This series of 74-minute TV westerns ran seven seasons, from 1962 to 1969, and though mostly boring it did recruit a large number of interesting guest stars who held the attention, despite leisurely production and strong family ambience. It had little to

THE VIRGINIAN, a popular 74-minute series, was less about that character than about assorted goings-on at the old Shiloh ranch, where guest stars on mysterious missions were apt to pop in every week. Here are three of the regulars: Charles Bickford, Sara Lane, Don Quine.

do with the original story: the Virginian (James Drury) was a slightly mysterious but impeccably natured ranch foreman, Trampas (Doug McClure) was an impulsive pal rather than a villain, and most of the stories centred on the judge, played first by Charles Bickford, then by Lee J. Cobb. Executive producer: Norman MacDonnell; producers: Howard Christie, Paul Freeman, Jim McAdams. Here is a selection of the more interesting episodes and guest stars:

THE BRAZEN BELL: George C. Scott
IMPASSE: Eddie Albert
THE DREAM OF STAVROS KARAS: Michael Constantine
ROAR FROM THE MOUNTAIN: Jack Klugman
THE EXECUTIONERS: Hugh O'Brian
THE SMALL PARADE: David Wayne
THE ACCOMPLICE: Bette Davis
IT TAKES A BIG MAN: Ryan O'Neal
THE EVIL THAT MEN DO: Robert Redford
THE BIG DEAL: Ricardo Montalban
THE NOBILITY OF KINGS: Charles Bronson
MEN WITH GUNS: Telly Savalas
OLD COWBOY: Franchot Tone
THE INVADERS: Ed Begley
A TIME REMEMBERED: Yvonne de Carlo
STRANGERS AT SUNDOWN: Harry Morgan
DUEL AT SHILOH: Brian Keith
IT TOLLS FOR THEE: Lee Marvin
THE FORTUNES OF J. J. JONES: Pat O'Brien

Visions*
aka: *Visions of Death*

US 1972   73m   colour   TVM
Leonard Freeman

A clairvoyant professor has a vision of a building being dynamited, and though the police scoff he is suspected when it comes true.
Adequate, predictable TV suspenser.

w Paul Playdon   *d* Lee Katzin

Monte Markham, Barbara Anderson, Telly Savalas, Tim O'Connor

Viva Valdez
US 1976   × 25m   colour
Columbia/Rothman–Wohl/Stan Jacobson

Mishaps of a Chicano family in Los Angeles.
Forgettable ethnic comedy.

cr Jacobson, Rothman, Wohl   *d* Alan Rafkin

Carmen Zapata, Rodolfo Hoyos, James Victor

vox pop. TV jargon for the familiar kind of sequence in which people in the street are asked their views on a certain topic and the results are edited together.

The Voyage of the Yes*
US 1972   73m   colour   TVM
Fenady–Crosby

Teenagers embark on a dangerous sea journey.
Mildly pleasing adventure with racial overtones.

w William Stratton   *d* Lee H. Katzin

Desi Arnaz Jnr, Mike Evans, Beverly Garland, Skip Homeier, Della Reese

Voyage to the Bottom of the Sea ＊＊
US 1964–7   110 × 50m   colour
TCF/Irwin Allen

An atomic submarine scours the ocean bed for villains and monsters.

Among the best-produced juvenile series of its kind, this very watchable slice of hokum also benefited from agreeably zany script ideas and kept its tongue firmly in its cheek.

cr IRWIN ALLEN   *m/d* Lionel Newman

Richard Basehart, David Hedison, Robert Dowdell, Terry Becker

VTR. Video Tape Recording.

W

The Wackiest Ship in the Army
US 1965 29 × 50m colour
Columbia/Harry Ackerman (Herbert Hirschman)

During World War II in the Pacific an officer finds himself in charge of the only ship ever commissioned by the army.
Rather tired version of a rather tired film. It would have been funnier at half an hour.

cr Danny Arnold

Jack Warden, Gary Collins, Mike Kellin

† One episode title demands to be quoted: 'I'm Dreaming of a Wide Isthmus'.

Wacky Races
US 1968–9 52 × 25m colour
Hanna–Barbera

Stories of a cross country car race, with villain Dick Dastardly trying to outdo all the other contestants.

Moderately pleasing cartoon series obviously inspired by *The Great Race*.

Wagner, Robert
(1930–). Durable American leading man of many films. TV series: *It Takes a Thief*, *Colditz*, *Switch*.

Wagon Train **
aka: *Major Adams, Trailmaster*
US 1957–61 approx. 195 × 50m bw
US 1963 32 × 74m colour
NBC (later ABC)/Revue

Stories of the people on an 1840s wagon train heading west.
A highly popular family series which showed that the western can be bent to any purpose: its scripts included rewrites of *Pride and Prejudice* and *Great Expectations*. It tended to be studio bound, and one tired of the same shot of four wagons rounding a bend; the interest was

WAGON TRAIN featured a guest star every week. Here, Barbara Stanwyck, then in her late fifties, shows that you can't keep a good star down; and in 1978 at seventy-three, she was contracted to make a comeback.

in character, and luckily a stranger turned up every week, played by a famous star. The colour longforms didn't work at all: they looked too realistic for the material.

ROBERT HORTON (later Robert Fuller), WARD BOND (who died and was replaced by John McIntire)

†The last of the 50m episodes was directed by John Ford and featured John Wayne as General Sherman.

Wait 'Til Your Father Gets Home**
US 1972–3   48 × 22m   colour
Hanna–Barbera

Domestic problems of a suburbanite.
This cartoon half-hour, drawn with UPA-like economy, is also an agreeable satirical comedy with more than a passing reference to *All in the Family*. Thoroughly amusing, and not for kids.

Waite, Ralph (*c* 1937–). American general purpose actor, hardly known until he became a national figure as Dad in *The Waltons*.

Wake Me When the War Is Over
US 1969   74m   colour   TVM
Spelling–Thomas

In the closing days of World War II an American is captured by a German baroness, who keeps him in luxury long after the war.
Smoking room story, a little funnier than *Situation Hopeless But Not Serious*; though not much.

w Frank Peppiatt, John Aylesworth   *d* Gene Nelson

Ken Berry, Eva Gabor, Werner Klemperer, Jim Backus, Hans Conried

Walk Up and Die: see Banyon

Walk with Destiny
US title: *The Gathering Storm*
GB 1974   75m   colour (VTR)
BBC/Jack Le Vien (Andrew Osborn)

The life of Winston Churchill in the years preceding his appointment as prime minister.
Interesting but much decried drama documentary with impersonations of historic figures too much the centre of attention.

w Colin Morris   *d* Herbert Wise

Richard Burton, Virginia McKenna, Angharad Rees (Sarah), Clive Francis (Randolph), Robert Beatty (Beaverbrook), Robin Bailey (Chamberlain), Thorley Walters (Baldwin), Ian Bannen (Hitler), Ian Ogilvy (Edward VIII)

Walker, Clint (1927–). Massive American leading man who came to fame via TV in the series *Cheyenne*; later in *Kodiak*. Also in many films.

Walker, Nancy (1921–) (Ann Swoyer). Pint-sized American comedienne who appeared in a handful of seventies series. *McMillan and Wife*, *Rhoda*, *The Nancy Walker Show*, *Mrs Blansky's Beauties*.

Wallace, Mike (1918–). American newscaster and host who became known in the fifties for his abrasive interviews.

Walston, Ray (1917–). American comedy character actor, star of TV series *My Favorite Martian*.

Walter, Jessica (1944–). Stylish American leading lady, busy in films and TV. Series: *Amy Prentiss*, *Wheels*.

Walters, Barbara (–). American interviewer and newscaster who made headlines in 1977 when she left NBC's *Today* for a million-a-year contract with ABC.

The Waltons***
US 1972–   × 50m   colour
Lorimar

Problems of a family in the Appalachian mountains during the Depression years.
The original novel by Earl Hanmer Jnr also formed the basis of a film, *Spencer's Mountain*, and a TV movie, *The Homecoming*. The series rapidly became the seventies equivalent of the Hardy family movies, and one could not fault the writing or production.

Ralph Waite, Michael Learned, Will Geer, Ellen Corby, Richard Thomas

† The series included a number of episodes combined to make longforms under such titles as *The Waltons' Crisis*.

Wambaugh, Joseph (1937–). American novelist, an ex-cop who writes exclusively about what he knows. *The New Centurions* formed the basis for *Police Story*, which spun off into *Police Woman*; meanwhile he had got a long TV movie and a series out of *The Blue Knight*.

Wanted Dead or Alive*
US 1958–60   98 × 25m   bw
Four Star/Malcolm

Adventures of a western bounty hunter.
Competent series which helped to create one of the sixties' biggest stars.

Steve McQueen

Wanted, the Sundance Woman*
US 1976   75m   colour   TVM
ABC/TCF (Ron Preissman)

The wife of the Sundance Kid tries to find another identity in the old west.

Pretty good action pilot, certainly better than the previous attempt at this subject, *Mrs Sundance*.

w Richard Fielder   *d* Lee Philips   *m* Fred Karlin

Katharine Ross, Steve Forrest, Stella Stevens, Michael Constantine, Hector Elizondo

War and Peace***
GB 1963   150m approx. (bw) VTR
Granada

Tolstoy's novel compressed and adapted for the studio, with a master of ceremonies. Trail-blazing, Emmy-winning compendium of television technique

w R. D. MacDonald   *d* Silvio Narizzano

John Franklyn Robbins, Kenneth Griffith (as Napoleon), Daniel Massey, Clifford Evans, Valerie Sarruf

War and Peace*
GB 1972   20 × 45m   colour (VTR)
BBC

Solemn, expensive, beautiful, reverent adaptation. Unfortunately it was too slow, too complex and too long.

w Jack Pulman   *d* John Howard Davies

Rupert Davies, Anthony Hopkins, Faith Brook, Morag Hood

The War between the Tates*
US 1977   75m   colour   TVM
NBC/Talent Associates (Frederick Brogger)

A study of a marriage on the point of breaking up. Good solid matrimonial drama with satisfactory performances.

w Barbara Turner, *novel* Alison Lurie   d Lee Phillips
m John Barry

Richard Crenna, Elizabeth Ashley, Granville Van Dusen

A War of Children*
US 1973   73m   colour   TVM
Tomorrow (Roger Gimbel)

Problems of an Irish family in the present troubles.

WAR AND PEACE was a prestigious studio production of 1963. This shot shows the parsimony of the settings, but clever direction made it work on the box. Daniel Massey holds the standard.

Well-made but astonishingly anti-British lowlife drama.

w James Costigan *d* George Schaefer

Vivien Merchant, Jenny Agutter, John Ronane, Anthony Andrews

Ward, Burt (1945–) (Herbert Jervis). American juvenile actor who became famous as Robin in *Batman*.

Ward, Jay (–   ). American animator and producer, creator of *Bullwinkle* and *Fractured Flickers*.

Warden, Jack (1920–). American character actor. TV series: *The Asphalt Jungle*, *The Wackiest Ship in the Army*, *NYPD*.

Waring, Richard (*c* 1930–). British comedy writer whose series include *The Marriage Lines*, *Not in Front of the Children*, *Bachelor Father*, *Miss Jones and Son*.

Warner, Jack (1895–) (Jack Waters). British character actor, the beloved *Dixon of Dock Green*. He also made light entertainment appearances as a comedian and singer.

Warship
US 1973–5   × 50m   colour (VTR)
BBC (Anthony Coburn)

Stories of the men on a modern battleship.
Adequate, unexciting anthology series.

Donald Burton, Michael Cochrane, David Savile

Washington: Behind Closed Doors **
US 1977 6 × 96m   colour
Paramount (Norman Powell)

A fictionalization of the Nixon regime.
Parts of this extension of John Erlichman's book *The Company* are as gripping and well produced as anything made for TV, and the acting is of a high standard, but in the end one wonders whether the mixing of fact

WASHINGTON: BEHIND CLOSED DOORS. There were no prizes for guessing that Jason Robards Jnr (front) looked and behaved rather like Richard Nixon; or that Andy Griffith reminded one of Lyndon Johnson or Robert Vaughn (right) of H. R. Haldeman. The origin of Cliff Robertson (back centre), who played the head of the CIA, is just a little more open to doubt.

and fiction can in any way be justified, especially as the plot does not vary sufficiently from the known facts to be worth considering on its own account.

w David W. Rintels with Eric Bercovici   *d* Gary Nelson

JASON ROBARDS JNR, Cliff Robertson, Stefanie Powers, Robert Vaughn, Barry Nelson, Andy Griffith, Lois Nettleton, Harold Gould, Tony Bill, John Houseman

Water World
US 1973–4   52 × 25m   colour
Syndicast

Film snippets of water sports, linked by Lloyd Bridges (first 26) and James Franciscus (second 26). The hosts occasionally participate.

Waterfront
US 1954–5   78 × 25m   bw
Roland Reed

Adventures of a tugboat captain in San Pedro harbour.
Adequate low-key melodrama with a family background.

Preston Foster

Watford, Gwen (*c* 1929–). British leading actress, in the sixties one of the most popular on TV, in many single plays including *The Greeting, A Provincial Lady, Aren't We All.*

Watkins, Peter (1937–). Controversial British writer–director whose influential specials include *Culloden, The War Game.*

Waverly's Wonders. Lorimar half-hour series for the 1978 season, about a baseball team; hastily cancelled.

Wayne, David (1914–) (Wayne McKeekan). American character actor with many film credits. TV series: *Norby, The Good Life* (US), *Ellery Queen, Dallas.*

Weaver, Dennis (1924–). American character star, one of TV's busiest actors and almost exclusive to the medium. Series: *Gunsmoke, Gentle Ben, Kentucky Jones, McCloud.* Also in many TV movies.

The Web
US 1956   13 × 25m   bw
Columbia/Goodson–Todman

Stories of people trapped by circumstantial evidence. Unremarkable suspense series.

W. E. B.
US 1978   96m   colour   TVM
TCF (Lin Bolen)

Struggles of an ambitious young woman producer in the TV jungle.
Adequately bitchy backstairs look at TV.

w David Karp   *d* Harvey Hart

Alex Cord, Richard Basehart, Pamela Bellwood, Andrew Prine, John Colicos

† The projected series was cancelled after this episode, which was played as a two-parter.

Webb, Jack (1920–). Busy American character actor who turned producer. Internationally known as the flat-talking Joe Friday ('All we want is the facts, ma'am') in *Dragnet*, he seldom acted thereafter but turned out via his Mark VII Productions such series as *True, Pete Kelly's Blues, Adam 12, Emergency, O'Hara US Treasury* and *Hec Ramsey.*

The Weekend Nun
US 1972   74m   colour   TVM
Paramount

A young nun is a parole officer during the week.
Beyond comment: some people will like it.

w Ken Trevey   *d* Jeannot Szwarc

Joanna Pettet, Vic Morrow, Beverly Garland, Ann Sothern, James Gregory, Barbara Werle, Kay Lenz

Weekend of Terror *
US 1970   74m   colour   TVM
Paramount

Two young killers accidentally kill a hostage and search for a lookalike to replace her.
Fast-moving suspenser.

w Lionel E. Siegel   *d* Jud Taylor

Robert Conrad, Lois Nettleton, Lee Majors, Carol Lynley, Jane Wyatt

Welcome Back Kotter
US 1975–   × 25m   colour   (VTR)
David Wolper (James Komack)

A Jewish primary school teacher has trouble with tough kids.
Formalized 'realistic' comedy with a marked resemblance to *Please Sir.* The studio audience makes it seem funnier than it is: the characters are really a bunch of morons.

cr Gabriel Kaplen, Alan Sacks, Peter Myerson   *m* John B. Sebastian

Gabriel Kaplen, John Travolta, Marcia Strassman, John Sylvester White

Welcome Home Johnny Bristol **
US 1971   100m   colour   TVM
Cinema Center 100 (Arthur Joel Katz)

A wounded Vietnam veteran seeks the hometown he dreamed of, but finds only mystery.

DENNIS WEAVER, here seen as Marshal McCloud, has been one of TV's most ubiquitous and reliable actors, right from the days when he played the limping aide in *Gunsmoke*.

A good, gripping puzzler.

w Stanley R. Greenberg *d* George McCowan *ph* Robert L. Morrison *m* Lalo Schifrin

Martin Landau, Jane Alexander, Brock Peters, Forrest Tucker, Martin Sheen, Pat O'Brien, Mona Freeman

Welk, Lawrence (1902–). American bandleader whose old-fashioned but enjoyable show was popular on ABC from 1955 until 1970.

We'll Get By

US 1975   5 × 25m   colour (VTR)
CBS

Problems of a New Jersey lawyer and his family. Modestly pleasing upper-crust comedy.

cr Alan Alda

Paul Sorvino, Mitzi Hoag

Welland, Colin (1934–). Chubby British actor who became popular in *Z Cars* but later more or less de-

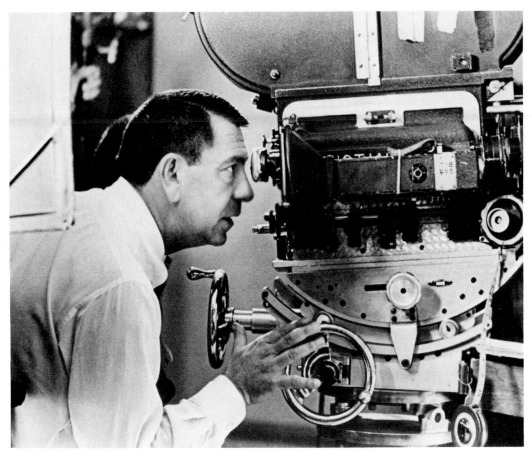

JACK WEBB is as active behind the camera as before it, but the world will remember him as Sergeant Joe Friday, the patient cop who always got his man by sticking rigidly to police procedural rules.

serted acting for writing plays such as *Bangelstein's Boys, Kisses at Fifty, Say Goodnight to Your Grandma.*

Wells Fargo: see Tales of Wells Fargo

Wendy and Me *
US 1964   34 × 25m   bw
Warner/Natwill (George Burns)

An apartment house owner has one particularly dizzy lodger.
The star takes kind of a back seat to a substitute Gracie. The result is mildly appealing and quite stylish.

George Burns, Connie Stevens, Ron Harper

West, Adam (1929–) (William Anderson). American light leading man who scored an unexpected success as *Batman.* Also appeared in *The Detectives.*

The Westerner *
US 1960   13 × 25m   bw
Four Star/Winchester (Sam Peckinpah)

Experiences of a wandering ranch-hand in the 1870s. Intelligent low-key western which didn't take.

Brian Keith

'An unusually good show.' – Don Miller

Weston, Jack (1926–). Roly-poly American character comedian. Series: *Rod Brown of the Rocket Rangers, The Hathaways.*

We've Got Each Other
US 1977   22 × 25m   colour
Viacom

Misadventures of two married misfits.
Less endearing than was intended.

Oliver Clark, Beverly Archer

What Are Best Friends For?
US 1973   74m   colour   TVM
ABC Circle

A man thrown out by his wife moves in with his best friends.

Underwritten treatment of a pleasant idea.

w Rubin Carson, J. A. Vapors   *d* Jay Sandrich

Ted Bessell, Lee Grant, Larry Hagman, Barbara Feldon, Nita Talbot

What the Papers Say*. A 15-minute British programme in which since 1955, by courtesy of Granada TV, a leading journalist each week has wittily reviewed the performance of his colleagues.

Whatever Happened to the Likely Lads? British comedy series which won BAFTA's 1973 award for producer James Gilbert. See *The Likely Lads.*

What's a Nice Girl Like You ... ?*
US 1971   73m   colour   TVM
Universal (Norman Lloyd)

A working girl impersonates a socialite and is drawn into an elaborate plot.
Sharply written and acted gangster comedy.

w HOWARD FAST, *novel* E. V. Cunningham   *d* Jerry Paris

BRENDA VACCARO, Vincent Price, Jack Warden, Roddy McDowall, Edmond O'Brien, Jo Ann Worley

What's My Line?**. A Goodson–Todman game show, immensely popular in the fifties, in which the panel had to guess the occupation of the contestant by asking roundabout questions. The American host was John Daly, with Dorothy Kilgallen, Arlene Francis and Bennett Cerf as panellists. In Britain (where the show was briefly revived in the seventies) Eamonn Andrews was in the chair, and residents included Isobel Barnett, David Nixon, Gilbert Harding and Barbara Kelly.

Wheeler and Murdoch*
US 1970   70m   colour   TVM
Paramount

Seattle private eyes take on an assignment to guard money that proves to belong to the Syndicate.
Routine cops and robbers with an agreeably fresh and rainy location and a whiff in the script of *The Maltese Falcon.* It didn't make a series for all that.

w Jerry Ludwig, Eric Bercovici   *d* Joseph Sargent

Jack Warden, Christopher Stone, Van Johnson, Charles Cioffi, Jane Powell, Diane Baker

Wheeler, Sir Mortimer (1890–1976). British archaeologist and TV personality of the fifties, especially on the panel game *Animal, Vegetable or Mineral?*

Wheels*
US 1978   6 × 96m   colour
Universal/Roy Huggins

Lots of problems crop up for Adam Trenton, senior executive in a Detroit car factory.

Busy, competent but somehow not very interesting novelization. Good production, boring characters and situations, good performances.

w Millard Lampell, Hank Searls, *novel* Arthur Hailey   *d* Jerry London

Rock Hudson, Lee Remick, Blair Brown, Ralph Bellamy, Tim O'Connor, Gerald S. O'Loughlin, Tony Franciosa, John Beck, James Carroll Jordan

The Wheeltappers and Shunters Social Club (GB 1974–7). Rough-edged Granada variety series set in a working men's club, with highly resistible hosts in the shape of Colin Crompton and Bernard Manning. Not one for export.

Wheldon, Sir Huw (1916–). Welsh producer and performer who in the fifties hosted *Monitor*, the BBC arts programme. Subsequently was elevated to Director of Television, but on retirement returned to hosting with *Royal Heritage.*

When Day Is Done
GB 1974   78m   colour (16mm)   TVM
Thames/Euston Films (Reg Collin)

A disillusioned musician finds that life holds too many problems, and his wife tries to bring him back to optimism.
Rather muddled character drama with good acting.

w John Kershaw   *d* Reg Collin

Edward Woodward, Rosemary Leach, Patricia Maynard, Jeremy Hawk, Julia Goodman

When Every Day Was the Fourth of July*
US 1978   96m   colour   TVM
Dan Curtis

A small town is rocked by a brutal murder.
Interesting reconstruction of a real murder case.

Dean Jones, Louise Sorel

When Havoc Struck: see Havoc

When Michael Calls**
US 1971   74m   colour   TVM
TCF (Gil Shiva)

A woman is terrorized by phone calls which appear to come from a dead child.
Chilling suspenser which plays pretty fair and moves smartly along.

w James Bridges   *d* Philip Leacock

Michael Douglas, Ben Gazzara, Elizabeth Ashley, Karen Pearson

When the Boat Comes In*
GB 1975–7   26 × 50m   colour (VTR)
BBC (Leonard Lewis/Andrew Osborn)

Life for the Seaton family in the north-east during the Depression.

THE WHEELTAPPERS AND SHUNTERS SOCIAL CLUB proved that television light entertainment need not be extravagantly budgeted. The set was even tattier than working men's clubs usually are, and the presentation was usually clumsy, but audiences revelled all the same in the beer-swilling atmosphere and the blue jokes. The resistible Bernard Manning lorded it over all.

Love on the Dole in another setting: impressive serial drama for those who care to remember.

w James Mitchell (with episodes from Sid Chaplin, Tom Hathaway, Alex Glasgow)

James Bolam, Susan Jameson, John Nightingale, James Garbutt, Jean Heywood

'A thrill of pleasure is consistently renewed at the sheer consistency of the performances.' – *The Times*

When Things Were Rotten
US 1974   13 × 25m   colour
Paramount/Mel Brooks

Robin Hood has more than his share of trouble with the idiocies of his merry men as well as with King John.
Campy spoof which is neither campy, spoofy nor funny enough; usually just embarrassing.

cr Mel Brooks

Dick Gautier, Misty Rowe, Bernie Kopell, Dick Van Patten, Richard Dimitri

Where's Raymond?: see The Ray Bolger Show

Whicker, Alan (*c* 1920–   ). British commentator with a distinctive voice and chatty manner. First popular in the fifties on BBC's *Tonight*, he went over to Yorkshire TV and has produced many series of *Whicker's World* and is fast running out of places to visit.

Whiplash
GB 1960   34 × 25m   bw
ATV

In the 1840s, an American forms Australia's first stage-coach line.
Quite well made, rather unjustly derided down-under western.

Peter Graves

Whirlybirds
US 1954–8   111 × 25m   bw
Desilu/CBS (N. Gayle Gitterman)

Two young pilots own and operate a charter service.
Adequate juvenile action series.

Kenneth Tobey, Craig Hill

ALAN WHICKER, a man at home in any society, has a fairly enviable job, travelling the world in search of eccentrics to interview. He found plenty in Palm Beach, where this modest residence would hardly even get its owner into the top 400.

Whispering Smith
US 1958   25 × 25m   bw
Whispering Smith Company

Cases of the old west's first private detective.
A promising but rather disappointing series.

Audie Murphy, Guy Mitchell

The Whistler*
US 1954   39 × 25m   bw
Columbia

Anthology of suspense stories with twist endings.
Not a bad collection on a purely hokum level. The title merely referred to a theme tune which was whistled briefly at the beginning of each story.

White, Betty (1926–). American character comedienne who has been around as long as TV and had her own show as recently as 1977.

White Hunter
GB 1958   39 × 25m   bw
Bernard L. Schubert

Hero vs villain in the African bush.
Abysmally made and acted hokum adventures.

Rhodes Reason

Whitehouse, Mary (1910–). British moral reformer who became well known in the sixties and seventies for her attacks on the corrupting influence of TV. Her influence was generally beneficial.

Whitelaw, Billie (1932–). Spunky British character actress with instant popular appeal. BAFTA award 1972 for *The Sextet*; also in many single plays.

The Whiteoaks of Jalna
Canada 1972   13 × 50m   colour (16mm)
CBC

Four generations of the Whiteoaks family.
The popular stories by Mazo de la Roche are made unnecessarily complicated by intercutting present and past, and despite the general high quality there is some decidedly bad acting. On the whole the series lacked the Ancient Mariner touch.

Paul Harding, Kate Reid

Whitfield, June (c 1933–). British comedy actress, a stalwart of radio's *Take it from Here* and a highly professional worker with all the major comedians. Got her own series in the seventies: *Happy Ever After*.

Whitmore, James (1921–). Leading American character actor with long film career and penchant for one-man shows in which he impersonates famous figures (Harry Truman, Will Rogers). TV series: *The Law and Mr Jones*, *My Friend Tony*, *Temperatures Rising*.

Who Do You Do? A variety format devised by Jon Scoffield for London Weekend in the seventies: impressionists' acts are intercut so that joke follows joke with great rapidity and freshness; trains of thought and running gags can also be arranged. The contributors included Freddie Starr, Paul Melba, Little and Large, Peter Goodwright.

Who Is the Black Dahlia? *
US 1975 96m colour TVM
Douglas S. Cramer

The unsolved 1947 murder case of a 22-year-old girl found dead on waste ground.
Interesting and well made, but like all unsolved cases a bit of a let-down.

w Robert W. Lenski   *d* Joseph Pevney

Lucie Arnaz, Efrem Zimbalist Jnr, Ronny Cox, Macdonald Carey, Linden Chiles, Mercedes McCambridge, Tom Bosley, Gloria de Haven, John Fiedler, Rick Jason, Henry Jones, June Lockhart, Donna Mills

Who Killed Miss USA? *
aka: *McCloud: Who Killed Miss USA?*
GB title: *Who Killed Merri-Ann?*
US 1971 98m colour TVM
Universal (Leslie Stevens)

A New Mexican marshal loses a murder suspect in New York, but recovers him and stays for further training in metropolitan methods.
Based on the cinema film *Coogan's Bluff*, this is the pilot for one of *Mystery Movie*'s more popular segments; the plot makes no great sense, but technically it is well put together.

w Stanford Whitmore, Richard Levinson, William Link   *d* Richard A. Colla

Dennis Weaver, Craig Stevens, Mark Richman, Diana Muldaur, Julie Newmar

Who Killed the Mysterious Mr Foster?
aka: *Sam Hill: Who Killed the Mysterious Mr Foster?*
US 1973 98m colour TVM
Universal (Jo Swerling Jnr)

A western sheriff finds the body of the town's new minister.
Failed comedy western pilot which never really gets going.

w Richard Levinson, William Link   *d* Fielder Cook

Ernest Borgnine, Judy Geeson, Will Geer, J. D. Cannon, Bruce Dern, Sam Jaffe, John McGiver, Slim Pickens, Jay C. Flippen

Who, Me? **
GB 1959 55m bw (VTR)
BBC

Three men are interviewed by police after a robbery. Trim little dramatic set piece, one of the pilots which led to the long-running *Z Cars*.

w Colin Morris   *d* Gilchrist Calder

Brewster Mason, Lee Montague, Maxwell Shaw, Neil McCarthy

Who Were the British? * (GB 1966). Six half-hours of archaeology from Anglia TV; an excellent piece of popular research.

Who's Who? One-hour peak-time magazine show tried out unsuccessfully by CBS in the 1976 season. It usually consisted of three rather slackly handled interviews with people of passing interest.

Wichita Town
US 1959 39 × 25m bw
NBC

Marshal Mike Dunbar keeps law and order.
Adequate potted western of its time.

Joel McCrea, Jody McCrea

The Wide Country
US 1962 28 × 50m bw
MCA/Revue/Gemini

A rodeo rider tries to prevent his young brother, who travels with him, from following in his footsteps.
Boring modern western.

Earl Holliman, Andrew Prine

Widmark, Richard (1914–). Cold-eyed American leading man and character actor with extensive film career. TV series: *Madigan*.

Widow *
US 1975 96m colour TVM
Lorimar

The first year of widowhood for an attractive woman with a family.
Glossy but moving domestic drama.

w Barbara Turner, *book* Lynn Caine *d* J. Lee-Thompson

Michael Learned, Bradford Dillman, Robert Lansing, Louise Sorel, Farley Granger, Carol Rossen

Wilcox, Desmond (1931–). British anchorman, long on *Nationwide* and *Man Alive*; more recently had his own series, *Americans*. BAFTA awards 1967 and 1971.

Wilcox, Paula (*c* 1950–). Saucer-eyed British leading actress, a comedy specialist. Series: *The Lovers, A Man About the House, Miss Jones and Son*.

Wild and Woolly

US 1978 96m colour TVM
Aaron Spelling/Douglas Cramer (Earl W. Wallace)

Three female convicts escape from Yuma in 1903 and expose a plot to kill the President.
An alleged adventure comedy with precious little of either commodity; very unprofessionally thrown together in the apparent hope of creating 'Charlie's Angels Out West'.

w Earl W. Wallace d Philip Leacock

Elyssa Davalos, Susan Bigelow, Christine de Lisle, Vic Morrow, Doug McClure, David Doyle, Paul Burke, Charles Siebert

Wild Bill Hickok

US 1951–4 113 × 35m bw (39 colour)
Columbia

Sheriff Hickok fights for law and order.
Cheerful, competent juvenile western.

Guy Madison, Andy Devine

The Wild Wild West *

US 1965–8 104 × 50m colour (26 bw)
CBS/Fred Freiburger, John Mantley (Bruce Lansbury)

Special government agents in the old west have their own specially equipped train.
A James Bond spoof which outlasted its welcome and had some terribly dud episodes; but people kept watching in the hope of a stunt or a laugh.

Robert Conrad, Ross Martin

Wild Women

US 1970 74m colour TVM
Aaron Spelling

Army engineers on a secret mission disguise themselves as a wagon train and use women borrowed from the local jail.
Oddball comedy western, not really very good.

w Vincent Fotre d Don Taylor

Hugh O'Brian, Anne Francis, Marilyn Maxwell, Marie Windsor

Will Shakespeare

GB 1978 6 × 50m colour (VTR)
ATV (Lorna Mason, Peter Roder, Cecil Clarke)

Shakespeare's adventures in and around the Globe Theatre.
An extremely ill-advised concept which, with all its undisciplined noise and bustle, and lack of sympathy

WILL SHAKESPEARE suffered from the English masses' aversion to their national poet, but even if promotion had conquered that it suffered from too much bustle and too many rhubarbing extras. There were few complaints however about the performances of Tim Curry as Will or Patience Collier as Queen Elizabeth I.

for its leading character, must have set back the Shakespeare cause quite a bit.

w John Mortimer   *d* Peter Wood

Tim Curry, Ian MacShane, André Morell, Nicholas Gray, Patience Collier

William Tell: see The Adventures of William Tell

Williams, Andy (*c* 1930–   ). American ballad singer who through the sixties and seventies had several musical series to himself.

Williams, Van (–   ). American leading man who didn't get far in films but on TV played *The Green Hornet.*

Willis, Ted (*c* 1918–) (Lord Willis). British 'working-class' TV playwright notable for *Woman in a Dressing Gown* and *Dixon of Dock Green.*

Wilson, Dennis Main (–   ). British producer of comedy series including *Till Death Us Do Part.* BAFTA award 1969.

Wilson, Donald (1910–). British producer, especially of BBC drama serials. BAFTA award 1967 for *The Forsyte Saga.*

Wilson, Flip (1933–) (Clerow Wilson). Black cabaret comedian who was a number one TV attraction in a one-hour musical series in the early seventies, after which his appeal faded somewhat.

Winchell, Paul (1924–). American ventriloquist popular in the fifties with his dummy Jerry Mahoney.

Winchell, Walter (1897–1972). American columnist of the fast-talking, hard-hitting school, a national institution through the thirties and forties. He made several less successful forays into TV, and will be best remembered in this medium as commentator for *The Untouchables.*

Windom, William (1923–). American character actor who must have played in more TV guest spots than anyone. Series include *The Farmer's Daughter, My World and Welcome to It.*

Window on Main Street
US 1961   36 × 25m   bw
FKB (Robert Young)

A novelist returns to write about his home town.
Modest, agreeable drama.

Robert Young, Constance Moore

Windsor, Frank (1926–). Forthright north country British actor who rose to fame as Inspector Watt in *Z Cars.*

Wine, Women and War: see The Six Million Dollar Man

Wings
GB 1976–7   26 × 50m   colour (VTR)
BBC (Peter Cregreen)

Stories of the Royal Flying Corps in World War I.
Rather dull series with good flying sequences.

cr Barry Thomas   *m* Alexander Faris

Tim Woodward, John Hallam, Nicholas Jones, Michael Cochrane

Wings of Fire
US 1967   99m   colour   TVM
Universal (David Lowell Rich)

The daughter of an air freight service owner enters an air race.
Moderate old-fashioned romantic drama with aerial trimmings; rather a bore.

w Stirling Silliphant   *d* David Lowell Rich

Suzanne Pleshette, James Farentino, Lloyd Nolan, Juliet Mills, Jeremy Slate, Ralph Bellamy

Winkler, Henry (1946–). American character actor who unexpectedly became a national celebrity as the bumptious but likeable Fonzie in *Happy Days;* otherwise rather difficult to cast.

Winner Take All
US 1975   100m   colour   TVM
Jozak

A housewife becomes addicted to gambling.
Domestic drama moving in well-defined grooves.

w Caryl Ledner   *d* Paul Bogart

Shirley Jones, Laurence Luckinbill, Sam Groom, Joan Blondell, Joyce Van Patten, Sylvia Sidney

Winner Take All
US 1977   50m   colour
CBS/Quinn Martin (John Wilder)

A police lieutenant is helped by an insurance investigator.
So-so crime pilot which didn't go.

w Cliff Gould   *d* Robert Day   *m* John Elizalde

Michael Murphy, Joanna Pettet, Clive Revill, Mark Gordon, David Huddleston, Signe Hasso

Winter Kill**
US 1974   100m   colour   TVM
MGM

Inexplicable but connected murders strike a mountain resort community.
This fairly gripping, nicely photographed and vividly narrated murder mystery was intended as a pilot for a series which never happened, *Adams of Eagle Lake.* It

was inspired by the movie *They Always Kill their Masters* but took its plot without permission from an old Sherlock Holmes movie *The Scarlet Claw*.

w John Michael Hayes   *d* Jud Taylor

Andy Griffith, Sheree North, John Larch, John Calvin, Tim O'Connor, Louise Latham, Joyce Van Patten

Winters, Mike (1930–) **and Bernie** (1932–). British music hall crosstalk act patterned after Abbott and Costello (and Martin and Lewis). TV appearances sporadic. The act split up in 1978.

Wire Service
US 1956   39 × 50m   bw
Sharpe–Lewis

Adventures of international reporters.
The stars alternated, but the stories were the same old hokum.

George Brent, Mercedes McCambridge, Dane Clark

'Not very far removed from the Grade B movie melodramas of the 1930s.' – Don Miller, 1957

Wise, Ernie (1925–). British comedian, the less zany half of Morecambe and Wise and the one with the short fat hairy legs.

Wise, Herbert (*c* 1920–). British director of long standing. Recent credits: *Walk with Destiny*, *I, Claudius*, *The Norman Conquests*, *Rumpole of the Bailey*.

Wiseman, Frederick (–   ). American documentarist who specializes in *cinéma vérité* looks at life's less attractive side, and especially at American institutions such as schools, hospitals and law. His films were all commissioned by public television. *Titicut Follies* 1967. *High School* 1968. *Law and Order* 1969. *Hospital* 1970. *Basic Training* 1971. *Juvenile Court* 1973. *Welfare* 1975; etc.

With This Ring *
US 1978   96m   colour   TVM
Paramount/Jozak (Bruce J. Sallan)

Three couples about to get married have second thoughts.
Intercut comedies apparently inspired by *Plaza Suite*. Quite witty on occasion.

w Terence Mulcahy   *d* James Sheldon   *ph* Roland S. Smith   *m* George Allison Tipton

Joyce de Witt, Scott Hylands, Tony Bill, Betty White, John Forsythe, Tom Bosley, Deborah White

Withers, Googie (1917–) (Georgette Withers). Stately British character actress with a long early career as movie heroine. Her most notable TV appearance was as the prison governor in *Within These Walls*.

Within These Walls * (GB 1974–7). British one-hour drama series (from LWT) about life in a prison for women. In general, responsible stuff, but pretty heavy going as entertainment. The governors were played successively by Googie Withers, Katharine Blake and Sarah Lawson.

Wolper, David (1928–). American documentarist who turned executive and formed the Wolper Organization to make non-fiction programmes, a few movies and eventually half-hour comedies (*Welcome Back Kotter*, *Chico and the Man*), TV movies and the smash success *Roots*. Merged with Warner in 1976.

The Woman Hunter
US 1972   74m   colour   TVM
Jerome L. Epstein

An international jewel thief and murderer seems to be on the trail of a wealthy woman.
Crime in the luxury classes, suffering from obscure narration.

w Brian Clemens   *d* Bernard L. Kowalski

Barbara Eden, Robert Vaughn, Stuart Whitman, Sydney Chaplin, Larry Storch

Woman of the Year
US 1975   100m   colour   TVM
MGM (Hugh Benson)

A sports writer tames and marries a politically conscious lady.
Disappointing TV remake of the cinema film . . . as what remake wouldn't be?

w Joseph Bologna, Renee Taylor, Bernie Kahn   *d* Gene Kelly

Renee Taylor, Joe Bologna, Dick O'Neill, Anthony Holland

Women in Chains
US 1971   74m   colour   TVM
Bernard Kowalski (Edward J. Mikis)

A probation officer has herself imprisoned to help research, but her only confidant dies . . .
Not exactly a new plot, but the old melodramatics suffice.

w Rita Lakin   *d* Bernard Kowalski

Ida Lupino, Lois Nettleton, Jessica Walter, Belinda Montgomery, John Larch, Penny Fuller

Wonder Woman
US 1974   75m   colour   TVM
Warner

Wonder Woman leaves Paradise Island to undertake a special mission for the CIA.
Abysmal comic strip adventures lacking in logic or even action.

w John D. F. Black   *d* Vincent McEveety

Cathy Lee Crosby, Ricardo Montalban, Andrew Prine, Kaz Garas

† The subsequent one-hour series started very hesitantly, changed both its format and its network after one season, and was much derided, but struggled on for several seasons.

Woobinda, Animal Doctor: see Animal Doctor

Wood, Peggy (1892–1978). American character actress whose TV pinnacle was as *Mama* in the early fifties.

Woodward, Edward (1930–   ). British general purpose actor who scored a major hit as *Callan* and found later roles few and far between because he was so identified with the character. 1978: *1990, The Bass Player and the Blonde.*

Woody Woodpecker. The cartoon bird with the maniacal laugh, created for the cinema by Walter Lantz, turned up on TV in half-hours which were collections of the old cartoons with new bridges.

working title. One which is used during production but is likely to be changed.

The World About Us. Long-standing umbrella title for BBC2's Sunday evening one-hour documentary about animals or exploration.

The World at War***
GB 1975   26 × 50m   bw
Thames (Jeremy Isaacs)

A history of World War II.
Major in undertaking and achievement, this great enterprise was impeccably executed. If it had a fault it was that it somehow missed the elation which was felt by the winning side even in the midst of the horror.

World in Action***. A title devised in 1963 by Granada for its Monday night half-hours of investigative journalism in a punchy, hard-hitting style comparable with that of the popular press (but rather better informed). The series has run for the best part of each year since.

WORLD IN ACTION has been British television's equivalent of the investigative report in the popular press. In this case Mike Scott (right) accompanied various interested parties on a tour of factories where it was claimed workers' lives were being made happier and more productive.

The World of Darkness
US 1977   50m   colour
CBS/Warner/David Susskind

A sportswriter becomes involved in solving supernatural problems.
Occult series never go, but producers keep trying.

w Art Wallace   *d* Jerry London   *m* Fred Karlin

Granville Van Dusen, Beatrice Straight, Gary Merrill

World of Sport. ITV's Saturday afternoon sports
compendium, hosted by Dickie Davies.

World Première. An umbrella title given by NBC to
its 96m TV movies which filled two-hour slots in the
late sixties. *Movie of the Week* covered the 90m slots.

Worldvision. Distribution company formed after the
demise in 1971 of ABC Films, the networks having been
forced to divest themselves of subsidiaries.

Worth, Harry (1920–). British variety and sketch
comedian who in the sixties perfected his character of
an amiable bumbler who confused not only himself but
everyone with whom he came in contact.

Wrather, Jack (1918–). American independent
producer particularly associated with *Lassie* and *The
Lone Ranger*.

WRKP in Cincinnati. New half-hour comedy for the
1978 season, from MTM. Life in a radio station which
is slightly out of touch.

Wyatt Earp: see The Life and Legend of Wyatt Earp

Wyatt, Jane (1912–). American leading lady who
after a rather desultory movie career became famous in
the long-running *Father Knows Best*.

Wyman, Jane (1916–) (Sarah Jane Faulks).

WORLD OF SPORT. The Saturday afternoon sports magazine is a constant feature of British television on both
BBC and ITV (and a bugbear to those who, like the writer, can't stand sport in any of its organized forms and
would much prefer a good movie). The success of ITV's *World of Sport* is very much to the credit of its presenter,
Dickie Davies.

American star actress with a long and satisfying Hollywood career. Series: *The Jane Wyman Show*.

Wynn, Ed (1886–1966) (Isaiah Edwin Leopold). American vaudeville comedian known as 'the perfect fool'. His many appearances in TV's early years included a domestic comedy series *The Ed Wynn Show*.

Wynn, Keenan (1916–). American character actor, son of Ed Wynn. Series: *Trouble Shooters, The Westerns*.

Wynn, Tracy Keenan (–). American writer, son of Keenan Wynn. His best-known TV scripts include *Tribes, The Autobiography of Miss Jane Pitman, The Glass House, The Quest*.

Y

Yancey Derringer
US 1958 34 × 25m bw
Sharpe–Lewis

Experiences of an adventurer in post-Civil-War New Orleans.
Competent and quite forgettable.

Jock Mahoney, X Brands

Yanks Go Home
GB 1976 13 × 25m colour (VTR)
Granada (Eric Prytherch)

Stories of a USAF base in Lancashire during World War II.
A good idea which somehow didn't take: the interplay was all too forced and strident to be funny.

w various *d* Eric Prytherch

Lionel Murton, Stuart Damon, Richard Oldfield, Alan MacNaughton, Bruce Boa, Meg Johnson

Yarwood, Mike (1941–). Favourite British impressionist of the seventies.

Yes, Honestly: see No, Honestly

Yes, Yes, Nanette
aka: *The Nanette Fabray Show*
US 1961 26 × 25m bw
NBC/BJ

Stories of a Hollywood writer and his ex-actress wife.
Mild comedy series supposedly inspired by the star's own life with husband Ranald McDougall, and written by him.

Nanette Fabray, Wendell Corey, Doris Kemper

Yesterday's Child
US 1977 74m colour TVM
Paramount (William Kayden)

A woman returns to claim her inheritance and finds her life in danger.
A hoary plot dusts off quite entertainingly.

w Michael Gleason *d* Corey Allen

Shirley Jones, Geraldine Fitzgerald, Claude Akins, Ross Martin, Stephanie Zimbalist

Yesterday's Witness. Generic title of an occasional series of documentaries produced by Stephen Peet for BBC2. The general aim is to put on record the recollections of days gone by from elderly people who led interesting lives.

Yogi Bear*
US 1958–62 123 × 25m colour
Hanna–Barbera

Cartoon series featuring a friendly bear in Jellystone National Park; also *Snagglepuss* and *Yakky Doodle Duck*.

† Yogi became the most popular Hanna–Barbera character of all.

Yogi's Gang
US 1973 19 × 22m colour
Hanna–Barbera

Yogi and his friends set out on a crusade to protect the environment.
Inferior workmanship marks this sequel.

Yorkin, Bud (1926–) (Alan Yorkin). American producer–director who after years in light entertainment teamed with Norman Lear in Tandem Productions to make the smash hits *All in the Family*, *Maude* and *Sanford and Son*.

You Are There**
US 1954–6 65 × 25m bw
CBS

Re-enactments of historical incidents in terms of modern reporting: the trial of Joan of Arc, the death of John Dillinger, etc.
Carefully researched information series in a format which was certainly an influential TV first. It was briefly revived in the early seventies, but by then the freshness had worn off.

host Walter Cronkite

You Bet Your Life. A so-called quiz show which, cheaply made, was really an excuse for Groucho Marx to interview and mildly insult a variety of contestants. The impromptu humour was a little strained at times, but the show became a national institution. (A British version, *Groucho*, failed miserably.) The show ran from 1956 to 1961, was produced by John Guedel and hosted by George Fenneman.

You Lie So Deep My Love
US 1975 74m colour TVM
Universal (David Lowell Rich)

Murder results when a girl is convinced that her husband is a crook and philanderer.
Muddled and slow-starting suspenser.

w William K. Stuart, Robert Hammer, John Neufeld   *d* David Lowell Rich

Barbara Anderson, Don Galloway, Walter Pidgeon, Angel Tompkins

You'll Never Get Rich****
aka: *The Phil Silvers Show; Bilko*
US 1955–8   138 × 25m   bw
CBS

At a remote army post, the fast-talking motor pool sergeant is full of clever schemes.
Smartly written and performed vehicle for a star who as Ernie Bilko created an unforgettable comic character and became a national institution.

cr NAT HIKEN   *m* John Strauss

PHIL SILVERS, PAUL FORD (Colonel Hall), MAURICE GOSFIELD (Doberman), Elizabeth Fraser (Sgt Hogan), Joe E. Ross (Ritzik), Harvey Lembeck (Barbella), Allan Melvin (Henshaw), Billy Sands (Paparelli), Hope Sansberry (Mrs Hall)

You'll Never See Me Again
US 1973   74m   colour   TVM
Universal (Harve Bennett)

A wife disappears after a quarrel and may have been murdered.
Standard suspenser.

w William Wood, Gerald di Pego   *d* Jeannot Szwarc

David Hartman, Joseph Campanella, Jane Wyatt, Ralph Meeker, Jess Walton, Bo Swenson

Young, Alan (1919–) (Angus Young). British character comedian in America: after some success as nervous type in films he became a variety star on TV and especially scored in the series *Mister Ed*.

The Young and the Restless. CBS daily soap opera which premièred in 1973 and puts its main focus on teenage problems.

Young, Sir Brian (1922–). British executive, director-general since 1970 of the Independent Broadcasting Authority.

Young, Collier (1908–). American writer–producer who created *The Rogues*, *One Step Beyond* and *Ironside*.

The Young Country*
US 1970   74m   colour   TVM
Universal (Roy Huggins)

A young gambler gets worried when he finds a fortune in a saddlebag and no one will acknowledge ownership.
Pleasant light western.

w/d Roy Huggins

Roger Davis, Walter Brennan, Joan Hackett, Wally Cox, Pete Duel

Young Dan'l Boone
US 1977   8 × 50m   colour
TCF

An attempt to refurbish an old warhorse with youth appeal, this location adventure series failed rather miserably.

Rick Moses, John Joseph Thomas, Devon Ericson

Young Dr Kildare
US 1972   24 × 25m   colour (VTR)
MGM

A cheap taped retread of a famous series.

Gary Merrill, Mark Jenkins

Young, Gig (1913–78) (Byron Barr). Debonair American leading man of the fifties, latterly character actor, especially associated with tipsy roles. TV series: *The Rogues, Gibbsville*.

Young Joe, the Forgotten Kennedy
US 1977   96m   colour   TVM
ABC Circle (William McCutchen)

The eldest son of Joseph Kennedy, killed in World War II, is presented as an ambitious and romantic young man.
So-what biopic leaves us not much the wiser and very thinly entertained.

w M. Charles Cohen, *biography The Lost Prince* by Hank Searls   *d* Richard T. Heffron   *ph* Stevan Larner   *m* John Barry

Peter Strauss, Barbara Parkins, Stephen Elliott, Darleen Carr, Simon Oakland, Asher Brauner, Gloria Strook

'Torn between his family, who demanded greatness, and a woman who wanted only his love, he risked it all in one defiant moment of glory.' – publicity

The Young Lawyers
US 1969   74m   colour   TVM
Paramount

A Boston corporation lawyer takes over a legal aid office run by students.
A very predictable pilot.

w/d Harvey Hart

Jason Evers, Louise Latham, Keenan Wynn, Michael Parks, Anjanette Comer

† The ensuing series lasted 24 × 50m films and starred Lee J. Cobb with Judy Pace and Zalman King.

Young, Muriel (*c* 1928–). British presenter, especially associated with children's programmes. In the seventies she became head of children's programmes for Granada TV.

Young Pioneers*
US 1975 100m colour TVM
ABC Circle

In 1873, newlywed teenagers travel west.
Standard pioneering saga, well enough made.

novels Rose Wilder Lane *d* Michael O'Herlihy

Roger Kern, Linda Purl

† A second 96m episode, *The Young Pioneers'
Christmas*, was aired in 1977, and in 1978 two one-hour
films were made but no series resulted.

The Young Rebels
US 1970 15 × 50m colour
Columbia/Aaron Spelling (Jon Epstein)

During the War of Independence, a young guerrilla
band fights the British.
Unappetizing historical adventure.

cr Harve Bennett

Rick Ely, Lou Gossett, Philippe Forquet, Alex
Henterloff, Will Geer

'Together they operate as a kind of "colonial" Mod
Squad, working to create their own kind of world.' –
promotion

Young, Robert (1907–). American movie star of
the thirties and forties who also had great TV success
with *Father Knows Best, Window on Main Street* and
Marcus Welby.

Young, Stephen (*c* 1931–) (Stephen Levy).
Canadian leading man, occasionally in Hollywood.
Series: *Seaway, Judd for the Defence*.

Your Money or Your Wife
US 1972 74m colour TVM
Bentwood

A scriptwriter's plot turns into an almost perfect crime.
Rather talkative comedy suspenser.

w J. P. Miller, *novel If You Want to See Your Wife
Again . . .* by John Gay *d* Allen Reisner

Ted Bessell, Elizabeth Ashley, Jack Cassidy, Betsy Von
Furstenberg

Your Show of Shows. American variety show
which ran on NBC on Saturday nights from 1949 to
1954 and made stars of Sid Caesar and Imogene Coca.
Among the writers were Neil Simon, Mel Brooks and
Woody Allen; producer–director was Max Leibmann.
Some grainy kinescopes were edited into a 1976 movie
release, *Ten from Your Show of Shows*.

Yuma*
US 1970 70m colour TVM
Aaron Spelling

A tough lawman tackles the wildest town in the old
west.
Conventional, enjoyable western.

d Ted Post

Clint Walker, Barry Sullivan, Edgar Buchanan,
Kathryn Hays

Z

Z Cars*. A BBC series which emerged from Elwyn Jones's drama documentary department and ran from 1960 until 1978, covering 667 one-hour episodes. When it began, with a simple play called *Jacks and Knaves*, based on the experiences of Liverpool detective Jack Prendergast (the series format based on the crime cars was by Troy Kennedy Martin) it seemed to have all the hallmarks of the new realism, showing crime and low-life from the police point of view in two kinds of Liverpool suburb. The leading policemen, played by Stratford Johns, Frank Windsor, Joseph Brady, Jeremy Kemp, James Ellis, Terence Edmond, and later Brian Blessed and Colin Welland, soon became familiar faces. Leading writers over the years were John Hopkins, Robert Barr, Alan Plater, Allan Prior. Spin-offs included *Softly Softly* and *Barlow*; the influence on other crime series was immense.

Z Channel. One on which, for a fee, the American viewer can see up-to-date uncut movies without commercials.

Zane Grey Theatre*
US 1956–60 156 × 25m bw
Four Star

Western anthology, hosted by Dick Powell.
A competent production with excellent guest stars, providing the kind of middlebrow entertainment hard to find in the seventies.

Zero One*
GB 1962 39 × 25m bw
MGM/BBC

Cases of an airline detective.
Polished crime entertainment.

Nigel Patrick, Katya Douglas

Ziegfeld: The Man and His Women
US 1978 150m colour TVM
Columbia/Mike Frankovich (Buzz Kulik)

The women in the life of the great showman give their assessment of him.
Despite a large budget by TV standards, this hefty biopic looks like a dry run, notably lacking in slickness and professionalism. Its facts appear to be accurate, but its presentation of them seems shifty, and the performances leave much to be desired. Only the musical numbers raise a mild flicker of interest.

w Joanna Lee *adviser* Patricia Ziegfeld *d* Buzz Kulik *ph* Gerald Perry Finnerman *a/d* John de Cuir *m/d* Dick de Benedictis *choreo* Miriam Nelson

Paul Shenar, Samantha Eggar (Billie Burke), Barbara Parkins (Anna Held), Pamela Peadon (Marilyn Miller), Valerie Perrine (Lillian Lorraine), David Opatoshu, Nehemiah Persoff, Richard B. Shull, Inga Swenson (Nora Bayes), David Downing (Bert Williams), Richard Shea (Eddie Cantor), Dan Tullis Jnr (singer of 'Old Man River'), Catherine Jacoby (Fanny Brice)

Zimbalist, Efrem Jnr (1918–). American star actor of comfortable presence. Series: 77 *Sunset Strip*, *The FBI*.

Zoo Gang*
GB 1973 6 × 50m colour
ATV (Herbert Hirschman)

Members of a wartime resistance group meet again 30 years later to use their special skills in combating modern crime.
Curiously abortive star-studded series which had good things but failed to catch the imagination.

cr Paul Gallico, from his novel *m* Paul and Linda McCartney

Lilli Palmer, John Mills, Brian Keith, Barry Morse

Alternative Titles for TV Movies

(not including pilots for subsequent series – these are cross-referenced in the text)

Alias Sherlock Holmes *see* The Return of the World's Greatest Detective
The Art of Crime *see* Roman Grey
As I Rode Down from Laredo *see* The Return of the Gunfighter
The Aspen Murder *see* Aspen

The Big Dragnet *see* Dragnet
The Big Train *see* Alcatraz Express
Brahmin *see* The Invasion of Johnson County

The Cable Car Murders *see* Crosscurrent
The Caper *see* The Heist
Cat and Mouse *see* Mousey
Circumstantial Evidence *see* Mallory
The Companion *see* The Betrayal

Danger Grows Wild *see* The Poppy Is Also a Flower
The Deadly Game *see* Serpico
Deadly Roulette *see* How I Spent My Summer Vacation
Death Dive *see* Fer de Lance
Doberman Patrol *see* Trapped

The Egghead on Hill 656 *see* The Reluctant Heroes
End of the Line *see* A Cry for Help
Enter Horowitz *see* Conspiracy of Terror
Escape of the Birdmen *see* The Birdmen

The Faceless Man *see* The Counterfeit Killer
The FBI versus the Ku Klux Klan *see* Attack on Terror
Fitzgerald and Pride *see* Heat of Anger

The Gravy Train *see* The Dion Brothers
The Guardians *see* Incident on a Dark Street

Hildegarde Withers *see* A Very Missing Person
The Hunter *see* Scream of the Wolf

Incident in a Dark Alley *see* Incident on a Dark Street
Inside Job *see* The Alpha Caper

Joshua Tree *see* The Courage and the Passion

The Last Key *see* Crime Club (1975)
Law of the Land *see* The Deputies
The Legend of Machine Gun Kelly *see* Melvin Purvis G-Man

Man at the Crossroads *see* A Great American Tragedy
The Man Who Wanted to Live Forever *see* The Only Way Out Is Dead
Midnight Oil *see* Now You See It, Now You Don't
Mrs R *see* Death Among Friends
My Darling Daughters' Anniversary *see* All My Darling Daughters' Anniversary

New Orleans Force *see* Dead Man on the Run
Nick Carter *see* The Adventures of Nick Carter

Ohanian *see* The Killer Who Wouldn't Die
One Hour to Doomsday *see* City Beneath the Sea
Only One Day Left Before Tomorrow *see* How to Steal an Airplane

The Paramedics *see* The New Healers
The Power and the Passion *see* The Courage and the Passion

The Rivermen *see* The Runaway Barge

Sam Hill: Who Killed the Mysterious Mr Foster? *see* Who Killed the Mysterious Mr Foster?
Sarge: The Badge or the Cross *see* The Badge or the Cross
Set This Town on Fire *see* The Profane Comedy
Shamus *see* A Matter of Wife and Death
The Sixth Column *see* The Love War
The Soldier Who Declared Peace *see* Tribes
A Special Kind of Love *see* Special Olympics
SST: Death Flight *see* SST: Disaster in the Sky
The Storm *see* The New Healers
The Storm *see* The Victim
Streets of Fear *see* To Kill a Cop
The Strong Man *see* The 500 Pound Jerk
Suspected Person *see* The Heist

Three Faces of Love *see* Rex Harrison Presents Three Stories of Love
Today Is Forever *see* Griffin and Phoenix: A Love Story
Truman at Potsdam *see* Meeting at Potsdam

The UFO Incident *see* The Interrupted Journey

Visions of Death *see* Visions